NATIONAL SECURITY IN SAUDI ARABIA

NATIONAL SECURITY IN SAUDI ARABIA

Threats, Responses, and Challenges

Anthony H. Cordesman and Nawaf Obaid

PUBLISHED IN COOPERATION WITH
THE CENTER FOR STRATEGIC AND INTERNATIONAL STUDIES
WASHINGTON, D.C.

PRAEGER SECURITY INTERNATIONAL
WESTPORT, CONNECTICUT · LONDON

Library of Congress Cataloging-in-Publication Data

Cordesman, Anthony H.
  National security in Saudi Arabia : threats, responses, and challenges / Anthony H.
  Cordesman and Nawaf Obaid.
    p. cm.
    Includes bibliographical references.
    ISBN 0-275-98811-2 (alk. paper)
    1. National security—Saudi Arabia.   2. Saudi Arabia—Military policy.
    I. Obaid, Nawaf E., 1974- II. Title.
  UA853.S33C664 2005
    355.0330538—dc22   2005016847

British Library Cataloguing in Publication Data is available

Library of Congress Catalog Card Number: 2005016847
ISBN: 0-275-98811-2

First published in 2005

Praeger Security International, 88 Post Road West, Westport, CT 06881
An imprint of Greenwood Publishing Group, Inc.
www.praeger.com

Printed in the United States of America

The paper used in this book complies with the
Permanent Paper Standard issued by the National
Information Standards Organization (Z39.48-1984).

10   9   8   7   6   5   4   3   2   1

Contents

Tables and Figures

Acknowledgments

This book was made possible through repeated visits to Saudi Arabia and extensive talks with Saudi officials, security experts, and military officers; as well as Saudi citizens, and through the aid of various U.S. and British officials and experts. The authors relied heavily on the work of Khalid al-Rodhan.

Introduction

Both Saudi Arabia's security situation and its security apparatus are undergoing major changes. Saudi Arabia does not currently face a major threat from Iraq, but it must deal with potential conventional threats from Yemen and Iran as well as the growing risk that Iran will become a nuclear power. This confronts Saudi Arabia with hard strategic choices as to whether to ignore Iran's efforts to proliferate, to seek U.S. military assistance in deterring Iran and possibly in some form of missile defense, or to acquire more modern missiles and its own weapons of mass destruction.

The Kingdom's most urgent security threats, however, no longer consist of hostile military forces; these threats have been replaced by the threat of Islamic extremism and terrorism. Saudi Arabia faces a direct internal threat from Islamic extremists, many affiliated with al Qaeda and similar extremist groups, and it must pay far more attention to internal security than in the past. At the same time, the Saudi government must deal with the reality that this threat is also regional, extends throughout the Islamic world, and has cells throughout the rest of the globe. The religious legitimacy of Saudi Arabia and its neighbors and allies is being challenged, and the scale of this threat may also take on new scope and meaning if instability continues in Iraq, if Iraq comes under a hostile regime, and/or Iraq becomes a new source of terrorist attacks on the Kingdom.

Changing Nature of Alliances

Saudi Arabia must also make major adjustments in its alliances. The events of 9/11, the backlash from the Israeli-Palestinian conflict, differences over how to deal with terrorism, and differences over the Iraq War have all combined to complicate Saudi Arabia's security relations with the United States, and to force the Kingdom to distance itself from Washington in some ways.

At the same time, the al Qaeda terrorist attacks on Saudi Arabia in May 2003 made it brutally clear that Saudi Arabia was a full participant in the same war on Islamic terrorism that the United States was fighting and gave Saudi Arabia even stronger incentives to cooperate with the United States in antiterrorism. Similarly, Saudi Arabia has not found any substitute for U.S. power-projection capabilities in dealing with Iran, instability in Iraq or Yemen and needs U.S. technical assistance with its massive and continuing deliveries of U.S. military equipment.

Regional security is largely a myth, not a military reality. The Gulf Cooperation Council (GCC) has made some advances in military cooperation and internal security, but it largely remains a hollow shell. There is no true integration of security efforts and only symbolic progress toward collective security. Interoperability remains poor at every level, there is little progress toward effective power projection and sustainability, and there virtually has been no meaningful progress toward the creation of the kinds of information technology, C⁴I (Command, Control, Communications, Computers, and Intelligence), IS&R (Intelligence, Surveillance, and Reconnaissance), and net-centric systems that could tie together the forces of the GCC, as well as make Saudi cooperation with U.S. forces far more effective.

At the same time, petty rivalries continue to divide the Southern Gulf states, and Saudi Arabia faces serious problems in dealing with Yemen and in obtaining Yemeni cooperation in blocking the infiltration of terrorists and the smuggling of arms and narcotics.

Saudi Arabia also maintains military ties with Europe, particularly with Britain and France. Some Saudi officials see efforts to expand the role of NATO in the Middle East as a possible way of reducing Saudi de facto dependence on the United States, and/or of using NATO as a more politically acceptable cover for Saudi military ties to Washington. Saudi strategists and policymakers, however, are all too aware of the real world limits on European power-projection capabilities as well as to the limitations of the power-projection forces NATO and the EU are trying to build. They understand that Europe will not be able to replace the United States in assisting Saudi Arabia to deal with serious foreign threats at any time in the foreseeable future.

THE BROADER NATURE OF THE SAUDI SECURITY EFFORT

All of these factors interact with a longer-term set of threats to Saudi stability that are largely economic and demographic but that may well be more important than any combination of outside military threats and the threat of Islamic extremism and terrorism. Saudi Arabia has embarked on a process of political, economic, and social reforms that reflect a growing understanding by the governing members of the royal family, Saudi technocrats, and Saudi businessmen that Saudi Arabia must reform and diversify its economy, and must create vast numbers of new jobs for its growing and young population.

There is a similar understanding that economic reform must be combined with some form of political and social reform if Saudi Arabia is to remain stable in the face of change, and that the Kingdom must be far more careful about the ways in which it uses the revenues from its oil exports and other revenues. This means hard decisions about future arms imports and investments in military and security forces. Massive changes are needed in Saudi military planning, and especially in military procurement and arms imports, to create balanced and effective forces at far lower cost.

As yet, Saudi Arabia's security apparatus has only begun to react to these changes. Its military forces are only beginning to adapt to the fact that the Iraqi threat has largely disappeared, that Iran's threat is a mix of proliferation and capabilities for asymmetric warfare and not the buildup of conventional forces, and that it is engaged in a generational struggle against domestic and foreign Islamic extremism.

Similarly, the Kingdom has begun the process of deeper political, economic, and social reform, but it has only made a beginning; its plans are still half formed, and no aspect of reform as yet has the momentum necessary to succeed. Like much of the Arab and Islamic world, Saudi Arabia also seems culturally unable to honestly address the scale of its demographic problems and rapid population growth, and the decline in oil wealth in per-capita terms that come with population growth. It is focused on the symptoms, but not one of the key causes.

Given this background, the current structure of the Saudi security apparatus is only one key to security. It is Saudi ability to formulate and execute policies that can cope with the major changes that must be made in the Saudi approach to strategy. The finer details of governance are really of passing interest at best, and are necessarily transitional. The real question is how quickly Saudi Arabia can change and adapt its overall approach to security, and how successful it will be in the process.

SAUDI SECURITY AND THE ROLE OF THE WEST

At the same time, no analysis of the Saudi security apparatus can, however, focus on Saudi Arabia alone. The West must be far more careful in the future in pressing for military sales in ways that do not meet vital Saudi security needs, and that do not take Saudi Arabia's domestic economic problems and social needs into account. Saudi Arabia has long been the largest single customer for U.S. and European military exports. Saudi purchases had the benefit of increasing interoperability and sustainability with British, French, and U.S. forces and reduction of the unit cost of equipment used by Western forces. It is clear, however, that Saudi Arabia faces serious long-term constraints on what it can buy in the future and that it will often have to make hard choices between the military desirability of standardization with Western power-projection forces and the political need to buy arms from a range of friendly states.

Defense contractors will be defense contractors; they exist to sell regardless of need or merit. Governments, however, must act as governments and think first of their strategic interests. It is time that the governments of Europe and the United States make it clear to the Saudi people that they emphasize Saudi security, military readiness, and effectiveness rather than exports and sales. They need to make it clear that they are not pressuring Saudi Arabia to buy unnecessary arms, to recognize Saudi Arabia's need to limit its purchases to the level Saudi Arabia can afford, and act to prevent corruption and ensure that arms buys are part of packages that include the proper support, training, munitions stocks, and sustainability.

It is also clear that the time has come to put an end to client and tutorial relations. The United States and European governments must treat Saudi Arabia as a partner, as they do the other friendly states in the region. This requires a U.S. and European focus on creating effective Saudi forces for both defense and counterterrorism. It means that if NATO is to play a role in the region, it cannot be in a form that sees the Southern Gulf states as bases rather than partners. It means an emphasis on interoperability and on consultation in both planning and operations that require Saudi and regional support.

It certainly does not mean measures that block Saudi military training in the United States, or actions that sustain the climate of tension and hostility that has grown up since 9/11. Gulf security, the war on terrorism, and the security of some 60 percent of the world's oil reserves require a level of cooperation and mutual understanding that has been inadequate in the past; true partnership is the only way to build and sustain it in the future.

Chapter 1

The New Balance of Threats in the Gulf Region

T he fall of Saddam Hussein and the Ba'ath regime has removed a critical set of military threats from the Gulf. At the same time, the end of Saddam's regime has scarcely transformed the Middle East or brought security and stability to the Gulf. No one knows how stable Iraq will be in the future, what its government will be like, what its strategic goals will be, or how it will eventually rebuild its military forces and rearm. Furthermore, there are other types of threats that affect the region and Saudi Arabia's planning for defense and counterterrorism:

- Local threats from conventional military forces and proliferation;
- Regional threats from terrorism and Islamic extremism;
- Self-inflicted threats created by poor military planning and inadequate attention to economic reform on the part of the Southern Gulf states; and
- Threats imposed by policy failures on the part of the United States.

The end of the Iran-Iraq War, the impact of the Gulf War, the end of the Yemeni civil war, and the U.S.-led invasion of Iraq all combined to drastically slow the conventional arms race that drove military developments in the Gulf from the late 1960s to the early 1990s. Saudi Arabia has never faced a serious threat from the other Southern Gulf states and fellow members of the Gulf Cooperation Council (GCC). It has resolved all of its significant border disputes, and its mild political tensions with Qatar present no risk of war. It does not face a threat from the Red Sea states or from Syria and Jordan. Israel only poses a threat if it feels Saudi Arabia is likely to intervene massively in some future Arab-Israeli conflict or is acquiring weapons of mass destruction that could threaten Israel. For all of its rhetoric, Israel does not see Saudi Arabia as a significant threat or plan to fight it. Thus, in Saudi perceptions, the primary potential threats to it in the region are Yemen, and Iran—and possibly a resurgent Iraq.

Instability in Iraq

Saudi Arabia has good reasons to be concerned about any potential threat from Iraq. It shares an 814-kilometer border with Iraq and is within five minutes flying time from air bases in Southern Iraq. Most of the Saudi-Iraqi border region is empty desert, and substantial portions can be easily crossed by Iraqi armor. Many of Saudi Arabia's most critical oil fields, oil export facilities, electric power, and desalination plants are within a few minutes' flying time, and could be reached within roughly one or two days from Iraq by an unopposed armored unit.

The U.S.- and British-led Coalition have aided Gulf security to the extent that they have removed Iraq's ability to mount a near-term threat using conventional forces or weapons of mass destruction. However, the Coalition may well have created a new threat in the process. At best, Iraq seems likely to face years of insurgency and instability. At worst, Iraq may emerge as a state hostile to Saudi Arabia and the other Southern Gulf states. It could emerge as a Shiite-dominated state with close ties to Iran, that disenfranchises the Sunni minority, and that becomes a source of new tensions with its neighbors. Furthermore, there is a fear that Iraq may replace Afghanistan as a center for Islamic extremists and terrorist activities.

Saudi Arabia already faces problems with Islamist and other hostile infiltrators coming into the country from Iraq. Many Saudis feel that the invasion of Iraq increased the recruitment of extremists. Brig. Gen. Mansour al-Turki, the Saudi Ministry of Interior's spokesman, was quoted as saying that the extremists "wanted to spread their war against the United States and found that doing this was easier in their own country. But it wasn't until the invasion of Iraq that they could convince others in the country to share their goals. For that reason, the invasion was very important to them." One of their alleged frustrations was that the Saudi government should have been able "to prevent America from invading Iraq without justification."[1]

The Saudis have made their concerns about an unstable Iraq apparent. Saudi Arabia has provided aid to Iraq and discussed debt relief and reparations issues with the new government in Baghdad. It has also made its own proposals to try to bring stability to Iraq. During Secretary of State Colin Powell's visit to Jeddah in the summer of 2004, the Kingdom proposed the creation of a "Muslim force" to help secure Iraq under the UN. The United States rejected the idea and stated the White House was worried about the chain of command under this plan.[2] It is far from clear when Iraq will be stable enough to permit such an approach, but it is a concept that is well worth examining over the next few years if Iraqi military and security forces cannot make the transition to providing security and stability within Iraq.

The Decline of Iraq's Military Forces

The Coalition invasion of Iraq in 2003 largely destroyed Iraq's military forces, which had gone into decline long before the Coalition invasion. At the time it invaded Kuwait in 1990, Iraq had over one million men in uniform. Its army had 955,000 men in seven corps, which was equivalent to 51–61 divisions. It had some 5,500 main battle tanks (MBTs), 2,800–3,700 other armored fighting vehicles (AFVs), 7,100 armored personnel carriers (APCs), 3,700 artillery weapons, and 160 armed helicopters. Its small 5,000-man Navy had 5 frigates, 4 corvettes, 8 missile patrol craft, 6 torpedo boats, 20 inshore patrol boats, 8 mine warfare ships, and 6 amphibious ships. Its relatively modern Air Force had some 513 combat aircraft, with 2 bomber, 17 attack, 16 fighter, and one reconnaissance squadron. Some 10,000 of the men in its Air Force were assigned to land-based air defense forces with one of the largest and most densely deployed air defense systems in the world. It had over 4,000–6,500 air defense guns and some 120 SA-2, 150 SA-3, 60 Roland, and large numbers of SA-6, SA-7, SA-8, SA-13, and SA-15 surface-to-air missile launchers.

The Gulf War destroyed some 40 percent of this force, and Iraq could not overtly import arms during the period from August of 1990 to Saddam's fall in April 2003. By 2000 Iraq's forces had declined to some 429,000 men in uniform. Its Army had 375,000 men and seven corps with 21–24 division equivalents. It had some 2,200 worn and aging MBTs, 1,700–2,000 AFVs, 2,400 APCs, 2,500 artillery weapons, and 120 armed helicopters—most no longer operational. Its Navy had shrunk to 2,000 men, with one missile patrol craft, four inshore patrol boats, and four amphibious ships. Its worn and aging Air Force had some 310 combat aircraft, of which roughly half normally were operational, and its pilots had little flight time. Its land-based air defense forces had risen to some 17,000 men—in part, because they were its only relatively survivable force element. It still had thousands of air defense guns and many surviving SA-2, SA-3, Roland, and SA-6, SA-7, SA-8, SA-13, and SA-15 surface-to-air missile launchers. It had, however, lost much of its air defense system and was reliant on weapons whose technology dated back to the 1960s and 1970s.

Although Iraq did not have weapons of mass destruction at the time of the Coalition attack, it was still engaged in its research and development efforts. It also maintained some 400,000 men under arms and nearly another 100,000 paramilitary and security combatants. While it demonstrated little conventional war fighting capability against U.S. and British forces, it did still have some 2,600 MBTs, 3,600 AFVs and APCs, 2,300 artillery weapons, and over 300 combat aircraft and 62 attack helicopters, as well as a large land-based air defense system.[3] Within a few weeks, however, its land forces had been shattered and dispersed, the remnants of its navy had been destroyed, and its land-based air defenses had been destroyed and suppressed. Its air force was so inferior that it never flexed in combat.

Iraq's Military Capabilities in the Post-Saddam Era

As of late 2004, the Iraqi armed forces were just beginning to rebuild as light motorized forces tailored to internal counterinsurgency missions. Their strengths are summarized in Table 1.1 as follows:[4]

Table 1.1: The Emerging New Iraqi Military and Security Forces

Force Element	Current Strength	On Duty, Trained, and Equipped	Total Authorized
Police	87,133	47,342	135,000
Special Police Commando Battalions	2,019	900	2,019
Border Enforcement	16,237	14,593	29,360
Highway Patrol	925	370	6,300
Bureau of Dignitary Protection	484	484	500
Intervention Force	6,584	1,816	6,859
Emergency Response Force	168	168	270
Civil Intervention Force	1,091	1,091	3,720
National Guard[a]	43,318	41,409	55,921
	(41,261)	?	(61,904)
Special Operations Force	604	590	1,967
Army	16,634	4,507	27,000
Air Force	206	167	502
Coastal Defense Force	409	536	582
TOTAL	175,812	113,973	270,000
Military Forces	(17,249)	(5,210)	(28,084)
Military and Elite Paramilitary (less National Guard)	(29,124)	(10,491)	(49,719)

a. Data from MNSTC-1 are not clear. Data in parenthesis are taken from U.S. Embassy Weekly Status Report of November 3, 2004.

By the end of January 2005, Iraq was seeking to create a force of 27 Regular Army or Intervention Force battalions (including six more from the Intervention Force). Sixteen light National Guard battalions were conducting operations at the company level or above, with a number conducting operations effectively at the battalion level. Current plans were to expand the National

Guard from its previous authorized strength of 45 battalions and 6 brigades to 6 division HQs, 21 brigade commanders, and 65 battalions.

The key components of Iraq's forces include:

- *Special Police Commando Battalions.* The Special Police Commando Battalions represent the Iraqi Ministry of Interior's (MOI's)strike-force capability. The commandos—ultimately to be composed of six full battalions—are highly vetted Iraqi officers and rank-and-file servicemen largely made up of prior service Special Forces professionals and other skilled servicemen with specialty unit experience.

  All members of the unit are chosen based on loyalty to Iraq and its new democratic model. The unit focuses primarily on building raid operations and counterterrorist missions, including anti-airplane hijacker, kidnapping, and other similar missions.

  The force resembles more a paramilitary army-type force, complete with heavy weapons, rocket-propelled grenades, AK-47 assault rifles, mortars, and 9 mm Glock pistols. The commando battalions give the MOI a high-end strike force capability similar to Special Forces units and was quickly stood up to capitalize on previously existing skill sets in Iraq.

- *Iraqi Police Service Emergency Response Unit.* An elite 270-man team trained to respond to national-level law enforcement emergencies. Team members undergo a robust eight-week specialized training course spawned from the current wave of anti-Iraqi forces actions.

  The mission of the emergency response unit is to provide a national, high-end, rapid-response law enforcement tactical unit responsible for high-risk search, arrest, and hostage-rescue and crisis-response operations. The emergency response unit is the predominant force for national-level incidents calling for a DELTA/SWAT capability and will only be used in extreme situations by local and national authorities.

  The $64.5 million effort is part of a larger mission to create national-level law enforcement investigative and special operations capability within the Iraqi MOI to counter terrorism, large-scale civil disobedience and insurgencies throughout Iraq. The capability will eventually include a counterterrorism investigative unit and a special operations unit. Volunteers for the force must first complete the standard eight-week basic training course or three-week transition integration program course for prior service officers before entering the specialized emergency response unit training modeled after the U.S. State Department's Anti-Terrorism Assistance (ATA) and Bureau of Alcohol, Tobacco and Firearms' training programs.

Of the total force, 235 eligible candidates received rigorous instruction based on the ATA Crisis Response Team training program, while the balance of 35 recruits are part of the Special Operations Explosive Ordinance Team, based on the State Department's ATA Explosive Incident Countermeasures training course.

Team members receive instruction on terrorist incidents, kidnappings, hostage negotiations, explosive ordnance, high-risk searches, high-risk assets, weapons of mass destruction, and other national-level law enforcement emergencies. Officers also have an opportunity to receive supplementary training in hostage negotiation, emergency medical procedures, and counterterrorism task force coordination.

- *Iraqi Intervention Forces.* The Iraqi Intervention Force (IIF) is the counterinsurgency wing of the Iraqi Army. Ultimately to be combined into nine battalions, organized into three brigades, these forces negotiate the standard eight-week basic training all Iraqi soldiers go through learning basic soldiering skills, such as weapons, drill, and ceremony.

  After graduation, IIF battalions spend several weeks and months in intensive military operations in urban terrain follow-on training—otherwise know as "MOUT" training. In this period, soldiers work through instruction in the art of street fighting and building-clearing operations typical to anti-insurgent operations in cities and towns. Units work in close coordination with other Iraqi Army battalions and will be completely stood up to the nine-battalion force by early 2005.

- *Iraqi Special Operations Force.* The Iraqi Special Operations Force—the Iraqi Armed Forces' high-end strike force resembling U.S. Special Forces units—continues training and operations in the country with multinational force assistance.

  Consisting of two trained battalions, including the 36th Commando Battalion—an infantry-type strike force—and the Iraqi Counterterrorism Battalion, the force has been involved in many operations throughout the country fighting anti-Iraqi forces with great distinction while continuing the stand-up effort of the unit. The force will add a third "support" battalion to its ranks in the coming months. Training is conducted at an undisclosed location.

  Selection for the force begins in the Iraqi National Guard and Iraqi Army units already operating in the country, much like typical multinational Special Forces' recruiting efforts in their own countries. Outstanding recruits successfully negotiating the vetting process, including exhaustive background checks, skill evaluations, and unit evaluations along with literacy, psychological, and physical tests, are run through various team-building and physical events meant to lean down the recruit pool. The selection process runs roughly 10 to 14 days.

The Iraqi Special Forces undergo intense physical, land navigation, small-unit tactics, live-fire, unconventional warfare operations, direct-action operations, airmobile operations, counterterrorism, survival, evasion, resistance, and escape training. Special Forces soldiers are an army's unconventional warfare experts, possessing a broad range of operational skills. The unit was formed based on a conversation between Prime Minister Ayad Allawi and multinational force personnel to give the Iraqi Armed Forces a high-end strike force in its ongoing security mission against anti-Iraqi forces operating in the country.

- *Iraqi Army.* Iraqi Army soldiers negotiate a standard eight-weeks of basic training, including basic soldiering skills instruction in weapons, drill and ceremony, soldier discipline, and physical training. Units negotiate advanced follow-on infantry, land navigation, and other operational training after graduation before deployment.

The Iraqi Army will ultimately be composed of 27 battalions of infantry, including 9 special Iraqi Intervention Force battalions, and 3 transportation battalions. The army will be organized into nine brigades and three divisions. The bulk of the force is slated to be in place by early 2005. Plans to create heavier and better armored forces are still in flux, but there are now 259 soldiers in the 1st Mechanized Brigade, preparing to train with 10 MTLB armored personnel carriers. These vehicles were drawn from a pool of over 300 armored vehicles the Iraqis intend to make ready as the unit grows. The brigade already has 50 T-55 tanks, 48 BMP-1s, 57 MTLBs, 36 Spartans, and 30 BTR-94s. Iraq hoped to have a combat-ready armored battalion by the end of January 2005, with others to follow.

- *Iraqi Coastal Defense Force.* The Iraqi Coastal Defense Force is the Iraqi Armed Forces' (IAF's) naval component. Ultimately, to number just more than 400 servicemen, the force also includes a land-based Coastal Defense Regiment resembling Western-type "Marine" infantry forces. Land- and sea-based forces negotiate IAF eight-week basic training courses before moving on to follow-on training and sea training for the boat crews.

Boat crews learn the basics in seamanship before moving on to instruction in advanced seamanship, towing, gunnery, sea rescue, chart reading, navigation, antismuggling, operations, and rigid inflatable boat integration and small boat drill instruction. Training is put in the context of a democratically based maritime sea force.

Primary duties include protecting the country's roughly 50-mile coastline from smuggling and foreign fighter infiltration operations as well as the port assets at Umm Qasr in Southern Iraq and oil assets in the Persian Gulf. The force patrols out to the 12-mile international water boundary in the Persian Gulf with five 27-meter-long, Chinese-made patrol boats and various other support craft.

The Emergence of a New Iraqi Threat?

These force numbers and descriptions show that the Iraqi military and security forces will be too weak to perform a serious war-fighting mission for years to come. However, Saudi Arabia will face different kinds of threats from Iraq unless that country becomes more stable, and something approaching a moderate and pluralistic government comes to power. These are all significant ifs.

It is far too early to predict that Iraqi Coalition efforts at nation building will fail, that a moderate Iraqi government will not emerge, or that Iraq will be a long-term source of instability. The fact remains, however, that poor U.S. preparations for stability and nation-building operations helped create a level of insurgency that has become a war after the war and that has greatly increased the risk of failure. The success of the Coalition effort in Iraq, and Iraq's ability to create a stable and secure new government, are now too close to call. Moreover, there is at least some risk that Iraq may divide on sectarian lines and that a Shiite-dominated regime may come to power that will create serious tensions with its Sunni neighbors, ally itself with Iran, and be overtly or covertly hostile to Saudi Arabia.

It also seems likely that Iraq will have to concentrate on internal counterinsurgency missions for some years to come. As a result, any Iraq threat to Saudi Arabia now consists largely of the threat of infiltration and asymmetric attacks from groups based in Iraq, rather than any tangible threat from Iraq's conventional forces or efforts at proliferation. This does not, however, mean that Saudi Arabia's security planning can ignore the mid- to long-term risk that Iraq may acquire a regime that is more actively hostile to Saudi Arabia, rebuild its military forces, and acquire significant capabilities for asymmetric warfare.

THREAT FROM YEMEN

While the Yemeni government and military still poses a potential threat to Saudi Arabia, this threat has changed strikingly in recent years, and is now one posed by terrorist infiltration across the Saudi-Yemeni border rather than the potential that Yemen will use direct military force. Saudi Arabia and Yemen have largely resolved their territorial claims and border issues, and Yemen no longer seems to face the kind of risk of civil war that might have spilled over into Saudi Arabia.

This settlement of Yemeni internal tensions may well have ended a problem that has existed for more than three decades. Yemen was divided into two countries when South Yemen achieved independence in 1967 as the People's Democratic Republic of Yemen (PDRY). The PDRY emerged as a deeply divided Marxist state, whose history was filled with coups and civil fighting, and which was the chief supporter of the Dhofar Rebellion in Oman. North Yemen saw a coup against its ruling imam and became the Yemeni Arab Republic (YAR) after a long civil war that saw active Egyptian military intervention and occasional attacks across the Saudi border. From roughly the late 1960s onward, the two countries were rivals involved in a local arms race that occasionally escalated to border clashes.

This history, border disputes and smuggling, past Yemeni claims to part of Saudi Arabia, and various tribal tensions led Saudi Arabia to see both Yemens as serious potential threats from the 1960s until the 1990s. The PDRY largely disintegrated in a civil war in the late 1980s, however, which led to the formal unification of the two countries as the Republic of Yemen on May 22, 1990. The largely North Yemeni leadership of the country put down a southern secessionist movement in 1994, and the country became significantly more stable. Saudi Arabia and Yemen began serious negotiations to resolve their differences and agreed to a delimitation of their mutual border in 2000.

Nevertheless, Yemen remains politically unstable, and there are significant Islamist extremist elements in the country, and there are still tensions between Yemen and Saudi Arabia. They share a 1,458-kilometer border, in a region that is largely desert and mountains and much of which is unpatrolled. This has led to significant infiltration of terrorist elements into Saudi Arabia in recent years.

This situation is at least partially beyond the control of the Yemeni government. Tribal groupings that occupy areas in both countries have long been a source of major smuggling activity, including drugs, arms and explosives. Yemen has a population of over 20 million and a depressed economy with something approaching 50 percent direct and disguised unemployment, and a per capita income that is only a fraction of that of Saudi Arabia's. While many Yemenis still work in Saudi Arabia, Riyadh fears that Yemen's economic and demographic problems may eventually lead to political troubles that could make it hostile to the Kingdom.

Yemen's Conventional Forces

Yemen no longer can pose a serious conventional military threat. It has no access to significant military assistance from either the West or the East, and its recent military expenditures have been relatively low. The U.S. State Department provides declassified statistics for the united Yemens for the period from 1990 to 1999 that estimate Yemeni military expenditures in current dollars ranged from $368 million to $492 million and averaged around $400 million. There was a slow decline in spending measured in constant 1999 dollars. Yemen was spending around $450 million to $490 million a year during 1990–92, and spending levels dropped to around $415 million to $370 million in 1989–90. According to the State Department estimates, military spending dropped from around 10 percent of Yemen's. GNP in 1990 to less than 6 percent in 1999, and from 30 percent of all central government expenditures to 22 percent in 1999.[5]

The International Institute for Strategic Studies (IISS) uses different definitions of military spending, which indicate that while Yemen raised its expenditures after 1999, it still recorded a comparatively low level of effort. IISS estimates that spending was $499 million in 2000, $542 million in 2001, $731 million in 2002, and $798 million in 2003. Yemeni expenditures dropped from 2.4 percent of GDP in 2000 to 2.1 percent in 2003, and averaged $30 to $42 per capita. To put these figures in perspective, the IISS estimates that Saudi Arabia spent $21.055 billion in 2001, $18.502 billion in 2002, and $18.747 billion in 2003, and from 8.9 to 11.3 percent of its GDP. Its per capita military spending ranged from $832 to $984.[6]

Yemen had very low levels of arms imports from the late 1980s to the end of the 1990s. The U.S. State Department provides declassified estimates for the period from 1989—the year after the Iran-Iraq War ended—to 1999. It estimates that Yemen's arms imports in current dollars ranged from $470 million to $5 million a year and declined slowly from peak levels of $470 million in 1989, to levels around $30 million in 1999. This decline was sharper in constant 1999 dollars. Iran was spending around $600 million a year in 1989, and spending levels dropped to around $30 million in 1989–90.[7]

According to declassified U.S. intelligence estimates, Yemen received only $400 million worth of arms deliveries during 1996–99 and $600 million worth during 2000–2003, and these included only limited numbers of advanced weapons: 6 Vigilante patrol boats (1999), 10 in-shore patrol boats (2003), 14 Su-27s (1999), and 15 MiG-29s (2001). While it ordered some $1.3 billion worth of new arms during 1996–2003, these orders will at most allow it to replace its aging inventory of older weapons.[8]

Yemen still had some 66,700 men in its armed forces in early 2005 along with some 40,000 reserves. Training levels were very low, however, and the reserves were largely a "paper" force with no real organization, equipment, and structure. Its force structure included eight armored brigades, 16 infantry brigades, six mechanized brigades, and two airborne and commando brigades, but this is a total force of over 10 division equivalents. It has the equipment strength for fewer than two modern mechanized division equivalents. Most of its active force structure was at best suited for light motorized operations and asymmetric warfare.

Most of Yemen's 790 main battle tanks are worn and/or obsolete. Its only relative modern tanks—none first line—consist of 50 M-60A1s and 60 T-72s. It has only 330 aging AFVs, although these do include 200 moderately capable BMP-1s and BMP-2s. It has some 150–210 operational APCs out of an inventory of over 700. Most are aging or obsolete Soviet-bloc wheeled types, and only 60 are tracked M-113s. There is little serious armored warfare, combined arms, and battle training.

Yemen has a limited inventory of modern antitank weapons, with 35 AT-3s, 12 TOWs, and 24 Dragons. It has 310 towed artillery weapons, but only 25 are self-propelled weapons. The operational status of its 30 obsolete SU-100 assault guns is unclear. It does have 33 surface-to-surface missiles and long-range rockets. These include 12 FROG-7s, 10 SS-21s, and 6 Scud-Bs, but they only have conventional warheads, and their operational status is unclear. Yemen does not have modern artillery computers, fire-control systems, artillery radars, or targeting systems. Overall command, control, and communications capabilities are weak, and communications equipment seems to suffer from serious maintenance and availability problems.

The Yemeni Navy has some 1,700 actives and bases in Aden, Al Hudaydah, Al Mukalla, Perim Island, and Socotra. Its small fleet of six aging missile craft and six mine warfare craft has limited operational status.

The Yemeni Air Force has an active strength of some 4,000–5,000 men, including the land-based air defense force. Roughly 40 of its 106 combat aircraft are in storage, and only 40 of its 72 operational fighters are relatively modern: 10 MiG-29s and 28–30 Su-20/22s. Pilot training is limited, and joint warfare capability is negligible. The air force has an obsolete mix of air defense command, control, and warning systems, oriented around ineffective ground-controlled intercept techniques. Yemen's land-based air defense is obsolete and has very low overall readiness and training. It consists of large numbers of aging man-portable light air defense missiles (MANPADS), large numbers of unguided and towed antiaircraft guns, some 100 radar-guided ZSU-23-4s of unknown operational status, and a mix of heavier surface-to-air missiles. These include SA-2, SA-3, SA-6s, and SA-9s. The vast majority are decades-old systems with minimal or no updating.

Border Issues and Defenses

This mixture of improved Saudi-Yemeni relations, and Yemen's conventional weaknesses, helps explain why Saudi Arabia now faces a more serious threat from infiltration across the Yemeni border than from the Yemeni military forces. Finding a solution to securing the border, however, is anything but easy. Yemen's government has never been in firm control of the tribal areas, and the country's uneasy political history has long made it a refuge for political extremists. Yemen is fighting its own war against terrorists and has its own religious divisions.

The border is mountainous in many areas. It is heavily populated in the Najran area, and some villages lie across the border, while key tribes exist on both sides, routinely crossing the border and earning money from smuggling and helping illegal Yemeni workers enter Saudi Arabia. This smuggling activity has included explosives, weapons, and terrorists. Low-level tribal violence remains endemic and led to minor attacks on the German teams emplacing cement border markers after Saudi Arabia and Yemen agreed on the demarcation of their border.

Yemeni unemployment averages around 50 percent among young men, and some 30,000 Yemenis were detained in the border area in July 2004 alone. Yemenis often beg in the streets of Saudi Arabia, and Yemen's growing population and weak economy ensures that the pressure on the Saudi border will increase for at least the next decade.

Saudi Arabia has considered creating an extensive border sensor net and barriers, and plans were developed for an expensive French-supplied system. This has been halted, or at least delayed, at the request of the Yemeni government. At least for the time being, Saudi Arabia is seeking to stabilize Yemen with aid and by bringing it into the GCC. It also maintains a major part of its forces at the air base and military city in Khamis Mushayt, and is building new bases near the border and Red Sea coast. It is also strengthening the border and coast guard forces in the area.

Saudi Vulnerability in the Red Sea Area

The current period of stabilization of Saudi-Yemeni relations could change, however, if Yemen ever came under an Islamist extremist or other hostile government. While Yemen has relatively weak military forces, it can still put pressure on Saudi Arabia in the border area, and even limited Yemeni air and naval capabilities can play a strategic role in the Red Sea area.[9]

Yemen is at the eastern entrance to the Red Sea and can threaten the Strait of Bab el Mandab, a natural bottleneck at this entrance. According to the U.S. Energy Information Agency (EIA), some 3.2–3.3 million barrels of oil per day

(MMBD) flow through this strait.[10] Its closure could block all east-west shipping, except for limited trade within the Red Sea region, and keep tankers from the Gulf from reaching the Suez Canal/Sumed Pipeline complex. This would force shipping to go around the southern tip of Africa (the Cape of Good Hope), add greatly to the transit time and cost for much of the world's shipping, and put a service strain on the world's tanker capacity.

Saudi Arabia can bypass the need to ship through the Bab el Mandab to some extent by using its east-west oil pipeline, which traverses Saudi Arabia and has a capacity of about 4.8 MMBD. This, however, could only allow shipping to the northwest and Suez Canal/Sumed Pipeline complex, and traffic to the Indian Ocean and Asia would still be blocked. In addition, closing of the Bab el Mandab would effectively block non–oil shipping from using the Suez Canal.[11]

The overall security of the Red Sea is also an issue. Libya showed in the past that even limited mining of the Red Sea shipping channels could have considerable political and economic effect. Any ship could be used to release free floating or bottom mines, and Yemen has had naval clashes with some of its other neighbors. An EIA analysis of risks to shipping in the Red Sea notes that:

> Security remains a major concern of foreign firms doing business in the region, particularly after the French-flagged tanker Limburg was attacked off the coast of Yemen by terrorists in October 2002. The Canadian oil company Nexen, which operates the ash-Shihr oil export terminal, agreed in January 2003 to provide assistance to the Yemeni government in improving security. Prior to this, the region had faced different security concerns. In December 1995 and again in August 1996, Eritrean and Yemeni forces clashed over control of the Hanish Islands, located just north of the Bab el Mandab. In October 1996, the two countries signed an agreement over the islands.[12]

There is also a problem with maritime smuggling on both the Red Sea and Gulf coasts. This includes narcotics and alcohol and could be a further source of infiltration and smuggling by terrorists.

THE THREAT FROM IRAN

Iran is a nation with a mixed record in terms of Gulf and regional security. It claims it no longer actively seeks to export its religious revolution to other Islamic states. It reached a rapprochement with Saudi Arabia and the other Southern Gulf states in the late 1990s and has since avoided further efforts to try to use the annual Hajj pilgrimage to Mecca to attack the Kingdom or to exploit Shiite versus Sunni tensions in Saudi Arabia and other Gulf countries like Bahrain. Iran maintains an active presence in the Gulf, conducts large-scale military exercises, and maintains an active intelligence and surveillance presence in both the Gulf and neighboring states. It has avoided provocative military action, however, and there is no evidence of active hostile attacks on Southern Gulf targets or U.S. targets since the Al Khobar bombings.

Conversely, Iran no longer seems to be evolving toward a more moderate and democratic regime. It deals at least at low levels with outside terrorist groups. It actively supports the Hezbollah in Lebanon and hard-line groups like Hamas and the Palestinian Islamic Jihad in attacking Israel. Iran is also well aware that Sunni and Shiite tensions are rising throughout the Islamic world, driven in part by Salafi extremist and terrorist groups like al Qaeda.

Iran plays at least some role in the political instability in Iraq and may take a more aggressive role in trying to shape Iraq's political future and security position in the Gulf.

Jordan's King Abdullah claimed that more than 1 million Iranians moved into Iraq to influence the Iraqi election. The Iranians, King Abdullah argued, have been trying to build pro-Iranian attitudes in Iraq by providing salaries to the unemployed. The king has also said that Iran's Revolutionary Guards are helping the militant groups fighting the United States in Iraq. He was quoted as saying, "It's in Iran's vested interest to have an Islamic republic of Iraq."[13] The same sentiment has been echoed by the interim Iraqi president, Ghazi al-Yawar. "Unfortunately . . . Iran has very obvious interference in our business [with] a lot of money, a lot of intelligence activities."[14]

While such claims are far from verified, Iranian officials have at least hinted that any U.S. use of force against Iran could lead Iran to take action in Iraq. On December 3, 2004, Iran also conducted war games in its five western provinces, near the Iraqi border, involving 120,000 air and ground troops. A spokesman for the Iranian Army claimed that tanks, APCs, fighters, and helicopters took part in the exercise.[15]

Iran is a far less modern military power in comparative terms than it was during the time of the shah, or during the Iran-Iraq War. Nevertheless, it is slowly improving its conventional forces and is now the only regional military power that poses a serious conventional military threat to Gulf stability. Iran has significant capabilities for asymmetric warfare and poses the additional threat of proliferation. There is considerable evidence that it is developing both a long-range missile force and a range of weapons of mass destruction. It has never properly declared its holdings of chemical weapons, and the status of its biological weapons programs is unknown. The disclosures made by the International Atomic Energy Agency (IAEA) since 2002 indicate Iran likely will continue to covertly seek nuclear weapons.

Iranian Conventional Forces

Most of Iran's military equipment is aging or second rate and much of it is worn. Iran lost some 50–60 percent of its land order of battle in the climatic battles of the Iran-Iraq War, and it has not since then had large-scale access to the modern weapons and military technology necessary to replace them. It also has lacked the ability to find a stable source of parts and supplies for most of its Western-supplied equipment and has not had access to upgrades and modernization programs since the fall of the shah in 1979.

IRANIAN MILITARY EXPENDITURES. Iran's military expenditures have been comparatively limited in recent years. The U.S. State Department estimates indicate that military expenditures in current dollars ranged from $4.93 billion to $8.26 billion and declined slowly from average levels of $7.5 to $8 billion in 1989–90 to levels around $7 billion in 1999. This decline was much sharper in constant 1999 dollars. Iran was spending around $10 billion a year in 1989 and 1990, and spending levels dropped to around $7 billion in 1999. According to the State Department estimates, military spending dropped from well in excess of 6 percent of Iran's GNP in 1989 to less than 3 percent in 1999 and from 36 percent of all central government expenditures in 1989 to less than 12 percent in 1999.[16]

The IISS uses different definitions of military spending, and indicates that Iran has an even lower level of effort. It estimates that spending was $4 billion in 2000, $3.218 billion in 2001, $3.077 billion in 2002, and $3.051 billion in 2003. Expenditures did not increase with a major increase in Iran's oil export revenues during this period, and as a result, they dropped from 5.4 percent of Iran's GDP in 2000 to 2.4 percent in 2003. They have averaged only $46 to $50 per capita in recent years. To put these figures in perspective, the IISS estimates that Saudi Arabia spent $21.055 billion in 2001, $18.502 billion in 2002, and $18.747 billion in 2003, and from 8.9 to 11.3 percent of its GDP. Its per capita military spending ranged from $832 to $984.[17]

IRANIAN ARMS IMPORTS. Iran is still dependent on large numbers of aging, worn, and obsolescent or obsolete weapons. It has, however, been able to rebuild some of its conventional capabilities during 1988–2003 and to make progress toward acquiring weapons of mass destruction and long-range missiles.

Iran was able to make massive arms imports during the Iran-Iraq War and to obtain substantial supplies from the smaller European countries, China, and other communist suppliers. It was slow to understand the need to place massive orders, however, and many orders were only delivered toward the end of the war. Ironically, the end result was that when Iraq successfully counterattacked in 1988, Iran lost massive amounts of new equipment rushed into the battlefield. These losses equaled some 40–60 percent of its total inventory of armor and significant amounts of its other land weapons inventory.

Iran also was unable to buy cutting-edge weapons from the Former Soviet Union and to obtain significant amounts of modern arms from its suppliers at the time of the shah. Most of its deliveries during 1988–92 were relatively low-grade weapons, although Russia did supply some modern armor and aircraft. Iran faced major financial problems until the mid-1990s and could not obtain resupply or new weapons from most Western states.

Iran did not carry out a major arms import effort once the Iran-Iraq War was over and it received the backlog of arms imports from the orders it placed during the war. According to declassified U.S. intelligence estimates, Iran imported $8.8 billion worth of arms between 1988 and 1991, but only $3 billion during the 1992–95 period, $2 billion between 1996 and 1999, and $600 million between 2000 and 2003.[18]

These trends are reinforced when one looks at the annual patterns in Iranian expenditures. U.S. State Department estimates for the period from 1989—the year after the Iran-Iraq War ended—to 1999 indicate Iran's annual arms imports in current dollars declined slowly from $1.9 billion for the 1989–90 period to around $150 million in 1999. This decline was much sharper in constant 1999 dollars. Iran was spending around $2.3–2.4 billion a year in 1989 and 1990, and spending levels dropped to around $150–400 million in 1989–90.[19]

However, Iran has been able to gradually acquire significant numbers of capable and advanced weapons over time, particularly land-based and naval weapons. The following sections also describe a number of areas where Iran has sought to produce or assemble its own weapons systems.

Nevertheless, Iran's current level of arms import and arms production is only about 35 percent to 50 percent of the level of imports necessary to recapitalize and modernize all of its forces. It also helps explain why Iran lacks advanced new C^{4}I systems and has not been able to modernize its air forces and ground-based air defenses or to develop major amphibious warfare capabilities. Iran is seeking to compensate in part through domestic military production, but as yet, its present defense industry is not producing either the quality or quantity necessary to solve its problems.

OTHER PROBLEMS IN MILITARY MODERNIZATION. Iran's problems in military modernization have been compounded by a number of factors. The vast majority of the combat-trained manpower Iran developed during the Iran-Iraq War left military service by the mid-1990s. Iran now has a largely conscript force with limited military training and little combat experience. The deep divisions between "moderates" and "hard-liners" in Iran's government inevitably politicized the armed forces, which remain under the command of the supreme religious leader, the Ayatollah Khamenei. Iran retained divided armed forces, split between the regular forces that existed under the shah, and the Revolutionary Guards created under the Ayatollah Khomeini. This split was compounded by a highly bureaucratic and "stovepiped" command structure, which made limited progress in joint warfare.

Nevertheless, Iran is still a significant conventional military power by Gulf standards. It has some 540,000 men under arms, and over 350,000 reserves. These include 120,000 Iranian Revolutionary Guards trained for land and naval asymmetric warfare. Iran's military also includes holdings of 1,613 main battle tanks, 1,500 other armored fighting vehicles, 3,200 artillery weapons, 306 combat aircraft, 50 attack helicopters, 3 submarines, 59 surface combatants, and 10 amphibious ships.

The Iranian Army

The Iranian Army is large by regional standards. It has some 350,000 men (220,000 conscripts), organized into four corps, and with a total of four armored divisions, six infantry divisions, two commando divisions, an airborne division, and other smaller independent formations. These latter units include independent armored, infantry, and the six artillery groups of the commando brigades, and army aviation units.

In practice, each Iranian division has a somewhat different organization. For example, only one Iranian division (the 92nd) is equipped well enough in practice to be a true armored division and two of the armored divisions are notably larger than the others. Two of the infantry divisions (the 28th and 84th) are more heavily mechanized than the others.[20] The lighter and smaller formations in the regular army include the 23rd Special Forces Division, which was formed in 1993–94, and the 55th paratroop division. According to one source, the 23rd Special Forces Division has 5,000 full-time regulars and is one of the most professional units in the Iranian Army.

The airborne and special forces are trained at a facility in Shiraz.[21] The regular army also has a number of independent brigades and groups. These include some small armored units, one infantry brigade, one airborne and two to three special forces brigades, coastal defense units, a growing number of air defense groups, five artillery brigades/regiments, four to six army aviation units, and a growing number of logistic and supply formations. The land forces have six major garrisons and 13 major casernes. There is a military academy at Tehran, and a signal-training center in Shiraz.[22]

IRANIAN TANK STRENGTH. Iran has steadily rebuilt its armored strength since the Iran-Iraq War. It has some 1,613 main battle tanks, and the number has risen steadily in recent years. Iran had a total of 1,135 in 2000 and 1,565 in 2003. The IISS estimates that Iran's inventory of main battle tanks now includes some 150 M-47/M-48s and 150–160 M-60A1s, 100 Chieftain Mark 3/5s, 250 T-54/T-55s, 150–250 T-59s 75 T-62s, 480 T-72/T-72Ss, and 100 Zulfiqars. Its T-72 strength has increased from 120 in 2000. (Other estimates indicate that Iran may have as many as 300 Type 59s and/or 150–250 T-69IIs.)

Only part of Iran's tank inventory is fully operational. It is uncertain how many Chieftains and M-47/M-48s are really operational, although its Chieftains include the remainder of 187 improved FV4030/1 versions of the Mark 5 Chieftain that were delivered to Iran before the fall of the shah. Smaller problems seem to exist in the rest of the force, and some experts estimate that Iran's sustainable *operational* tank strength may be fewer than 1,000 tanks. Furthermore, Iran's Chieftains and M-60s are at least 16–20 years old, and the T-72 and Zulfiqar are Iran's only tanks with advanced fire-control systems, sights, and armor-piercing ammunition.

Iran's T-72Ss are export versions of the Soviet T-72B. Some have been built under license in Iran, and are armed with a 125 mm 2A46M smoothbore gun. They have a relatively modern IA40-1 fire-control system and computer, a laser range finder, and a night and day image-intensifying sighting system. The T-72S is powered by an 840-horsepower V-84MS diesel engine and has an upgraded suspension and mine protection and a combat weight of 44.5 tons. Russian sources indicate that Iran has ordered a total of 1,000 T-72s from Russia.

Iran has developed a main battle tank called the Zulfiqar, with a 125 mm smoothbore gun and welded steel turret of Iranian design. According to one report, the Zulfiqar is powered by a V-46-6-12 V-12 diesel engine with 780 horsepower and uses a SPAT 1200 automatic transmission. This engine is used in the Soviet T-72, but the tank transmission design seems to be closer to that of the U.S. M-60. It seems to have a relatively modern fire-control system, and Iran may have improved its T-72s with a similar upgrade. The Zulfiqar's combat weight is reported to be 36 tons, and it is reported to have a maximum speed of 65 kilometers per hour and a power-to-weight ratio of 21.7 horsepower per ton. It has a 7.62 mm coaxial and a 12.7 mm roof-mounted machine gun.[23]

According to some reports, the Zulfiqar uses the Fontana (EFCS)-3-72 Enhanced Fire Control System. Slovenian analysts indicate, however, that the system was exported to Iran via Austria in the mid-1990s, when it was intercepted by Austrian customs. There is the possibility that it was later exported via a third party to Iran or that the former Yugoslavia exported some parts of the former Yugoslav MBT M-84's Fire Control System called SUV-84, which is very similar, at least in outside appearance to the EFCS-3-72 and is produced by factory called Rudi Cajevec that originally was in Bosnia but was evacuated to Serbia at the beginning of the 1990s.

The Zulfiqar uses a modern Slovenia Fontana EFCS-3 computerized fire-control system to provide a fully stabilized fire-on-the-move capability. It may have a roof-mounted laser-warning device, and it could use the same reactive armor system discussed earlier. Roughly 100 Zulifqars seem to be in service.

Iran has extended the life of some of its T-54s, T-55s, and T-59s by improving their armor and fire-control systems and by arming them with an Iranian-made M-68 rifled 105 mm gun similar to the one used on the M-60A1. This weapon seems to be made by the Armament Industries Division of the Iranian Defense Industries Organization. The Revolutionary Guard is reported to have a special conversion of the T-54 called the Safir-74. Iran has developed explosive reactive armor add-ons for its tanks, although the effectiveness of such armor and the extent of such uparmoring of any given model of tank is unclear.

Iran's 168 M-47/M-48s include Iran's surviving upgraded M-47Ms. These M-47s were upgraded by the American firm of Bowen-McLaughlin York between 1970 and 1972. This company also built a vehicle manufacturing plant in Iran. They have many of the components of the M-60A1, including the diesel engine, automatic transmission, suspension, and gun-control and fire components. The conversion extended the operating range of the M-47 from 130 to 600 kilometers and increased space to hold 79 rounds by eliminating the bow-mounted machine gun and reducing the crew to four. A total of about 150 conversions seem to have been delivered to Iran.

In spite of its tank deliveries and production since the Iran-Iraq War, Iran's total operational main battle tank holdings are only sufficient to fully equip five to seven of its divisions by Western standards, and Iran could only sustain about half this force for any period of extended maneuver warfare. At present, however, the tanks are dispersed in relatively small lots among all of its Regular Army and some of its Islamic Revolutionary Guards Corps (IRGC) combat units—all the IRGC units generally only have small tank force cadres, and it is unclear how heavy these forces will really be in the future. The 92nd Armored Division is the only Iranian division that has enough tanks to be a true armored division, even by regional standards.

OTHER IRANIAN ARMOR. Iran seems to have about 1,000 to 1,360 AFVs and APCs in its operational inventory, although counts are contradictory and it is difficult to estimate what parts of Iran's holdings are fully operational and/or sustainable for any length of time in combat. The IISS, for example, estimates 80 light

tanks, 610 armored infantry fighting vehicles, and 640 APCs. Virtually all estimates indicate, however, that Iran only has about half of the total holdings that
it would need to fully mechanize its forces.[24] This total compares with around
3,000 to 3,600 such weapons for Saudi Arabia.

Iran has some 865 AFVs, of which some 650 are active, including 210 BMP-
1s and 400 BMP-2s. This compares with a total of 555 such weapons in 2000,
which then included only 140 BMP-2s. Iran appears to retain 70–80 British-
supplied Scorpions out of the 250 it received before the fall of the shah. These
are tracked weapons equipped with 76 mm guns. However, the Scorpion is
more than 20 years old, and as few as 30 may be fully operational. These problems may explain why Iran has developed a new light tank called the Tosan
(Towsan, "Wild Horse," or "Fury") with a 90 mm gun, some of which may now
be in service.[25]

Iran's BMPs are Soviet-designed systems, but the BMP-1s, in particular, have
serious ergonomic and weapons suite problems. They are hard to fight from,
hard to exit, and too slow to keep pace with modern tanks. They lack thermal
vision systems and modern long-range fire-control systems, and their main
weapons are hard to operate in combat even from static positions. Nevertheless, many have smoothbore antitank guns and guided missiles. Iran also has at
least 35 EE-9 Cascavel ARVs; one estimate indicates it has 100. The Cascavel is
an acceptable design for Third World combat, although it lacks modern sensors and weapons.

Iran is much less well equipped to provide its forces with adequate armored
mobility. It has 550–670 APCs. No more than 600 are operational, and most are
worn and aging BTR-50s and BTR 60s (300–320) or M-113s (230–250) that are
over a quarter of a century old and have not be updated.

Iran is producing an armored fighting vehicle called the Boragh (Boraq) and
a lighter APC called the Cobra or BMT-2. Some 40 to 120 of these are in service, depending on the source of the report. There are different views over
whether such weapons should be classed as AFVs or APCs. The Boragh seems
to be a copy of a Chinese version of the BMP-1. It is a fully tracked and amphibious and has a combat weight of 13 tons. It can carry 8–12 people, plus 2 crew.
Reports differ as to its armament—perhaps reflecting different variants. Initial
reports indicated that it has a turret armed with a 73 mm smoothbore gun and
antitank guided-missile launcher. It may, however, lack the commander's position that exists in the BMP-1 and be armed with a 12.7 mm machine gun. Iran
has developed an armor package designed to fit over the hull of the Boragh to
provide protection against 30 mm armor-piercing ammunition.[26] Variants with
120 mm mortars, one-man turrets with Iranian-made Toophan ATGMs, and

AT-4 ATGMs, and others with 73 mm BMP-2 turrets guns also seem to be deploying.

The Cobra or BMT-2 is clearly an APC. It is a low profile, wheeled troop carrier, which can hold seven people. Some versions may have twin 23 mm AA guns.

Iran has an unknown number of British Chieftain bridging tanks, a wide range of specialized armored vehicles, and some heavy equipment transporters. It is steadily improving its ability to support armored operations in the field and to provide recovery and field-repair capability. However, its exercises reveal that these capabilities are still limited relative to those of U.S. forces and that a lack of recovery and field-repair capability, coupled with poor interoperability, will probably seriously limit the cohesion, speed, and sustainability of Iranian armored operations.

Iran's armored warfare doctrine seems to be borrowed from U.S., British, and Russian sources without achieving any coherent concept of operations. Even so, Iran's armored doctrine is improving more quickly than its organization and exercise performance. Iran's armored forces are very poorly structured, and Iran's equipment pool is spread between far too many regular and IRGC units. Iran has only one armored division—the 92nd Armored Division—with enough tanks and other armor to be considered a true armored unit.

IRANIAN ANTITANK WEAPONS. Iran has large holdings of antitank guided weapons and has been manufacturing copies of Soviet-systems, while buying missiles from China, Russia, and the Ukraine. It has approximately 50–75 TOW and 20–30 Dragon antitank guided-missile launchers that were originally supplied by the United States, although the operational status of such systems is uncertain. It has Soviet and Asian versions of the AT-2, AT-3, AT-4, and AT-5. Iran seems to have between 100 and 200. AT-4 (9K111) launchers, but it is impossible to make an accurate estimate, because Iran is producing its own copies of the AT series called the Towsan. According to some reports it's also making copies of the Dragon (Saeqhe) and TOW (Toophan).

Iran has some 750 RPG-7V, RPG-11, and 3.5-inch rocket launchers, and roughly 150 M-18 57 mm, 200 M-20 75 mm and B-10 82 mm, and 200 M-40 106 mm and B-11 107 mm recoilless guns.

Iran makes a number of antitank weapons. These include an improved version of the man-portable RPG-7 antitank rocket, with an 80 mm tandem HEAT warhead instead of the standard 30 mm design, the NAFEZ antitank rocket, and a copy of the Soviet SPG-9 73 mm recoilless antitank gun. Iran also makes a copy of the Russian AT-3 9M14M (Sagger or Ra'ad) antitank guided missile. This system is a crew-operable system with a guidance system that can be linked to a launcher holding up to four missiles. It has a maximum range of 3,000 meters, a minimum range of 500 meters, and a flight speed of 120 meters per second. Iran is also seeking more advanced technology from Russian arms firms, and some reports indicate it may be able to make copies of the AT-4 and/ or AT-5. The United States maintains that a firm sold Iran Krasnopol artillery shells, although the company denies any connection with Iran.[27] Prospective sanctions are likely to deter arms manufacturers from filling the many needs of the Iranian military.

The Iranian copy of the AT-3 is made by the Shahid Shah Abaday Industrial Group in Tehran. There are reports that it may be an early version of the missile that lacks semiautomatic guidance that allows the operator to simply sight the target, rather than use a joystick to guide the missile to the target, by using the light from the missile to track it. These same reports indicate that the Iranian version seems to have a maximum armored-penetration capability of 500 mm, which is not enough to penetrate the forward armor of the latest Western and Russian main battle tanks.

Russia has, however, refitted most of its systems to semiautomatic line-of-sight guidance and with tandem warheads capable of penetrating 800 mm. Iran may have or be acquiring such capabilities, which would significantly improve the lethality of its antiarmor forces. Recent reporting on Iranian arms transfers to Lebanon indicates that it does have AT-3s with advanced guidance systems and either an advanced Russian warhead or one designed by Raad engineers in Iran.[28]

IRANIAN ARTILLERY STRENGTH. Iran has some 3,000 to 3,200 operational medium and heavy artillery weapons and multiple-rocket launchers and some 5,000 mortars. Its towed artillery consists largely of effective Soviet designs. Its self-propelled artillery includes 60 2S1 122 mm weapons and some Iranian copies. It has some 180 aging M-109 155 mm weapons and is seeking to produce its own weapons as part of the Thunder series. It has some 60 aging 170 mm, 165 mm, and 203 mm weapons. Iran also has large numbers of multiple rocket launchers, including some 700 107 mm weapons, 150–200 122 mm weapons, 20-odd 240 mm weapons, and some 333 mm weapons. It manufactures its own multiple-rocket launchers, including the long-range Fajr series.

This total is very high by regional standards and reflects Iran's continuing effort to build up artillery strength that began during the Iran-Iraq War. Iran used artillery to support its infantry and IRGC in their attacks on Iraqi forces. It had to use artillery as a substitute for armor and airpower during much of the Iran-Iraq War and generally used relatively static massed fires. However,

Iran's reliance on towed artillery and slow-moving, multiple-rocket launchers limits Iran's combined arms maneuver capabilities, and it has failed to develop effective night and beyond-visual-range targeting capability.

Some 2,085 of Iran's weapons are towed tube artillery weapons, versus 310 self-propelled tube weapons and 700 to 900 vehicle-mounted or towed multiple-rocket launchers. Iran's holdings of self-propelled weapons still appear to include a substantial number of U.S.-supplied systems, including 25–30 M-110 203-mm howitzers, 20–30 M-107 175-mm guns, and 130–150 M-109 155-mm howitzers. These U.S.-supplied weapons are worn, have not been modernized in over 15 years, and lack modern fire-control systems and artillery radars. Many lack sustainability, and a number may not be operational.

Iran understands that it has less than a quarter of the self-propelled artillery it needs to properly support its present force structure, and that maneuverable artillery is critical to success in dealing with Iraqi and other maneuver forces. It is attempting to compensate for the resulting lack of modern artillery and artillery mobility by replacing its U.S. self-propelled weapons with other self-propelled systems. Iran has purchased 60–80 Soviet 2S1 122-mm self-propelled howitzers and has developed an Iranian-made design called the Raad (Thunder 1) and Raad (Thunder 2). The Thunder 1 is a 122-mm weapon similar to Russian designs. The Thunder 2 is a "rapid-fire" 155-mm self-propelled weapon. Both systems are now in deployment.

Iran bought large numbers of mortars during the Iran-Iraq War for the same reasons it bought large numbers of towed tube artillery weapons. Iran has some 5,000 such weapons. These include 107-mm and 120-mm heavy mortars and 800-900 81-mm and 82-mm mortars. Iran mounts at least several hundred of its heavy mortars on armored vehicles.

Iran's emphasis on massed, static area fire is also indicated by its possession of 700–900 multiple-rocket launchers. It is difficult to estimate Iran's inventory in these, but its holdings include roughly 10 M-1989 240-mm multiple-rocket launchers, 500–700 Chinese Type 63 and Iranian Haseb and Fadjir-1 107–mm multiple-rocket launchers, and more than 100 Soviet BM-21, Soviet BM-11 122-mm launchers.

Iran has produced its own multiple-rocket launchers. These include some 50 122-mm, 40-round Hadid rocket-launcher systems. In addition, Iran is producing variants of Chinese and Russian 122-mm rockets called the Arash and Noor. The Iranian state television announced the production of the DM-3b seeker for the Noor. The DM-3b is an active radar sensor that is used in the final stages of flight to acquire and home in on ship targets. A joint program between Iran's Aerospace Industries Organization (AID) and the China

Aerospace Science and Industry Corp developed the Noor.[29] The Falaq 1 and 2 series are examples of vehicle-mounted unguided rocket systems in the Iranian arsenal. The Falaq 1 fires a 240-mm rocket with 50 kilograms of explosives and can reach a target up to 10 kilometers away. The Falaq 2 is slightly larger, carries 10 more kilograms of explosives, and flies almost a full kilometer further.[30]

Iran's land forces operate a number of Iranian-made long-range unguided rockets, including the Shahin 1 and 2, Oghab, and Nazeat. They also include some 10 large 240-mm artillery rockets, with a range of up to 40–43 kilometers, called the Fadjr 3. The key longer-range systems seem to include:

- The Shahin 1 (sometimes called the Fadjr 4) is a trailer-launched 333-mm caliber unguided artillery rocket. Two rockets are normally mounted on each trailer; these have a solid-propelled rocket motor, a maximum range of 75 kilometers, and a 175-kg conventional or chemical warhead. The Shahin evidently can be equipped with three types of warheads: a 180 kilogram high-explosive warhead, a warhead using high-explosive submunitions, and a warhead that uses chemical weapons. There is a truck-mounted version, called the Fajr 5, with a rack of four rockets. A larger Shanin 2, with a range of 20 kilometers, is also deployed.

- The Fadjr-3 is a truck-mounted system with a 12-round launcher for 240-mm rockets. It has a maximum range of 43 kilometers, and a 45-kilogram payload in its warhead.

- The Fadjr-5 is truck-mounted 333-mm-caliber unguided artillery rocket with a solid-propelled rocket motor, a maximum range of 75 kilometers, and a 175-kg conventional or chemical warhead. It carries four rockets, which evidently can be equipped with three types of warheads: a kilogram high-explosive warhead, a warhead using high-explosive submunitions, and a warhead that uses chemical weapons.

- The Oghab is a 320 mm-caliber unguided artillery rocket that is spin stabilized in flight, has a maximum range of 34 kilometers, and a 70-kg high-explosive fragmentation warhead, although chemical warheads may be available. While it may have a chemical warhead, it has an operational Command Experience Point (CEP) that has proved to be in excess of 500 meters at maximum range. Further, Iran has no way to target accurately the Oghab or any other long-range missile against mobile or point targets at long ranges, other than a limited ability to use RPVs.

- The Nazeat is a TEL-launched system with conventional and possibly chemical and biological warheads. The full details of this system remain unclear, but it seems to be based on Chinese technology and uses a solid fuel rocket, with a simple inertial guidance system. Nazeat units are equipped with communications vans, meteorological vans, and a global-positioning system for surveying the launch site. Some reports indicate there are two variants of the Nazeat solid-fueled rocket system—a 355.6 mm-caliber rocket, with a 105 kilometers range and a 150-kilogram warhead, and a 450 mm-caliber rocket, with a reported range of 130–150 kilometers and a 250-kilogram warhead. Both systems have maximum closing velocities of Mach 4–5, but both also appear to suffer from poor reliability and accuracy. Other reports indicate that all Nazeats are 335.6 mm and that there are four versions of progressively larger size, with ranges from 80 to 120 kilometers. It is claimed to have a CEP within 5 percent of its range.

- The Zelzal 2 is a 610-mm long-range rocket, with a warhead with a 600-kilogram payload and a maximum range of up to 210 kilometers. A single rocket is mounted on a launcher on a truck. It is unguided, but is spin stabilized and is claimed to have a CEP within 5 percent of its range.

- The Fateh A-110 is a developmental system believed to be similar to the Chinese CSS-8, which is a surface-to-surface system derived from the Russian SA-2 surface-to-air missile.[31]

Iran has only limited artillery fire-control and battle management systems, counterbattery radar capability, and long-range target acquisition capability (although it does have some RPVs) to support its self-propelled weapons. Iran has actively sought more modern fire-control and targeting systems since the mid-1980s. It has had some success in deploying and testing RPVs as targeting systems and has obtained some additional counterbattery radars, but it is unclear how many it obtained or put in service.

Iran has transferred large numbers of Fadjr rockets to the Hezbollah in Lebanon.[32]

IRANIAN SURFACE-TO-SURFACE MISSILES. Iran continues to deploy surface-to-surface missiles and has its own systems in development. The number assigned to the army versus the IRGC is unclear, but this force, rather than the Regular Army, seems to hold and operate most long-range missiles. Iran seems to have some 12–18 Scud B/C launchers and 250–350 missiles as well as 30 land-based CSS-8 launchers, with 175 missiles. Iran refers to the Scud-B as the Shahab-1 and the Scud C as the Shahab-2.

Iran's Scud B Missiles. The Soviet-designed Scud B (17E) guided missile currently forms the core of Iran's ballistic missile forces:

- Iran acquired its Scuds in response to Iraq's invasion. It obtained a limited number from Libya and then obtained larger numbers from North Korea.

It deployed these units with a special Khatam ol-Anbya force attached to the air element of the Pasdaran. Iran fired its first Scuds in March 1985, firing as many as 14 Scuds in that year, 8 in 1986, 18 in 1987, and 77 in 1988. Iran fired 77 Scud missiles during a 52-day period in 1988, during what came to be known as the "war of the cities." Sixty-one were fired at Baghdad, nine at Mosul, five at Kirkuk, one at Tikrit, and one at Kuwait. Iran fired as many as five missiles on a single day and once fired three missiles within 30 minutes. This still, however, worked out to an average of only about one missile a day, and Iran was down to only 10–20 Scuds when the war of the cities ended.

- Iran's missile attacks were initially more effective than Iraq's attacks. This was largely a matter of geography. Many of Iraq's major cities were comparatively close to its border with Iran, but Tehran and most of Iran's major cities, that had not already been targets in the war, were outside the range of Iraqi Scud attacks. Iran's missiles, in contrast, could hit key Iraqi cities like Baghdad. This advantage ended when Iraq deployed extended-range Scuds.

- The Scud B is a relatively old Soviet design that first became operational in 1967, designated as the R-17E, or R-300E. The Scud B has a range of 290–300 kilometers with its normal conventional payload. The export version of the missile is about 11 meters long and 85–90 centimeters in diameter and weighs 6,300 kilograms. It has a nominal CEP of 1,000 meters. The Russian versions can be equipped with conventional high-explosive, fuel-air-explosive, runway penetrator, submunition, chemical, and nuclear warheads.

- The export version of the Scud B comes with a conventional high-explosive warhead weighing about 1,000 kilograms, of which 800 kilograms are the high-explosive payload and 200 are the warhead structure and fusing system. It has a single-stage storable liquid rocket engine and is usually deployed on the MAZ-543 eight-wheel transporter-erector-launcher (TEL). It has a strap-down inertial-guidance system, using three gyros to correct its ballistic trajectory, and uses internal graphite jet vane steering. The warhead hits at a velocity above Mach 1.5.

- Most estimates indicate that Iran now has 6–12 Scud launchers and up to 200 Scud B (R-17E) missiles, with a 230–310 kilometer range.

- Some estimates give higher figures. They estimate Iran bought 200–300 Scud Bs from North Korea between 1987 and 1992 and may have continued to buy such missiles after that time. Israeli experts estimate that Iran had some 250–300 Scud B missiles, and some 8–15 launchers on hand in 1997.

- U.S. experts also believe that Iran can now manufacture virtually all of the Scud B elements, with the possible exception of the most-sophisticated components of its guidance system and rocket motors. This makes it difficult to estimate how many missiles Iran has in inventory and can acquire over time, as well as to estimate the precise performance characteristics of Iran's missiles, because it can alter the weight of the warhead, adjust the burn time and improve the efficiency of the rocket motors.

Iran's Scud C Missiles. Iran also has longer-range North Korean Scuds, with ranges near 500 kilometers. According to some reports, Iran has created shelters and tunnels in its coastal areas that it could use to store Scuds and other missiles in hardened sites to reduce their vulnerability to air attack.

- The North Korean missile system is often referred to as a "Scud C." Typically, Iran formally denied the fact it had such systems long after the transfer of these missiles became a fact. Hassan Taherian, an Iranian foreign ministry official, stated in February 1995, "There is no missile cooperation between Iran and North Korea whatsoever. We deny this."[33]

- In fact, a senior North Korean delegation traveled to Tehran to close the deal on November 29, 1990, and met with Mohsen Rezaei, the former commander of the IRGC. Iran either bought the missile then or placed its order shortly thereafter. North Korea then exported the missile through its Lyongaksan Import Corporation. Iran imported some of these North Korean missile assemblies using its B-747s, and seems to have used ships to import others.

- Iran probably had more than 60 of the longer-range North Korean missiles by 1998, although other sources report 100, and one source reports 170.

- Iran may have 5–10 Scud C launchers, each with several missiles. This total seems likely to include four new North Korean TELs received in 1995.

- Iran seems to want enough missiles and launchers to make its missile force highly dispersible.

- Iran has begun to test its new North Korean missiles. There are reports it has fired them from mobile launchers at a test site near Qom about 310 miles (500 kilometers) to a target area south of Shahroud. There are also reports that units equipped with such missiles have been deployed as part of Iranian exercises like the Saeqer-3 (Thunderbolt 3) exercise in late October 1993.

- The missile is more advanced than the Scud B, although many aspects of its performance are unclear. North Korea seems to have completed development of the missile in 1987, after obtaining technical support from the People's Republic of China. While it is often called a "Scud C," it seems to differ substantially in detail from the original Soviet Scud B. It seems to be based more on the Chinese-made DF-61 than on a direct copy of the Soviet weapon.

- Experts estimate that the North Korean missiles have a range of around 310 miles (500 kilometers), a warhead with a high-explosive payload of 700 kg, and relatively good accuracy and reliability. While this payload is a bit limited for the effective delivery of chemical agents, Iran might modify the warhead to increase payload at the expense of range and restrict the using of chemical munitions to the most lethal agents such as persistent nerve gas. It might also concentrate its development efforts on arming its Scud C forces with more lethal biological agents. In any case, such missiles are likely to have enough range-payload to give Iran the ability to strike all targets on the southern coast of the Gulf and all of the populated areas in Iraq, although not the West. Iran could also reach targets in part of eastern Syria, the eastern third of Turkey, and cover targets in the border area of the former Soviet Union, western Afghanistan, and western Pakistan.

- Accuracy and reliability remain major uncertainties, as does operational CEP. Much would also depend on the precise level of technology Iran deployed in the warhead. Neither Russia nor the People's Republic of China seems to have transferred the warhead technology for biological and chemical weapons to Iran or Iraq when they sold them the Scud B missile and CSS-8. However, North Korea may have sold Iran such technology as part of the Scud C sale. If it did so, such a technology transfer would save Iran years of development and testing in obtaining highly lethal biological and chemical warheads. In fact, Iran would probably be able to deploy far more effective biological and chemical warheads than Iraq had at the time of the Gulf War.

- Iran may be working with Syria in such development efforts, although Middle Eastern nations rarely cooperate in such sensitive areas. Iran served as a transshipment point for North Korean missile deliveries during 1992 and 1993. Some of this transshipment took place using the same Iranian B-747s that brought missile parts to Iran. Others moved by sea. For example, a North Korean vessel called the *Des Hung Ho*, bringing missile parts for Syria, docked at Bandar Abbas in May, 1992. Iran then flew these parts to Syria. An Iranian ship coming from North Korea, with a second North Korean ship following, carried missiles and machine tools for both Syria and Iran. At least 20 of the North Korean missiles have gone to Syria from Iran, and production equipment seems to have been transferred to Iran and to Syrian plants near Hama and Aleppo.

- Iran can now assemble Scud B and Scud C missiles using foreign-made components. It may soon be able to make entire missile systems and warhead packages in Iran.

Iran's Shahab Missiles. Iran's new Shahab-3 (Shahab, Sehob) series is a much larger missile that seems to be based on the design of the North Korean No Dong 1 or A and No Dong B missile, which some analysts claim were developed with Iranian financial support. It is based on North Korean designs and technology, but is developed and produced in Iran. This development effort is controlled and operated by the IRGC.

The Shahab-3 is a single-stage, liquid-fueled missile. It is road mobile and is believed to be 16 meters long and 1.32 meters in diameter and to have a launch weight of 16,250 kilograms. Iran has discussed payloads using submunitions, but it seems more likely to be designed to carry a chemical, nuclear, or biological weapon.[34]

Its range-payload, accuracy, and reliability are matters of speculation. Its nominal range is believed to be 1,300 kilometers—long enough to hit virtually any target in the Gulf as well as Israel—and its payload to be 1,000–1,200 kilograms. It can carry a warhead with a 550–700 kilogram payload. An analysis by John Pike of Global Security points out,[35] however, that missiles—like combat aircraft—can make trade-offs between range and payload. For example, the No Dong B has a range of 1,560 kilometers with a 760-kilogram warhead and 1,350 kilometers with a 1,158-kilogram warhead.

The Shahab-3 may now be in deployment, but possibly only in "test-bed" units. Some reports have claimed it was operational as early as 1999. Other reports have claimed that development of the Shahab-3 was completed in June 2003 and that it underwent "final" tests on July 7, 2003. However, the Shahab-3 underwent a total of only nine tests from inception through late 2003, and only four of them could be considered successful in terms of basic system performance. The missile's design characteristics also continued to evolve during these tests. A CIA report to Congress,[36] dated November 10, 2003, indicated that upgrading of the Shahab-3 was still under way, and some sources indicate that Iran is now seeking a range of 1,600 kilometers.

Iran conducted further major Shahab-3 tests on August 11, 2004, deploying it with a new, smaller, and "bottle neck" warhead. This kind of warhead has a slower reentry than a cone-shaped warhead and has advantages using warheads containing chemical and biological agents. Another test took place on September 19, 2004, and the missile was paraded on September 21st covered in banners saying, "We will crush America under our feet" and "Wipe Israel off the map."[37]

Nasser Maleki, the head of Iran's aerospace industry, stated on October 7, 2004, that, "Very certainly we are going to improve our Shahab-3 and all of our other missiles." Tehran also claimed in September that the Shahab-3 could now reach targets up to 2,000 kilometers away, presumably allowing the missiles to be deployed a greater distance away from Israel's Air Force and Jericho-2 ballistic missiles.[38] IRGC political bureau chief, Yadollah Javani, stated that the Shahab-3 could be used to attack Israel's Dimona nuclear reactor.[39]

Iran performed another test on October 20, 2004, and this time Iran's defense minister, Ali Shamkani, claimed it was part of an exercise. On November 9, 2004, he also claimed that Iran was now capable of mass producing the Shahab-3 and that Iran reserved the option of preemptive strikes in defense of its nuclear sites. Shamkani also claimed shortly afterward that the Shahab 3 now had a range of more than 2,000 kilometers (1,250 miles).[40]

Since that time, the Mojahedin Khalq Organization (MEK) has claimed that Iran is developing a version of the Shahab with a 2,400-kilometer range (1,500 miles). Mortezar Ramandi, an official in the Iranian delegation to the UN, has denied that Iran is developing a missile with a range of more than 1,250 miles (2,000 kilometers); the MEK has an uncertain record of accuracy in making such claims, and they cannot be confirmed in this case.[41]

Discussions of the Shahab-3's accuracy and reliability are largely speculative. If the system used older guidance technology and warhead separation methods, its CEP could be anywhere from 1,000–4,000 meters. If it uses newer technology, such as some of the most advanced Chinese technology, it could have a CEP as low as 250–800 meters. In any case, such CEP data are engineering estimates, and missile accuracy and reliability cannot be measured using technical terms like CEP, which are based on simulations and models, not tests. Such tests assume the missile can be perfectly targeted at launch and performs perfectly through its final guidance phase and then somewhat arbitrarily define CEP as the accuracy of 50 percent of the systems launched. True performance can only be derived from observing reliability under operational conditions and correlating actual point of impact to a known aim point.

As is the case with virtually all unclassified estimates of missile performance, the estimates of accuracy and CEP available from public sources are matters of speculation, and no such source has credibility in describing performance in real-world, war-fighting terms. This is not a casual problem, since actual weaponization of a warhead requires extraordinarily sophisticated systems to detonate a warhead at the desired height of burst and to reliably disseminate the munitions or agent. Even the most sophisticated conventional submunitions are little more than area weapons if the missile accuracy and target location has errors in excess of 250–500 meters, and a unitary conventional explosive warhead without terminal guidance is little more than a psychological or terror weapon almost regardless of its CEP.

The effective delivery of chemical agents by either spreading the agent or the use of submunitions generally requires accuracies under 1,000 meters to achieve lethality against even large point targets. Systems with biological weapons are inherently area weapons, but a 1,000-kilogram nominal warhead can carry so little agent that accuracies under 1,000 meters again become desirable. Nuclear weapons require far less accuracy, particularly if a "dirty" ground burst can be targeted within a reliable fallout area. There are, however, limits. For example, a regular fission weapon of some 20 kilotons requires accuracies under 2,500–3,000 meters for some kinds of targets like sheltered airfields or large energy facilities.

The CIA report, dated November 10, 2003, also reported that the Islamic Republic was developing a "Shahab-4" ballistic missile with a range of 2,000 kilometers and possibly up to 3,000 kilometers with a small warhead. Such a missile could reach targets in Europe and virtually any target in the Middle East.

Various experts have claimed that the Shahab-4 is based on the North Korean No Dong 2 or three-stage Taepodong-1 missile, or even some aspects of the Russian SS-4, but that it has a modern digital guidance package rather than the 2,000–3,000 meter CEP of early missiles like the SS-4. Russian firms are believed to have sold Iran special steels for missile development, test equipment, shielding for guidance packages, and other technology. Iran's Shahid Hemmet Industrial Group is reported to have contracts with the Russian Central Aerohydrodynamic Institute, Rosvoorouzhenie, the Bauman Institute, and Polyus. It is also possible that Iran has obtained some technology from Pakistan.

There have also been Israeli reports of an Iranian effort to create a Shahab-5, with a 4,900–5,000 kilometer range. These reports remain uncertain, and Israeli media and official sources have repeatedly exaggerated the nature and speed of Iranian efforts.

The Iranian government stated as early as 1999 that it was developing such a large missile body or launch vehicle for satellite launch purposes, however, and repeatedly denied that it is upgrading the Shahab-3 for military purposes. Iran also continued to claim that the program that the West refers to as "Shahab-4" is a program aimed at developing a booster rocket for launching satellites into space. In January 2004, Iran's defense minister claimed that Iran would launch a domestically built satellite within 18 months.[42]

As of December 2004, some U.S. intelligence experts were firmly convinced that Iran was aggressively seeking to develop a nuclear warhead for the Shahab series. They mentioned that Iran was actively working on the physic package for such a warhead design and cited Secretary of State Colin Powell's warning on November 17, 2004, that Iran was working on such developments. Powell had stated that Iran was "actively working on (nuclear delivery) systems. . . . You don't have a weapon until you put it in something that can deliver a weapon."[43] U.S. officials stated that this information did not come from Iranian opposition sources like the MEK.

Iranian Army Air Defense Systems. Iranian land forces have a total of some 1,700 antiaircraft guns, including 14.5 mm ZPU-2/4s, 23 mm ZSU-23-4s and ZU-23s, 35 mm M-1939s, 37 mm Type 55s, and 57 mm ZSU-57-2s. Iran also has 100-180 Bofors L/70 40 mm guns and moderate numbers of Skyguard 35 mm twin anti-aircraft guns (many of which may not be operational). Its largest holdings consist of unguided ZU-23-2s (which it can manufacture) and M-1939s.

It is unclear how many of these systems are really operational as air defense weapons, and most would have to be used to provide very short-range "curtain fire" defense of small point targets. They would not be lethal against a modern aircraft using an air-to-ground missile or a laser-guided weapon. The only notable exception is the ZSU-23-4 radar-guided antiaircraft gun. Iran has 50–100 fully operational ZSU-23-4s. The weapon is short ranged and vulnerable to electronic countermeasures (ECM) but is far more lethal than Iran's unguided guns.

Iran has large numbers of SA-7 (Strela 2M), and SA-14 (Strela) man-portable surface-to-air missiles, and some SA-16s and HN-5/HQ-5 man-portable surface-to-air missiles. It had some U.S.-made Stinger man-portable surface-to-air missiles it bought from Afghan rebels, but these may no longer be operational or may have been used for reverse engineering purposes. Iran also has some RBS-70 low-level surface-to-air missiles and seems to be producing some version of the SA-7, perhaps with Chinese assistance. It is not clear whether Iran can do this in any large number. Iran's land-based air defense forces are also acquiring growing numbers of Chinese FM-80s, a Chinese variant of the French-designed Crotale.

Iranian Army Aviation. Iran pioneered the regional use of army aviation and attack helicopters during the time of the shah, but it built up its holdings of helicopters far more quickly than it expanded its training and maintenance capability. As a result, it had a hollow force at the time the shah fell. Its inability since that time to obtain adequate spare parts and help in modernizing the air-craft has long made Iranian operational helicopter holdings uncertain.

The Iranian Army seems to retain 50 AH-1J Sea Cobra attack helicopters and 20 CH-47C, 110–130 Bell-214A, 30–35 AB-214C, 35–40 AB-205A, 10 AB-206, and 25 Mi-8/Mi-27 transport and utility helicopters. There are also reports that it signed orders for 4 Mi-17s in 1999 and 30 Mi-8s in 2001.

These Western-supplied transport and support helicopters have low operational readiness and little sustained sortie capability.

Iran is also seeking to create a significant RPV force that borrows in many ways from Israeli technical developments and doctrine. It has produced some such RPVs, such as the Mohajer series—and several exercise reports refer to their use. It has sold some of these systems to the Hezbollah, but insufficient data are available to assess this aspect of Iranian capabilities.

IRANIAN ARMY COMMAND, CONTROL, COMMUNICATIONS, COMPUTERS, AND INTELLIGENCE (C^4I). Iranian Army communications have improved, as have Iranian battle management and communications exercises. They are now capable of better coordination between branches, the density of communications equipment has improved, and the functional lines of communication and command now place more emphasis on maneuver, quick reaction, and combined arms. However, Iranian battle management and communications capabilities seem to remain relatively limited.

Iran's holdings still consist largely of aging VHF radio with some HF and UHF capability. This equipment cannot handle high-traffic densities, and secure communications are poor. Iran still relies heavily on analog data handling and manually switched telephone systems. It is, however, acquiring a steadily growing number of Chinese and Western encryption systems and some digital voice, fax, and telex encryption capability.

OTHER ASPECTS OF IRANIAN ARMY CAPABILITY. Iran's Army has improved its organization, doctrine, training, and equipment for land-force operations. Iran still, however, is a slow-moving force, with limited armored maneuver capability and artillery forces better suited to static defense and the use of mass fires than the efficient use of rapidly switched and well-targeted fire. Sustainability is limited, as is field recovery and repair capability. Overall manpower quality is mediocre because of a lack of adequate realistic training and a heavy reliance on conscripts.

The army has some capability for power projection and armored maneuver warfare, but it does not train seriously for long-range maneuver and does little training for amphibious warfare or deployment by sea. Its logistics, maintenance, and sustainment system is largely defensive and designed to support Iranian forces in defending Iran from local bases. It does not practice difficult amphibious operations, particularly "across the beach" operations. It could, however, deploy into Kuwait and cross the border into Iraq. It can also move at least brigade-sized mechanize units across the Gulf by amphibious ship and ferry, if it does not meet significant naval and air opposition to any such movement. It lacks the air strength and naval air and missile defense capabilities to be able to defend such an operation.

The Islamic Revolutionary Guards Corps (Pasdaran)

The Iranian Revolutionary Guards add some 120,000 additional men to Iran's forces. Roughly 100,000 are ground forces, including many conscripts. There is a large naval branch, and a small air branch. Estimates of its equipment strength are highly uncertain. The IISS estimates that it has some 470 tanks, 620 APCs, 360 artillery weapons, 40 multiple-rocket launchers, and 150 air defense guns, but these estimates are now several years old.

The naval branch has some 20,000 men. According to the IISS, this total includes Iran's marine force of some 5,000 men and a combat strength of one brigade. Other sources show this force subordinated to the Navy. It has at least 40 light patrol boats, 10 Houdong guided-missile patrol boats armed with C-802 antiship missiles, and a battery of HY-2 Seersucker land-based antiship missiles. It has bases in the Gulf, many near key shipping channels and some near the Strait of Hormuz. These include facilities at Al-Farsiyah, Halul (an oil platform), Sirri, Abu Musa, Bandar Abbas, Khorramshahr, and Larak. It also controls Iran's coastal defense forces, including naval guns and an HY-3 Seersucker land-based antiship missile unit deployed in five to seven sites along the Gulf coast.

These forces can carry out extensive raids against Gulf shipping, can carry out regular amphibious exercises with the land branch of the IRGC against objectives like the islands in the Gulf, and could conduct raids against Saudi Arabia or other countries on the Southern Gulf coast. They give Iran a major capability for asymmetric warfare. The Guards also seem to work closely with Iranian intelligence and to be represented unofficially in some embassies, Iranian businesses and purchasing offices, and other foreign fronts.

IRGC elements do seem to run training camps inside Iran for outside "volunteers." Some 400 IRGC personnel seem to be deployed in Lebanon and actively involved in training and arming the Hezbollah, other anti-Israeli groups, and other elements.[44] The IRGC has been responsible for major arms shipments to the Hezbollah, including large numbers of AT-3 antitank guided missiles, long-range rockets, and some Iranian-made Mohajer UAVs.[45] Some reports indicate Iran has sent thousands of 122 mm rockets and Fajr 4 and Fajr 5 long-range rockets, including the ARASH, which has a range of 21–29 kilometers. These reports give the Fajr 5 a range of 75 kilometers with a payload of 200 kilograms. Iran seems to have sent arms to various Palestinian movements, including some shiploads of arms to the Palestinian Authority.[46]

As has been touched on earlier, the air branch is believed to operate Iran's three Shahab-3 IRBM units and may have had custody of its chemical weapons and any biological weapons. While the actual operational status of the Shahab-3 remains uncertain, Iran's supreme leader, Ayatollah Ali Khamenei, announced in 2003 that Shahab-3 missiles had been delivered to the Islamic Revolutionary Guards Corps. In addition, six Shahab-3s were displayed in Tehran during a military parade in September 2003.[47]

Sources differ sharply on the organization of the IRGC, and its combat formations seem to be much smaller than the title implies, and to differ sharply from unit to unit. The IISS reports a strength of 2 armored, 5 mechanized, 10 infantry, and 1 Special Forces division, plus 15–20 independent brigades, including some armed and paratroop units. In practice, its manning would support three to five real divisions, and many of its divisions have an active strength equivalent to large brigades.

The IRGC has a complex structure that is both political and military. It has separate organizational elements for its land, naval, and air units, which include both military and paramilitary units. The Basij and the tribal units of the Pasdaran are subordinated to its land-unit command, although the commander of the Basij often seems to report directly to the commander in chief and minister of the Pasdaran and through him to the leader of the Islamic Revolution. The IRGC has close ties to the foreign operations branch of the Iranian Ministry of Intelligence and Security (MOIS), particularly through the IRGC's Qods force. The Ministry of Intelligence and Security, which was established in 1983, has an extensive network of offices in Iranian embassies. It is often difficult to separate the activities of the IRGC, Vezarat-e Etteláat Va Amniat-e Keshvar (VEVAK) or Ministry of Intelligence, and Foreign Ministry, and many seem to be integrated operations managed by a ministerial committee called the "Special Operations Council," which includes the leader of the Islamic Revolution, president, minister of intelligence and security, and other members of the Supreme Council for National Defense.[48]

The IRGC's growing involvement in Iran's military industries, and its lead role in Iran's efforts to acquire surface-to-surface missiles and weapons of mass destruction, give it growing experience with advanced military technology. As a result, the IRGC is believed to be the branch of Iran's forces that plays the largest role in Iran's military industries.[49] It also operates all of Iran's

Scuds, controls most its chemical and biological weapons, and provides the military leadership for missile production and the production of all weapons of mass destruction.

The IRGC plays a major role in internal security. Nevertheless, it seems best to treat the IRGC primarily as a military land force that parallels the Iranian Regular Army and that would operate with it in most contingencies. As has been discussed earlier, the IRGC has been placed under an integrated command with Iran's regular armed forces at the general staff level. It retains an independent command chain below this level, however, and generally continues to exercise as an independent force. It rarely exercises with the regular Iranian Army—and then usually in large, set piece exercises, which do not require close cooperation.[50]

It is difficult to estimate the proficiency of IRGC units. It seems likely, however, that they vary sharply by unit and that only a portion of the IRGC land forces are intended to participate in joint operations with the regular army in regular combat. These forces seem to have improved steadily in their training, organization, and discipline since the early 1990s and have also expanded their joint training with the Regular Army, Navy, and Air Force.

The IRGC would probably be capable of providing an extensive defense capability in the event of any invasion of Iran. This force is also light enough so that units could rapidly deploy as "volunteers" to Iraq or any Southern Gulf country where they could obtain local support and access to a seaport or airport. It seems likely that they could move into a country like Iraq in significant force—at least several brigade equivalents and possibly at the division level—if they were invited to do so by some friendly faction. They could also infiltrate in significant numbers. It seems unlikely that the IRGC could deploy and sustain more than a force of several brigades if it were invited into a secure port by some Southern Gulf faction and were not opposed by air and sea. They could certainly mount a significant attack on any island or offshore facility in the Gulf, and covertly or overtly introduce large numbers of free-floating or bottom mines into any shipping channel.

The Quds (Qods) Forces. The IRGC has a large intelligence operations and unconventional warfare component. Roughly 5,000 of the men in the IRGC are assigned to the unconventional warfare mission. The IRGC has the equivalent of one Special Forces "division," plus additional smaller formations, and these forces are given special priority in terms of training and equipment. In addition, the IRGC has a special Quds force, which plays a major role in giving Iran the ability to conduct unconventional warfare overseas, using various foreign movements as proxies. This force is under the command of Gen. Ahmad Wahidi, who used to head the information department in the IRGC General Command and had the mission of exporting the revolution.[51]

The budget for the Quds forces is classified and is directly controlled by Khamenei. It is not reflected in the Iranian general budget. The force operates primarily outside Iran's borders, although it has bases inside and outside of Iran. The Quds troops are divided into specific groups, or "corps," for each country or area in which they operate. There are directorates for Iraq; Lebanon, Palestine, and Jordan; Afghanistan, Pakistan, and India; Turkey; the Arabian Peninsula; the Asiatic republics of the FSU; Western Nations (Europe and North America); and North Africa (Egypt, Tunisia, Algeria, Sudan, and Morocco).

The Quds has offices or "sections" in many Iranian embassies that are closed to most embassy staff. It is not clear whether these are integrated with Iranian intelligence operations or that the ambassador in such embassies has control of, or detailed knowledge of, operations by the Quds staff. However, there are indications that most operations are coordinated between the IRGC and offices within the Iranian Foreign Ministry and MOIS. There are separate operational organizations in Lebanon, Turkey, Pakistan, and several North African countries. There also are indications that such elements may have participated in the bombings of the Israeli embassy in Argentina in 1992 and the Jewish Community Center in Buenos Aires in 1994—although Iran has strongly denied this.[52]

The Quds force seems to control many of Iran's training camps for unconventional warfare, extremists, and terrorists in Iran and countries like the Sudan and Lebanon. It has at least four major training facilities in Iran. The Quds forces have a main training center at Imam Ali University that is based in the Sa'dabad Palace in Northern Tehran. Troops are trained to carry out military and terrorist operations and are indoctrinated in ideology. There are other training camps in the Qom, Tabriz, and Mashhad governorates as well as in Lebanon and the Sudan. These include the Al Nasr camp for training Iraqi Shiites and Iraqi and Turkish Kurds in northwest Iran, and a camp near Mashhad for training Afghan and Tajik revolutionaries. The Quds seems to help operate the Manzariyah training center near Qom, which recruits from foreign students in the religious seminary and which seems to have trained some Bahraini extremists. Some foreigners are reported to have received training in demolition and sabotage at an IRGC facility near Esfahan, in airport infiltration at a facility near Mashhad and Shiraz, and in underwater warfare at an IRGC facility at Bandar Abbas.[53]

The Basij and Other Paramilitary Forces. The rest of Iran's paramilitary and internal security forces seem to have relatively little war-fighting capability. The Basij (Mobilization of the Oppressed) is a popular reserve force of about 90,000 men, with an active and reserve strength of up to 300,000 and a mobilization capacity of nearly 1,000,000 men.

It is controlled by the Islamic Revolutionary Guards Corps and consists largely of youths, men who have completed military service, and the elderly. It has up to 740 regional battalions with about 300–350 men each, which are composed of three companies or four platoons plus support. These include the former tribal levies and are largely regional in character.

Many Basij have little or no real military training or full-time active manning. However, Iran has used the Basij to provide local security ever since the popular riots of 1994. It called up over 100,000 men in 19 regions in September 1994 and began far more extensive training for riot control and internal security missions. It also introduced a formal rank structure and a more conventional system of command and discipline and created specialized Ashura battalions for internal security missions. Some reports indicate that 36 of these battalions were established in 1994. The primary mission of the Basij now seems to be internal security, monitoring the activities of Iranian citizens, acting as replacements for the military services, and serving as a static militia force tied to local defense missions.

Iran also has 45,000–60,000 men in the Ministry of Interior serving as police and border guards, with light utility vehicles, light patrol aircraft (Cessna 185/310s and AB-205s and AB-206s), 90 coastal patrol craft, and 40 harbor patrol craft.

The Iranian Navy

The Iranian Navy has some 18,000 men. According to the IISS, this total includes a two-brigade marine force of some 2,600 men and a 2,000-man naval aviation force. It has bases at Bandar Abbas, Bushehr, Kharg Island, Bandar-e Anzelli, Chah Bahar, Bandar-e Mahshahar, and Bandar-e Khomeini. This gives it bases opposing most of the Saudi coast.

It has 3 submarines, 3 frigates, 2 corvettes, 10 missile patrol craft, 7 mine warfare ships, 44 coastal and inshore patrol craft, and 9–10 amphibious ships. Its naval aviation branch is one of the few air elements in any Gulf navy and has 5 maritime patrol aircraft and 19 armed helicopters. When combined with the IRGC naval branch, this is a total maritime strength of 38,000 men with significant capabilities for both regular naval and asymmetric naval warfare.

Iran has given the modernization of its naval forces high priority, although its major surface ships are all old vessels with limited refits and aging weapons and fire-control systems. Since the end of the Iran-Iraq War, Iran has obtained new antiship missiles and missile patrol craft from China, midget submarines from North Korea, submarines from Russia, and modern mines. Iran has expanded the capabilities of the naval branch of the IRGC, acquired additional mine warfare capability, and upgraded some of its older surface ships. Iran's exercises have included a growing number of joint and combined arms exercises with the land forces and Air Force.

Iran has also improved its ports and strengthened its air defenses, while obtaining some logistic and technical support from nations like India and Pakistan. In August 2000, the Islamic Republic announced that it had launched its first domestically produced light submarine, which is called the Al-Sabiha 15. It can be used for reconnaissance and laying mines.[54]

IRANIAN ANTISHIP MISSILES AND MISSILE CRAFT. Iran depends heavily on its ability to use antiship missiles to make up for its lack of airpower and modern major surface vessels. Iran's Western-supplied missiles are now all beyond their shelf life, and their operational status is uncertain. Iranian forces are now operating four systems that Iran has obtained from China:

- *The Seersucker* is a long-range, mobile antiship missile, which is designated the HY-2 or Sea Eagle-2 by the People's Republic of China. It is a large missile with a 0.76-meter diameter and a weight of 3,000 kilograms. It has an 80–90 kilometer range and a 450-kilogram warhead. There are two variants. One uses radar active homing at ranges from the target of eight kilometers (4.5 nautical miles). The other is set to use passive IR homing and a radar altimeter to keep it at a constant height over the water.

- *The CS-801* antiship missile, also called the Yinji (Hawk) missile, is a solid-fuel missile, which can be launched from land and ships. It has a range of approximately 74 kilometers in the surface-to-surface mode and uses J-Band active radar guidance. It has a 512-kilogram warhead and cruises at an altitude of 20–30 meters.

- *The CS-802* is an upgraded CS-801, which uses a turbojet propulsion system with a rocket booster instead of the solid-fuel booster in the CS-801. It has a range of 70–75 miles, has a warhead of up to 363 pounds, and can be targeted by a radar deployed on a smaller ship or aircraft operating over the radar horizon of the launching vessel.[55]

- *The CS-801K* is a Chinese-supplied, air-launched antiship missile and variant of the CS-801. It too is a sea-skimming, high-subsonic cruise missile and has a range in excess of 20 nautical miles. It has been test fired by Iran's F-4Es, but Iran may be able to use other launch aircraft. This air-delivery capability gives Iran what some analysts have called a "360 degree" attack capability, because aircraft can rapidly maneuver to far less predictable launch points than Iranian combat ships can.[56]

Iran has sought to buy advanced antiship missiles from Russia, North Korea, and China; to buy antiship missile production facilities; and possibly even to acquire Chinese-made missile armed frigates. Some sources have claimed that Iran has bought eight Soviet-made SS-N-22 "Sunburn" or "Sunburst" antiship missile launch units from Ukraine and has deployed them near the Strait of Hormuz. However, U.S. experts have seen no evidence of such a purchase and doubt that Iran has any operational holdings of such systems. The "SS-N-22" is a title that actually applies to two different modern long-range supersonic sea-skimming systems—the P-270 Moskit (also called the Kh-15 or 3M80) and P80, or P-100 Zubi/Onika.

Iran's main launch platforms for antiship missiles include three British-supplied Vosper Mark 5 Sa'am-class frigates—called the *Alvand, Alborz,* and *Sabalan.* These ships date back to the time of the shah, and each is a 1,100-ton frigate with a crew of 125–146 and maximum speeds of 39 knots. Each was originally armed with one five-missile Sea Killer Mark II surface-to-surface missile launcher and one Mark 8 4.5-inch gun mount. They have since had their Sea Killers replaced with C-802 antiship missiles and new fire-control radars. The Sea Killer has a relatively effective beam-riding missile with radio command or optical guidance, and a maximum range of 25 kilometers.

All three ships are active, but the *Sabalan* took serious damage from the U.S. Navy during the tanker war of 1987–88, and the ships have not had a total refit since the early 1990s. The ASW capabilities of these ships seem to be limited or nonfunctioning. Iran has two US PF-103 (*Bayandor*-class) corvettes called the *Bayandor* and the *Naghdi.* These ships are 900-ton vessels, with crews of 140, two 76 mm guns, and a maximum speed of 18 knots. They were laid down in 1962 and delivered in 1964. The *Bayandor* and the *Naghdi* are probably the most active large surface ships in the Iranian Navy. However, neither is equipped with antiship and antiair missiles, sophisticated weapons systems, sonars, or advanced electronic warfare equipment and sensors.[57]

Iran is slowly building a 1,500-ton corvette, but its status is uncertain as is its equipment and armament. It has two old PF-103-class corvettes, the *Bayandor* and *Naghdi,* which the United States transferred to Iran in 1966. These are 900-ton vessels that are very active in the patrol role but that do not have modern radars and fire control, and are only armed with 76 mm guns and not with missiles. They lack any effective antiaircraft and antimissile defenses.[58]

The rest of Iran's major surface vessels consist of missile patrol boats. These include 10 68-ton Chinese-built *Thnodor* (*Hudong*)-class fast-attack craft or missile patrol boats. The *Hudong*-class fast-attack craft are equipped with I-band search and navigation radars, but they do not have a major antiair missile system. Iran ordered these ships for the naval branch of its Iranian Revolutionary Guards Corps in 1992, and all 10 were delivered to Iran by March 1996. The vessels have a crew of 28, carry four antiship missiles, and are armed with the CS-801 and CS-802 missile.

Iran now has at least 100 CS-801s and CS-802s. Iran's missile patrol boats also include 10 275-ton French-made Combattante II (*Kaman*-class) fast-attack boats, out of an original total of 12. These boats are armed with antiship missiles and one 76 mm gun, and have maximum speeds of 37.5 knots. They were originally armed with four U.S. Harpoon missiles, but their Harpoons may no longer be operational. At least five had been successfully converted with launchers that can carry two to four CS-801/CS-802s.

Iran has a number of large patrol craft and fast-attack craft. The operational ships of this type include three North Korean-supplied 82-ton *Zafar*-class (*Chaho*-class) fast-attack craft with I-band search radars and armed with 23 mm guns and a BM-21 multiple-rocket launcher; two *Kavian*-class (U.S. *Cape*-class) 148-ton patrol craft armed with 40 mm and 23 mm guns; and three Improved PGM-71 *Parvin*-class 98-ton patrol craft supplied in the late 1960s and armed with 40 mm and 20 mm guns.

There are more than 35 other small patrol boats plus large numbers of small boats operated by the IRGC. Most of these craft are operational and can be effective in patrol missions. They lack, however, sophisticated weapons systems or air defenses, other than machine guns and SA-7s and SA-14s. Iran has 5–6 BH-7 and 7–8 SRN-6 Hovercraft, believed to be operated by the IRGC. About half of these Hovercraft may be operational. They are capable of speeds of up to 60–70 knots. They are lightly armed and vulnerable, but their high speed makes them useful for many reconnaissance and unconventional warfare missions, and they can rapidly land troops on suitable beaches.

IRANIAN MINE WARFARE CAPABILITIES. Mine warfare, amphibious warfare, antiship missiles, and unconventional warfare offer Iran other ways of compensating for the weakness of its conventional air and naval forces. Iran's mine warfare vessels include two or three operational *Shahrock*-class MSC-292/268 coastal minesweepers (one used for training in the Caspian Sea). Two of these three ships, the *Shahrock* and *Karkas*, are known to be operational. They are 378-ton sweepers that can be used to lay mines as well as sweep, but their radars and sonars date back to the late 1950s and are obsolete in sweeping and countermeasure activity against modern mines.

Iran has one or two operational *Cape*-class (*Riazzi*-class) 239-ton inshore minesweepers and seems to have converted two of its *Iran Ajar*-class LSTs for mine warfare purposes. Many of its small boats and craft can also lay mines. Both the Iranian Navy and the naval branch of the IRGC are expanding their capability for mine warfare. While Iran has only a limited number of specialized mine vessels, it can also use small craft, LSTs, Boghammers, helicopters, and submarines to lay mines. As a result, it is impossible to determine how many ships Iran would employ to plant or lay mines in a given contingency, and some of its mines might be air dropped or laid by commercial vessels, including dhows.

Iran has a range of Soviet-, Western-, and Iranian-made moored and drifting contact mines, and U.S. experts estimate that Iran has at least 2,000 mines. Iran has significant stocks of antiship mines and has bought Chinese-made and North Korean-made versions of the Soviet mines. It has claimed to be making its own nonmagnetic, acoustic, free-floating and remote-controlled mines and has had Chinese assistance in developing the production facilities for such mines. It may have acquired significant stocks of nonmagnetic mines, influence mines, and mines with sophisticated timing devices from other countries.[59]

There also are reports that Iran has negotiated with China to buy the EM-52 or MN-52 rocket-propelled mine. The EM-52 is a mine that rests on the bottom until it senses a ship passing over it and then uses a rocket to hit the target. The maximum depth of the Strait of Hormuz is 80 meters (264 feet), although currents are strong enough to displace all but firmly moored mines.[60] Combined with modern submarine-laid mines and antiship missile systems like the CS-801/802 and SS-N-22, the EM-52 would give Iran considerable capability to harass Gulf shipping and even the potential capability to close the Gulf until U.S. naval and airpower could clear the mines and destroy the missile launchers and submarines.

Even obsolete moored mines have proven difficult to detect and sweep when intelligence does not detect the original laying and size of the minefield, and free-floating mines can be used to present a constant hazard to shipping. Bottom-influence mines can use acoustic, magnetic, or pressure sensors to detect ships passing overhead. They can use multiple types of sensor/actuators to make it hard to deceive the mines and force them to release and can be set to release only after a given number of ships pass. Some can be set to attack only ships of a given size or noise profile. Such mines are extremely difficult to detect and sweep, particularly when they are spaced at wide intervals in shipping lanes.

IRANIAN AMPHIBIOUS ASSETS. Iran has significant amphibious assets by Gulf standards, and the regular Navy and naval branch of the IRGC have independent marine forces. These assets are large enough to move a battalion-sized force relatively rapidly and include three *Hengam*-class (*Larak*-class) LST amphibious support ships (displacement of 2,940-tons loaded) that can carry up to six tanks, 600 tons of cargo, and 227 combatants; three *Iran Hormuz*-class (South Korean) LSTs (2,014 tons loaded) that can carry up to nine tanks and berth 140 combatants, three *Hormuz-21*-class 1,80-ton LSTs, and three *Fouque*-class 176-ton LSLs.

Iran's amphibious ships give it the theoretical capability to deploy about 1,000 combatants, and theoretically about 30–40 tanks in an amphibious assault—but Iran has never demonstrated that it has an effective over-the-shore capability. Iran might use commercial ferries and roll on-roll off ships if it felt they could survive. Iran has also built up its capability to hide or shelter small ships in facilities on its islands and coastline along the Gulf as well as the ability to provide them with defensive cover from antiair and antiship missiles. However, all of Iran's training to date has focused on amphibious raiding and not on operations using heavy weapons or larger operations. Iran lacks the air and surface power to move its amphibious forces across the Gulf in the face of significant air/sea defenses or to support a landing in a defended area.

Iran has support ships, but these are generally insufficient to sustain "blue water" operations and support an amphibious task force. It has 1 *Kharg*-class 33,014-ton replenishment ship, 2 *Bandar Abbas*-class 4,673-ton fleet supply ships and oilers, 1 14,410-ton repair ship, 2 12,000-ton water tankers, 7 1,300-ton *Delva*-class support ships, 5 or 6 *Hendijan*-class support vessels, 2 floating dry docks, and 20 tugs, tenders, and utility craft to help support a large naval or amphibious operation.

IRANIAN NAVAL AIR. The Iranian Navy's air capability consists of two to three operational P-3F Orion maritime patrol aircraft out of an original inventory of five. According to reports from the Gulf, none of the surviving P-3Fs have fully operational radars, and their crews often use binoculars. It also has up to 12 Sikorsky SH-3D ASW helicopters, 2 RH-53D mine-laying helicopters, and 7 Agusta-Bell AB-212 helicopters. It uses air force AH-1J attack helicopters, equipped with French AS.12 missiles, in naval missions and has adapted Hercules C-130 and Fokker Friendship aircraft for mine laying and patrol missions. The most significant recent development in Iran's capabilities to use airpower to attack naval targets has been the acquisition of the CS-801K for its regular Air Force.

Iran's Submarine Forces. Iran has attempted to offset the weakness of its major surface forces by obtaining three Type 877 EKM *Kilo*-class submarines. The Kilo is a relatively modern and quiet submarine that first became operational in 1980. The Iranian Kilos are Type 877EKM export versions that are about 10 meters longer than the original Kilos and are equipped with advanced command and control systems.

Each Type 877EKM has a teardrop hull coated with anechoic tiles to reduce noise. It displaces approximately 3,076 tons when submerged and 2,325 tons when surfaced. It is 72.6 meters long, 9.9 meters in beam, has a draught of 6.6 meters, and is powered by three 1,895 HP generator sets, one 5,900 SHP electric motor and one six-bladed propeller. It has a complement of 52 men and an endurance of 45 days. Its maximum submerged speed is 17 knots, and its maximum surface speed is 10 knots.

Each Kilo has six 530 mm torpedo tubes, including two wired guided torpedo tubes. Only one torpedo can be wire guided at a time. The Kilo can carry a mix of 18 homing and wire-guided torpedoes or 24 mines. Russian torpedoes are available with ranges of 15–19 kilometers, speeds of 29–40 knots, and warheads with 100-, 205-, and 305-kilogram weights. Their guidance systems include active sonar homing, passive homing, wire guidance, and active homing. Some reports indicate that Iran bought over 1,000 modern Soviet mines with the Kilos and that the mines were equipped with modern magnetic, acoustic, and pressure sensors. The Kilo has a remote antiaircraft launcher with one preloaded missile in the sail, and Soviet versions have 6 SA-N-5 (Igla/SA-16) surface-to-air missiles stored inside. However, Russia only supplied Iran with the SA-14 (Strela). It can be modernized to carry Chinese YJ-1 or Russian Novator Alfa surface-to-surface missiles.[61]

The Kilo has a maximum surface speed of 10 knots, a maximum submerged speed of about 17 knots, a minimum submerged operating depth of about 30 meters, an operational diving depth of 240 meters, and a maximum diving depth of 300 meters. The submarine also has a surface cruise range of 3,000–6,000 nautical miles and a submerged cruise range of 400 nautical miles—depending on speed and combat conditions.[62]

Iran's ability to use its submarines to deliver mines and fire long-range wake-homing torpedoes give it a potential capability to strike in ways that make it difficult to detect or attack the submarine. Mines can be laid covertly in critical areas before a conflict, and the mines can be set to activate and deactivate at predetermined intervals in ways that make mining difficult to detect and sweep. Long-range homing torpedoes can be used against tanker-sized targets at ranges in excess of 10 kilometers as well as to attack slow-moving combat ships that are not on alert and/or that lack sonars and countermeasures.

At the same time, many Third World countries have found submarines to be difficult to operate. For example, Russia delivered the first two Kilos with two 120-cell batteries designed for rapid power surges, rather than power over long periods. They proved to last only one to two years in warm waters versus five to seven years for similar batteries from India and the UK. Iran had to turn to India for help in developing batteries that are reliable in the warm waters of the Gulf. Iran has also had problems with the air conditioning in the ships, and their serviceability has been erratic. There are serious questions about crew capability and readiness, and all three submarines already need significant refits.

Iran faces significant operational problems in using its submarines in local waters. Many areas of the Gulf do not favor submarine operations. The Gulf is about 241,000 square kilometers in area and stretches 990 kilometers from the Shatt al-Arab to the Strait of Hormuz. It is about 340 kilometers wide at its maximum width, and about 225 kilometers wide for most of its length. While heat patterns disturb surface sonars, they also disturb submarine sonars, and the advantage seems to be slightly in favor of sophisticated surface ships and maritime patrol aircraft.

The deeper parts of the Gulf are noisy enough to make ASW operations difficult, but large parts of the Gulf, including much of the Southern Gulf on a line from Al Jubail across the tip of Qatar to about half way up the UAE, are less than 20 meters deep. The water is deeper on the Iranian side, but the maximum depth of the Gulf—located about 30 kilometers south of Qeys Island—is only 88 meters. This means that no point in the Gulf is deeper than the length of an SN-688 nuclear submarine. The keel-to-tower height of such a submarine alone is 16 meters. Even smaller coastal submarines have maneuver and bottom suction problems and cannot hide in thermoclines or take advantage of diving for concealment or self-protection. This may explain why Iran is planning to relocate its submarines from Bandar Abbas, inside the Gulf, to Chah Bahar in the Gulf of Oman and is deepening the naval facility at Chah Bahar.[63]

The Strait of Hormuz at the entrance to the Gulf is about 180 kilometers long, but it has a minimum width of 39 kilometers, and only the two deep-water channels are suitable for major surface ship or submarine operations. Further, a limited flow of fresh water and high evaporation makes the Gulf extremely salty. This creates complex underwater currents in the main channels at the Strait of Hormuz and complicates both submarine operations and detection. There are some areas with considerable noise, but not of a type that masks submarine noise from sophisticated ASW detection systems of the kind operated by the United States and UK.

Furthermore, the minimum operating depth of the Kilo is 45 meters, and the limited depth of the area around the strait can make submarine operations difficult. Submarines are easier to operate in the Gulf of Oman, which is noisy enough to make ASW operations difficult, but such deployments would expose the Kilos to operations by U.S. and British nuclear attack submarines. It is unlikely that Iran's Kilos could survive for any length of time if hunted by a U.S. or British Navy air-surface-SSN hunter-killer team.[64]

In any case, the effectiveness of Iran's submarines is likely to depend heavily on the degree of Western involvement in any ASW operation. If the Kilos did not face the U.S. or British ASW forces, the Iranian Kilos could operate in or near the Gulf with considerable impunity. If they did face U.S. and British forces, they might be able to attack a few tankers or conduct some mining efforts but would be unlikely to survive extended combat. This makes the Kilos a weapon that may be more effective in threatening Gulf shipping, or as a remote minelayer, than in naval combat. Certainly, Iran's purchase of the Kilos has already received close attention from the Southern Gulf states and convinced them that they must take Iran more seriously.

THE ROLE OF THE NAVAL BRANCH OF THE IRGC. Finally, any analysis of the capabilities of the Iranian Navy cannot ignore the fact that Iran's unconventional warfare capabilities include the naval branch of the Islamic Revolutionary Guards Corps that operates Iran's land-based antiship missiles and coastal defense artillery. In addition to its land- and sea-based antiship missile forces, the naval guards can use large numbers of small patrol boats equipped with heavy machine guns, grenade launchers, antitank guided weapons, man-portable surface-to-air missies, and 106 mm recoilless rifles.

The IRGC also uses small launches and at least 30 Zodiak rubber dinghies to practice rocket, small arms, and recoilless rifle attacks. Its other small craft were armed with a mix of machine guns, recoilless rifles, and man- and crew-portable antitank guided missiles. These vessels are difficult to detect by radar in anything but the calmest seas. Iran bases them at a number of offshore islands and oil platforms, and they can strike quickly and with limited warning. The Naval Branch of the IRGC also has naval artillery, divers, and mine-laying units. It had extensive stocks of scuba equipment and an underwater combat center at Bandar Abbas.[65] Iran is also improving the defenses and port capabilities of its islands in the Gulf, adding covered moorings, more advanced sensors, and better air defenses.

Iran can use IRGC forces to conduct the kind of low-intensity/guerrilla warfare that can only be defeated by direct engagement with land forces and can filter substantial reinforcements into a coastal area on foot or with light vehicles, making such reinforcement difficult to attack. Iran can use virtually any surviving small craft to lay mines and to place unmoored mines in shipping lanes. Its IRGC forces can use small craft to attack offshore facilities and raid coastal targets.

Finally, it is important to note that the United States did not successfully destroy a single land-based Iraqi antiship missile launcher during the Gulf War, and the IRGC now has many dispersal launch sites and storage areas over a much longer coast. It also has a growing number of caves, shelters, and small hardened facilities. Such targets are sometimes difficult to detect until they are used and present added problems, because they usually are too small and too numerous to attack with high-cost ordnance until it is clear they have valuable enough contents to merit such an attack.

NAVAL FORCE DEPLOYMENTS. The main forces of the Iranian Navy are concentrated in the Gulf. Iran gives more importance to the security of its territorial sea in the Gulf area, because in this direction, it has highly complicated relations with various Arab nations, the United States, and Israel. After the collapse of the Soviet Union, however, Iran's policy toward the Caspian has changed. According to the contracts between the Soviet Union and Iran, Tehran was not allowed to station its navy in the Caspian Sea. After the disintegration of the USSR, however, the fourth naval regional forces started representing the Iranian Navy in the Caspian.[66]

The Islamic Republic has almost 3,000 personnel in the Caspian. The forces include up to 50 fighting ships and support vessels, the Marine Corps, coastal guard forces, and the sea aircraft. There are also training vessels in the fleet, including one Shahrokh MSC minesweeper, two Hamzeh ships, and others. Currently, Iran has the second largest fleet in the Caspian after Russia. The fleet, however, is outdated. This is why Tehran has been trying to strengthen its naval forces in the Caspian through various programs. The government reportedly has numerous plans to modernize its fleet. According to these projects, the future fleet will include several divisions and separate battalions of ships and submarines.[67]

OVERALL NAVAL CAPABILITIES. Iran's efforts have steadily improved Iran's capabilities to threaten Gulf shipping and offshore oil facilities, its capability to support unconventional warfare, and its ability to defend Iran's offshore facilities, islands, and coastline. They have not, however, done much to help Iran to act as an effective "blue water" navy.

At the same time, the military capability of Iranian naval forces should not be measured in terms of the ability to win a battle for sea control against U.S.

and British naval forces, or any combination of Southern Gulf states supported by U.S. and British forces. For the foreseeable future, Iran's forces are likely to lose any such battle in a matter of days. As a result, it is Iran's ability to conduct limited or unconventional warfare, or to threaten traffic through the Gulf, that gives Iran the potential ability to threaten or intimidate its neighbors.

The Iranian Air Force

The Iranian Air Force has some 52,000 men: 37,000 in the Air Force per se and 15,000 in the Air Defense Force, which operates Iran's land-based air defenses. It has over 300 combat aircraft in its inventory (the IISS estimates 306). Many of these aircraft, however, are either not operational or cannot be sustained in air combat. This includes 50–60 percent of Iran's U.S.- and French-supplied aircraft and some 20–30 percent of its Russian- and Chinese-supplied aircraft. It has nine fighter ground-attack squadrons, with 162–186 aircraft; seven fighter squadrons, with 70–74 aircraft; a reconnaissance unit, with 4–8 aircraft; and a number of transport aircraft, helicopters, and special-purpose aircraft. It operates most of Iraq's land-based air defenses, including some 150 I Hawks, 45 HQ-21s, 10 SA-5s, 30 Rapiers, and additional forces equipped with light surface-to-air missiles.

The Iranian Air Force is headquartered in Teheran with training, administration, and logistics branches, as well as a major central Air Defense Operations Center. It has a political directorate and a small naval coordination staff and three major regional headquarters: Northern Zone (Badl Sar), Central Zone (Hamaden), and Southern Zone (Bushehr). Each regional zone seems to control a major air defense sector with subordinate air bases and facilities. The key air defense subzones and related bases in the Northern Zone are at Badl Sar, Mashhad, and Shahabad Kord. The subzones and bases in the Central Zone are at Hamadan and Dezful, and the subzones and bases in the Southern Zone are at Bushehr, Bandar Abbas, and Jask. Iran has large combat air bases at Mehrabad, Tabriz, Hamadan, Dezful, Bushehr, Shiraz, Esfahan, and Bandar Abbas. It has smaller bases at least at eleven other locations. Shiraz provides interceptor training and is the main base for transport aircraft.

Iranian Air Strength. As is the case with most aspects of Iranian military forces, estimates differ by source. The IISS estimates the Air Force has 18 main combat squadrons. These include nine fighter ground-attack squadrons, with 4/55-65 U.S.-supplied F-4D/E and 4/55-65 F-5E/FII, and 1/27-30 Soviet-supplied Su-24. Iran had 7 Su-25K and 24 Mirage F-1 Iraqi aircraft it seized during the Gulf War, and some may be operational. Some reports indicate that Iran has ordered an unknown number of TU-22M-3 "Backfire C" long-range strategic bombers from either Russia or the Ukraine.[68] Discussions do seem to have taken place, but no deliveries or purchases can be confirmed.

Iran had seven air defense squadrons, with 2/20-25, -60 U.S.-supplied F-14, 2/25-30 Russian/Iraqi-supplied MiG-29, and 1/25-35 Chinese supplied F-7Ms.[69] The Iranian Air Force had a small reconnaissance squadron with three to eight RF-4Es. It has five C-130H MP maritime reconnaissance aircraft, one RC-130, and other intelligence/reconnaissance aircraft, together with large numbers of transports and helicopters.

Most Iranian squadrons can perform both air defense and attack missions, regardless of their principal mission—although this was not true of Iran's F-14 (air defense) and Su-24 (strike/attack) units. Iran's F-14s have not been able to use their Phoenix air-to-air missiles since the early 1980s. Iran has claimed that it is modernizing its F-14s by equipping them with I-Hawk missiles adapted to the air-to-air role, but it is far from clear that this is the case or that such adaptations can have more than limited effectiveness.[70]

Iran has made ambitious claims about aircraft production than it cannot, as yet, back up. Russian firms and the Iranian government tried to reach an agreement over license-production of the MiG-29, but repeated attempts have failed. Likely because of the difficulty the regime has had in procuring new aircraft, Iran has been developing three new attack aircraft. The indigenous design and specifics of one of the fighters in development, the Shafagh, were unveiled at the Iran Air Show in 2002. Engineers hope to have a prototype by 2008, though it is unclear what the production numbers will be and what the real-world timetable for deployment may be.[71]

Little is known about the other two fighters in development, the Saeghe and the Azarakhsh, other than they have been reportedly derived from the F-5F. Claims have been made that the Azarakhsh is in low-rate production and has had operational weapons tests. There are also some indications that Iran is experimenting with composites in the Azarakhsh and is seeking to give it a locally modified beyond-visual-range radar for air-to-air combat.[72]

In practice, Iran is making light turboprop aircraft and a light utility helicopter. It is making enough progress so that it will probably be able to produce a jet trainer and heavier helicopters, but it is unclear how effective it can be in producing modern combat aircraft.[73]

Iran has moderate airlift capabilities for a regional power. The Iranian Air Force's air transport assets included 3 B-707 and 1 B-747 tanker transports and five transport squadrons with 4 B-747Fs, 1 B-727, 18C-130E/Hs, 3 Commander 690s, 10 F-27s, 1 Falcon 20A, and 2 Jetstars. Iran will have 14 Xian Y-7 transports by 2006.[74] Its helicopter strength includes 2 AB-206As, 27–30 Bell 214Cs, and 2 CH-47, 30 Mi-17 and Iranian-made Shabaviz 206-1, and 2–75 transport helicopters.

The IRGC also has some air elements. It is not clear what combat formations exist within the IRGC, but the IRGC may operate Iran's 10 EMB-312 Tucanos.[75] It seems to operate many of Iran's 45 PC-7 trainers, as well as some Pakistani-made trainers at a training school near Mushhak, but this school may be run by the regular Air Force. It has also claimed to manufacture gliders for use in nonconventional warfare. The IRGC has not recently expanded its air combat capabilities.[76]

IRANIAN LAND-BASED AIR DEFENSE. Iran seems to have assigned about 12,000–15,000 men in its Air Force to land-based air defense functions, including at least 8,000 regulars and 4,000 IRGC personnel. It is not possible to distinguish clearly between the major air defense weapons holdings of the regular air force and IRGC, but the air force appeared to operate most major surface-to-air missile systems. Total holdings seem to include 30 Improved Hawk fire units (12 battalions/150+ launchers), 45–55 SA-2 and HQ-2J/23 (CSA-1) launchers (Chinese-made equivalents of the SA-2), and possibly 25 SA-6 launchers. The Air Force also had three Soviet-made long-range SA-5 units with a total of 10–15 launchers—enough for six sites. Iran has developed and deployed its own domestically manufactured SAM dubbed the Shahab Thaqeb. The SAM requires a four-wheeled trailer for deployment and closely resembles the R440 SAM.[77]

Iran's holdings of lighter air defense weapons include five Rapier squadrons with 30 Rapier fire units, 5–10 Chinese FM-80 launchers, 10–15 Tigercat fire units, and a few RBS-70s. Iran also holds large numbers of man-portable SA-7s, HN-5s, and SA-14s, plus about 2,000 antiaircraft guns—including some Vulcans and 50–60 radar-guided and self-propelled ZSU-23-4 weapons.[78] It is not clear which of these lighter air defense weapons were operated by the Army, the IRGC, or the Air Force. The IRGC clearly had larger numbers of man-portable surface-to-air launchers, including some Stingers that it had obtained from Afghanistan. It almost certainly had a number of other light air defense guns as well.

There are no authoritative data on how Iran deploys air defenses, but Iran seems to have deployed its new SA-5s to cover its major ports, oil facilities, and Tehran. It seems to have concentrated its Improved Hawks and Soviet- and Chinese-made SA-2s around Tehran, Esfahan, Shiraz, Bandar Abbas, Kharg Island, Bushehr, Bandar-e Khomeini, Ahvaz, Dezful, Kermanshah, Hamadan, and Tabriz. Iran's air defense forces are too widely spaced to provide more than limited air defense for key bases and facilities, and many lack the missile launcher strength to be fully effective. This is particularly true of Iran's SA-5 sites, which provide long-range, medium-to-high altitude coverage of key coastal installations. Too few launchers are scattered over too wide an area to prevent relatively rapid suppression. Iran also lacks the low-altitude radar coverage, overall radar net, command and control assets, sensors, resistance to sophisticated jamming and electronic countermeasures, and systems integration capability necessary to create an effective air defense net. Its land-based air defenses must operate largely in the point defense mode, and Iran lacks the battle management systems and data links are not fast and effective enough to allow it to take maximum advantage of the overlapping coverage of some of its missile systems—a problem further complicated by the problems in trying to net different systems supplied by Britain, China, Russia, and the United States. Iran's missiles and sensors are most effective at high-to-medium altitudes against aircraft with limited penetrating and jamming capability.

IRANIAN AIR FORCE READINESS AND EFFECTIVENESS. In spite of Iran's efforts, readiness and force quality remain major issues. The Iranian Air Force still has many qualitative weaknesses, and it is far from clear that its current rate of modernization can offset the aging of its Western-supplied aircraft and the qualitative improvements in U.S. and Southern Gulf forces. The Air Force also faces serious problems in terms of sustainment, command and control, and training. Iran has a pilot-quality problem. Many of its U.S.-trained pilots were purged at some point during the revolution. Its other U.S.-trained pilots and ground-crew technicians are aging to the point where many should soon retire from service. These pilots also have not had advanced air-to-air combat and air-attack training for more than 15 years.

While Iran practices realistic individual intercept training, it fails to practice effective unit or force-wide tactics and has shown only limited capability to fly large numbers of sorties with its U.S.-supplied aircraft on even a surge basis. It has limited refueling capabilities, although it has four B-707 tanker/transports and may have converted other transports. The Iranian Air Force lacks advanced training facilities and has only limited capability to conduct realistic training for beyond-visual-range combat and standoff attacks with air-to-surface munitions. Ground crew training and proficiency generally seem mediocre, although the layout of Iranian air bases, aircraft storage and parking, the deployment of equipment for maintenance cycles, and the other physical signs of air unit activity are generally better organized than those of most Middle Eastern air forces.

The Iranian Air Force must also deal with the fact that its primary challenge now consists of the U.S., British, and Saudi air forces. They are high technology air forces that operate the AWACS airborne control system, have some of the most advanced electronic warfare and targeting systems in the world, and have full refueling capability. They use sophisticated, computer-aided aggressor training and have all of the range and training facilities for beyond-visual-range combat and standoff attacks with air-to-surface munitions. Iran has no airborne control system, although it may be able to use the radars on its F-14s to support other aircraft from the rear. Its overall C⁴I system is a totally inadequate mix of different sensors, communications, and data processing systems. It has limited electronic warfare capabilities by U.S. standards, although it may be seeking to acquire two Beriev A-50 Mainstay AEW aircraft and has converted some aircraft to provide a limited ELINT/SIGINT capability.

Iran is slowly improving its capability for joint land-air, and air-sea operations. Iranian exercises and statements provide strong indications that Iran would like to develop an advanced air defense system, the ability to operate effectively in long-range maritime patrol and attack missions, effective joint warfare capabilities, and strike/attack forces with the ability to penetrate deep into Iraq, the southern Gulf states, and other neighboring countries. Iran's exercises, military literature, and procurement efforts also make it clear that its air planners understand the value of airborne early warning and C⁴I systems, the value of airborne intelligence and electronic warfare platforms, the value of RPVs, and the value of airborne refueling. Iran has even sought to create its own satellite program.[79] Further, the Air Forces' efforts at sheltering and dispersal indicate that it understands the vulnerability of modern air facilities and the standoff attack capabilities of advanced air forces like those of the United States.

Iranian Capabilities to Carry Out Attacks in the Gulf

The conventional military threat from Iran may be limited, but it could still launch asymmetric attacks in the Gulf that would have a strategic effect out of proportion to the size and capability of its forces. Iran is a potential threat to Gulf shipping as well as to shipping in the Gulf of Oman. It can also attack targets throughout the Gulf Coast, and the Gulf contains 715 billion barrels of proven oil reserves, representing over half (57 percent) of the world's oil reserves, and 2,462 Tcf of natural gas reserves (45 percent of the world total). Saudi Arabia alone has more than 20 percent of the world's proven oil reserves, and Saudi Arabia exported some 49 percent of Gulf exports in 2003.[80]

THE STRAIT OF HORMUZ AND GULF SHIPPING CHANNELS. Iran's territory includes the northern coast of the Strait of Hormuz and the coast on either side. Oman occupies the islands in the strait and Goat Island and the Musandam Peninsula to the south. The strait is the world's most important oil choke point. As has been noted earlier, it is 180 kilometers long and 39 kilometers wide at its narrowest passage. The strait has channels for inbound and outbound tanker traffic that are only two miles wide, plus a two-mile wide buffer zone. Some 40 percent of all world oil exports (15–15.5 MMBD now pass daily through the Strait of Hormuz EIA and International Energy Agency IEA projections indicate this total will increase to around 60 percent of all world oil exports by 2025–2030).[81]

Iran has serious vulnerabilities of its own, but this does not mean there is any guarantee it would not attack Saudi or other Gulf facilities. As has been discussed earlier, Iran occupies a number of Islands in the main shipping channels to the strait on the Gulf side. These include the Tunbs, Abu Musa, Qeshem, Larak, Hormuz, Sirri, and Bani Forur. It has a major naval and air base on the coast above the strait at Bandar Abbas.

Abu Musa and the Greater and Lesser Tunb Islands present special problems, because they are located in the main shipping channels just to the west of the strait. They are disputed territory between Iran and the UAE that Iranian troops seized in 1992. The Iranian Foreign Ministry claimed that the islands are "an inseparable part of Iran" in 1965, and Iran rejected a proposal by the GCC in 1996 to have the International Court of Justice resolve the dispute. It has since strengthened its presence in the islands by starting up a power plant on Greater Tunb and opening an airport on Abu Musa. It has said it will construct a new port on Abu Musa.[82]

While it has not fortified the islands in the shipping channels, it has deployed Revolutionary Guards to some of these islands, and a number of them have airfields or airstrips and limited naval facilities. It is within a few minutes flight time of the strait, and has other bases on the Gulf coast extending to locations near its border with Kuwait. It is within a five-to-seven-minute flight time of targets on the coast of Saudi Arabia and the Gulf Coast of every other Southern Gulf state, and its mountains make a natural radar shield for "pop up" air attacks with limited warning unless an AWACS is patrolling in the area. Revolutionary Guards and Iranian naval forces can deploy to the shipping channels and Saudi waters in a matter of hours, and Iran showed during the Iran-Iraq War that it could deploy free-floating mines in the shipping channels in ways that were very difficult to detect. Iran can also attack shipping in the Strait of Hormuz and the Gulf of Oman.

THE GULF COAST AND KEY FACILITIES. Saudi Arabia and the other Gulf states have substantial vulnerabilities to attacks on shipping inside the Gulf as well as the tanker loading facilities and power and desalination plants along the Gulf coast. While vulnerability studies often focus on petroleum exports, the Gulf states are acutely vulnerable to attacks on their water and power facilities. Saudi Arabia alone gets 60 percent of its water from some 30 desalination plants with a capacity of some 3.4 million cubic meters a day, although many are on its Red Sea coast.[83] Virtually all future increase in Gulf water use must come from such desalination plants, and output must rise at an average rate of at least 3 percent a year for the foreseeable future. Saudi Arabia, for example, plans to increase capacity to 4.4 million cubic meters a day by 2010 and 5.5 million cubic meters a day by 2020.[84]

There are many major offshore oil facilities, including Safaniya (the world's largest offshore oilfield, with estimated reserves of 35 billion barrels). The EIA reports that Saudi offshore production includes Arab Medium crude from the Zuluf (over 500,000 MMBD capacity) and Marjan (270,000 MMBD capacity) fields and Arab Heavy crude from the Safaniya field.

Saudi Arabia shares the Neutral Zone with Kuwait, which contains about 5 billion barrels of proven oil reserves, and has two offshore fields (Khafji and Hout) producing some 300,000 MMBD. There is also a large natural gas field, called Dorra, located offshore near the Khafji oil field. The development of this field presents problems because it is also claimed by Iran (which calls the field Arash). Saudi Arabia did reach an agreement with Kuwait to share Dorra equally in July 2000, but the maritime border between Kuwait and Iran remains undemarcated. Iran and Kuwait have held boundary discussions since 2000, but Iran continues to oppose Saudi and Kuwaiti efforts to develop the field.[85]

SAUDI EXPORT FACILITIES. The EIA provides the following description of Saudi oil export facilities and Saudi Arabia's overall dependence on the security of the Gulf and access through the Strait of Hormuz:

> Most of Saudi Arabia's crude oil is exported from the Persian Gulf via the huge Abqaiq processing facility, which handles around two-thirds or so of the country's oil output. Saudi Arabia's primary oil export terminals are located at Ras Tanura (6 million bbl/d capacity; the world's largest offshore oil loading facility) and Ras al-Ju'aymah (3 million bbl/d) on the Persian Gulf, plus Yanbu (as high as 5 million bbl/d) on the Red Sea. Combined, these terminals appear capable of handling around 14 million bbl/d, around 3.5–4.0 million bbl/d higher than Saudi crude oil production capacity (10–10.5 million bbl/d), and about 6 million bbl/d in excess of Saudi crude oil production in 2002. Despite this excess capacity, there have been reports that the Saudis are planning to conduct a feasibility study on construction of an oil pipeline from the Empty

Quarter of southeastern Saudi Arabia through the Hadramaut in Yemen to the Arabian Sea.

Saudi Arabia operates two major oil pipelines. The 5-million bbl/d East-West Crude Oil Pipeline (Petroline), operated by Aramco since 1984 (when it took over from Mobil), is used mainly to transport Arabian Light and Super Light to refineries in the Western Province and to Red Sea terminals for export to European markets. The Petroline was constructed in 1981, with initial capacity of 1.85 million bbl/d on a single, 48-inch line (AY-1). The Petroline was expanded in 1987, during the height of the Iran-Iraq war (and specifically the so-called "tanker war" in the Gulf), to 3.2 million bbl/d, with the addition of a parallel ("looped"), 56-inch line (AY-1L). Finally, in 1993, Petroline capacity was increased to 5.0 million bbl/d by adding significant pumping capability on the line. Reportedly, the Saudis expanded the Petroline in part to maintain Yanbu as a strategic option to Gulf port facilities in the event that exports were blocked at that end. A study in 1997 by the Baker Institute indicated that capacity on the Petroline could be expanded significantly by using so-called "drag reduction agents" (DRAs), and that this could enhance the line's strategic value.

In purely economic terms, Yanbu remains a far less economical option for Saudi oil exports than Ras Tanura. Among other factors, shipments from Yanbu add about 5 days roundtrip travel time for tankers through the Bab el Mandab strait to major customers in Asia compared to Ras Tanura (via the Strait of Hormuz). In addition, according to Oil Minister Ali al-Naimi, the Petroline is only utilized at half capacity. Given this fact, as well as the desire to boost natural gas usage (see below), Saudi Aramco has begun converting the AY-1 (48-inch) line to natural gas pumping capability. The natural gas will supply Yanbu's petrochemical and power facilities.

Running parallel to the Petroline is the 290,000-bbl/d Abqaiq-Yanbu natural gas liquids pipeline, which serves Yanbu's petrochemical plants. The Trans-Arabian Pipeline (Tapline) to Lebanon is mothballed, and the 1.65-million-bbl/d, 48-inch Iraqi Pipeline across Saudi Arabia (IPSA), which runs parallel to the Petroline from pump station #3 (there are 11 pumping stations along the Petroline, all utilizing on-site gas turbine electric generators) to the port of Mu'ajjiz, just south of Yanbu, was closed indefinitely following the August 1990 Iraqi invasion of Kuwait (also, in June 2001, Saudi Arabia seized ownership of IPSA "in light of the Iraqi government's persistence in its stands"). Theoretically, IPSA could be used for Saudi oil transport to the Red Sea, although the Saudis have stated that "there are no plans" to do so. According to Oil Minister al-Naimi, Saudi Arabia has "surplus oil export and pipelines capacity . . . [including the] East-West oil pipeline system [which] can carry and deliver 5 million bbl/d" but is being run at "only half capacity."

SABIC, the Middle East's largest non-oil industrial company (and expected to become one of the world's top five ethylene producers by 2005), accounts for around 10% of world petrochemical production. In February 2001, SABIC completed a $1 billion expansion at the Yanbu petrochemical facility, making it the largest polyethylene plant in the world. . . . In early January 2002, SABIC agreed to a $1.15 billion loan to fund a new petrochemicals plant in the eastern Saudi Arabian industrial city of Jubail. The complex is scheduled to come online in the second half of 2004, and to produce 1 million tons per year of ethylene, plus olefins, polyethylene, and glycol ethylene. . . .

Aramco's shipping subsidiary Vela has the world's largest fleet of oil tankers, including 19 VLCC's (very large crude carriers) and 4 ULCC's (ultra large crude carriers). Overall, Vela carries around half of Saudi oil exports. In addition to tankers, Aramco owns or leases oil storage facilities around the world, in places like Rotterdam, Sidi Kerir (the Sumed pipeline terminal on Egypt's Mediterranean coast), South Korea, the Philippines, the Caribbean, and the United States.[86]

INCREASING GLOBAL DEPENDENCE ON GULF EXPORTS. To put this situation in broader perspective, the security of the Gulf and exports out of the Gulf are critical to Saudi Arabia and all of the world's oil importers. Moreover, global dependence on such exports will increase steadily with time. Projections by the International Energy Agency indicate that Middle Eastern exports will total some 46 MMBD by 2030 and represent more than two-thirds of the world total.

This means that the daily traffic in oil tankers will increase from 15 MMBD and 44 percent of global interregional trade in 2002, to 43 MMBD and 66 percent of global interregional trade in 2030. The daily traffic in LNG carriers will increase from 28 BCM and 18 percent of global interregional trade in 2002 to 230 carriers and 34 percent of global interregional trade in 2030.[87]

The International Energy Agency also estimates that imports will rise from 63 percent of total OECD demand for oil in 2002 to 85 percent in 2030. Some $3 trillion dollars must be invested in the oil sector from 2003 to 2030 to meet world demand for oil, and something approaching half of this total must be invested in the Middle East. Some $234 billion will be required for tankers and oil pipelines, and again, a substantial amount must go to the Middle East and North Africa (MENA) area.[88]

Iranian Proliferation and Weapons of Mass Destruction

Iran has many reasons for acquiring weapons of mass destruction, although it has never openly declared its intentions or admitted to a nuclear weapons program. This makes it impossible to determine Iran's precise motives and intentions, but it is seems likely that they include a mix of the following factors:

- A defensive political ruling elite that has survived the Iran-Iraq War, lost the "tanker war" of 1987–88 to the United States, and seen the impact of U.S. conventional superiority in the Gulf War of 1991 and the Iraqi War of 2003.

- U.S. policy-level discussions of regime overthrow in Iran; attacks on Iran for its support of the Hezbollah, Hamas, and other enemies of Israel; and preemptive strikes on Iran's nuclear facilities. President George Bush's description of Iran as part of the "axis of evil."

- Iran's problems in modernizing its conventional forces.

- The legacy of the shah's ambitious efforts to make Iran a major military power and the high probability that he started and maintained a covert nuclear weapons program.

- The legacy of the Iran-Iraq War and Iraq's extensive use of chemical weapons against Iran, plus its use of conventionally armed ballistic missiles against Iranian cities.

- The legacy of the Gulf War, and the lesson that Iraq could use missiles against targets in Saudi Arabia and Israel.

- The broad lesson that weak conventional forces cannot deter or defend against the United States.

- The potential threat posed by a hostile Israel, with its own long-range strike systems and nuclear weapons.

- The example set by nations like India, Pakistan, and North Korea.

- The fact that nuclear weapons provide a unique level of military status and prestige and could potentially make Iran something approaching a regional superpower.

- The potential ability to use long-range missiles and possession of nuclear weapons not only to deter the United States and Iran's neighbors, but also to intimidate and pressure Iran's neighbors to support its policies and/or to deter interference in limited Iranian military operations in areas like Iraq or the Gulf.

- A belief that Iran must be able to retaliate against any U.S. or regional attack that threatens its regime or the defeat of its conventional forces.

It should be noted that it is impossible to determine what combination of these motives will drive Iran's behavior, and it is dangerous to assume that Iran has fixed plans for proliferation or the use of the forces it develops. Iran faces so much opposition to acquiring such weapons that it is forced to proliferate on a target of opportunity basis and constantly to adapt its approaches to acquiring weapons and delivery systems. Even if it has force plans, it will almost certainly change them over time—and, necessarily, its doctrine, war plans, and targeting as well.

It is also extremely dangerous to assume that Iran would behave as a perfect "rational bargainer" in an actual war or crisis. Iran has not acted aggressively in the past in military terms, and its ruling elite has been cautious in taking risks. History provides warning after warning, however, that behavior can change radically, and that international actors can take unpredictable risks in the face of a major crisis. The history of the West in the 20th century is filled with such examples, and is ample proof that this takes place regardless of nation and culture.

As for Iran's current efforts, its missile developments have already been discussed. In terms of Iran's efforts to acquire weapons of mass destruction, Iran has declared it has the capacity to make chemical weapons. The details of its biological warfare efforts are unknown, but it continues to import suspect biotechnology. It is also moving forward in the nuclear dimension. The IAEA has discovered a number of disturbing details about its uranium enrichment program that are similar to Libya's nuclear weapons program, including the ability to produce P-2 centrifuges. Iran has conducted experiments with uranium hexafluoride that could fuel a weapons-oriented enrichment program and has worked on a heavy water plant that could be used in a reactor design that would produce fissile material far more efficiently than its Russian-supplied light water reactor.

While it is not yet confirmed, Iran may well have received the same older Chinese design data for a 1,000–2,000 pound nuclear weapon that Libya acquired through Pakistani sources. U.S. Secretary of State Colin Powell declared on November 17, 2004, that Iran was preparing its missiles to carry nuclear weapons, although he did not provide details.[89] The United States also announced the next day that Iran was rushing its processing of uranium hexafluoride forward to complete the processing before its negotiations with Europe might force it to halt.

The Status of the Iranian Chemical Weapons Program. Iran has pursued chemical weapons since at least the time it first came under Iraqi chemical attack early in the Iran-Iraq War. It purchased large amounts of chemical defense gear from the mid-1980s onward. Iran also obtained stocks of nonlethal CS gas, although it quickly found such agents had very limited military impact, because they could only be used effectively in closed areas or very small open areas. Acquiring poisonous chemical agents was more difficult. Iran did not have any internal capacity to manufacture poisonous chemical agents when Iraq first launched its attacks with such weapons. While Iran seems to have made limited use of chemical mortar and artillery rounds as early as 1985— and possibly as early as 1984—these rounds were almost certainly captured from Iraq.

Iran had to covertly import the necessary equipment and supplies, and it took several years to get substantial amounts of production equipment and the necessary feedstocks. Iran sought aid from European firms like Lurgi to produce large pesticide plants and began to try to obtain the needed feedstock from a wide range of sources, relying heavily on its embassy in Bonn to manage the necessary deals. While Lurgi did not provide the pesticide plant Iran sought, Iran did obtain substantial support from other European firms and feedstocks from many other Western sources.

By 1986–87, Iran developed the capability to produce enough lethal agents to load its own weapons. The director of the CIA as well as informed observers in the Gulf made it clear that Iran could produce blood agents like hydrogen cyanide, phosgene gas, and/or chlorine gas. Iran was also able to weaponize limited quantities of blister (sulfur mustard) and blood (cyanide) agents beginning in 1987 and had some capability to weaponize phosgene gas, and/or chlorine gas. These chemical agents were produced in small batches, and evidently under laboratory scale conditions, which enabled Iran to load small numbers of weapons before any of its new major production plants went into full operation. These gas agents were loaded into bombs and artillery shells and were used sporadically against Iraq in 1987 and 1988.

Reports regarding Iran's production and research facilities since that time are highly uncertain:

- Iran seems to have completed a major poison gas plant at Qazvin, about 150 kilometers west of Tehran. This plant is reported to have been completed between November 1987 and January 1988. While supposedly a pesticide plant, the facility's true purpose seems to have been poison gas production using organophosphorous compounds.

- It is impossible to trace all the sources of the major components and technology Iran used in its chemical weapons program during this period. Mujahideen sources claim Iran also set up a chemical bomb and warhead plant operated by the Zakaria Al-Razi chemical company near Mahshar in southern Iran, but it is unclear whether these reports are true.

- Reports that Iran had chemical weapons plants at Damghan and Parchin that began operation as early as March 1988, and may have begun to test fire Scuds with chemical warheads as early as 1988–89, are equally uncertain.

- Iran established at least one large research and development center under the control of the Engineering Research Centre of the Construction Crusade (Jahad e-Sazandegi), and had established a significant chemical weapons production capability by mid-1989.

- Debates took place in the Iranian parliament, or Majlis, in late 1988 over the safety of Pasdaran gas plants located near Iranian towns, and that former President Hashemi Rafsanjani described chemical weapons as follows: "Chemical and biological weapons are poor man's atomic bombs and can easily be produced. We should at least consider them for our defense. Although the use of such weapons is inhuman, the war taught us that international laws are only scraps of paper."

Post Iran-Iraq War estimates of Iran chemical weapons production are largely speculative:

- U.S. experts believe Iran was beginning to produce significant mustard gas and nerve gas by the time of the August 1988 cease-fire in the Iran-Iraq War, although its use of chemical weapons remained limited and had little impact on the fighting.

- Iran's efforts to equip plants to produce V-agent nerve gases seem to have been delayed by U.S., British, and German efforts to limit technology transfers to Iran, but Iran may have acquired the capability to produce persistent nerve gas during the mid 1990s.

- Production of nerve gas weapons started no later than 1994.

- Began to stockpile of cyanide (cyanogen chloride), phosgene, and mustard gas weapons after 1985. Recent CIA testimony indicates that production capacity may approach 1,000 tons annually.

- On August 2, 2002, the NSC's director for the Near East indicated that Iran is producing and stockpiling blister, blood, and choking agents.

- The Defense Department's 2001 Report "Proliferation: Threat and Response" suggests that Iran, in addition to producing and stockpiling blister, blood, and choking agents, has weaponized these agents for use with artillery shells, mortars, rockets, and bombs. The report also states that Iran is continuing its research into nerve agents.

- Weapons include bombs and artillery. Shells include 155 mm artillery and mortar rounds. Iran also has chemical bombs and mines. It may have developmental chemical warheads for its Scuds and may have a chemical package for its 22006 RPV (doubtful).

• There are reports that Iran has deployed chemical weapons on some of its ships. Training for Iranian naval forces suggests that they are preparing for the possibility of operating in a contaminated environment.

• Iran has increased chemical defensive and offensive warfare training since 1993.

Iran has sought to buy more advanced chemical defense equipment and has sought to buy specialized equipment on the world market to develop an indigenous capability to produce advanced feedstocks for nerve weapons.

• CIA sources indicated in late 1996 that China might have supplied Iran with up to 400 tons of chemicals for the production of nerve gas.

• One report indicated in 1996 that Iran obtained 400 metric tons of chemicals for use in nerve gas weapons from China—including carbon sulfide.

• Another report indicated that China supplied Iran with roughly two tons of calcium-hypochlorate in 1996 and loaded another 40,000 barrels in January or February of 1997. Calcium-hypochlorate is used for decontamination in chemical warfare.

• Iran placed several significant orders from China that were not delivered. Razak Industries in Tehran, and Chemical and Pharmaceutical Industries in Tabriz ordered 49 metric tons of alkyl dimethylamine, a chemical used in making detergents, and 17 tons of sodium sulfide, a chemical used in making mustard gas. The orders were never delivered, but they were brokered by Iran's International Movalled Industries Corporation (Imaco) and China's North Chemical Industries Co. (Nocinco). Both brokers have been linked to other transactions affecting Iran's chemical weapons program since early 1995, and Nocinco has supplied Iran with several hundred tons of carbon disulfide, a chemical used in nerve gas.

• Another Chinese firm, only publicly identified as Q. Chen, seems to have supplied glass vessels for chemical weapons.

• The United States imposed sanctions on seven Chinese firms in May 1997 for selling precursors for nerve gas and equipment for making nerve gas—although the United States made it clear that it had "no evidence that the Chinese government was involved." The Chinese firms were the Nanjing Chemical Industries Group and Jiangsu Yongli Chemical Engineering and Import/Export Corporation. Cheong Yee Ltd., a Hong Kong firm, was also involved. The precursors included thionyl chloride, dimethylamine, and ethylene chlorohydril. The equipment included special glass lined vessels, and Nanjing Chemical and Industrial Group completed construction of a production plant to manufacture such vessels in Iran in June 1997.

- Iran sought to obtain impregnated alumina, which is used to make phosphorous oxychloride—a major component of VX and GB—from the United States.

- Iran has obtained some equipment from the Israelis. Nahum Manbar, an Israeli national living in France, was convicted in an Israeli court in May 1997 for providing Iran with $16 million worth of production equipment for mustard and nerve gas during the period from 1990 to 1995.

- CIA reported in June 1997 that Iran had obtained new chemical weapons equipment technology from China and India in 1996.

- India is assisting in the construction of a major new plant at Qazvin, near Tehran, to manufacture phosphorous pentasulfide, a major precursor for nerve gas. The plant is fronted by Meli Agrochemicals, and the program was negotiated by Dr. Mejid Tehrani Abbaspour, a chief security adviser to Rafsanjani.

- A number of reports indicate that China has provided Iran with the ability to manufacture chemical weapons indigenously as well as providing precursors since at least 1996.[90]

- A recent report by German intelligence indicates that Iran has made major efforts to acquire the equipment necessary to produce Sarin and Tabun, using the same cover of purchasing equipment for pesticide plants that Iraq used for its Sa'ad 16 plant in the 1980s. German sources note that three Indian companies—Tata Consulting Engineering, Transpek, and Rallis India—have approached German pharmaceutical and engineering concerns for such equipment and technology under conditions where German intelligence was able to trace the end user to Iran.

Iran ratified the Chemical Weapons Convention (CWC) in June 1997, but it is far from clear what this means. It submitted a statement in Farsi to the CWC secretariat in 1998, but this consisted only of questions as to the nature of the required compliance. It has not provided the CWC with detailed data on its chemical weapons program. Iran also stridently asserted its right to withdraw from the convention at any time.

- The CIA stated that Chinese entities sought to supply Iran with chemical warfare CW-related chemicals during 1997–98 period. The U.S. sanctions imposed in May 1997 on seven Chinese entities for knowingly and materially contributing to Iran's CW program remain in effect.

- The CIA estimated in January 1999 that Iran obtained material related to CW from various sources during the first half of 1998. It already has manufactured and stockpiled chemical weapons, including blister, blood, and choking agents and the bombs and artillery shells for delivering them. However, Tehran is seeking foreign equipment and expertise to create a more advanced and self-sufficient CW infrastructure.

- On May 2, 2003, the Iranian news agency, IRNA, issued a report stating that Iran called on all world countries to take serious and coordinated measures to obliterate chemical weapons.

- In mid-May 2003, the Bush administration released a statement to the Organization for Prohibition of Chemical Weapons in which the United States accused Iran of continuing to pursue production technology, training, and expertise from abroad. The statement asserts that Iran is continuing to stockpile blister, blood, choking, and some nerve agents.

- The CIA reported in November 2003 that Iran is a party to the Chemical Weapons Convention (CWC). Nevertheless, during the reporting period it continued to seek production technology, training, and expertise from Chinese entities that could further Tehran's efforts to achieve an indigenous capability to produce nerve agents. Iran likely has already stockpiled blister, blood, choking, and probably nerve agents—and the bombs and artillery shells to deliver them—which it previously had manufactured.

There are a number of sites in Iran that are alleged to be related to Iran's chemical warfare effort:

- *Abu Musa Island:* Iran holds a large number of chemical weapons, principally 155 mm artillery shells, in addition to some weaponized biological agents.

- *Bandar-e Khomeini:* Allegedly the location of a chemical weapons facility, run by the Razi chemical corporation, established during the Iran-Iraq war to manufacture chemical weapons.

- *Damghan:* Either a chemical weapons plant or warhead assembly facility. Primarily involved in 155 mm artillery shells and SCUD warheads.

- *Esfahan:* Suspected location of a chemical weapons facility, possibly operated by the Poly-Acryl Corporation.

- *Karaj:* Located about 14 km from Tehran, this is the site of an alleged storage and manufacturing facility for chemical weapons. Reports suggest that this facility was built with Chinese assistance.

- *Marvdasht:* The Chemical Fertilizers Company is suspected to have been a manufacturing facility for mustard agents during the Iran-Iraq War.

- *Parchin:* The location of at least one munitions factory and is suspected of being a major chemical weapons production facility. Reports of uncertain reliability indicate that the plant was in operation no later than March 1988. In April 1997, a German newspaper reported that, according to the German Federal Intelligence Service, the factories at Parchin were producing primary products for chemical warfare agents.

- *Qazvin:* A large pesticide plant at this location is widely believed to produce nerve gas.

- *Mashar:* Iranian opposition groups have made allegations, of uncertain reliability, that a warhead filling facility is operated at this location.[91]

It seems likely that Iran retains some chemical weapons and could employ them in combat. It does not, however, overtly train for offensive chemical warfare, and its current and future war fighting capabilities are unknown.

THE STATUS OF THE IRANIAN BIOLOGICAL WEAPONS PROGRAM. Any analysis of Iran's biological weapons effort must be speculative. Iran does have extensive laboratory and research capability, and steadily improving industrial facilities with dual-use production capabilities. Whether it has an active weapons development program, however, is a controversial matter.

Reports first surfaced in 1982—during the Iran-Iraq War—that Iran had imported suitable type cultures from Europe and was working on the production of mycotoxins—a relatively simple family of biological agents that require only limited laboratory facilities for small-scale production. Many experts believe that the Iranian biological weapons effort was placed under the control of the Islamic Revolutionary Guards Corps, which is known to have tried to purchase suitable production equipment for such weapons.

U.S. intelligence sources reported in August 1989, that Iran was trying to buy two new strains of fungus from Canada and the Netherlands that can be used to produce mycotoxins. German sources indicated that Iran had successfully purchased such cultures several years earlier. Some universities and research centers may be linked to biological weapons program. The Imam Reza Medical Center at Mashhad Medical Sciences University and the Iranian Research Organization for Science and Technology were identified as the end users for this purchasing effort, but it is likely that the true end user was an Iranian government agency specializing in biological warfare.

Since the Iran-Iraq War, Iran may have conducted research on more lethal active agents like anthrax, hoof and mouth disease, and biotoxins. Iranian groups have repeatedly approached various European firms for equipment and technology that could be used to work with these diseases and toxins.

Unclassified sources of uncertain reliability have identified a facility at Damghan as working on both biological and chemical weapons research and production, and believe that Iran may be producing biological weapons at a pesticide facility near Tehran.

Reports surfaced in the spring of 1993 that Iran had succeeded in obtaining advanced biological weapons technology in Switzerland and containment equipment and technology from Germany. According to these reports, this led to serious damage to computer facilities in a Swiss biological research facility by unidentified agents. Similar reports indicated that agents had destroyed German biocontainment equipment destined for Iran. More credible reports by U.S. experts indicate that Iran might have begun to stockpile anthrax and botulinum in a facility near Tabriz, can now mass manufacture such agents, and has them in an aerosol form. None of these reports, however, can be verified.

The CIA has reported that Iran has "sought dual-use biotech equipment from Europe and Asia, ostensibly for civilian use." It also reported in 1996 that Iran might be ready to deploy biological weapons. Beyond this point, little unclassified information exists regarding the details of Iran's effort to "weaponize" and produce biological weapons.

The CIA reported in 1996 that "We believe that Iran holds some stocks of biological agents and weapons. Tehran probably has investigated both toxins and live organisms as biological warfare agents. Iran has the technical infrastructure to support a significant biological weapons program with little foreign assistance."

Iran announced in June 1997 that it would not produce or employ chemical weapons including biological toxins. However, the CIA reported in June 1997 that Iran had obtained new dual use technology from China and India during 1996.

The CIA reported in January 1999 that Iran continued to pursue dual-use biotechnical equipment from Russia and other countries, ostensibly for civilian uses. Its biological warfare (BW) program began during the Iran-Iraq War, and Iran may have some limited capability for BW deployment. Outside assistance is both important and difficult to prevent, given the dual-use nature of the materials and equipment being sought and the many legitimate end uses for these items.

In 2001 an allegation from the former director of research and development at the Cuban Center for Genetic Engineering and Biotechnology surfaced that claimed Cuba had assisted the Iranian bioweapons program from 1995 to 1998. The authenticity of the director's claims has not been established.[92]

A report produced by the Iranian insurgent group, the Mojahedin Khalq Organization, asserted in 2003 that Iran had started producing weaponized anthrax and was actively working with at least five other pathogens, including small pox. The Mojahedin Khalq Organization was the same organization that produced early evidence of Iran's noncompliance with the terms of the Nuclear Non-Proliferation Treaty. Iran issued a vehement denial of these charges in a May 16, 2003, press release. The accuracy of either set of statements is uncertain.

The CIA reported in November 2003 that, even though Iran is part of the Biological Weapons Convention (BWC), Tehran probably maintained an offensive BW program. Iran continued to seek dual-use biotechnical materials, equipment, and expertise. While such materials had legitimate uses, Iran's biological warfare (BW) program also could have benefited from them. It is likely that Iran has capabilities to produce small quantities of BW agents, but has a limited ability to weaponize them.

Russia remains a key source of biotechnology for Iran. Russia's world-leading expertise in biological weapons makes it an attractive target for Iranians seeking technical information and training on BW agent production processes. Iran may have the production technology to make dry storable and aerosol weapons. This would allow it to develop suitable missile warheads, bombs, and covert devices.

THE STATUS OF THE IRANIAN NUCLEAR PROGRAM. As has been noted earlier, Iran has denied that it is developing nuclear weapons since such reports first surfaced in the early 1970s, at the time of the shah. Since that time, evidence has surfaced again and again that Iran may be lying and that many of its "peaceful" nuclear activities are actually under the direct or indirect control of the IRGC. However, there has never been conclusive evidence Iran was developing a weapon.

There also have been long periods since the fall of the shah when very little data have been available on any aspect of Iran's nuclear efforts, leaving serious gaps in the historical flow of the evidence. Iran has also always claimed to comply with arms control agreements and has always found an explanation for each new discovery that claims its actions were peaceful and either were connected research programs or were efforts to create a national nuclear power program.

The end result is a long list of nuclear programs and facilities that are at best ambiguous in character. Taken as a body of evidence, they provide strong indications that Iran began a nuclear weapons program under the shah and that the Ayatollah Khomeini revived this program after Iraq began to use chemical weapons against Iran during the Iran-Iraq War. While Iran has continued to state that it is not developing nuclear weapons, and some of its clerics have said such weapons are against Islamic principles, senior Iranian officials and clerics have also asserted Iran's right to have nuclear weapons and the kind of nuclear fuel cycle that Iran could use to produce weapons-grade materials.

THE UNCERTAIN CHARACTER OF NUCLEAR FACILITIES. Iran has a long list of known and suspect nuclear facilities, many of which have raised serious questions regarding their character and Iran's nuclear research, development, and production facilities. Iran also has a large and well-dispersed mix of state industries and military facilities it can use to hide its activities or to shelter and disperse them.

There are no accurate unclassified lists of such Iranian facilities, and claims have been made in various press and opposition sources over the years that Iran is carrying out parts of a nuclear weapons program in a wide range of sites—only some of which have turned out to be real or probable. Work by Global Security has examined these various reports and claims in depth.[93] The following list is drawn from this work and is combined with recent reporting by the International Atomic Energy Agency on what is and is not known about the nature of Iran's activities in each facility.[94] This material shows how difficult it is to understand the overall structure of Iran's activities and the scale of Iran's activities, to know whether or not they are weapons related, and to know enough to target them:

- *Anarak: Waste storage site:* Iran has stated that small amounts of imported UO2 were prepared for targets at Jabr Ibn Hayan Multipurpose Laboratories (JHL), irradiated at TRR, and sent to a laboratory belonging to the MIX Facility in Tehran for separation of I-131 in a lead-shielded cell. Iran has informed the IAEA that the remaining nuclear waste was solidified and eventually transferred to a waste disposal site at Anarak. There reportedly is uranium ore near Anarak, not far from Yazd. The Talmessi Mine (Talmesi Mine), near Anarak has produced Seelite, which occurs with Uranospinite.

- *Arak:* The IAEA reports that:

    Iran is in the process of constructing the IR-40 reactor at Arak (although originally planned to be built at Esfahan, a decision is said to have been taken in 2002 to build the reactor at Arak instead). The basic design of the IR-40 was completed in 2002 and provides for the use of natural uranium oxide as fuel. It is planned to go into operation in 2014. The IR-40 is said to have been based on indigenous design. The purpose of the reactor was declared to be research and development and the production of radioisotopes for medical and industrial use.

Iran is also building a heavy water production plant (HWPP) at Arak and has said that it intends to start producing heavy water there in 2004.

In its letter of 21 October 2003, Iran acknowledged that two hot cells had been foreseen for the reactor project. In that letter, Iran also made reference to its plans for nine hot cells for the production of radioisotopes (molybdenum, iodine, xenon, cobalt-60 and iridium-192); specifically, "four for the production of radioisotopes, two for the production of cobalt and iridium and three for waste management processing" (along with 10 backup manipulators). According to the information provided in that letter, however, neither the design nor detailed information about the dimensions or the actual layout of the hot cells were available yet, because the Iranian authorities did not know the characteristics of the manipulators and lead-glass shielding windows they could procure. . . .

In the IR-40 design information provided by Iran in November 2003, Iran confirmed that it had tentative plans for a building, in the proximity of the IR-40 facilities, with hot cells for the production of "long lived radioisotopes." Iran agreed to submit the relevant preliminary design information with respect to that building in due course. In May 2004, Iran provided updated design information for the reactor, in which it noted that the planning of hot cells for "long lived radioisotopes" was no longer under consideration in light of difficulties with the procurement of equipment.[95]

Iran has informed the IAEA that it conducted laboratory-scale experiments to produce heavy water at the Esfahan Nuclear Technology Centre, that two hot cells had been foreseen for its project at Arak, and that yet another building with hot cells is planned for the production of radioisotopes. Iran appears to be at least five years away from completing the heavy water reactor at Arak. According to reports published in Russia, apparently based on information developed by the Russian Federal Security Service, facilities located at Arak are involved in R&D of unguided missiles and modifications of the Scud-S missile.

• *Ardekan [Ardakan] Nuclear Fuel Site:* This site is reportedly scheduled to be completed in mid-2005, and some reports indicate that a uranium mill with an annual capacity of 120,000 metric tons of ore and an annual output of 50 metric tons of uranium is being built 35 kilometers north of Ardakan city. The IAEA reported on November 15, 2004, that:

The ore is to be processed into uranium ore concentrate (UOC/yellowcake) at the associated mill at Ardakan, the Yellowcake Production Plant. The design capacity of the mill corresponds to that of the mine (50 tons of uranium per year). The mill startup is forecast to coincide with the start of mining at Saghand. The mill site is currently at an early stage of development; the installation of the infrastructure and processing buildings has been started. In the south of Iran, near Bandar Abbas, Iran has constructed the Gchine uranium mine and its co-located mill. The low but variable grade uranium ore found in near-surface deposits will be open-pit mined and processed at the associated mill. The estimated production design capacity is 21 t of uranium per year. Iran has stated that, as of July 2004, mining operations had started and the mill had been hot tested, during which testing a quantity of about 40 to 50 kg of yellowcake was produced.[96]

- *Bushehr: Nuclear facility and 1,000 Mwe light water nuclear power reactor:* Unit 1 of BNPP is a 1000 MW(e) light water reactor designed to use low enriched uranium oxide (up to 5 percent U-235). According to IAEA estimates made in November 2004, it is scheduled to reach first criticality in 2006. The reactor is being built by Russia. Some 600–1,000 Russians are now working on the project. Some 750 Iranian technicians, trained in Russia, will take over the plan once it becomes operational.

  It will use some 90 tons of Russian-supplied enriched uranium and is located at the site of a German-built reactor project the shah commissioned in the 1970s and which was bombed during the Iran-Iraq War. The new reactor is being built to Russian designs. There are two reactor sites at Bushehr, but no work is taking place on the second site. The reactor's design is not suited to produce high levels of plutonium, as long as it operates as designed, and would present problems because of the amount of Pu-240 produced relative to Pu-239. It can, however, be used to produce more weapons-grade materials by changing the fuel-loading cycle of the reactor and to develop the skills and technology necessary to produce other reactor designs better suited to producing weapons-grade plutonium.[97] Iran is considering the construction of three to five more power reactor facilities, which may or may not be located at Bushehr. Press reports indicate that several batteries of U.S.-made Hawk (Improved) surface-to-air missiles have been placed around Bushehr.

- *Chalus:* Chalus has been reported as a potential location for an underground nuclear weapons development facility located inside a mountain south of this coastal town. The facility has been variously reported as being staffed by experts from Russia, China, and North Korea.

- *Covert Reactor?* Unconfirmed reports have been made of a covert reactor(s) at Arak, Chalus, Darkhovin, and Tabas. Debates exist over any plans to create such reactors and whether their heat profiles could be concealed from satellite and other infrared sensors.

- *Darkhovin:* (Also referred to as Ahvaz, Darkhouin, Esteghlal, and Karun) is a suspected underground nuclear weapons facility of unspecified nature reported to be under the control of the Islamic Revolution Guard Corps and located on the Karun River south of the city of Ahvaz.

- *Esfahan (Isfahan) Nuclear Technology/Research Center (ENTC):* This facility is operated by the University of Esfahan, is Iran's largest nuclear research center and is said to employ as many as 3,000 scientists. Facilities are said to include a fuel fabrication laboratory (FFL), uranium chemistry laboratory (UCL), uranium conversion facility (UCF) and fuel manufacturing plant (FMP). Two reactors, subject to IAEA inspection are located at the ENTC: the Miniaturized Neutron Source Reactor (MNSR), a 30 kilowatt light water reactor in operation since the mid-1990s, which uses U/Al fuel enriched to 90.2 percent U-235; and the Heavy Water Zero Power Reactor (HWZPR), also located at ENTC—a 100 W heavy water reactor, in operation since the mid-1990s, which uses natural uranium metal fuel. Iran also has a light water subcritical reactor (LWSCR) using uranium metal fuel, which operates a few days out of the year, and a decommissioned graphite subcritical reactor (GSCR) that also uses uranium metal fuel.

According to some sources, this is the primary location of the Iranian nuclear weapons program, with its main buildings located at Roshandasht, 15kilometers southeast of Esfahan. At one point, Iran sought to build a uranium hexafluoride (UF6) conversion plant at the center with Chinese assistance. The IAEA did find that Iran performed at least some unreported plutonium-separation experiments at this facility. Esfahan is where Iran's largest missile assembly and production plant is located, and it is reported to be the location of a chemical weapons production facility. (Other rumored locations are at Damghan, Parchin and Qazvin.) Many conventional military facilities are in the area, including facilities for munitions productions, tank overhaul, and helicopter and fixed-wing aircraft maintenance. The main operational facilities for the army's aviation units are located at Esfahan, presumably at Khatamin Air Base northeast of the city.

The IAEA has made the facilities at Esfahan a key focus of its investigations. Its November 2004 report noted that:

> Iran carried out most of its experiments in uranium conversion between 1981 and 1993 at TNRC and at the Esfahan Nuclear Technology Centre (ENTC), with some experiments (e.g., those involving pulse columns) being carried out through early 2002. In 1991 Iran entered into discussions

with a foreign supplier for the construction at Esfahan of an industrial-scale conversion facility. Construction on the facility, UCF, was begun in the late 1990s. UCF consists of several conversion lines, principal among which is the line for the conversion of UOC to UF_6 with an annual design production capacity of 200 tons of uranium as UF_6. The UF_6 is to be sent to the uranium-enrichment facilities at Natanz, where it will be enriched up to 5 percent U-235 and the product and tails returned to UCF for conversion into low enriched UO_2 and depleted uranium metal. The design information for UCF provided by Iran indicates that conversion lines are also foreseen for the production of natural and enriched (19.7 percent) uranium metal, and natural UO_2. The natural and enriched (5 percent U-235) UO_2 are to be sent to the Fuel Manufacturing Plant (FMP) at Esfahan, where Iran has said it will be processed into fuel for a research reactor and power reactors. In March 2004, Iran began testing the process lines involving the conversion of UOC into UO_2 and UF_4, and UF_4 into UF_6. As of June 2004, 40 to 45 kilograms of UF_6 had been produced therefrom. A larger test, involving the conversion of 37 tons of yellowcake into UF_4, was initiated in August 2004. According to Iran's declaration of October 14, 2004, 22.5 tons of the 37 tons of yellowcake had been fed into the process and that approximately 2 tons of UF_4, and 17.5 tons of uranium as intermediate products and waste, had been produced. There was no indication as of that date of UF_6 having been produced during this later campaign. Iran has stated that UCF was to have been constructed under a turnkey contract with a foreign supplier, but that when the contract was canceled in 1997, Iran retained the engineering designs and used them as the basis to construct UCF with Iranian resources. Iran provided preliminary design information to the IAEA in July 2000, which has been carrying out continuous design information verification (DIV) since that time. The IAEA's enquiry into the chronology and scope of Iran's uranium conversion activities has focused on two central issues: (a) assessment of Iran's statements concerning the basis for its design of UCF (including conversion experiments), with a view to ascertaining whether Iran has declared all of its activities involving nuclear material; and (b) assessment of the declared intended uses for the products of the various UCF process lines.

In 1985, Iran brought into operation a Fuel Fabrication Laboratory (FFL) at Esfahan, about which it informed the Agency in 1993 and for which design information was provided to the Agency in 1998. It is still in operation, and is suitable for producing, on a small scale, fuel pellets. The fuel manufacturing plant to be constructed at Esfahan (FMP) is scheduled to be commissioned in 2007. According to the preliminary design information that has been provided by Iran, the facility is planned to produce 40 tons per year of UO_2 fuel (with a maximum enrichment of 5%) for research and power reactors. Iran is also building a Zirconium Production Plant (ZPP) at Esfahan which, when complete, will have a capacity to produce 10 tons of zirconium tubing per year. . . . In a letter dated 5 May 2003, Iran informed the Agency of its plan to commence in 2003 the construction of FMP. On 1 November 2003, Iran submitted preliminary design information for FMP stating that the plant capacity would be 30 t UO_2 per year. On 31 August 2004, Iran submitted updated design information which reflected an increase in plant capacity to 40 t UO_2 per year, declared to have been to accommodate the fuel needs for the Bushehr Nuclear Power Plant (BNPP) (about 25 t UO_2 per year) and the 40 MW pressurized heavy water research reactor (IR-40) (about 10 t UO_2 per year).[98]

- *Gchine uranium mine:* The IAEA reported on November 15, 2004 that:

  Iran has constructed the Gchine uranium mine and its co-located mill. The low but variable grade uranium ore found in near-surface deposits will be open-pit mined and processed at the associated mill. The estimated production design capacity is 21 t of uranium per year. Iran has stated that, as of July 2004, mining operations had started and the mill had been hot tested, during which testing a quantity of about 40 to 50 kg of yellowcake was produced. . . . Iran provided information to the Agency on the location, operational status and estimated annual production capacity of the Gchine mine and mill, the Saghand Mine and the Yellowcake Production Plant. The Agency carried out complementary access at Gchine on 17 July 2004, at the Saghand Mine on 6 October 2004 and at the Ardakan Yellowcake Production Plant on 7 October 2004, in the course of which the Agency was able to confirm the declared status of these operations.

  Iran also explored potential uranium production through the production of yellowcake using percolation leaching. Iran produced an estimated several hundred kilograms of yellowcake using temporary facilities, now dismantled, located at the Gchine mining site.[99]

- *Karaj/Karai/Hashtgerd: Nuclear Research Center for Agriculture and Medicine:* This facility is some 160 kilometers northwest of Tehran, includes a building with a dosimetry laboratory and an agricultural radiochemistry laboratory. Other buildings will house a calutron electromagnetic isotope separation system purchased from China for obtaining target materials to be radiated with neutron streams in a 30-million electron volt cyclotron. These are research systems that are not easily adaptable to nuclear weapons design efforts. There may also be a facility nearby for rocket R&D and production.

  The IAEA reports that:

  In its letter dated 21 October 2003, Iran finally acknowledged that, between 1975 and 1998, it had concluded contracts related to laser enrichment using both AVLIS and MLIS techniques with four foreign entities.[13] In the letter, Iran provided detailed information on the various contracts and acknowledged that it had carried out laser-enrichment experiments using previously undeclared imported uranium metal at TNRC between 1993 and 2000, and that it had established a pilot plant for laser enrichment at Lashkar Ab'ad, where it had also carried out experiments using imported uranium metal. According to information provided subsequently by the Iranian authorities, the equipment used there had been dismantled in May 2003 and transferred to Karaj for storage together with the uranium metal used in the experiments, before the IAEA was permitted to visit Lashkar Ab'ad in August 2003. The equipment and material were presented to IAEA inspectors at Karaj on 28 October 2003.

During the IAEA's complementary access to the mass spectrometry laboratories at Karaj in December 2003, it examined two mass spectrometers that had not been included in Iran's declaration of October 21, 2003. Iran acknowledged that the mass spectrometers had been used at Karaj in the past to provide analytical services (isotope enrichment measurements) to the AVLIS program and gave the IAEA a list of samples that had been analyzed. The IAEA collected environmental samples from the mass spectrometers; no uranium particles were found in these samples. As requested by the IAEA following complementary access at Karaj, Iran submitted additional information to it on January 5, 2004, to clarify the role of the mass spectrometers in relation to Iran's uranium enrichment program. The laboratory containing the equipment is now part of the safeguarded facility at Karaj. [100]

- *Kolahdouz:* (Kolahdouz, Kolahdooz, or Kolahdoz nuclear facility; 14 kilometers west of Tehran): The location of some of Iran's armored weapons production facilities, Kolahdouz is a large complex that the MEK claims has a concealed nuclear weapons plant, including uranium enrichment, and operates as a supplement to the uranium enrichment site in Natanz. A technical team of the IAEA visited the industrial complex in Kolahdouz; no work was seen at those locations that could be linked to uranium enrichment, but environmental samples were taken.

- *Lashkar Ab'ad pilot plant for isotope separation:* The IAEA reports that:

  Iran established a pilot plant at Lashkar Ab'ad in 2002, where it conducted laser-enrichment experiments in December 2002 and January 2003. Iran dismantled the equipment in May 2003. Iran has stated that it currently has no plans to resume the enrichment of uranium using laser isotope separation. It has indicated that it is continuing with its R&D on laser activities, such as those involving copper vapor lasers (CVLs) and Nd:YAG lasers, but that that work is not part of a program to use such lasers for uranium enrichment. . . .

While the contract for the AVLIS facility at Lashkar Ab'ad was specifically written for the delivery of a system that could demonstrably achieve enrichment levels of 3.5 percent to 7 percent, it is the opinion of IAEA experts that the system, as designed and reflected in the contract, would have been capable of highly enriched uranium (HEU) production had the entire package of equipment been delivered. In response to IAEA questions in connection with this assessment, Iran referred to the contract and the design parameters contained therein and provided information demonstrating the very limited capabilities of the equipment actually delivered to Iran under this contract to produce HEU (i.e., only in gram quantities). Iranian AVLIS researchers maintain that they were not aware of the significance of these features when they negotiated and contracted for the supply and delivery of the Lashkar Ab'ad AVLIS facility. . . .

The IAEA has completed its review of Iran's AVLIS program and has concluded that Iran's descriptions of the levels of enrichment achieved using AVLIS at the TNRC CSL and at Lashkar Ab'ad and the amounts of material used in its past activities are consistent with information available to the IAEA to date. Iran has presented all declared key equipment, which has been verified by the IAEA. If, as stated by Iran, the evaporated uranium and some collectors were discarded as waste, mainly at the Qom disposal site, recovery of the small quantities of nuclear material involved would not be feasible, and therefore accurate nuclear material accountancy is not possible. The IAEA will continue to monitor laser related activities in Iran as a routine safeguards implementation matter.

• *Lavizan I and II: Nuclear Weapons Development Center*: (Northeastern Tehran) Some analysts claimed in December 2004 that Iran was testing conventional explosives at a Lavizan site in ways that indicated they might be to simulate nuclear explosions and text high-explosive lenses and warheads. The IAEA has satellite photos that seem to support this possibility but cannot inspect without Iran's permission, because this is not a declared facility.[101]

• *Meysami Research Center*: (kilometer 27 of Karaj Special road) This research center's principal activity is chemical agent detector and chemicals. It may have a role in chemical and nuclear weapons efforts.

• *Natanz [Kashan] facility (between Isfahan and Kashan in central Iran, some 100 miles north of Esfahan, in old Kashan-Natanz):* This is reported to be a covert facility for heavy water production and centrifuge enrichment activity. The IAEA had found particles of highly enriched uranium in environmental samples taken at Natanz in August 2003. The machines the IAEA found at the pilot fuel enrichment plant [PFEP] were early European designs of Pakistani origin. Iran stated it did not carry out enrichment and that no nuclear material was introduced to the PFEP prior to IAEA sampling. The IAEA sampling found two types of highly enriched uranium, and some 1,000 centrifuges under construction.

There is a fuel enrichment plant (FEP) here of some 100,000 square meters, which the MEK claims has two 25,000-meter halls, built 8 meters deep into the ground and protected by a concrete wall 2.5 meters thick. According to some estimates, it could house as many as 50,000 centrifuges, producing enough weapons-grade uranium for 20 weapons per year. Other estimates suggest a total of 5,000 centrifuges capable of producing enough enriched uranium for several nuclear weapons a year. By mid-2004 the Natanz centrifuge facility was hardened with a roof of several meters of reinforced concrete and buried under a layer of earth some 75 feet deep.

The MEK claims that parts for centrifuges were imported and that others were built at a plant in Esfahan. They were then tested at the Kalaye plant in Ab-Ali and sent to Natanz for final assembly. Two villages near Natanz—called Lashkar Ab'ad and Ramandeh—have uranium enrichment plants hidden behind trees in orchards, are surrounded by security guards, and function as a backup to the Natanz site in case that facility comes under military attack. The labs are reported to be in the Hasthgerd region near Karaj, about 40 kilometers (25 miles) west of Tehran. There are also reports of Laser lstop Separation (LIS) experiments at Nantaz, as well as at Ramandeh (part of the Karaj Agricultural and Medical Centre) and a laser laboratory at Lashkar Ab'ad.

The IAEA describes a far more modest effort. It reports that:

> In 2001, Iran began the construction of two facilities at Natanz: the smaller scale PFEP, planned to have some 1000 centrifuges for enrichment up to 5 percent U-235; and the large scale commercial FEP, which is planned to contain over 50 000 P-1 centrifuges for enrichment up to 5 percent U-235. On 25 June 2003, Iran introduced UF6 into the first centrifuge at PFEP. As of October 2003, the installation of a 164-machine cascade was being finalized. In November 2003, the cascade was shut down. As of the IAEA's latest inspection on 11 October 2004, the cascade had not been operated and no further UF6 gas had been fed into centrifuges at PFEP. FEP has been scheduled to start receiving centrifuges in early 2005, after

the design is confirmed by the tests to be conducted in PFEP. According to Iran, the only work that has been done on the P-2 design was carried out between 2002 and 2003, largely at the workshop of a private company under contract with the Atomic Energy Organization of Iran (AEOI), and the work was limited to the manufacture and mechanical testing of a small number of modified P-2 composite rotors. Iran has stated that "no other institution (including universities), company or organization in Iran has been involved in P-2 R&D" and that "no P-2 R&D has been undertaken by or at the request of the Ministry of Defence." Iran has also said that all R&D on P-2 centrifuges had been terminated and that no other work on that, or any other centrifuge design, was conducted before 2002 or has been done since 2003. However, in its Additional Protocol declarations, Iran has foreseen P-2 R&D activities for the future.[102]

- *Parchin:* (Southeast of Tehran) Some analysts claimed in December 2004 that Iran was testing conventional explosives at this site in ways that indicated they might be able to simulate nuclear explosions and test high-explosive lenses and warheads. The IAEA has satellite photos that seem to support this possibility but cannot inspect without Iran's permission, because this is not a declared facility.[103]

- *Qatran Workshop in Central Iran:* MEK sources have claimed that a secret nuclear facility exists at the Qatran Workshop in Central Iran, some 150 miles south of Tehran. A plant has been under construction that appears to be designed to produce heavy water. Heavy water is used to moderate the nuclear chain reaction in one type of nuclear reactor, but the nuclear reactor at Bushehr does not use heavy water. State Department spokesman Richard Boucher stated in a 13 December 2002 briefing that there was "hard evidence" that Iran appeared to be constructing a uranium enrichment plant at Natanz, as well as a heavy water plant. "The suspect uranium-enrichment plant . . . could be used to produce highly-enriched uranium for weapons. The heavy-water plant could support a reactor for producing weapons-grade plutonium. These facilities are not justified by the needs of Iran's civilian nuclear program." Iran rejected the allegations and reiterated that the two plants were intended to generate electricity, but Iran has no known heavy-water reactor and no need for an indigenous source of heavy water. Heavy-water moderated reactors are better suited for plutonium production than are light water reactors.

- *Saghand [Sagend] uranium ore deposit in Yazd:* This ore deposit is said to cover an area of 100–150 square kilometers, with reserves estimated at 3,000–5,000 tons of uranium oxide. Some reports indicate a reserve of at least 1.58 million metric tons of uranium ore, with an average grade of 533 ppm (0.0533 percent U). This translates into a total uranium contents of 842 metric tons. The IAEA reported in November 2004 that:

> Iran has a long-standing program of exploration for uranium deposits, and has selected two locations for development as mines. At the Saghand Mine, located in Yazd in central Iran, low-grade hard rock ore bodies will be exploited through conventional underground mining techniques. The annual estimated production design capacity is forecast as 50 t of uranium. The infrastructure and shaft sinking are essentially complete, and tunneling towards the ore bodies has started. Ore production is forecast to start by the end of 2006. The ore is to be processed into uranium ore concentrate (UOC/yellowcake) at the associated mill at Ardakan, the Yellowcake Production Plant. The design capacity of the mill corresponds to that of the mine (50 t of uranium per year). The mill startup is forecast to coincide with the start of mining at Saghand. The mill site is currently at an early stage of development; the installation of the infrastructure and processing buildings has been started in the south of Iran, near Bandar Abbas.[104]

- *Tehran Nuclear Research Center and Kalaye Electric Company:* The research program of the Tehran-based Center for Theoretical Physics and Mathematics of the Atomic Energy Organization of Iran includes theoretical physics and other R&D related to high-energy physics, including particle physics, mathematical physics, astrophysics, theoretical nuclear physics, statistical mechanics, theoretical plasma physics, and mathematics. There is a research reactor, the TRR, located at the TNRC—a 5 megawatt pool-type light-water research reactor, which has been in operation since the late 1960s; it originally used high-enriched uranium aluminum (U/Al) alloy fuel but was reconfigured in the early 1990s and now uses fuel of U_3O_8/Al enriched to around 20 percent U-235, Iran's main missile program office is in the southwestern suburbs of Tehran.

The IAEA notes that:

> Iran has explored two other potential uranium production routes. One was the extraction of uranium from phosphoric acid. Using research scale equipment, small quantities of yellowcake were successfully produced at the Tehran Nuclear Research Centre (TNRC) laboratories. Iran has stated that there are no facilities in Iran for separating uranium from phosphoric acid other than the research facilities at TNRC. . . . Iran carried out most of its experiments in uranium conversion between 1981 and 1993 at TNRC and at the Esfahan Nuclear Technology Centre (ENTC), with some experiments (e.g., those involving pulse columns) being carried out through early 2002. . . . In February 2003, Iran acknowledged that it had imported in

1991 natural uranium, in a variety of forms, which it had not previously reported to the Agency, and that it had used some of these materials, at locations which had not previously been reported to the Agency, for testing certain parts of the UCF conversion process (i.e., uranium dissolution, purification using pulse columns and the production of uranium metal). On a number of occasions between February and July 2003, Iran stated that this information, along with documentation provided by the foreign supplier, had been sufficient to permit Iran to complete indigenously the detailed design and manufacturing of the equipment for UCF. Iran repeatedly stated that it had not carried out any research and development (R&D) or testing, even on a laboratory scale, of other more complex processes (e.g. conversion of UO_2 to UF_4 and conversion of UF_4 to UF_6) using nuclear material.[105]

. . . Following the discovery by the Agency of indications of depleted UF_4 in samples of waste taken at the Jabr Ibn Hayan Multipurpose Laboratories (JHL) at TNRC, Iran acknowledged, in a letter dated 19 August 2003, that it had carried out UF_4 conversion experiments on a laboratory scale during the 1990s at the Radiochemistry Laboratories of TNRC using depleted uranium which had been imported in 1977 and exempted from safeguards upon receipt, and which Iran had declared in 1998 (when the material was de-exempted) as having been lost during processing. In October 2003, Iran further acknowledged that, contrary to its previous statements, practically all of the materials important to uranium conversion had been produced in laboratory and bench scale experiments (in kilogram quantities) carried out at TNRC and at ENTC between 1981 and 1993 without having been reported to the Agency. The information provided in Iran's letter of 21 October 2003 stated that, in conducting these experiments, Iran had also used yellowcake imported by Iran in 1982 but only confirmed in 1990. . . .

In its letter of 21 October 2003, Iran acknowledged that the uranium metal had been intended not only for the production of shielding material, as previously stated, but also for use in its laser enrichment program (the existence of which, as discussed below, Iran had previously not acknowledged, and which was only declared to the Agency in that same letter of 21 October 2003). Iran stated that the uranium metal process line at UCF had been developed by Iranian scientists at the TNRC laboratories, and that a small quantity of the metal produced at TNRC during the development tests (about 2 kg) had been given to the laser group for its evaluation.

. . . In 1985, Iran initiated its efforts in gas centrifuge enrichment with a search of available technical literature. In 1987, Iran acquired through a clandestine supply network drawings for a P-1 centrifuge, along with samples of centrifuge components. According to Iran, gas centrifuge R&D

testing began at TNRC in 1988 and continued there until 1995, when those activities were moved to a workshop of the Kalaye Electric Company, a company in Tehran belonging to the Atomic Energy Organization of Iran (AEOI). Between 1994 and 1996, Iran received another—apparently duplicate—set of drawings for the P-1 centrifuge design, along with components for 500 centrifuges. According to Iran, it was at this time as well when Iran received design drawings for a P-2 centrifuge through the same network. Between 1997 and 2002, Iran assembled and tested P-1 centrifuges at the Kalaye Electric Company workshop where Iran says it fed UF_6 gas into a centrifuge for the first time in 1999 and, in 2002, fed nuclear material into a number of centrifuges (up to 19 machines).

. . . Given the inherent difficulties with investigating activities that ended over a decade ago, it is not possible to verify in detail the chronologies and descriptions of the experiments that took place in Iran. Thus, the Agency's activities have had to focus on assessing the consistency of the information provided by Iran and examining the remaining equipment and nuclear material. . . .

Iran also acknowledged that the Kalaye Electric Company workshop in Tehran had been used for the production of centrifuge components, but stated that there had been no testing of centrifuges assembled from these components involving the use of nuclear material, either at that workshop or at any other location in Iran. . . . According to information provided at that time by Iran, the design, research and development work, which it said had been started only five years earlier (i.e., 1997), had been based on information available from open sources and extensive computer modeling and simulation, including tests of centrifuge rotors without nuclear material. . . .

In June 2003, Iran reiterated that its centrifuge R&D had commenced only in 1997, with centrifuge testing having taken place in the Plasma Physics buildings of TNRC. The Agency was shown the areas within the buildings where the testing was said to have been conducted, and was again told that no nuclear material had been used during the test program. Based on their own observations and their discussions with Iranian authorities, the Agency enrichment technology experts concluded that it was not possible for Iran to have developed enrichment technology to the level seen at Natanz based solely on open source information, computer simulation and mechanical testing. . . . In August 2003, Iran amended these statements, informing the Agency that the decision to launch a centrifuge enrichment program had actually been taken in 1985, and that Iran had in fact received drawings of the P-1 centrifuge through a foreign intermediary around 1987. Iran stated that the centrifuge R&D program had been situated at TNRC between 1988 and 1995, and had been moved to the Kalaye Electric Company workshop in 1995. According to Iran, the centrifuge R&D activities were carried out at the Kalaye Electric Company workshop between 1995 and 2003, and were moved to Natanz in 2003.

During its August 2003 visit to Iran, the IAEA was shown electronic copies of the centrifuge engineering drawings (including the general arrangement, subassembly and component drawings). IAEA inspectors were also able to visit and take environmental samples at the Kalaye Electric Company workshop, where they noted that, since their first visit to the workshop in March 2003, considerable renovation had been made to one of the buildings on the site. As was anticipated by the IAEA at the time, the renovation, which was carried out in connection with Iran's attempt to conceal the activities carried out there, has interfered with the IAEA's ability to resolve issues associated with Iran's centrifuge enrichment program, because the IAEA was unable to see the equipment in site and could not take environmental samples while the equipment was there.

In its letter of October 21, 2003, Iran finally acknowledged that "a limited number of tests, using small amounts of UF_6, had been conducted in 1999 and 2002 at the Kalaye Electric Company workshop." In October/November 2003 and again in October 2004, Agency inspectors interviewed a former official of the AEOI, said by Iran to have been involved in its centrifuge R&D work from 1987 until he left the Kalaye Electric Company in 2001. During the latter meeting, he provided, in particular, details on the negotiations which had resulted in Iran's procurement around 1987 of the P-1 design (and sample components), and on the supply of the duplicate set of P-1 designs and the components for 500 P-1 centrifuges, delivered through intermediaries to Iran in two shipments said to have taken place in March 1994 and July 1996, and the supply of bellows in 1997 to replace previously provided poor quality bellows. He also confirmed that meetings with the intermediary continued after 1996, and included discussions on technical issues. According to the information provided by Iran, 13 official meetings took place with the clandestine supply network between 1994 and 1999. Iran has been requested to provide information on what, if any, meetings related to Iran's centrifuge program took place prior to 1994. The Agency has also requested Iran to present the shipping documents associated with the 1994 and 1996 deliveries, and to provide information on the content of the technical discussions held with the intermediaries and explain why no meetings involving AEOI officials took place after June 1999.

In January 2004, in response to a follow-up inquiry by the Agency on Iran's centrifuge enrichment program, Iran acknowledged, for the first time, that it had received in 1994 P-2 centrifuge drawings from foreign sources. Iran also stated that the AEOI had concluded a contract with the owner of a private company located in Tehran to develop a P-2 centrifuge, and that some mechanical tests had been conducted, without nuclear material, on a small number of domestically manufactured rotors based on a modified P-2 design. In its communication of 5 March 2004, Iran indicated that R&D activities on P-2 centrifuges had not been mentioned in its 21 October 2003 declaration because Iran intended to submit information on P-2 along with further declarations it is required to provide in accordance with its obligations under the Additional Protocol within the timetable established by the IAEA.

In clarifications provided in April and May 2004, Iran stated that the P-2 drawings had been received around 1995, but that, due to a shortage in professional resources and changes in AEOI management, priority was placed at that time on resolving difficulties being encountered by Iran in connection with the P-1 centrifuge, and that no actual work on the P-2 centrifuge had commenced until after the contract was concluded in early 2002. . . . The Agency has been able to interview the owner of the private company on a number of occasions since then. According to the contractor, he first saw the design for the P-2 centrifuge in early 2002, and after having received copies and reviewing them, he had decided that, since in his view Iran was not capable of manufacturing maraging steel cylinders with bellows, work should proceed with a shorter, sub-critical carbon composite rotor. He explained further that he had manufactured seven rotors and had performed some mechanical tests on them, but without using nuclear material. He said that the contract was terminated in March 2003, but that he continued to work on his own until June 2003, and that all of the centrifuge equipment had been moved to Pars Trash. In October 2004, the Agency also interviewed the former AEOI official referred to above, who was said to have originally received the P-2 centrifuge design. During these discussions, he described the negotiations that had led to the supply of the P-2 design drawings, which he recalled as having taken place around 1995 or 1996, as well as the reasons for the apparent gap of seven years before the R&D test work on the P-2 design had begun. . . .

The Iranian authorities have stated that Iran did not obtain any P-2 centrifuges from abroad, and that the components that it did have had been produced domestically in the contractor's workshop, with the exception of some raw materials and minor items supplied to the contractor by the P-1 R&D team and a few items which had been purchased from abroad in connection with the P-2 contract, such as bearings, oils, and magnets.

The contractor acknowledged that he had made enquiries with a European intermediary about the procurement of 4000 magnets with specifications suitable for use in P-2 centrifuges and that he had also mentioned to the intermediary the possibility of much higher numbers to attract the supplier and to get a good price by suggesting that larger orders would follow. The Iranian authorities have stated that no magnets were actually delivered by that intermediary to Iran, but that imported magnets relevant to P-2 centrifuges had been procured from other foreign suppliers in 2002. . . .

The IAEA has reiterated its previous requests for further information from Iran, along with supporting documentation, on the procurement of magnets for the P-2 centrifuges (in particular, on the sources of all such magnets), including attempted procurement and enquiries about procurement, and the procurement of any other relevant components, with a view to facilitating completion by the IAEA of its assessment of the P-2 experiments said to have been carried out by the private contractor. In October 2004, Iran provided the IAEA with more information in this regard, which is currently being assessed. However, there remains further information requested by the IAEA that has yet to be provided. After a number of requests by the IAEA, on October 19, 2004, Iran finally provided the IAEA with copies of the contract and the report, which had been informally translated by Iran in April 2004. These documents appear to confirm the Iranian statements about the nature of the work requested of and carried out by the contractor between 2002 and 2003. Iran has reiterated that no work was carried out on the P-2 design (or any centrifuge design other than the P-1 design) before 2002. The reasons given by Iran for the apparent gap between 1995 and 2002, however, do not provide sufficient assurance that there were no related activities carried out during that period, particularly given that the contractor was able to make the modifications necessary for the composite cylinders within a short period after early 2002, when, according to Iran, he had seen the drawings for the first time. The IAEA is attempting to verify this information, inter alia, through the network of suppliers. . . .

Between 1975 and 1998, Iran concluded with four foreign supplier's contracts related to laser enrichment using both atomic vapor laser isotope separation (AVLIS) and molecular laser isotope separation (MLIS) techniques. In connection with the first two contracts, the Agency has confirmed that the AVLIS spectroscopy equipment Iran received never properly functioned, and that Iran did not receive all of the components of the MLIS equipment. . . . In connection with the third contract, Iran carried out testing in the supplied Laser Separation Laboratory (LSL) and Comprehensive Separation Laboratory (CSL) at TNRC between 1993 and 2000, and dismantled the supplied equipment between 2000 and 2003. . . .

Between 1988 and 1993, Iran carried out plutonium separation experiments at TNRC. The shielded glove boxes in which these experiments were carried out were dismantled in 1993, relocated to JHL and used for other purposes. In 1995, Iran started constructing the MIX Facility. However, as the neutron flux of TRR is not sufficient for the production of the radioisotopes referred to above using natural uranium targets, the facility has not yet been commissioned. In its letter of 21 October 2003, Iran acknowledged the irradiation of depleted UO_2 targets at TRR and subsequent plutonium separation experiments in shielded glove boxes in the Nuclear Safety Building of TNRC. Neither the activities nor the separated plutonium had been reported previously to the Agency. . . .

In meetings held in Iran between 27 October and 1 November 2003, Iran provided additional information about these experiments. According to Iranian officials, the experiments took place between 1988 and 1993 and involved pressed or sintered UO_2 pellets prepared at ENTC using depleted uranium that had been exempted from safeguards in 1978. Iran stated that the capsules containing the pellets had been irradiated in TRR in connection with a project to produce fission product isotopes of molybdenum, iodine, and xenon and that some of the capsules had been processed and the plutonium separated. The plutonium separation was carried out at TNRC in three shielded glove boxes, which, according to Iran, were dismantled in 1993 and moved to the JHL building, where the glove boxes were used for iodine production until 1999. They were dismantled in 1999, decontaminated and sent to ENTC in 2000, where they have been stored along with related equipment since then. Iran has stated that these experiments were carried out to learn about the nuclear fuel cycle, and to gain experience in reprocessing chemistry. . . .

On November 8, 2003, the IAEA was able to take samples from the separated plutonium, which was presented to the IAEA in the form of plutonium solution contained in two bottles, one of which had completely leaked out of its container. During their inspection at JHL, IAEA inspectors were also shown four heavily shielded containers said by Iran to contain the unprocessed irradiated targets. The containers had been buried on the site of TNRC but were dug up and presented to the IAEA for verification. Using available nondestructive analysis equipment, IAEA inspectors were able to confirm that one of the containers (selected at random) contained highly radioactive material characteristic of irradiated targets. All four containers have been placed under IAEA seal for future examination. . . .

On the basis of information available to it as of November 2003, the Agency concluded: that the amount of separated plutonium declared by

Iran had been understated (quantities in the milligram range rather than the microgram range as stated by Iran); that the plutonium samples taken from a glove box said to have been involved had plutonium-240 (Pu-240) abundance higher than that found in the plutonium solution bottles presented; that there was an excess amount of americium-241 (Am-241) in the samples; and that the age of the plutonium solution in the bottles appeared to be less than the declared 12–16 years. . . .   On the basis of a subsequent recalculation carried out by it using corrected irradiation data and a corrected equation, Iran acknowledged in May 2004 that its theoretical estimations of the quantities of plutonium produced had been understated (micrograms rather than milligrams) and accepted the Agency's estimate of about 100 mg as having been correct. . . .

In early August 2004 the IAEA explained in detail the methodology it had used for dating the plutonium that had been separated and additional on going work to validate the results. The Iranian officials reiterated their previous statement that the experiments had been completed in 1993 and that no plutonium had been separated since then. The IAEA agreed to further analyze the available data. On September 15, 2004, a new set of samples was taken from the plutonium solution. The preliminary results of the analyses of the samples thus far are the same as those previously obtained, indicating that the plutonium could have been separated after 1993. On October 29, 2004, the IAEA requested additional clarifications, which are needed for a final assessment. . . .

Between 1989 and 1993, Iran irradiated two bismuth targets, and attempted to extract polonium from one of them, at TRR as part of a feasibility study for the production of neutron sources. Iran has stated that it does not have a project either for the production of Po-210 or for the production of neutron sources using Po-210, and that there [had] not been in the past any studies or projects on the production of neutron sources using Po-210. . . . In September 2003, the Agency noticed from TRR operating records that bismuth metal samples had been irradiated during the same general period as the reprocessing experiments had been carried out (1989–1993). Although bismuth is not nuclear material requiring declaration under a comprehensive safeguards agreement, the irradiation of bismuth is of interest to the Agency as it produces polonium-210 (Po-210), an intensely radioactive alpha emitting radioisotope that can be used not only for certain civilian applications (such as radioisotope thermoelectric generators (RTGs), in effect, nuclear batteries), but also, in conjunction with beryllium, for military purposes (specifically, as a neutron initiator in some designs of nuclear weapons). . . .

In the meeting on 21 May 2004, Iranian authorities continued to maintain that the purpose of the bismuth irradiation had been to produce pure Po-210 on a laboratory scale, noting that, if production and extraction of Po-210 were successful, it could be used in radioisotope thermoelectric batteries, as was the case in the SNAP-3 application (a US developed power source for use in space probes). . . . The Agency has requested access to the glove box used for the Po-210 separation; however, according to Iran, the glove box has been discarded. The Agency has also requested to see the original project proposal by the scientists involved seeking permission to carry out the project. Iran has stated that the original documentation could not be found, and has provided instead a document that it has certified as being a correct and authentic copy.

- *Uranium Mines/Facilities:* Since 1988, Iran has reportedly opened as many as 10 uranium mines, including the Saghand uranium mine in Yazd province, as well otherwise unspecified locations in Khorassan, Sistan va Baluchestan, and Hormozgan Provinces, and in Bandar-Abbas and Badar-e-Lengeh Provinces along the Gulf. Iran, however, is not rich in uranium resources, and only has proven reserves of about 3,000 tons, although its resources could be as high as 20,000–30,000 tons of U3O8.

Reports by the director general of the IAEA—dated September 1, 2004, and October 15, 2004—show that there has been low and highly enriched uranium contamination in Iranian nuclear sites. They also provide significant indications that Iran continues its nuclear development program. They indicate it has already sought to create centrifuge enrichment facilities, has experimented with laser isotope separation, and may have a design for more advanced P-2 centrifuges. They do not confirm that Iran is actively pursuing nuclear weapons and cite a number of other explanations for its activities. They do, however, cite case after case where major questions remain and Iran may well remain committed to a nuclear weapons program in spite of its agreements in late November 2004 to cease its most controversial research and development efforts, and to comply with the Nuclear Non-Proliferation Treaty and all IAEA inspection requirements.

IAEA reports indicate that Pakistan has helped Iran in its enrichment program since 1995 and may have delivered the P-2 design to the Iranians. The IAEA has warned that Iran intended to "turn 37 tons of nearly raw uranium called yellowcake, into uranium hexafluoride." Experts contend that this could be enough to create five or six atomic weapons.[106]

The future nature of Iran's efforts is uncertain. On November 15, 2004, Iran and the EU reached an agreement that read in part:

> To build further confidence, Iran has decided, on a voluntary basis, to continue and extend its suspension to include all enrichment related and reprocessing activities, and specifically: the manufacture and import of gas centrifuges and their components; the assembly, installation, testing or operation of gas centrifuges; work to undertake any plutonium separation, or to construct or operate any plutonium separation installation; and all tests or production at any uranium conversion installation. The IAEA will be notified of this suspension and invited to verify and monitor it. The suspension will be implemented in time for the IAEA to confirm before the November Board that it has been put into effect. The suspension will be sustained while negotiations proceed on a mutually acceptable agreement on long-term arrangements.[107]

This change in the Iranian position seems to have been motivated by fear of sanctions imposed by the UN Security Council and triggered Iran's agreement to suspend its nuclear program three days before the IAEA met in Vienna on November 25, 2004. On November 22, 2004, the Iranians announced "to build confidence and in line with implementing the Paris Agreement, Iran suspended uranium enrichment (and related activities) as of today." The *Associated Press* quoted the Iranian's Foreign Ministry's spokesman, Hamid Reza Asefi, as saying that "Iran's acceptance of suspension is a political decision, not an obligation, [which is] the best decision under the current circumstances."[108]

The head of the IAEA, Mohamed El Baradei said at the time of the agreement that he thought, "everything has come to a halt."[109] However, the report the IAEA had issued a few weeks earlier did not exonerate Iran of its nuclear ambitions. In fact, the report pointed out that "based on all the information currently available to the Agency, it is clear that Iran has failed in a number of instances over an extended period of time to meet its obligations under its Safeguards Agreement with respect to the reporting of nuclear material, its processing and its use, as well as the declaration of facilities where such material has been stored." The IAEA also summarized the failures of Iran as failure to report, failure to declare, failure to provide design information, and finally a failure to facilitate the implementation of the safeguards.[110]

To quote the summary in the IAEA report of October 30, 2004:

> Based on all information currently available to the Agency, it is clear that Iran has failed in a number of instances over an extended period of time to meet its obligations under its Safeguards Agreement with respect to the reporting of nuclear material, its processing and its use, as well as the declaration of facili-

ties where such material has been processed and stored. In his June, August and November 2003 reports to the Board of Governors (GOV/2003/40, GOV/2003/63, and GOV/2003/75), the Director General identified a number of instances of such failures and the corrective actions that were being, or needed to be, taken with respect thereto by Iran.

86. As assessed in light of all information available to date, these failures can now be summarized as follows:

a. Failure to report:

(i) the import of natural uranium in 1991, and its subsequent transfer for further processing;

(ii) the activities involving the subsequent processing and use of the imported natural uranium, including the production and loss of nuclear material where appropriate, and the production and transfer of waste resulting therefrom;

(iii) the use of imported natural UF6 for the testing of centrifuges at the Kalaye Electric Company workshop in 1999 and 2002, and the consequent production of enriched and depleted uranium;

(iv) the import of natural uranium metal in 1993 and its subsequent transfer for use in laser enrichment experiments, including the production of enriched uranium, the loss of nuclear material during these operations and the production and transfer of resulting waste;

(v) the production of UO2, UO3, UF4, UF6 and ammonium uranyl carbonate (AUC) from imported depleted UO2, depleted U3O8 and natural U3O8, and the production and transfer of resulting wastes; and

(vi) the production of natural and depleted UO2 targets at ENTC and their irradiation in TRR, the subsequent processing of those targets, including the separation of plutonium, the production and transfer of resulting waste, and the storage of unprocessed irradiated targets at TNRC.

b. Failure to declare:

(i) the pilot enrichment facility at the Kalaye Electric Company workshop; and

(ii) the laser enrichment plants at TNRC and the pilot uranium laser enrichment plant at Lashkar Ab'ad.

c. Failure to provide design information, or updated design information, for:

(i) the facilities where the natural uranium imported in 1991 (including wastes generated) was received, stored and processed (JHL, TRR, ENTC, waste storage facility at Esfahan and Anarak);

(ii) the facilities at ENTC and TNRC where UO2, UO3, UF4, UF6 and AUC from imported depleted UO2, depleted U3O8 and natural U3O8 were produced;

(iii) the waste storage at Esfahan and at Anarak, in a timely manner;

(iv) the pilot enrichment facility at the Kalaye Electric Company workshop;

(v) the laser enrichment plants at TNRC and Lashkar Ab'ad, and locations where resulting wastes were processed and stored, including the waste storage facility at Karaj; and

(vi) TRR, with respect to the irradiation of uranium targets, and the facility at TNRC where plutonium separation took place, as well as the waste handling facility at TNRC.

d. Failure on many occasions to cooperate to facilitate the implementation of safeguards, as evidenced by extensive concealment activities.

87. As corrective actions, Iran has submitted inventory change reports (ICRs) relevant to all of these activities, provided design information with respect to the facilities where those activities took place, and presented all declared nuclear material for Agency verification, and it undertook in October 2003 to implement a policy of cooperation and full transparency.

Nuclear Developments in 2003 and 2004. The latest round of serious charges and claims of innocence led Iran to agree with Britain, France, and Germany in October 2003 that it would (1) sign the IAEA Additional Protocol allowing improved inspection; (2) continue to cooperate with the IAEA, (3) voluntarily suspend all uranium enrichment and reprocessing activities as defined by the IAEA, and (4) engage in full cooperation with the IAEA to address and resolve all outstanding issues.[111]

Iran did sign the protocols on December 18, 2003, but did not ratify them and has severely restricted the IAEA's inspections to known and declared nuclear facilities or inspection only by prior agreement on limited terms. It also became clear during 2004 that Iran was not prepared to fully cooperate, that there were many new issues that remained unresolved, and that Iran's actions were anything but "transparent." Furthermore, on June 24, 2004, Iran declared it would continue to manufacture centrifuges and experiment with uranium hexaflouride, two of the activities of most concern to the IAEA.[112]

Baqer Zolqadr, the commander of the IRGC, also stated in August 2004 that any Israeli attack on Iran would have "terrifying consequences," and that Israel would have to "permanently forget" about its nuclear research center and reactor at Dimona. He also warned that, "the entire Zionist territory . . . is now within the range of Iran's advanced missiles."[113]

On November 17, 2004, the U.S. Secretary of State, Colin Powell, reiterated that Iran has not given up its determination to acquire a nuclear weapon or a delivery system that is capable of carrying such a weapon. "I have seen some information that would suggest that they have been actively working on delivery systems . . . You don't have a weapon until you put it in something that can deliver a weapon. . . . I am not talking about uranium or fissile material or the warhead; I'm talking about what one does with a warhead," Secretary Powell announced.[114]

In early December 2004, some U.S. intelligence experts gave a background briefing that followed upon Secretary Powell's statements. They indicated that they were convinced that Iran was aggressively seeking to develop a nuclear warhead for Iran's Shahab series of missile and that Iran was actively working on the physics package for such a warhead design.[115] The U.S. officials stated that this information did not come from Iranian opposition sources like the MEK.

IRAN'S NUCLEAR WEAPONS DEVELOPMENT OPTIONS. It is far from clear whether Iran will stop its pursuit of nuclear weapons, and it may be only a matter of time before it acquires nuclear weapons. However, it is very unclear what kind of a nuclear power Iran is or will seek to be. No plans have ever surfaced as to the number and type of weapons it is seeking to produce or the nature of its delivery forces.

Iran might be content to simply develop its technology to the point it could rapidly build a nuclear weapon. It might choose to create an undeclared deterrent and limit its weapons numbers and avoid a nuclear test. It might test and create a stockpile but not openly deploy nuclear-armed missiles or aircraft. It also, however, might create an overt nuclear force. Each option would lead to a different response for Saudi Arabia and Iran's other neighbors, as well as provoke different responses from Israel and the United States—creating different kinds of arms races, patterns of deterrence, and risks in the process.

As a result, Iran could pursue a wide range of nuclear weapons development options—many of which could be effective even if Iran was subject to many forms of preemptive attack:

- Simply carry out enough ambiguous activity to convince outside nations it has an active nuclear weapons effort, seeking to use the threat of development to create some degree of nuclear ambiguity.

- Carry out a low-level research and development effort that was covert enough to steadily move it toward a breakout capability to rapidly create weapons production capabilities, but not actually build production facilities. It could maintain ambiguity by using small redundant efforts, canceling efforts when uncovered, or pausing when acute pressure came from the outside. Developing truly advanced centrifuges or LIS facilities, and completing bomb design and simulation, before beginning development of production facilities are particularly attractive options.

- Covertly develop a highly dispersed set of small and redundant production facilities, combing covert facilities like small "folded centrifuge" operations with sheltered or underground facilities. Slowly acquire actual production capability and begin stockpiling.

- Rely on covert simulation to test bomb designs and their weaponization; test a fractional weapon undergone under the cover of an earthquake, or overtly conduct a surface test as proof of Iran's nuclear capability.

- Appear to cancel most of its ambiguous activities and wait until its civil nuclear reactor and technology program advances to the point where it is no longer dependent on outside supply, and, possibly, it can use some of its power reactors to obtain plutonium. Use compliance with the Nuclear Non-Proliferation Treaty to proliferate.

- Deploy its Shahab missiles with conventional warheads and create a launch on warning/launch under attack capability mixed with sheltering and mobility. Arm the missiles with weapons of mass destruction once this capability is ready. Alternatively, covertly arm some missiles as soon as the Shahab missiles and warheads are ready and/or seek at least limited missile defenses like the SA-400. Combine Shahab forces with air units and sea-based cruise missile units to create survivable and redundant forces. Either announce nuclear capability once a survivable/retaliatory force is in being or rely on nuclear ambiguity.

- Stop at fission weapons, or go on to develop "boosted" and true thermonuclear weapons.

- Stop building up a force at the level of minimal assured deterrence; participate in an open-ended arms race, seek "parity" with other regional power like Israel—at least in terms of weapons numbers.

- Rely on an area targeting capability or develop a point target capability as well.

- Deploy satellites to improve targeting, damage assessment, and C⁴I capabilities.

- Develop small weapons, and/or radiological weapons, for possible covert delivery or use by extremist and/or proxy organizations. Use the threat of transfer as a further deterrent, execute strikes in ways where deniability of responsibility has some credibility, or use actual transfer to aid in attacks or for retaliatory purposes.

It is also impossible to dismiss the possibility that Iran could respond to any decision to give up nuclear weapons by developing and producing advanced biological weapons, or that it may already have biological and nuclear efforts going on in parallel. It might also choose to develop and use radiological weapons. Such weapons might take three forms—all of which would interact with its potential use of chemical and biological weapons.

- *The first would be a "dirty weapon"* using fissile material with contaminated or low enrichment levels that would have limited heat and blast effects but still produce yields of three to five kilotons and which would effectively poison a city if detonated near the ground. Such a device would reduce some of the manufacturing and design problems inherent in creating clean or efficient nuclear weapons.

- *The second would be to use a weapon that had not been tested, that was felt to be unreliable, or that was on an inaccurate missile* and detonate it near the ground so that radiation effects compensate for a failure to reach design efficiency or accuracy of the delivery system.

- *The third would be to use radioactive material in micropowder or liquid form as a terror or unconventional weapon.* It would be very difficult to get substantial lethality from the use of radioactive material, and such a weapon would be less efficient than biological weapons in terms of weight and lethality. It would, however, have the capacity to contaminate a key area and to create panic.

While the United States and Russia have rejected radiological weapons because they have the ability to precisely control the yield from their nuclear weapons, such options might be attractive to Iran or Iraq. As is the case with chemical and biological weapons, even the prospect of Iran's acquiring any such nuclear weapons has increased its ability to intimidate its neighbors.

Iran could deliver chemical, biological, or nuclear weapons on any of its fighter bombers, use covert delivery means, or use its missiles. It could use its Scuds and some types of antiship missiles to deliver such warheads relatively short distances. Its Shahab-3 missiles could probably reach virtually all of the targets in Gulf countries, including many Saudi cities on the Red Sea coast and in western Saudi Arabia.

As has been discussed earlier, Iran's Shahab-3s are probably too inaccurate and payload limited to be effective in delivering conventional weapons. This does not mean that conventionally armed Shahab missiles would not use terror weapons, or weapons of intimidation, but they could only have a major military impact—even against area targets—if they were armed with warheads carrying weapons of mass destruction. Moreover, Saudi Arabia faces the possibility of an Iranian transfer of weapons of mass destruction to some anti-Saudi extremist group or proxy. These currently do not seem to be probable scenarios, but Saudi Arabia is worried.

Senior Saudi officials have said that Saudi Arabia has examined its options for responding to such an Iranian threat, including an effort to acquire its own nuclear weapons, but has rejected such an option. The Saudi media has also recognized the threat. For example, a Saudi writer, Abdurrahman Alrashid, in an article in *Al-Sharq Al-Awsat,* stated: "Yes, we are afraid of the Iranian Uranium." He went on to argue that the Iranians are not building the bomb only to threaten Israel and the United States, but also the Gulf countries.[116] Iran has tried to dominate the Gulf region since the revolution, and continues to this day.

POSSIBLE DATES FOR IRAN'S ACQUISITION OF NUCLEAR WEAPONS. There is no way to estimate when Iran will get nuclear weapons or to be certain that Iran will push its nuclear programs forward to the point where it has actual weapons. In fact, there is a long history of estimates of possible dates that does little more than warn that such estimates are either extremely uncertain or have limited value.

Lt. Gen. Binford Peay, the commander of USCENTCOM, stated in June, 1997, "I would predict to you that it would be some time at the turn of the next century. . . . I wouldn't want to put a date on it. I don't know if its 2010, 2007, 2003. I am just saying its coming closer. Your instincts tell you that that's the kind of speed they are moving at."[117] Robert Gates, then director of central intelligence, testified to Congress in February 1992 that Iran was "building up its special weapons capability as part of a massive . . . effort to develop its military and defense capability."[118] In 1992 press reports on the U.S. Central Intelligence Agency National Intelligence Estimates (NIE) on this subject indicated that the CIA estimated Iran could have a nuclear weapon by the year 2000. Reports coming out of Israel in January 1995, also claimed that the United States and Israel estimated Iran could have a nuclear weapon in five years.[119]

During the same period, U.S. intelligence sources denied the reports coming out of Israel and estimated that it might take 7 to 15 years for Iran to acquire a nuclear weapon.[120] As has been mentioned earlier, John Holum testified to Congress in 1995 that Iran could have the bomb by 2003. In 1997 he testified that Iran could have the bomb by 2005–2007.[121] Although two years had passed in which Iran might have made substantial progress, the U.S. estimate of the earliest date at which Iran could make its own bomb slipped by two to four years.

U.S. Secretary of Defense William Perry stated on January 9, 1995, "We believe that Iran is trying to develop a nuclear program. We believe it will be many, many years until they achieve such a capability. There are some things they might be able to do to short-cut that time."[122] In referring to "short cuts," Secretary Perry was concerned with the risk that Iran could obtain fissile material and weapons technology from the former Soviet Union or some other nation capable of producing fissile material.

In 1996, John M. Deutch—then the director of central intelligence—testified to Congress that: "We judge that Iran is actively pursuing an indigenous nuclear weapons capability. . . . Specifically, Iran is attempting to develop the capability to produce both plutonium and highly enriched uranium. In an attempt to shorten the timeline to a weapon, Iran has launched a parallel effort to purchase fissile material, mainly from sources in the former Soviet Union." He indicated that Iran's indigenous uranium-enrichment program seemed to be focused on the development of gas centrifuges and that Iran's nuclear weapons program was still at least 8 to 10 years away from producing nuclear arms, although this time could be shortened significantly with foreign assistance.[123]

A detailed Department of Defense report on proliferation was issued in 1997. It did not comment on the timing of Iran's nuclear efforts. It did, however, draw broad conclusions about the scale of the Iranian nuclear program and how it fit into Iran's overall efforts to acquire weapons of mass destruction. What is striking about this report is that some eight years later, its conclusions still seem to broadly reflect the department's views regarding Iran's efforts to acquire both weapons of mass destruction and long-range missiles:

> Iran's national objectives and strategies are shaped by its regional political aspirations, threat perceptions, and the need to preserve its Islamic government. Tehran strives to be a leader in the Islamic world and seeks to be the dominant power in the Gulf. The latter goal brings it into conflict with the United States. Tehran would like to diminish Washington's political and military influence in the region. Iran also remains hostile to the ongoing Middle East peace process and supports the use of terrorism as an element of policy. Within the framework of its national goals, Iran continues to give high priority to expanding its NBC weapons and missile programs. In addition, Iran's emphasis on pursuing independent production capabilities for NBC weapons and missiles is driven by its experience during the 1980-1988 war with Iraq, during which it was unable to respond adequately to Iraqi chemical and missile attacks and suffered the effects of an international arms embargo.

Iran perceives that it is located in a volatile and dangerous region, virtually surrounded by potential military threats or unstable neighbors. These include the Iraqi government of Saddam Hussein, Israel, U.S. security agreements with the Gulf Cooperation Council (GCC) states and accompanying U.S. military presence in the Gulf, and instability in Afghanistan and the Central Asian states of the former Soviet Union.

Iran still views Baghdad as the primary regional threat to the Islamic Republic, even though Iraq suffered extensive damage during the Gulf War. Further, Iran is not convinced that Iraq's NBC programs will be adequately restrained or eliminated through continued UN sanctions or monitoring. Instead, the Iranians believe that they will face yet another challenge from their historical rival.

Tehran is concerned about strong U.S. ties with the GCC states because these states have received substantial amounts of modern Western conventional arms, which Tehran seeks but cannot acquire, and because U.S. security guarantees make these states less susceptible to Iranian pressure. While Tehran probably does not believe GCC nations have offensive designs against the Islamic Republic, it may be concerned that the United States will increase mistrust between Iran and the Arab states. It also likely fears that the sizable U.S. military presence in the region could lead to an attack against Iran. Iran may also be concerned by Israel's strategic projection capabilities and its potential to strike Iran in a variety of ways. For all these reasons, Tehran probably views NBC weapons and the ability to deliver them with missiles as decisive weapons for battlefield use, as deterrents, and as effective means for political intimidation of less powerful neighboring states.

In recent years, Iran's weak economy has limited the development of its NBC weapons and missile programs, although oil price increases in 1996 may have relieved the pressure at least temporarily. Tehran's international debt exceeds $30 billion, although Iran is meeting its debt repayment obligations. Iran also is facing a rapidly growing population that will exact greater future demands from its limited economy. Despite these internal problems, Iran assigns a high priority to attaining production self-sufficiency for NBC weapons and missiles. Therefore, funding for these efforts is likely to be a high priority for the next several years.

Tehran has attempted to portray U.S. containment efforts as unjust, in an attempt to convince European or Asian suppliers to relax export restrictions on key technologies. At the same time, foreign suppliers must consider the risk of sanctions or political embarrassment because of U.S.-led containment efforts.

Iran's nuclear program, focusing on electric power production, began during the 1970s under the Shah. Research and development efforts also were conducted on fissile material production, although these efforts were halted during the Iranian revolution and the Iran-Iraq war. However, the program has been restarted, possibly in reaction to the revelations about the scope of Iraq's nuclear weapons program.

Iran is trying to acquire fissile material to support development of nuclear weapons and has set up an elaborate system of military and civilian organizations to support its effort. Barring outright acquisition of a nuclear weapon from a foreign source, Iran could pursue several other avenues for weapon development. The shortest route, depending on weapon design, could be to purchase or steal fissile material. Also, Iran could attempt to produce highly enriched uranium if it acquired the appropriate facilities for the front-end of the nuclear fuel cycle. Finally, Iran could pursue development of an entire fuel cycle, which would allow for long-term production of plutonium, similar to the route North Korea followed.

Iran does not yet have the necessary infrastructure to support a nuclear weapons program, although is actively negotiating for purchase of technologies and whole facilities to support all of the above strategies. Iran claims it is trying to establish a complete nuclear fuel cycle to support a civilian energy program, but this same fuel cycle would be applicable to a nuclear weapons development program. Iran is seeking foreign sources for many elements of the nuclear fuel cycle. Chinese and Russian supply policies are key to whether Iran will successfully acquire the needed technology, expertise, and infrastructure to manufacture the fissile material for a weapon and the ability to fashion a usable device. Russian or Chinese supply of nuclear power reactors, allowed by the NPT, could enhance Iran's limited nuclear infrastructure and advance its nuclear weapons program.

Iran has had a chemical weapons production program since early in the Iran-Iraq war. It used chemical agents to respond to Iraqi chemical attacks on several occasions during that war. Since the early 1990s, it has put a high priority on its chemical weapons program because of its inability to respond in kind to Iraq's chemical attacks and the discovery of substantial Iraqi efforts with advanced agents, such as the highly persistent nerve agent VX. Iran ratified the CWC, under which it will be obligated to eliminate its chemical program over a period of years. Nevertheless, it continues to upgrade and expand its chemical warfare production infrastructure and munitions arsenal.

Iran manufactures weapons for blister, blood, and choking agents; it is also believed to be conducting research on nerve agents. Iran has a stockpile of these weapons, including artillery shells and bombs, which could be used in another conflict in the region.

Although Iran is making a concerted effort to attain an independent production capability for all aspects of its chemical weapons program, it remains dependent on foreign sources for chemical warfare-related technologies. China is an important supplier of technologies and equipment for Iran's chemical warfare program. Therefore, Chinese supply policies will be key to whether Tehran attains its long-term goal of independent production for these weapons.

Iran's biological warfare program began during the Iran-Iraq war. The pace of the program probably has increased because of the 1995 revelations about the scale of Iraqi efforts prior to the Gulf War. The relative low cost of developing these weapons may be another motivating factor. Although this program is in the research and development stage, the Iranians have considerable expertise with pharmaceuticals, as well as the commercial and military infrastructure needed to produce basic biological warfare agents. Iran also can make some of the hardware needed to manufacture agents. Therefore, while only small quantities of usable agent may exist now, within 10 years, Iran's military forces may be able to deliver biological agents effectively. Iran has ratified the BWC.

Iran has an ambitious missile program, with SCUD B, SCUD C, and CSS-8 (a Chinese surface-to-surface missile derived from a surface-to-air missile) missiles in its inventory. Having first acquired SCUD missiles from Libya and North Korea for use during the Iran-Iraq war, the Iranians are now able to produce the missile themselves. This has been accomplished with considerable equipment and technical help from North Korea. Iran has made significant progress in the last few years toward its goal of becoming self-sufficient in ballistic missile production.

Iran produces the solid-propellant 150-kilometer range Nazeat 10 and 200-kilometer range Zelzal unguided rockets. Iran also is trying to produce a relatively short-range solid-propellant missile. For the longer term, Iran's goal is to establish the capability to produce medium range ballistic missiles to expand its regional influence. It is attempting to acquire production infrastructure to enable it to produce the missiles itself. Like many of Iran's other efforts, success with future missile capabilities will depend on key equipment and technologies from China, North Korea, and Russia.

Iran's missiles allow it to strike a wide variety of key economic and military targets in several neighboring countries, including Turkey, Saudi Arabia, and the other Gulf states. Possible targets include oil installations, airfields, and ports, as well as U.S. military deployment areas in the region. All of Iran's missiles are on mobile launchers, which enhance their survivability. Should Iran succeed in acquiring or developing a longer-range missile like the North Korean No Dong, it could threaten an even broader area, including much of Israel.

Iran has purchased land-, sea-, and air-launched short-range cruise missiles from China; it also has a variety of foreign-made air-launched short-range tactical missiles. Many of these systems are deployed as anti-ship weapons in or near the Gulf. Iran also has a variety of Western and Soviet-made fighter aircraft, artillery, and rockets available as potential means of delivery for NBC weapons.

In the future, as Iran becomes more self-sufficient at producing chemical or biological agents and ballistic missiles, there is a potential that it will become a supplier. For example, Iran might supply related equipment and technologies to other states trying to develop capabilities, such as Libya or Syria. There is precedent for such action; Iran supplied Libya with chemical agents in 1987.[124]

Martin Indyck, assistant secretary for Near East affairs, testified to the Senate Foreign Relations Committee on July 28, 1998, that Iran's Shahab-3 and Shahab-4 programs were clearly linked to its efforts to acquire nuclear weapons. He made it clear that the missiles would give Iran the range to hit targets in Israel, Turkey, and Saudi Arabia. In regard to Iran's nuclear program, Indyck stated that Iran had a "clandestine nuclear weapons program. People tend to say that a nuclear weapons capability is many years off. Our assessments vary. I would want to be a bit cautious about that because I believe there are large gaps in our knowledge of what is going on there because it's a clandestine program."[125]

There has been relatively little new formal testimony on the nature of U.S. estimates of the timing of Iran's nuclear program, and the director of the CIA did not address this subject in his testimony to Congress on the "World Wide Threat" on February 2, 2000. U.S. intelligence has, however, continued to flag the Iranian nuclear threat as part of its broader assessments of Iran's efforts to proliferate. Since 1997 the Nonproliferation Center of the Office of the Director of Central Intelligence has issued a series of unclassified reports on Iran's efforts to acquire nuclear weapons technology. The most recent version of the report was issued in February 2000, and focuses on developments in Iran since 1998:

> Iran remains one of the most active countries seeking to acquire WMD and ACW technology from abroad. In doing so, Tehran is attempting to develop an indigenous capability to produce various types of weapons—nuclear, chemical, and biological—and their delivery systems. During the reporting period, Iran focused its efforts to acquire WMD- and ACW-related equipment, materials, and technology primarily on entities in Russia, China, North Korea and Western Europe.
>
> For the first half of 1999, entities in Russia and China continued to supply a considerable amount and a wide variety of ballistic missile-related goods and technology to Iran. Tehran is using these goods and technologies to support current production programs and to achieve its goal of becoming self-suffi-

cient in the production of ballistic missiles. Iran already is producing Scud short-range ballistic missiles (SRBMs) and has built and publicly displayed prototypes for the Shahab-3 medium-range ballistic missile (MRBM), which had its initial flight test in July 1998 and probably has achieved "emergency operational capability"—i.e., Tehran could deploy a limited number of the Shahab-3 prototype missiles in an operational mode during a perceived crisis situation. In addition, Iran's Defense Minister last year publicly acknowledged the development of the Shahab-4, originally calling it a more capable ballistic missile than the Shahab-3, but later categorizing it as solely a space launch vehicle with no military applications. Iran's Defense Minister also has publicly mentioned plans for a "Shahab-5."

For the reporting period, Tehran continued to seek considerable dual-use bio-technical equipment from entities in Russia and Western Europe, ostensibly for civilian uses. Iran began a biological warfare (BW) program during the Iran-Iraq war, and it may have some limited capability for BW deployment. Outside assistance is both important and difficult to prevent, given the dual-use nature of the materials, the equipment being sought, and the many legitimate end uses for these items.

Iran, a Chemical Weapons Convention (CWC) party, already has manufactured and stockpiled chemical weapons, including blister, blood, and choking agents and the bombs and artillery shells for delivering them. During the first half of 1999, Tehran continued to seek production technology, expertise, and chemicals that could be used as precursor agents in its chemical warfare (CW) program from entities in Russia and China. It also acquired or attempted to acquire indirectly through intermediaries in other countries equipment and material that could be used to create a more advanced and self-sufficient CW infrastructure.

Iran sought nuclear-related equipment, material, and technical expertise from a variety of sources, especially in Russia, during the first half of 1999. Work continues on the construction of a 1,000-megawatt nuclear power reactor in Bushehr, Iran, that will be subject to International Atomic Energy Agency (IAEA) safeguards. In addition, Russian entities continued to interact with Iranian research centers on various activities. These projects will help Iran augment its nuclear technology infrastructure, which in turn would be useful in supporting nuclear weapons research and development. The expertise and technology gained, along with the commercial channels and contacts established-even from cooperation that appears strictly civilian in nature-could be used to advance Iran's nuclear weapons research and developmental program.

Russia has committed to observe certain limits on its nuclear cooperation with Iran. For example, President Yel'tsin has stated publicly that Russia will not provide militarily useful nuclear technology to Iran. Beginning in January

1998, the Russian Government took a number of steps to increase its oversight of entities involved in dealings with Iran and other states of proliferation concern. In 1999, it pushed a new export control law through the Duma. Russian firms, however, faced economic pressures to circumvent these controls and did so in some cases. The Russian Government, moreover, failed in some cases regarding Iran to enforce its export controls. Following repeated warnings, the US Government in January 1999 imposed administrative measures against Russian entities that had engaged in nuclear- and missile-related cooperation with Iran. The measures imposed on these and other Russian entities (which were identified in 1998) remain in effect.

China pledged in October 1997 not to engage in any new nuclear cooperation with Iran but said it would complete cooperation on two ongoing nuclear projects, a small research reactor and a zirconium production facility at Esfahan that Iran will use to produce cladding for reactor fuel. The pledge appears to be holding. As a party to the Nuclear Nonproliferation Treaty (NPT), Iran is required to apply IAEA safeguards to nuclear fuel, but safeguards are not required for the zirconium plant or its products.

Iran is attempting to establish a complete nuclear fuel cycle for its civilian energy program. In that guise, it seeks to obtain whole facilities, such as a uranium conversion facility, that, in fact, could be used in any number of ways in support of efforts to produce fissile material needed for a nuclear weapon. Despite international efforts to curtail the flow of critical technologies and equipment, Tehran continues to seek fissile material and technology for weapons development and has set up an elaborate system of military and civilian organizations to support its effort.[126]

Unofficial or leaked estimates have, however, appeared to grow more pessimistic in recent years. The *New York Times* and *Washington Post* published reports in January 2000 that the CIA now estimated that it could not characterize the timing of the Iranian nuclear weapons program and that Iran might already have a bomb. These reports, however, seem to have dealt with an intelligence report that focused on the inherent uncertainties in estimating Iranian capabilities, rather than to have been the result of any radical change in an estimate of how rapidly Iran could produce a weapon.[127]

Further leaks—following the *New York Times* report—indicated the CIA had concluded that Iran was capable of completing the design and manufacture of all aspects of a nuclear weapon except the acquisition of fissile material—an accomplishment that Iraq had also mastered by 1990. While the details of the report were never leaked, it seems likely that it concluded that Iran could now design medium-sized plutonium and uranium weapons and manufacture the high-explosive lens, neutron initiators, high-speed capacitors, and other components of the weapon. It could conduct fissile simulations of the explosive behavior of such designs using modern test equipment in ways similar to the Iraqi and Pakistani nuclear programs and could rapidly assemble a weapon from these components if it could obtain illegal fissile material.

It seems likely that the report concluded that Iran now had the technology for processing highly enriched plutonium simply because no country that has ever seriously attempted such processing has failed, but Iran would need fissile or borderline fissile uranium to make a bomb. As a result, the key uncertainty was whether the United States could monitor all potential sources of fissile material with enough accuracy to ensure that Iran did not have a weapon and the answer was no.

Although any such conclusions are speculative, it also seems likely that the U.S. intelligence community concluded that it is not possible to perfectly identify the level of Iranian nuclear weapons efforts, the specific organizations involved, the location and nature of all facilities, the foreign purchasing offices, and Iran's technical success. U.S. intelligence certainly knows far more than it makes public, but Iran has been carrying out a covert program since the shah without one known case of a major defector or public example of a reliable breakthrough in human intelligence (HUMINT). It also learned during the Iran-Iraq War that it needed to ensure its facilities were not centralized and vulnerable and had to conceal its activities as much as possible from any kind of intelligence surveillance. The strengthening of the Nuclear Non-Proliferation Treaty inspection regime, and Iran's search for a more moderate effort, has almost certainly reinforced these efforts to conceal its programs.[128]

Then CIA Deputy Director for Intelligence John McLaughlin made the following broad comments on the uncertainties in estimating the nature of efforts to proliferate in an interview in January 2000:

> I would say the problem of proliferation of weapons of mass destruction is becoming more complex and difficult. . . . We're starting to see more evidence of what I might call kind of secondary proliferation. That is more evidence of sharing of information and data among countries that are striving to obtain weapons. . . . As the systems mature in the obvious countries like North Korea and Iran, they themselves have the potential to start becoming sources of proliferation as distinct from aspirants. And that begins to complicate the whole picture. . . . In the intelligence business (denial and deception) is an art form unto itself, it is how do you deny information to the other side and how do you deceive the other side? . . . Countries that are building such weapons are learning more and more about how to do that, making our job harder. . . . So if there is an issue that is to me personally worrying, it's the increasing complexity of the proliferation challenge. . . . To some degree we're dealing with

problems that are fuelled by hundreds of years of history. At the same time this past is colliding with the future, because you have these same people now using laptop computers and commercial encryption . . . You're not going to find that information on their Web sites. You're going to have to go out and get it somewhere clandestinely, either through human collection or through technical means.[129]

A recent unclassified CIA report on Iran's efforts covers developments through the end of 2003 and was issued in the spring of 2004. It makes the following judgments about Iran's nuclear weapons efforts and other programs, and while these do not take account of the developments in 2004 that have been discussed earlier, they still seem to broadly reflect current U.S. intelligence assessments:

> Iran continued to vigorously pursue indigenous programs to produce nuclear, chemical, and biological weapons. Iran is also working to improve delivery systems as well as ACW. To this end, Iran continued to seek foreign materials, training, equipment, and know-how. During the reporting period, Iran still focused particularly on entities in Russia, China, North Korea, and Europe. Iran's nuclear program received significant assistance in the past from the proliferation network headed by Pakistani scientist A.Q. Khan.

> *Nuclear.* The United States remains convinced that Tehran has been pursuing a clandestine nuclear weapons program, in contradiction to its obligations as a party to the Nuclear Non-proliferation Treaty (NPT). During 2003, Iran continued to pursue an indigenous nuclear fuel cycle ostensibly for civilian purposes but with clear weapons potential. International scrutiny and International Atomic Energy Agency (IAEA) inspections and safeguards will most likely prevent Tehran from using facilities declared to the IAEA directly for its weapons program as long as Tehran remains a party to the NPT. However, Iran could use the same technology at other, covert locations for military applications.

> Iran continues to use its civilian nuclear energy program to justify its efforts to establish domestically or otherwise acquire the entire nuclear fuel cycle. Iran claims that this fuel cycle would be used to produce fuel for nuclear power reactors, such as the 1,000-megawatt light-water reactor that Russia is continuing to build at the southern port city of Bushehr. However, Iran does not need to produce its own fuel for this reactor because Russia has pledged to provide the fuel throughout the operating lifetime of the reactor and is negotiating with Iran to take back the irradiated spent fuel. An Iranian opposition group, beginning in August of 2002, revealed several previously undisclosed Iranian nuclear facilities, sparking numerous IAEA inspections since February 2003. Subsequent reports by the IAEA Director General revealed numerous failures

by Iran to disclose facilities and activities, which run contrary to its IAEA safe-guards obligations. Before the reporting period, the A.Q. Khan network provided Iran with designs for Pakistan's older centrifuges, as well as designs for more advanced and efficient models, and components.

The November 2003 report of the IAEA Director General (DG) to the Board of Governors describes a pattern of Iranian safeguards breaches, including the failure to: report the import and chemical conversion of uranium compounds, report the separation of plutonium from irradiated uranium targets, report the enrichment of uranium using both centrifuges and lasers, and provide design information for numerous fuel cycle facilities. In October 2003, Iran sent a report to the DG providing additional detail on its nuclear program and signed an agreement with the United Kingdom, France, and Germany that included an Iranian promise to suspend all enrichment and reprocessing efforts. On 18 December 2003, Iran signed the Additional Protocol (AP) to its IAEA Safeguards Agreement but took no steps to ratify the Protocol during this reporting period.

Ballistic Missile. Ballistic missile-related cooperation from entities in the former Soviet Union, North Korea, and China over the years has helped Iran move toward its goal of becoming self-sufficient in the production of ballistic missiles. Such assistance during 2003 continued to include equipment, technology, and expertise. Iran's ballistic missile inventory is among the largest in the Middle East and includes some 1,300-km-range Shahab-3 medium-range ballistic missiles (MRBMs) and a few hundred short-range ballistic missiles (SRBMs)—including the Shahab-1 (Scud-B), Shahab-2 (Scud C), and Tondar-69 (CSS-8)—as well as a variety of large unguided rockets. Already producing Scud SRBMs, Iran announced that it had begun production of the Shahab-3 MRBM and a new solid-propellant SRBM, the Fateh-110. In addition, Iran publicly acknowledged the development of follow-on versions of the Shahab-3. It originally said that another version, the Shahab-4, was a more capable ballistic missile than its predecessor but later characterized it as solely a space launch vehicle with no military applications. Iran is also pursuing longer-range ballistic missiles.

Chemical. Iran is a party to the Chemical Weapons Convention (CWC). Nevertheless, during the reporting period it continued to seek production technology, training, and expertise from foreign entities that could further Tehran's efforts to achieve an indigenous capability to produce nerve agents. Iran may have already stockpiled blister, blood, choking, and, possibly nerve agents—and the bombs and artillery shells to deliver them—which it previously had manufactured.

Biological. Even though Iran is part of the Biological Weapons Convention (BWC), Tehran probably maintained an offensive BW program. Iran continued to seek dual-use biotechnical materials, equipment, and expertise that could be used in Tehran's BW program. Iran probably has the capability to produce at least small quantities of BW agents.

Advanced Conventional Weapons. Iran continued to seek and acquire conventional weapons and production technologies, primarily from Russia, China, and North Korea. Tehran also sought high-quality products, particularly weapons components and dual-use items, or products that proved difficult to acquire through normal governmental channels.[130]

Maj. Gen. Aharon Zeevi Farkash, the head of Israeli Military Intelligence (AMAN), stated in August 2004 that, "once they have the ability to produce enough enriched uranium, we estimate that the first bomb will be constructed within two years—i.e., the end of 2006 or the beginning of 2007."[131]

At present, most experts feel that Iran has all the basic technology it needs to build a bomb but lacks any rapid route to getting fissile uranium and plutonium unless it can steal or buy it from another country. They also believe that Iran is increasingly worried about preemptive strikes by Israel or the United States. As a result, some feel that Iran has deliberately lowered the profile of its activities and only conducts a low-to-moderate-level weapons design and development effort.[132] As a result, many feel that Iran is at least five to seven years away from acquiring a nuclear device using its own enriched material, and is six to nine years away from acquiring the ability to design a nuclear weapon that can be fitted in the warhead of a long-range missile system.

There are experts, however, who feel that Iran is working actively on the design of missile warheads and bombs at a level of activity that indicates it may well be significantly closer to having a bomb. These experts also feel that Iran has a covert nuclear weapons design and enrichment effort that is developed in parallel with its more-overt nuclear research and power activities, and that the elements of this program are well dispersed and designed to have denial covers that can claim they are peaceful research or efforts conducted in the past. They state that the information they rely on has not been provided by opposition sources.[133]

Much hinges on the level of centrifuge development Iran has made and its covert ability to acquire/manufacture centrifuges and to assemble them into chains that can be hidden and deployed either in large underground/sheltered facilities, or buildings that appear to have other uses. Experts disagree over the level of technology Iran has, which can make the difference between chains of hundreds and thousands of centrifuges, and whether it has moved beyond the limited levels of efficiency found in the P2 centrifuges being manufactured for Libya. Rotor design and overall efficiency is critical in determining the size of the facilities needed to spin uranium hexaflouride into enriched uranium and how quickly Iran could acquire a weapon. There are significant time gaps and uncertainties in the data Iran has provided to the IAEA, and it may have advanced beyond the designs of the 20 centrifuges it has declared to the IAEA. This is, however, a major "wild card" in estimating Iran's progress.[134]

Another "wild card" in these estimates is that the deadlines would change so radically if Iran could buy fissile material from another nation or source—such as the 500 kilograms of fissile material the United States airlifted out of Kazakhstan in 1994. This was enough material to make up to 25 nuclear weapons, and the United States acted primarily because Iran was actively seeking to buy such material.[135] If Iran could obtain weapons-grade material, a number of experts believe that it could probably develop a gun or simple implosion nuclear weapon in 9 to 36 months and might be able to deploy an implosion weapon suited for missile warhead or bomb delivery in the same period.

The risk of such a transfer of fissile material is significant. U.S. experts believe that all of the weapons and fissile material remaining in the former Soviet Union are now stored in Russian facilities. The security of these facilities is still erratic, however, and there is a black market in nuclear material. While the radioactive material sold on the black market by the Commonwealth Independent States (CIS) and Central European citizens to date has consisted largely of plutonium 240, low-grade enriched uranium, or isotopes of material that have little value in a nuclear-weapons program, this is no guarantee for the future. There are also no guarantees that Iran will not be able to purchase major transfers of nuclear weapons components and nuclear ballistic missile warhead technology.

Iran's Nuclear War–Fighting Doctrine and Capabilities. Little meaningful data are available on Iranian nuclear doctrine and targeting—to the extent current plans would even be relevant in the future. The same is true of Iranian plans to limit the vulnerability of its weapons and facilities—and whether Iran would try to create a launch-on-warning or launch-under-attack capability. It is easy to speculate at vast length on what Iran would do with nuclear weapons. However, it is impossible to determine how aggressively Iran would exploit such a capability in terms of threatening or intimidating its neighbors or putting pressure on the West. Trying to guess at Iran's war-fighting doctrine and actions in using weapons of mass destruction simply lacks meaningful data.

It is also quite possible that Iran has not yet looked far enough beyond its nuclear weapons acquisition efforts to work out detailed plans for possession. There is no way to know if Iran would choose a relatively stable model of deterrence or aggressively exploit its possession politically. It is equally difficult to guess whether Iran would develop an aggressive doctrine for use, consider developing a launch on warning/launch under attack capability, or reserve the use of such a weapon as a last resort.[136]

As for war-fighting capability, any working nuclear device Iran is likely to develop will be sufficient to destroy any hardened target, area target, or city in the Middle East if the delivery vehicle is accurate enough. Nuclear weapons do, however, differ sharply in their effect as they grow in size. If Iran had to rely on inaccurate delivery systems, it not only would have to target area targets like cities and major energy facilities, it might also have either to use multiple strikes or to develop more advanced and higher-yield nuclear weapons like boosted weapons. Alternatively, it might rely on ground bursts and fallout.

Iran's nuclear efforts will also interactive heavily with the progress Iran makes in biological and chemical weapons programs and its efforts to improve its delivery capabilities. By the time Iran has significant nuclear capability, it may have significant missile, cruise missile, and long-range strike aircraft capability as well—although it may not have cruise missiles capable of carrying a nuclear weapon. It may also have rebuilt much of its conventional capabilities to the point where it has significant war-fighting capabilities.

Regardless of which weapons of mass destruction Iran develops and deploys, it will encounter certain practical problems:

- Unless Iran acquires satellites, it will have limited dynamic targeting capability and limited ability to assess the impact of any strikes it launches. Even if it does acquire satellites, it will experience serious problems in trying to assess damage and its target and escalatory options in the event of a chemical and biological strike or in terms of nuclear fallout.

- It would take a major surface testing effort to be certain of the reliability and yield of its weapons designs and testing of actual bombs and warheads to know the success of its weaponization effort—although a nuclear devise could be tested using noncritical materials to determine that its explosive and triggering systems functioned.

- Quite aside from theoretical accuracy problems, long-range missiles are subject to some loss of accuracy depending on the vector they are fired in, as well as potential weather effects. Combined with targeting, weapons design, and other accuracy problems—plus reliability problems—a significant number of Iranian strikes might miss their targets and some might hit unintended targets.

- Past tests have shown that efforts to apply chemical and biological lethality data based on laboratory or limited human testing simply do not provide anything approaching an accurate picture of area lethality. Nominal lethality data can be wrong by more than an order of magnitude—so far, by exaggerating lethality. The impact of nuclear strikes on large, semihard, area targets is very hard to predict. So is the effect of unusual winds and weather.

- Iranian C⁴I systems might not be adequate and survivable enough to maintain cohesive control over Iran's weapons and launch forces. Any reliance on launch on warning or launch under attack virtually precludes such control, and could trigger Iranian action based on false alarms or serious misunderstanding of the developing tactical situation. If Iran was preempted or subject to a first strike, its ability to characterize the result could be equally uncertain.

- Iran might well have equal problems in characterizing enemy responses and retaliatory strikes once exchanges begin.

- For all these reasons, Iranian command and control might well have to operate on the basis of grossly inadequate information in both planning operations and conducting them. The "fog of war" might well be exceptionally dense.

What is clear is that if Iran acquired a working nuclear device, this would suddenly and radically change perceptions of the military balance in the region. Iran is likely to acquire such weapons at about the same time it acquires MRBMs, and this would be a volatile combination. Iran could then destroy any hardened target, area target, or city within the range of its delivery systems. Iran's Southern Gulf neighbors are extremely vulnerable to attacks on a few cities, and even one successful nuclear attack might force a fundamental restructuring of their politics and/or economy. They are effectively "one bomb" countries. The same is true of Israel, although it has limited missile defenses and is steadily improving them and could launch a massive retaliatory nuclear-armed missile strike against virtually all of Iran's cities.

Iranian nuclear capabilities would raise major midterm and long-term challenges to Saudi Arabia, the other Southern Gulf states, Iraq, Israel, and to the West in terms of deterrence, defense, retaliation, and arms control. Iran can almost certainly continue to disguise most of the necessary research and development effort to go on developing improved enrichment and weapons design and manufacture technology regardless of the limits placed on it by IAEA inspection and its agreements with Europe. These could include the ballistic testing of weapons and warheads with the same weight, size, and balance as real weapons, and the use of complex simulation and testing with nuclear weapons designs that are workable in every respect except that they substitute material with lower levels of enrichment for Pu-239 or highly enriched uranium.

There is the possibility that Iran's efforts could lead to U.S. and Israeli preemption against Iran's developing nuclear-weapons production facilities if either country felt confident it could destroy them with conventional weapons and that there was an urgent need to do so. This, however, presents serious problems for the United States and Israel. Iran has extensive numbers of known nuclear facilities and is a large country that could conceal many more.

Even if a preemptive strike was initially successful, Iran could continue its efforts by placing them in many dispersed small and redundant facilities and/or putting them deep underground. Even P-2 centrifuge enrichment facilities can be deployed in small chains that can be "folded" to fit in virtually any building and that can be made redundant by having multiple small chains and moving steadily more enriched material from one building to another.

Iran can proceed to deploy its Shahab missiles as conventionally armed missiles and give them mobility to hide them or organize them with suitable warning and command and control system so they can launch on warning (LOW) or launch under attack (LUA). It can instantly convert part of its air force to an LOW or LUA capability simply by arming them with nuclear weapons and putting them on alert. Even a few nuclear deployments of this kind could act as a powerful deterrent to both Israel and the United States and do serious damage to any Gulf state or major Gulf energy facility.

Saudi Arabia and its neighbors can respond with accelerated efforts to deploy theater missile defenses—although such systems seem more likely to be "confidence builders" than leakproof. It would almost certainly lead the United States to consider counterproliferation strikes on Iran and to work with its Southern Gulf allies in developing an adequate deterrent. Given the U.S. rejection of biological and chemical weapons, this raises the possibility of creating a major U.S.-theater nuclear deterrent, although such a deterrent could be sea and air based and deployed outside the Gulf. If the United States failed to provide such a deterrent and/or missile defenses, it seems likely that the Southern Gulf states would be forced to accommodate Iran or seek weapons of mass destruction of their own.

Chapter 2

Asymmetric Threats and Islamist Extremists

S audi Arabia still faces significant uncertainties regarding potential external threats from Iran, Iraq, and Yemen. Since May 2003, however, it has been all too clear that its primary security threats now come from terrorism, and specifically from a movement and cells affiliated with al Qaeda and Osama bin Laden.

Terrorism is not new to Saudi Arabia. Saudi Arabia has been the target of sporadic terrorist activity since the 1960s, when Gamal Abdul Nasser made repeated attempts to create groups that could overthrow the Saudi government and to subvert the Saudi military.

Saudi Arabia had a major clash with radical Islamists on November 20, 1979, when Sunni militants seized control of the Grand Mosque in Mecca, one of the holiest sites in Islam. The Saudi military, along with the special counterterrorism forces of an allied country, regained control of the mosque several weeks later. More than 200 soldiers and militants were killed, and 60 militants were subsequently executed.[1] Saudi Arabia also experienced Shiite riots in the Eastern Province, and some sporadic incidents and petty sabotage.

Saudi Arabia only began to experience serious internal security problems, however, when Osama bin Laden and al Qaeda actively turned against the monarchy in the mid-1990s and began to launch terrorist attacks in an effort to destroy it. The Kingdom was the first target of al Qaeda, when, in November 1995 the U.S.-operated National Guard Training Center in Riyadh was attacked, killing five Americans. This subsequently led to the arrest and execution of four men, who purportedly had been inspired by Osama bin Laden.

These attacks remained sporadic, however, until May 2003, when cells affiliated with al Qaeda began an active terror campaign directed both at foreigners, especially Americans, and the regime. Until that time, the security services had only had to deal with isolated incidents for more than two decades and could rely largely on co-option and limited measures by individual service. Al Qaeda fundamentally changed both the level of the threat and the way in which the Kingdom's security forces had to respond.

Origins and Nature of the Threat

The al Qaeda organization evolved from a network of Arab Mujahideen, who had gone to Afghanistan in the 1980s to fight against the Soviet occupation under the banner of Islam. The Makhtab al Khadimat (Office of Order) (MAK), commonly known as the Afghan Bureau, trained and recruited non-Afghani Muslims in the war against the Soviets. The MAK was cofounded by Osama bin Laden and Palestinian militant, Abdullah Yusuf Azzam, between 1982 and 1984. The MAK's primary function was to channel funds from various sources, including charities in the Middle East and North America. The money was used largely to fund training facilities for Islamic militants, many of who were senior operatives, in Afghanistan (later, funds were used to fund operations in places such as Bosnia, Kosovo, Chechnya, the Philippines, and Indonesia).

Osama bin Laden was born in 1957, the son of a wealthy Yemeni father and a Syrian mother. Bin Laden first became active in Pakistan, helping to finance the Mujahideen and establish the MAK. He later went to Afghanistan to directly participate in the Afghan jihad. He operated in an environment where Islamist extremists expelled from Egypt and other countries began to play a major role in the fighting in Afghanistan.

Pakistan's leader, Gen. Mohammad Zia ul-Haq, used his intelligence service, the ISI, to actively support Pashtun Islamic extremists that Pakistan felt would be loyal to Pakistan and act as a buffer against Afghani freedom fighters from other factions, like the Uzbeks, Tajiks, and Heraza. While Saudi money was used to fund some of the religious training schools and other facilities that helped indoctrinate young Saudi men in violent religious extremism and terrorism, it is important to note that it was Pakistan that created most of the movement and that the schools and training centers were largely neo-Salafi and not Saudi Ahab in character.

Organizing al Qaeda

Although negotiations for Soviet withdrawal from Afghanistan began in 1982, withdrawal did not formally begin until February 1989. Near the end of the Soviet occupation, some Mujahideen began to extend their activities to include Islamist causes worldwide and a variety of organizations with convergent interests were established to further these aims.

Osama bin Laden established al Qaeda as one of these organizations about 1988. Bin Laden sought to expand the conflict to include nonmilitary terrorist activities in other regions. Azzam, however, wanted to stay the course, choosing instead to concentrate on military operations. After Azzam's assassination in a car bomb explosion in 1989, MAK split, with a considerable number joining bin Laden's organization.

Following the Soviet withdrawal in 1989, bin Laden returned to Saudi Arabia, but fled in 1991 to Sudan after being detained in Jeddah and banned from travel for arms smuggling. In Sudan, bin Laden also began financing terrorist training facilities.

In Sudan, bin Laden built on the organization he founded in Afghanistan. The organization had its own "membership roster" and committee structure to supervise procedures such as terrorist training, recommending targets, financing operations and issuing decrees, ostensibly justified by Islamic law. (See Figure 2.1.)

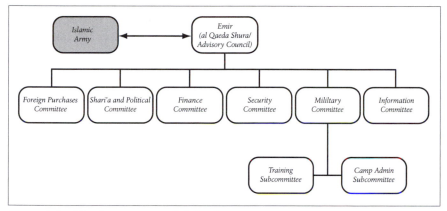

Figure 2.1: The Organization of al Qaeda

Al Qaeda's structure included:

- The Shura (Advisory Council), a close circle of bin Laden's associates; including a Shari'a and Political Committee in charge of issuing *fatwas*.

- The *Military Committee*, responsible for recommending targets and supporting operations.

- The *Finance Committee*, responsible for fund-raising and budgetary provisions for the training camps.

- A *Foreign Purchases Committee*, responsible for weapons and explosives acquisitions, as well as technical equipment.

- The *Security Committee*, in charge of protection, intelligence gathering and counterintelligence.

- The *Information Committee*, responsible for generating and disseminating propaganda.

The organization underwent a fundamental transformation after the 2001–2002 U.S.-led war destroyed al Qaeda's headquarters in Afghanistan. It changed from a quasi command and control structure under bin Laden to a more loosely configured network based on individual cells dispersed throughout the world, using technology and affiliated groups to achieve its aims. Al Qaeda is now more of a "movement" and an "idea" than it is an established organization, "in that its supporters now plan attacks independently of any centralized organization."[2]

The al Qaeda Organization in the Arabian Peninsula

Bin Laden had always counted overthrowing the Saudi monarchy and dividing Saudi Arabia from the West and internal reform among his major goals. The global anger at his attacks on 9/11 and the subsequent American invasion of Afghanistan helped lead al Qaeda to shift its focus back against Saudi Arabia.

An organization that called itself the al Qaeda Organization in the Arabian Peninsula began setting up an infrastructure that included safe houses, ammunitions depots, cells, and support networks. This organization was able to create a substantial structure while the Saudi government focuses on the outside threat and backlash from the events of 9/11 and concentrated on bringing weapons and explosives through Yemen, thus strengthening its presence in the Kingdom.

Initial Organization and Structure

At the beginning, Yusef al-Ayeri was the chief of al Qaeda in the Arabian Peninsula and reported directly to bin Laden (al-Ayeri's was the only regional al Qaeda operation to report directly to bin Laden). Al-Ayeri's lieutenants, in turn, reported directly to him. They were responsible for setting up five autonomous cells focusing exclusively on operations within Saudi Arabia. Since all terrorists' activities in the Kingdom are derived from these cells, it was imperative for the Saudis to infiltrate and destroy them.

The first cell was the largest and strongest and was responsible for the May 2003 attacks that announced the fact that al Qaeda in the Arabian Peninsula had become a major threat. It was headed by Turki al-Dandani. Most of al Qaeda's resources were allocated to this cell, allowing individuals to set up independent networks that made them autonomous from one another.

The second cell was headed by Ali Abd-al Rahman al-Fagasi al-Ghamdi (aka Abu Bakr al-Azdi), considered to be the mastermind behind the 12 May attacks in Riyadh. Khaled al-Hajj, who was in charge of the third cell, was a Yemeni national and thought by some to be the "real chief" of al Qaeda in Saudi

Arabia. Abdulazziz al-Muqrin, leader of the fourth cell, was largely responsible for organizing the November 2003 bombings.

After the infiltration of the first cell, one by one, the other cells were compromised and consequently destroyed. Members, including the key leadership, were forced to take refuge in a fifth cell. Although the fifth cell was never fully established, by default, it became the most prolific cell in Saudi Arabia, responsible for most major attacks throughout 2004—including the 29 December attack targeting the Interior Ministry and security recruitment center.

Even in Afghanistan, there were disagreements among the leadership regarding the timing and potential targets of attack. Al-Ayeri maintained that al Qaeda members were not yet ready and lacked the time, resources and necessary supply routes from Yemen.

Furthermore, recruitment proved to be more difficult than expected. Ayman al-Zawahiri, the Egyptian surgeon who is the theological adviser and likely successor to bin Laden, dismissed these objections, arguing that the time was right for operations to begin. Al-Zawahiri made the case that attacking soft targets and Americans (who would flee the Kingdom) would paralyze and consequently topple the Saudi government. This position won out against the standard al Qaeda approach of patience, building support networks and launching a spectacular attack.

Abdul Kareem al-Majati, a Moroccan national and main deputy and general strategist of al-Ayeri agreed with his commander's assessment, but was overruled by bin Laden. Soon after, Majati left Saudi Arabia with the belief that attacking prematurely was a huge miscalculation and would compromise the existence and establishment of future al Qaeda cells. Moreover, he expressed grave doubts that the attacks would be successful, further hindering the recruitment efforts and eroding support for the organization.

The Cell Structure Is Attacked and Weakened

The first cell was infiltrated immediately following the May 12, 2003, attacks in Riyadh. Saudi intelligence had received enough credible information to know who the leaders of the cells were, and from this, the government was able to draw up a list of senior operatives connected to Al-Ayeri. Subsequently, Al-Ghamdi surrendered, Al-Dandani was killed, and the remaining members were scattered among nascent cells. The dispersion of members undermined the autonomy of the cells, and they were forced to share resources. The loss of independence, however, made it easier for the government to infiltrate remaining cells, because, when one member was captured, he could provide valuable information concerning the identities and activities of his confederates.

The leaders appointed after Al-Ghamdi surrendered were unable to establish their own cells. In June 2003, Al-Ayeri was killed at a roadblock in a shootout with Saudi security forces. On March 16, 2004, Khaled Ali Hajj was ambushed and killed by security forces in Riyadh en route to an undisclosed mission. He was succeeded by Abdulaziz al-Muqrin, the self-proclaimed leader of al Qaeda operations in Saudi Arabia, until his death on June 18, 2004.

Once the top tier of the leadership was gone, less-practiced militants took charge, thus further compromising the cells. This development, in addition to increased Saudi security measures, led to a series of botched attacks, culminating in the November 2003 attack on the Al Muhayya residential compound that killed mainly Arabs and Muslims.

One of the major problems confronting al Qaeda in Saudi Arabia—its Achilles' heel—has been its weak recruitment effort. It expected a much larger cadre of able and willing young men to replenish the ranks as the Saudi government attacked and killed its members. This expectation proved to be a serious miscalculation, because few high-quality candidates were willing to answer the call to jihad. Subsequently, al Qaeda was forced to enlist the services of very young and inexperienced men.

As Yusef al-Ayeri and Majati revealed, the organization felt that it did not have the time or the resources to do the important work of creating strong viable cells. By 2003 they were not prepared for the government's vigorous counterstrike, and both of these men expressed reservations about an early attack. The actual problem was that al Qaeda had not been able to justify its dogmatism and call for murder and suicide with religious arguments. This became especially problematic when it advocated attacking Saudis. It was only the battle-hardened legions from Afghanistan that were amenable to following bin Laden's instructions to attack Saudi security officers.

ORGANIZATION AND PATTERNS OF ATTACKS

Al Qaeda strategies have included suicide attacks, assassinations, bombings, hijackings, and kidnappings. Furthermore, numerous reports indicate that bin Laden has an interest in acquiring or making chemical, biological, and nuclear weapons. The organization has attacked American and other Western interests, as well as Muslim governments it considered to be corrupt or immoral, especially Saudi Arabia.[3]

As the chronology below shows,[4] targets tend to be selected for their symbolic value and include embassies, military installations, and public buildings in the United States and allied countries.

1995

- *November 13:* Saudi Arabia National Guard (SANG) HQ in Riyadh bombed. First of the new wave of terror attacks and the start of the wind down of the U.S. presence in KSA. Seven U.S. killed: one military, six civilians.

1996

- *June 25:* Bomb kills 19 U.S. soldiers, wounds nearly 400 people at U.S. military housing complex in Al Khobar.

2003

- *May 12:* Suicide bombers attack housing compounds for foreign workers in Riyadh. Thirty-five are killed, including nine bombers, and 200 wounded. Al Hamra, Vinnell, and Jedewahl compounds.
- *June 14:* Raid in Mecca kills five Islamic militants and two security agents.
- *July 28:* Raid on farm in Al Qassim kills six militants and two police.
- *September 23:* Raid in Jizan kills al Qaeda operative wanted by the FBI.
- *November 3:* Clash with terrorists in Mecca kills two and finds large weapons cache.
- *November 8:* Suicide bombers blow up Riyadh compound housing foreigners and Saudis, killing at least 18. Old B1 Boeing compound, now called Al Muhayya compound.

2004

- *January 28:* Gun battle in Riyadh kills one al Qaeda and five police.
- *April 21:* Suicide bomber kills five, including two senior police officers in attack on government building in Riyadh. The al Haramain Brigades claim responsibility.
- *May 1:* Gunmen kill five Westerners in attack on oil office in Yanbu; four attackers and one policeman die. Some 50 people are injured.
- *May 20:* Police battle militants near Burada, killing four.
- *May 22:* Terrorists kill German ex-pat, Herman Dengel, head chef of Saudi Catering Company, on a Riyadh street.

- *May 29–30:* Militants attack oil company and housing compounds in Al Khobar. Seven Saudi policemen and 22 civilians are killed; 50 hostages are taken.

- *June 6:* Simon Cumbers, an Irish cameraman working for the BBC, is shot dead in Riyadh.

- *June 8:* Gunmen kill American Robert Jacob, of Vinnell Corp., in Riyadh.

- *June 12:* American Kenneth Scroggs is shot dead in Riyadh. Al Qaeda claims responsibility.

- *June 18:* Kidnappers behead Lockheed Martin employee Paul M. Johnson Jr. in Riyadh.

- *August 3:* An Irish civil engineer, Tony Christopher, is shot dead in Riyadh.

- *August 30:* Gunmen fire on U.S. consulate vehicle in Jeddah.

- *September 15:* Edward Muirhead-Smith, a British engineer, is killed in Riyadh in an attack claimed by al Qaeda.

- *September 26:* Frenchman Laurent Barbot is shot dead in Jeddah.

- *October 18:* Top-ranking militant, Abdel Majed al-Muneeh, is among three terrorists killed in Riyadh.

- *November 4:* Saudi security forces arrest seven people, including a wanted terrorist suspect. The seven are apprehended during a raid on a cyber café in Buraida. Two security personnel are wounded in a shootout preceding the arrest.

- *November 6:* Twenty-six Saudi religious scholars sign and release an open letter calling on Iraqis to fight Americans and considering it jihad. Two days later the Saudi ambassador to the United States, Prince Abdul Aziz bin Bandar bin Abdul Aziz, released an official statement making it clear that the letter from these scholars represented neither the government of Saudi Arabia nor the senior religious scholars of the country.

- *November 9:* In a predawn raid, security forces kill one wanted terrorist and capture three others after a shootout in Jeddah. The daily *Al-Riyadh* quotes a witness as saying that Sultan al-Otaibi, from Saudi Arabia's list of 26 most-wanted terrorists, was killed in the confrontation. A substantial arms cache is found in the house where the suspected terrorists were found. The cache includes machine guns, hand grenades, and various types of ammunition. According to local press reports, the four-member group planned to attack a Jeddah compound coinciding with fireworks celebrations during Eid Al-Fitr. Additionally, security forces arrest three suspects north of Riyadh on the highway to Al Qassim.

- *November 11:* The Interior Ministry announces that King Fahd bin Abdul Aziz al-Saud ordered the release of those militants who surrendered to security authorities as a result of the June amnesty offer.

- *November 12:* Saudi security forces arrested five suspected terrorists in two operations in Riyadh and Zulfi. Three of the suspects were detained in Riyadh and two in Zulfi. Weapons and ammunition were reportedly seized in these operations. The next day an Interior Ministry spokesman stated that these individuals were not directly involved in violence, but were suspected of supporting extremist thought.

- *November 13:* The U.S. embassy releases Warden Message to remind of security concerns surrounding the death of Palestinian Authority chairman Yasser Arafat.

- *November 17:* A security officer is killed and eight officers wounded during a raid on a terrorist hideout in Al Qassim. Five suspects are arrested. Two of the suspects were wanted by authorities and linked to al Qaeda. One reportedly belonged to the list of the 26 most-wanted. He was not identified by name.

- *November 27:* Saudi security forces in Jeddah kill a terrorist suspect later identified as Essam Siddiq Mubaraki. This man was linked to plotters of the Al Muhayya housing compound attack the previous November in Riyadh. One additional suspect is arrested in conjunction with the killing of Mabaraki. Additionally, police find a cache of arms in Mabaraki's car.

- *December 2:* Saudi security forces announce arrest of four suspected terrorists in various parts of the country. Two suspects are arrested in Artawiya. The two others are captured in vicinity of Hafr Al Baten and Buraidah.

- *December 6:* Militants storm the U.S. consulate in Jeddah. Five U.S. employees and three gunmen are killed.

- *December 29:* Ministry of Interior and special forces recruitment office bombed; bystander killed. Seven suspected al Qaeda shot dead later in the evening.

As this chronology also shows, many al Qaeda-affiliated attacks on civilians were directed at destabilizing the Kingdom by targeting the 6 million foreign workers on whom the Saudi economy partially relies. They also were focused on Americans, in an effort to compound the tensions created by 9/11 and to split Saudi Arabia and the United States. In many cases, however, Saudis were killed as well.

The coordinated car bombings on May 12, 2003, targeted Riyadh housing complexes and killed 34 Saudis and foreign Arabs. A November 8, 2003, car bombing killed at least 17. Al Qaeda's ultimate target is the Saudi royal family. After the 8 November bombing, Richard Armitage, U.S. deputy secretary of state, stated[5] that the terror network aimed "to bring down the Saudi government as well as to create fear and spread terror." Osama bin Laden has long called for the overthrow of the royal family in retaliation for the Saudi government's allowing the United States to establish military bases in the Kingdom.

Saudi officials gleaned important information from the Saudi-based members of al Qaeda during these attacks, particularly regarding their methods of operation in the Kingdom. Among other things, militants rented houses and cars using stolen IDs and disguised themselves as women or "hip" young men. In addition, the money purportedly raised for Iraqi prisoners in U.S. custody actually went to fund terrorist operations.[6]

Confessions by captured militants also shed light on al Qaeda operations within the Kingdom. According to Abdul Rahman al-Rashoud (cousin of Abdullah al-Rashoud, who's on the most-wanted list and Khaled al-Farraj, approximately 95 percent of al Qaeda operatives are "ignorant," and most do not observe basic Islamic teachings. They also stated that the organization recruited especially from the young. "Young ones are recruited because they do not have sufficient knowledge of the religion or a wise mind that can tell right from wrong," they said. Al-Rashoud went on to say that al Qaeda members spend a great deal of money and that most of it comes from "charitable donations." In some cases, members convince donors they are collecting money for poor Iraqi families.[7]

Both these interrogations and the behavior of al Qaeda indicate that the Saudi government response took time but began to severely affect the terrorist organization's capabilities after mid 2004. Al Qaeda was forced to rely on less-organized surrogates to carry out its activities, ones who were not directly under the control of bin Laden or any senior operative capable of sophisticated planning and execution.

One key example of such problems is that a housing complex al Qaeda attacked on November 8, 2004, had once housed U.S. nationals employed by the Boeing Company, but few Americans were living there at the time of the attack. The end result was an attack on Saudis and other foreigners, further adding to al Qaeda's unpopularity. The Riyadh attack also appeared to lack the planning and surveillance expertise that are the established hallmarks of a bin Laden-orchestrated attack.

Another example occurred on December 7, 2004, in which five militants attacked the U.S. consulate in Jeddah, killing 5 consulate employees and injuring 10 others. Security forces killed four of the militants. The new more stringent security measures implemented by the Saudi government seem to be working. Although the militants were able to breach the compound, no Americans were killed or seized in the raid, and the militants' car was unable to enter the compound. It appeared that the attackers did not have the same capabilities they had only 18 months previously, because they fell short of their objectives in killing as many Americans as possible. All the militants were either killed or captured, and the attack was poorly orchestrated and executed.

On December 29, 2004, the Ministry of Interior and a security recruiting center was attacked in a double suicide car bombing. There were two car bomb explosions that killed the bombers but no security personnel or civilians. The Ministry of Interior reported that tons of explosive materials were used in the bombings. The vehicle used in the attack near the Interior Ministry building was laden with around 1.5 tons of explosive mixes, including ammonal and other commercial explosives. Another car carrying 1.3 tons of the same explosive mixes detonated 380 meters away from the Special Forces base. Al Qaeda claimed later that the goal of the attack was to kill the minister of the interior and his deputy, clearly showing that al Qaeda actively targeted Saudi officials and members of the royal family, as well as foreigners.[8]

The operation was anything but a success. The vehicles were unable to get close enough to their intended targets and killed only the three suicide bombers. The five terrorists who carried out the attack were quickly identified, and seven terrorists were killed soon after the blasts in a gun battle with security forces in Riyadh.

According to Brig. Gen. Mansour al-Turki, the militants were forced to carry out the operation earlier than planned, because a member was captured after a shootout in Riyadh a day earlier. "It is for sure that the terrorist operation was executed hastily," he said. "It seemed to be programmed to be executed at a different time and in a different fashion." Ten more militants were also killed in two shootouts on the same day—three right before the bombings and seven immediately afterward. Among those killed was Sultan al-Otaibi and Bandar Abdel Rahman al-Dikeel, both on the 26 most-wanted list.[9] Of the original 26 most-wanted, only 7 remain at large. In the past year alone, Saudi security forces have scored numerous impressive successes against al Qaeda operations in the Kingdom.

On December 31, 2004, a statement posted on the Internet, signed by the Al Qaeda Organization in the Arabian Peninsula, claimed that the attack on the Ministry of Interior was an assassination attempt against the interior minister and his son. The statement read in part "A brigade prepared a complex operation to kill the head of apostasy in the Arabian Peninsula, (Interior Minister) Nayef bin Abdul-Aziz al-Saud, his son and entourage and also striking the headquarters of the emergency forces. . . . A number of crusader trainers were killed in the training headquarters and several of the forces were wounded."[10] The December 29 attack was the second strike against a government installation. The first was on 21 April, when al Qaeda attacked a police building in Riyadh.[11] Some experts argue that these attacks may represent a shift of al Qaeda's strategy in Saudi Arabia from focusing on striking Western targets to attacking Saudi leaders, Saudi security agencies, and the country's infrastructure as well. Others argue, however, that the attacks represent a somewhat desperate effort to strike at Saudi Arabia's steadily more effective security forces and to find some way to either intimidate the Saudi government or capture the world's attention through a single dramatic act.

It is far from clear that the al Qaeda organization in Saudi Arabia now has, or can pursue, a consistent strategy. Its efforts to strike at the Ministry of Interior and security forces are further indications that it is under pressure. It is likely, however, that al Qaeda is still providing the funding, training, and encouragement for these operations.[12] There also are substantial numbers of radicalized young Saudis in other countries, and more are still being recruited by various Islamist groups to go to Iraq, Chechnya, and other areas.

It is also clear from the tapes being circulated by bin Laden—or in his name—that Saudi Arabia remains a prime target. A tape that bin Laden seems to have circulated on December 17, 2004, shows how committed he remains to trying to overthrow the Saudi government by force.[13] The tape was nearly an hour long and repeated many of Osama bin Laden's classic themes as well as expanded the scope of his targets.

As in past tapes and messages, bin Laden attacked the supposed financial and religious corruption, and pro-Americanism, of the Saudi royal family. "We are talking about apostasy and subservience to the infidels. . . . As there is no difference between [U.S. Administrator Paul] Bremer, the former U.S. ruler in Baghdad, and [current Iraqi Prime Minister Iyad] Allawi in the implementation of America's policy . . . So there is no difference between Bremer and the rest of the rulers of the region in implementing U.S. policy."

Bin Laden effectively called the Saudi royal family "infidels" and called on every Muslim to overthrow them by violent means, "How can (even) an insane person see an infidel ruler and his heavily armed soldiers and then claim that he wants reforms through peaceful means? This is completely false. This is meant to frustrate the efforts to establish justice."

Bin Laden called education reform one of "the most dangerous interference in our affairs." He continued to say that "It is evident that the outcome of changing the religious curricula is damaging both to religion and to material interests. As for [the damage to] religion, you already know that it is blatant apostasy, and as for material interests, the [altered curricula] will eventually produce educated slaves in our country, who will be loyal to America, sell the interests of the country and smile in the face of the Americans, while they conquer the land and defile the [Muslin's] honor, under the pretext of liberty, equality, and the laws of the United Nations. This is one example of the American intervention in domestic policy."[14]

He recommended striking at Saudi oil facilities, because "Targeting America in Iraq in terms of economy and loss of life is a golden and unique opportunity . . . One of the most important reasons that our enemies control our land is the pilfering of our oil . . . prevent them from getting the oil and conduct your operations accordingly, particularly in Iraq and the Gulf."

Bin Laden's rhetoric, and the continuing strikes by al Qaeda in Saudi Arabia, are warnings that the threat may take years to entirely eliminate, but the terror campaign since May 2003 does seem to have produced few new recruits and won little popular support. In fact, it has resulted in a backlash among the Saudi population, including many Saudis critical of the government. "People want government reforms and changes, but they are more scared of al-Qaeda extremists," said Mansour Nogaidan, a former Islamic militant and government critic. "The common people—those people who thought their life might improve if the government changed—they are not ready to lose all this for what some teenagers have in their minds as a utopia."[15]

While al Qaeda still enjoys support from some quarters in Saudi Arabia and among some religious figures, the government campaign to sway Saudi public opinion away from Islamic extremism seems to be gaining momentum. Many Saudis now refer to the militants as "the grim reapers" and believe that they are bent on ruining the country. The family of one militant complicit in the U.S. consulate attack condemned the act and refused to accept condolences for his death. The family of another attacker, Fayez bin Awad al-Juhaini, refused to hold a wake for him, "as a sign of their rejection for the criminal act their son carried out." The Kingdom's most prominent religious figure, Grand Mufti Abdul Aziz al-Sheikh, called the attack a "great sin."[16]

One thing is clear. None of al Qaeda's present problems mean that Saudi Arabia is secure against some successful attacks in the future. While Saudi security is steadily improving in expertise, coordination, and training, Saudi Arabia is a relatively open society. It cannot protect every public building, area where foreigners go or live, or areas where ordinary Saudis can be attacked. It is obvious that bin Laden and al Qaeda remain committed; they have many resources outside Saudi Arabia, and there is enough religious and political turmoil in the region to aid in fund-raising and recruiting. Security will always be relative under these conditions.

The Saudi Response

The structure and evolution of Saudi internal security efforts is discussed in detail in the following chapters of this book. To understand the threat that Saudi Arabia faces, however, it is necessary to understand that Saudi Arabia began to respond to the threat posed by bin Laden and al Qaeda years before the events of September 2001 and May 2003. In 1993–94 Saudi Arabia froze bin Laden's assets. The Kingdom was one of the first countries to take such action. On April 9, 1994, the government publicly revoked his citizenship. After the 1995 assassination attempt against Egyptian president Hosni Mubarak, to which bin Laden was linked, he was expelled from Sudan. In 1996 he returned to Afghanistan, where the extremist Taliban had come to power. The November 1995 bombing of the Saudi National Guard Training Center in Riyadh that killed five Americans and resulted in the arrest and execution of four men was purportedly inspired by Osama bin Laden.

The events of September 11, 2001, brought a considerable increase in attention to Saudi Arabia. On that day, Saudi Arabia issued a statement characterizing the attacks on the World Trade Center and the Pentagon as "regrettable and inhuman." On September 20, Foreign Minister Prince Saud al-Faisal told Colin Powell and President George Bush that the Kingdom wanted to be a part of the antiterror coalition being formed, saying, "We will do everything in our capacity to fight the scourge of terrorism."

A few weeks later, the government of Saudi Arabia signaled that it would allow U.S. planes and troops stationed in that country to participate in military action against bin Laden during the war in Afghanistan by granting use of the Prince Sultan Air Base's Command and Control infrastructure in Kharj. On 20 September, the Kingdom announced that it would sever diplomatic relations with the Taliban on the grounds that the Taliban government "continues to use lands to harbor, arm, and encourage those criminals [al Qaeda] in carrying out terrorist atrocities which horrify those who believe in peace and the innocent and spread terror and destruction in the world."

Internal Security Action

According to Saudi Arabia's ambassador to the United Kingdom, Prince Turki al-Faisal, the government has arrested and detained more than 600 individuals and questioned over 2,000 with suspected ties to terrorism since September 11, 2001. In addition, dozens of suspects have been extradited from other countries. Finally, as detailed above, the Kingdom has dismantled the major al Qaeda cells operating in the Kingdom.

On April 26, 2004, in his address to the National Guard and security forces, Minister of Defense Prince Sultan warned terrorists to surrender for the sake of their own safety and security, saying, "Those who surrender will be safe and those who resist will lose." Prince Sultan went on to describe the terrorists as "a misled and brainwashed few working against their religion, their rulers and their people." Shortly after al-Muqrin was killed, Crown Prince Abdullah bin Abdul Aziz al-Saud offered an amnesty for those al Qaeda supporters who had not directly taken part in the killing. At that same time, he gave the militants an ultimatum: "We tell this deviant group and others that if they do not return to the right path, they will meet the same fate [as al-Muqrin] or worse."

The events of September 11, 2001 and the May 12 and November 9, 2003, attacks in Riyadh all reaffirmed the Kingdom's commitment to fighting the terrorist threat on all fronts and that commitment has resulted in a great deal of cooperation between Saudi Arabia, the United States, and other nations. Measures have been implemented to monitor and secure the financial infrastructure against illegal activities such as money laundering, and the government has taken aggressive steps to freeze the assets of individuals suspected of terrorist activity.

The Kingdom has also improved security measures at a range of locations throughout the country, such as public buildings and residential facilities. In May and December 2003 the government began to publish its counterterrorism initiatives, including a list of individuals most wanted by security forces for involvement in terrorist-related activities.

The most wanted list is shown in Table 2.1 and predates the May 12, 2003, Riyadh bombings. The Saudi government demonstrated that it already had a good understanding of some key elements of the threat and of the individuals involved. At the time of its publication, the 26 most-wanted list included the leaders of all five cells. Saudi security and intelligence officials not only knew who the al Qaeda leaders were, they also accurately judged their relative importance in the al Qaeda hierarchy. It is important to note that no individual who has claimed leadership in Saudi Arabia al Qaeda has been outside this list.

To enhance the quality and performance of security and intelligence forces, King Fahd issued a royal decree calling for a 25 percent pay increase for these forces and all supporting units. More significant, the Kingdom reorganized its security efforts to develop better training programs and provide better equipment. It sought lessons from the experience of other countries and began to improve the coordination of the security and police forces of the Ministry of Interior, the National Guard, and the regular military forces. A new command authority was established to fight terrorism in the Ministry of Interior, and the ministry was given the task of coordinating the overall effort on an interservice level.

Progress necessarily was slow, and several attacks revealed a lack of expertise, training, and coordination. While the Saudi response improved over time, it became clear to the Saudi government that it would take years to train and equip the forces needed, recast the role of the military and National Guard, and strengthen key elements of the security services.

Fortunately, it became clear with time that al Qaeda had very little luck in penetrating the military, National Guard, and security services, or even the ordinary police. Some recruitment was inevitable, but it occurred at so limited a level that most of the few cell members with any ties to the military or security services had only limited previous service and training and have held only minor positions.

The Political Dimension

Al Qaeda also could not create a popular base to challenge the government. Like other Muslims, the great majority of Saudis rejected the criminal acts perpetrated by extremist organizations such as al Qaeda, regarding them as contrary to Islamic values. A poll published in November 2003 indicated that while most Saudis are suspicious of Western intentions in Islamic countries, few believe that the methods used by al Qaeda are justifiable. As one interviewee commented, "When we hear bin Laden railing against the West, pointing out the humiliation of the Arab Peoples and the suffering of the Palestinians, it is like being transported to a dream . . . [but] when we see images of innocent people murdered for this ideology, it's as if we've entered a nightmare."[17]

Crown Prince Abdullah consistently cautioned Saudi citizens against showing sympathy toward terrorists, saying that even silence can constitute support and pledging to stem the tide of terrorism: "I warn and caution . . . everyone not to be silent, as silence means he is one of them. . . . God willing, we are following them, and with God's help we will get them, no matter how long it takes, even if that means 20 or 30 years."[18]

Saudi government and religious officials endorsed a message of tolerance and moderation, explaining that Islam and terrorism are incompatible. Crown Prince Abdullah, in speeches at the Organization of Islamic Conference Summit in Malaysia and Pakistan, underscored this position, recommending solid steps to combat extremism and improve relations between Muslims and non-Muslims.

Saudi Arabia repeatedly called for a global fight against terrorism and has urged an all-out war on terror. In a message to Hajj pilgrims in Mecca in February 2004, King Fahd stated:

> The Kingdom's stance against terrorism is fundamental. It earlier urged the international community to confront the menace of terrorism, and has supported all peace-loving countries in their efforts to uproot terrorism. It calls on all peace-loving countries to adopt a comprehensive program within the framework of international legitimacy for combating terrorism so as to enhance the pillars of security and stability.

During the first half of 2004, the Kingdom fired 44 Friday preachers, 160 imams, and 149 muezzins (prayer callers) for "incompetence." Another 1,357 religious officials were put on suspension and ordered to undergo training. This total included 517 imams, 90 Friday preachers, and 750 muezzins.[19] Saudi officials also deal with the difficult issue of purging and reforming radicals in the clergy.

The Amnesty Program

In June 2004, the Saudi government implemented a controversial, one-time amnesty program aimed primarily at undercutting support for al Qaeda. The one-month amnesty, announced by King Fahd, was open only to those who had not been directly involved in carrying out terrorist attacks.

The objective of the program was to defuse the cycle of violence by offering individuals a chance to reflect on their course of action, renounce it, and return to the "Islamic fold." Prince Nayef, insisting that the amnesty was a sign of the Kingdom's strength, said, "the [amnesty] granted by Custodian of the Two Holy Mosques King Fahd is a sign of strength. It was intended to tell these errant people to come to their senses and return to their parents, families and homes and to their religion."[20]

This initiative not only had a profound psychological effect on the militants, but it had such an effect on Saudi society and the Muslim community at large as well. It took advantage of the fact that a family-driven society, in which family values and the extended family were critical, could be persuaded to put intense pressure on many of the young men that families know supported al Qaeda.

It also had a practical effect. Al Qaeda had long accused the Saudi regime of being un-Islamic for cooperating with the United States and not fully implementing Shari'a law. In the speech announcing the amnesty, King Fahd included a chapter from the Qur'an that highlighted the importance of the concept of forgiveness in Islam. By demonstrating that the Kingdom was governed by the law of God, the government reasserted its religious authority. This maneuver had the effect of undermining the legitimacy of al Qaeda that has long used Islam to justify its actions.

The program netted 31 militants who were later pardoned and released in November 2004 after authorities were assured that "the deviants [had] rectified their ideology and attitudes toward their nation and society."[21] In a related initiative, the Saudi government implemented a two-month amnesty for the handover of unlicensed weapons without penalty. Those who did not comply by the August 29, 2004 deadline would be punished.[22]

It should, however, be noted that the progress also had its drawbacks. In a number of cases, the families were not capable of keeping their sons from going back to extremist movements or playing the role of terrorists. The Saudi amnesty program also had its downside.

The government also responded to al Qaeda's use of illegitimate fatwas to justify its views and behavior with legitimate fatwas. The Saudi mufti general issued a fatwa calling on "citizens and residents to inform about each and every one who plans or prepares for committing destructive actions so as to protect the people and the country." This had the effect of depriving al Qaeda of needed logistical support, making it more difficult to carry out operations.[23]

Using the Media

The government has also made more effective use of the media as a weapon in counterterrorism. On October 22, 2004, a Saudi newspaper published the confession of an unidentified militant originally posted on an Internet Web site. Although he denied involvement in any bombings, he did admit that he was guilty of "incitement" to violence. The "repentant" member confessed he had ties to the al-Haramain Islamic Foundation and "had prior information about the bombing in Al Muhayyah neighborhood" in Riyadh. He also implicated Sa'd al-Faqih, the Saudi dissident leader of Movement For Islamic Reform in Arabia (MIRA), in the attempted assassination plot against a Saudi official.[24]

As part of the government's campaign against militants who have carried out attacks against Westerners in the Kingdom, on December 4, 2004, Saudi national television aired interviews with the fathers of five militants, denouncing their own sons for complicity in the terrorist attacks. The father of top al Qaeda militant, Abdulaziz Issa Abdul-Mohsin al-Muqrin said he had wanted to take down his son himself. Ahmed Jamaan al-Zahrani, father of captured militant cleric, Faris Ahmed Jamaan al-Zahrani, who was on the most-wanted list, contacted authorities when he knew his son was wanted, saying, "he has a wife and children whom he should have been taking care of better than staying in Afghanistan."[25]

On December 14, 2004, several jailed militants made a televised appeal from al-Hayer prison to al Qaeda sympathizers in an effort to persuade them to surrender to authorities. Characterizing his jailers "like family," and denying reports of torture and abuse, one seemingly repentant militant Abdulrahman al-Amari told the program that, "anyone who has experienced the reality finds a big difference between the many cases of torture we heard about and what we found. The dealings of the prison administration, the sympathy for the prisoners' wishes. . . . I can call it a family connection."[26] Another militant, who is on the list of the 26 most-wanted, said that his jailers were nicer than his parents. This glowing picture of prison life, apparently given freely by those who participated, is another part of the government's media campaign to further undermine support for al Qaeda in the Kingdom.

Antiterrorism Measures in the Financial Sector

The Saudi Government took deliberate measures to safeguard the financial system against unlawful activities long before September 11, 2001. In 1988, Saudi Arabia joined the United Nations Convention Against Illicit Trafficking of Narcotics and Psychotropic Substances. In 1995, units were established at the Ministry of Interior, the Saudi Arabian Monetary Agency (SAMA) and commercial banking institutions to counter money-laundering activities. SAMA issued "Guidelines for the Prevention and Control of Money-Laundering Activities" to Saudi banks to apply stringent "Know Your Customer" rules, to monitor records of dubious transactions, and to report them to law enforcement authorities and SAMA.

Saudi Arabia is a member of the Financial Action Task Force (FAFT) established by the G-7 in 1988 and has approved and completed two FAFT self-assessment questionnaires—one regarding FAFT recommendations on the prevention of money laundering (known as the FAFT 40 + 8 Recommendations) and the other regarding special recommendations on terrorist financing. SAMA exchanges information with other banking authorities and law-enforcement agencies regarding money laundering and terrorist financing and has created a committee to undertake self-assessment for compliance with FAFT rules. The Kingdom invited FAFT to conduct a mutual evaluation in April 2003. It is also an active participant in international seminars, conferences, and symposia dedicated to combating terrorist activities globally.

In February 2003, SAMA began implementation of a program to train judges and investigators on legal matters involving terrorism financing and money laundering.In August 2003, the Council of Ministers approved legislation to impose severe penalties for money laundering and terror financing. The new law requires maintenance of banking records, establishes intelligence units to investigate transactions, sets up international cooperation on money laundering issues with countries that have formal agreements with the Kingdom, and bans financial transactions with unidentified parties.

In July 2004, the Financial Task Force released its evaluation of Saudi Arabia's laws, regulations, and systems combating money laundering and terrorist financing. According to this evaluation: "Saudi authorities have focused heavily on systems and measures to counter terrorism and the financing of terrorism. Specifically, they have taken action to increase the requirements for financial institutions on customer due diligence, established systems for tracing and freezing terrorist assets, and tightened the regulation and transparency of charitable organizations." It concluded that Saudi Arabia "meets almost all of the general obligations of the FATF 40 + 8 Recommendations."

Although the Saudi government willingness to cooperate has been encouraging, clearly more work lies ahead. According to a September 29, 2004, Senate Banking Commission report, Saudi Arabia has yet to fully implement its new laws and regulations, and opportunities for the "witting or unwitting" financing of terrorist activity remain. In addition, there is little evidence that the Kingdom has taken any substantial retaliatory actions against organizations or individuals engaged in terror financing. Consequently, Saudi Arabia has yet to hold anyone personally accountable for terrorist funding and, in the process, delegitimize these activities.[27]

Monitoring Charitable Organizations

Saudi Arabia took a wide range of actions to ensure greater oversight of charitable organizations and safeguard against possible abuse and misuse of the system. In March 2002, Saudi Arabia froze the accounts of the Somalia and Bosnia branches of the Al-Haramain Islamic Foundation.

Similarly, on December 22, 2002, the Saudi government took measures to designate the Bosnia-based Vazir and the Liechtenstein-based Hochburg AG as financiers of terrorism under UN Security Council Resolution 1267 (1999). The Vazir representative, Mr. Safet Durguti, was also designated a terrorism financier under the resolution. The Saudi government concluded that the two branches supported terrorist activities and organizations such as al Qaeda and al-Itihaad al-Islamiya (AIAI) and others.

In May 2003, SAMA distributed an update specifically targeted at illegal banking activities related to charitable organizations, titled, "Rules Governing Anti-Money Laundering and Combating Terrorist Financing." This update was issued to all banks and financial institutions in Saudi Arabia requiring implementation of new policies and procedures:

Consolidation of all bank accounts of charitable or welfare organizations into a single account for each organization.

- Identification required for all deposits.
- No ATM or credit cards can be issued for these accounts.
- No cash withdrawals.
- No overseas fund transfers.
- Accounts must be approved by SAMA.

Only two individuals authorized by the board of a charitable institution will be allowed to operate the primary account.

On January 22, 2004, a joint press conference was held in Washington, D.C., to announce that Saudi Arabia and the United States had asked the UN Sanctions Committee to designate the Kenya, Pakistan, Tanzania, and Indonesia branches of the Al-Haramain Islamic Foundation as supporters of terrorism. On January 29, the UN complied with the request.

Then, on June 2, 2004, Saudi Arabia announced that it had dissolved the Al-Haramain Islamic Foundation, five of its branches, and other private groups and established a new organization, the Saudi National Commission for Relief and Charity Work Abroad. This new entity is intended to be the sole means for private contributions raised in the Kingdom. It will operate with total transparency with accounting and audited statements issued every three months. Although the Al-Haramain Islamic Foundation has been notified of the government's decision to close it, as of yet, no actions have officially been taken. The government had ordered the charity disbanded and its operations dissolved by October 15, 2004. Officials maintain that the foundation is "as good as closed" and no new donations were being accepted.[28]

Saudi Arabia took steps to freeze the assets of close bin Laden associates. These included Wa'el Hamza Julaidan, who is believed to have been a financial conduit for al Qaeda. Julaidan served as the director general of the Rabita Trust, an nongovernmental organization designated by President Bush's Executive Order 13224 as an organization that provided logistical and financial support for al Qaeda.

During the month of Ramadan in 2004, the Saudi government stepped up monitoring of charitable organizations, fearing that some of the donations were being funneled to al Qaeda and its affiliates. A strict ban on dropping cash into boxes at entrances of mosques and shopping centers was put in place along with the appointment of a committee of accountants to audit the financial statements of 299 registered charities.[29]

As in most other areas of counterterrorism, there is still much to be done. Although the Kingdom has made significant progress toward impeding the ability of terrorists to use the financing mechanisms previously available to them, the systemic measures implemented will take time to yield results. Also, according to the House Financial Services Subcommittee on Oversight and Investigations, Saudi Arabia has not yet complied with the UN requirement to set up financial investigative units (FIU) to track charitable giving.

The Kingdom has not yet assigned personnel to the office to monitor the progress of tracking terrorist money. However, Juan Zarate, assistant secretary of treasury of terrorist financing, noted that Saudi Arabia had begun setting up an FIU and commended the important steps the government had taken in conjunction with the United States to halt terrorist funding. He also noted that, the new restrictions on the financial activities of charitable organizations represented a "concrete step" by the government to deal with terrorist financing.[30]

International Cooperation

Saudi Arabia occupies a major role in regional and international affairs through membership in various international organizations and it is using this role to help combat terrorism. The Kingdom cooperates with the United Nations, Interpol, and others to combat terrorism and supports a host of international initiatives through its implementation of multilateral and bilateral agreements. Saudi Arabia is an active and regular participant in G-20 meetings and has signed a multilateral agreement under the auspices of the League of Arab States as well as a number of bilateral agreements and protocols with non-Arab countries. The government is also mindful of maintaining vigilance over the activities of those working at the institutions it funds. In a joint U.S.-Saudi effort in January 2004, the diplomatic visas of 16 people affiliated with the Islamic Institute in Virginia were revoked.

The Saudi Government has combined its resources with the governments of the United States, the European Union, and Asian countries to devise a means for sharing information quickly and effectively. In 1996 the Kingdom established a joint counterterrorism committee with the United States to exchange information on al Qaeda. In the wake of the events of September 11, 2001, the committee was reinvigorated, and the Kingdom redoubled its efforts to become a major partner in the war on terror.

On September 10, 2003, Prince Saud al-Faisal stated:[31]

> Whatever justification [for terrorism] Saudis understood before, now they see they are at war with these terrorists. It is not true that the extremists are gaining the upper hand. We are fighting terrorists, pursuing them everywhere, closing the net on them. The government has arrested many of the Ulema. The war, as the Crown Prince said, is a war against those who wage it, who encourage it, who support it, and even those who tacitly accept it. If there are in the pulpits of the mosques those who urge violence, they are removed immediately. In the schools, the books have been changed for the new school

year. The instructions to the teachers have been changed. The [terrorist] money aspect is now completely controlled and the government knows it.

WHAT THE SAUDI GOVERNMENT DID NOT DO: THE FINDINGS OF THE 9/II COMMISSION

Despite allegations in the media and elsewhere that the Kingdom furnished material support to al Qaeda, the independent and bipartisan 9/11 Commission formed to investigate the attacks of 11 September concluded that no such support existed. Specifically, the 9/11 Commission confirmed that there is no evidence that the government of Saudi Arabia funded al Qaeda, nor any evidence that the 9/11 hijackers received funding from Saudi citizen Omar al-Bayoumi, or from Princess Haifa al-Faisal, wife of Saudi ambassador to the United States Prince Bandar bin Sultan.

The commissioners wrote: "We have found no evidence that the Saudi government as an institution or senior Saudi officials individually funded [al Qaeda]." Foreign Minister Prince Saud al-Faisal lauded the report, saying it had put to rest "false accusations" about Saudi Arabia's stand against terrorism. He continued:[32]

> The 9/11 Commission has put to rest the false accusations that have cast fear and doubt over Saudi Arabia. For too long Saudi Arabia stood morbidly accused of funding and supporting terrorism. In contrast to the insinuations of the infamous congressional report . . . which aimed at perpetuating these myths instead of investigating them seriously, now there are clear findings by an independent commission that separate fact from fiction.

The commission's report also denied that Saudi nationals were inappropriately allowed to leave the United States in the days following 9/11. According to the commission, there was "no evidence that any flights of Saudi nationals, domestic or international, took place before the reopening of national airspace on the morning of September 13, 2001." It also affirmed, "the FBI interviewed all persons of interest on these flights prior to their departures. They concluded that none of the passengers was connected to the 9/11 attacks and have since found no evidence to change that conclusion. Our own independent review of the Saudi nationals involved confirms that no one with known links to terrorism departed on these flights."

In December 2004, Prince Turki, the Saudi ambassador to Britain, was awarded substantial libel damages and issued a public apology from *Paris Match*. The October 2003 issue of the French magazine ran an article that "pinned" the September 11 attacks directly on the prince and included an interview with Laurent Murawiec along with excerpts from his book, *La Guerre d'Apres*, which details the author's account of the dangers posed by Saudi Arabia to the United States. Murawiec described Prince Turki as having a close involvement with al Qaeda and using it as his military organization—allegations that the prince termed "outrageous." These views have been rejected by the U.S. government and the 9/11 Commission. French authorities have also distanced themselves from the Murawiec controversy.[33]

Although the 9/11 report clearly absolves Saudi Arabia from any direct connection to al Qaeda financing and the September 11 attacks, the commission does acknowledge that there was a failure by the government to properly supervise Islamic charities in the Kingdom. Consequently, some responsibility existed at the lower level. Radical clergy, employed by government charities, as well as prominent associates of the royal family, have been found culpable for providing encouragement, if not outright material assistance, for the terror campaign.

AL QAEDA'S SITUATION IN 2005

The al Qaeda organization in Saudi Arabia has done some damage to the Kingdom's economy and has killed many innocent people. It has scored a kind of victory in that it has forced the government to make massive expenditures on internal security and has created a general climate of insecurity in the Kingdom.

This has had little impact on the day-to-day life of ordinary Saudis. It has, however, made many foreign workers leave, has forced foreign diplomats and businessmen to spend much of their time in secure compounds, and has reduced foreign investment. Almost inevitably, the end result has also fueled exaggerated fears about the Kingdom's internal instability. While the al Qaeda attacks have brought Saudi and U.S. officials together in cooperating in counterterrorism measures in the many areas, the resulting fears have helped to widen the distance between ordinary Saudis and Americans created by 9/11.

Nevertheless, al Qaeda has been ineffective in achieving its main goals for a number of reasons. First, it was unsuccessful in its recruitment efforts; second, it failed to articulate a viable alternative to the existing government; and third, it lacked funding and was forced to channel resources into the one existing cell—thus unable to establish other independent cells.

Despite the popular notion of al Qaeda as a hydra that can constantly grow new heads, there are indications that the organization has not been able to recover from government attacks. At its peak, Saudi al Qaeda claimed between 500 and 600 members scattered among the cells. Of these, roughly 250 were diehards. By the end of 2004, between 400 and 500 militants had been captured or killed, including all of the leaders—this is in addition to the thousands of sympathizers who were arrested and interrogated, most of whom have been freed.

Al Qaeda underestimated the efficacy of Saudi intelligence and security forces and their ability to adapt to new types of threat and attack. While ordinary police were not equipped to deal with new threat, Saudi intelligence was able to accurately identify those militants who composed the original 26 most-wanted list as leaders of al Qaeda relatively quickly, and the security services were able to hunt many down and disrupt most of the cells they headed.

Finally, in 2004 Saudi border guards detained nearly a million people attempting to gain illegal entry into the Kingdom and captured more than 10 tons of drugs (the sales of which are often used to fund terrorist operations). In addition, 2,000 weapons were seized and, in all, 19,000 smuggling attempts were foiled and 8,000 smugglers arrested.[34]

Most important, the organization could not win popular support. While it was able to exploit popular feeling and anger on some issues such as the Arab-Israeli issue, it could not win significant support for its actual activities from either the Saudi people or the Saudi clergy. Above all, its emphasis on violence failed to resonate with the people. Saudis were shocked by the initial attacks, and those that targeted Muslims and Arabs further alienated and diminished support for the organization.

Nevertheless, Saudi Arabia is at a critical juncture in its fight against terrorism. The threat is unlikely to disappear for years to come. Al Qaeda can draw on Saudis in Afghanistan, Pakistan, Yemen, and Central Asia, as well as other members of al Qaeda who may be able to enter Saudi Arabia. The Iraqi and Yemeni borders present serious problems in terms of infiltration.

Saudi Arabia has hundreds of miles of porous border. In July 2004 alone some 30,000 men were detained in the Yemeni border area.

The Yemeni border is particularly hard to secure. Much of it is in mountain areas or open desert that is very difficult to secure. Some tribes exist across the border and some towns straddle it without any barriers. Smuggling not only is a way of life, it is sometimes the key economic activity. Saudi security officers speculate that much of the more than 1.3 tons of explosives used in the attacks on the Ministry of Interior in late December 2004 came from across the Yemeni border.

As has been touched upon earlier, the Iraq war has also posed new security challenges for Saudi Arabia, and while relatively few Saudi young men who have joined the Sunni insurgent groups in Iraq are not clearly tied to recruitment by al Qaeda, most have been recruited by Islamist extremists.

At a high-level security meeting in Tehran in December 2004, Iraqi interior minister Fallah Hassan al-Naqib called on regional ministers and security chiefs to prevent infiltrators and money from flowing into Iraq. Commenting on the problem, Prince Nayef said, "Iraq must not be a place for training terrorists, and they could be Saudis, like what happened in Afghanistan . . . the situation in Iraq endangers not only the country and its people, but has also become a clear and dangerous threat to security and stability in the region."[35]

Although the government can point to significant strides in rooting out militant activity, the fact remains that over 90 people have been killed in terrorist incidents since May 2003, and al Qaeda remains a threat both inside and outside Saudi Arabia.[36]

DEALING WITH THE UNDERLYING CAUSES OF SUPPORT FOR AL QAEDA

As is discussed in later chapters, these trends of terrorism in the region are serious enough so that the government must address the underlying causes of unrest and of recruitment by extremist organizations. The government needs to demonstrate a broader commitment to expediting the reform efforts now in place and move forward in new areas. Keeping violent opposition at bay requires a more open and representative Saudi political system, reductions in corruption and favoritism within the public sector, and less concentration of wealth and power within the royal family and other leading families. This can be accomplished by increasing popular political participation, giving Saudi citizens a more active voice and a stake in the system, allowing free association, strengthening political institutions, and rooting out corruption.[37]

Similar efforts are needed in economic reform, in diversifying the economy, in Saudization, in making education more relevant to job skills and employment, and in the overall effort to create jobs and careers for young Saudi men and women. Terrorism and instability never have a single or predictable set of causes. Ensuring internal stability requires a broad-based effort to remove as many of the underlying causes of terrorism as possible and giving more attention to issues like education, employment, and career expectations, which draw more attention in Saudi public opinion polls and surveys than politics.

Similarly, human rights and the rule of law—including business law and property rights—affect far more people on a day-to-day basis than elections. Legitimacy is far more a matter of meeting these expectations than rushing toward democracy without the proper institutions, experience, and development of moderate and stable political parties. This can present a serious problem when the Saudi government must also carry out effective and continuing

Table 2.1: Al Qaeda in Saudi Arabia—The Most Wanted List

1	Abdulaziz al-Muqrin	KILLED (Riyadh)	18 Jun 2004
2	Rakan ibn Mohsen al-Seikhan Rakan Sakhan	KILLED (Riyadh)	13 Apr 2004
3	Khaled al-Hajj	KILLED (Riyadh)	16 Mar 2004
4	Abdul Kareem al-Majati	KILLED (Al Rass)	05 Apr 2005
5	Saleh al-Aufi	AT LARGE	
6	Talib Saud al-Talib	AT LARGE	
7	Saud al-Otaibi	KILLED (Al Rass)	05 Apr 2005
8	Ahmad al-Fadhli	KILLED (Jeddah)	22 Apr 2004
9	Sultan al-Otaibi	KILLED (Riyadh)	29 Dec 2004
10	Abdullah Saud Abu-Nayan al-Sobaie	KILLED (Riyadh)	29 Dec 2004
11	Faisal al-Dakheel	KILLED (Riyadh)	18 Jun 2004
12	Faris Ahmed Jamaan al-Zahrani	CAPTURED (Abha)	05 Aug 2004
13	Khaled al-Qurashi	KILLED (Jeddah)	22 Apr 2004
14	Issa al-Aushan	KILLED (Riyadh)	20 Jul 2004
15	Mustapha Mubaraki	KILLED (Jeddah)	22 Apr 2004
16	Abdul Majeed ibn Muhammad Abdullah al-Munie	KILLED (Riyadh)	12 Oct 2004
17	Nasser ibn Rashid al-Rashid	KILLED (Riyadh)	13 Apr 2004
18	Bandar Abdel Rahman al-Dikeel	KILLED (Riyadh)	29 Dec 2004
19	Othman Hadi al-Maqbul al-Amri	SURRENDERED (Abha)	28 Jun 2004
20	Talal Anbari	KILLED (Jeddah)	22 Apr 2004
21	A'amir al-Zaidan al-Shihri	KILLED (Riyadh)	23 Dec 2003
22	Abdullah al-Rashoud	AT LARGE	
23	Abdul Rahman al-Yaziji	KILLED (Riyadh)	06 Apr 2005
24	Hassan al-Hassaki	CAPTURED (Belgium)	26 Oct 2004
25	Ibrahim Mohammad Abdullah al-Rayyes	KILLED (Riyadh)	08 Dec 2003
26	Mansour ibn Muhammad Faqeeh	SURRENDERED (Najran)	30 Dec 2003

counterterrorism operations, and it is critical that the government find the right balance.

The best solution to terrorism and internal security is ultimately for the Saudi government to respond to the aspirations of its reform-minded citizens, which include many leading Saudi princes, officials, technocrats, and businessmen. Progress in a conservative and traditional society must be measured and evolutionary, and should be driven by Saudi reformers and not the priorities of outside nations and advocates. If, however, the government hesitates to make real, tangible progress in instituting reform, the Kingdom will lose a critical opportunity.

Chapter 3

External Strategic Pressures

S audi national security must respond to a wide range of external strategic pressures in addition to potential threats. Saudi Arabia must respond to strategic pressures from its Gulf allies and the United States, the impact of regional conflicts like the Israeli-Palestinian war, and a wide range of other problems. In many ways, the problem of alliances is as difficult for Saudi Arabia as the problem of potential threats.

FAILURES IN INTEROPERABILITY, COOPERATION, AND THE DEVELOPMENT OF THE GULF COOPERATION COUNCIL

The Kingdom must deal with the result of a decades-long failure to create effective regional security structures. There have been token forces and token exercises, many meetings, and many speeches, reports, and documents. However, there has been little progress in integrating the security efforts of the South Gulf states and in making their forces more interoperable. Saudi Arabia and its Gulf neighbors may not have committed self-inflicted wounds, but they have certainly created self-inflicted vulnerabilities.

The Impact of the Gulf Cooperation Council

The most serious self-inflicted military vulnerability is the failure to create a better integrated approach to defense planning and operations through the Gulf Cooperation Council (GCC). Although the GCC was formed in 1980, in reaction to the Iran-Iraq War and the fall of the shah, there has been a consistent failure to develop proper mission specialization and interoperability and a continuing tendency on the part of many individual states to buy weapons and technology for their "glitter factor." Member states have underfunded manpower quality, readiness, sustainability, and projection/maneuver capability.

PROGRESS WITHOUT PROGRESS. The problem has not been that there is no progress; it is rather the *rate* of progress and the resulting ineffectiveness and waste. Every development in military cooperation between the GCC members has been slow in coming, and the developments have had only limited impact after more than two decades.

The GCC command and Peninsula Shield force was so ineffective during the buildup for the first Gulf War in 1991 that the Arab commander, Gen. Khalid bin-Sultan, was forced to disband its elements and commanders on a de facto basis and disperse them back to their national units.

Since that time, there have been several useful initiatives to improve naval exercises and cooperation in mine warfare. The Saudi defense minister, Prince Sultan bin Abdul Aziz al-Saud, did open a new Peninsula Shield compound near Hafr Al Baten in December 2003, which has the facilities to train 6,000 personnel. Furthermore, *Jane's Sentinel Security Assessment* reported that the GCC's armed forces deliberated, during their meeting in Bahrain in October 2001, the purchase of "a high-resolution military reconnaissance satellite." They hoped that it would add to their early-warning capabilities, and $500 million was approved for the project.

However, overall progress has been largely cosmetic or driven by exercises conducted by outside powers. There is still no cohesive effort in vital mission areas like mine warfare, maritime patrol, surveillance, intelligence and counterterrorism, air combat, or land-based air defense. The most that has been accomplished is to create an expensive secure command communications system with little war-fighting value in an era when real- or near-real-time netting of the information technology necessary for battle management and interoperability is critical to success.

GCC Cooperation versus an Unnecessary Degree of Dependence on Outside Allies. Unless radical shifts take place in virtually every military aspect of the GCC—particularly in command and control, intelligence, information technology, mission and procurement planning, cross basing and sustainability, combat interoperability, large-scale exercise training on a joint level, and command and control—talk about regional military security concepts is a well-meaning fantasy.

Saudi Arabia and the Gulf may have to continue to rely on help from the United States and outside powers, particularly if Iran does build and deploy nuclear forces. At the same time, Southern Gulf military forces in the GCC now are large enough so that they could take on most of the tasks of regional defense and deterrence if the forces of the GCC states were more integrated and more interoperable and each nation focused on key military missions.

This would be especially true if they created joint command, control, communications, computer, and intelligence (C⁴I); battle management (BM); and intelligence, surveillance, and reconnaissance systems to integrate air and maritime defense, deal with infiltration and amphibious attacks, and create a true, sustainable rapid deployment capability.

There are also plans for critical improvements in C⁴I/BM. On February 25, 2001, the development of a joint air defense system, named Hizam Al-Tawaun (HAT), was commissioned. This system, which is linked to the GCC air defense structure, would include tracking capabilities that would enable the council countries to track any airplane in their air space to help them synchronize defensive actions. The head of the UAE Air Force, Brig. Gen. Khalid Abu Ainnain, introduced a proposal to improve warning of attack by missile through the deployment of S-band radars on three fronts: northern Saudi Arabia, the UAE, and Oman.[1]

Saudi Arabia has a wide range of assets around which such joint planning and C⁴I/BM capabilities could be built. And they could easily be made compatible with U.S., British, and other forces, when required in an emergency. Military planning groups within the GCC have recognized this for years, as have many outside military advisers. *The problem is not the need or capability to act; it is the lack of any realistic collective decision to act.*

The Coming Military Recapitalization Crisis

The level of waste caused by the lack of such cooperation is indicated by the fact that no Southern Gulf county today has balanced and effective forces, but the GCC states cumulatively spend some $37 billion a year on military forces and at least another $3 billion on paramilitary forces and pay for security forces of over 220,000 men.

At the same time, the data in Table 3.1 show that most Southern Gulf states cannot individually afford to recapitalize their present force structure. They are only spending about half as much on new arms transfers as they did in the early 1990s. Total expenditures on new arms agreements were only $15.3 billion during 2000–2003 versus $29.3 billion in deliveries, and new arms agreements only totaled $33.5 billion over the entire period of 1996–2003, versus a total of $78.7 billion in new deliveries. The gap between the rate of new orders and actual deliveries would be far greater except for some $15.7 billion in new UAE orders during 1996–2003. The Southern Gulf states must either make serious force cuts or sharply slow their past pace of modernization and procurement.[2]

In spite of the current boom in oil export revenues, Qatar and the UAE now seem to be the only Gulf countries able to afford to sustain their past levels of military spending and arms imports—given their needs for domestic spending for both investment and for entitlements and operating expenditures. Qatar's forces, however, are of token strength at best, and the UAE seems determined to make expensive showpiece purchases rather than develop real military capabilities.

Oil wealth is proving to be increasingly relative for Gulf nations whose populations are increasing rapidly. The slow pace of economic reform and diversification, and of job creation, is becoming more of a medium- to long-term threat to most Southern Gulf states than any foreign threat, as well as a serious potential cause of terrorism. Saudi Arabia and the other Gulf states face limits on their present and future income and need to make hard trade-offs between military forces and development and internal stability.

If the Southern Gulf states do limit their military budgets, they will either have to make significant force cuts or fall behind in force modernization over time. The scale of such pressures on their ability to fund their security apparatuses will depend on how well Gulf nations do in diversifying their economies, reducing dependence on foreign labor, and creating new jobs for their own citizens.

The Problem of Saudi and U.S. Strategic Relations

The failure to create effective regional security structures has left Saudi Arabia dependent on the United States for its ultimate security guarantees in the effect of some major conflict with Iran, or any sustained rebirth of the Iraqi threat. The United States contributes important strengths to Saudi Arabia's security and to the security of the Gulf region as a whole. U.S. forward-deployed military power, and power-projection capabilities essentially checkmate Iran and outside threats. They provide a basis for improved training and military assistance as well as for counterproliferation and missile defense.

At the same time, Saudi Arabia has long been a key partner to the United States. It has long been a moderate diplomatic and political voice in the Arab and Islamic worlds, and it actively supported the United States during the cold war. It also supported the United States during the "tanker war" against Iran in 1987–88, and it was the key Arab ally during the 1990–91 Gulf War. It provided bases for U.S. operations to contain Iraq between 1991 and 2003, and it quietly provided the United States with extensive support and facilities during the Iraq War in 2003—even though Saudi Arabia opposed the Coalition invasion.

Saudi Arabia provided basing facilities for U.S. Special Forces at Arar, refueling facilities and cheap fuel, and overflight rights during the Iraq War in 2002–2003. It made the Combined Aerospace Operations Center (CAOC) at Prince Sultan Air Base available for U.S. use in supporting the war in Afghanistan and Iraq.[3]

Saudi Arabia is dependent on the United States to secure its economic lines of communication and the security of Gulf petroleum exports. It also continues to need American military support and resupply. Saudi Arabia now operates well over $50 billion worth of U.S. military equipment. Some $22.9 billion of a total of $61.1 billion in arms deliveries during 1996–2003 came from the United States. Saudi Arabia placed new arms orders during that period that mean another $7.3 billion is now in the process of delivery.[4] Saudi Arabia does not require an American military presence on Saudi soil, but it will need U.S. military advisers and contract support for some years to come.

Growing U.S. and Saudi Divisions

Both Saudi Arabia and the United States have failed to maintain an effective strategic partnership in recent years. Saudi Arabia was slow to react to the threat posed by Islamic terrorism and acted more in denial than effectively after al Qaeda launched its 9/11 attacks in the United States. Many of these problems are being corrected, and Saudi counterterrorism efforts have gathered momentum, but the events of 9/11 have left a legacy of public anger and bitterness on both sides that will take years of cooperation to overcome.

As the following chapters show, Saudi Arabia has seen all too clearly since May 2003 just how painful and damaging terrorist attacks can be when they involve much smaller casualties than in the World Trade Center and the Pentagon. Many Saudis still, however, find it easier to blame Islamic extremism and terrorism on conspiracy theories and issues like U.S. ties to Israel than to admit that Saudi Arabia did make mistakes in education and dealing with religious hatred and intolerance that helped create Osama bin Laden and violence.

Saudi Arabia has also been slow to confront the fact that religion is a key issue. While its counterterrorism efforts have improved, it has been reluctant to ask its clergy to join in what has become a broad ideological struggle to maintain Islamic legitimacy both in Saudi Arabia and the world.

Saudi Arabia needs to meet the threat of Islamic extremism head on and proactively. Like every other Islamic state, it must take every possible step to encourage its clergy to attack the kind of perversion of Islam advanced by Osama bin Laden and the preaching and writing of religious intolerance and hatred. Counterterrorism is critical, as are the other forms of reform necessary to fight the causes of terrorism, but key Islamic leaders and nations must meet voices like bin Laden head on. Only those who truly practice and preach Islam can deal with this aspect of the threat, and none can afford to stand aside at this point in time.

The United States has been slow to see that the political impact of a visible deployment of U.S. combat forces in the Kingdom was creating growing resentment among Saudi Arabia's Islamic population and internal political problems in the Kingdom. This problem has been solved by the withdrawal of U.S. forces following the Iraq War. The United States has exaggerated Saudi Arabia's role in the support of extremist and terrorist movements, although this problem has been greatly reduced by the Islamist attacks on the Kingdom that began in May 2003 and growing Saudi cooperation with the United States in counterterrorism.

The United States has been slow to realize that it needs to take a more nuanced approach to counterterrorism. It cannot afford to engage every terrorist movement by itself, and its intervention in Iraq has shown that it risks alienating and radicalizing peoples and movements in nations throughout the Islamic world if it does so. It needs to create local partnerships with key nations like Saudi Arabia and Indonesia. It needs to focus systematically on just how different the various Sufi, Salafi, neo-Wahhabi, and Shiite movements are and then deal with each separately on the terms best tailored to defeating violence and extremism in each separate case.

A more visible U.S. effort is needed to make it clear that the United States understands these realities and understands that it is fighting against a relatively small minority of extremists, and not the Arab world and Islam as a whole. In the process, the United States must also make it clear that it will persuade other countries that it is suggesting the adoption of "universal values" and not seeking to impose "Western values." The United States also needs to start thinking in terms of decades. It needs to understand that it must make a long-term effort to work with the nations of the Arab and Islamic worlds to both fight terrorist movements and encourage the full range of well-defined evolutionary reforms best suited to a given country at a given time.

THE NEED FOR NEW FORMS OF SAUDI AND U.S. COOPERATION IN FIGHTING COUNTERTERRORISM. Other measures are needed. The United States has taken necessary steps to improve the security of its visa and immigration policies, but the U.S. State Department and its consular service have failed to implement these with anything like the efficiency necessary to maintain the flow of Saudi contact with the United States necessary to U.S. and Saudi military cooperation, training effective Saudi forces, and business. The U.S. Congress has further complicated this situation badly by creating overrestrictive laws and regulation and failed to provide the resources necessary to allow quick and effective action on visa applications.

In Saudi Arabia's case, this has virtually put a halt to the training of Saudi regular military officers in the United States, although National Guard personnel do continue to be sent to the United States. The United States has seen effective immigration controls as a weapon against terrorism, but not as a political weapon to support counterterrorism. It also focuses far too much on bureaucratic convenience and concepts of equity and far too little on using the visa process to serve the national interest.

Saudi Arabia and the United States also need to cooperate in creating the kind of agreed security arrangements in Saudi Arabia necessary to allow American businessmen and workers to live and operate safely in the Kingdom and to invest in Saudi Arabia's economic development and economic diversification. Risk cannot be eliminated, but it can be reduced. This same effort is obviously needed to create similar security for all key foreign workers, but the United States is the prime target.

The burden of the former effort must fall on Saudi Arabia, but a further step is needed. The U.S. media and Congress have helped to create an emphasis on security and force protection in U.S. embassies and military facilities that poses a serious threat to the U.S. national interest. Embassies have tended to become isolated fortresses, and contact is being lost with local populations.

A focus on unaccompanied tours has led to one-year tours in countries like Saudi Arabia, ensuring that personnel lack expertise, contacts with the Saudis, and the personnel relationships critical to their mission. This compounds the chronic problems created by the State Department's lack of effective personnel management in terms of rotations and area expertise and emphasis on producing *generalists* at the expense of producing *competents*.

Strong Saudi-U.S. relations, like relations in most areas threatened by violence or terrorism, require more tolerance of risk, and risk management rather than risk management. It is also necessary for U.S. government civilians to take on much of the same burden in an era of counterterrorism and asymmetric warfare that the military takes on in high-threat areas. Recruitment, promotion, and retention of State Department and other U.S. government personnel serving overseas is going to have to change to operate on this basis.

The Failure to Come to Grips with the Arab-Israeli Conflict

Saudi security is dependent on regional stability and security, and this cannot be achieved as long as Arab-Israeli relations are shaped by war and not by a peace process. No issue does more to polarize the region than the Israeli-Palestinian conflict. It encourages popular support for Islamic extremism and divides the Arab world from the West.

The Arab-Israeli conflict has long been a force that threatens Saudi-U.S. security relations. Poll after poll has also shown that there is no greater source of hostility to the United States than the Arab and Islamic perception that it is a cobelligerent with Israel. The United States is Israel's ally and its main source of aid and military equipment. It is seen throughout most of the Arab and Islamic world as being responsible for Israel's actions.

A struggle that the United States and Israel perceive as against terrorism and extremism is perceived by Gulf Arabs and Iran as against Palestinians using the only means they have to struggle for liberation and independence. The United States is seen, furthermore, to value Israeli lives more than those of the Palestinians.

Far too often Arab media are anything but objective and tend to play to the crowds. Worse, the U.S. "occupation" in Iraq is increasingly perceived in Saudi Arabia and the Arab world as the mirror image of the Israeli occupation in Gaza and the West Bank. There is a flood of conspiracy theories charging that the United States is copying Israeli tactics or that its actions in Iraq are somehow dictated by Israel.

The United States does not have good options. It cannot abandon Israel or sacrifice its security, but it must deal with two failed leaderships and two peoples who no longer have faith in each other or are capable of seeing the world through the other's eyes. The United States will be at a major disadvantage in Iraq, in the war on terrorism, and in the Arab and Islamic worlds as long as the Israeli-Palestinian conflict continues.

Saudi Arabia faces equal problems. It cannot abandon its support for the Palestinians because of its need for a security relationship with the United States or because of the problems created by its own war against terrorism. Its legitimacy lies in its support for Islamic and Arab causes, both in the view of its own population and in the perceptions of other Islamic and Arab nations.

There is no way out of this dilemma other than a continuing and highly visible Saudi-U.S. effort to create a just Israeli-Palestinian peace regardless of how many times new initiatives fail. Moreover, this is the only way Saudi Arabia can bring full security to its Western border and minimize the risk of some kind of strategic exchange between Israel and Iran or the broadening of the Israeli-Palestinian conflict to include other Arab states. This aspect of security cannot be achieved by military means.

Saudi, U.S., Palestinian, and Israeli interests can only ultimately be served by a just peace. Crown Prince Abdullah has taken the lead in advancing an Israeli-Palestinian peace proposal. These proposals, which have been accepted in large part by the Arab League, are an important step in this process. So are the proposals the U.S. and the Quartet (US, EU, Russia, and UN) advanced in their "road map" for peace.

Arafat's death, Palestinian elections, Ariel Sharon's withdrawal plans, and a new coalition government in Israel may offer new opportunities to move forward in reaching peace during the next few years. The end result, however, may take more than Saudi words and political action. It has been clear since the time of Camp David that massive new economic aid will be needed over a period of a decade to both a new Palestinian state and to Jordan in order to ensure the success of any peace process and provide the necessary "nation building."

The Need for Saudi and Regional Reform

Saudi Arabia can only deal with its full range of security issues if it looks beyond its military and internal security situation and acts on the need to deal with both Islamic extremism and terrorism and internal reform.

Broader efforts at reform are a critical element of any long-term effort to deal with terrorism and extremism, both inside and outside Saudi Arabia. While it is tempting to focus on the immediate threat posed by leaders like bin Laden and groups like al Qaeda, the forces that shape the rising threat of terrorism and insurgency in the Middle East and North Africa are broad based and ideological, rather than tied to a given leader or movement.

The Economic and Demographic Pressures that Drive the Region toward Terrorism and Extremism

Saudi Arabia must deal with both internal and external forces that are generational in character and that will play out over decades:

- *The Middle East and North Africa are a long-term demographic nightmare.* The U.S. Census Bureau estimates that the Middle East is a region where the population will nearly double between now and 2030. The total population of the Gulf has grown from 30 million in 1950 to 39 million in 1960, 52 million in 1970, 74 million in 1980, 109 million in 1990, and 139 million in 2000. Conservative projections put it at 172 million in 2010, 211 million in 2020, 249 million in 2030, 287 million in 2040, and 321 million in 2050. The Middle East and North Africa had a population of 112 million in 1950. The population is well over 415 million today and is approaching a fourfold increase. It will more than double again, to at least 833 million, by 2050.

  The need to come firmly to grips with population growth is all too clear. Some of the most important, and sometimes most troubled, countries in the region will experience explosive population growth. Algeria is projected to grow from 31 million in 2000 to 53 million in 2050. Egypt has a lower population growth rate than many of its neighbors, but it is still projected to grow from 68 million in 2000 to 113 million in 2050. The Gaza Strip is projected to grow from 1.1 to 4.2 million, and the West Bank from 2.2 to 5.6 million. Iran is estimated to grow from 65 to 100 million, and Iraq from 23 to 57 million. Morocco is projected to grow from 30 to 51 million. Oman will grow from 2.5 to 8.3 million. Saudi Arabia will grow from 22 to 91 million, and Syria from 16 to 34 million. Yemen's population growth rate is so explosive that it is projected to grow from 18 to 71 million.

- *Population growth is creating a "youth explosion."* This growth has already raised the size of the young working-age population (ages 20 to 24) in the Gulf area from 5.5 million in 1970 to 13 million in 2000. Conservative estimates indicate it will grow to 18 million in 2010 and to 24 million in 2050. If one looks at the Middle East and North Africa region as a whole, the numbers of those who are between the ages of 20 and 24 have grown steadily from 10 million in 1950 to 36 million today and will grow steadily to at least 56 million by 2050. The World Bank estimates that some 36 percent of the total population of this region is less than 15 years old versus 21 percent in the United States and 16 percent in the European Union countries. The ratio of dependents to each working-age man and woman is three times that in a developed region like the EU. The U.S. State Department has produced estimates that more than 45 percent of the population is under 15 years of age.

- *Population growth presents major problems for future infrastructure development.* Major problems now exist in every aspect of infrastructure from urban services to education. At the same time, population pressure is exhausting natural water supplies in many countries, leading to growing dependence on desalination and forcing permanent dependence on food imports. Demand for water already exceeds the supply in nearly half the countries in the region, and annual renewable water supplies per capita have fallen by 50 percent since 1960 and are projected to fall from 1,250 square meters today to 650 square meters in 2025—about 14 percent of today's global average. Groundwater is being overpumped, and "fossil water" depleted.

- *Much of the region cannot afford to provide more water for agriculture at market prices, and in the face of human demand; much has become a "permanent" food importer.* The resulting social changes are indicated by the fact that the percentage of the work force in agriculture has dropped from around 40 percent to around 10 percent over the last 40 years. At the same time, regional manufacturers and light industry have grown steadily in volume, but not in global competitiveness.

- *Employment and education will be critical challenges to regional stability.* The Gulf already is an area where approximately 70 percent of the population already is under 30 years of age and nearly 50 percent is under 20. It is also a region where real and disguised unemployment averages at least 25 percent for young males, where no real statistics exist for women, and where the number of young people entering the work force each year will double between now and 2025. This creates an immense "bow wave" of future strains on social, educational, political, and economic systems whose effect is compounded by a lack of jobs and job growth, practical work experience, and competitiveness. The failure to achieve global competitiveness, diversify economies, and create jobs is only partially disguised by the present boom in oil revenues. Direct and disguised unemployment range from 12 percent to 20 percent in many countries, and the World Bank projects the labor force as growing by at least 3 percent per year for the next decade.

- *Hyperurbanization and a half-century decline in agricultural and traditional trades impose high levels of stress on traditional social safety nets and extended families.* The urban population seems to have been under 15 million in 1950. It has since more than doubled from 84 million in 1980 to 173 million today, and some 25 percent of the population will soon live in cities of one million or more.

- *Broad problems in integrating women effectively and productively into the work force.* Female employment in the Middle East and North Africa region has grown from 24 percent of the labor in 1980 to 28 percent today, but that total is 15 percent lower than in a high-growth area like East Asia.

- *The World Bank does not report trends for the Gulf region, but the Middle East and North Africa have had limited or no real growth in per capita income, and growing inequity in the distribution of that income, for more than two decades.* This is reflected in the fact that growth in per capita income in constant prices dropped from 3.6 percent during 1971–80 to –0.6 percent during 1981–90 and was only 1 percent from 1991 to 2000. During this entire period, the disparity between the income of rich and poor tended to increase. The Middle East and North Africa region has a regionwide average per capita income of around $2,200 versus $26,000 in the high-income countries in the West.

- *Overall economic growth is too low.* The World Bank's report on *Global Economic Development* for 2003 shows a sharp decline in economic growth in GDP in the Middle East and North Africa region in constant prices from 6.5 percent during 1971–80 to 2.5 percent during 1981–90. While growth rose to 3.2 percent during 1991–2000, it barely kept pace with population growth.

- *The Middle East is not competitive with the leading developing regions.* While interregional comparisons may be somewhat unfair, the economic growth in East Asia and the Pacific was 6.6 percent during 1971–80, 7.3 percent during 1981–90, and 7.7 percent during 1991–2000. The growth in real per capita income in East Asia and the Pacific was 3 percent during 1971–80, 4.8 percent during 1981–90, and 5.4 percent during 1991–2000.

- *The region is not competitive in trade.* The Middle East and North Africa is a region whose share of the world's GNP and world trade has declined for nearly half a century, where intraregional trade remains limited, and where nearly all states have states outside the region as their major trading partners. The rhetoric of Arab unity and regional development has little relation to reality.

- *Radical economic changes are affecting regional societies. Agricultural and rural communities have given way to hyperurbanization and slums.* Most Middle East and North Africa countries are now net food importers and must devote a growing portion of their limited water supplies to urban and industrial use. The region cannot eliminate food import dependence at any foreseeable point in the future, and demographics inevitably mean its water problems force economic and social change.

- *"Oil wealth" has always been relative, and can no longer sustain any country in the region except for Qatar, the UAE, and possibly Kuwait.* The present boom in oil revenues has greatly eased the financial pressures on many oil-exporting states, but such developments are cyclical and uncertain. Real per capita oil wealth is now only about 15 percent to 30 percent of its peak in 1980. For example, Saudi Arabia's per capita petroleum exports in 2002 had less than one tenth of their peak value from $24,000 in 1980 to $2,300 in 2002.

- *In spite of decades of reform plans and foreign aid, there are no globally competitive economies in any of the Middle East and North Africa states.* Productivity has been inhibited by problems in education, bureaucratic barriers, a focus on state industry, a lack of incentives for foreign direct investment, a strong incentive to place domestic private capital in investments outside the region, problems in the role of women that sharply affect productivity gain, and corruption. There are beginnings in nations like Tunisia, Jordan, and Dubai, but there are no real successes as yet, and many states have little more than ambitious plans.

- *Far too many countries have a sustained debt and budget crisis.* Most states already cannot afford many of the expenditures they should make or have national budgets under great strain. The end result is to cut back entitlements and investment in infrastructure and allow state industries to decline. At the same time, many countries still spend far too much on military forces, continue to fail to effectively modernize their forces, and now must spend more on internal security.

- *Immigration is being driven by such forces and creates new challenges of its own.* It is hardly surprising therefore that the Arab Development Report should mention surveys where 50 percent of the young Arab males surveyed stated their career plan was to immigrate.

The Pressures Created by a Lack of Political Reform and Stabilizing Political Ideology

Demographic and economic pressures are only part of the story. There are tremendous cultural, societal, political, and ideological pressures that operate within and around the Kingdom as well. Saudi Arabia and all of the countries in the region must also deal with serious ethnic and confessional differences, as well as differences resulting from education, tribalism, and class. The end result is that Saudi efforts to create national security must deal with the following additional issues:

- *The Middle East is a region with a long history of failed secularism.* Pan Arabism, Arab socialism, the cult of the leader, and exploitative capitalism, have all had their day and failed. Most states have patriarchal and authoritarian leaders, one or no real political parties, and elites unprepared for truly representative government. Far too often democracy is a word rather than a practical option.

- *Vast changes in communications—such as satellite TV News channels like Al Jazeera and the regional content of the Internet—produce serious cultural alienation and expose the public to the outside world.* Such exposures have made the public aware of the failure of their current political and economic systems in comparison to other systems.

- *This alienation is compounded by the Arab-Israeli conflict, the military dominance and intervention of the United States, and often careless and extreme U.S. and Western criticism of Islam and the Arab world.* The image of crusaders, of neo-imperialism, and Western contempt or disregard for the values of the region and the Islamic world is grossly exaggerated. So too is the blame assigned to Israel and to the United States for supporting Israel. It is, however, a reality in terms of regional perceptions, and there are enough underlying elements of truth behind these perceptions so that no one in the United States should ignore them.

- *It is hardly surprising, therefore, that many in the region have turned back to what they regard as their roots in Islam and ethnicity.* They see their future in terms of religion, a broad Arab identity mixed with reliance on extended family and tribe. The end result is sometimes extremism, anger, hatred, and violence.

It is equally unsurprising that American calls for reform and democracy are seen as outside interference, as motivated by selfish U.S. interests or even "Zionist plots," and that U.S. efforts at nation building are greeted with so many conspiracy theories and so much suspicion. Growing internal security problems are often far more serious than external threats.

- *Governments are generally failing to modernize their conventional military forces at the rate required and to recapitalize them.* This failure is forcing regional states to reshape their security structures and is pushing some toward proliferation.

This mix of complex forces has already created military and internal security threats that are all too tangible, but no amount of Saudi military and internal security activity can be an adequate response. Saudi Arabia must accompany its security efforts with matching efforts at economic, demographic, social, and political reforms.

The Saudi royal family, Saudi technocrats and educators, and many Saudi businessmen recognize the seriousness of these problems. The Kingdom is making at least some progress in many areas. Saudi economic plans call for reform, and efforts are being made to address Saudi demographic problems through Saudization. Saudi Arabia is strengthening its Majlis, moving toward local elections, and encouraging Islam and interfaith dialog.

At the same time, the pace of reform still lags far behind the need. Political cultures and economic and social structures take time to evolve. This means that the underlying forces behind extremism and terrorism will endure for years to come, and any assessment of the threats to Saudi Arabia must look beyond traditional security threats and consider the broader forces at work.

TENSIONS OVER REFORM. The U.S. efforts to encourage reform have been another source of Saudi and U.S. tensions and have sometimes acted to exacerbate Saudi Arabia's security problems rather than to help solve them. U.S. calls for instant political reforms have been more counterproductive than useful. If the United States is to maintain the Saudi and regional political support it needs to sustain its current security role in the Gulf, it must accept the fact that change must be evolutionary and must be driven largely based on local values and reform efforts.

The United States cannot succeed in dealing with Saudi Arabia or any other Arab state if it continues to make vague calls for democracy rather than well-planned nation-by-nation efforts to achieve evolutionary reform. In fact, the current U.S. approach threatens to turn "democracy" into a four-letter word, a synonym for half-reasoned U.S. efforts to force its own political system on other countries or simply serve its own interests through regime change.

The United States also needs to show Saudi Arabia and its other Arab allies and friends the respect they deserve. The United States cannot afford to deal with Islam or the Arab world in terms of ideological prejudice. The United States does not need either neo-conservatism or neo-liberalism. It needs pragmatism, neo-realism, and a return to the "internationalism" that has shaped its most successful national security policy efforts ever since World War II.

The United States should focus on supporting Saudi reformers to make reforms on Saudi terms. In the Kingdom's case, this may well mean beginning by encouraging efforts to improve human rights and the quality of the rule of law. At the same time, it means helping Saudi Arabia to achieve economic reform, and dealing honestly with their demographic problems should have equal priority.

Political evolution will take time. Saudi Arabia needs to create elected consultative institutions, move through a process where its population learns what voting and elections really mean, develop political parties, create media capable of supporting an honest elective process, and learn how to debate how the Kingdom uses its resources and manages the state. There are essential real-world preconditions to effective pluralism.

Chapter 4

The Saudi Security Apparatus

T he current Saudi security apparatus that must deal with this mix of
strategic threats and pressures is a complex mix of regular military
forces in the Ministry of Defense and Aviation (MODA), a separate
Saudi Arabian National Guard (SANG), and various internal security and intelligence services in the Ministry of Interior (MOI). Saudi Arabia's military forces
are only one element of the Saudi security structure and are currently divided
into five major branches: the Army, the National Guard, the Navy, the Air
Force, and the Air Defense Force. Saudi Arabia also has large paramilitary and
internal security forces and a small strategic missile force.

Saudi Arabia has made significant progress in creating modern and effective
military forces, but it still faces major problems in the leadership and organization of its armed forces. These include the traditional problems all states face in
organizing and commanding large military forces and in shaping and funding
the future structure of its armed forces. At the same time, the Kingdom faces
newer problems in dealing with significant problems in manpower quality,
advanced military technology, readiness, sustainability, and managing an
advanced force structure that must have the option of being interoperable with
both region allies and those from outside the Gulf.

Saudi Arabia also must recast the mission of many elements of it forces to
focus on "jointness." It must adopt many of the advances in joint warfare pioneered by the United States and other Western nations, and improve cooperation between the Army, Navy, Air Force, and Air Defense Force. It must also
redefine the mission of jointness to link the regular services, the National
Guard, and the internal security and police forces under the Ministry of Security into a coherent structure that can prevent and respond to terrorism.

Saudi Arabia has made major advances in internal security and counterterrorism since it came under more intense terrorist attack in May 2003. It has
given the deputy minister of the Ministry of Interior the interagency lead in this
role and has effectively dual-hatted him in dealing with the forces of the Ministry of Defense. Nevertheless, it will be several years before Saudi Arabia can
plan and implement all of the measures required.

The Leadership of the Saudi Security Apparatus

Civilian control of the Saudi security apparatus is extended through the royal family and not through the methods common in the West. Saudi military forces are formally under the direct control of King Fahd bin Abdul Aziz al-Saud. King Fahd is the prime minister of Saudi Arabia, Custodian of the Two Holy Mosques (since adopting the title in 1986 to substitute for "His Majesty") and the commander in chief of the Saudi Armed Forces. He is one of the sons of the Kingdom's founder and assumed power of the Kingdom on June 13, 1982, after the death of King Khalid bin Abdul Aziz. Before his current appointment, King Fahd became Saudi Arabia's first minister of education in 1953; he was appointed minister of interior in 1962. He held this post until he became crown prince in 1975.[1]

Crown Prince and First Vice Prime Minister Abdullah bin Abdul Aziz al-Saud (half-brother to the monarch and crown prince since 13 June 1982) has acted as regent since January 1996. He has steadily played a more leading role in shaping the country's security policy. Major policy decisions are normally made by a group of senior members of the royal family, especially two major princes play a critical role: Prince Sultan bin Abdul Aziz al-Saud and Prince Nayef bin Abdul Aziz al-Saud, the minister of the interior.

Prince Sultan bin Abdul Aziz makes most decisions affecting the regular armed forces. He has been the minister of defense and aviation since 1963 and the second vice prime minister since 1982. Before being named to these positions, Prince Sultan held numerous government posts, including governor of Riyadh, minister of agriculture and minister of communications. He has now spent four decades shaping and modernizing Saudi Arabia's armed forces, shaping most critical policy decisions relating to military procurement, and supervising the construction of modern military bases and cities throughout the Kingdom.[2] His son, Prince Khalid bin Sultan, is the assistant minister of defense for military affairs and now plays a leading role in shaping defense policy, and in managing the day-to-day decisions of the Ministry of Defense and Civil Aviation (MODA).

The Saudi National Guard remains under a separate chain of command. Crown Prince Abdullah bin Abdul Aziz, the first vice prime minister, has commanded the National Guard since 1962. Prince Mitiab bin Abdullah, the assistant vice commander for military affairs, acts as the de facto commander of the National Guard for his father.

Prince Nayef has been the minister of interior since 1975. He controls the General Security Services (internal intelligence services), the Public Security Administration Forces (the police), the Civil Defense Administration (fire service), the Border Guard, the Passport & Immigration Department, the

Mujahideen Forces, the Drug Enforcement Agency, and the Special Security Forces. Like the other senior princes, Prince Nayef has held prior gubernatorial and ministerial posts, such as governor of Riyadh, vice minister of interior, and minister of state for security affairs. His son, Prince Muhammed, acts as his assistant for security affairs and has played a key role in leading the fight against terrorism.

Saudi Arabia has a number of intelligence services, and the three leading princes who hold government positions have their own intelligence support (Crown Prince Abdullah: National Guard Intelligence Directorate; Prince Sultan: Military Intelligence, which is composed of officers from the four major branches of the armed services; Prince Nayef: General Security Service, the domestic intelligence service).

The most important intelligence service is the General Intelligence Directorate. It is relatively well known in the West, because it was formerly controlled by the Prince Turki al Faisal, who was appointed director general of the General Intelligence Directorate by King Khalid bin Abdul Aziz in 1977. Prince Turki held this position until he was replaced by Prince Nawaf bin Abdul Aziz on September 1, 2001. The service was renamed "The General Intelligence Presidency" during Prince Nawaf's tenure. The service focuses on external intelligence matters affecting Saudi Arabia and its mission is to gain a better understanding of the relationship between extremist groups in Saudi Arabia and the flow of currency both within the Kingdom and beyond its borders.[3]

THE IMPORTANCE OF CONSENSUS AND CONSULTATION

While separate royal chains of command divide some aspects of the control of the Saudi security apparatus by senior princes, it is important to understand that the cooperation between them has steadily improved since the Gulf War in 1990–91, and particularly since the series of terrorist attacks that began in May 2003.

Moreover, the senior leaders of the royal family normally operate by a consensus reached at a number of levels. It is rare for a major decision not to be discussed informally by the most senior princes. This discussion generally includes consultation and advice from all of the relevant princes at the ministerial level, supported by a mix of outside advisers and technocrats within the key security ministries. Interviews indicate that there is nothing rigid about this process, however, and that senior ministers can act quickly and with minimal amounts of technical advice. Such actions are rare, however, and the senior princes often staff their decision-making process with analyses of options, budget implications, and advice on the internal political, social, and religious impact of their decisions.

A lack of administrative structure and clear and well-established procedures for collective planning and review do, however, present problems. This is particularly true when decisions cut across the lines of responsibility from one senior prince to another, when they are not part of the normal flow of annual decision making, and when hard choices have to be made in analyzing the effectiveness and cost of given decisions and options.

The coordination of all counterterrorism efforts under the MOI since 2004 is an important start, but Saudi leaders and officers recognize that more must be done. At the operational level, they recognize that there is a need for joint commands that include all of the regular military services, the National Guard, and the key elements of the security services under the MOI. There is also a need for a joint approach to creating a national command; control, communications, computer, and intelligence system (C^4I); and joint battle management capabilities. Plans to begin this process by creating a suitable joint command and control system may help create such capabilities.

At the planning level, there is a need for a coordination planning, programming, and budgeting level. The need to put major new resources into internal security is having an impact on procurement and modernization in the military services, and the Kingdom has long needed a longer-term and more integrated approach to shaping and funding its force development. Similar "jointness" is needed in intelligence, in acquiring suitable military and information technology, and in creating a national intelligence system. Preventing and responding to terrorist attacks makes the "fusion" of various intelligence efforts even more time sensitive.

Consultation at the top also is not a substitute for systematic coordination throughout the security apparatus, and the coordination between planning, policy, and budget decisions for the regular armed forces, national guard, internal security services, and intelligence branches is inadequate and sometimes tenuous. The Kingdom has talked about creating a national security council for decades and even once built a building for such a body, but it does not have either a staff that integrates all of its security efforts or even something approaching an adequate interagency process.

The remaining problems in interagency cooperation have also been compounded by other aspects of the terrorist threat. Coordination must now be far more effective at levels that go beyond the MODA, SANG, and MOI. Other princes act as governors and play a major role in shaping internal security at the regional level. Equally important, dealing with Islamic extremism involves a wide range of other ministries and religious leaders and requires a coordinated approach to issues like education and countering the attacks extremists like Osama bin Laden make on Islam.

The Command Structure and Leadership of Saudi Military Forces

The Saudi military command structure has improved over the years. As has been noted earlier, three highly competent junior princes have taken on much of the command, management, planning, and budgeting effort in the MODA, MOI, and National Guard. Many senior Saudi officers have trained in U.S. and other Western staff and war colleges. While Saudi Arabia does not have a formal war college, it does have a modern Armed Forces Command and Staff College that combines all four services and teaches joint operations in a combined course with advanced instruction in each of the four services. This staff college also has students from the National Guard, the GCC states, and other Arab countries. The King Abdul Aziz Military College provides college-level training for officer candidates.

The Saudi forces are adopting more management, planning, and operational methods, but they still lack some of the elements necessary for a modern command structure. Leadership is an issue. Many outside observers have felt that the military chain of command has tended to be cautious, overcompartmented, and too reliant on decisions from the top. For cultural and other reasons, command relationships are highly personal and informal relationships often define real authority and promotion. The senior princes and commanders of their respective services maintain tight control over operations, deployments, procurement, and all other aspects of Saudi military spending, and this sometimes discourages initiative at lower levels, although the MODA has developed an annual overall review of the funding and modernization needs of all of the four regular services.

In the past, the Saudi high command rewarded longevity, conservatism, and personal loyalty rather than performance. Saudi Arabia was slow to develop systems of rotation that retire senior officers and systems that modernize the higher levels of command. There were many good high-ranking officers, but there are also many mediocre and overcautious loyalists. Senior officers often served too long and blocked the promotion of younger and more capable officers below them. Some treated their positions as sinecures or as positions they could exploit for profit.

These problems led Prince Khalid bin Sultan to shake up the higher levels of command within each regular military service after he came back to the MODA as the assistant minister of defense for military affairs in 2001. He brought in younger and more aggressive officers to many of the top command slots as well as to the area command.

The military forces are also less political. Many senior commanders come from families with long ties to the Saudi royal family, and many mid-level officers come from families and tribes that are traditionally loyal to the Al-Saud family. These officers must now meet the full training and education qualifications suitable for their ranks, however, and the base for promotion must be steadily expanded. There are royal family members in a number of senior command positions, but many officers outside the royal family do hold command slots, and this includes the vast majority of senior generals.

At the same time, a "generational" improvement has long been taking place within the officer corps and other ranks. The overall level of education and experience of Saudi officers has improved strikingly since the mid-1950s— when most officers had a traditional background. The majority of mid-level and senior officers do have the proper level of advanced training. Younger Saudi officers may still have a largely traditional cultural background, but they are increasingly well educated, and many have considerable technical proficiency. The Saudi military services have also developed impressive ultramodern headquarters training facilities and management systems and have had the support of Western advisers and technicians, training overseas, and exercises with other countries. As a result, there is a steadily growing degree of military proficiency as younger level officers have risen to higher ranks.

Another positive aspect of recent development in Saudi military leadership is particularly important in dealing with counterterrorism. There have been few overt signs of political activism in the Saudi military in recent years, although there have been extensive reviews of the political loyalty of both regular and National Guard personnel since a series of terrorist attacks in Riyadh in May 2003. These reviews found only a few officers with ties to Islamist ideologies and very small groups that had been nonviolent sympathizers. There were few arrests and no purges, and only a handful of the terrorists that have been detected, captured, or killed have any background in the military or National Guard. Bin Laden, al Qaeda, and other Islamist extremists have not attracted any significant support whatsoever in the armed forces—which shows few signs of the broader level of politicization that was a problem at the time of Nasser.

The Problem of Creating Synergy between the Regular Services and National Guard

In the past, the fact that Saudi Arabia has both a Regular Army and National Guard has created somewhat duplicative forces without defining roles and missions and creating the level of specialization necessary to meet the Kingdom's needs. This does not necessarily mean that the Army and National Guard should be integrated—any more than the U.S. Army and Marine Corps should be integrated. The regular forces and National Guard cooperated comparatively well in the first Gulf War, although after a somewhat slow start. However, this experience was not followed by continued cooperation in peacetime, and problems remained that needed to be solved by better defining the roles and missions of each of the Saudi forces and by rationalizing the roles of the Army and National Guard.

The recent shifts in both forces to meet the new mission of counterterrorism have led to further steps in this area. However, the two sets of forces remain somewhat isolated from each other, and it's not apparent that there is a coherent longer-term plan to produce full synergy and interoperability.

There have also been past differences in the emphasis that the regular services and the SANG put on readiness. In the past, the Saudi National Guard has had a better reputation than the regular services within the Kingdom, and among its foreign advisers, for promoting on the basis of merit, for setting training standards and insisting that they be met, for budgeting and financial controls, and for avoiding corruption. The MODA has improved its efforts in recent years, however, and has always faced a far more challenging set of tasks. The National Guard does not have to make the use the advanced weapons and technology that complicate the training and readiness problems of the regular armed services.

THE SEARCH FOR "JOINTNESS"

Saudi Arabia has become steadily more aggressive in its efforts to create true jointness in the operations of all four of its regular military services. It found during the preparation and execution of its operations in the first Gulf War that its Army, Navy, Air Force, and Air Defense Force had little joint training and doctrine and that many of their command and information systems could not properly communicate. The Saudi Air Force was also not properly prepared to support the Army with close air support (CAS), airlift, reconnaissance, and information transfer.

Accordingly, Saudi Arabia established a National Defense Operations Center to coordinate command activity, intelligence, and information. It began joint training at its airbase at Khamis Mushayt in the south, where it brought together army and air force instructors. Forward Air Controllers (FACs) trained with the army. Mid-level commanders were given training in joint operations, a continuous course program was set up, and suitable training programs and equipment began to be put in place.

Slow Improvement in Jointness in the Regular Services

This, however, was only a start, and it was clear at higher levels at the MODA that more had to be done. At the same time, it was apparent that Saudi Arabia could not simply adopt a U.S. doctrine and concept of operations that emphasize global power projection and preparation for all kinds of warfare.

As a result, Saudi Arabia surveyed the doctrine of other countries, including France, Egypt, and Israel. It also began to develop a set of joint doctrine plans and documents based largely on a defensive approach to operations. Saudi Arabia established a formal joint doctrine in 2001, and is steadily reevaluating its doctrine and ways to improve joint operations. It has begun to exercise joint operations in exercises like the Peace Sword series and to use such exercises to test and review what needs to be done. It conducted exercises of this kind with outside observers in 2004.

The Saudi forces have taken other tangible steps, like providing FACs to all brigades, more air-land training, and more training between the Air Force and the Navy. They have improved the "connectivity" and data transfer between the Air Force's E-3A AWACS airborne warning and control systems and the land forces and Navy. The Navy now takes much more advantage of the maritime surveillance capabilities of the E-3A, and both the Navy and Army can fully communicate with the Saudi E-3A. During the first Gulf War, technical interface problems meant that the Saudi ground and air forces often found it easier to communicate through the USAF E-3As. The Saudi Army has established an educational institute to examine ways to improve joint and combined warfare activity and is seeking to create a fully computerized joint training center established with many of the features of the U.S. Army center at Fort Irwin.

Saudi officers recognize, however, that progress has been slow, that the scale of joint exercise training remains far too small, and that the Saudi forces must scale up its exercises, training, and doctrine to the brigade and major air formation level to be effective. Jointness must be adapted to both the defensive character of Saudi planning and the need to be able to deal with different mission needs in different areas. Saudi Arabia has found that a joint interservice presence at command centers is the key to effective "jointness" in actual operations and is establishing joint command links between the regular forces and National Guard. It plans to create a new C⁴I/battle management system and architecture to fully implement such capabilities in the future.

In addition to adapting to the counterterrorism missions discussed shortly, jointness must develop air-land battle concepts that call for rapid redeployment of airpower from bases in forward areas throughout the Kingdom to support air-land operations on any given border and make up for the inability to rapidly redeploy land forces from the "corners" of a country the size of the United States east of the Mississippi.

Air-navy operations must adjust to the different conditions in the Gulf and Red Sea. The Gulf is a dense, congested area, with many countries operating near Saudi Arabia and with critical flows of commerce and oil. The Red Sea is a large area, where Saudi Arabia has a very long coast, there is far less traffic, and maritime surveillance presents different problems from the Gulf. It also presents different coastal security problems because of the influx of illegal immigrants from Eritrea and Ethiopia seeking jobs in the Kingdom. Air-land-sea operations must also be capable of counterinfiltration and smuggling activity in any region, particularly the Iraqi and Yemeni borders and Gulf and Red Sea coasts.

All of these measures require a degree of integrated command and control capability that is still in development. This includes the ability to handle near-real-time operations far more efficiently and provide better integration of intelligence, targeting, battle damage, and "joint situational" awareness data. In many of these areas, Saudi Arabia must still transform concepts into operational capabilities. Like most countries other than the United States, Saudi Arabia must also find solutions to the problem of "netcentric" warfare that are affordable, easy to maintain and operate, and place as much emphasis on the skill of "humancentric" operators as complex IT systems.

Much also depends on Saudi capability to work with U.S., British, and outside reinforcements in an emergency and to be capable of joint interoperability on an international level. They face the problem that while Saudi Arabia provided the United States with significant support in the attack on Saddam Hussein, coordination with the United States has suffered badly since 9/11.

Establishing Broader Jointness for Counterterrorism

As has been mentioned earlier, the Saudi forces, National Guard, and Ministry of Interior security and police forces have also begun to be much more effective in working together in counterterrorism operations. Saudi Arabia had sought to establish an integrated approach to civil defense during the first Gulf War, but Iraq never provided any meaningful test of the system, and its few Scud strikes were little more than an irritant. The scattered acts of terrorism between 1995 and 2001 did little to test the coordination between the Saudi regular forces, National Guard, and Ministry of Interior security and police forces.

Serious problems also existed in the training, readiness, coordination, interoperability, and jointness of the various forces in the Ministry of Interior. The police forces had little preparation, training, and equipment for counterterrorism. The security forces had never had to deal with a serious threat, intelligence was compartmented, and the Border Guard and Coast Guard forces were not really trained and equipped for such missions and operated virtually independently of each other, the security services, and regular forces. These problems were compounded by the fact the National Guard was trained largely as a light mechanized force to deal with foreign threats, rather than force area defense, counterterrorism, and to supplement the various security forces protecting critical facilities.

As a result, Saudi counterterrorism efforts exhibited serious coordination problems from the first major attacks in May 2003 through the attack on the Oasis Compound in May 2004. Saudi forces did not coordinate in dealing with a hostage situation, and untrained forces had elementary problems in exiting from helicopters.

It was this experience that led to the creation of a Joint Counterterrorism Center in the Ministry of Interior. A separate Counterterrorism Operations Center was also created in MODA to strengthen, better train, and equip the different services of the armed forces involved in the ongoing war against terrorism such as the Defense Facilities Protection Forces. Furthermore, a National Joint Counterterrorism Command (NJCC) was also established to enhance the cooperation and Command and Control capabilities between MODA, SANG and MOI. The NJCC is headed by the assistant minister of interior for security affairs, Prince Muhammed bin Nayef.

The regular services, National Guard, and Ministry of Interior have redefined their internal security missions to allow more cooperation without having overlapping responsibility or dual command. Each element has been given a clearly defined new set of responsibilities, with the Ministry of Interior retaining primary responsibility for security in all populated areas, and the regular services and National Guard taking on well-defined responsibilities for area defense and to back up the protection of critical infrastructure facilities and energy facilities.

The regular services now have well-defined roles in supporting the Ministry of Interior security forces and clear guidance on key missions like providing helicopter support. The Special Security Forces and the Special Emergency Forces have also been retrained to deploy more rapidly and with more flexibility, operate better with other force elements like the Border Guard and the General Security Service in counterterrorism operations, and be better prepared for independent counterterrorism missions. The end result was much better performance during the attacks on the U.S. consulate in Jeddah in December 2004.

Saudi officers fully acknowledge, however, that much still needs to be done. As was the case in the United States after 9/11, creating fully effective coordination and jointness among so many force elements in three major different ministerial equivalents, as well as other civil ministries with critical facilities to protect, will take years. Just as creating a fully effective Homeland Defense function in the United States will take a minimum of half a decade, Saudi officers and officials fully understand that Saudi Arabia still has a long way to go before it can develop an optimal level of efficiency and coordination.

MANAGEMENT, BUDGETING, LEADERSHIP, AND CIVILIAN CONTROL AND MANAGEMENT OF THE REGULAR ARMED SERVICES

In the past, the Ministry of Defense and Aviation often seemed to find it easier to talk about grand strategy and to make dramatic new arms purchases than take the kind of hard, consistent, and systematic decisions necessary to translate strategic ideas into operational and mission-oriented war-fighting capability. The end result is that Saudi arms purchases—which have totaled some $85 billion since the Gulf War in 1991—have sometimes created turbulence in the Saudi military, and conversion problems.[4]

The Need for Fiscal Restraint

Through the late 1990s, the ministry seemed unready to recognize the manpower and financial constraints on the expansion of Saudi military forces, although it has made progress in recent years. Saudi Arabia experienced major cash flow problems in its oil revenues in the mid-1990s. Nevertheless, Prince Sultan gave a speech in 1996, stating that, "We have great plans to modernize the armed forces during the next five-year plan. The broad headlines have been made starting with the training of the individual to securing modern equipment. The sixth plan for our armed forces, which may begin next year, will be, God willing, a plan of expansion not only in purchases but in men and attracting Saudi school and university graduates."[5]

In practice, the financial constraints imposed by low oil revenues did curb Saudi force expansion and modernization plans after the mid-1990s. The Kingdom established tighter overall financial controls and policies and kept them in place even when it experienced a massive surge in oil revenues after 1999. For example, it paid off much of the debt for its massive Al Yamamah arms deals rather than buy new arms.

The Need to Create Truly Effective Planning, Programming, and Budgeting Systems

Nevertheless, the Kingdom has been slow to create fully realistic annual budgets and five-year plans that stress investment in balanced war-fighting capabilities rather than emphasizing procurement. Key military activities like manpower quality, training and exercises, sustainment, and maintenance have been underfunded. At least some outside observers feel this helps explain problems like a high rate of accidents in the Air Force, and in expanding the levels of exercise training in the Army.

In the past, Saudi Arabia tended to allow each service to develop different levels of capability by branch. Only limited effort was made to develop cohesive plans to ensure suitable progress in interservice cooperation or jointness, in combined arms, and in balancing the development of combat arms with suitable sustainment and support capabilities. Cost savings in many areas critical to military capability were used to fund equipment orders that should have been downsized and renegotiated. When years of high oil revenues did occur, the ministry sometimes sharply overspent its budget by making new arms purchases.

The individual services did have a planning, programming, and budgeting system (PPBS), and a future-year defense plan (FYDP). They had to present annual justifications of their force requirements, and more recently have had to prepare a review of joint requirements as well. However, the ministry still needed to develop fully effective planning, programming, and budgeting systems that were effective enough to ensure that there were effective fiscal controls over procurement, manpower, and operating and maintenance systems. The lack of them made it difficult to plan and control cash flow for major arms buys. It also encouraged "stovepiped" funding of different elements of the military forces and makes it harder to control waste and corruption.

Senior officials like Prince Khalid bin Sultan—assistant minister for military affairs—have recognized that the Ministry of Defense and Aviation needs to shift from a focus on force buildup to a focus on force effectiveness and to introduce tight top-down budget and program management. The Ministry of Defense and Aviation has also taught its officers and planners to pay much more attention to resource limits in recent years, and the Saudi Ministry of Finance has begun to set tighter limits on Saudi spending on conventional forces. The MODA has improved the ways in which it exerts central management over the services to ensure that they maintained readiness and convert to new equipment since 2001, but further improvement is clearly still necessary.

Creating Balanced Forces

At a broader level, there is a need for more coherent and stable force modernization and force expansion goals or efforts to shape and fund balanced warfighting capabilities. There seems to be no centralized system to assess the warfighting capability and readiness of Saudi forces and to monitor measures of effectiveness. There also is no public transparency of the kind that ensures funds are spent effectively or that allows Saudis inside and outside the Ministry of Defense and Aviation to assess what the five-year plan is, how the budget is allocated, or how money is actually spent.

In fairness, such problems affect every military force in the Middle East. It is also clear from discussions with senior Saudi officers that there is a new spirit of realism in the way they think about resource constraints and far more consideration of the need to think in terms of the overall and joint needs of all services. There are a number of high-level officers, including some junior members of the royal family, who hope that future new equipment buys will be carefully managed in order to concentrate on military effectiveness and fund a proper level of readiness and sustainment for the Army, Air Force, Air Defense Force, and Navy.

Saudi forces also face problems that make their task exceptionally difficult. They have a mix of weapons and technology that is more advanced than that in most Middle Eastern or developing countries. Saudi Arabia has one of the most complex force postures of any developing nation and operates some of the most advanced military technology in the world. In several cases, Saudi military technology is as—or more—advanced than that in many developed NATO countries. Furthermore, Saudi Arabia has just completed the final stages of massive infrastructure programs that have created some of the world's most modern facilities out of empty desert. It is beginning to produce its second generation of ranks with modern military training. Only a little more than a generation ago most of its troops were traditional villagers with only limited education and technical background.

The people who criticize the Saudi military often ignore both the challenges the military has faced and how much it has already accomplished. Saudi Arabia's military planning and management is clearly imperfect, but so is that of every other country that has tried to cope with the ongoing revolution in military affairs. Saudi Arabia has already overcome massive challenges in terms of manpower, infrastructure, and technology transfer. It has a solid mix of infrastructure and existing equipment holdings to build on and a relatively high level of overall tactical proficiency for a major developing nation.

Saudi Arabia has also recently been fortunate in its potential enemies. As has been discussed in Chapter 1, Iran has never fully rebuilt its conventional forces since it experienced massive losses at the end of the Iran-Iraq War. Iraq suffered a devastating defeat in the Gulf War, and its military forces and weapons of mass destruction were eliminated in the Iraq War of 2003. Yemen's forces have been weakened by civil war, and the government's lack of funds has prevented major arms imports since the end of the cold war. Saudi Arabia may have its military problems, but its most serious potential threats have had military disasters.

Saudi Arabia faces difficult challenges in determining and providing the proper levels of military spending, in effectively managing its funds and in deciding on the proper level of arms imports. Uncertain oil revenues and steadily expanding civil demands for entitlements, and civil investment, have greatly reduced the ease with which the Kingdom can sustain high levels of defense expenditures.

This leads some Saudi officers to speculate that Saudi Arabia could save money by focusing on lighter forces and by modernizing the best of Saudi Arabia's existing platforms with new battle management and information technology (IT) systems, and for advanced precision guided weapons, rather than the big arms packages and buys of new tanks, aircraft, and ships of the past.

The future is always uncertain, however, and the Kingdom must deal with potential new challenges. For example, the United States announced it is lifting the 14-year-old ban on military equipment sales to Yemen.[6] The United States believes that Yemen has been a reasonable partner in the fight against al Qaeda, and this move is Yemen's reward. More seriously, U.S. lawmakers have shown a new willingness to limit military exports to Saudi Arabia through legislation such as the Saudi Accountability Act of 2003. Finally, Iran has played a constant cat and mouse game with the International Atomic Energy Agency (IAEA), and most observers believe that its nuclear weapons program is becoming steadily more advanced. In addition, its deployment of Shahab-3 missiles could threaten most Saudi cities.

Saudi Military Expenditures

Figures 4.1 to 4.3 provide a broad comparison of Saudi and other Gulf state military expenditures. There are a number of different estimates of Saudi expenditures, and of the burden they impose on the Saudi economy, but most agree to the extent they report extremely high levels of spending. U.S. Department of Defense estimates show that Saudi spending peaked during the Gulf War, then dropped in the mid-to-late 1990s as Saudi Arabia came under increasing financial pressure because of comparatively low oil revenues and increased civil spending burdens caused by major population increases. In fact, 1995 was a year of Saudi fiscal crisis and led to cuts that reduced Saudi spending by 33 percent between 1990 and 2000. Other Department of Defense sources indicate, however, that Saudi expenditures leaped back up in 2001 as a result of a sudden "boom" in oil expenditures.

Reporting by the U.S. State Department indicates that Saudi Arabia spent $8.3 billion on defense during January 1 to December 31, 1999.[7] It notes, however, that the Saudi government data it drew upon did not provide separate

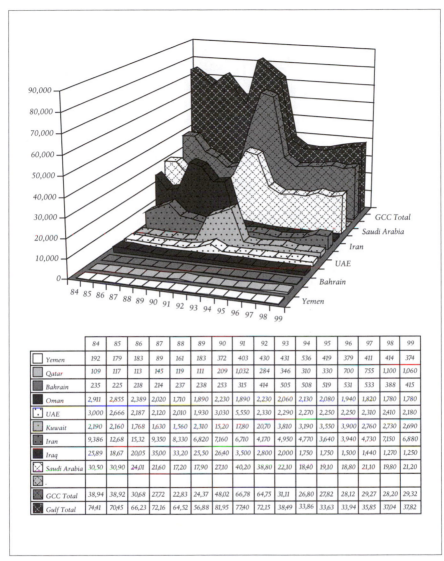

	84	85	86	87	88	89	90	91	92	93	94	95	96	97	98	99
☐ Yemen	192	179	183	89	161	183	372	403	430	431	536	419	379	411	414	374
▢ Qatar	109	117	113	145	119	111	209	1,032	284	346	310	330	700	755	1,100	1,060
▨ Bahrain	235	225	218	214	237	238	253	315	414	505	508	519	531	533	388	415
■ Oman	2,911	2,855	2,389	2,020	1,710	1,890	2,230	1,890	2,230	2,060	2,130	2,080	1,940	1,820	1,780	1,780
⬚ UAE	3,000	2,666	2,187	2,120	2,010	1,930	3,030	5,550	2,330	2,290	2,270	2,250	2,250	2,310	2,410	2,180
Kuwait	2,190	2,160	1,768	1,630	1,560	2,310	15,20	17,80	20,70	3,810	3,190	3,550	3,900	2,760	2,730	2,690
Iran	9,386	12,68	15,32	9,350	8,330	6,820	7,160	6,710	4,170	4,950	4,770	3,640	3,940	4,730	7,150	6,880
Iraq	25,89	18,67	20,05	35,00	33,20	25,50	26,40	3,500	2,800	2,000	1,750	1,750	1,500	1,440	1,270	1,250
⊠ Saudi Arabia	30,50	30,90	24,01	21,60	17,20	17,90	27,10	40,20	38,80	22,10	18,40	19,10	18,80	21,10	19,80	21,20
▧																
▩ GCC Total	38,94	38,92	30,68	27,72	22,83	24,37	48,02	66,78	64,75	31,11	26,80	27,82	28,12	29,27	28,20	29,32
▨ Gulf Total	74,41	70,45	66,23	72,16	64,52	56,88	81,95	77,40	72,15	38,49	33,86	33,63	33,94	35,85	37,04	37,82

Figure 4.1: Comparative Military Expenditures of the Gulf Powers: 1984–1999 (in constant $US 1999 Millions)

Source: Adapted by Anthony H. Cordesman from ACDA, *World Military Expenditures and Arms Transfers, 1995*, (Washington, DC: ACDA/GPO), 1996, and U.S. State Department, *World Military Expenditures and Arms Transfers, 1999–2000* (Washington, DC: U.S. State Department Bureau of Arms Control, 2001).

* GCC: Bahrain, Kuwait, Oman, Qatar, Saudi Arabia, and the VAE.

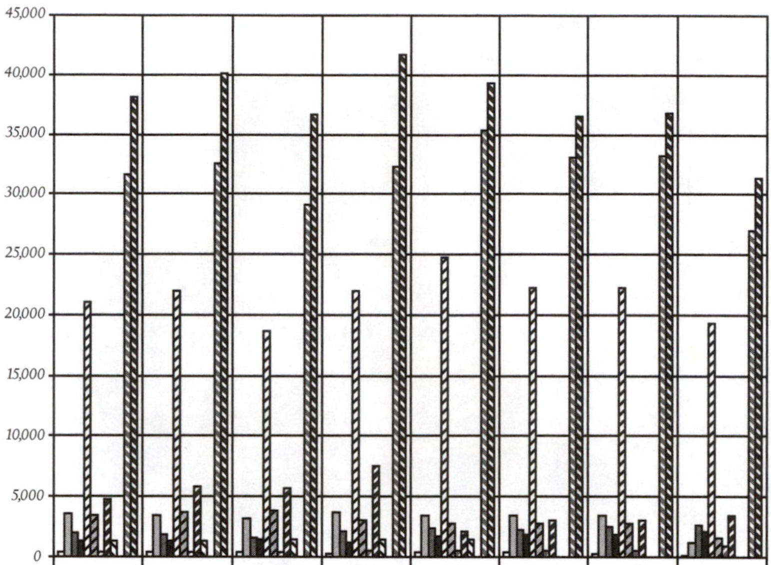

	1997	1998	1999	2000	2001	2002	2003	2004*
Bahrain	364	402	444	322	334	331	329	180
Kuwait	3,600	3,400	3,200	3,700	3,400	3,500	3,500	1,200
Oman	2,000	1,800	1,600	2,100	2,400	2,300	2,500	2,600
Qatar	1,300	1,300	1,400	1,200	1,700	1,900	1,900	2,100
Saudi Arabia	21,000	22,000	18,700	22,000	24,700	22,200	22,200	19,300
UAE	3,400	3,700	3,800	3,000	2,800	2,800	2,800	1,600
Yemen	411	396	429	498	536	515	561	885
Iran	4,700	5,800	5,700	7,500	2,100	3,000	3,000	3,500
Iraq	1,300	1,300	1,400	1,400	1,400	?	?	?
.								
GCC Total	31,664	32,602	29,144	32,322	35,334	33,031	33,229	26,980
Gulf Total	38,075	40,098	36,673	41,720	39,370	36,546	36,790	31,365

Figure 4.2: *Southern Gulf Military Expenditures by Country: 1997–2004*
         (in $US current millions)

Source: International Institute of Strategic Studies, Military Balance, various editions.

* The IISS did not report military expenditures for 2004. The number for 2004 represents the military budget, which does not include procurement costs.
* GCC: Bahrain, Kuwait, Oman, Qatar, Saudi Arabia, and the VAE.

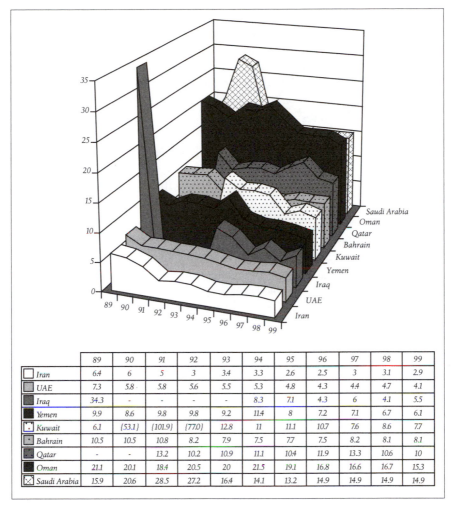

	89	90	91	92	93	94	95	96	97	98	99
☐ Iran	6.4	6	5	3	3.4	3.3	2.6	2.5	3	3.1	2.9
▨ UAE	7.3	5.8	5.8	5.6	5.5	5.3	4.8	4.3	4.4	4.7	4.1
▨ Iraq	34.3	-	-	-	-	8.3	7.1	4.3	6	4.1	5.5
■ Yemen	9.9	8.6	9.8	9.8	9.2	11.4	8	7.2	7.1	6.7	6.1
⊡ Kuwait	6.1	(53.1)	(101.9)	(77.0)	12.8	11	11.1	10.7	7.6	8.6	7.7
▨ Bahrain	10.5	10.5	10.8	8.2	7.9	7.5	7.7	7.5	8.2	8.1	8.1
▨ Qatar	-	-	13.2	10.2	10.9	11.1	10.4	11.9	13.3	10.6	10
■ Oman	21.1	20.1	18.4	20.5	20	21.5	19.1	16.8	16.6	16.7	15.3
⊠ Saudi Arabia	15.9	20.6	28.5	27.2	16.4	14.1	13.2	14.9	14.9	14.9	14.9

*Figure 4.3:   Comparative Military Expenditures of the Gulf Powers as a Percentage of
GNP: 1989–1999*

Source: Adapted by Anthony H. Cordesman from ACDA, *World Military Expenditures and Arms
Transfers, 1995* (Washington DC: ACDA/GPO, 1996) and U.S. State Department, *World Military
Expenditures and Arms Transfers, 1999–2000* (Washington, DC: Bureau of Arms Control, 2001).

line-item budgets for defense and national security. As a result, such estimates
of defense spending include Ministry of Interior expenditures and are therefore
somewhat misleading. According to this estimate, Saudi Arabia spent 13
percent of its GDP and 41.65 percent of its national budget on military forces
during this period.[8]

The International Institute of Strategic Studies (IISS) uses Saudi budget data to calculate the total Saudi security budget, including internal security, using data provided by the Saudi Arabian Monetary Agency (SAMA). According to the IISS, this spending totaled $18.4 billion in 1999 (69 billion riyals), $20 billion (74.9 billion riyals) in 2000, $24.7 billion (92.7 billion riyals) in 2001, and $22.2 billion (83.2 billion riyals) in 2002. The Saudi budget generally fell well below the level of actual spending. According to the IISS, the budget called for spending levels of $21.1 billion (78.9 billion riyals) in 2001, $18.5 billion (69.4 billion riyals) in 2002, $18.4 billion (68.9 billion riyals) in 2003, and $19.3 billion (72.3 billion riyals) in 2004.[9]

These figures indicate that Saudi Arabia spent 40 percent of its total budget on national security in 2000, 37 percent in 2001, 34 percent in 2002, 33 percent in 2003, and approximately 36 percent in 2004. A detailed examination of the Saudi budget data indicates that national security spending is kept relatively high even in low budget years, but that Saudi Arabia is slowly increasing the percentage of its budget going to the civil sector.

It is impossible to assess how Saudi military and security expenditures are spent in any detail by using unclassified reports. The Saudi budget provides only an undefined "top line" total. Furthermore, it does not include all purchases of military equipment, construction, and services. Saudi Arabia does not report all of the relevant costs in its budget documents—particularly costs of defense relating to the purchase of foreign defense goods and services. Saudi Arabia has often increased its defense expenditures after the budget was issued without reporting them, and has never publicly reported the actual cash flow it has spent on arms imports or on the value of the oil it has sometimes used in complex barter deals.

This lack of transparency in the Ministry of Defense and Aviation, National Guard, and other Saudi security-related budgets reflects broad problems in the management of Saudi defense resources. It makes it impossible for Saudis inside and outside military and security activities to provide intelligent criticism of the way the Kingdom spends its resources.

Perhaps more important, it is impossible to determine the extent that problems in creating an effective planning, programming, and budgeting system in the Ministry of Defense and Aviation (MODA) have or that still prevent matching plans to available resources. This same lack of transparency makes it difficult to determine the extent to which problems exist in exerting the proper fiscal controls in reviewing arms orders and procurement spending.

Finding the Proper Level of Expenditure

Some things are clear. The total cost of Saudi military efforts since the early 1970s has exceeded several hundred billion dollars, even if the cost of the Gulf War is excluded. The Kingdom spent from $14 to $24 billion a year on defense during the later 1970s and the 1980s and its full-time active military manpower increased from 79,000 in the 1970s to 199,500 in 2005.[10] Much of this expenditure—probably on the order of 60-65 percent—was spent on infrastructure, foreign services and maintenance, and basic manpower training. Saudi Arabia had to create entire military cities, new ports, and major road networks. It had to create modern military bases in the middle of its deserts and pay for far more extensive training than most of the military manpower in the Third World receives.

There were good reasons for many of these expenditures during the period Saudi Arabia had to create a modern military force. Saudi recruits, whether nomad or townie, had to be brought to the point where they could operate modern military equipment and buy a pool of equipment and munitions large and modern enough to give Saudi Arabia the ability to deter Iran and Iraq. Since the mid-1980s, Saudi Arabia has been able to shift from creating basic military capabilities and infrastructure to a slower and less-expensive buildup of combat capabilities.

The cost of the Gulf War placed a massive new burden on the Kingdom, however, and such expenses had to take place at the cost of "butter" and helped lead to chronic Saudi budget deficits.[11] In fact, the Gulf War pushed Saudi military and security expenditures to the crisis level. Saudi security expenditures rose from 36 percent of the total national budget in 1988, and 39 percent in 1989, to nearly 60 percent in 1990. Although any such estimates are highly dependent on exactly what aspects of the cost of Saudi support to allied military forces during the Gulf War should be included, the percentage rose to around 70 percent in 1991–92, including the cost of aid to allied governments during Desert Storm. It declined to around 30 percent after 1992 and has remained at the 30–40 percent level ever since.

What is not clear is why Saudi military expenditures remained so high for so long after the Gulf War. One explanation is the need to pay for the long pipeline of arms deliveries ordered in reaction to the war. However, the data available indicate that such costs should have tapered off more rapidly by the mid-1990s than the figures shown indicate and should have bought more major combat systems, readiness, and sustainability for the money. In fact, both the size of Saudi arms deliveries after 1995 and the ratio of deliveries to new agreements after 1995 are higher than can easily be explained by either the volume of actual deliveries of major weapons or Saudi needs.

Saudi military expenditures have also consumed a very high percentage of GDP and as a percentage of total government expenditures and have put serious strain on the Saudi budget and pressure on the Saudi economy. U.S. State Department estimates indicate that Saudi Arabia spent about 20 percent of its GDP on defense during 1983–86. They ranged from 16 percent to 23 percent of the GNP during the 1980s, peaked at 27–29 percent in 1990–92, and have since dropped to around 14 percent. The percentage was only about 8.5 percent in 1996, however, if GDP is measured in purchasing power parity.[12] The Department of Defense has somewhat different estimates. As a percentage of GDP, these reports estimate that Saudi defense spending was 25.9 percent in 1990, 13.5 percent in 1995, 13.9 percent in 1996, 11 percent in 1997, 14.3 percent in 1998, 13.4 percent in 1999, 11.7 percent in 2000, 13.3 percent in 2001, and 13.3 percent in 2002.[13]

Saudi military expenditures averaged around 40 percent of all central government expenditures (CGE) before the Gulf War and rose to a peak of 60–73 percent during the Gulf War. As the previous data have shown, they then dropped back to around 35–40 percent. U.S. officials estimate that Saudi expenditures accounted for approximately 35–40 percent of all Central Government Expenditures and 12.9 percent of the GNP in 2000.[14] Even so, this is still an exceptionally high percentage for a Saudi government that must fund so large a mix of welfare, entitlement, and civil investment expenditures.

There is no way to establish a "golden rule" as to what share Saudi military and security expenditures should consume of the GNP or total budget in the future. It is clear, however, that past levels of spending placed a strain on the Saudi budget and economy. At the same time, military spending is not easy to cut. The past history of Saudi spending indicates that Saudi Arabia must spend about $13 to $15 billion a year, in 2002 dollars, if it is to maintain its present forces and rate of modernization. It should be noted that the military is making an effort to save some money by taking such steps as increasing its repair capabilities, which would reduce the number of spares normally required to be stockpiled while systems are en route for overseas repair.[15]

Saudi Arms Imports

Figures 4.4 to 4.6 provide a broad comparison of Saudi and other Gulf state arms imports. Saudi Arabia has long been dependent on other nations for virtually all of its arms and military technology. Saudi Arabia is making some limited slow progress in developing an indigenous arms industry. Saudi Arabia has made progress in the support, supply, and operations and maintenance areas. It can produce some small arms, automatic weapons, and munitions, but much of the Saudi portion of the work consists of assembling imported parts rather than real manufactures.

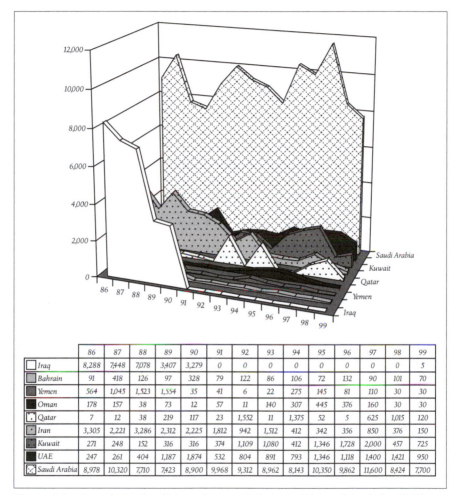

	86	87	88	89	90	91	92	93	94	95	96	97	98	99
Iraq	8,288	7,448	7,078	3,407	3,279	0	0	0	0	0	0	0	0	5
Bahrain	91	418	126	97	328	79	122	86	106	72	132	90	101	70
Yemen	564	1,045	1,523	1,554	35	41	6	22	275	145	81	110	30	30
Oman	178	157	38	73	12	57	11	140	307	445	376	160	30	30
Qatar	7	12	38	219	117	23	1,552	11	1,375	52	5	625	1,015	120
Iran	3,305	2,221	3,286	2,312	2,225	1,812	942	1,512	412	342	356	850	376	150
Kuwait	271	248	152	316	316	374	1,109	1,080	412	1,346	1,728	2,000	457	725
UAE	247	261	404	1,187	1,874	532	804	891	793	1,346	1,118	1,400	1,421	950
Saudi Arabia	8,978	10,320	7,710	7,423	8,900	9,968	9,312	8,962	8,143	10,350	9,862	11,600	8,424	7,700

Figure 4.4: Cumulative Saudi Arms Imports Relative to Those of the Other Gulf States: 1986–1999
(Value of Deliveries in Constant $US Millions)

Source: Adapted by Anthony H. Cordesman from State Department, *World Military Expenditures and Arms Transfers* (Washington, DC: GPO), various editions.

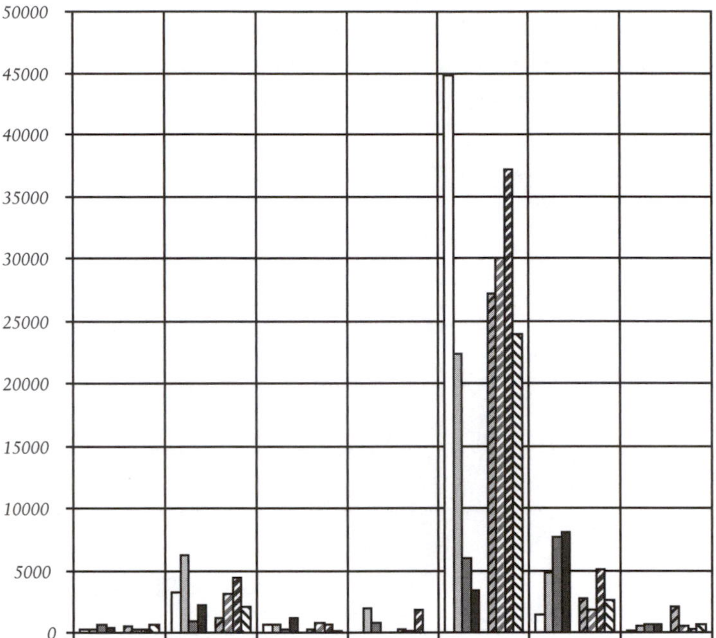

	Bahrain	Kuwait	Oman	Qatar	Saudi Arabia	UAE	Yemen
☐ Agreements: 88-91	300	3300	700	0	44800	1400	100
▨ Agreements: 92-95	200	6200	600	2000	22300	4800	500
▨ Agreements: 96-99	600	900	300	800	6,000	7,600	700
■ Agreements: 00-03	400	2,200	1,200	0	3,400	8,100	600
▨ .							
▨ Deliveries: 88-91	500	1,200	200	300	27,200	2,700	2,100
▨ Deliveries: 92-95	300	3,100	800	100	30,000	1,800	500
▨ Deliveries: 96-99	300	4,400	600	1,800	37,200	5,100	200
◩ Deliveries: 00-03	600	2,100	100	0	23,900	2,600	600

Figure 4.5: Southern Gulf Arms Agreements and Deliveries by Country: 1988–2003 (In $US Current Millions)

0 = less than $50 million or nil. All data rounded to the nearest $100 million.

Source: Richard F. Grimmett, *Conventional Arms Transfers to the Developing Nations* (Washington, DC: Congressional Research Service), various editions.

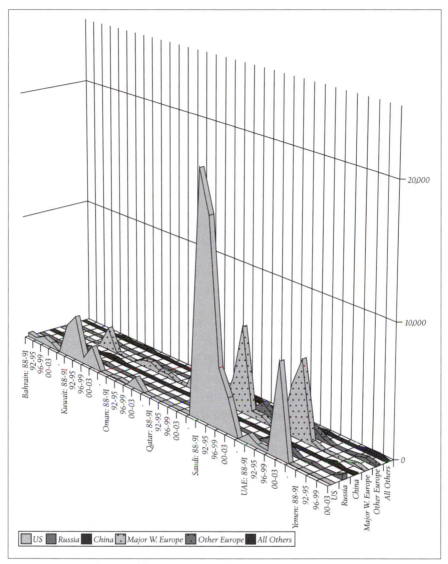

US   Russia   China   Major W. Europe   Other Europe   All Others

Figure 4.6:   *Southern Gulf New Arms Orders by Supplier Country: 1988–2003*
               (Arms Agreements in $US Current Millions)

0 = less than $50 million or nil. All data rounded to the nearest $100 million.

Source: Adapted by Anthony H. Cordesman, CSIS, from Richard F. Grimmett, *Conventional Arms Transfers to the Developing Nations* (Washington, DC: Congressional Research Service), various editions.

A number of other programs consist of efforts where a foreign arms supplier has agreed to set up defense-related industrial efforts in Saudi Arabia to "offset" Saudi spending on arms imports. Some of these "offset" efforts have been useful in reducing the need to import technology, services, and parts, but many others are more symbolic efforts to employ Saudis than substantive efforts to aid the Saudi military or industrial base. It is scarcely surprising, therefore, that Saudi Arabia's military buildup and modernization has led to massive expenditures on military imports.[16]

Saudi Arabia has no reason to try to build major weapons systems, particularly when it can now buy some of the most advanced military technology available from diverse suppliers in the United States, Europe, and Russia. Saudi Arabia's recent arms purchases reflect this fact. During 1996–2000, it placed new orders for $4.6 billion worth of U.S. arms, $500 million worth of arms from major European powers, and $900 million worth of arms from other European states.

During 2001–2003, it placed new orders for $2.7 billion worth of U.S. arms, $500 million worth of arms from major European powers, and $200 million worth of arms from other European states. During 1996-2000, it took delivery on $16.6 billion worth of U.S. arms, $17.6 billion worth of arms from major European powers, and $3 billion worth of arms from other European states. During 2001-2003, it took delivery on $6.3 billion worth of U.S. arms, $16.6 billion worth of arms from major European powers, and $1 billion worth of arms from other European states.[17]

Saudi Arabia does, however, have a great deal to gain from rationalizing its military industries and equipping them to produce more spares and handle major equipment upgrades and overhauls. This would reduce Saudi life cycle costs, help sustainability, and ensure that the Kingdom could afford major upgrades and extend the life cycle of its weapons. It is also clear that this is the best way to ensure Saudi Arabia's independence from any one supplier of key weapons. Simply diversifying the sources of weapons and technology to reduce dependence on any one country is expensive, reduces interoperability, raises training and readiness costs, and still leaves Saudi Arabia dependent on a given supplier for a critical part of its arsenal in any sustained or high-intensity conflict.

Saudi spending on arms imports also helps explain why Saudi Arabia ranked as one of the world's 10 largest military importers in every year for much of the last two decades. It ranked first in both new arms agreements and in actual arms deliveries during 1989–92, and 1993–96, and it ranked first in arms deliveries during 1996–99, although it ranked third in terms of new orders—behind the UAE and India and only marginally above Egypt.[18]

This situation has changed strikingly, however, since the mid-1990s. Saudi Arabia ranked seventh in terms of new agreements during 2000–2003, although it stayed first in arms deliveries during the same period, because deliveries lag years behind orders. Saudi new orders during 2000–2003 were half of what they were during 1996–99, and only 14 percent of what they were during 1991–94.[19] Saudi Arabia no longer is one of the top 10 arms importers.[20]

It is not easy to make an accurate analysis of Saudi arms buys. Saudi Arabia does not provide statistics on its military imports, and most outside estimates are of limited analytic reliability. Two useful sources of unclassified intelligence estimates are, however, available from the U.S. government: The Bureau of Arms Control in the State Department (formerly the Arms Control and Disarmament Agency [ACDA]), and the Congressional Research Service. These estimates are based on unclassified intelligence data that make a detailed effort to include all weapons and produce comparable estimates.

These sources provide a more reliable picture than academic and nongovernmental organization (NGO) estimates of arms sales. They are certainly accurate in reflecting the steady increase in Saudi arms imports that has taken place in reaction to the massive buildup of Iraqi and Iranian forces, the threats and uncertainties posed by the Iran-Iraq War, the cost of fighting the Gulf War, and other current threats.[21]

The Impact of the Gulf War

Saudi Arabia took delivery on $48.1 billion worth of arms during 1983–89 and purchased 14.1 percent of all Third World military import agreements during 1982–89.[22] The Gulf War did, however, lead Saudi Arabia to make major additional purchases of military imports. Saudi Arabia ordered $18.6 billion worth of military imports in 1990 and took delivery on $6.749 billion worth. Saudi Arabia cut its new orders to $7.8 billion in 1991, but deliveries rose to $7.1 billion as its backlog of increased orders began to raise deliveries. Both new orders and deliveries dropped to $4.5 billion in 1992. Saudi military imports then began to rise again because of the perceived threat from Iran and Iraq. Saudi Arabia ordered $9.6 billion worth of arms in 1993, and took delivery on $6.4 billion. In 1994 it ordered $9.5 billion worth of military imports and took delivery on $5.2 billion.

The end result of these orders was a bill that strained Saudi Arabia's financial capabilities at a time its oil revenues were declining and it was involved in a massive "pipeline" of ongoing arms deliveries that it could not effectively absorb. The Kingdom had problems with meeting its payment schedules for several ongoing arms deals. It had signed a multistage deal with Britain, called Al Yamamah, that costs the Kingdom up to three billion dollars per year, but that was not integrated into its normal budget process. A similar agreement for the upgrade of the Saudi Navy, Sawari, was penned with France. While the Kingdom could meet some of its obligation with oil, these deals still imposed a major financial burden. The United States had to be paid in cash, which imposed even more of a burden.

There were reasons to diversify the Kingdom's arms purchases. Saudi Arabia found it could not rely on the United States because of U.S. ties to Israel and internal political pressure from Israel's supporters. It made sense for the Kingdom not to become too dependent on one supplier. Second, major arms purchases were a diplomatic tool in ensuring support from supplier nations. Finally, arms imports were a way of "recycling" oil export revenues and preserving market share. However, the Kingdom failed to pay proper attention to interoperability and standardization. Like most Gulf countries, it often focused on buying the most effective or advanced system and paid little attention to the practical problems of integrating weapons from different suppliers into overall force structures that minimized the problems in operating systems designed by different countries, the maintenance problems involved, and the difficulties in supplying and sustaining systems with different maintenance and ammunition needs in combat.

Aside from the National Guard, Saudi Arabia paid too little attention to the training burden involved, problems in combined arms and joint operations, and difficulties in command and control. It also underestimated the inevitable rivalry between foreign military advisory teams and the natural competitive bias of foreign contract support teams toward favoring systems made by their companies or countries. Saudi Arabia also underestimated the tendency of supplier countries to focus on sales per se and ignore the Kingdom's strategic interests, even though most supplier countries were dependent on the security of Saudi oil exports.

Excessive arms spending also led to a budget crisis in the mid-1990s. The Kingdom's problems in paying for its existing arms orders in 1994 led it to make much more modest new purchases after this time. The Kingdom ordered $2.1 billion worth of arms in 1995 and took delivery on $2.1 billion in arms. New orders totaled $1.9 billion in 1996, and deliveries totaled $6.3 billion. Saudi Arabia placed $2.7 billion in new orders in 1997 and took $11.0 billion worth of deliveries.[23]

Arms Imports since the Late 1990s

The "oil crash" in late 1997 reinforced Saudi Arabia's need to limit its new arms imports. As a result, it placed $2.9 billion in new orders in 1998 and took $8.7 billion worth of deliveries, and placed $1.6 billion in new orders in 1999 and took $6.9 billion worth of deliveries.[24] The scale of the decline in new Saudi arms import agreements is indicated by the fact that new orders during 1991–94 were only about two-thirds of the total during 1987–90. Saudi new orders for the four-year period from 1994 to 1997 were substantially less than half the new orders Saudi Arabia placed during the four-year period before the Gulf War, even measured in current dollars.[25]

The Kingdom's new arms orders also suffered from planning management problems that reinforced the problems in Saudi military sustainment and modernization.

- First, the Kingdom focused on major new arms purchases during the period immediately after the Gulf War, rather than sustainment, and then did not shift its purchases to focus on sustainment when it had to make major cutbacks after the mid-1990s. As a result, Saudi Arabia was flooded with weapons but seriously underfunded in terms of the investment in maintenance and sustainment that was necessary to keep its existing weapons effective and properly absorb its new ones.

- Second, the flood of new deliveries during the 1990s added to the Kingdom's problems in effectively recapitalizing and maintaining its overall force posture. As a rough rule of thumb, every major weapons system costs at least as much in terms of the arms imports needed to maintain and upgrade it during its life cycle as it does to buy, and often twice as much. The Kingdom now faces a major future cost problem in making and in keeping its new weapons effective that will add to the problem of sustaining its existing weapons. While no precise figures are available, some U.S. advisers estimate that the Kingdom needed to restructure its arms import program to focus on sustainment half a decade ago and needs to spend three to four times more on support equipment, training systems, and so forth than it does today, even if this means major additional cuts in spending on new arms.

- Third, the Kingdom never really developed a clear strategy for both improving interoperability and setting affordable long-term force goals. It went from year to year solving its payments problems as they occurred. It did not develop effective future year plans, and the spending fixes it adopted for any one year tended to compound its overall problems in standardization and interoperability.

The patterns of Saudi arms imports since its funding crunch in the mid-1990s have been different. Saudi Arabia imported $37.2 billion worth of arms during 1996–99, and $23.9 billion during 2000–2003. In contrast, it signed only $6.0 billion worth of new arms agreements during 1996–99, and only $3.4 billion in new arms agreements per year during 2000–2003.[26] New orders were less than one-sixth of deliveries during 1996–99 and roughly one-seventh during 2000–2003.[27]

Table 4.1:   Southern Gulf New Arms Orders by Supplier Country: 1988–2003
(Arms Agreements in $US Current Millions)

Country	Date	United States	Russia	China	Major W. Europe	Other Europe
Yemen	00–03	0	400	100	0	100
	96–99	0	0	0	200	300
	92–95	0	0	200	0	100
	88–91	0	100	0	0	0
UAE	00–03	7,100	400	0	300	300
	96–99	200	400	0	6,100	800
	92–95	300	500	0	3,900	100
	88–91	700	0	0	200	0
Saudi Arabia	00–03	2,700	0	0	500	200
	96–99	4,600	0	0	500	900
	92–95	15,600	0	0	6,600	100
	88–91	18,800	200	300	2,300	2,300
Qatar	00–03	0	0	0	0	0
	96–99	0	0	0	800	0
	92–95	0	0	0	2,000	0
	88–91	0	0	0	0	0
Oman	00–03	900	0	0	300	0
	96–99	0	0	0	300	0
	92–95	100	0	0	600	0
	88–91	0	0	0	500	0
Kuwait	00–03	1,700	100	200	0	0
	96–99	500	0	200	100	0
	92–95	3,500	800	0	1,800	0
	88–91	2,500	200	0	200	200

Table 4.1: *Southern Gulf New Arms Orders by Supplier Country: 1988–2003*
(Arms Agreements in $US Current Millions)

Country	Date	United States	Russia	China	Major W. Europe	Other Europe
Bahrain	00–03	400	0	0	0	0
	96–99	600	0	0	0	0
	92–95	200	0	0	0	0
	88–91	300	0	0	0	0

0 = less than $50 million or nil, and all data rounded to the nearest $100 million.
Source: Adapted by Anthony H. Cordesman, CSIS, from Richard F. Grimmett, *Conventional Arms Transfers to the Developing Nations* (Washington, DC: Congressional Research Service), various editions.

Chapter 5

Saudi Military Forces

T he quantitative trends in Gulf military forces are summarized in Table 5.1 and Figures 5.1 through 5.4. These figures show that Saudi armed forces dominate the strength of Southern Gulf and Gulf Cooperation Council (GCC) forces. This makes Saudi military capabilities critical to the security of some 60 percent of the world's oil reserves and over 35 percent of its gas. It also makes the balance of power in the Gulf at large a balance of the forces that Saudi Arabia and the GCC states can deploy, the force of Iran, and the power projection forces available from the United States and Britain.

Saudi military forces are modern, high-technology forces by regional standards, but manpower is a problem. Saudi military manpower is compared to that of other Gulf states in Figures 5.2 through 5.4. Saudi regular forces now total some 124,500 men, plus some 95,000–100,000 actives in the National Guard and another estimated 130,000 men in the various paramilitary forces (excluding the different police forces), some 30,000 in the Border Guard, 20,000 in the Drug Enforcement Agency, 25,000 in the Civil Defense Administration, 30,000 in the Special Emergency Forces, 5,000 in the Mujahideen, 10,000 in the Petroleum Installation Security Force, and some 10,000 in the Special Security Forces. These totals do not include the internal intelligence service, the General Security Service, and the different police forces in the Ministry of Interior. Moreover, the Royal Guard and the General Intelligence Presidency are also not included in the above tally.

As has been discussed in Chapter 1, Saudi forces must deal with two significant potential threats: Iran and Yemen, and Iran is acquiring long-range missiles and may become a nuclear power. Saudi Arabia must also deploy forces to cover its borders with Iraq, Jordan, and Syria and to defend both its Gulf and Red Sea Coasts. This means Saudi Arabia's regular military services must defend a territory roughly the size of the United States east of the Mississippi. The mix of potential threats Saudi Arabia faces also means that Saudi Arabia cannot concentrate its forces to meet a single threat and must normally disperse its forces over much of the Kingdom.

At the same time, Chapter 2 has shown that Saudi Arabia's regular military forces must also make major changes in their mission. The Kingdom's primary active threat comes from internal and external Islamic extremists and not from the regular armies, navies, and air forces the Saudi Arabia organized to fight in the past. This means a shift is needed to a support role to the Ministry of Interior in fighting the threat of al Qaeda and independent extremist groups, developing new counterterrorism capabilities, and preparing for the threat of low-level counterinsurgency warfare.

The Saudi Army

The Saudi Army has about 75,000–100,000 actives, an inventory of some 1,055 medium tanks, plus over 3,000 other armored vehicles, and 500 major artillery weapons. It is headquartered in Riyadh and has five staff branches: G1 Personnel, G2 Intelligence and Security, G3 Operations and Training, G4 Logistics, and G5 Civil and Military Affairs. It also has field commands organized into six area commands under military zone commanders, which are located at Riyadh, King Khalid Military City, Tabuk, Khamis Mushayt, Dhahran, and Jeddah.

Since the Gulf War, the Saudi Army has developed, modernized, and increased in size. It has nearly doubled its manpower, battle tanks, APCs, transport helicopters, and SAM launchers. Table 5.2 provides the details of the development of the force structure in the Saudi Army since the end of the Gulf War in 1991, levels of manpower, and numbers and types of major weapons.

It is clear from Table 5.2 that the Saudi Army has expanded significantly in manpower. It is also clear that it has increased its combat unit strength and has modernized many categories of key weapons. At the same time, the number of different equipment types compounds its interoperability problems, and the Army retains significant numbers of older or obsolescent systems. Army readiness and maintenance have improved since the late 1990s, but the Saudi Army's diversity of weapons also contributes to the fact it has serious maintenance and sustainability problems if its forces have to operate away from the their main bases or military cities.

Much of the Saudi Army is now deployed in military cities at least 500 miles from the Kingdom's main oil facilities in the Eastern Province, although a brigade is stationed in the new King Fahd military city in the Eastern Province, and combat elements of another brigade were deployed to the new Saudi Army base at King Khalid Military City, near Hafr Al Baten, in 1984. For the foreseeable future, the Saudi Army will be dispersed so that much of its strength will

Table 5.1: *Gulf Military Forces in 2005*

	Iran	Iraq[a]	Bahrain	Kuwait	Oman	Qatar	Saudi Arabia[b]	UAE	Yemen
Manpower									
Total active	540,000	424,000	11,200	15,500	41,700	12,400	219,500	50,500	66,700
Regular	350,000	375,000	11,200	15,500	25,000	12,400	124,500	50,000	66,700
National Guard & other	120,000	0	0	0	6,400	0	95,000	0	0
Reserve	350,000	650,000	0	23,700	0	0	20,000	0	40,000
Paramilitary	40,000	42,000+	10,160	6,600	4,400	0	15,500+	1,100	70,000
Army and Guard manpower	540,000[a]	375,000	8,500	11,000	31,400	8,500	170,000	50,500	60,000
Regular Army manpower	350,000	375,000	8,500	11,000	25,000	8,500	75,000	50,500	60,000
Reserve	350,000	650,000	0	0	0	0	20,000	0	40,000
Total main battle tanks[c]	1,613	2,200	180	385	117	30	1,055	461	790
Active main battle tanks	1,300	1,900	120	293	100	25	710	330	650
Active AIFV/recce, lt. tanks	724	1,300	71	355	167	80	1,270+	780(40)	330
Total APCs	640	2,400	235	321	204	190	3,190	730	710
Active APCs	540	1,800	205	281	185	162	2,630	570	240
ATGM launchers	75	100+	15	118	48	148	2000+	305	71
Self-propelled artillery	310	150	13	68(18)	24	28	170	181	25
Towed artillery	2,010	1,900	26	0	108	12	238(58)	93	310
MRLs	876+	200	9	27	?	4	60	72(48)	164
Mortars	5,000	2,000+	21	78	101	45	400	155	502
SSM launchers	51	56	0	0	0	0	10	6	28
Light SAM launchers	?	1,100	78	0	78	0	1,000+	100	800
AA guns	1,700	6,000	27	1	26	0	0	62	530
Air Force manpower	52,000	20,000	1,500	2,500	4,100	2,100	18,000	4,000	5,000
Air Defense manpower	15,000	17,000	0	0	0	0	16,000	0	2,000
Total combat aircraft	306	316	33	80	40	18	291	106	72(40)
Bombers	0	6	0	0	0	0	0	0	0

(continued)

Table 5.1: *Gulf Military Forces in 2005 (continued)*

	Iran	Iraq[a]	Bahrain	Kuwait	Oman	Qatar	Saudi Arabia[b]	UAE	Yemen
Fighter/attack	163+	130	12	39	12	18	171	48	40
Fighter/interceptor	74+	180	22	14	0	0	106	22	26
Recce/FGA recce	6	5	0	0	12	0	10	8	0
AEW C⁴I/BM	1	0	0	0	0	0	5	0	
MR/MPA[b]	5	0	0	0	0	0	0	0	0
OCU/COIN/CCT	0	0	0	28	16	0	14	28	0
Other combat trainers	35	157	0	0	0	0	50	0	6
Transport aircraft[d]	68	12	4	4	16	6	45	22	18
Tanker aircraft	4	2	0	0	0	0	15	0	0
Total helicopters	628	375	47	28	30	23	178	115	25
Armed helicopters[e]	104	100	40	20	0	19	22	59	8
Other helicopters[d]	524	275	7	8	30	4	156	56	17
Major SAM launchers	250+	400	15	84	40	9	106	39	57
Light SAM launchers	95	1,100	-	60	28	90	1,709	134	120
AA Guns	2	6,000	-	60	-	-	340	-	-
Total Navy manpower	38,000[a]	2,000	1,200	2,000	4,200	1,800	15,500	2,500	1,700
Regular Navy	15,400	2,000	1,200	2,000	4,200	1,800	12,500	2,500	1,700
Naval Guards	20,000	0	0	0	0	0	0	0	0
Marines	2,600	-	-	-	-	-	3,000	-	-
Major surface combatants									
Missile	3	0	3	0	0	0	8	4	0
Other	0	0	0	0	0	0	0	0	0
Patrol craft									
Missile	10	1	6	10	6	7	9	8	6
(Revolutionary Guards)	10	-	-	-	-	-	-	-	-
Other	42	5	4	0	7	-	17	8	5
Rev. Guards (boats)	40	-	-	-	-	-	-	-	-

Table 5.1: *Gulf Military Forces in 2005 (continued)*

	Iran	Iraq[a]	Bahrain	Kuwait	Oman	Qatar	Saudi Arabia[b]	UAE	Yemen
Submarines	3	0	0	0	0	0	0	0	0
Mine vessels	7	3	0	0	0	0	7	0	6
Amphibious ships	10	0	0	0	1	0	0	0	1
Landing craft	9	-	4	2	4	0	8	5	5
Support ships	25	2	5	4	4	-	7	2	2
Naval air	2,000	-	-	-	-	-	-	-	-
Naval aircraft									
Fixed-wing combat	5	0	0	0	0	0	0	0	0
MR/MPA	10	0	0	0	(7)	0	0	0	0
Armed helicopters	19	0	0	0	0	0	21	7	0
SAR helicopters	-	0	0	0	0	0	4	4	0
Mine warfare helicopters	3	0	0	0	0	0	0	0	0
Other helicopters	19	-	2	-	-	-	19	-	-

Note: Equipment in storage shown in the higher figure in parenthesis or in range. Air Force totals include all helicopters, including Army-operated weapons and all heavy surface-to-air missile launchers.

Source: Adapted by Anthony H. Cordesman from interviews, International Institute for Strategic Studies, *Military Balance* (London: IISS); *Jane's Sentinel*; *Periscope*; and Jaffee Center for Strategic Studies, *The Military Balance in the Middle East* (Tel Aviv: JCSS).

a. Iranian total includes roughly 100,000 Revolutionary Guard actives in land forces and 20,000 in naval forces. Iraqi totals are preconflict counts.

b. The source for the Saudi National Guard and paramilitary manpower numbers are from the Saudi National Security Project. The IISS numbers for SANG = 75,000 and for paramilitary = 15,000+. Saudi totals for reserve include National Guard Tribal Levies. The total for land forces includes active National Guard equipment. These additions total 450 AIFVs, 730(1,540) APCs, and 70 towed artillery weapons.

c. Total tanks include tanks in storage or conversion.

d. Includes Navy, Army, National Guard, and royal flights, but not paramilitary.

e. Includes in Air Defense Command.

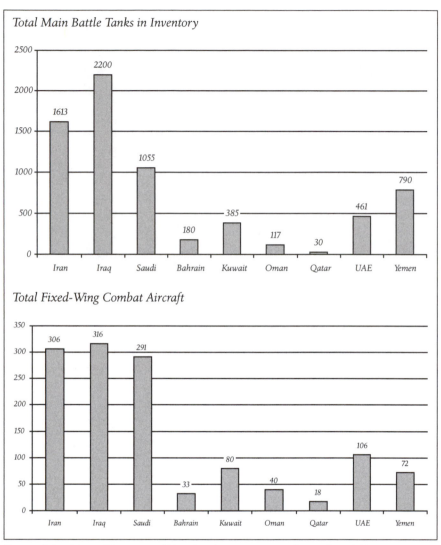

Figure 5.1: Major Measures of Key Combat Equipment Strength in 2005

Source: Adapted by Anthony H. Cordesman from various sources and IISS, The Military Balance, 2004–2005 (London: IISS).

be deployed near Saudi Arabia's borders with the angles located at Tabuk, Hafr Al Baten, and Sharurah-Khamis Mushayt.

Force Strength and Structure

The combat strength of the Saudi Army consists of four armored brigades, five mechanized infantry brigades, three light motorized rifle brigades, and one

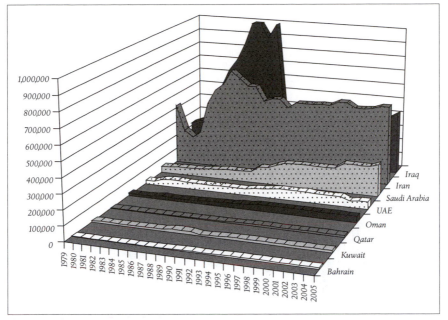

Figure 5.2: Comparative Trends in Gulf Total Active Military Manpower: 1979–2005

Note: Saudi totals include full-time active National Guard, Omani totals include Royal Guard, Iranian totals include Revolutionary Guards, and Iraqi totals include Republican Guards and Special Republican Guards as of March 2003.

Source: Estimated by Anthony H. Cordesman using data from various editions of the IISS *Military Balance* (London: IISS); *Jane's Sentinel* and *Military Technology*; and the Saudi National Security Project.

airborne brigade. It also has five independent artillery brigades and an aviation command. The Saudi Army deployed the 12th Armored Brigade and 6th Mechanized Brigade at King Faisal Military City in the Tabuk area. It deployed the 4th Armored Brigade, and 11th Mechanized Brigade at King Abdul Aziz Military City in the Khamis Mushayt area. It deployed the 20th Mechanized Brigade and 8th Mechanized Brigade at King Khalid Military City near Hafr Al Baten. The 10th Mechanized Brigade is deployed at Sharawrah, which is near the border with Yemen and about 150 kilometers from Zamak.

A typical Saudi armored brigade has an armored reconnaissance company; three tank battalions, with 42 tanks each; two tank companies, with a total of 30 tanks; three tank troops, with a total of 12 tanks; a mechanized infantry battalion, with 54 AIFVs/ APCs; and an artillery battalion, with 18 self-propelled guns. It also has an army aviation company, an engineer company, a logistic battalion, a field workshop, and a medical company.

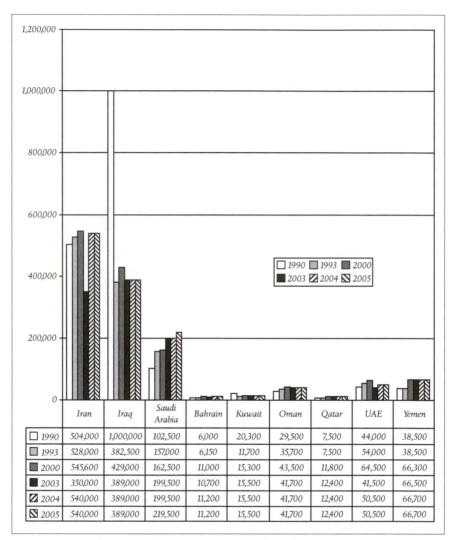

		Iran	Iraq	Saudi Arabia	Bahrain	Kuwait	Oman	Qatar	UAE	Yemen
☐	1990	504,000	1,000,000	102,500	6,000	20,300	29,500	7,500	44,000	38,500
▨	1993	528,000	382,500	157,000	6,150	11,700	35,700	7,500	54,000	38,500
▦	2000	545,600	429,000	162,500	11,000	15,300	43,500	11,800	64,500	66,300
■	2003	350,000	389,000	199,500	10,700	15,500	41,700	12,400	41,500	66,500
▨	2004	540,000	389,000	199,500	11,200	15,500	41,700	12,400	50,500	66,700
◨	2005	540,000	389,000	219,500	11,200	15,500	41,700	12,400	50,500	66,700

Figure 5.3: Total Active Military Manpower in All Gulf Forces: 1990–2005

Note: Saudi totals include full-time active National Guard, Omani totals include Royal Guard, Iranian totals include Revolutionary Guards, and Iraqi totals include Republican Guards and Special Republican Guards.

Note: the IISS number for the SANG is 75,000, while Saudi officials say that the SANG manpower is 95,000–100,000.

Source: Estimated by Anthony H. Cordesman, using data from various editions of the IISS *Military Balance, Jane's Sentinel,* and *Military Technology.*

A typical Saudi mechanized brigade has an armored reconnaissance company; one tank battalion, with 37–42 tanks; three mechanized infantry bat-

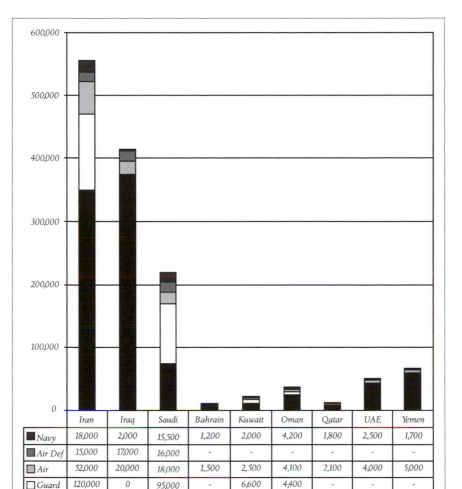

	Iran	Iraq	Saudi	Bahrain	Kuwait	Oman	Qatar	UAE	Yemen
■ Navy	18,000	2,000	15,500	1,200	2,000	4,200	1,800	2,500	1,700
■ Air Def	15,000	17,000	16,000	-	-	-	-	-	-
□ Air	52,000	20,000	18,000	1,500	2,500	4,100	2,100	4,000	5,000
□ Guard	120,000	0	95,000	-	6,600	4,400	-	-	-
■ Army	350,000	375,000	75,000	8,500	11,000	25,000	8,500	44,000	60,000

Figure 5.4: Total Gulf Military Manpower By Service in 2005

Note: the IISS number for the SANG is 75,000, while Saudi officials say that the SANG manpower is 95,000–100,000.

Source: Estimated by Anthony H. Cordesman, using data from the IISS, *Military Balance,* various editions.

talion, with 54 AIFVs/APCs each; two infantry companies, with a total of 33 APCs; three infantry platoons, with a total of 12 APCs; and an artillery battalion, with 18 self-propelled guns. It also has an army aviation company, an engineer company, a logistic battalion, a field workshop, and a medical company. It has 24 antitank guided weapons launchers and four mortar sections, with a total of eight 81 mm mortars.

Table 5.2: Saudi Royal Army: Force Structure

	1991	2000	2005
Manpower	40,000	75,000	75,000
Active	40,000	75,000	75,000
Reserves	0	0	0
Combat units			
Armored brigade	2	3	3
Mechanized brigade	4	5	5
Airborne brigade	1	1	1
Royal Guard brigade	1	1	1
Artillery battalion	5	8	8
Army Aviation command	0	1	1
Infantry brigade	1	0	0
MBT	550	1,055	1,055
M-1A2 Abrams	0	315(200)	315(200)
AMX-30	300	290(145)	290(145)
M-60A3	200	450	450
M-60A1	50	0	0
AIFV/recce, lt. tanks	740	1,270+	1,270+
AML-60\-90	240	300	300
AMX-10P	500+	570+	570+
M-2 Bradley	0	400	400
APC	1,280	1,900	3,190
M-133	1,100	1,750	3,000
Panhard M-3	150	150	150
EE-11 Urutu	30	0	0
Al-Fahad	0	0	40
Towed artillery	134(110)+	248(58)+	238(148)
105 mm: Model 56	24+	0	0
105 mm: M-101/-120	40(40)	100	100(100)
155 mm: FH-70	70(70)	50(50)	40(40)
155 mm:M-198	66	90	40
155 mm:M-114	0	?	50
203 mm: M-115	0	8(8)	8(8)
SP artillery	275	200	170
155 mm: M-109A1B/A2	224	110	110
155 mm:GCT	51	90	60
MRL	14	60	60
ASTROS II	14	60	60
MOR	330	400	400
81 mm: ?	0	?	70+
107 mm: 4.2in M30	330	?	150+
120 mm: Brandt	0	110	110
SSM launchers	30	10	10
CSS-2	30	10	10

Table 5.2: Saudi Royal Army: Force Structure (continued)

	1991	2000	2005
ATGW	290+	1,300+	2,000+
BGM-71A TOW	200+	0	0
TOW/-2A	0	200+	900
M-47 Dragon	?	1,000	1,000
HOT	90+	100+	100+
RL & RCL	450+	1550	1550
75 mm: M-20	?	0	0
84 mm: Carl Gustav	450	300	300
90 mm: M-67	?	100	100
106 mm: M-40A1	?	50	50
112 mm: APILAS	0	0	200
Attack helicopter	0	12	12
AH-64	0	12	12
Transport helicopter	34	55	52
S-70A-1	0	12	12
UH-60A	12	22	22
SA365N	22	6	6
Bell 406CS	0	15	12
SAM launchers	500+	500+	1,000+
Stinger	?	?	500
Redeye	500	500	500
Crotale	?	?	?
SURV	0	?	?
AD guns	15+	0	0
40 mm: M-42 SP	?	0	0
90 mm: 15 M-117	15	0	0

Source: Adapted by Anthony H. Cordesman from various sources and IISS, Military Balance, various editions.

The Airborne Brigade is normally deployed near Tabuk. The Airborne Brigade has two parachute battalions and three Special Forces companies. The three light motorized brigades include the 17th, 18th, and 19th. Saudi Arabia is expanding its special forces and improving their equipment and training to help deal with the threat of terrorism. The Special Forces have been turned into independent fighting units to help deal with terrorists. They report directly to Prince Sultan.

The Army also has an Army Aviation Command, which was formed in 1986 and operates Saudi Arabia's Bell 406 armed helicopters and AH-64s. There are also security garrisons at most major Saudi cities, including Dhahran, Jeddah, and Riyadh.

There also are the Royal Guards unit, which is an independent force located near Riyadh. The Royal Guard Brigade has three battalions and is equipped with light-armored vehicles. It reports directly to the king and is recruited from loyal tribes in the Najd.

This is an impressive land force order of battle for a country the size of Saudi Arabia, but the Saudi Army only has around 75,000–100,000 full time actives for a force structure and equipment holdings that require up to at least twice as many men. As Figure 5.5 shows, its manpower is also much smaller than that of Iran. The current level of Saudi active Army manpower is adequate to man about two to three U.S. division "slices," with minimal manning for combat, combat support, and service support units. In the U.S. Army, it could support a total force with a maximum of around 600 tanks and 1,000 other armored vehicles. In practice, however, the Saudi Army's manpower must be divided into a force structure that has an order of battle equivalent to around three heavy divisions, and with an equipment pool at least that size. This requires more manpower than Saudi Arabia has available.

The Saudi Army's problems in expansion, planning, manpower, organization, and deployment have been compounded by the need to absorb the massive equipment buildup that took place before and after the Gulf War. As has been noted earlier, the Army faces the need to operate a complex mix of equipment supplied by many nations and then be able to operate effectively with the equipment mixes in the forces of regional allies, the United States, and Britain. The diversification of the Saudi Army's sources of army equipment has reduced its dependence on the United States, but it has also increased its training and support burden and has raised its operations and maintenance costs.

Saudi Armored Forces

Saudi armored strength is compared to that of other Gulf armies in Figures 5.6 through 5.12. Saudi Army weapons and equipment numbers are more than adequate now that Iraq has ceased to be a threat. Saudi Arabia has an inventory of 1,055 main battle tanks and more than 300 tank transporters. Its tanks included 315 M-1A2s, 450 M-60A3s, and 290 French-made AMX-30s. The Saudi Army now concentrates on maintaining, training, and operating its M-60s and M-1A2s, and it regularly upgrades them as the U.S. Army develops modifications and improvements. It has shifted its lightly armored and aging AMX-30s to its light brigades.

Some experts feel that half of its AMX-30s are in storage, however, and only about 700–765 of Saudi Arabia's main battle tanks are fully operational. Saudi Arabia was also experiencing major problems in converting to the M-1A1 tanks, leaves it with a reliable core strength of around 380 well-manned M-60A3s, about 200–275 M-1A2s that were combat ready with good crew proficiency, and a residual force of around 160–170 AMX-30s.

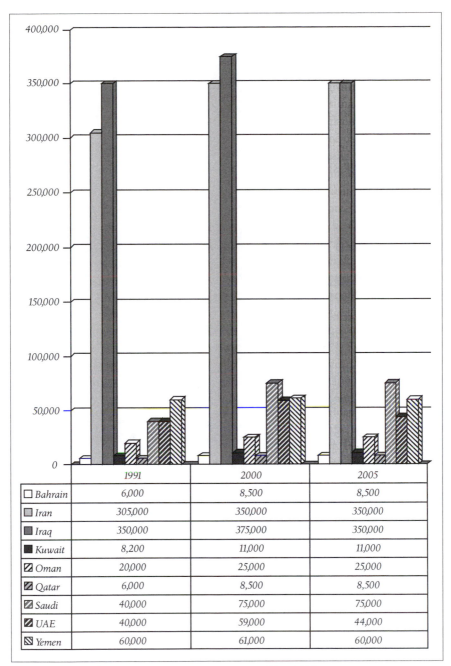

	1991	2000	2005
☐ Bahrain	6,000	8,500	8,500
▨ Iran	305,000	350,000	350,000
▨ Iraq	350,000	375,000	350,000
■ Kuwait	8,200	11,000	11,000
▨ Oman	20,000	25,000	25,000
▨ Qatar	6,000	8,500	8,500
▨ Saudi	40,000	75,000	75,000
▨ UAE	40,000	59,000	44,000
▧ Yemen	60,000	61,000	60,000

Figure 5.5: Gulf States Active Army Manpower: 1991–2005

Note: The Iraq numbers are those before March 2003.

Source: Adapted by Anthony H. Cordesman from various sources and IISS, *Military Balance*, various editions.

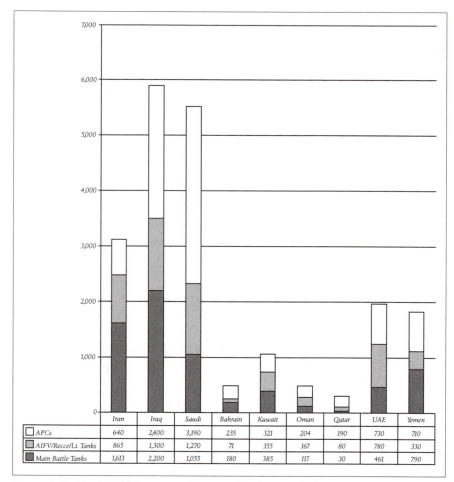

	Iran	Iraq	Saudi	Bahrain	Kuwait	Oman	Qatar	UAE	Yemen
☐ APCs	640	2,400	3,190	235	321	204	190	730	710
▨ AIFV/Recce/Lt. Tanks	865	1,300	1,270	71	355	167	80	780	330
■ Main Battle Tanks	1,613	2,200	1,055	180	385	117	30	461	790

Figure 5.6: Total Gulf Operational Armored Fighting Vehicles in 2005

Note: Iraq totals are for March 2003, before the Iraq War.

Source: Estimated by Anthony H. Cordesman, using data from various editions of the IISS *Military Balance* and *Jane's Sentinel*.

Saudi Arabia has a large inventory of other mechanized armored equipment. It has roughly 2,600 armored vehicles in addition to its tanks (300 reconnaissance, 970 armored infantry fighting vehicles, and 1,900 armored personnel carriers), and it has a ratio of about 27 actives per other armored vehicle. In contrast, Iran has 1,455 other armored vehicles for 325,000 actives (450,000, if the Revolutionary Guards are included), and Iraq has about 2,700 for 375,000 men.[1] These comparisons are shown in more detail in Figure 5.6. The Saudi Army also has large numbers of French and U.S.-made armored recovery vehicles, armored bridging units, and large numbers of special purpose armored vehicles.

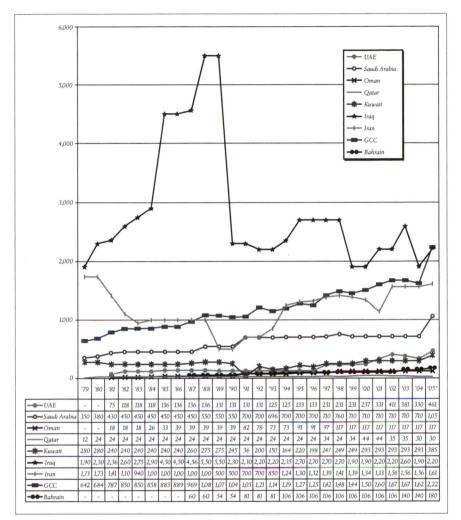

Figure 5.7: Total Operational Main Battle Tanks in All Gulf Forces: 1979–2005

	'79	'80	'81	'82	'83	'84	'85	'86	'87	'88	'89	'90	'91	'92	'93	'94	'95	'96	'97	'98	'99	'00	'01	'02	'03	'04	'05*
UAE	-	-	75	118	118	118	136	136	136	136	131	131	131	131	125	125	133	133	231	231	231	237	331	411	381	330	461
Saudi Arabia	350	380	430	450	450	450	450	450	450	550	550	550	700	700	696	700	700	700	710	760	710	710	710	710	710	710	1,05
Oman	-	-	18	18	18	26	33	39	39	39	39	39	82	78	73	91	91	97	117	117	117	117	117	117	117	117	117
Qatar	12	24	24	24	24	24	24	24	24	24	24	24	24	24	24	24	24	24	34	24	34	44	44	35	35	30	30
Kuwait	280	280	240	240	240	240	240	240	260	275	275	245	36	200	150	164	220	198	247	249	249	293	293	293	293	293	385
Iraq	1,90	2,30	2,36	2,60	2,75	2,90	4,50	4,50	4,56	5,50	5,50	2,30	2,30	2,20	2,20	2,35	2,70	2,70	2,70	2,70	1,90	1,90	2,20	2,20	2,60	1,90	2,20
Iran	1,73	1,73	1,41	1,10	940	1,00	1,00	1,00	1,00	1,00	500	500	700	700	850	1,24	1,30	1,32	1,39	1,41	1,39	1,34	1,13	1,56	1,56	1,61	
GCC	642	684	787	850	850	858	883	889	969	1,08	1,07	1,04	1,05	1,21	1,14	1,19	1,27	1,25	1,42	1,48	1,44	1,50	1,60	1,67	1,67	1,62	2,22
Bahrain	-	-	-	-	-	-	-	-	60	60	54	54	81	81	81	106	106	106	106	106	106	106	106	106	140	140	180

* The data for 2005 represent the total number of MBTs

Note: Iranian totals include Revolutionary Guards, and Iraqi totals include Republican Guards and Special Republican Guards. Iraq totals are for March 2003, before the Iraq War.

Source: Estimated by Anthony H. Cordesman, using data from the IISS, *Military Balance,* various editions.

It is not possible to separate all of the Saudi Army's holdings of other armored vehicles (OAFVs) from those of the National Guard, Border Guard, and other paramilitary forces. According to the IISS *Military Balance,* the Saudi Army's holdings of armored infantry fighting and command vehicles seem to

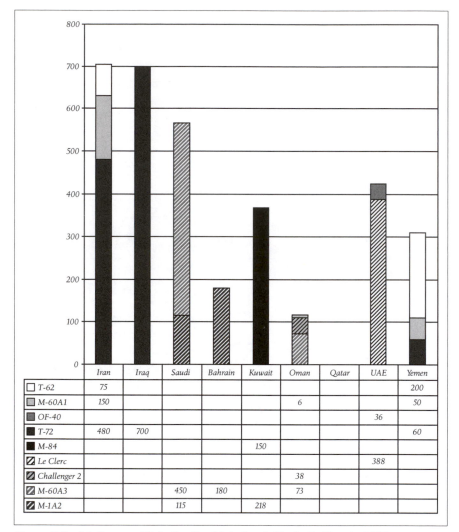

	Iran	Iraq	Saudi	Bahrain	Kuwait	Oman	Qatar	UAE	Yemen
□ T-62	75								200
▦ M-60A1	150					6			50
■ OF-40								36	
■ T-72	480	700							60
■ M-84					150				
▨ Le Clerc								388	
▨ Challenger 2						38			
▨ M-60A3			450	180		73			
▨ M-1A2			115		218				

Figure 5.8: Medium- to High-Quality Main Battle Tanks By Type in 2005

Note: Iraq totals are for March 2003, before the Iraq War

Source: Estimated by Anthony H. Cordesman, using data from the IISS, *Military Balance,* various editions.

have included 400 M-2A2 Bradleys, 150 M-577A1s, and 570+ AMX-10Ps as of late 2004.[2] According to *Jane's Sentinel Security Assessment—The Gulf States,* Saudi Arabia had 300AML-60, AML-90, and AML-245 reconnaissance vehicles, of which roughly 280 remained in active service.[3]

In terms of armored personnel carriers, various sources indicate that the Saudi Army had up to 3,000 M-113s in various configurations (the operational

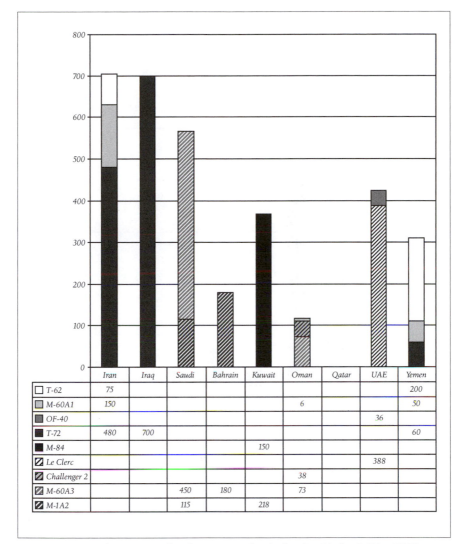

	Iran	Iraq	Saudi	Bahrain	Kuwait	Oman	Qatar	UAE	Yemen
☐ T-62	75								200
▨ M-60A1	150					6			50
▩ OF-40								36	
■ T-72	480	700							60
■ M-84					150				
▨ Le Clerc								388	
▨ Challenger 2						38			
▨ M-60A3			450	180		73			
▨ M-1A2			115		218				

Figure 5.9: Total Operational Other Armored Vehicles (Lt. Tanks, LAVs, AIFVs, APCs, Recce) in Gulf Forces: 1990–2005

Note: Iranian totals include active forces in the Revolutionary Guards. Saudi totals include active National Guard. Omani totals include Royal Household Guard. Iraq totals are for March 2003, before the Iraq War.

Source: Adapted by Anthony H. Cordesman from various sources and IISS, *Military Balance,* various editions.

inventory may be closer to 1,750–2000). Saudi Arabia is experimenting with upgrading its M-113s and is studying the upgrades developed by the Turkish Army. It also had 150 Panhard M-3s, 40 Al-Fahads, 440 Piranhas, and 290

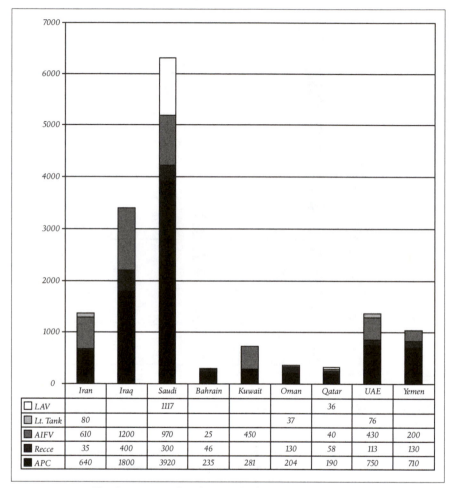

Figure 5.10: Gulf Other Armored Fighting Vehicles (OAFVs) by Category in 2005

Note: Iranian totals include active forces in the Revolutionary Guards. Saudi totals include active National Guard. Omani totals include Royal Household Guard. Iraq totals are for March 2003, before the Iraq War.

Source: Adapted by Anthony H. Cordesman from various sources and IISS, *Military Balance*, various editions.

V150s (810 more in store) in early 2005. It is obvious from these totals that the Saudi Army's holdings of OAFVs include enough U.S.-supplied equipment to provide reasonable levels of standardization for all of the Saudi Army's full-time active manpower, as well as a high degree of interoperability with U.S. forces. The Piranha has also proved to be effective in Saudi exercises and trials.

At the same time, the Saudi Army's total inventory of armored weapons not only presents problems in interoperability, standardization, and moderniza-

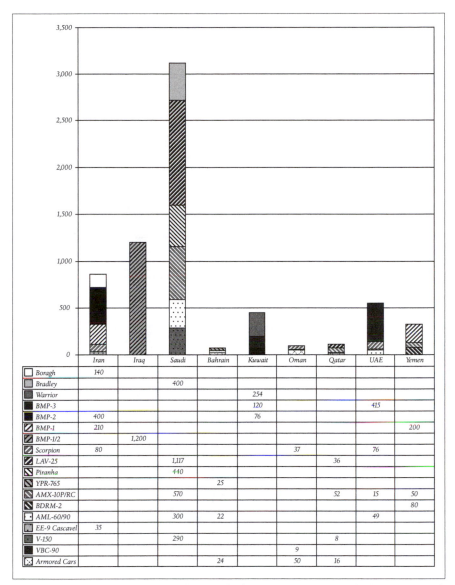

	Iran	Iraq	Saudi	Bahrain	Kuwait	Oman	Qatar	UAE	Yemen
Boragh	140								
Bradley			400						
Warrior					254				
BMP-3					120			415	
BMP-2	400				76				
BMP-1	210								200
BMP-1/2		1,200							
Scorpion	80					37		76	
LAV-25			1,117				36		
Piranha			440						
YPR-765				25					
AMX-10P/RC			570			52		15	50
BDRM-2									80
AML-60/90			300	22				49	
EE-9 Cascavel	35								
V-150			290				8		
VBC-90						9			
Armored Cars				24		50	16		

Figure 5.11: Armored Infantry Fighting Vehicles, Reconnaissance Vehicles, LAVs, and Light Tanks by Type in 2005

Note: Iranian totals include active forces in the Revolutionary Guards. Saudi totals include active National Guard. Omani totals include Royal Household Guard. Iraq totals are for March 2003, before the Iraq War.

Source: Adapted by Anthony H. Cordesman from various sources and IISS, *Military Balance,* various editions.

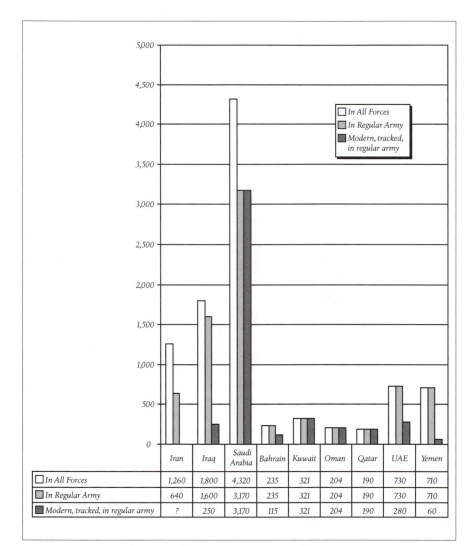

Figure 5.12: Armored Personnel Carriers (APCs) in Gulf Armies in 2005

Note: Iranian totals include active forces in the Revolutionary Guards. Saudi totals include active National Guard. Omani totals include Royal Household Guard. Iraq totals are for March 2003, before the Iraq War.

Source: Adapted by Anthony H. Cordesman from various sources and IISS, *Military Balance*, various editions.

tion, but there also are many variants with the various types of armor listed above that are highly specialized and difficult to properly integrate into Saudi forces in small numbers. Some purchases are also the result of past political efforts to give foreign suppliers a share of the Saudi market, regardless of military needs.

The end result also further complicates the problems the Army would have in moving forces from their widely dispersed peacetime locations in military cities near the Kingdom's different borders to concentrate them to defend against a given enemy. Saudi Arabia still exercises almost exclusively at the battalion level and does not conduct long-distance brigade-sized exercises. Its armored training is largely firing range and daytime training, and not maneuver and night warfare training. The Saudi Army did learn during the Gulf War that it can draw on its civilian fleet of transporter to move tanks and on trucks for logistic supply, but it has little meaningful practice in such operations and does not seem to have detailed contingency plans for such operations.

Saudi officers note that the destruction of Iraq's Army, Iran's lack of major amphibious lift, and Yemen's military limits make a requirement for concentrating the Kingdom's heavy armor uncertain. They feel there is now much more emphasis on moving lighter and easier-to-move formations for missions like border security against infiltration and to support the Ministry of Interior in fighting terrorists. Nevertheless, the combination of a lack of interoperability, maintenance and sustainment problems, large-scale exercise training, and reliance on civilian lift for rapid long-distance armored movement is a significant force limitation.

Whether there also is a requirement for Saudi Arabia to develop urban warfare capabilities for its heavy forces is an open question. Saudi officers note that Saudi Army's missions are defensive and that any security operations in Saudi cities are the function of the Ministry of Interior security forces. They do not see a potential threat requiring such training and preparation.

Saudi Antitank Weapons

The Saudi Army has a good mix of small arms, light weaponry, and antitank weapons. These include massive stocks of mobile, crew-portable, and man-portable TOW, HOT, and Dragon antitank guided missiles. Saudi Arabia has a total of some 950 TOW launchers, with some 200 TOW launchers mounted on VCC-1 armored fighting vehicles, and an additional 300 mounted on M-113A1s or other U.S.-supplied armored vehicles. It had 100 HOT launchers mounted on AMX-10P armored fighting vehicles. The Army also has large numbers of TOW crew-portable and roughly 1,000 Dragon man-portable antitank guided weapons systems.

It also has 300 Carl Gustav rocket launchers, 400 M-20 3.5-inch rocket launchers, thousands of M-72 LAWs, and extensive numbers of 75 mm, 84 mm, 90 mm (100) and 106 mm (300) rocket launchers and recoilless rifles.

Saudi Arabia is replacing its LAWs with more effective antiarmor rockets. It is replacing its TOW-1A antitank guided missiles with TOW-2As. Unlike the older antitank guided weapons in some Gulf armies, the Saudi Army TOW-2A missiles are very effective in killing T-72A, T-72M1, T-80, and other modern tanks. It is seeking to replace its Dragons with the more modern Javelin.

Saudi Artillery

Saudi artillery strength is compared to that of other Gulf armies in Figures 5.13 through 5.15. The Saudi Army has large numbers of modern artillery weapons. The Saudi Army inventory includes 60 Astros II multiple rocket launchers and 110 M-109A1B/A2 and 60 GCT 155 mm self-propelled howitzers.[4]

The Army had 24 Model 56 and 90–100 M-101/M-102 105 mm towed howitzers and 40 FH-70 105 mm towed howitzers, in storage. It had 40 M-198 and 50 M-114 155 mm towed howitzers in service and 5–10 M-115 203 mm towed howitzers and some other older towed weapons in storage. Its total mortar strength included over 400 120 mm and 4.2-inch weapons, over 1,000 81 mm weapons, and large numbers of light 60 mm weapons. It had 70 81 mm, and 150 M-30 4.2-inch mortars on M-106 and M-125A1 armored vehicles, and roughly 200 81mm–120 mm towed mortars.

Saudi artillery units are being equipped with better targeting, command and control, and battle management capabilities, but they do suffer from training, mobility, and support problems. Training is range oriented, and some experts report that many units only shoot in serious training exercises every one and a half years. The Saudi Army needs more and better ballistic computers, mobile fire-control and ammunition-supply equipment, and it desperately needs new target-acquisition radars—such as the AN/PPS-15A, MSTAR, or Rasit 3190B. It also needs a modern and fully integrated mix of counterbattery radars and fire-control systems to rapidly mass and shift fires and to practice night operations in combination with the armored and light forces.

In spite of these problems, the Saudi Army has more effective artillery than most Middle Eastern and developing armies do. It has the advantage that the Saudi Air Force is much better equipped to provide firepower for the army in joint operations than most regional air forces are, and it is seeking to develop more advanced concepts for combined arms, joint, and maneuver warfare that most regional armies still ignore. Nevertheless, the Saudi Army presently has limited-to-moderate ability to use artillery in maneuver and combined arms warfare, to target effectively in counterbattery fire or at targets beyond visual range, and to shift and concentrate fires. Unless the Kingdom takes combined arms and maneuver warfare more seriously in terms of brigade-size maneuvers

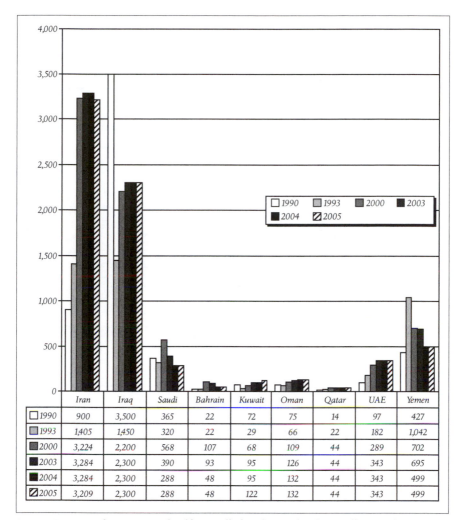

	Iran	Iraq	Saudi	Bahrain	Kuwait	Oman	Qatar	UAE	Yemen
☐1990	900	3,500	365	22	72	75	14	97	427
▨1993	1,405	1,450	320	22	29	66	22	182	1,042
▨2000	3,224	2,200	568	107	68	109	44	289	702
■2003	3,284	2,300	390	93	95	126	44	343	695
■2004	3,284	2,300	288	48	95	132	44	343	499
▨2005	3,209	2,300	288	48	122	132	44	343	499

Figure 5.13: Total Operational Self-propelled and Towed Tube Artillery and Multiple-Rocket Launchers in Gulf Forces: 1990–2005

Note: Iranian totals include active forces in the Revolutionary Guards. Saudi totals include active National Guard. Omani totals include Royal Household Guard. Iraq totals are for March 2003, before the Iraq War.

Source: Adapted by Anthony H. Cordesman from various sources and IISS, *Military Balance,* various editions.

and joint warfare exercises, its artillery units will have significant limitation in maneuver warfare.

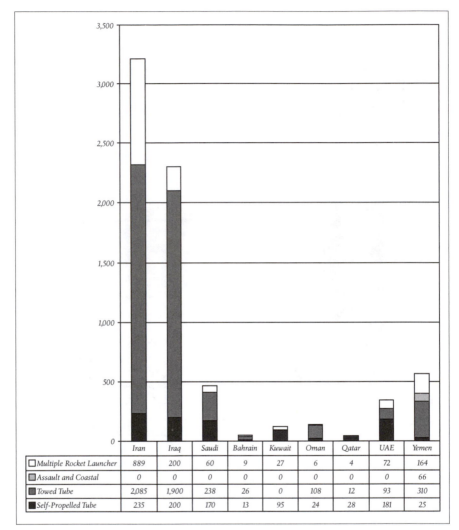

	Iran	Iraq	Saudi	Bahrain	Kuwait	Oman	Qatar	UAE	Yemen
☐ Multiple Rocket Launcher	889	200	60	9	27	6	4	72	164
▨ Assault and Coastal	0	0	0	0	0	0	0	0	66
▦ Towed Tube	2,085	1,900	238	26	0	108	12	93	310
■ Self-Propelled Tube	235	200	170	13	95	24	28	181	25

Figure 5.14: Total Operational Gulf Artillery Weapons in 2005

Note: Iranian totals include active forces in the Revolutionary Guards. Saudi totals include active National Guard. Omani totals include Royal Household Guard. Iraq totals are for March 2003, before the Iraq War.

Source: Adapted by Anthony H. Cordesman from various sources and IISS, *Military Balance,* various editions.

Saudi Light and Medium Air Defense Weapons

Saudi Arabia has relatively large numbers of modern air defense weapons by Gulf standards. It is not easy to separate the Saudi Army's air defense assets from those in the Saudi Air Defense Force, and sources disagree over which

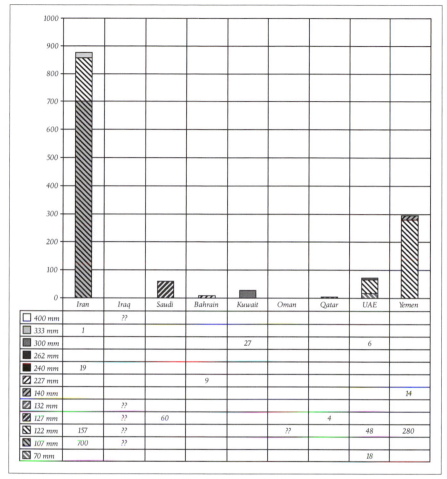

	Iran	Iraq	Saudi	Bahrain	Kuwait	Oman	Qatar	UAE	Yemen
☐ 400 mm		??							
☐ 333 mm	1								
■ 300 mm					27			6	
■ 262 mm									
■ 240 mm	19								
▨ 227 mm				9					
▨ 140 mm									14
▨ 132 mm		??							
▨ 127 mm		??	60			4			
▧ 122 mm	157	??					??	48	280
▧ 107 mm	700	??							
▧ 70 mm								18	

Figure 5.15: Gulf Inventory of Multiple Rocket Launchers by Caliber in 2005

Note: Iranian totals include active forces in the Revolutionary Guards. Saudi totals include active National Guard. Omani totals include Royal Household Guard. Iraq had a total of approximately 200 multiple-rocket launchers before the Iraq War in March 2003.

Source: Adapted by Anthony H. Cordesman from various sources and IISS, *Military Balance,* various editions.

force operates given systems. The Saudi Army seems to have 33 SAM batteries and 17 AM/FPS-117 radars and is organized and equipped to protect its maneuver forces in combat. Total Saudi holdings of short-range air defenses include 73 Crotale (Shahine) radar-guided missiles on tracked armored vehicles and 17 with 68 Shahine firing units, some mounted on AMX-30 tank bodies.

Saudi Arabia also has man-portable surface-to-air missiles. Its current holdings include 500 Mistrals. It is upgrading its Mistrals with better rocket motors and possibly better sensors and countermeasures. It once had around 500 Stingers, which it destroyed in 2002 because of maintenance and security issues; it had previously destroyed holdings of 500 obsolescent Redeye man-portable surface-to-air missiles. Saudi Arabia may have an unknown number of Kolomna KBM Igla (SA-16 Gimlet) weapons. Saudi Arabia bought 50 Stinger launchers and 200 Stinger missiles on an emergency basis in August 1990 and ordered additional Crotales and 700 French Mistral launchers and 1,500 missiles.

It is equally difficult to separate the Army's air defense gun holdings from those of the National Guard, but Saudi Arabia's total holdings of light antiaircraft weapons seems to include 10 M-42 40 mm and 92 Vulcan M-163 20 mm antiaircraft guns. It also seems to have 150 Bofors L-60/L-70 40 mm and 128 Oerlikon 35 mm towed guns, and possibly 15 M-117 90 mm towed antiaircraft guns.

This is a reasonable mix of air defense assets, but training and readiness levels are moderate to low. The separate Saudi Air Defense Force—which controls Saudi Arabia's heavy surface-to-air missiles and fixed air defenses—is also a relatively static force that cannot easily support the Army in mobile operations. The Army's air defense units consist largely of independent fire units, rather than an integrated system of netted C⁴I/BM capabilities, although Saudi officers indicate such capabilities are planned.

A broader question affects the future of this force, as it does the future of most short-range air defense units (SHORADS). The Afghan and Iraq wars have shown that a truly modern air force can strike land units with extraordinary lethality, using weapons like laser and GPS-guided weapons at standoff ranges that SHORADS cannot target, that radar-guided air defense systems are easy to locate and bypass or strike with antiradiation missiles, and that optical and IR systems are subject to countermeasure and tracking problems.

This does not mean that disperse systems that conceal their presence and "pop up" cannot be effective, that dense or "curtain" fire will not occasionally hit an aircraft with a lucky or "magic" bullet, or that the very existence of such force does not force aircraft to operate at much longer strike ranges and degrade their effectiveness. It does, however, raise issues about the kind of air defense forces the Saudi Army must plan for in the future.

Saudi Army Aviation

Saudi Army helicopter forces are important areas for future force improvement, and the Saudi Army has developed a comprehensive army aviation modernization plan that it will seek to implement as funds become available.

As has been noted earlier, the Saudi Army is highly dispersed, and much of its strength is deployed near Saudi Arabia's borders at Tabuk, Hafr Al Baten, and Sharurah-Khamis Mushayt. Helicopters offer a partial solution to providing rapid concentration of force and help Saudi Arabia to make up for its lack of experience in large-scale maneuver. They also allow the Army to support the Ministry of Interior security forces in counterterrorism missions as well as the National Guard, throughout the Kingdom, by providing both lift and firepower.

These factors first led the Saudi Army to seek attack helicopters in the early 1980s. Saudi Arabia initially experienced political problems in obtaining such helicopters from the United States, and this led the Saudi Army to obtain an option to buy 88 Sikorsky-designed S-70 Blackhawk helicopters from Westland in Britain. Roughly 80 of these Westlands were to be attack helicopters equipped with TOW-2. The rest were to be configured for SAR missions. The order was divided into batches of 40 and 48 aircraft.

The Gulf War changed this situation and created the political conditions in which Saudi Arabia could buy the AH-64 from the United States. The AH-64s began to enter Saudi service in 1993. Saudi Arabia eventually took delivery on 12 AH-64 Apache attack helicopters, 155 Hellfire missiles, 24 spare Hellfire launchers, 6 spare engines, and associated equipment from the United States.

In 2005 the Saudi Army had a helicopter strength that included 12 AH-64 attack helicopters, 15 Bell 406CS armed helicopters, 12 S-70A1 Sikorsky Blackhawk transport helicopters, 6 SA-365N medical evacuation helicopters, 10 UL-60 Blackhawk medical evacuation, and 12 UH-60 transport helicopters. The Saudi Army has had maintenance problems with its helicopter fleet, although standards seem to be much higher than in Iran and Iraq. It also tends to use helicopters more for search and rescues, light transport, service, and medical evacuation functions than to achieve tactical mobility. This could present problems in terms of training and readiness to compensate for the dispersal of the Saudi Army and in deploying forward defenses.

The Army would like to buy more attack helicopters and sees them as a key future system for both regular military counterterrorism operations. It is studying the use of UAVs for reconnaissance and targeting missions, as are all of the Saudi military services. It also is working with the Saudi Air Force and Air Defense Force to develop better plans to joint operations, deconflicting fixed-

and rotary-wing aircraft in combat operations, and improved air space control—which is managed by the Air Force.

Facilities and Infrastructure

The Saudi Army has all the facilities, infrastructure, and equipment necessary to support its forces in peacetime. It has a full series of training facilities for officers and other ranks, and most of its combat forces are in large, self-contained, military cities. These cities have modern housing, good equipment facilities, and adequate maintenance and support facilities for peacetime and limited combat operations near base. There is ongoing construction of facilities near Yemen. This latter effort now seems oriented largely toward border control and the prevention of infiltration or operations by terrorists, although low-level tribal violence still takes place sporadically in the area.

The Army has excellent support facilities, although it underfunded logistic and support vehicles and equipment between the mid-1990s and 2001. Nevertheless, the Saudi Army has made major purchases of support equipment, along with the purchase of its M-1A2s and M-2A2s. It is improving its field support vehicle strength and ordered 10,000 support vehicles from the United States on September 27, 1990, including 1,200 High Mobility Multipurpose Wheeled Vehicles (HMMWVs). The Saudi Army still has extensive foreign support in spite of cutbacks in foreign manpower and support contracts.

The Saudi Army has not, however, created the sustainment and support capabilities necessary to support mobile combat operations in the field. While it did make progress toward converting to maneuver warfare during the Gulf War, it then reverted to a largely static and caserne-oriented pattern of peacetime behavior. As a result, it has failed to give sustainability the same priority as firepower and mobility.

The lack of standardization within the Saudi Army adds to these problems, as does excessive dependence on base facilities and foreign civilian support. So would the lack of progress in these areas in the rest of the Southern Gulf, in any joint warfare involving regional allies. There are exceptions like attack helicopters, but the Saudi Army now needs the specialized training, organization, and manpower necessary to improve its support structure, as well as the ability to sustain its existing forces in combat, far more than it needs more weapons.

The Saudi Army is still an army that normally operates near its peacetime casernes and that will experience serious problems in redeploying its major combat forces unless it has extensive strategic warning. While Saudi Arabia can move a brigade set of armor relatively rapidly, it would take the Saudi Army a minimum of 7–10 days to redeploy a combat sustainable brigade to a new front.

Interoperability within the Saudi Army would then be an even broader problem than the previous discussion of armor indicates. Saudi Arabia operates three types of tanks and five different types of major armored fighting vehicles and armored personnel carriers, with an inventory of more than 20 subtypes. It has major artillery holdings from five different countries, antitank weapons from four, and helicopters from two. This equipment is broadly interoperable, and there is no reason not to buy from a variety of foreign suppliers. However, Saudi Arabia's unique weather, terrain, and desert warfare conditions create special demands in terms of support and sustainability, and each additional type of weapon increases any army's training and sustainability problems.

Much of the equipment the Saudi Army has purchased has required modification, or extensive changes to its original technical and logistic support plan, before it could be operated in large numbers. New problems may arise the moment the Saudi Army is forced to operate away from its bases, conduct sustained maneuvers, and deal with combat damage. Contractor support is not a substitute for uniformed Saudi combat support and service support capabilities that can deploy and fight in the field, and the Saudi Army's standardization and interoperability problems are compounded by the need to support equipment in remote and widely dispersed locations. The Saudi Army has tried to reduce such problems by creating an advanced logistic system, but some experts feel this effort has been overly ambitious and has lacked proper advisory management.

Military advisory teams generally provide relatively unbiased advice but do tend to push their own nation's manufactures. Contract teams—Saudi or foreign—are profit- and sales-oriented groups. The Kingdom should use advice, not rely on it, carefully carrying out its own independent assessment, and seek to Saudiize contract efforts wherever cost effective. Saudi planners should examine what Western countries and Israel do, compare the systems, and select the best elements tailored to Saudi needs—seeking competitive bids for what must be bought from the outside. "Trust, but verify" applies to more than arms control.

Foreign contractors are also expensive and are noncombatants who may not be willing to support military operations in the field. The Kingdom now has the manpower pool and skills to create its own major overhaul and maintenance facilities, provide the necessary maintenance and sustainment capabilities in the field, and provide recovery, service, and repair units that will enable it to maneuver in the field. It also has developed to the point where it can still benefit from foreign advice on such issues but does not need to rely on it. It should be able to create its own plans and make its own choices about logistics, sustainment, and repair systems.

It may initially be more expensive to create Saudi-managed and -manned capabilities, but they will employ Saudis and develop essential skills and military capabilities. Recent wars have shown that field repair and sustainment is as important as initial combat strength and is critical to rapid and effective maneuver. Moreover, one of Israel's advantages over Arab troops in past wars has been that it concentrated on the recovery of damaged equipment in combat and rapidly brought weapons like tanks back into service, while Arab forces tend to abandon equipment with limited combat damage or field-repairable maintenance problems.

The creation of Saudi-manned major maintenance and overhaul facilities might offer several other advantages. Buying from different suppliers does not by itself guarantee independence or sustainability. Dependence on foreign suppliers is not an issue after the equipment and weapons are delivered if Saudi Arabia has the capability to repair and refit equipment and has bought the necessary stocks of parts and specialized equipment. Turnaround and repair times are shorter and can be peaked in preparation for war and sustaining operations without political issues and delays for delivery from the supplier country.

Field exercises become far more realistic if emergency repair can be made part of the exercise without adding to foreign contractor costs. Commanders come to see repair and sustainability as an integral part of combat operations and not a task contracted out to foreigners. Developing such capabilities also creates an enhanced ability to modify and modernize equipment and to make modifications tailored to Saudi needs that can be bought from a range of foreign suppliers.

These are issues the Saudi Army must now address in the light of the fact Saddam Hussein's Iraq has ceased to be a threat, and lighter and more mobile forces may be needed to deal with the problems of infiltration and terrorism. It should be possible to consolidate Saudi forces around the mission of defending against any incursions by Iran or Yemen, cut major equipment purchases and eliminate older and less capable equipment, and stress training and readiness. The Saudi Army also fully recognizes that its need to focus on developing additional light and heavily mobile forces, Special Forces and counterterrorism units will require new forms of support at every level.

Saudi Arabia should make its own choices and create its own operations research (OR) and test and evaluation (T&E) teams, focusing on interoperability, joint warfare performance, and sustainability—and not simply technical specifications and individual equipment performance. It should buy independent sustainability with its weapons in terms of stocks on in-Kingdom service and repair facilities to minimize dependency. Iraq's defeat and the slow rate of Iranian improvement give the Kingdom time in which to adopt a slower rate of modernization based on its own choices as to what equipment best meets its needs.

Overall Capabilities

The preceding comments judge the Saudi Army by a very demanding standard: How it compares with U.S., British, Israeli, and other advanced land forces. Three points need to be stressed in summarizing such judgments for the Saudi Army and all of the services reviewed in this study. First, Saudi Arabia has made immense progress in the last thirty years and has regained the momentum it lost during the 1990s since Prince Khalid bin Sultan became assistant minister of defense in 2001. Two, such standards are absolute and do not take account of the destruction of the Iraqi threat and acute limitations of potential threats like Iran and Yemen. Third, global military standards for readiness are relatively low, and the Saudi armed forces not only compare favorably to those of regional power, but to those of many NATO countries—many of which have not fought a meaningful military action in well over half a century.

That said, the Saudi Army does need to press ahead with a focus on readiness, training, and sustainability focused on maneuver warfare, night combat operations, combined arms, and joint warfare. No force can afford to stand still or not seek excellence regardless of today's known threats and mission requirements. The risk of becoming a "garrison force" is too great; forces that do not progress, regress.

Key concepts the Saudi Army is examining include creating its own equivalent of the advanced training facilities the U.S. Army has developed at Fort Irwin, creating a similar mix of automated capabilities for large-unit joint warfare training, and demanding "red-blue" exercises with highly capable "threat forces." These are almost certainly the best investments the Saudi Army could make at this time. It is also seeking to expand to brigade-sized exercises with the U.S. Army. This kind of exercise training with friendly and allied forces has equally high priority.

THE SAUDI NATIONAL GUARD

Saudi Arabia divides its land-force manpower between the Army and the Saudi Arabian National Guard (SANG). The National Guard is the successor of the Ikhwan, or White Army. It is still largely a tribal force forged out of tribal elements loyal to the Saud family. It was created in 1955 and was originally administered directly by the king until King Faisal appointed the current Crown

Prince Abdullah its commander in 1962. A year later, Crown Prince Abdullah requested a British military mission to help modernize the guard.

Since the late 1970s, however, the U.S.-Saudi Arabian National Guard Program (SANG) and U.S. contractors have provided most of the SANG's advisory functions.[5] In fact, in 1973 Prince Abdullah signed an agreement with the U.S. ambassador to set up the Office of the Program Manager-Saudi Arabian National Guard Modernization Program (OPM-SANG).[6] The recent shifts in the organization, manpower, and equipment strength of the National Guard are shown in Table 5.3.

Table 5.3:   Saudi National Guard: Force Structure

	1991	2000	2005
Manpower	55,000	95,000	110,000
Active	35,000	75,000	95,000
Reserve	20,000	20,000	20,000
Combat units			
Mechanized infantry brigade	2	3	3
Infantry brigade	2	5	5
Ceremonial cavalry	1	1	1
LAV	0	1,117	1,117
LAV-25	0	384	384
LAV-CP	0	182	182
LAV-AG	0	130	130
LAV-AT	0	111	111
LAV-M	0	73	73
LAV	0	47	47
Support vehicle	0	190	190
APC	1,100	730	730
V-150 Commando	1,100	290 (810)	290 (810)
Piranha	0	440	440
Towed Artillery	68	70	70
105 mm: M-102	50	40	40
155 mm: M-198	18	30	30
MOR	0	73+	73+
81 mm: ?	0	?	?
120 mm: ?	0	73+	73+
RL & RCL	?	?	?
106 mm: M-40A1	?	?	?
ATGW	?	111+	111+
TOW-2A	?	111+	111+

Note: The Iraq numbers are those before March 2003. The IISS number for the SANG is 75,000, while Saudi officials say that the SANG manpower is 95,000–100,000.

Source: Adapted by Anthony H. Cordesman from various sources and IISS, *Military Balance,* various editions.

The National Guard is sometimes viewed as a counterweight to the regular military forces, where reliance on recruiting from loyal tribes creates a force the regime could count on to checkmate a coup by the regular forces. In practice, however, it has served more to ensure the continued loyalty of various tribes and has evolved steadily toward becoming a more modern force in its own right. Over time, it has become a steadily more effective internal security force, as well as a force that can provide rear area security for the Army and can help defend the major urban areas and critical petroleum infrastructure.

The five major current missions of the Guard are:

- Maintain security and stability within the Kingdom.
- Defend vital facilities (religious sites, oil fields).
- Provide security and a screening force for the Kingdom's borders.
- Provide a combat-ready internal security force for operations throughout the Kingdom.
- Provide security for Crown Prince Abdullah and the senior members of the royal family.

Since May 2003, the Guard has focused on counterterrorism and support of the Ministry of Interior's security, facilities protection, counterfiltration in border areas, and counterterrorism operations in built-up areas.

Strength and Organization

The National Guard got its first real modern combat experience during the Gulf War in 1991. It has since steadily improved its readiness and training and has grown into a 95,000-man force. While it retains tribal elements, its modern combat elements have added 1,117 LAV, more than 73 mortars, and more than 111 antitank guided weapons to its arsenal. The manpower and equipment developments in the Saudi National Guard are shown in Table 5.3.

Estimates of the current full time strength of the National Guard differ sharply. The IISS reports it had 75,000 actives and 25,000 tribal levies in 2005. A senior U.S. expert quoted a strength of 105,000 in February 2001. Some estimates put the range at 100,000 actives and 30,000 tribal levies. Regardless of the exact numbers, it is clear that the guard is now far larger than it was at the time of the Gulf War and that it has a full-time active strength approaching that of the Saudi Army.

The guard is organized into three mechanized brigades and five infantry brigades. These brigades had modern light armored vehicles (LAVs), and each brigade had some 800 men each and some 360 vehicles. There were also five light infantry brigades, equipped primarily with V-150s. These forces were deployed so that there were two mechanized brigades, and another forming, near Riyadh, plus one light infantry brigade. The Western Sector had three light infantry brigades, and the Eastern Sector has one mechanized and one light infantry brigade.

Major Combat Equipment

The National Guard does not have a complex or sophisticated mix of equipment and has chosen to standardize on some of the best wheeled-armored weapons available. The Guard's operational forces are equipped with about 1,117 LAVs in its mechanized units. According to the IISS, these include 394 LAV-25s, 184 LAV-Cps, 130 LAV-Ags, 111 LAV-ATs, 73 LAV-Ms, 47 LAVs, plus 190 LAV support vehicles.

It also has 290 V-150 Commando armored vehicles in active service in its light infantry forces, plus 810 more V-150s in storage and 440 Piranhas. The guard prefers wheeled vehicles because of their superior speed, endurance, and ease of maintenance. The guard also had a significant number of towed artillery weapons.

Modernization and New Mission Requirements

The National Guard is still modernizing, but it continues to improve its support and sustainability. Saudi Arabia has agreed to a contract to supply the guard with replacement parts for its LAVs and APCs, as well as additional vehicles, artillery pieces, and training. The contract, according to *Jane's Defence Weekly*, would include a support service for the period January 1, 2004– December 31, 2008 and would be a joint venture with Vinnell Cooperation. Its value could total over $900 million.

The guard's present goal is to become a modernized, 100,000-man force. The U.S. Defense Security Cooperation Agency's statement on November 22, 2003, describes this goal as follows, "The [SANG] Modernization Program ensures necessary training, logistics, support, doctrine, development and force integration for the continuing expansion and uses of their weapons systems. These services will remain the cornerstone of an effort to upgrade and enhance the future infrastructure of the SANG organization."[7]

Overall Capabilities

Just as the regular military services need to comprehensively revise their future plans to take account of the fall of Saddam Hussein and the destruction of Iraq's armed forces, reexamine the potential threat from Iran, and develop better capabilities for asymmetric warfare, the National Guard needs to reexamine its roles and missions. It has evolved more as a result of history than to meet a clear national need. That need has emerged with the rise of the terrorist threat inside Saudi Arabia.

This means the guard needs better training for counterinsurgency, urban warfare, and counterterrorism; to protect Saudi Arabia's critical infrastructure; and to protect its petroleum facilities. It needs a better ability to protect borders against infiltration by elements too well armed for normal border guards, and to reinforce Ministry of Interior forces when they need light mechanized forces.

This also means adopting tactics for using its LAVs suited to such missions, which may involve dealing with RPGs, improvised explosive devices, and even ATGMs in the hands of terrorists and insurgents. At the same time, the Saudi Army has the heavy armor for the kind of urban fighting described above, and may also—as did the U.S. Army—need retraining and organizational chances for missions of this kind. The military balance in the Gulf has changed fundamentally over the period since Iran's defeat in 1988, and the Kingdom may need to make the same shifts toward force transformation as U.S. and British forces make.

Finally, while some steps have been taken to improve jointness and create a central command for counterterrorism under the MOI, joint operations are still a problem. The National Guard may send officers for training in the Armed Forces Command and Staff College, but there is still little joint exercise training and coordination.

One oddity of the visa problems that have developed between the United States and Saudi Arabia since 9/11 is that the guard has taken advantage of the slots given up by the regular armed services to send more and more officers and personnel to the United States for training. This has obvious advantages, but it is also helping to maintain the gap between the guard and regular forces.

Furthermore, efforts to integrate the guard into the overall C⁴I/battle management system of the regular forces are waiting on the creation of a new Saudi C⁴I/battle management system for all the services that will, even if funded, take years to implement.

THE SAUDI NAVY

The trends in the strength and modernization of the Saudi Navy are shown in Table 5.4. The Saudi Navy has slowly improved its readiness and effectiveness, but it still has major problems. Only its fleet on the Gulf coast is regarded as having made significant progress as a war-fighting force. Its force on the Red Sea is seen more as a work in progress than a war-fighting force. Joint warfare capabilities are still in development, and the Navy is not integrated into either a GGC or Saudi-U.S.-UK concept of operations.

The Saudi Navy must restructure its plans and capabilities to focus on Iran, now that Iraq has ceased to be a threat, and on defense of the Red Sea. It still has a potential surface warfare, antimine warfare, and ASW threat from nations like Iran. In practice, however, its more immediate threats are potential terrorist attacks, infiltration, and asymmetric warfare.

Table 5.4:　Saudi Royal Navy: Force Structure

	1991	2000	2005
Manpower	9,500	15,500	15,500
Navy	8,000	12,500	12,500
Marines	1,500	3,000	3,000
Frigates with GM	4	4	6(1)
Madina: Fr F-2000	4	4	4
Makkah: Mod La Fayette F300S	0	0	1
Al-Riyadh: Mod La Fayette F3000S	0	0	1
Al-Dammam: Mod La Fayette F3000S	0	0	(1)
Corvettes	4	4	4
adr: U.S. Tacoma FSG	4	4	4
Missile craft	9	9	9
Al-Siddiq: US 58m PFM	9	9	9
Torpedo craft	3	0	0
Jubail: FRG Jaguar	3	0	0
Patrol craft	0	17	17
US Halter Marine PCI	0	17	17
Mine countermeasures	5	7	7
Al-Jawf: UK Sandown MHO	1	3	3
Addriyadh: U.S. MSC-322 MCC	4	4	4
Amphibious	16	8	8
LCU	4	4	4
LCM	12	4	4
Support & miscellaneous	3	7	7
Boraida: Mod Fr Durance	2	2	2
ST/F	0	3	3
ARS	0	1	1
Royal yacht	0	1	1
Ocean tugs	1	0	0
Helicopters	24	31	44
AS-565 SAR	4	4	4
AS-565 AS-15TT ASM	20	15	15
AS-323B/F: Transport	0	6	6
AS-323B/F: AM-39 Exocet	0	6	6
Bell 406CS	0	0	13
BMR-600P	140	140	140

Source: Adapted by Anthony H. Cordesman from various sources and IISS, *Military Balance*, various editions.

Strength and Organization

The manpower strength of the Saudi Navy and other Gulf navies is shown in Figure 5.16. The Saudi Navy has a nominal strength of 15,500–17,000 men, including 3,000–4,500 Marines. It has added more than 6,000 men to its naval power in the past decade.

The Saudi Navy is headquartered in Riyadh and has major bases in Jeddah, Jizan, Al Wajh in the Red Sea, and in Jubail, Dammam, Ras al Mishab, and Ras al Ghar in the Gulf. The size of the Saudi Navy is compared to that of other regional navies, as shown in Figures 5.17 to 5.21.

Main Surface Combatants

Its combat strength includes four *Madina*-class (F-2000) frigates, three *Alriyad*-class (F-3000S) guided-missile frigates, four *Badr*-class missile corvettes, and nine *Al Siddiq*-class guided-missile ships.[8] The *Madina*-class has already been refitted and modernized.

The Saudi Navy has commissioned three multipurpose antiair warfare frigates, which were scheduled to enter the service between 2004 and 2006. The three frigates are: *Makkah,* commissioned in July 2001, *Al-Riyadh,* commissioned in July 2002, and *Al-Damman,* commissioned in September 2002. *Al-Riyadh* and *Makkah* were delivered to the Kingdom on November 7, 2004, and *Al-Damman* was scheduled to be delivered later in 2005. The Sawari II accord between France and Saudi Arabia, signed in 1994, includes logistics, training, and infrastructure development. The training mission involves as many as 200 personnel from NAVFCO to train Saudi naval forces in the King Faisal Naval Base in Jeddah. The first of their training mission will start a nine week course, including 30 sea days for the *Al-Riyadh*-class frigate.[9]

The Sawari II frigates will be 25 percent larger than the French *La Fayette*-class with enhanced antiair warfare and antisubmarine capabilities. They will have the design of Director of Naval Construction (DCN's)[10] stealth frigates, with highly automated combat management systems based on the Thales' Tavitac 2000. They are shaped to decrease radar cross-section (RCS). Furthermore, to reduce vulnerability, the frigates will be designed with double bulkheads, armoured around sensitive parts, firefighting capabilities, ventilation structure, and redundancy in the systems.[11]

The Sawari-II systems will include the following:

• Missiles:
   — Eight anti-ship missiles, Exocet MM40 Block II SSM, with 165kg shaped charge warhead and a range of 70km, which travel at approximately 0.95 Mach.

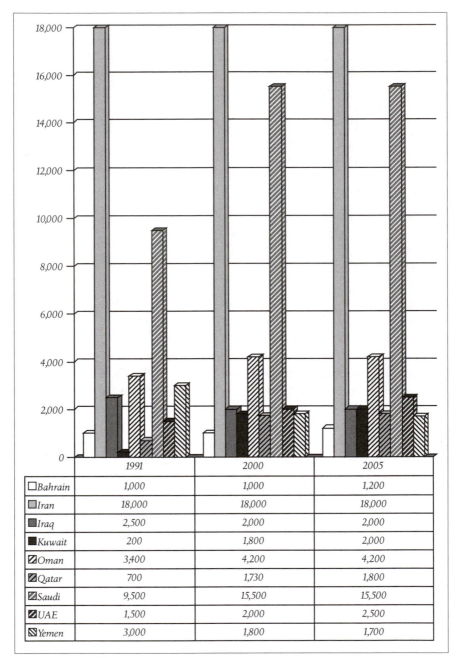

	1991	2000	2005
□Bahrain	1,000	1,000	1,200
▨Iran	18,000	18,000	18,000
▨Iraq	2,500	2,000	2,000
■Kuwait	200	1,800	2,000
▨Oman	3,400	4,200	4,200
▨Qatar	700	1,730	1,800
▨Saudi	9,500	15,500	15,500
▨UAE	1,500	2,000	2,500
▨Yemen	3,000	1,800	1,700

Figure 5.16: Gulf States Active Naval Manpower: 1991–2005

Note: The Iraq numbers are those before March 2003.

Source: Adapted by Anthony H. Cordesman from various sources and IISS, *Military Balance*, various editions.

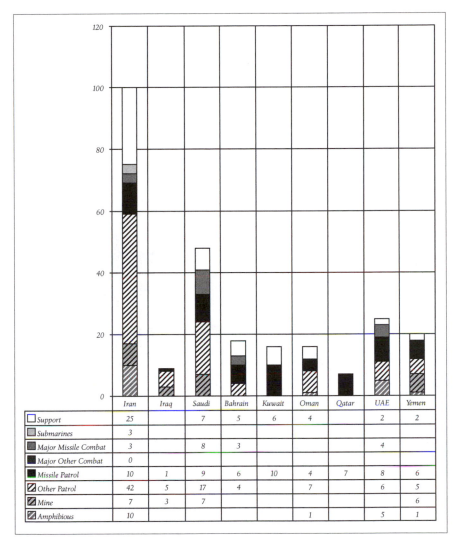

	Iran	Iraq	Saudi	Bahrain	Kuwait	Oman	Qatar	UAE	Yemen
☐ Support	25		7	5	6	4		2	2
▦ Submarines	3								
▪ Major Missile Combat	3		8	3				4	
▪ Major Other Combat	0								
▪ Missile Patrol	10	1	9	6	10	4	7	8	6
▨ Other Patrol	42	5	17	4		7		6	5
▨ Mine	7	3	7						6
▨ Amphibious	10					1		5	1

Figure 5.17: Gulf Naval Ships by Category in 2005

Note: Iraq totals are for March 2003, before the Iraq War.

Source: Adapted by Anthony H. Cordesman from IISS, *Military Balance,* various editions.

— The guidance system on the SAM is equipped with data uplink and active radar terminal homing. For increased maneuverability in the terminal phase, the missile uses a "PIF-PAF" direct thrust control system with gas jets.

— Two eight-cell Sylver vertical launch systems for Aster 15 SAM, which is effective from 1.7km to 30km and to an altitude of 15,000m.

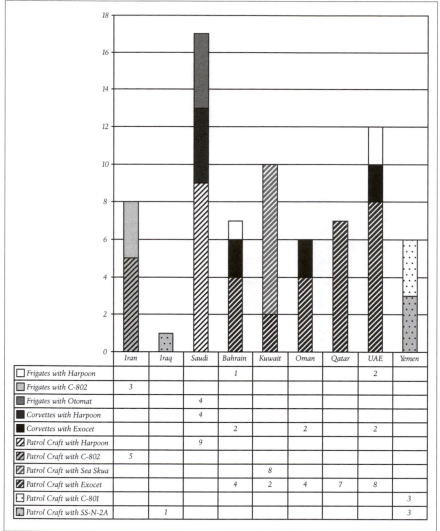

Figure 5.18: Gulf Warships with Antiship Missiles in 2005

Note: Iraq totals are for March 2003, before the Iraq War.

Source: Adapted by Anthony H. Cordesman from IISS, *Military Balance,* various editions and material provided by U.S. experts.

- Guns: an Oto Melara 76/62 and two Giat 15B guns. The Oto Melara 76/72 can fire up to 120 rounds per minute with a range of 20km. A heavyweight anti-submarine torpedo.

- Sonar: a sonar suite is the Thales Underwater Systems CAPTAS 20 towed array sonar.

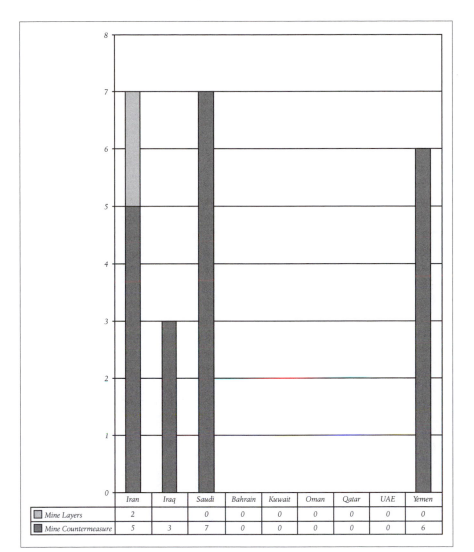

	Iran	Iraq	Saudi	Bahrain	Kuwait	Oman	Qatar	UAE	Yemen
Mine Layers	2	0	0	0	0	0	0	0	0
Mine Countermeasure	5	3	7	0	0	0	0	0	6

Figure 5.19: Gulf Mine Warfare Ships in 2005

Note: Iraq totals are for March 2003, before the Iraq War.

Source: Adapted by Anthony H. Cordesman from IISS, *Military Balance*, various editions and material provided by U.S. experts.

- Radars: The round radome of the Thales Arabel 3D I-band surveillance and fire control radar. Thales long-range air search radar, DRBV 26D Jupiter operating at D-band, is forward of the main radar mast. Two Sperry Marine Decca navigation and helicopter control radars are also fitted.

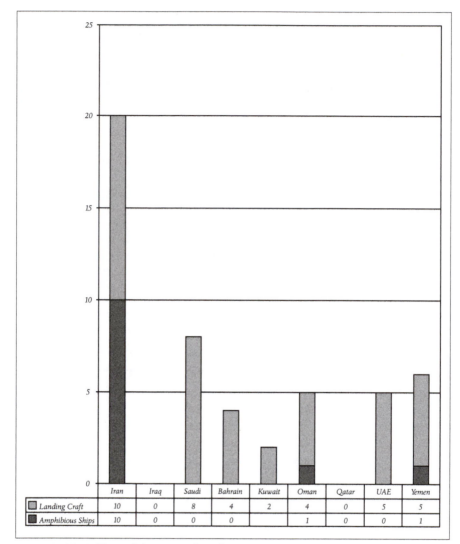

	Iran	Iraq	Saudi	Bahrain	Kuwait	Oman	Qatar	UAE	Yemen
Landing Craft	10	0	8	4	2	4	0	5	5
Amphibious Ships	10	0	0	0		1	0	0	1

Figure 5.20: Gulf Amphibious Warfare Ships in 2005

Note: Iraq totals are for March 2003, before the Iraq War.

Source: Adapted by Anthony H. Cordesman from IISS, *Military Balance*, various editions and material provided by U.S. experts.

- EW: DR 3000 electronic support measures (ESM), Altesse communications intercept system, Salamander B2 radar jammer and TRC 281 communications jammer. Two EADS Dagaie decoy launchers are also fitted.
- The deck at the stern has a single landing spot for a medium size helicopter and has a fully equipped hangar to accommodate one helicopter.

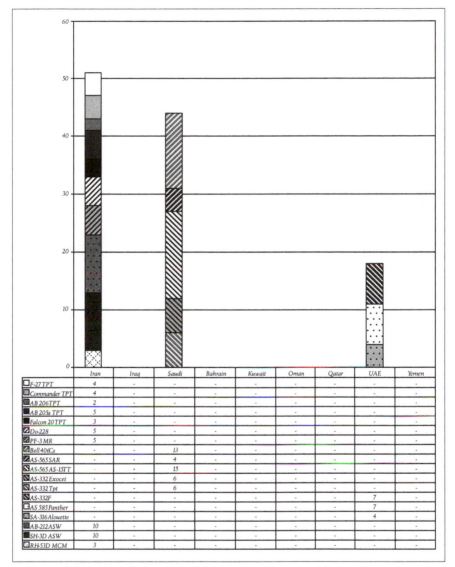

	Iran	Iraq	Saudi	Bahrain	Kuwait	Oman	Qatar	UAE	Yemen
☐ F-27 TPT	4	-	-	-	-	-	-	-	-
☐ Commander TPT	4	-	-	-	-	-	-	-	-
☐ AB 206 TPT	2	-	-	-	-	-	-	-	-
■ AB 205a TPT	5	-	-	-	-	-	-	-	-
▨ Falcon 20 TPT	3	-	-	-	-	-	-	-	-
▨ Do-228	5	-	-	-	-	-	-	-	-
▨ PF-3 MR	5	-	-	-	-	-	-	-	-
▨ Bell 406Cs	-	-	13	-	-	-	-	-	-
▨ AS-565 SAR	-	-	4	-	-	-	-	-	-
◪ AS-565 AS-15TT	-	-	15	-	-	-	-	-	-
◪ AS-332 Exocet	-	-	6	-	-	-	-	-	-
◪ AS-332 Tpt	-	-	6	-	-	-	-	-	-
◪ AS-332F	-	-	-	-	-	-	-	7	-
☐ AS 585 Panther	-	-	-	-	-	-	-	7	-
▨ SA-316 Alouette	-	-	-	-	-	-	-	4	-
▨ AB-212 ASW	10	-	-	-	-	-	-	-	-
■ SH-3D ASW	10	-	-	-	-	-	-	-	-
◪ RH-53D MCM	3	-	-	-	-	-	-	-	-

Figure 5.21: Gulf Naval Aircraft and Helicopters Aircraft in 2005

Note: Iraq totals are for March 2003, before the Iraq War.

Source: Adapted by Anthony H. Cordesman from the IISS, *Military Balance*.

- Engines: The diesel engines drive two shafts with Rolls-Royce Kamewa controllable pitch propellers.[12]

One of the frigates ran aground in the Jeddah area and has proved difficult to free. It may require a major refit by the manufacturer, and the future status of its vertical launch system is unclear.[13]

The Navy's major surface ships are still a developing force. Actual at-sea performance is increasing, as is exercise activity. It is still low by Western standards, however, particularly in the Red Sea area.

Modernization plans are uncertain, and no major surface ship purchases seem to be planned in the near future. Some Saudi experts feel the future emphasize should be on smaller ships with less detectable superstructures, high levels of firepower, and "a compact, AEGIS-like" sensor and battle management capability.

Smaller Combat Ships, Mine Warfare, and Support Forces

The Saudi Navy also has 3 *Damman*-class (German Jaguar) torpedo boats, 20 Naja 12 inshore fast craft, 17 Halter-type coastal patrol craft (some in the Coast Guard), and 3 Al Jawf (British Sandown) and four *Safwa* (*Addriyah*)-class (ex-US MSC-322 Bluebird) mine warfare ships.[14]

The mine warfare mission is potentially critical. It also presents major problems. Libya once laid mines covertly in the Red Sea, using a commercial vessel. Iran showed in 1987–88 that it could disrupt some aspects of Gulf shipping simply by releasing freefloating mines, and a wide range of Iranian Navy and IRGC naval branch forces practice minelaying, including laying freefloating mines. This kind of minelaying can be done by any ship, from a tanker to small craft, and virtually any type of mine from the oldest contact mine to the most modern influence mine can be used.

The Saudi mine warfare force is far too small to practice defense against this kind of random threat, and the limited GCC cooperation in mine warfare is hampered by the small size of mine warfare forces in other navies.

Although the Saudi Navy does have relatively modern mine vessels, there are also significant technical challenges. The U.S. and British Navy could not initially detect an Iraqi minefield during the first Gulf War, relying on very similar vessels. U.S. IS&R assets also failed to detect that the field was being laid. This is a warning that structured minefields could present as much of a threat as random minelaying.

Auxiliary ships include three *Radhwa*-class ocean-going tugs, three *Radhwa*-class coastal tugs, two *Buraida*-class replenishment oilers (French *Durance*-class), one *Al-Riyadh* royal yacht, and the *Al Azizah* hydrofoil yacht tender. The royal yachts are based at Dammam.

Submarines?

Saudi naval planners differ over the need for a submarine force. Some feel this mission should be left to other forces and that the U.S. and British navies can deal with the ASW threats in the Gulf, Red Sea and other nearby waters. They note the Saudi Navy already has maintenance and readiness problems and needs forces that are simple and easy to maintain. They see submarines as expensive and very difficult to operate and as a misuse of money.

Nevertheless, other officers disagree—as much for prestige reasons as because of validated mission requirements. Reports indicate that Saudi Arabia is considering acquiring up to four diesel-electric submarines. Reportedly, the Saudis are looking into the Swedish Kockums Type 471, the German IKL 200, and an undetermined French submarine.[15]

Marine and Amphibious Forces

The Saudi Navy has doubled its Marine force in the past decade. The 3,000–4,500-man force is organized into a brigade with six battalions. There are now three battalions deployed in the west (near Jeddah) and three more in the east (near Ras al-Ghar). The Marines are now being organized and trained for counterterrorism missions as well as asymmetric warfare.

Saudi Special Forces have a small SEAL (sea-land-air) component. King Faisal's great grandson commands this force.

The Marine force was initially equipped with 140 BTR-60Ps. It is now equipped with 140 Spanish Santa Barbara SBB BMR-600 6x6 amphibious APCs. It seems to have received nearly 100 Al Fahd 8x8 Armored personnel carriers during 2001.

The Saudi Navy has 4 *Afif*-class LCU amphibious craft, 4 LCMs, 2 other amphibious craft, 2 10,500-ton *Boraida*-class (French *Durance*) support ships, 4 smaller support vessels, 14 tugboats, and large numbers of small patrol boats, including 40 Simmoneau Type 51 inshore patrol boats.

While the Navy has lost 8 of its LCM amphibious vessels in recent years, it has kept its 4 Badr Corvette, and added 17 U.S.-made Halter Marine FCI patrol crafts. Saudi Arabia is considering buying more modern LCUs and/or LCMs.

Naval Aviation

Saudi naval aviation is based at Al Jubail. Various sources report different holdings for Saudi naval aviation. It seems to have included 15 operational SA-565F Dauphin ASW and antiship missile helicopters, with AS-15TT missiles, and 4 SA-565s equipped for the search and rescue mission.

The SA-365Fs have only limited ASW capability and are configured primarily for the surface search-and-attack roles. Each combat-equipped SA-365F carries four missiles and has an Agrion search/attack system. They have Crouzet MAD systems and can carry two Mark 46 torpedoes.

The Saudi Navy also has 3 Westland Sea King Mark 47 ASW helicopters, 12 land-based AS-332SC(B/F) Super Puma helicopters, and 13 Bell 406CS. Some reports indicate the AS-332s included 12 aircraft with Omera search radars, 9 with Giat 20 mm cannon, and 12 with Exocet or Sea Eagle air-to-ship missiles. Other reports indicate the AS-332s included only six transport aircraft, plus another six with Exocet air-to-ship missiles.[16]

Reports that NH-90 helicopters are being purchased for Saudi frigates are not confirmed, and may only be a contingency study.[17]

Border Guard

The Saudi Border Guard is a branch of the Ministry of Interior; its mission is to defend Saudi Arabia's land borders. It has an estimated 30,000 men and has its main base at Azizam.

Its main equipment includes 2 large *Yarmouk*-class patrol boats; 2 fast missile attack craft, with AS-15TT missiles; 4 large *Al-Jouf*-class patrol boats; 2 large *Al Jubaiel*-class patrol boats; 25 *Skorpion*-class patrol boats; 13 other coastal patrol boats; 4 SRN-6, Model 4 Hovercraft; 16 Slingsby SAH 2200 Hovercraft; large numbers of inshore patrol craft; 3 royal yachts; 3 small tankers; firefighting craft; and 3 tugs.

Saudi Arabia is buying new, very fast patrol craft from the Philippines with 14.5 mm guns. These seem to be for the Border Guard. Consideration is being given to either giving the Border Guard helicopters with suitable sensors to extend its range and coverage, or to supporting it with Saudi Navy helicopters.

The Border Guard's primary mission has been antismuggling in the past, but it has shifted to internal security, counterinfiltration, counterterrorism, and the defense of critical coastal facilities against terrorism and covert strikes.[18] In theory, the Border Guard can draw on the Navy and Air Force for support, as well as the National Guard and other land services in dealing with serious threats. The Ministry of Interior has the authority to request such support and maintains a joint command and control committee to coordinate such efforts. Saudi naval officers and the Saudi Navy already supplements the Border Guard in patrolling the Red Sea area.

In practice, the Border Guard's real-world surveillance and combat capabilities against such threats are unclear. It is an untested force, and while it is reorganizing to meet new threats, there is no way to judge its actual progress. The adequacy of the mission tasking of the Border Guard and Navy is unclear, as is the interface they have with other security forces in defending critical targets like desalination plants, ports, oil facilities, and offshore facilities. It is easy to claim that suitable capabilities and plans for coordination and joint operations exist. It is less clear that such claims can be made good in practice.

Roles, Missions, and Capability

The Saudi Navy has substantial amounts of modern, expensive ships and equipment, but it lacks a clearly defined set of roles and missions and needs improved training and readiness. It also needs to develop a clear picture of what its role is as an independent force, in support of outside powers, and as the core of a potential GCC force.

It the past, the Saudi Navy has been overshadowed by the dominant role the U.S. and British navies have played in the Gulf, particularly since the "tanker war" against Iran in 1987–88. Like other Southern Gulf navies, the Saudi Navy has never had to develop the level of effectiveness and coordination that would be vital if they could not depend on the navies of other powers. The Red Sea has also been a "quiet zone," except for a low-level Libyan mine warfare attack now long in the past and limited clashes between Yemen and Eritrea over several islands.

A force as large, well-equipped, and expensive as the Saudi Navy, however, must be able to perform important roles and missions, and its effectiveness is the key to any future serious effort to create effective GCC forces that are not almost totally dependent on the U.S. Navy in dealing with a potential threat the size of Iran.

There are several obvious areas where changes could take place that would enhance the value of the Saudi Navy and justify its present strength and cost:

- *Protection of critical facilities*: The Saudi Navy may never need to directly engage the Iranian Navy, but sabotage or sudden strikes on offshore oil facilities, ports, and critical shoreline facilities like desalination plants are both possible and a form of asymmetric warfare that could do serious damage to the Kingdom.

- *Mine warfare*: Both the "tanker war" and Gulf War showed the danger mines pose, even if laid in covert operations or as freefloating mines. This is an important mission in conventional war and asymmetric conflicts.

- *Ship protection and escort*: Iran's Revolutionary Guard is well equipped to launch strikes against tankers and commercial shipping, and terrorists in Yemen have already shown that terrorists can attack in ports and other facilities.

- *Joint land/air operations*: Saudi Arabia has never fully exploited the maritime reconnaissance capabilities of its E-3A, and there is little jointness in Saudi Navy, Air Force, and Air Defense Force operations. The Saudi Navy would be far more effective as part of a joint team, able to use direct intervention with sea power when needed, relying on air strikes when more desirable, and carrying out maritime surveillance against both combat ships and potential covert and unconventional infiltration and operations.

- *A maritime role in air and missile defense*: Saudi E-3As have limits to their low-altitude coverage and endurance. The ability to provide a forward screen of pickets and radar coverage could help provide warning of air- and cruise-missile attacks, particularly if netted into the Saudi Air Force and Saudi Air Defense Force warning and control system.

- *Antiamphibious raid and operations capability*: Iran has limited amphibious lift, but extensive ferry and Revolutionary Guard raid capabilities. These can attack offshore facilities, raid shoreline areas, and potentially transfer forces to a port in the event of a coup or upheaval in a Southern Gulf country.

It should be noted that in all these missions, the Saudi Navy would benefit from a force multiplier effect if there was far closer and more realistic cooperation among all of the Southern Gulf navies, and if the Saudi Navy participated in more demanding and realistic exercises with the U.S. and British navies, such as an expansion of the Red Reef exercise series.

It is equally clear that "jointness" with the Saudi Air Force, Border Guard and possibly the Air Defense Force is critical to both conventional warfare and to meeting the threat of infiltration, terrorism, and asymmetric warfare.

The Saudi Air Force

The Royal Saudi Air Force (RSAF) is one of the most technically advanced air forces in the Middle East. It also has the potential to be the most decisive single element of both Saudi forces and the military forces of the Gulf Cooperation Council. However, it developed significant shortcomings during the 1990s that it is now struggling to overcome.

Between 1994 and 2001, the Air Force suffered from poor leadership that mishandled overall training and readiness, underfunded readiness, and mismanaged procurement. The resulting shortcomings included:

- A lack of overall readiness and poor aircrew and maintenance-to-aircraft ratios severely reduced the effectiveness of its F-15s and Tornados. Monthly training hours for the F-15, for example, dropped to six hours. They have since risen back to 9, but need to be 12–18. Long-range mission and refueling training also dropped sharply but is slowly being brought up to standard.

- Mistakes in managing the Saudization of contract maintenance and support personnel led high-quality personnel to leave. This and poor contractor management helped bring readiness to the point of near crisis and led to an increase in the Air Force's accident rate.

- An overemphasis on air defense at the expense of offensive air capabilities, and particularly capabilities designed to deal with advancing Iraqi armor or the naval threat from Iran.

- A failure to develop effective joint warfare capabilities and realistic joint warfare training capabilities and to transform joint warfare doctrine into fully effective war fighting plans to support the land-based Air Defense Force, and the Army, National Guard, and Navy.

- A failure to develop a truly integrated air defense and war-fighting capability with other Southern Gulf states.

- A failure to rapidly modernize the RSAF C⁴I/SR and battle management system, to develop high-capacity secure communications, and to expand the role of sensor, electronic warfare, and intelligence aircraft to support offensive and joint warfare missions.

- A failure to modernize training to support realistic offensive and joint warfare missions.

This situation is being corrected. Since 2001, the Royal Saudi Air Force has seen a significant new emphasis on readiness, combat effectiveness, and joint warfare and has improved its cooperation with the other services. It takes time to recover an "edge," however, and it will be at least several years before RSAF readiness, training, and maintenance can be increased to the point where the Air Force can exploit its equipment and technology effectively.

The RSAF still needs to set more demanding standards at every level in terms of meeting training qualifications and performance, and particularly to both eliminate pilots who cannot fly demanding flight profiles and meet the required number of training hours and to either force contract maintenance to meet high standards or find a new source of contract support.

Strength and Structure

The trends in the strength, organization, and modernization of the Saudi Air Force are summarized in Table 5.5. The RSAF has about 18,000 men, not including another 16,000 men in the Air Defense Force. The comparative manpower strength of the Saudi and other Gulf air forces is shown in Figure 5.22.

Table 5.5:   Saudi Royal Air Force: Force Structure

	1991	2000	2005
Manpower	22,000	36,000	34,000
Air Force	18,000	20,000	18,000
Air Defense	4,000	16000	16,000
Total combat aircraft	189	417	291
Fighter-ground attack	5/99	7/225	4/171
F-5B/F/RF	21	21	15
F-5E	53	56	53
Tornado IDS	25	76	85
F-15S	0	72	71
Fighter-interceptor	5/76	9118	9/106
Tornado ADV	19	24	22
F15C	42	70	66
F15D	15	24	18
RECCE	1/10	1/10	?/10
Tornado IDS	0	0	10
RF-5E	10	10	0
Airborne early warning	1/5	1/5	1/5
E-3A	5	5	5
Tanker aircraft	1/16	1/16	1/15
KE-3A	8	8	7
KC-130H	8	8	8
Operational conversion units	2/14	2/14	2/14
F-5B	14	14	14
Transport aircraft	70	3/39	3/45
C-130	30	36	38
L-100-30HS	5	3	3
CN-235	0	0	4
C-212	35	0	0
Helicopters	2/48	2/104	2/78
AB-205	8	22	22
AB-206A	13	13	13
AB-212	27	17	17
AB-412	0	40	16
AS-532A2	0	12	10
KV-107	7	0	0
Training aircraft	?/60	7/114	7/122
Hawk	29	50	43
PC-9	30	50	45
Jetstream	1	1	1
Cessna 172	0	13	13
Super Mushshaq	0	0	20
BAC-167	35	0	0
Air-to-surface missile	?	?	?
AGM Maverick	?	?	?
Sea Eagle	0	?	?
ALARM	0	?	?
AS-15	?	0	0

Table 5.5:   Saudi Royal Air Force: Force Structure (continued)

	1991	2000	2005
Air-to-air-missile	?	?	?
AIM-9J/L/L/M/P Sidewinder	?	?	?
AIM-7F Sparrow	?	?	?
Skyflash	0	?	?
AD guns	420	420	340
20 mm: M-163 Vulcan	92	92	92
30 mm: AMX-20SA	50	50	50
35 mm	128	128	128
40 mm: L/70	150	150	70
Surface-to-air missile	269	309	1,709
Shahine	141	141	141
MIM-23B I Hawk	128	128	128
Crotale	0	40	40
Stinger	0	0	400
Redeye	0	0	500
Mistral	0	0	500

Source: Adapted by Anthony H. Cordesman from various sources and IISS, *Military Balance*, various editions.

According to one source, the RSAF's combat forces were organized into six wings with a total of 15 combat squadrons and about 256–259 operational first-line, fixed-wing combat aircraft, and 39 combat capable trainers. The IISS estimates that in 2005 Saudi Arabia maintains a total inventory of about 291 active combat aircraft.

The Saudi Army operates an additional force of 12 AH-64 attack helicopters, and the Navy has 21 more armed helicopters. These armed naval helicopters include 19 AS-56 helicopters, of which 4 are equipped for the search and rescue mission, and 15 AS-15TT antiship missiles, 6 AS-332B transports, and 6 AS-332Bs equipped with Exocet antiship missiles.[19]

Combat Aircraft

The combat air strengths of the Saudi and other Gulf air forces are shown in Figures 5.23 to 5.27, and Tables 5.6 and 5.7. Saudi Arabia's total inventory of major combat aircraft in 2005 is estimated to include 68–71 F-15Ss, 66 F-15Cs, 18 F-15Ds, 85 Tornado IDSs (10 Tornado GR.1 recce-attack equipped), 22 Tornado ADVs, and 5 E-3 AWACS.

The RASF also has 56 F-5Es, 21 F-5Fs, and 15 F-5Bs that it has been trying to sell for several years. By early 2001, most of its F-5s were grounded and in storage, including 53 F-5Es. The RSAF has 10 RF-5Es and continues to fly these as its main reconnaissance aircraft. The RF-5Es flying out of Taif play a critical role in providing surveillance over the Yemeni border area. Another 15

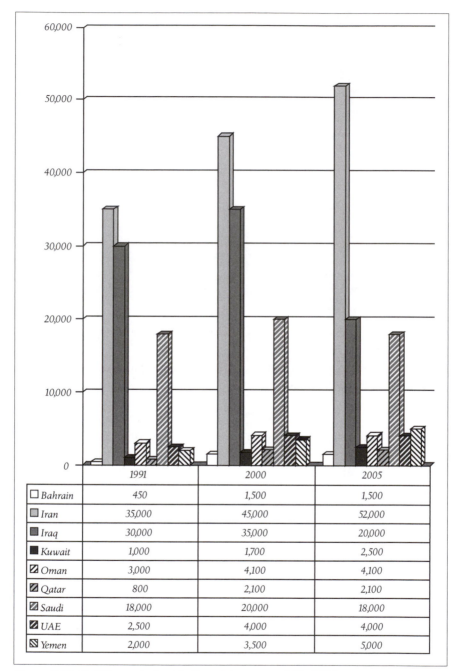

	1991	2000	2005
☐ Bahrain	450	1,500	1,500
☐ Iran	35,000	45,000	52,000
☐ Iraq	30,000	35,000	20,000
■ Kuwait	1,000	1,700	2,500
▨ Oman	3,000	4,100	4,100
▨ Qatar	800	2,100	2,100
▨ Saudi	18,000	20,000	18,000
▨ UAE	2,500	4,000	4,000
▨ Yemen	2,000	3,500	5,000

Figure 5.22: Gulf States Active Air Force Manpower: 1991–2005

Note: The Iraq numbers are those before March 2003.

Source: Adapted by Anthony H. Cordesman from various sources and IISS, *Military Balance,* various editions.

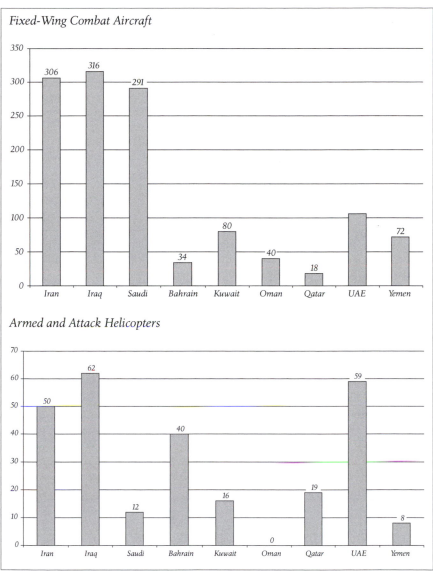

Figure 5.23: Total Gulf Holdings of Combat Aircraft in 2005

Note: Only armed or combat-capable fixed-wing combat aircraft are counted, not other trainers or aircraft. Note: Yemen has an additional 5 MiG-29S/UB on order. Iraq totals are for March 2003, before the Iraq War.

Source: Adapted by Anthony H. Cordesman from IISS, *Military Balance,* various editions.

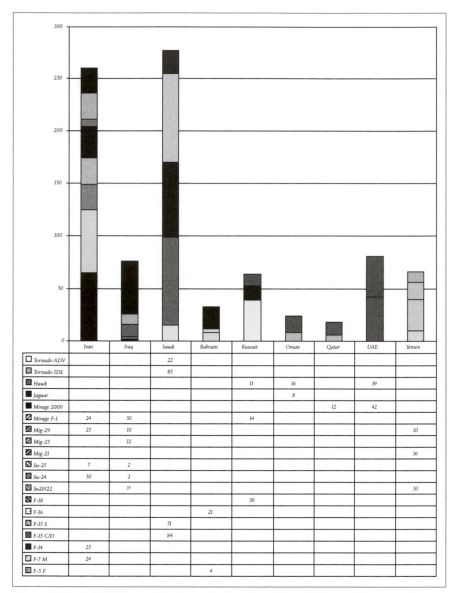

	Iran	Iraq	Saudi	Bahrain	Kuwait	Oman	Qatar	UAE	Yemen
☐ Tornado ADV			22						
☐ Tornado IDS			85						
▦ Hawk					11	16		39	
■ Jaguar						8			
■ Mirage 2000							12	42	
▨ Mirage F-1	24	50			14				
▨ Mig-29	25	10							10
▨ Mig-25		12							
▨ Mig-21									16
◲ Su-25	7	2							
◲ Su-24	30	2							
◲ Su20/22		??							30
◲ F-18					39				
⊡ F-16				21					
▦ F-15 S			71						
▦ F-15 C/D			84						
■ F-14	25								
▣ F-7 M	24								
▦ F-5 F				4					

Figure 5.24: Gulf High- and Medium-Quality Fixed-Wing Fighter, Fighter-Attack, Attack, Strike, and Multirole Combat Aircraft, By Type, in 2005

(Totals do not include combat-capable recce but do include OCUs and Hawk combat-capable trainers)

Note: Yemen has an additional 5 MiG-29S/UB on order. Iraq totals are for March 2003, before the Iraq War.

Source: Adapted by Anthony H. Cordesman from various sources and IISS, *Military Balance*, various editions.

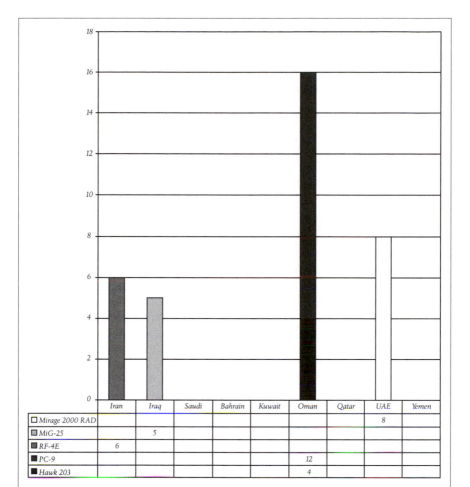

Figure 5.25: Gulf Reconnaissance Aircraft in 2005

Note: Iraq totals are for March 2003, before the Iraq War.

Source: Adapted by Anthony H. Cordesman from IISS, Military Balance, various editions.

F-5Bs still seem to be operational in a combat-capable training unit.[20] In theory, there are still three squadrons, with up to 53 F-5Es, but virtually all of these aircraft were grounded.

There are four fighter-attack squadrons, three with Tornado IDS, and one with 15 F-15Bs. The IDS squadrons had dual-capable trainer aircraft, and 10 had a dual-mission capability in the reconnaissance role, although it is unclear they are actually used in this role. These squadrons were equipped with a wide range of attack munitions, including laser and GPS-guided bombs, and the AS-15, AS-30, AGM-45 Shrike, and AGM-65 Maverick air-to-surface missiles.

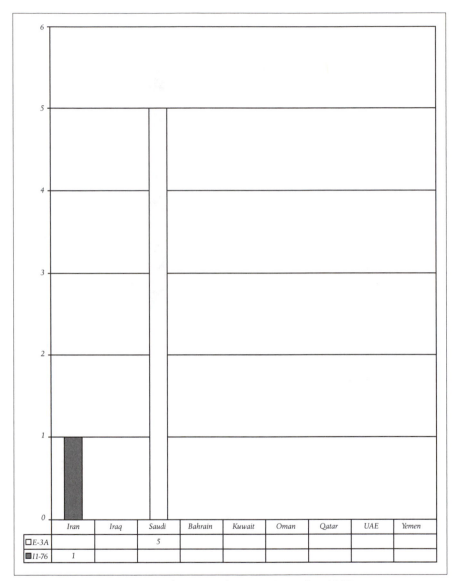

Figure 5.26: Sensor, AWACS, C⁴I, EW, and ELINT Aircraft in 2005

Note: Iraq totals are for March 2003, before the Iraq War.

Source: Adapted by Anthony H. Cordesman from IISS, *Military Balance*, various editions.

There is a large inventory of dumb bombs and cluster munitions, including the Rockeye. The Sea Eagle and Alarm air-to-ground weapons are aging and proved expensive to support. They have been withdrawn from service, and Saudi Arabia is seeking more advanced air-to-surface weapons like the JDAM.

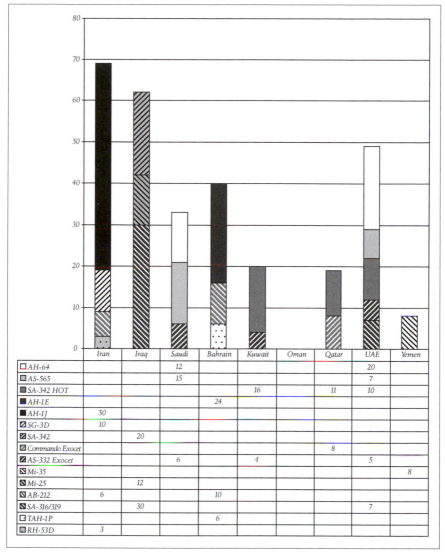

	Iran	Iraq	Saudi	Bahrain	Kuwait	Oman	Qatar	UAE	Yemen
☐ AH-64			12					20	
▣ AS-565			15					7	
▦ SA-342 HOT					16		11	10	
■ AH-1E				24					
■ AH-1J	50								
▨ SG-3D	10								
▨ SA-342		20							
▨ Commando Exocet							8		
▨ AS-332 Exocet			6		4			5	
◣ Mi-35									8
◣ Mi-25		12							
◣ AB-212	6				10				
◣ SA-316/319		30						7	
☐ TAH-1P				6					
▣ RH-53D	3								

Figure 5.27: Gulf Attack, Antiship, and ASW Helicopters in 2005

Note: Iraq totals are for March 2003, before the Iraq War.

Source: Adapted by Anthony H. Cordesman from IISS, *Military Balance*, various editions.

The Tornado IDS squadrons provide much of the potential offensive strength of the Saudi Air Force. The Tornado is used in both low- and medium-altitude attack missions. The Tornado does have superior low-altitude flight performance in attack missions to the F-15S, and the Tornado was specifically designed to fly nap-of-the earth missions, while the F-15S is subject to buffeting because of its large wing area. The RSAF has largely abandoned training in this mission profile, however, and now relies almost exclusively on using the IDS in medium-altitude strike profiles.

Table 5.6: Saudi Air Defense Force: Force Structure

	1991	2000	2005
Manpower	4,000	16,000	16,000
SAM batteries	33	33	33
With 128 I Hawk	16	16	16
With 68 Shahine fire units	17	17	17
With 160 PAC-2 launchers	0	0	2-4
Shahine fire units as static defense	73	73	73
AD guns			
20 mm: 92 M-63 Vulcan	?	?	?
30 mm: 50 AMX-20SA	?	?	?
35 mm: 128	?	?	?
40 mm: L/70	(150)	(150)	(70)
SAM launchers	269	309	1709
Shahine	141	141	141
MIM-23B I Hawk	128	128	128
Crotale	0	40	40
Stinger	0	0	400
Redeye	0	0	500
Mistral	0	0	500

Source: Adapted by Anthony H. Cordesman from various sources and IISS, *Military Balance*, various editions.

Table 5.7: Gulf Land-based Air Defense Systems in 2005

Country	Major SAM	Light SAM	AA guns
Bahrain	8 I Hawk	60 RBS-70 18 Stinger 7 Crotale	15 Oerlikon 35 mm 12 L/70 40 mm
Iran	16/150 I Hawk 3/10 SA-5 45 HQ-2J (SA-2) ? SA-2	SA-7/14/16, HQ-7 HN-5 30 Rapier FM-80 (Ch Crotale) 15 Tigercat SA-7 Stinger (?)	1,700 guns ZU-23, ZSU-23-4, ZSU-57-2, KS-19 ZPU-2/4, M-1939, Type 55
Iraq	SA-2 SA-3 SA-6	Roland 1,500 SA-7 850 (SA-8 (SA-9 (SA-13 (SA-14, SA-16	6,000 guns ZSU-23-4 23 mm, M-1939 37 mm, ZSU-57-2 SP, 57 mm 85 mm, 100 mm, 130 mm

Table 5.7: *Gulf Land-based Air Defense Systems in 2005 (continued)*

Country	Major SAM	Light SAM	AA guns
Kuwait	4/24 I Hawk 4-5/40 Patriot	6/12 Aspede 48 Starburst	6/2X35 mm Oerlikon
Oman	None	Blowpipe 2 Mistral SP 34 SA-7 20 Javelin 40 Rapier	10 GDF 35 mm/Skyguard 4 ZU-23-2 23 mm 12 L-60 40 mm
Qatar	None	10 Blowpipe 12 Stinger 9 Roland 20 SA-7, 24 Mistral	?
Saudi Arabia	16/128 I Hawk 4-6/16-24 Patriot 17/68 Shahine Mobile 2-4/160 PAC-2 launch- ers 17 ANA/FPS-117 radar	40 Crotale 500 Stinger (ARMY) 500 Mistral (ADF) 500 Redeye (ARMY) 500 Redeye (ADF)50 AMX-30SA 30 mm 73-141 Shahine static 500 Stinger (ADF)	92 M-163 Vulcan 20 mm 150 L-70 40 mm (in store)
UAE	5/30 I Hawk Bty.	20+ Blowpipe 20 Mistral 12 Rapier 9 Crotale 13 RBS-70 Javelin Igla (SA-16)	42 M-3VDA 20 mm SP 20 GCF-BM2 30 mm
Yemen	Some SA-2, SA3, SA-6 SA-7, SA-9, SA-13 SA-14	Some SA-7, SA-9, SA13, SA-14 800 SA-7/9/13/14	50 M-167 20 mm 20 M-163 Vulcan 20 mm 100 ZSU-23-4 23 mm 150 M-1939 23 mm 120 S-60 37 mm 40 KS-12 85 mm

Note: Iraq totals are for March 2003, before the Iraq War.
Source: Adapted by Anthony H. Cordesman from IISS, *Military Balance, Periscope,* JCSS, *Middle East Military Balance, Jane's Sentinel,* and *Jane's Defence Weekly.* Some data adjusted or esti-mated by the author.

The F-15S has accordingly become the most important offensive aircraft in the Saudi inventory, although it is also dual capable in the air-to-air role. It has notably more power and lift capability than the F-15C/D and much more modern avionics and flat-panel displays. Saudi pilots feel it is far superior to the IDS in practice in terms of stand-off precision strike capability at medium and high altitudes—mission profiles that now offer more precision and survivability than low-altitude strike profiles. Both the F-15S and IDS aircraft can deliver laser-guided and GPS-guided bombs and can self-illuminate their targets, and the F-15S is again superior in this role. Both aircraft are being steadily improved as the USAF and RAF implement multistage improvement plans (MSIPs).

The RSAF has nine interceptor squadrons for defensive missions. There are five squadrons, with a total of 84 F-15C/Ds (66 F-15Cs and 18 F-15Ds), and more squadrons with 71 F-15Ss. F-15Ds were deployed to each F-15 squadron to perform both training and operational missions. There is one Tornado ADV squadron, with 22 aircraft, which also includes dual-capable trainer aircraft. Saudi pilots feel the ADV is not a successful air-combat design (which has also been the experience of the RAF), and this aircraft was deployed to Khamis Mushayt, which the RSAF feels is an area with a relatively low air-combat threat, when Saudi F-15C/Ds replaced phased out F-5s at Taif and Tabuk.

Saudi fighters are equipped with modern air-to-air missiles, including AIM-9L and AIM-9P infrared-guided missiles, AIM-7F Sparrow, and Sky flash radar-guided missiles. The RSAF is taking delivery on the AMRAAM air-to-air missile, which is giving it substantial beyond visual range (BVR) all-weather air-combat capability.

Saudi F-15 fighter units are capable in the air defense role, but most aircrews now lack adequate advanced-fighter combat training. As has been noted earlier, the training of Saudi aircrews became weak to the point during the mid and late 1990s where it presented serious safety problems in advanced mission profiles and led to a number of fatal accidents. The level of accidents no longer is high relative to force numbers, but is still high in terms of hours flown. Mission training is also slowly becoming more demanding, and more-advanced training efforts are under way at King Khalid and Prince Sultan bases.

Saudi Arabia also needs to examine ways to speed up the tempo of its offensive air operations. It relies largely on the relatively slow-reacting cycle of target-acquisition-sortie allocation-mission execution-battle damage assessment used during the Gulf War. This air traffic order (ATO) system was vastly speeded up in the Iraq War, and both the Afghan and Iraq conflicts have shown the value of near-real-time and in-flight mission tasking and retasking and have on-call strike airpower ready to respond to ground force needs and target illumination. Both Saudi Air Force and Army officers see a shift to near-real-time strike operations as being of major importance.

Dropping the F-5E presented special problems that led Saudi Arabia to obtain U.S. permission to deploy some of its F-15s to Tabuk in western Saudi Arabia in 2003, although it had previously agreed not to do so because of Israeli security concerns. This deployment has little, if any, practical impact on

Israel's security, but it has significantly improved the RSAF's ability to cover Saudi Arabia's western border.

Reconnaissance and Early Warning

Saudi Arabia has been the only Southern Gulf air force with meaningful numbers of reconnaissance aircraft. The RSAF must, however, rely heavily on two aging reconnaissance squadrons, with a total of 10 RF-5Es. These aircraft have reached obsolescence in terms of their sensors and survivability, however, and most are now deadlined or in storage. The RSAF is seeking to replace them by adding advanced reconnaissance packages to its F-15s, including reconnaissance and electronic warfare pods. The 10 Tornado IDS-Rs in the fighter-ground attack force can perform some missions, but their current role and capability is unclear.

The RSAF has an airborne early-warning squadron, with four E-3As and one E-3B communications intelligence (COMINT) aircraft. These aircraft now have Saudi crews, but the crews are still acquiring all of the training and mission capability necessary to manage complex air battles, and the RSAF must rely on the USAF for help in such missions. The Saudi E-3As need better secure communications and data links, although this may come along with the upgrading of their software and improved electronic support measures.

The Saudis have improved the connectivity of their E-3As with the air defense command center as well as with the Saudi Navy. During the Gulf War in 1991, these connectivity problems forced the Saudi Navy to rely on USAF E-3As. The departure of the United States from the command center at Prince Sultan Air Force Base after the Iraq War did, however, leave the RSAF without a truly advanced air-command center and overall C⁴I battle management center and system, and one that allows it to shift effectively from preplanned to near-real-time mission planning. Acquiring such a capability is a high priority for the RSAF for both the air defense and offensive missions.

As has been mentioned earlier, the Kingdom is discussing the purchase of 14 AEW&C planes. One key candidate is based on Sweden's Saab 2000 and equipped with the Erieye radar and sensor suite by Ericsson Microwave Systems.

Saudi Arabia has MQM-74C Chukar II and Banshee remotely piloted vehicles for training, reconnaissance, and target acquisition. It does not have modern unmanned aerial vehicles (UAVs) or use its drones in this role.

Training Aircraft

The remaining multipurpose squadron, with 14 F-5Bs, has both training and combat missions, but it has had little real operational capability in combat.

The RSAF has roughly 25 armed Hawk Mark 65 jet trainers and 20 armed Hawk Mark 65A jet trainers. Saudi holdings of 36 BAC-167 turboprop COIN and training aircraft were phased out of service in the late 1990s. The Hawk units are technically capable of performing COIN and light attack functions with machine guns, cannons, and rockets, in addition to training missions, but the limited combat mission training of the Hawk aircrews prevents the RSAF from using them in that role.

The RSAF also has 13 Cessna 172s, 1 Jetstream, and 50 PC-9 aircraft in training units that were not armed for combat. The RSAF have purchased Super Mushshaq from Pakistan, and IISS estimates that the RSAF has received the first 20.

Refueling, Transport, and Support

The RSAF is the only Gulf air force with an effective mid-air refueling capability. Its support units include a tanker squadron, with 8 KE-3A tanker/transports and 8 KC-130H tankers. Along with the extremely high mission support capacity of Saudi air bases, tanker refueling capability is critical to the RSAF's ability to rapidly deploy its forces from one end of the Kingdom to another and mass airpower from different bases over the same area of operations. Tanker upgrades and modernization are a high priority for the RSAF.

The Air Force has three transport squadrons, with 38 C-130 cargo transports (7 E, 29 H, and 2 H-30), 1 KE-3B (EW), 3 L-100-30HS hospital aircraft, and 4 CN-235s. The C-130 is the workhorse of the RSAF and is of increasing value in providing mobility for light forces to fight terrorism. Upgrading the C-130 fleet is a high priority.

There are also two helicopter squadrons, with 22 AB-205s, 13 AB-206s, 17 AB-212s, 40 AB-41EPs (SAR), and 10 AS-5323A2s (SAR). Three AS-532A2 Cougar search and rescue helicopters were ordered from France in September 1996 at a cost of $590 million.[21] The Royal Flight provided substantial additional airlift assets, including two B-747SPs, one B-737-200, four BAE 125-800s, two Gulfstream IIIs, two Learjet 35s, four VC-130Hs, and five utility helicopters.

Munitions and Spares

Saudi Arabia has moderate but aging inventories of air munitions and spares—a marked decline from the large inventories of cutting-edge munitions and high inventories it had at the time of the Gulf War. The Kingdom has not continued to properly maintain and modernize its munitions inventory, however, and has not procured all of the air-to-ground and antiship ordnance necessary for joint warfare.

Support, Training, Logistics, and Sustainment

Saudi Air Force facilities remain excellent. No U.S. or NATO base has sheltering or hardening equal to the Saudi bases at Dhahran and Khamis Mushayt, and similar facilities are being built at all of Saudi Arabia's main operating bases. Saudi bases also have significant modern maintenance and service facilities, including advanced F-15 services facilities at Khamis Mushayt.

As has been noted earlier, however, maintenance and sustainment still present problems. Up until the mid-1990s, the Saudi Air Force had excellent foreign support. The Kingdom did, however, face growing financing and payment problems after the mid-1990s, and these problems worsened after the "oil crash" of late 1997. This created a climate where readiness and sustainment were not properly funded.

Efforts to force the rate of Saudization in contractor maintenance and support without adequate resources and standards have not helped. Foreign contractors have often been replaced with Saudis selected more for their contacts than for their skills, and training programs for Saudis have not enforced the proper qualification standards.

Some U.S. experts and Saudis blame the main maintenance contractor for these problems, but several Saudi unit commanders feel the problem has been the funding and flow of spare parts and equipment orders. They note that the flow of parts and equipment has become much slower since 9/11, that it is much harder to maintain readiness with long lead times for orders, that reexport of serviced equipment experiences serious delays, and that the United States and U.S. manufacturers refuse to license key service and maintenance activities.

The RSAF has failed to make adequate use of its offset programs. These have some important successes, but they have not developed the level of maintenance, major repair, and other capabilities the RASF needs to support sustained operations and maintain readiness.

Overall Capabilities

Training and readiness are the most serious problems the RSAF faces at several different levels. As has been discussed earlier, Saudi flight hours per aircrew have improved strikingly over the last few years from an average monthly low of only 6 hours to 12–14, but these still need to be raised, and the realism of the training missions flown remains a problem.

Above all, the RSAF must move forward to ensure that all of the pilots it trains, retains, and promotes actually fly suitable numbers of hours. Moreover, flight hours must be spent in truly demanding training profiles for the use of precision weapons in interdiction and close-support missions as well as in integrated air defense training using large numbers of fighters, its E-3As, and Air Defense Forces in demanding "aggressor" exercises.

The RSAF and other Saudi services, especially the Air Defense Force and Navy, also need a modern C⁴I/battle management system to replace the one the United States withdrew from Prince Sultan Air Force Base south of Riyadh after the Iraq War. No U.S. facilities remain other than the office furniture, and Saudi Arabia badly needs an advanced system to replace it that is both tailored to Saudi needs and interoperable with the relocated U.S. capabilities now located in Qatar. This is also a key modernization priority for the GCC, but there seems to be little chance the GCC can agree on an effective system and a very good chance it could waste more money on efforts of little more than symbolic value for actual war fighting.

The Gulf War, Kosovo conflict, and Iraq War all demonstrate that integrated, joint air operations can be decisive, but are extraordinarily difficult to conduct. They require extensive preconflict training between all elements of the armed forces, and particularly in air-land battle exercises. These wars also show that meaningful air training must be conducted primarily on a task force basis and must integrate all elements of targeting, strike planning, damage assessment, and "jointness" with the land forces.

Put differently, the RSAF must ask itself why the Iraqi Air Force collapsed after a few days in 1991 and failed to fight in 2003. It must ask why the Syrian Air Force has become something of a military joke, and why Israel has acquired such an "edge." The answer is that effective C⁴I/BM and IS&R integration of the air force is the key to modern air warfare. Without it, military spending can only produce a third-rate or ineffective force.

Once again, the destruction of the Iraqi threat and slow pace of Iranian modernization give Saudi Arabia a window of opportunity in which it can concentrate on effectiveness rather than modernization and force building. The Saudi Air Force's most important challenges are the improvement of its readiness, training, and capability for joint operations. Iraq's defeat has greatly reduced the potential threat, as has the slow rate of Iranian air modernization. As a result, Saudi Arabia has no immediate need for replacement of its F-5Es or for any other major procurement. It can consolidate around its most advanced aircraft, creating a smaller and more effective force.

Saudi Land-Based Air Defenses

Saudi Arabia has extensive land-based air defenses, some under a separate Air Defense Force and some integrated into other services. The recent trends in the strength, organization, equipment holdings, and modernization of this force are shown in Table 5.6. The comparative strength of the Saudi Air Defense Force and other Gulf land-based air defenses is shown in Table 5.7.

The Air Defense Force

The Saudi Air Defense Force (ADF) had a nominal strength of 16,000 men in 2005 and some 33 surface-to-air missile batteries. Some reports indicated its total major surface-to-air missile strength included 16 Improved Hawk batteries, with 128 fixed and mobile fire units; 9 Crotale batteries, with 48 Crotale fire units (currently being modernized); 16 air defense batteries, with 72 Shahine fire units; and 50 AMX-30SA 30 mm self-propelled guns.

The IISS reported a strength 16 Improved Hawk batteries, with 128 fire units; 17 air defense batteries, with 68 Shahine fire units and AMX-30SA 30 mm self-propelled guns; and 73 Crotale and Shahine fire units in static positions, 2–4 with 160 PAC-2 launchers. It also reported a total inventory of 50 AMX-30SAs, 141 Shahine launchers, and 40 Crotale launchers. It also reported 92 M-163 20 mm Vulcan antiaircraft guns and 50 AMX-30SA antiaircraft guns, plus 70 L/70 40 mm antiaircraft guns in storage. The Saudi ADF has also added 400 Stingers, 500 Redeyes, and 500 Mistrals to its arsenal. The ADF force structure development, since the Gulf War, can be seen in more details in figure 5.33.

Most of Saudi Arabia's Shahine units were deployed in fixed locations for the defense of air bases and key targets. All of the Shahine systems have been upgraded as the result of an agreement with France signed in 1991. These units provide short-range defense capability for virtually all of Saudi Arabia's major cities, ports, oil facilities, and military bases.

The Patriot and the IHawk

While the IHawk still plays a major role in Saudi air defense, it is an aging system, and the Patriot has become Saudi Arabia's main land-based air defense system. Saudi Arabia now has five major operational MIM-104 Patriot fire units; the fifth unit was brought on line in 2004. A sixth unit has been procured and is in storage while suitable manpower is trained. The United States deployed an additional Patriot battalion near Riyadh in 2001 but withdrew it after Iraq ceased to be a threat in 2003.

The Patriot was bought after the Gulf War, but it has taken some years to come on line. Live fire exercises began to take place in the fall of 2000, and mobile operations took some years to develop. The first mobile deployment approaching a combat exercise was a road march from Dhahran to a site near King Khalid Military City in the fall of 2000.

Both Patriot and IHAWK defenses are concentrated along the Gulf coast, with some point defense of major cities and Red Sea ports and facilities. Saudi

Arabia has continued to buy MSIP improvement programs for both the Patriot and IHawk, but a number of experts feel the IHawk is beginning to move toward obsolescence. Efforts to integrate the air defense command and the control and information technology system for the Patriot and IHawk have not been successful, and some experts feel such contracts are an expensive waste. The option of modifying the C⁴I/battle management systems to integrate the Patriot and Shahine seems to be under study, but there is no way to evaluate its practicality with the data available.

Saudi officers indicate that the Air Defense Force plans to buy the PAC-3 variant of the Patriot. This provides a major upgrade of its ballistic and cruise missile defense capabilities and heightens its ability to deal with the emerging threat from UAVs and unmanned combat aerial vehicles (UCAVs). The PAC-3 does have area coverage limitations, however, which makes it usable only as a point defense system against long-range ballistic missiles with very high closing velocities like the Iranian Shahab.

Other Land-based Air Defenses

Total Saudi Army holdings of man-portable surface-to-air missiles, as estimated by IISS, include 500 Mistrals, 400 Stingers, and 500 Redeyes. U.S. experts indicate that the Stingers and Redeyes are no longer in active service.

The number and type of antiaircraft guns currently operational is uncertain. Some reports state that Saudi Arabia has 35 35 mm Oerlikon-Contraves twin AA guns, with Skyguard fire control systems; 72 40 mm L-70 AA guns; 53 30 mm AMX-30 DCA twin antiaircraft guns; and an unknown number of 20 mm Vulcan M163 guns. Other reports indicate it had had 92 M-163 Vulcan 20 mm antiaircraft guns; 30 V-150s, with Vulcan 20 mm guns; 30 towed 20 mm Vulcans; 128 35 mm AA guns; and 150 L/70 40 mm guns (most in storage).

Overall Capabilities

The end of the threat from Saddam Hussein, and the slow modernization of the Iranian Air Force, greatly ease the potential air defense burden on both the Saudi Air Force and Army. The Air Defense Force's Patriot units have improved Saudi Arabia's low- to high-level air defense capability along its Gulf coast, while providing some defense against medium-range and theater ballistic missiles.

The Saudi Air Defense Force has also made important progress in developing an air defense doctrine and plan developed to Saudi needs and in learning how to use Saudi Arabia's radar net and existing C⁴I system more effectively. It now has a limited capability to develop and modify its air defense software and has its own programming and support center. It has a modified Mark IV identification of friend or foe (IFF) that also offers Saudi Air Force and Air Defense Force considerable security against electronic warfare.

At the same time, the Saudi Air Defense force needs to improve its capability for joint operations with the Saudi Air Force and Army. The fact that active U.S. air forces and army forces have left Saudi Arabia requires that Saudi Arabia develop far more effective Air Defense Force and Air Force capabilities and C⁴I and IS&R assets to net all of their air defense assets and use them more effectively. Both air defense and air-land battle training should be joint as a rule, not an exception and should be based on more demanding standards in peacetime than war. Joint commands and operations centers should be the major focus of all command activity.

Growing questions also exist regarding Saudi Arabia's mix of short-range air defenses (SHORADS) and how to integrate them into a common concept of joint operations. The Afghan and Iraq wars both illustrated how effective an advanced air force can be in launching medium range laser- and GPS-guided bombs from altitudes over 16,000 feet and outside the range of most SHORADS. At the same time, fixed- and rotary-wing attack aircraft operated at much more intense tempos and closer to ground forces.

Potential regional threats like Iran and Yemen currently lack both the sophistication and equipment to operate effectively outside the range of most Saudi SHORADS and the target acquisition and command and control systems necessary to locate Saudi SHORADS dynamically in combat. This may, however, change in the future. Saudi fixed- and rotary-wing attack aircraft already need to be able to operate in close support with ground forces and defended facilities covered by SHORADS as well as Patriots and IHawks.

SAUDI MISSILE FORCES AND THE POSSIBILITY OF SAUDI WEAPONS OF MASS DESTRUCTION

The Saudi interest in weapons of mass destruction has been the subject of far more rumor than fact. For example, many reports of Saudi nuclear activities from various Saudi opposition groups have never been confirmed, and many of their reports of visits of senior Saudi officials to Pakistan and other potential nuclear suppliers have either not occurred in the way reported or have not occurred at all.

Some relevant visits and discussions do, however, seem to have taken place with China and Pakistan. The Saudi chief of staff, Lt. Gen. Saleh Mohaya, and Prince Khalid Bin Sultan also seem to have begun discussing replacement of the CSS-2 with China in 1995.[22] Similarly, in 1999, after Pakistan's nuclear tests, Prince Sultan and other Saudi military officials toured Pakistan's nuclear weapons facilities. There was no firm evidence, however, that they ever considered buying any form of "Islamic bomb."

While there have been reports of a much more extensive Saudi nuclear program, the "evidence" advanced to date has been tenuous at best, and the charges involved seem to be more political in character and directed at trying to break up the U.S.-Saudi military relationship than inspired by any facts or actual knowledge.

The most disturbing aspect of Saudi talks with Pakistan has had nothing to do with the Kingdom but has resulted from the fact that some estimates indicate Pakistan's production of fissile material will begin to exceed its domestic military requirements at some point around 2005–2006. Similarly, there is no convincing data available on whether Saudi Arabia has had any discussions with China about the possible purchase of weapons of mass destruction or replacing its aging CSS-2s—which are now operated under the supervision of the Saudi Air Defense Force.

Saudi Arabia has never had any illusions about the problems Saudi proliferation would create in terms of its relations with the United States or the extent to which they would suddenly make the Kingdom a key target for Israel's nuclear forces. Saudi Arabia, however, has continued to study such options along with missile defense. Ironically, it also now faces a growing risk from Iran at a time that the potential threat from Saddam Hussein's Iraq has disappeared.

Saudi Arabia cannot possibly develop and build its own weapons of mass destruction for the foreseeable future. If it did try to obtain such weapons, its options would be to acquire a nuclear weapon from nations like China or Pakistan. Buying weapons from either country would create a host of political difficulties, even if they consented. One "wild card" option has been the idea of buying Pakistani nuclear weapons that could be rapidly deployed on Saudi missiles. This would not be an overt violation of the Nuclear Non-Proliferation Treaty.[23] However, Saudi Arabia cannot count on Pakistan. The government is not stable; recent revelations about Pakistani involvement in the Iranian program raise additional questions; and Pakistan might well not risk the tensions with the United States that would arise if such an arrangement became public.

In making its choices, Saudi Arabia has two important additional options. One is to buy missile defenses. The other is to seek some form of "extended deterrence" from the United States against any threat by Iran. These options could be combined, and such "extended deterrence" could be part of a broader, Gulf-wide, U.S. security guarantee. They would not necessarily require a new, formal agreement with the United States.

Modernizing the CSS-2

The Kingdom does, however, have to make hard choices at some point in the future about the future of its CSS-2 missiles, and the U.S. State Department published a report in August 2002 stating that Saudi Arabia held "discussions" with Pakistan regarding nuclear cooperation.[24] Some high-level visits did take place by Saudi leaders to Pakistan and China in 1999 and 2000, and the Chinese premier, Jiang Zemin, visited the Kingdom in 2000. Some have speculated that the Chinese approached the Kingdom with offers to modernize their CSS-2 that was purchased in 1988.[25]

Saudi Arabia claimed that it bought the CSS-2 to "propagate peace," but it actually bought them for a number of other reasons.[26] Its efforts to buy arms from the United States had reached a low point when the purchase was made, and Saudi Arabia felt the purchase would be a major demonstration of its independence. Equally, Saudi Arabia felt threatened by Iran's and Iraq's possession of long-range surface-to-surface missiles. Also, Yemen then had the SS-21, and Saudi Arabia did not. Saudi Arabia was particularly interested in acquiring systems that could hit Tehran, while being deployed outside the range of Iranian surface-to-surface missiles.[27]

However, Saudi Arabia's present CSS-2 missiles are not a meaningful response to the Iranian CBRN threat, and they have only token war-fighting capability. The CSS-2 has limitations that led Saudi Arabia to examine possible replacements beginning in the mid-1990s. It is an obsolete missile that was first designed in 1971. While an improved version has been deployed, most experts still estimate the missile has a CEP of nearly two to four kilometers and lacks the accuracy to hit anything other than large-area targets like cities or industrial facilities. Even with the improved warhead, each missile would still only have the effective lethality of a single 2,000-pound bomb. It requires large amounts of technical support and ground equipment and takes hours to make ready for firing.[28]

It is also far from clear that the CSS-2 missile can be properly calibrated for targeting purposes and be kept truly operational, without more frequent test firings and without test firings conducted at long ranges along the axis it would have to be fired in an actual strike. Saudi Arabia has never conducted a meaningful operational test of the CSS-8 and is incapable of conducting the tests necessary to refine the missile's targeting using the derived aim-point method.[29]

The CSS-2 missiles are extremely large 70-ton systems and have a special, large conventional warhead. Still, they are semimobile, and one-third are supposed to be kept armed and near-launch-ready on transporters, one-third are kept half fueled, and one-third are normally empty and being serviced. Saudi sources indicate that actual readiness rates are normally far lower.

The missiles are deployed in two battalions. One is located at the As-Sulayyil Oasis, roughly 475 kilometers south to southwest of Riyadh. As-Sulayyil will also be the site of one of Saudi Arabia's new air bases for its Tornado fighter-bombers. A second battalion is located at Al Juaifer near the Al Kharj Air Base south of Riyadh. A further training facility that may have a launch capability, seems to exist in southwestern Saudi Arabia at Al Liddam.[30]

Commercial satellite photos of the site at As-Sulayyil show a very large headquarter and transportation complex, with 60 buildings or tents; a transportation center; a command and control complex with roughly 40 buildings and tents; a secure area; a construction area; a bunker, which may be a fixed launcher site; other launch areas with bunkers for missile storage; an additional launch area, and three 150 meter-long white buildings that may be missile assembly facilities.[31] Saudi Arabia has only a limited technological base to support such programs, although it has begun to experiment with short-range artillery systems.

It is unclear whether the Saudi Air Defense Force can maintain or fire its CSS-2 missiles without Chinese technical support, and Chinese technicians are operating the missiles under Saudi supervision. Ballast Nedam, a subsidiary of British Aerospace, has recently extended the runway at the As-Sulayyil Air Base to 3,000 meters. There are some signs that Saudi Arabia may be deploying surface-to-air missiles to defend the facility.[32]

None of the Saudi missiles are now known to be armed with weapons of mass destruction. Saudi Arabia is a signatory of the Non-Proliferation Treaty, and Saudi Arabia and the PRC have provided U.S. officials with assurances that the missiles will remain conventional. The Saudi government has issued a written statement that "nuclear and chemical warheads would not be obtained or used with the missiles." U.S. experts believe that Saudi Arabia has largely kept its word, although the Saudis have refused a U.S. request to inspect the missile sites in Saudi Arabia, and Saudi Arabia's visits to nations like China and Pakistan do raise questions about their future intention.[33]

There are good reasons to question the military value of such missiles as long as they are only equipped with conventional warheads.[34] The CSS-2s deployed in the PRC are all nuclear-armed missiles. Each can carry one to three megaton warheads. They have a maximum range of about 2,200 miles (3,500 kilometers), an inertial guidance system, and a single-stage, refrigerated liquid-fuel rocket motor. The version of the CSS-2 that the PRC has sold to Saudi Arabia is very different. It is heavily modified and has a special large conventional warhead, which weighs up to 3,500 to 4,000 pounds. This added warhead weight cuts the maximum range of the missile to anywhere from 1,550 nautical miles (2,400 kilometers) to 1,950 nautical miles (3,100 kilometers).

A conventional warhead of this size is more effective than the warhead on a Scud, but it is hardly a weapon of mass destruction, or even an effective conventional weapon. Assuming an optimal ratio of high explosives to total weight, the warhead of the CSS-2 could destroy buildings out to a radius of 200–250 feet, seriously damage buildings out to a radius of 300–350 feet, and kill or injure people with projectiles to distances of up to 1,000 feet.[35] This is the damage equivalent of three to four 2,000-pound bombs, or about the same destructive power as a single sortie by a modern strike fighter.

The CSS-2s have aged to the point where they need to be replaced, and the need to find a new system is becoming steadily more pressing. Saudi Arabia does not, however, have any good short-term options for acquiring its own missile capabilities. Saudi Arabia has no capability to produce its own long-range ballistic missiles or weapons of mass destruction. The most it has done is develop an unguided rocket. In July 1997, Saudi Arabia test fired its first domestically produced surface-to-surface artillery rocket or missile at the Al Kharj complex. Defense Minister Prince Sultan stated that the missile has a range of between 35 and 62 kilometers.[36]

Pakistan's missile programs are still in development, as are those of North Korea. As a result, the Kingdom has three major choices in dealing with the CSS-2: (1) to establish a program with China to extend the life of the CSS-2, (2) to get a new MRBM, preferably a solid-fuel system like the CSS-5, which would eliminate all of the problems in using liquid fuels and the need for Chinese operators, and (3) to use Pakistan as a source of other missiles. Yet, China cannot make new sales of long-range missiles without openly violating its agreements relating to the Missile Technology Control Regime (MTCR), and Russia and the other Former Soviet Union states are bound by both the MTCR and the limits of the IRBM Treaty.

The Saudi holdings of the CSS-2 thus raise serious issues on several grounds:

- A costly weapons system is deployed in small numbers with relatively low lethality.

- As now configured, the missile system may do more to provoke attack or escalation than to deter attack or provide retaliatory capability. This point became clear to the Saudis during the Gulf War. King Fahd rejected advice to retaliate against Iraqi strikes, because he felt that strikes that simply killed civilians would have a provocative, rather than a deterrent effect;

• Conversely, Saudi acquisition of chemical or nuclear warheads would radically improve the value of the system as a deterrent or retaliatory weapon.

What Comes Next? Missiles, Missile Defenses, Civil Defense, Counterproliferation, Counterterrorism, and Deterrence

At best, the CSS-2 now acts as a low-level deterrent and a symbol of Saudi Arabia's willingness to retaliate against Iranian strikes. At worst, the missiles are a potential excuse for Iranian missile strikes, and their use could trigger a process of retaliation against which Saudi Arabia would have little real defense capability. Israel, which initially showed concern about the system, no longer seems to perceive Iran as a direct threat. Israel has the capability to launch air strikes against the Saudi missile sites, but it is unlikely to consider preemptive strikes unless radical changes take place in Saudi Arabia's political posture or regime.

The CSS-2 does, however, symbolize the risk that Saudi Arabia will buy a more capable missile and seek weapons of mass destruction. While nations like India, Iran, Israel, Pakistan, and Syria are the major proliferators in the region, Saudi possession of the CSS-2 does give other countries an added incentive and excuse to join the missile arms race, acquire weapons of mass destruction, or preempt in a conflict.

At some point, Saudi Arabia has to make hard choices as to whether it should invest in a symbolic and ineffective deterrent, buy new missiles armed with weapons of mass destruction, trust in extended deterrence by the United States, and/or invest in areas like theater missile defense, civil defense, and counterterrorism.

A few Saudi analysts outside government do advocate buying modern missiles and arming them with chemical, biological, or nuclear weapons. They believe that buying long-range missiles without such weapons has little purpose. It is unclear, however, that such thinkers as yet have any broad support or that Saudi Arabia really does have better options to acquire weapons of mass destruction than it does to buy missiles. It does not have the industrial base to produce biological and nuclear weapons or to compete in producing chemical weapons. It is very difficult to purchase "turn key" production capabilities and/or finished weapons abroad, and such purchases might well cut off Saudi Arabia from United States and other Western supplies of conventional arms.

Any missile purchase or development of weapons of mass destruction could also make Saudi Arabia a target for Israel. Even if Saudi Arabia could find ways to join Iran and Israel in proliferating, it is not clear whether it would reduce its vulnerability or simply raise the threshold of any attack on the Kingdom. Mere possession of weapons of mass destruction may be adequate for the purposes of prestige in peacetime, but they must be carefully structured to avoid encouraging preemption and escalation in wartime and accelerating the efforts of neighboring states to acquire even more chemical, biological, and nuclear arms.

It is also unclear how much Saudi Arabia is concerned with Iran emerging as a nuclear power. Although Saudi Arabia has long expressed its concerns over regional proliferation, it has never publicly expressed the kind of concern over Iran's efforts to arm itself that the United States has. In an interview with *Al-Sharq al-Awsat*[37], Crown Prince Abdullah defended Iran's right to arm itself, as well as the right of others to do so: "Iran has every right to develop its defense capabilities for its security without harming or damaging the rights of others. We also do the same. All countries follow the same policy." He also expressed concern about Israeli armament and weapons programs. Although Saudi views differ from those held by Washington, Saudi Arabia is not likely to enter any arrangements or relations with Iran that would compromise their defense links with the United States and the West.[38]

At the same time, Saudi Arabia can scarcely privately ignore such a major shift in the balance of power in the Gulf in its strategic planning, and measures like buying improved theater missile defense, civil defense, and counterterrorism may well not be enough to deal with the creeping proliferation in Iran.

The United States has agreed to share missile early-warning data with Saudi Arabia and other friendly Arab states, but it is unclear what this warning is worth. The U.S. Patriot missiles deployed in Saudi Arabia have only limited missile-intercept capability against advanced Scud missiles. While the Patriot 3 should provide more effective defense against such missiles—when and if the Patriot 3 becomes available—it has only limited effectiveness against more-advanced missiles with higher closure speeds. Iran is already testing such missiles, and Iraq is almost certain to develop them if it can break out of sanctions.

Developmental antitheather ballistic missile (ATBM) U.S. systems like the Navy Standard and the U.S. Army ATBM systems are designed to provide such defense capabilities—as are additional boost-phase intercept weapons—but these programs are lagging and deeply troubled. The United States currently has no ability to tell Saudi Arabia when it will be able to sell such weapons, and what their cost, effectiveness, and delivery dates will be.

Furthermore, U.S. efforts like the agreement to provide early warning of enemy missile launchers and discussing the potential sale of theater missile defense systems, offer little mid- to long-term security. Warning at best can have limited benefits in improving civil defense if it is not backed by active missile and air defense or retaliation in kind. The United States will not possess wide-area theater missile defenses until well after 2010, and their future cost, effectiveness, and delivery schedule is unclear. At least, at present, a determined proliferator is likely to acquire major offensive capabilities that outstrip any near-term options for defense.

As a result, Saudi Arabia may begin to believe that it needs a stronger form of deterrence, as do the other Southern Gulf states. If so, the main options for Saudi Arabia would likely be to create a major long-range strike capability that combines the assets of the Saudi Air Force with modern strike systems like cruise missiles—systems Saudi Arabia might arm with either conventional warheads or some imported weapon of mass destruction—and Saudi de facto or formal reliance on U.S. extended deterrence and counterproliferation capabilities.

These issues are not urgent as long as Iran's proliferation remains a possibility and not a reality. There scarcely, however, is any guarantee that these conditions will hold true long after the year 2005. Dealing with these issues may be one of Saudi Arabia's most difficult challenges in the years to come.

NBC Defense Capabilities

At a very different level, Saudi Arabia also faces the potential threat of nuclear, chemical, and/or biological (NBC) attacks at a number of different levels. Attacks could come in direct or covert form from a power like Iran, or from terrorist movements. They could range from tiny attacks designed largely to produce media impact and temporary panic to the actual use of nuclear weapons.

Saudi Arabia developed a civil defense force during the Iran-Iraq War and expanded it during the Gulf War. It now, however, is beginning to think how it must provide NBC protection for its military and security forces, and some kind of detection, defense, and response capability against terrorism and overt or covert attack. As is the case in most countries, these are issues that Saudi Arabia is only beginning to address.

Chapter 6

The Saudi Paramilitary and Internal Security Apparatus

A l Qaeda is scarcely the first internal threat that Saudi Arabia has faced. The Saudi monarchy has had to deal with a long series of internal challenges from Islamic extremists since the time of the Ikhwan in the 1920s, as well as from secular movements supported by other Arab states. These struggles were particularly serious during the peak of Nasserism and Pan Arabism in the 1950s and the first major Islamic backlash from oil wealth and modernization in the late 1970s.

These internal security challenges decreased during the 1980–90 period (following the Grand Mosque takeover in 1979 until the Gulf War in 1990), largely because of the Kingdom's oil wealth, rapid growth, and a focus on internal development.

As discussed in Chapter 2, however, they became a resurgent problem after the Gulf War because of the rise of new extremist movements hostile to any U.S. or other Western military presence on Saudi soil. After the mid-1990s, the Saudi government increasingly came under direct and indirect attacks by such Islamic extremist groups. As a result, it slowly strengthened its internal security and counterterrorist programs. It also cooperated with the United States in a number of investigations, including Al Khobar Towers bombing, the attack on the Saudi National Guard Headquarters, and the attack on the USS *Cole*.

Saudi Internal Security before 9/11

The Saudi reaction to Islamic extremist or "deviant" threats was relatively limited until the events of 9/11. The senior leadership quietly put pressure on the ulema. It arrested a wide range of extremists and publicly condemned terrorism. It exploited the fact that the Saudi clergy is funded by the government and there are no Madrassas in the Kingdom that provide religious education separate from the state educational system.

The Saudi Ministry of Islamic Affairs (MOIA) was first organized for the purpose of religious administration, but it has always had an internal security element as well. It has been used to provide both carrots and sticks for internal security purposes. In fact, MOIA was created after the Gulf War, when it became apparent that many hard-line Islamists opposed any Western presence on Saudi soil, and was slowly stepped up in the 1990s when Islamic extremists became more active.

The Ministry of Interior and the General Intelligence Presidency took steps to strengthen their counterterrorist and security operations. They arrested extremists within the Kingdom and continued to monitor the activities of out-side-based opposition and pressure foreign governments. After Osama bin Laden emerged as an open opponent of the monarchy in the mid-1990s, Saudi intelligence stepped up its fight against these extremists. The security services increased their monitoring of the activities of hard-line Saudi opposition groups overseas that attacked the government, exploiting divisions in their ranks, co-opting or bribing elements within them, and putting pressure on foreign governments to end their activities.

Failures to See the Problems before 9/11

Saudi security did not focus on al Qaeda and bin Laden alone. It dealt with two main groups that threatened the internal security in the Kingdom. First, Sunni extremists led by al Qaeda and other affiliated groups such as the Egyptian Islamic Jihad and what is left of the Muslim Brotherhood. Second, it dealt with Shiite groups, supported by Iran, that were angry at the perceived mistreatment of their fellow Shiites in the Eastern Province but that also resented that the Mecca and Medina holy places are under Sunni control.

Saudi society and authorities underestimated the extent to which such groups were growing and how lethal they were becoming. Looking back, there were several failures:

- *First, during the 1960s and the 1970s, members of the Muslim Brotherhood were driven out of mainly Egypt, Syria, and some Palestinian Areas. They found a sanctuary in the Kingdom as preachers and teachers.* This had great influence on the next generation of Imams, teachers, and, eventually, their students. The majority of teachers in Saudi Arabia were non-Saudis until very recently; in fact, they were mainly Egyptians or Syrians. They used their positions to spread their ideology, and a lot of what we see now can be traced back to them. Prince Nayef iterated this point in an interview with the Kuwaiti newspaper *Al-Siyasa* on November 29, 2002. He argued that the Muslim Brotherhood is the cause of most problems in the Arab world, and that they have "done great damage to Saudi Arabia."[1] In addition, the Saudi society was young. It lacked any established institutions like Al-Azhar in Egypt to withstand and counter the influences of such ideologies.

- *Second, fund transfers were not well regulated.* People were free to raise money for different causes, and spend it as they wished—and sometimes such causes were that of the extremists. People sympathetic to different organizations raised money directly from wealthy Saudis, or legitimate charities for genuine causes were used to finance groups that, in fact, threatened the existence of the Saudi state. This was a difficult issue to deal with because: (1) It is impossible to monitor every cash transaction, and most transactions in the region are still done by cash. In addition, there is no income tax in the Kingdom, which makes it hard to monitor what people do with their money. (2) Able Muslims are obligated to give, *Zakat*, 2.5 percent of their annual income and 5–10 percent of their land to the needy.

  Companies are obligated to pay their *Zakat* to the Ministry of Islamic Affairs, but individuals pay it directly to the needy. Given the religious nature of such action, it is usually done discreetly; hence, it is difficult to know to whom people give money, and even more difficult to question people's "noble motivations." (3) Causes such as that of the Palestinians and the Chechens are seen by Saudis as legitimate struggles against an occupying power, and the Saudi authorities cannot be seen as trying to prevent donation to such causes. (4) Many Saudi citizens have a lot of money in foreign banks; hence, not under the jurisdictions of the government. In addition, other neighboring countries, such as the UAE, have less strict banking rules than the Kingdom and often are used by people to make large cash transfers.

  The lack of a Saudi income tax; Saudi Arabia's highly patriarchal, tribal, and clan-oriented society and the resultant dependency on personal patronage and charity make Saudi Arabia a nation that places a heavy reliance on voluntary Islamic charity. As a result, large amounts of money flowed out of the Kingdom from the senior leadership and wealthy businessmen to groups and causes that would never have received the money if those asking for it had received even cursory review of what they were actually doing and saying. Senior members of the royal family, officials, and wealthy businessmen often left the task of allocating funds to junior staff that either cared nothing about where the money actually went or had far too little political sophistication to evaluate the groups asking for money.

- *Third, there was a laissez-faire attitude toward people and organizations that were not hostile to the Saudi government.* Sometimes this manifested itself in sermons, newspaper articles, and lectures. These tended to be xenophobic, inflammatory to other faiths, and sometimes called for violent actions.

The authorities feared the public reactions had they cracked down on such groups—especially when they had a perceived legitimate cause, for example, the Palestinian cause. Some groups were given plenty of time to establish networks inside and outside the Kingdom, and sometimes they turned against the Saudi leadership.

• *Fourth, the Saudi authorities failed to keep track of young Saudis leaving to fight in foreign wars to support Islamic causes and how many of the some 70,000 and 100,000 such volunteers were Saudi.* Such volunteering started with the war in Afghanistan against the Soviets and included the war in Bosnia, Kosovo, and Chechnya. People who left were either very religious persons who thought that it was a religious obligation to help their brethren or they were young, uneducated, and poor. The latter were perfect recruits for organizations who were sending people abroad.

In any case, they came back more radicalized—unable to get a job and unable to be accepted in the society, and more often than not, they stayed in touch with people with similar experience to form what will become "sleeping cells." They failed to assimilate back in society, and tended to blame their failing on the leadership, and most important, on the Saudi-U.S. alliance. The General Intelligence Presidency discovered after the National Guard and Al Khobar bombings of 1995 and 1996 that approximately 10,000 young Saudi men had some kind of contact with Islamic extremist groups, Afghanis, and paramilitary training facilities between 1979 and the mid-1990s.[2]

• *Fifth, the Shiites in Saudi Arabia felt left out of the political process and threatened by what they perceived was a "puritan" Sunni society.* The impact of this problem was compounded by the Iranian revolution and by Iranian incitements to rise against the royal family. There was a failure to integrate the Shiites and win them over before Iran exploited their situation. Lack of diplomatic relations with Iran also was a problem, because Iran had nothing to lose by supporting extremist groups that threatened the Kingdom.

• *Sixth, the Saudi security services failed to detect a significant flow of arms, explosives, and terrorist supplies into Saudi Arabia from neighboring countries like Yemen, Jordan, and Iraq.* They also failed to connect the many young Saudis coming back from Afghanistan and Bosnia with this inflow of weapons.

Such failures took a long time to have any effects. The disagreement with the presence of U.S. forces on Saudi soil was only that—a disagreement. However, it was taken a step further on November 13, 1995, when the American mission to train the Saudi National Guard was bombed, leaving 6 dead and 60 injured.

Then on June 25, 1996, a truck bomb ripped Al Khobar towers, where U.S. military personnel were staying, killing 19 and injuring 500.

Nevertheless, Saudi intelligence and diplomacy failed to assess just how rapidly the threat was growing and to deal effectively with al Qaeda and bin Laden in Afghanistan. The security services also failed to monitor the degree to which Saudis and Saudi money indirectly became involved in supporting al Qaeda and other extremist causes in Central Asia, Pakistan, Germany, and elsewhere.

To deal with bin Laden, al Qaeda, and Islamic extremism from the mid-1990s onward, the Saudi government continued to tolerate occasional problems with such extremists and ultraconservative forms of Wahhabi and Islamist teaching and textbooks in its educational system that encouraged extremism. The Saudi government was generally careful to monitor the activities of Islamic groups that directly criticized the Saudi government and royal family, but it failed to monitor the flow of money to causes and groups outside the Kingdom with the care and depth required until September 11, 2001, and was then slow to correct the situation.

These failures were compounded by other actions that affected internal security. The government tolerated sermons, teaching, and textbooks with a strong xenophobic character—sometimes attacking Christians, Jews and other religions—as long as they did not attack specific political targets in Saudi Arabia or call for specific violent actions. The government also made relatively little effort to monitor the activities of "Islamic" groups in secondary schools and colleges if they did not directly oppose the monarchy and made far too little effort to evaluate what Saudi and many foreign contract teachers were actually teaching their students.

The Saudi government did not oppose foreign and domestic efforts to raise money and obtain support for "pro-Islamic" movements in Bosnia, Kosovo, Afghanistan, and Central Asia, even when these represented extreme and sometimes violent causes. Little or no effort was made to monitor the extent to which foreign "charities" raised money for political movements in Europe, the Middle East, and Asia that were far more extreme (and sometimes violent) than would have been tolerated in Saudi Arabia. The government turned a blind eye to the flow of funds to movements like Hamas that mixed charitable with terrorist activities in Israel.

Extremists and terrorists learned to exploit this situation, using formal charities or personal requests for charitable aid to obtain money they would never have gotten if they announced their real purpose in seeking funds. At the same time, some real charities had a strong political orientation and often supported extremist movements, and some donors knowingly gave money to "charities" that were extremist fronts. This was particularly true in the case of money going to Palestinian causes, after the beginning of the Second Intifada in the fall of 2000. Saudis saw Israel as an occupying nation constantly using excessive force against Palestinian freedom fighters—virtually the opposite image from Americans who saw the Palestinian militants as terrorists. The exploitation of individualized charity resulted in massive amounts of money flowing out to extremists, and sometimes-terrorist movements, through sheer negligence, fraud, or under the guise of charity.

In retrospect, both the Ministry of Interior and the General Intelligence Presidency also failed to pay attention to the "youth explosion" caused by Saudi Arabia's high birth rate. They not only were slow to monitor the movement and activities of young Saudis outside the Kingdom, and to closely examine those Saudis that became involved in paramilitary training and movements in Afghanistan, Bosnia, Kosovo, and Chechnya; but they also paid too little attention to developments inside the Kingdom, activities in its schools and universities, and the impact of unemployment and underemployment.

Saudi Response to 9/11

On one level, the events of 9/11 served as a wake-up call to the government and royal family. On another, Saudi society and some officials reacted by going into a state of denial. The royal family, most of the ulema, and business leaders in Saudi Arabia condemned the attacks on September 11th. Saudis, like everyone in the world, were horrified, and it was brought home by the fact that there were many Saudis on those planes and that bin Laden himself was a Saudi.

The Saudi government issued a statement condemning the "regrettable and inhuman bombings and attacks" that "contravene all religious values and human civilized concepts; and extended sincere condolences to the families of the victims, to U.S. President George W. Bush and to the U.S. people in general." The Saudi statement reiterated the Kingdom's position condemning all forms of terrorism and its ongoing cooperation with the international community to combat it. Many senior members of the royal family also issue their own statements condemning the attacks. For example, the Minister of Foreign Affairs, Prince Saud al-Faisal, argued during the Islamic Conference meeting, on October 11th, that terrorism harmed the Islamic world, impairs just Islamic causes, and cited that terrorism and violence never advanced the Palestinian cause.

Senior Saudi religious and legal figures condemned the attacks with equal speed. Sheikh Abdul Aziz al-Sheikh, the grand mufti of Saudi Arabia and chairman of the Senior Council of Ulema, stated on September 15th, "The recent developments in the United States constitute a form of injustice that is not tolerated by Islam, which views them as gross crimes and sinful acts." In addition, the chairman of the Supreme Judicial Council, Sheikh Salih Al-

Luheidan, stated on September 14, "As a human community we must be vigilant and careful to oppose these pernicious and shameless evils, which are not justified by any sane logic, nor by the religion of Islam." Since that time, leading Saudi officials and clerics have repeatedly condemned the attack on the World Trade Center and the Pentagon as well as other terrorist activities.[3]

Yet, a considerable portion of the Saudi public remained in denial. They either did not accept the fact that so many Saudis were involved in the 9/11 atrocities, or they found conspiracy theories to put the causes and blame outside Saudi Arabia. They became preoccupied with trying to counter charges in the Western media about their "sect of Islam," their society, and their schools that led young Saudis to become extremists without objectively examining what was actually happening. The government was less worried about internal terrorism than external threats. Their focus was mainly political and diplomatic, and little was done to boost internal security. This attitude changed a year and a half later—when the first major terrorist attack on Saudi soil occurred.

While the priority for Saudi internal security activity changed after the attacks on the World Trade Center and the Pentagon on September 11, 2001, the Saudi government initially did more to try to improve relations with the United States, deal with terrorism outside the Kingdom, and counter the damage to its image than it did to strengthen the operations of the Saudi security apparatus.

What Saudi Arabia was still slow to understand, until major terrorist attacks began to occur in the Kingdom in May 2003, was that Saudi Arabia faced truly serious internal security issues as well as the need to deal with terrorism inside the country. The apparent lack of a significant number of cells and the comparatively low levels of activity in Saudi Arabia led the Kingdom to focus on such terrorism largely in terms of external rather than internal threats.

Saudi intelligence and security services paid too little attention to the growing and highly visible ties between hard-line Pakistani extremists in the Pakistani intelligence service, the ISI, and religious schools and the impact of Saudi-financed activities in Pakistan and Central Asia and the number of young Saudi men associated with Osama bin Laden and al Qaeda. Discussions with Saudi officials indicate that they had surprisingly little understanding of the difference between legitimate Islamic organizations in Central Asia, China, and East Asia and highly political action groups that used Islam as an ideological cry.

They paid too little attention to the fact that such groups were committed to the violent overthrow of governments in their region, which strongly opposed both modernization and reform and which were broadly anti-Western in character. They also failed to monitor Islamist extremist "missionary" and charity groups operating in Europe. Even though such extremist groups, particularly the neo-Salafi ones, showed little of the pragmatic tolerance and moderation common to mainstream Wahhabi practices in the Kingdom, they often took on an extremist character, particularly in the United Kingdom and Germany.

The Saudi security services failed to fully appreciate the threat posed by the flow of Saudi money to Palestinian groups like Hamas and the Palestinian Islamic Jihad, and other hard-line or violent Islamic elements in countries like Egypt and failed to detect a significant flow of arms, explosives, and terrorist supplies into Saudi Arabia from neighboring countries like Yemen.

The Saudi government was slow to understand the fact that so many young Saudis were directly involved in 9/11, as well as in the overall membership of Osama bin Laden's al Qaeda, reflected the failure of the Saudi security efforts to come firmly to grips with its Islamic extremists at many levels.

One key problem was that the Saudi intelligence community relied too much on human contacts and informers and signals intelligence, rather than on active counterterrorism efforts in the field. It also remained weak in dealing with the financial aspects of intelligence and internal security, which helps explain why it failed to properly monitor the flow of money to Saudi charities, religious organizations, and individuals in financing extremist groups—other than those that posed a direct threat to the rule of the Saudi royal family.

In fairness, such monitoring is not easy. Saudi banking rules are relatively strict in terms of tracking and identifying individual accounts, but little effort was made before September 11th to track the flow of money inside or outside the country to extremist causes and factions. It should be noted, however, that Saudi organizations and individuals have hundreds of billions of dollars of privately held money in Western and other foreign banks. Effective surveillance of such holdings is difficult, if not impossible.

The problem is further compounded by easy access to the financial institutions of other GCC countries, like the UAE. Many Gulf countries have financial institutions that make cash transfers extremely easy, which tolerate high levels of money laundering, smuggling, and narco-trafficking, and which have often been far more careless in allowing the flow of money to extremist causes than Saudi Arabia has. The leaders and citizens of countries like Kuwait and the UAE have also been as careless in their donations to "charities" as Saudis.

SAUDI ARABIA'S OWN 9/11: THE IMPACT OF MAY 2003

As was the case in the United States before September 2001, it was not until the threat of terrorism truly came home to Saudi Arabia that the Kingdom fully understood the seriousness of the threat and the nature of the challenges it faced. As the chronology below—which is largely adapted from work by the National Council on U.S.-Arab Relations—shows, Saudi Arabia should have seen what was coming. Nevertheless, it failed to do so until terrorists carried out a brutal attack on several housing compounds in Riyadh on May 12, 2003.[4]

The attackers carried out four suicide bombings on compounds housing many Western residents. The bombing resulted in 34 dead, including 7 Americans and 7 Saudis, plus 200 wounded. From that point onward, Saudi Arabia found itself fighting a repeated series of terrorist attacks on its own soil and having to deal with more terrorist cells with far larger stocks of arms and explosives than it had previously estimated. The Saudi government also found that it was dealing with serious infiltration problems, particularly across the Yemeni border.[5]

This time, the Saudi authorities took the challenge seriously, and implemented many steps to fix their internal security apparatus, reform parts of their educational system, and develop a system of tracking and regulating charities.

The Saudi Chronology of Terrorism and Counterterrorism

The chronology of developments in terrorism in Saudi Arabia can be summarized as follows:[6]

- *1970:* Shiites in the town of Qatif, Eastern Province, riot and demand more shares in the oil revenues. The town is sealed for months.

- *1978:* Shiites protest again in the city of Qatif. The Saudi National Guard is mobilized. As many as 50 are arrested and some are executed.

- *November 20, 1979:* About 200–500 armed Sunni extremists, led by Juhaiman al-Utaibai, seize control of the Grand Mosque in Mecca. The extremists accuse the royal family of corruption, imitating the West, and of being puppets of the United States. This is the same argument Juhaiman's grandfather, who was part of the Ikhwan army with King Abdul Aziz, argued 58 years earlier. This is also the same argument that Khomeini made against the shah. Because it is forbidden to fight inside the Grand Mosque, the Saudi authorities did not go in immediately. However, the ulema in the Kingdom approve of the Saudi military going into the mosque. The Saudi National Guard, with the help of French Special Forces, regains control of the mosque 10–14 days later.

- *December 3–5, 1979:* Shiites in Qatif riot in support of the Iranian revolution and demanding a higher share of the oil revenues. The Saudi National Guard are mobilized, they clash with protesters, and at least five people are killed.

- *December 24, 1979:* The Soviets invade Afghanistan—and shortly many Saudis, most notably bin Laden will travel to Afghanistan to fight the Soviets. Saudi intelligence, along with the United States, will train the Mujahideen in guerrilla warfare to fight the communists.
- *January 9, 1980:* Sixty male terrorists are executed after being convicted of the Grand Mosque seizure.
- *July 31, 1987:* Iranian pilgrims riot and protest against the Saudi authorities. As many as 402 get killed during those riots.
- *August 1, 1987:* Iranians attack the Saudi and Kuwaiti embassies in the Tehran as a response to the riots in Mecca.
- *August 25, 1987:* The Saudi government denounces the Iranian government as terrorists for causing the riots in Mecca.
- *May 15, 1988:* The Soviets start withdrawing troops from Afghanistan after nine years of war.
- *1988:* Shortly after the Soviets withdrawal, Osama bin Laden forms the al Qaeda network from people who fought in Afghanistan.
- *1988 and 1989:* A Shiite militants group, which will be called Saudi Hezbollah, takes credit for bombing oil and petrochemical installations and for assassinations of Saudi diplomats in Ankara, Bangkok, and Karachi.
- *July 9, 1989:* Two bombs explode in the vicinity of Mecca's Grand Mosque, causing the death of one pilgrim and injuring 16.
- *September 1989:* Sixteen Shiites, Kuwaiti nationals, are executed for their involvement in the explosions in Mecca.
- *1994:* Osama bin Laden is stripped of Saudi citizenship, and his family disowns him. Safar al-Hawaly and Salman al-Awdeh, two Ulemas who spoke against the Saudi leadership and the U.S. presence on Saudi soil, are jailed.
- *November 13, 1995:* The U.S. Office of the Personnel Manager, Saudi Arabian National Guard (OPM/SANG)—American training mission—is attacked with a 220-pound car bomb in a parking lot. Five Americans and two Indians are killed, and 60 people are injured. Two Saudi opposition groups, Tigers of the Gulf and the Islamist Movement for Change, claim responsibility.
- *April 22, 1996:* Saudi TV airs the confessions of four Saudi nationals who admit to planning and conducting the bombing of the OPM/SANG compound. Three are veterans of the conflicts in Afghanistan, Bosnia, and Chechnya.

- *May 31, 1996:* Three of the Saudis, who are involved in the OPM/SANG bombing, are executed in Riyadh.

- *June 25, 1996:* Truck containing about 5,000 pounds of fuel and explosives targets the U.S. military compound near King Abdul Aziz Air Base, in the city of Khobar, the Eastern Province. There are 19 deaths and about 500 injuries.

- *1996:* Hani al-Sayegh, a Saudi, leaves the Kingdom for Iran shortly after the bombing and is shown to have ties to Iranian intelligence. He then leaves to Kuwait, and finally to Canada.

- *June 1997:* Hani al-Sayegh is deported from Canada to the United States. Canadian officials say that he was the lookout person during the bombing.

- *October 10, 1999:* Hani al-Sayegh is returned to Saudi Arabia from the United States. The United States denies him political asylum and argues that he "was not entitled to remain in this country and that his removal to Saudi Arabia was appropriate."

- *1999:* Mohammad Hamdi al-Ahdal is arrested in Saudi and put in jail for 14 months. He is charged with having contact with Osama bin Laden in Afghanistan (fourteen months later, Al-Ahdal is deported to Yemen).

- *November 17, 2000:* A car bomb in Riyadh kills Christopher Rodway, a British engineer, and wounds his wife. Saudi authorities accuse Bill Sampson, a Canadian biochemist, of the bombing in connection with the illegal trade of alcohol.

- *November 22, 2000:* A car bomb explodes in Riyadh, wounding two men and a woman, which, again, the Saudi authorities blame on the illegal alcohol trade.

- *December 15, 2000:* A bomb, which was left on the windshield, explodes in Huber, severely injuring a British citizen.

- *February 4, 2001:* Bill Sampson appears on Saudi TV and confesses of the bombing against Rodway.

- *March 15, 2001:* Chechen rebels hijack a Russian airplane after leaving Turkey and divert it to Medina in Saudi Arabia.

- *March 16, 2001:* Saudi commandos storm the Russian hijacked plane and free the hostages. A flight attendant, a passenger, and a hijacker are killed in the raid.

- *May 2, 2001:* A Letter bomb injures an American doctor in Khubar.

- *September 23, 2001:* The GCC countries meet in Jeddah and declare they are joining the international coalition against terrorism.

- *September 25, 2001:* Saudi Arabia withdraws its recognition of the Taliban.
- *October 6, 2001:* A bomb explodes in Khubar, killing two people and injuring four.
- *October 15, 2001:* Hamoud bin Uqlaa al-Shuaibi, calls on Muslims to wage war on any one who supports the U.S. war in Afghanistan.
- *October 31, 2001:* The Bush administration announces that it has asked the Saudi government to freeze the assets of people involved in the September 11 attacks.
- *January 4–10, 2002:* Muslim scholars meet in Mecca and define terrorism as "any unjustified attack by individuals, groups or states against a human being . . . the environment, public or private facilities, and endangering natural resources."
- *March 11, 2002:* The U.S. Treasury Department and Saudi Arabia announce the freezing of the accounts of the Somali and Bosnian branches of the Al-Haramain Islamic Foundation.
- *April 25, 2002:* Crown Prince Abdullah meets President Bush in Texas regarding the war on terrorism, the Israeli-Palestinian issue, and the possible war on Iraq.
- *June 14, 2002:* Three Saudis, Zuher al-Tbaiti, Abdullah al-Ghamdi and Hilal Alissiri, appear in court in Casablanca. They are accused of plotting to blow up British warship in the Strait of Gibraltar.
- *June 18, 2002:* Saudi Arabia announces its arrest of 13 al Qaeda members—11 Saudis, an Iraqi, and a Sudanese—for plotting to down a U.S. airplane near Prince Sultan Air Base.
- *June 20, 2002:* A British citizen, John Venessm, is killed in a bomb explosion in Riyadh.
- *August 10, 2002:* Saudi foreign minister announces that Iran has turned 16 al Qaeda suspects to Saudi authorities in June.
- *September 6, 2002:* The assets of Wa'el Hamza Julaidan, who is accused of being an al Qaeda financier, are frozen in Saudi Arabia.
- *December 10, 2002:* Saudi dissidents start a new radio station, Sawt al-Islah, "to push for reforms."
- *February 17, 2003:* Deputy governor of Al-Jouf Province, Hamad Al-Wardi, is shot dead as he is driving to work.
- *February 18, 2003:* Saudi Arabia announces that it is referring 90 Saudis to trial for al Qaeda links and that 250 people are under investigation.

- *May 6, 2003:* After a raid and a gunfight with terrorists in Riyadh, the Saudi authorities find weapons and announce the hunt for 19 terrorists: 17 Saudis, an Iraqi, and a Yemeni.

- *May 2003:* Saudi Arabia asks the Al-Haramain Islamic Foundation and all Saudi charities to suspend activities outside Saudi Arabia until mechanisms are in place to adequately monitor and control funds so they cannot be misdirected for illegal purposes.

- *May 12, 2003:* Bombers simultaneously attack three compounds in Riyadh, housing mostly Westerners. There are 35 deaths, including 10 Americans and 7 Saudis. There are 200 injuries.

- *May 13, 2003:* Crown Prince Abdullah announces that the Saudi government and people will not be deterred by the 12 May terror attacks in Riyadh, "We will fight terrorism together. . . . These messages, which do not require any interpretation, provide clear evidence that the fate of those murderers is damnation on earth and the fury of Hell in the thereafter."

- *May 28, 2003:* Three clerics, Ali Fahd al-Khudair, Ahmed Hamoud Mufreh al-Khaledi and Nasir Ahmed al-Fuhaid, are arrested in Tabuk after calling for support to the terrorists who carried out the Riyadh attacks. Also, eleven suspects are taken into custody in the city of Medina. Weapons, false identity cards, and bomb-making materials are confiscated. In addition, Saudi national Abdulmonim Ali Mahfouz al-Ghamdi is arrested, following a car chase. Three non-Saudi women without identity cards are detained.

- *May 31, 2003:* Yusef Salih Fahad al-Ayeri, aka Swift Sword, a major al Qaeda operational planner and fundraiser, is killed while fleeing from a security patrol.

- *June 7, 2003:* Prince Nayef, interior minister, identifies 12 suicide bombers responsible for attacks on three Riyadh compounds and says 10 suspects are still at large. Nayef says 25 people have been arrested and that the attacks are the work of al Qaeda.

- *June 14, 2003:* Saudi security raided a terrorist cell in the Alattas building in the Khalidiya neighborhood of Mecca. The raid leaves two security agents dead. In addition, 5 suspects are killed and 12 are arrested. The authorities find a number of booby-trapped Qur'ans, 72 homemade bombs, weapons, ammunition, and masks.

- *June 20, 2003:* Security forces in Mecca arrest four Saudi women after a raid on a flat rented by a suspected terrorist.

- *June 26, 2003:* One of the men wanted in connection with the 12 May bombings, Ali Abd-al Rahman al-Fagasi al-Ghamdi, considered the top al Qaeda leader in the Kingdom, surrenders.

- *July 1, 2003:* President Bush comments on U.S.-Saudi cooperation in the war on terrorism, "America and Saudi Arabia face a common terrorist threat, and we appreciate the strong, continuing efforts of the Saudi government in fighting that threat."

- *July 3, 2003:* Turki Nasser Mishaal Aldandany, a top al Qaeda operative and mastermind of the May 12 bombings, is killed on July 3 along with three other suspects in a gun battle with security forces, in the northern city of Al Jouf.

- *July 21, 2003:* The Ministry of Interior announces that they have stopped terrorist operations against vital installations and the arrest of 16 members of terrorist cells after searching their hideouts in farms and houses in Riyadh, al-Qasim, and the Eastern Province. Underground storage areas are found containing chemicals that could have been used to make explosive.

- *July 25, 2003:* Three men are arrested at a checkpoint in Mecca for possessing printed material that included a "religious edict" in support of terrorist acts against Western targets.

- *July 28, 2003:* Saudi security forces kill six terror suspects and wound another in a gunfight at a farm in the Qasim Province. Two Saudi policemen are also killed in the gun battle.

- *August 10, 2003:* Saudi security forces detain 10 suspected militants after a gunfight outside Riyadh.

- *August 13, 2003:* Security personnel arrest five terrorists after four policemen and a militant are killed in a shootout in Riyadh two days earlier.

- *August 15, 2003:* 11 militants are arrested by the Saudi authorities in the southern city of Jizan. The authorities seize a large cache of weapons, rockets and explosive chemicals.

- *August 18, 2003:* The Council of Ministers approves a new money laundering and terror financing laws that include harsh penalties.

- *August 26, 2003:* Saudi Arabia and the United States are to create a joint task force aimed at combating the funding of extremist groups in the country. Agents from the FBI, IRS, and Treasury are to be stationed in Saudi Arabia.

- *August 29, 2003:* U.S. Attorney General John Ashcroft commends Saudi Arabia's efforts in the war on terrorism: "I believe that progress is being made and I think not only that it (cooperation) is good but it continues to improve."

- *September 17, 2003:* U.S. Treasury Secretary John W. Snow meets with officials in Saudi Arabia and notes that "We discussed our outstanding progress working together on the fight against terrorist financing. Saudi Arabia has been a strong ally to the United States in this essential matter. Their close oversight of charities to guard against money laundering and terrorist financing sets an example to all countries engaged in the war against terror."

- *September 23, 2003:* Security forces surround a group of suspected terrorists in an apartment in the city of Jazan. During a gun battle, one security officer is killed and four officers are injured. Two suspects are detained and three are killed. One of the militants detained, Sultan Jubran Sultan al-Qahtani, is wanted by the United States. The suspects are armed with machine guns, pistols, and a large quantity of ammunition.

- *October 5, 2003:* Security forces arrest three suspects during a raid in the desert to the east of Riyadh.

- *October 8, 2003:* Security forces raid a farm in the northern Muleda area of Qasim Province and are able to arrest a suspect. Three other suspects flee the scene. Two security officers are injured. Large amounts of materials to make explosives and light weaponry are found in the farm where the suspects had been hiding.

- *October 14, 2003:* Many Saudis take to the streets in Riyadh demanding reforms.

- *October 20, 2003:* Saudi security forces raid several terrorist cells in various parts of the country, including the Al Majma'a District in Riyadh, Mecca, Jeddah, and Qasim. Security forces confiscate many items, including C4 plastic explosives, homemade bombs, gas masks, and large quantities of assault rifles and ammunition.

- *November 2, 2003:* U.S. Defense Secretary Donald Rumsfeld says, "The Saudi government, particularly since they were attacked some weeks and months ago, has been very aggressive, more aggressive than ever in the past."

- *November 3, 2003:* Saudi police arrest six suspected al Qaeda militants after a shootout in the holy city of Mecca. Two suspected terrorists are killed, and one security officer is wounded. Saudi police seize a large cache of weapons they believe is stockpiled for attacks during the Muslim holy month of Ramadan. The militants had rented the apartment for just the month of Ramadan.

- *November 6, 2003:* Saudi security forces encircle two terrorists in Al Swaidi district in Riyadh. The terrorists fire at the security forces and try to flee. In the gunfight, the Saudi security officers kill one militant, but eight officers also injured. On the same day, Saudi authorities in Mecca surround two suspects; a gun battle continues until a homemade bomb explodes, killing the militants.

- *November 7, 2003:* The United States warns of terrorist strikes in the Kingdom.

- *November 9, 2003:* Just after midnight, suicide bombers attack Al Muhayya residential compound in Riyadh. The interior minister and other leaders blame al Qaeda for the attack. The attack leads to 17 deaths and 122 injuries.

- *November 10, 2003:* A report on Saudi Arabia's progress in the war on terrorism is released by the Saudi embassy in Washington.

- *November 20, 2003:* Abdullah bin Atiyyah bin Hudeid al-Salami, a terror suspect, surrenders to Saudi police.

- *November 25, 2003:* A car bomb is foiled in the Saudi capital of Riyadh. Two notorious terror suspects die in the raid. Abdulmohsin Abdulaziz al-Shabanat is killed in a gun battle and Mosaed Mohammad Dheedan al-Sobaiee also is killed when a hand grenade detonates. At least 10 suspects are detained in different parts of the country.

- *November 26, 2003:* A raid takes place in which a terrorist suspect, who is linked to the 9 Nov bombing, is arrested. A large cache of weapons is confiscated, including 1 SAM-7, 5 RPG launchers, 384 kilograms of explosives (RDX), 8 AK47s, 41 AK47 magazines, 20 hand grenades, and 16,800 rounds of ammunition. Money and communication devices are also found.

- *December 1, 2003:* The UK Foreign and the Commonwealth Office advises British nationals against all but essential travel to Saudi Arabia.

- *December 2, 2003:* A U.S. embassy issues a warning to the 37,000 U.S. citizens living in Saudi Arabia, saying that compounds housing Westerners have come under surveillance by terrorists, indicating the possibility of another attack.

- *December 4, 2003:* Brig. Gen. Abdulaziz al-Huwairini escapes an assassination attempt in Riyadh. The "Two Holy Mosques Brigade" claims responsibility and declares in a statement that "since our brothers in al Qaeda are busy fighting the crusaders, we took it upon ourselves to cleanse the land of the two holy mosques of the crusaders' agents"—a reference to the Saudi government.

- *December 6, 2003:* The Saudi Ministry of Interior releases a list and the photos of 26 wanted terrorist suspects. A reward of up to $1.9 million is also offered to anyone who would lead the authorities to the arrest of the 26 militants.

- *December 7, 2003:* Security forces arrest 25 suspects in connection with the 12 May bombings in Riyadh.

- *December 8, 2003:* One of the Kingdom's most wanted terrorists, Mohammad Abdullah al-Rayis, is killed. Another militant is arrested following a shootout with the security forces in Al Swaidi district in southern Riyadh. The Ministry of Interior praises the "citizen's cooperation."

- *December 17, 2003:* The United States says it will allow its nonessential diplomats to leave Saudi Arabia because of security concerns.

- *December 18, 2003:* Deputy Secretary of State Richard Armitage tells a television interviewer, "The Saudis have been going after these terrorists and trying to tear them out, root and branch . . . the Government of Saudi Arabia has been terrific, particularly since May 12th and their Riyadh bombing."

- *December 30, 2003:* Mansour ibn Muhammad Faqeeh, one of the most wanted terrorists in the Kingdom, surrenders to the security forces.

- *January 3, 2004:* Brig. Gen. Hadi Mabjer al-Sahli, chairman of the military council at the Border Guards command in the Jizan region, is killed in front of his house.

- *January 8, 2004:* Swiss police arrest eight suspects for their involvement in the 12 May attack in Riyadh.

- *January 12, 2004:* The Ministry of Interior announces the progress of the war against the militants. They announce the confiscation of 23,893 kilograms of explosive, 301 RPGs, 431 homemade grenades, 304 explosive belts, 674 detonators, 1,020 small arms, and 352,398 rounds of ammunition.

- *January 22, 2004:* U.S. Treasury Secretary John W. Snow tells a Washington news conference, "The United States and Saudi Arabia share a deep commitment to fighting the spread of terrorism in all its forms. . . . Like the United States, the Saudis have been victims of al Qaeda. They are an important partner in the war on terrorist financing and have taken important and welcome steps to fight terrorist financing."

- *January 30, 2004:* The Ministry of Interior announces a raid on a house in Al Siliye district of Riyadh. Seven people are arrested, and weapons cache and military uniforms are confiscated.

- *February 13, 2004:* The Interior Ministry warns residents in the capital against a possible terrorist attack. It says that a car laden with explosives registered to a wanted suspect could be used in the attack.

- *February 14, 2004:* Saudi Arabia's Interior Ministry offers an award of SR7 million for information leading to the recovery of a GMC Suburban loaded with explosives.

- *February 16, 2004:* British Airways cancels its flight from London to Riyadh for "security reasons."

- *February 22, 2004:* The Ministry of Interior confirms the death of A'amir al-Zaidan al-Shihri, one of the 16 most-wanted terrorists announced in last December. His buried body is recovered from outside Riyadh.

- *February 28, 2004:* A royal decree is announced to establish the Saudi National Commission for Relief and Charity Work abroad to ensure that terrorist organizations do not misuse Saudi donations for humanitarian projects worldwide.

- *March 15, 2004:* Two of Saudi Arabia's most wanted terror suspects, Khaled Ali Hajj, a Yemeni, and Ibrahim bin Abdul-Aziz bin Mohammad al-Mezeini, a Saudi, are shot dead in a shootout with Saudi police.

- *March 19, 2004:* U.S. Secretary of State Colin Powell meets Saudi officials in Riyadh, tells the press that the United States and Saudi Arabia are united in war on terror.

- *March 24, 2004:* J. Cofer Black, coordinator for counterterrorism, U.S. State Department, testifies to Congress, "The Saudis are a key ally in the Global War On Terror. Their performance has not been flawless, and they have a large task before them, but we see clear evidence of the seriousness of purpose and the commitment of the leadership of the Kingdom to this fight."

- *March 24, 2004:* Juan C. Zarate, deputy assistant secretary, Executive Office for Terrorist Financing & Financial Crimes, U.S. Department of the Treasury, testifies to Congress, "the targeting actions and systemic reforms undertaken by the Kingdom of Saudi Arabia clearly demonstrate its commitment to work with us and the international community to combat the global threat of terrorist financing."

- *March 24, 2004:* Thomas J. Harrington, deputy assistant director, Counterterrorism Division, Federal Bureau of Investigation, testifies to Congress, "The Kingdom of Saudi Arabia is an important partner in this international effort and has taken significant steps to deter global terrorism."

- *April 5, 2004:* Saudi security forces kill a suspected militant and wound another during a car chase in Al Rawdah, an eastern Riyadh neighborhood—after receiving fire from a stolen car.

- *April 8, 2004:* Al Qaeda chief in Saudi Arabia, Abulazziz al-Muqrin, puts out a video vowing to eject the United States from the Arabian Peninsula and arguing that the real battle against the United States is starting.

- *April 12, 2004:* A member of the security forces is killed, one militant is killed, and five policemen are wounded during a clash in eastern Riyadh.

- *April 13, 2004:* In the town of Uniza, Qasim Province, during a police patrol, the security forces come under attack from militants believed to be the same from the day before. Four Saudi policemen are killed. Two trucks filled with explosives are confiscated by Saudi security.

- *April 15, 2004:* The United States orders the evacuation of most U.S. diplomats and all U.S. family dependents from Saudi Arabia, and "strongly urges" all American citizens to leave because of "credible and specific" intelligence about terrorist attacks planned against U.S. and other Western targets.

- *April 18, 2004:* Eight terror suspects, linked to violent clashes with security forces in the capital, are arrested. Three large vehicle bombs—each with over a ton of explosives on board—are defused.

- *April 19, 2004:* Saudi security forces seize two SUVs loaded with explosives near a gas station on a highway north of Riyadh.

- *April 21, 2004:* Terrorists launch two suicide car bombs attacks against Saudi Arabian security headquarters in Riyadh. Five people are killed, and over 150 are wounded in the attack.

- *April 22, 2004:* Saudi Security forces kill five terror suspects, including two of the country's most wanted men, during raids in Al Safa district in Jeddah.

- *April 22, 2004:* The "Al Haramin (the holy sites) Brigades in the Arabian Peninsula" claim responsibility on Web sites for the 21 April Riyadh suicide bombing against "special security forces."

- *April 22, 2004:* Grand Mufti Abdul Aziz al-Sheikh, the kingdom's highest religious authority, condemns the attack "as one of the greatest sins" and says the attackers are "a lost minority under the cover of religion" and will be "burned in hell."

- *April 24, 2004:* King Fahd characterizes the 21 April attack as "the work of a deviant few who wanted to undermine the country, terrorize peaceful people and kill Muslims."

- *April 29, 2004:* U.S. State Department's annual report, "Patterns of Global Terrorism—2003," praises Saudi Arabia's commitment to the war against global terrorism, "I would cite Saudi Arabia as an excellent example of a nation increasingly focusing its political will to fight terrorism. Saudi Arabia has launched an aggressive, comprehensive, and unprecedented campaign to hunt down terrorists, uncover their plots, and cut off their sources of funding."

- *May 1, 2004:* Gunmen opens fire against oil contractors in Yanbu, kills at least six people and wounds a dozen. A naked body is dragged behind a car. The Saudi police chase the militants and kill all four. At least one of the attackers is number 10 on the Saudi most-wanted list, Abdullah Saud Abu-Nayan al-Sobaie. In a simultaneous attack in Yanbu, a pipe bomb is thrown into an international school, injuring the custodian.

- *May 20, 2004:* The security forces come under heavy fire from machine guns after locating five militants in a rest house in Khudairah, a village in the area of Buraidah. Saudi security forces kill four terrorist suspects and injure another. A Saudi policeman is killed and five are wounded.

- *May 27, 2004:* The top al Qaeda leader, Abulazziz al-Muqrin, in Saudi Arabia issues a battle plan for an urban guerrilla war in the Kingdom. He gives a detailed list of steps militants should take to succeed in their campaign against the Saudi government. He argues that the campaign should include urban warfare, assassinations, kidnapping, and bombing. The "execution group" or "strike force" in each four-tiered cell should be "trained to carry out operations inside cities, including assassinations, abductions, bombings, sabotage, raids and the liberation of hostages."

- *May 29, 2004:* Four gunmen attack the Osais compound housing oil workers in Al Khobar, Eastern Province, at about 7:30 AM. Between 20–60 hostages are being held at one compound.

- *May 30, 2004:* Saudi security commandos storm the Oasis compound and free the hostages. 22 people are killed in the attacks, including 7 Saudi security officers. Three of the attackers escape. Al Qaeda claims responsibility.

- *June 7, 2004:* Two BBC journalists are shot. Simon Cumbers is killed and security correspondent Frank Gardner is seriously injured in a gun attack in Riyadh.

- *June 8, 2004:* Robert C. Jacobs, an American defense contractor, is shot and killed in the Al Khaleej neighborhood in Riyadh.

- *June 12, 2004:* Paul Johnson, an American who works for Lockheed Martin, is kidnapped by al Qaeda. Kenneth Scroggs of Laconia, who worked for Advanced Electronics Co., is killed in his garage in Riyadh.

- *June 15, 2004:* A video of Paul Johnson is posted on an extremist Web site. They demand the release of all militants detained in Saudi jails.

- *June 18, 2004:* The beheading of American Paul Johnson is posted on the militants' Web site. Saudi security forces are able to track down and kill al Qaeda leader Abulazziz al-Muqrin and three of his associates. Twelve others are also arrested in Al Malaz district of Riyadh.

- *June 23, 2004:* King Fahd offers terrorists a limited amnesty, calling on them to turn themselves in or face the "full might" of the state. In a televised address read on his behalf by Crown Prince Abdullah, King Fahd said those who willingly surrender within 30 days will be secure and warned all those who don't will be subjected to a fierce crackdown.

- *June 24, 2004:* The Ministry of Interior announces that Saaban al-Shihri, a wanted terrorist, is the first to take advantage of the amnesty by surrendering to the police.

- *June 25, 2004:* Prince Nayef announces that Saudi Arabia will allow foreigners, who feel threatened by the wave of terrorist violence in the Kingdom, to carry guns for their protection.

- *June 28, 2004:* One of Saudi Arabia's most wanted terrorists surrenders, the second suspect to turn himself in under the amnesty. Othman Hadi al-Maqbul al-Amri, 37, a close associate of Saaban Al-Shihri, gives himself up after two years on the run.

- *July 1, 2004:* Saudi Security forces engage in a gun battle with terrorists killing one and wounding another. One Saudi police officer is killed in the fight and another is injured.

- *July 3, 2004:* The Saudi Arabian Interior Ministry identifies the terrorist killed in a gun battle on July 1 as Awad ibn Muhammad ibn Ali al-Awad and the one wounded as Abdul Rahman ibn Muhammad ibn Abdul Rahman al-Abdul Wahab.

- *July 4, 2004:* Saudi security investigations uncover the deaths of two senior terrorists who died from untreated wounds after clashes with security forces in April 2004. Rakan ibn Mohsen al-Seikhan and Nasser ibn Rashid al-Rashid—both on a list of 26 most wanted suspects—were wounded during the April 12 clashes in Riyadh.

- *July 14, 2004:* A disabled Saudi terror suspect, Khaled ibn Odeh ibn Mohammad al-Harbi, hands himself in to the Saudi embassy in Iran, the third to do so under a month-long partial amnesty announced in June. The man is suspected of being a top al Qaeda figure close to Osama bin Laden and had been hiding along the Iran-Afghan border. He is the disabled man shown in the video found in Afghanistan showing bin Laden confessing to the 9/11 attacks.

- *July 20, 2004:* Saudi Arabian security forces kill two terrorist suspects, including one on a most-wanted list, and capture six others in a gun battle late yesterday in the capital, Riyadh. Authorities also found the head of slain U.S. hostage Paul Johnson in a refrigerator in the suspects' hideout.

- *July 23, 2004:* The partial amnesty offered by the king expires.

- *July 26, 2004:* A message purportedly from an al Qaeda cell in Saudi Arabia surfaces, acknowledging that three of its militants were killed the previous week in a shootout with security forces.

- *July 30, 2004:* Abdurrahman Alamoudi pleads guilty in a Virginia court to moving cash from Libya and involvement in a plot to assassinate Saudi prince.

- *August 5, 2004:* Saudi security forces arrest Faris Ahmed Jamaan al-Zahrani, the number 11 on a list of 26 most-wanted terrorists published by the Interior Ministry last December.

- *August 16, 2004:* U.S. Secretary of State Colin Powell: "As a result, since September 11th, 2001, more than two-thirds of al Qaeda's top leadership have been killed or captured. More than 3,000 al Qaeda criminals have been detained in over 100 countries. Terrorist cells have been wrapped up in Singapore, in Italy, right here in the United States. The Saudis are going after them with vigor and are more successful with each passing day."

- *August 17, 2004:* Saudi Arabia's major battle with terrorism is over, and the Kingdom is chasing the last remaining militants, Saudi Crown Prince Abdullah bin Abdul Aziz al-Saud says in an interview.

- *August 29, 2004:* Saudi police arrest two wanted militants in the central city of Buraidah in Qasim Province.

- *August 30, 2004:* Gunmen opens fire at a U.S. diplomatic car near the U.S. consulate in the Red Sea port city of Jeddah, but there are no injuries.

- *September 2, 2004:* One policeman is killed and three others are wounded in clashes with militants in a town northeast of Riyadh.

- *September 3, 2004:* Abulazziz al-Muqrin, who planned the attacks in May in Khobar, surrenders to the Saudi authorities. He is a relative of the slain al Qaeda chief.

- *September 5, 2004:* Saudi security forces arrest seven suspects in Buraidah. Three policemen are killed in the engagement.

- *September 6, 2004:* A young man, who is accused of incitement of violence, is arrested near the Grand Mosque in Mecca.

- *September 15, 2004:* Edward Stuart Muirhead-Smith, 55, a British citizen, who works for the telecommunication corporation Marconi, is shot and killed at the Max shopping center in eastern Riyadh.

- *September 20, 2004:* Saudi security forces clash with militants in the northern city of Tabuk. The gun battle ends with the arrests of two militants and the injuries of three Saudi officers.

- *September 21, 2004:* Saudi TV airs "Special Facts from Inside the Cell." Two detained militants, Khaled al-Faraj and Abdul Rahman al-Rashoud, argue that al Qaeda cells recruited young men and once they are in the cell, they are threatened to stay in and many are afraid to leave.

- *September 22, 2004:* Al Qaeda in Saudi Arabia claims responsibility for the killing of Edward Muirhead-Smith, killed on September 15, 2004.

- *September 26, 2004:* Laurent Barbot, 41, who is a technician for the French defense and electronics company, Thales, which is negotiating a border security deal, is shot dead in Jeddah. After a car chase and a shootout in the streets of Riyadh in Al Shafa district, three suspects are injured, and one is arrested.

- *September 27, 2004:* Saudi Arabia announces plans to host an international conference on combating terrorism in Riyadh, which will take place in February 5–8.

- *October 1, 2004:* A man attacked a housing compound in Riyadh with a machine gun. Authorities report that there was little damage or injuries.

- *October 12, 2004:* Three terror suspects are killed in a shootout with Saudi security forces in Al Nahda district of Riyadh. The Interior Ministry statement said, "After the area was sealed off, the militants moved seven women and a child to the first floor of the building in order to deceive the security forces. The terrorists, using machine guns and hand grenades, opened fire on the security forces from the second floor of the building."

- *October 14, 2004:* The Ministry of Interior announces that the Saudi security forces killed Abdul Majeed ibn Muhammad Abdullah al-Munie, one of the Kingdom's 26 most-wanted list, during the gun battle with terrorists on 12 October. He is killed with two other extremists: Essam ibn Muqbil al-Otaibi and Abdul Hameed ibn Abdul Aziz al-Yahya.

- *October 17, 2004:* Two wanted terror suspects are arrested after a gun battle with Saudi security forces in Al Khaleej district of Riyadh at 2:05 AM. One of the militants is wounded in the exchange of fire.

- *November 7, 2004:* Militants open fire on Saudi security forces in the Al Jamia district of Jeddah The security forces respond. One militant is killed and two are wounded in the attack. Saudi authorities find weapons caches, including automatic rifles, ammunitions, and grenades.

- *November 11, 2004:* Prince Nayef quoted saying that the Kingdom is "stripping the terrorists of all means of carrying out criminal acts."

- *November 13, 2004:* The Ministry of Interior announces the arrest of three men in Al Zulfi, northwest of Riyadh. Two more people are arrested in Riyadh. Interior Ministry security spokesman, Brig. Gen. Mansour al-Turki, says, "They are suspected mostly of supporting the extremist thought. They were trying to spread it among the youth."

- *November 21, 2004:* "Today at dawn the security forces arrested a member of the deviant minority [al Qaeda] who admitted wanting to carry out an act in a neighboring country. . . . He said he had come here to consult his brothers and was arrested at 5 am," Prince Abdullah says, without specifying the targeted country.

- *November 22, 2004:* Saudi security forces seize weapons cache and ammunition from a suspected terrorist hideout in the city of Buraidah, in Qasim Province.

- *November 27, 2004:* In Al Jamia district of Jeddah at 6:30 PM, Saudi security attack a car that had been under surveillance for a few days. The Saudi forces and the suspected terrorists engage in a gun battle, resulting in the death of a suspected militant and the detention of another.

- *November 28, 2004:* The Interior Ministry announces that the person killed 27 November, Mustapha Mubaraki, was on the Kingdom's most-wanted list for his involvement in the Muhaya housing compound bombing in Riyadh in November 2003.

- *November 29, 2004:* Saudi border guards seize large quantities of weapons in the province of Asir on the Saudi-Yemeni border. The arms cache include hand grenades, rocket-propelled grenades, rocket launchers and dynamite sticks.

- *November 29, 2004:* Saudi security forces capture a suspected militant in Riyadh after he fails to stop at a police checkpoint.

- *November 30, 2004:* A suspected terrorist is surrounded by Saudi forces and captured north of Riyadh in the city of Buraidah in Qasim Province. The police face no resistance.

- *December 2, 2004:* Saudi security forces arrest two militants in Artawiya, and two others are captured in vicinity of Hafr Al Baten and Buraidah. Seven from the security forces are injured in the raids.

- *December 4, 2004:* Saudi security forces arrest a man in the city of Taif, western Saudi Arabia. The Ministry of Interior spokesman says that the detained man is the brother of one of the people on the Kingdom's 26 most-wanted list. He is suspected of supporting militants.

- *December 6, 2004:* The U.S. consulate in Jeddah is attacked. Five people are killed, including the three attackers, and two non-U.S. citizens who worked in the consulate. Two of the gunmen are injured and taken to the hospital (one would later die in the hospital). Four Saudi security officers are killed and several are wounded. Al Qaeda Organization in the Arabian Peninsula claims responsibility with a statement that is posted on its Web site. The statement says that the attack is revenge for the U.S. attack on Fallujah the previous month.

- *December 7, 2004:* Saudi authorities identify the people who carried the attack against the U.S. consulate: Fayez bin Awad al-Juhaini, Eid ibn Dakhilallah al-Jeheni and Hassan ibn Hamed al-Hazmi, none on the 26 most-wanted list.

- *December 28, 2004:* Saudi security forces engage in a gun battle with suspected militants in Al Deera district of Riyadh. Three gunmen are killed and one is injured in the fight.

- *December 29, 2004:* Saudi security forces kill a militant in a gun battle in Riyadh after he throws a hand grenade at Saudi officers while they are patrolling a residential district in Riyadh. Police later surround the car and kill the man in the shootout. Another militant is killed in Jeddah.

- *December 29, 2004:* Militants launch coordinated car bombings against the Ministry of Interior and a security forces recruitment center in Riyadh. The bomb next to the Interior Ministry injures several people, including five Saudi security officers and some bystanders. The security forces are able to stop the suicide bombing before detonating killing seven militants.

- *December 31, 2004:* Al Qaeda Organization in the Arabian Peninsula posts a statement on a Web site claiming responsibility and saying that their target was the interior minister, Prince Nayef, and his son and deputy, Prince Ahmad bin Nayef.

- *January 2, 2005:* The Ministry of Interior names the attackers of the 29 December attack. Three participated in the attack on the Interior Ministry: Ismael Ali Mohammad al-Khuzaim; Abdullah Saud Abu-Nayan al-Sobaie; who was on the Kingdom's most-wanted list and was the suicide bomber in the attack; and Mohammad Mohsen al-Osaimi. Two more people were named for their involvement in the attack on the recruitment center: Dakheel Abdul Aziz Dakheel Mohammad al-Obeid, and Nasser Ali Saad al-Motairi

- *January 9, 2005:* Saudi forces kill four gunmen in a gun battle in Al Zulfi, northwest of Riyadh. Three from Saudi security forces are injured. The police seize arms caches.

- *January 10, 2005:* The Ministry of Interior identifies three of the four militants killed the previous day as Muhammad al-Farraj, Mishaal Obaid Abdullah al-Hasiri, and Omar Abdullah al-Raid al-Qahtani.

- *January 18, 2005:* The Saudi Ministry of Interior announces they were able to trace the explosive to a neighborhood in Riyadh.

- *February 5–8, 2005:* Saudi Arabia hosts a four-day counterterrorism international conference, where delegates from about 50 nations debate how to coordinate the fight against terrorism. Prince Abdullah calls for an international effort in creating an antiterrorism center.

- *February 6, 2005:* A total of 221 people, including 92 suspected militants, have been killed in terror attacks in the Kingdom over the past two years, Interior Minister Prince Nayef said here yesterday.

- *March 12, 2005:* Saudi security forces arrested 18 terror suspects (17 Saudis and one Afghan) in a sweep of the northern town of Zulfi, according to Ministry of Interior. The raids are linked to incidents in January when security forces killed four wanted men, Muhammad al-Farraj, Mishaal Obaid Abdullah al-Hasiri, and Omar Abdullah al-Raid al-Qahtani The identity of the fourth was not known.

- *April 2, 2005:* Three Saudi criminals, who were said to be part of a terrorist group trained in Afghanistan, executed on 1 April in this northern Saudi Arabian town of al-Jouf. The three men were found guilty of kidnapping, robbery, murder, and shooting police, high officials, imams, and judges.

- *April 5, 2005:* The leader of the al Qaeda cell in Saudi Arabia, Saleh al-Aufi, who was reported killed earlier, is holed up in a villa, an informed source said. Talib Saud al-Talib, another most-wanted terrorist on the list of 26, was also with Al-Aufi.

- *April 5, 2005:* Seven members of "the deviant group" are killed, and an eighth is critically wounded, in the clash in Al Rass, some 320 kilometers northwest of Riyadh, the Interior Ministry said in a statement.

- *April 7, 2005:* Another top terrorist is killed the previous morning after security forces raided his hideout in the south of the capital. Abdul Rahman al-Yaziji, a terror suspect on the list of 26 most-wanted in Saudi Arabia, is shot dead in the Southern Industrial Area of Riyadh.

- *April 8, 2005:* Prince Nayef says he can not say the battle against militants is over. "I cannot say operations have ended, although members of the deviant group have been weakened. They may still surprise us anywhere in the Kingdom. We will continue to fight them."

- *April 10, 2005:* The Interior Ministry confirmed the previous day the death of Saud al-Otaibi, the leader of al Qaeda cell in Saudi Arabia, and Moroccan Abdul Kareem al-Majati, a terror suspect on the list of 26 most-wanted terrorists, in the previous week's gun battle in Al Rass.

- *April 10, 2005:* Crown Prince Abdullah calls for measures to combat deviant thoughts by carrying out cultural and educational programs, explaining the true teachings of Islam and driving home the merits of moderation and tolerance.

Changes in Post-May 2003 Reactions

Saudi Arabia's intelligence community has begun to make a major effort to track the activities of Saudi religious and charitable groups inside and outside the Kingdom and is now giving special attention to Pakistan and Central Asia. It is tightening security inside the Kingdom and increasing surveillance of young men with ties to extremist groups as well as religious figures who have made hard-line or extremist statements. Surveillance has also been increased over the activities of religious schools and teachers.

Furthermore, the Saudi authorities have realized that "emptiness leads to terrorism," as a consultative Shura Council member has said.[7] The authorities have realized that addressing economic and educational needs of the Saudi public is the most important element of the fight against terrorists. Although this was realized before the May 2003 bombing, it is more urgent now.

The government is pouring billions of dollars into training young Saudis for the technical and job-related skills to prepare them for the workforce. "The Saudi government has come to view putting more of its people to work as a matter of national security." This seems to be the realization of the authorities, and as the development director at the General Organization for Technical Education and Vocational Training argued, "I believe that not being able to get a job for young Saudis will lead to disaster, whether in security or moral terms."[8]

This Saudization program is only beginning to meet the needs of internal stability and security. Saudis fill only 13 percent of the private-sector jobs compared to a goal of 45 percent by this year.[9] There are many signs that this is heading in the right direction, but a lot more has to be done in both the training and the Saudization program. There ought to be a change in the attitudes toward taking private-sector jobs. This involves changes in the attitude of the Saudis. Culturally, they have tended to avoid low-paying jobs, especially those in the service sector. Clearly, this is disappearing slowly as many Saudis begin to take jobs as hotel concierges, supermarket cashiers, and taxi drivers.

The Problem of Corruption

Saudi Arabia also still needs to fully address another area of internal security that is not normally seen as part of the security apparatus but that certainly affects its operations. The level of corruption in Saudi Arabia is often exaggerated and is used to make broad, undocumented charges against the government and royal family. Corruption is, however, a serious problem, and exaggerated perceptions of corruption can be as important as reality.

Saudi Arabia has been slow to reform civil law and regulation to create the legal basis for large-scale private and foreign investment and commercial operations that can be based on secure rights to property, conducting business without interference or reliance on agents, and resolving commercial disputes. There has been progress in these areas, but there has not been enough, and Saudi security is growing increasingly dependent on the broad international perception that Saudi Arabia will reduce corruption, that members of the royal family and senior officials cannot intervene improperly in business affairs, and that investments and business activities are safe.

More and more Saudis are demanding transparency. They want to know where money is being spent. The senior leadership is heeding the call, and we see this in Crown Prince Abdullah's announcement about the Kingdom's plans for spending the budget surplus for 2004.[10] This will please the Saudi public, prevent squandering of funds, and improve the country's reputation in the world.

THE SHIITE PROBLEM AND IRAN

Fortunately, one threat to Saudi internal security seems to have diminished while the threat posed by al Qaeda grew. The threat Iran posed by exploited Saudi Shiite concerns and tensions seems to have diminished. In the past, Saudi Arabia had serious problems with Iranian intelligence agents and covert support of Shiite extremists after the fall of the shah in 1979, until it reached an accommodation with the Iranian government in the late 1990s. Weapons and explosives were intercepted in the Eastern Province, and there were numerous small acts of sabotage related to Iranian-sponsored activities. Iran trained a number of Saudi Shiites in low-intensity warfare and covert operations in Iran and Lebanon and regularly disrupted the Hajj to make political protests.

Saudi intelligence estimates have clearly linked Iran's Revolutionary Guard and certain officers of Iran's Ministry of Intelligence with the Al Khobar bombing. Iranian activity seems to have sharply diminished since the uncovering of the major covert Iranian networks operating in the Eastern Province, but Saudi intelligence officials note that Iran still attempts to maintain a significant intelligence presence in the Kingdom and still provides political, paramilitary, and religious training for at least some Saudi Shiites. However, because of the new capabilities of the Saudi counterintelligence and counterterrorism forces, it is proving more difficult for Iranian informants and operatives to establish new networks within the Kingdom.

While the threat Iran posed as an enabler of the Shiite opposition is under control, as mentioned above, the potential threat posed by a nuclear Iran is real. The Kingdom is worried, and again the country can: (1) live with a nuclear Iran by doing nothing, (2) build an antimissile defense system, or (3) acquire its own nuclear weapons. None of these choices is easy, but given that Iraq, as a military power, is out of the mix for at least the next 5–10 years, with the U.S. occupation, the only viable rival to Iran is Saudi Arabia. Doing nothing is not an option, especially during this period of transitional reforms the Kingdom is going through.

Although very unlikely, Iran could use its nuclear weapons to blackmail the Kingdom over its Shiite population, over its support of Bahrain, or over its control of the holy places, Mecca and Medina. Conventional weapons by themselves are not the answer. The questions, however, remain: Will the Saudis trust that the United States will be there for their protection? Is this enough to deter Iran from blackmailing the Kingdom? Do they have to look somewhere else for protection? Do they try to acquire their own deterrence?

The Evolving Saudi Security Apparatus

As has been described in Chapter 2, Saudi Arabia's security apparatus now deals with these issues using a complex mix of paramilitary and internal security forces as well as using an equally complex legal system for dealing with civil and security cases. This is a truly massive effort. The total internal security budget for 2003 topped $7 billion and in 2004 is estimated at $8–$8.5 billion (including security and intelligence), with a virtually open-ended capability to spend on any internal security purpose.

As has already been noted, a number of civil ministries like the Ministry of Islamic Affairs and Guidance play at least an indirect role in internal security because of their political impact. Others include the Ministry of Foreign Affairs, the Ministry of Communications, the Ministry of Finance, the Ministry of Culture and Information, the Ministry of Education, Ministry of Higher Education, Ministry of Justice, the Ministry of Petroleum and Mineral Resources, and the Ministry of Pilgrimage and Islamic Trusts. This kind of indirect role in internal security is typical of similar ministries in virtually every country in the developing world, as well as a number of countries in Europe.

The previous chapters have shown that Saudi security forces involve a mix of elements in the regular armed forces and the National Guard as well as a range of internal security and intelligence services, most of which are under the Ministry of Interior. The following charts show the various services. The regular army provides external security, but it is normally kept away from urban areas except for special forces and the helicopters it uses to support the MOI security services.

The National Guard—with its more than 100,000 combatants—provides internal security under a different chain of command, using both its regular forces and tribal levies. It protects the territory of the Kingdom and the approaches to its cities and critical facilities, acts as reinforcements for the regular forces, and can serve as an urban security force in an emergency. It does, however, have an Intelligence Directorate that focuses on counterintelligence within the National Guard itself and plays a limited role in counterterrorism operations. As of yet, it has no foreign intelligence operations capability.

The Pivotal Role of the Ministry of Interior

The key to the Saudi security apparatus is the Ministry of Interior. The internal security forces are centralized under Prince Nayef bin Abdul Aziz al-Saud, the minister of the interior.[11] Prince Nayef is a major political power in the Kingdom. He is one of the strongest figures in the royal family and has long played a critical role in Saudi security. His vice minister is Prince Ahmad bin Abdul Aziz, whose main function is to deal with the different provinces of the Kingdom and who also plays a major role as the main force behind the General Security Service. Prince Muhammad bin Nayef is the assistant minister for security affairs and handles all the uniformed services that fall under the Ministry of Interior.

These services and their troop totals are listed in Table 6.1.

Table 6.1:   Ministry of Interior Troop Totals in 2004

Department	Troop Level
General Security Service *(mabahith)*	CLASSIFIED
Passport & Immigration Department	7,500
Drug Enforcement Agency	20,000
General Prisons Service	15,000
Mujahideen	5,000
Border Guard (includes Coast Guard)	30,000
Civil Defense Administration	25,000
Special Security Forces	10,000
Public Security Administration	135,000
Various Police Forces—95,000	
Special Emergency Forces—30,000	
Petroleum Installation Security Force—10,000	

The Role of Prince Nayef

There are two prevailing schools of thought in the Kingdom on Prince Nayef. Some Saudis feel he is conservative and has underestimated the Kingdom's security problems. They feel he was too slow to react to the growth of Islamic extremist movements outside the Kingdom and to the role the Kingdom played in supporting such movements with money and Saudi volunteers, and saw outside pressure from the United States to crackdown on such activities as the result of exaggerated U.S. fears that were at least partly the result of pressure from Israel.

The other school of thought holds that he is the nerve center of the complex security network in Saudi Arabia and hence is the key actor in Saudi Arabia's ongoing war against terrorism, and they give him the credit for all the successes in that war (hundreds of arrests of suspected militants, killing of senior al Qaeda figures, foiling of major bombings both within and outside the Kingdom, and the uncovering of huge weapons and explosives caches).

Using the Wrong Words at the Wrong Time

The former view is given some support by Prince Nayef's own words, and it has been clear that the MOI has lacked an effective public relations strategy. Since September 11, 2001, Prince Nayef has made several political statements implying that the people who benefited the most from the attacks were the "Zionists." For example, he made statements in an interview with the Kuwaiti newspaper *Al-Siyasa* on November 29, 2002.

Prince Nayef did say, "We put big question marks and ask who committed the events of September 11 and who benefited from them. Who benefited from the events of September 11? I think they [the Zionists] are behind these events." He expressed the view that it was "impossible" that al Qaeda alone, or that 19 youths, of which 15 were Saudi, could have acted alone.

He then went on to attack the Muslim Brotherhood by saying, "All our problems come from the Muslim brotherhood. We have given too much support to this group. . . . The Muslim Brotherhood has destroyed the Arab world." He attacked a multinational spectrum of Islamic politicians for turning their backs on Saudi Arabia, forgetting the favors it had given them, and launching attacks on the Kingdom. He singled out Hassan al-Turabi of the Sudan as a case in point. He also mentioned Hamas, Jordan's parliamentary opposition, and the Islamic Action Front for their attacks on the Kingdom, and attacked Islamic scholars like Abdul Rahman Khalifa, Rashid Ghannouchi, Abdul Majeed al-Zidani, and Necmettin Erbakan for supporting the Iraqi invasion of Kuwait. He stated there were no dormant al Qaeda cells remaining in Saudi Arabia and that this threat no longer existed.[12]

In fairness, Prince Nayef used such language in a long interview stressing the need to crack down on terrorism, that the government was putting pressure on Saudi religious figures and mosques that the Kingdom has made numerous arrests, and that terrorism was fundamentally anti-Islamic. He was also reacting to a flood of poorly founded U.S. and Western press criticism of Saudi Arabia, linking the possibility that the wife of the Saudi ambassador to the United States gave money to a family that *might* have been linked to terrorists.[13]

Actions Are More Important than Words

Actions, not words, however, are the key to successful counterterrorism. Other Saudis feel that Prince Nayef has reacted strongly and effectively to the increases in the Islamist threat to the Kingdom since the attacks of May 2003 and feel he is often quoted out of context. It is also clear than many U.S. and other Western experts feel that Prince Nayef, his brother Prince Ahmad, and his son Prince Mohammad have been highly effective in reacting to the threat since May 2003.

The directors general of the respective services administratively all report to the minister and vice minister and are directly responsible to the minister; operationally, they are directly linked to the assistant minister for security affairs. They include the directors general of the Civil Defense Administration, Public Security Administration (all police forces fall under this service and, more important, the Special Emergency Forces, which have taken the lead in the domestic war against terrorism), Passports & Immigration Department, Border Guards, Mujahideen, the General Prisons Service, and the Special Security Forces. Because of the power of the General Security Service (GSS) and the sensitivity of its mission, its director general reports to Vice Minister Prince Ahmad.

The Public Security Force, Special Security Forces, Mujahideen, and GSS provide internal security at the political and intelligence levels and inside cities and deal with limited problems that require crowd control, SWAT-like operations, and counterterrorist capabilities. They also provide the Kingdom's primary counterterrorist force and played a major role in dealing with the bombings of the SANG headquarters and the USAF barracks at Al Khobar.

All of these activities are becoming steadily more coordinated and effective, and steps are being taken to build morale as well. Prince Nayef and Prince Ahmad are reported to pay massive bonuses to successful security officers, but they also have a reputation for honesty and using the massive security budget only for the mission and not to enrich themselves. And Prince Mohammad bin Nayef has also been very generous to the families of the security officers who have died combating the terrorist networks in the Kingdom. This generosity has made the three senior figures extremely popular among the officers of the Ministry of Interior.

The Police and Security Services

The police and security forces are still somewhat traditional in character, but they have been steadily modernized. Over the past two years, under the strong leadership of Prince Mohammad bin Nayef, there has been a major reorganization and development of these forces financed by huge budget increases. Early in Saudi Arabia's history there were no formal police, and local and tribal authorities administered justice. During the reign of King Abdul Aziz, more modern police, justice, and internal security organizations were developed. In 1950 he created a "general directorate" to supervise all police functions. He established the Ministry of Interior in 1951, which has since controlled police matters.

Saudi Arabia has received substantial technical advice from British, French, German, Jordanian, Pakistani, and U.S. experts. Substantial numbers of British and French advisers served in Saudi Arabia in the past, including seconded ex-government and military personnel, but it is unclear how many have continued to serve since the early 1990s.

The police security forces are now divided into regular police (which fall under public security) and special investigative and intelligence police of the General Security Service, which are called the *mabahith* (secret police). The GSS performs the domestic security and counterintelligence functions of the Ministry of Interior. The GSS has a large special investigation force, something like the British CID. The U.S. State Department reports that political detainees arrested by the GSS are often held incommunicado in special prisons during the initial phase of an investigation, which may last weeks or months. The GSS allows the detainees only limited contact with their families or lawyers.

There are approximately 135,000 paramilitary policemen in the Public Security Administration, which is equipped with the latest weaponry. They are assigned to provincial governors and are under the minister of interior. Public Security forces train at the King Fahd College for Security Studies located in Riyadh. The Public Security Administration forces have a police college in Mecca. Police uniforms are similar to the khaki and olive drab worn by the army except for the distinctive black beret. Policemen usually wear side arms while on duty.

The Public Security's Special Emergency Forces have taken the lead in combating the al Qaeda networks in the Kingdom. They have similar specialized training as the Special Security Forces in counterterrorism and counterinsurgency operations. Because of their mobility, they act as a rapid-deployment security force in case of an unexpected security threat. They number around 30,000 and are in the process of a large-scale modernization and development program. They operate basically as the defensive Special Security Force and antiterrorist service of the Kingdom. The Special Security Force is the Saudi equivalent of a special weapons assault team (SWAT) and acts as the offensive force in the Kingdom. It reports directly to the minister of interior, but its operational head is the assistant minister for security affairs. It was organized in response to the poor performance of the National Guard during the 1979 revolt at the Grand Mosque in Mecca.

The force is equipped with the latest light armored vehicles, automatic weapons, and nonlethal chemical weapons. Although its core personnel have been raised to 10,000, its total final strength remains unclear, because the threat level varies. Its antiterrorism units have been steadily expanded since 1990. In the past few years, enormous sums have been spent to reorganize and modernize this force. It is designed to deal with terrorism and hijacking and has SWAT capabilities and detachments in every major Saudi city and province.

The public security forces are recruited from all areas of the country and maintain police directorates at provincial and local levels. These forces, particularly the centralized Public Security Police, can be reinforced by the National Guard in an emergency or can get support from the regular armed forces. The director general for public security retains responsibility for police units, but, in practice, provincial governors exercise considerable autonomy.

The focus of police and security activity has also changed over the years. Saudi Arabia is now a highly urbanized society, and these formal state institutions carry out most internal security and criminal justice activity in urban areas. This has helped drive the effort to modernize the police and security forces. For example, state-of-the-art command and control systems have been acquired and deployed and new vehicles and radio communications equipment have enabled police directorates to operate sophisticated mobile units, particularly in the principal cities. The Special Security Forces and the Special Emergency Forces have acquired a sizable fleet of helicopters for use in urban areas and have been used against various terrorist cells operating in the Kingdom.

The Ministry of Interior now maintains one of the most sophisticated centralized computer systems in the world at the National Information Center in Riyadh. This computer network links some 1,100 terminals and maintains records on citizens' identity numbers and passports, foreigners' residence and work permits, Hajj visas, vehicle registrations, and criminal records. Reports from agents and from the large number of informants employed by the security services are also entered. Officials of the GSS and the General Intelligence Presidency (GIP) have authority to carry out wiretaps and mail surveillance. The Ministry of Interior also has a large electronic intelligence operation with a separate budget that is estimated at over $500 million per year.

Some security activities do, however, continue to be enforced on a tribal level in tribal areas. The king provides payments or subsidies to key sheikhs, and they are largely in charge of tribal affairs. Offenses and many crimes are still punished by the responsible sheikh. The National Guard acts as a support force to deal with problems that cannot be settled or controlled by the tribal authorities.

GENERAL SECURITY SERVICE

The General Security Service is the domestic intelligence service of the Ministry of Interior. It is the most important and sensitive service in the Kingdom. Although exact figures pertaining to the GSS are classified, informed estimates

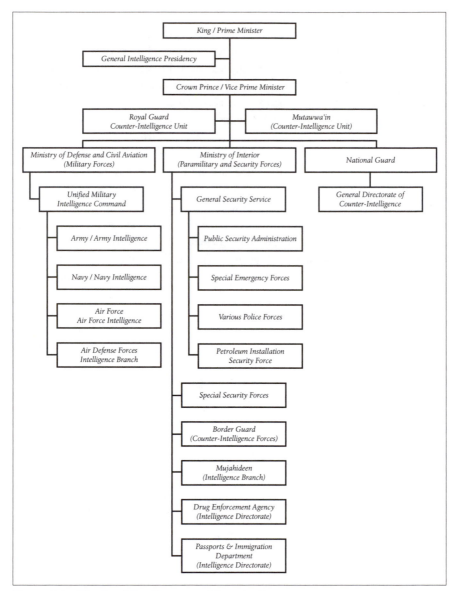

Figure 6.1: The Saudi Intelligence and Security Community

show that it has by far the largest budget of any domestic intelligence service in the Middle East. The numbers of its staff are likewise confidential.

Cooperation between the U.S. and Saudi intelligence communities has increased since the attacks in May 2003. Shortly thereafter, the FBI began to work with the GSS in earnest, and a close working relationship has developed.

Although shortcomings on both sides remain, their joint efforts have contributed to major successes in the war on terrorism in the Kingdom and abroad.

Under the strong leadership of Prince Ahmad and Prince Mohammad bin Nayef, the GSS has been successful at thwarting many plots and pressuring many Saudis not to join the militants. On August 30, 2004, Prince Nayef said that he "can say, confidently, that what happened does not exceed five or six per cent of what was foiled."[14] The GSS has remarkably improved the quality of its information gathering, the assessment of this data, and most important, its dissemination to troops on the ground.

GSS operations have been streamlined to adapt to new threats. In addition, budget increases have allowed for highly specialized training programs and acquisitions of the latest equipment, making the GSS one of the most professional intelligence services in the region. Furthermore, its interrogation methods have yielded actionable intelligence that has thwarted numerous attacks in the Kingdom and abroad.

As a result of this success, the senior officers of the service have become prime targets of the terrorists. There were at least two instances when they attempted assassinations against top security officials. First, in December 2003, Lt. Col. Ibrahim al-Dhaleh, of the GSS, was attacked by a car bomb. Second, there have been other attempts against Maj. Gen. Abdul Aziz al-Huweirini, the assistant director for interrogations at the GSS, and the senior officer in charge of debriefing captured al Qaeda terrorists in the Kingdom. He was shot and injured on December 4, 2003.[15] He has since recovered and returned to his post.

THE GENERAL INTELLIGENCE PRESIDENCY

Saudi Arabia's main foreign intelligence service is the General Intelligence Presidency. Its many responsibilities include foreign security operations, antiterrorism operations, foreign liaison functions, strategic analytical assessments, coordinating the foreign covert networks of the Kingdom, and, ultimately, foreign covert operations, if need be.

The president of the GIP reports directly to the prime minister (the king). Although the budget of the GIP is classified, it is roughly estimated at a minimum of $500 million per year. That would make it the highest-funded foreign intelligence service in the Middle East.

An Emerging Saudi Intelligence Community

In theory, the head of the General Intelligence Presidency is responsible for intelligence collection and analysis as well as for the coordination of intelligence tasks and reporting by *all* intelligence agencies, including those of the Ministry of Interior, Ministry of Defense and Civil Aviation, and the National Guard. In practice, at the operational level, there now is no real Saudi intelligence "community."

One is in the process of being formed, however, and a real effort is being made to ensure that the various services can function in a unified manner. Since 9/11, the senior Saudi leadership has realized that intelligence sharing—or "fusion"—is weak, coordination is poor, and the different services are filled with personal and bureaucratic rivalries and tensions. The problems are compounded by the fact that the research departments of the services—especially those at the GIP—are weak and that, in general, Saudi intelligence collection relies too heavily on personal contacts and briefings, rather than on systematic and structured analysis.

A pure Saudi intelligence community would be composed of the GIP, GSS, Border Guard, National Information Center, the three intelligence branches of the military (Army, Navy, and Air Force), the National Guard Intelligence Directorate, the Interior Minister's Bureau of Analysis and Studies, the Foreign Ministry's Information and Studies Center, and the National Guard's Specialized Studies Center.

The Changing Role of the GIP

Under Prince Turki al-Faisal's leadership, the GIP was successful in dealing with many internal and foreign threats that posed a direct menace to the Kingdom. It had a long history of cooperation with U.S. intelligence, although it has (along with its sister agency, the GSS) generally opposed any Western efforts to introduce law enforcement organizations like the CIA and FBI into Saudi security issues in ways that could embarrass the Saudi government. This led to acute tensions between the two main Saudi services and their American counterparts over such investigations as the Al Khobar bombing and helped lead to the charges that the Saudi government covered up Iranian involvement in the bombing.

In fairness to Saudi Arabia, however, the United States, Britain, and other Western countries failed to cooperate with Saudi intelligence in a number of past cases, because they felt that this might violate the rights of legitimate opposition movements or raise human rights issues. The U.S. and other Western intelligence services also turned a blind eye, or at least tolerated, Islamic extremist activity when it seemed to serve their interests in Afghanistan and Bosnia, or acted as a counterbalance to Russian influence in Central Asia and paid little attention to the potential threat posed by funds and manpower coming out of the Kingdom. If Saudi Arabia was slow to see the threat of extremism and terrorism and sometimes "exported" its problems, the U.S., British, and other European intelligence and security services made equally serious mistakes in monitoring and characterizing "Islamic" movements.

Major developments have taken place within the GIP since 11 September. Prince Turki al-Faisal was replaced in 2001 by Prince Nawaf bin Abdul Aziz.[16] This development was particularly striking, because Prince Turki al-Faisal had spent some 30 years in intelligence and had built a solid reputation for professionalism and effectiveness. He began his career as deputy director in the Office of Foreign Liaison at the age of 23.

Over the years, he reorganized and consolidated the office into a full-fledged intelligence service. He became director of intelligence in 1977, and it was at that time that the move toward a professional intelligence service began in earnest. Prince Turki had long been the main contact point for the U.S., British, French and other main Western and Arab services, among others. He was also responsible for dealing with operations in Afghanistan and Central Asia since the Soviet invasion in 1979. He was also the main point of contact with the U.S.-Saudi backed Mujahideen and the Pakistani Inter-Services Intelligence (ISI) service, with the various warring Afghan factions after the Soviet withdrawal, and with the Taliban and Osama bin Laden (along with other Arab Mujahideen).[17] He is considered by many inside Saudi Arabia as one of the Kingdom's leading strategic thinkers.

The Future Role and Capabilities of the GIP

The future of Saudi internal security will not be shaped by the leadership of the General Intelligence Presidency alone, but rather by the overall effectiveness of the government and the royal family in dealing with the broader mix of political, economic, social, and demographic issues that threaten Saudi Arabia's internal security. An important fact that has been missed by most foreign assessments is that the GIP, in its bylaws, does not have the right to make arrests; rather, it can track and monitor individuals in Saudi Arabia. At the same time, the General Security Service carries out any recommendations for arrests. Hence, its role is one of an early-warning advisory service, which, depending on the effectiveness of its head, can be extremely influential in Saudi security planning, or irrelevant, as is the case today.

Saudi Arabia clearly needs to do more to expand and modernize some aspects of its intelligence operations. In the past, Saudi intelligence has tended to rely heavily on interpersonal relations and human intelligence (HUMINT), supplemented by limited usage of surveillance equipment (SIGINT) and computerized records. It worked closely with the major Western and Arab intelligence services in some areas and had some access to more-advanced imagery and signal intelligence through such sources. Saudi intelligence did not, however, establish and organize for the kind of sophisticated domestic and foreign surveillance networks necessary to provide adequate coverage of small, dispersed Islamic terrorist groups and individual movements. It has tended to rely on information from traditional elites and to have limited data on urbanized Saudis and Saudi young males who become affiliated with extremist movements inside and especially outside of Saudi Arabia. Surveillance of financial transfers, charitable organizations, and activities like money laundering has been particularly weak, as no body within the GIP was set up to deal with those issues.

Moreover, the GIP had become markedly less effective since the departure of Prince Turki. Most of the sophisticated networks that had been established over many years have deteriorated, and hence the GIP's role in the global war on terrorism has been marginal at best. Thus, the Kingdom has had to rely heavily on only one truly professional security service, the GSS.

To address this deficiency, Crown Prince Abdullah appointed Prince Faisal bin Abdullah bin Mohammad as a new assistant president of the GIP in charge of administratively reorganizing the agency. He was a former deputy commander of the National Guard for the Western Region and brings a new administrative focus to the service, that along with the personal dynamism of Prince Abdulaziz bin Bandar bin Abdul Aziz, the other co-assistant president in charge of revamping the vitally important analysis and research directorate, has led some to hope that they can put back the GIP at the center of the Kingdom's international security relationships.

Hence, two new assistant presidents share the organizational day-to-day working of the service under the leadership of Prince Saud bin Fahd, King Fahd's son, who occupies the second slot as the vice president of GIP since Prince Nawaf bin Abdul Aziz, the president of GIP, retired from his post on January 26, 2005, and no successor has been named. It is hoped that the dynamism of the two assistant presidents under a new leader will lead to a reinvigoration of the service, especially if they surround themselves by a core group of capable new professional intelligence officers.

Border and Coastal Security

Border and coastline control is the responsibility of the Border Guard and has long been an important aspect of security operations. Smuggling is endemic, even across the Saudi border with Iraq. Saudi border guards arrested 777 smugglers crossing the border during 2001 and seized nearly three tons of hashish, more than 5,700 bottles of alcohol, more than 450 weapons, and 43,680 rounds of ammunition.[18] Since the fall of Saddam Hussein, smuggling across this border has dropped drastically. While Saudi Arabia does not announce the fact publicly, it regularly had to deal with Iraqi patrols that crossed into Saudi territory, and it is now clear that some Iraqi intelligence officers had been operating in the Kingdom prior to the Iraq War.

Saudi Arabia has taken diplomatic steps to greatly reduce its problems and tensions with Iran and Yemen and particularly to reduce Iranian efforts to exploit Saudi Arabia's problems with its Shiites and use the Hajj as a propaganda forum. The Kingdom has also, however, taken strong steps to improve its counterterrorism efforts in dealing with border and coastal security as well. It has improved its monitoring of foreign nationals and ability to track their movements and activities.

The Role of the Border Guard

The 30,000-man Border Guard covers Saudi Arabia's land and sea borders. It performs a host of patrol and surveillance missions and can act as a light defensive screen. It is equipped with four-wheel-drive vehicles and automatic weapons as well as a sizable fleet of helicopters. The Border Guard did much of the fighting with Yemen in the past and took casualties in doing so. It still must deal with the problem of smuggling and infiltration across the Saudi borders with Yemen, Jordan, and Iraq.

Some members of the Border Guard have been implicated in smuggling by sea, but this activity is severely punished and does not seem to be any more common than in other countries. Similar problems exist along the border with Yemen, although the border clashes that used to take place between Yemeni and Saudi security forces seem to have largely ended following the settlement of the Saudi-Yemeni border in June 2000.

The main problems are now smuggling and intertribal violence, which are still endemic. The Yemeni border has been the main source of the weapons and explosives used in the recent terrorist attacks against the Kingdom. This border is still the main conduit by which militants from Afghanistan enter the country. The Saudi borders with Kuwait, Bahrain, the UAE, and Oman are stable and secure except for smuggling. The movement of alcohol and narcotics is still a problem.

The Kingdom's strategic location and large territories makes its borders vulnerable to smuggling of arms and drugs. The various rugged terrains make surveillance difficult and provide hiding places for smugglers. Furthermore, the vastness of the borders makes it easier for terrorists and smugglers to train without being noticed by the authorities. The Kingdom has always been concerned with weapons and ammunition smuggling, especially since the May 2003 attacks. Table 6.2 provides the quantity of weapons and explosives the

Saudi Border Guard confiscated every year. The MOI also reported that the number of cases has declined in 2004 as a result of the use of surveillance systems at borders and coasts.[19]

In the same paper, the MOI provided a breakdown of weapons and explosives that were confiscated in the last five years. They totaled 16,389 weapons, 14,816,111 rounds of ammunition, 240 bombs, 1,282 materials, 355,191 digits, and 343,292 wire connections.[20]

The Option of a Border Surveillance and Defense System

Saudi Arabia has considered major changes in its security apparatus to deal with these issues. As early as the 1990s, Saudi Arabia considered building a border surveillance system that would use patrol aircraft, remotely piloted vehicles, and early-warning systems to detect intruders and border crossings. This would have involved a 12 kilometer-deep security zone around all 6,500 kilometers of the land and sea borders, with a mix of acoustic, seismic, radar, magnetic, and infrared sensors to detect movements of people and vehicles in the border area. It would have been supported by small manned patrol aircraft and unmanned remotely piloted vehicles wherever some threat from an intruder might exist.

Thomson CSF completed a $5 million feasibility study for this system in early 1990, and two consortiums—one led by E Systems and the other by Thomson CSF—submitted bids to Saudi Arabia in May 1991. The system was not funded in part because of its cost and in part because of the ease with which given sections could be penetrated before an effective response would be possible. Its estimated cost was around $3 billion, and it would have taken several years to complete.[21]

Putting in such a system has been put on hold at the request of the Yemeni government. If the government does put such a system in place, it is now likely to be through the installation of a much more technically sophisticated system.

MIKSA: Saudi Border Guard Development Program. In October 2002, the Border Guard was reported to have added thermal cameras, radars, and other detection systems to their arsenal.[22] The Kingdom, however, has also announced plans to upgrade its border surveillance systems, especially on the Saudi-Yemeni borders. MIKSA, Ministry of Interior Kingdom of Saudi Arabia, is a contract with France to build C^{4}I and IS&R systems on the Saudi-Yemeni border. Known also as the Saudi Border Guard Development Program, MIKSA has been under negotiations since 1994 following the signing of a MoU between Prince Nayef, the Saudi minister of interior, and his French counterpart, Charles Pasqua. It was reported that French president Jacques Chirac personally discussed MIKSA with the crown prince during his state visit to France in May 2004.[23]

According to press reports, President Chirac took "charge" of the negotiations himself, taking them away from the French minister of the interior, Nicholas Sarkozy, because he felt the process was taking too long and put his diplomatic adviser, Maurice Gourdault-Montagne, in charge of the negotiations. According to the French press, Mr. Sarkozy was "sidelined," because under his leadership, the French Ministry of Interior did not provide the necessary transparency and legal framework for the contract. Crown Prince Abdullah, according to the same press reports, voiced his opposition to the "payment of any commission," demanded more transparency, and asked that the contract be signed "state to state" by "highest authority" in France.[24]

Under the insistence of the Elysee, the consortium bidding has been taken away from Thales, and the French Advanced Systems Export Company, SOF-RESA, which has close ties to President Chirac, has taken the lead in the negotiations.[25]

MIKSA is estimated to take up to 12 years and cost between $5 billion and $9 billion to complete. If finalized the program would:

- Build a 3,000 mile electronic surveillance and detection system;
- Install ACROPOLE, a Communication System that was created for the French police. The system has databanks on wanted persons, stolen vehicles, and so forth;
- Install 400 frontier posts and barracks to house 20,000 soldiers;
- Train the 20,000 border guards;
- Provide 20 reconnaissance aircraft and helicopters;
- Build 225 radar stations and link them by satellite to a central command center; and[26]
- Provide unmanned aerial vehicles (UAVs).[27]

During Crown Prince Abdullah's visit to Paris in April 2005, an Elysee spokesman said that "Jacques Chirac and Prince Abdullah raised these two projects (Thales and Dassault) within the framework of a wide-ranging conversation." The Elysee reiterated that nothing was signed with regard to MIKSA.[28] However, it was reported that Thales' CEO hinted in late April of 2005 that the program is on a fast track.[29]

The Expanding Mission of the Border Guard

The Border Guard historically has been concerned with smuggling, but this has now become a growing internal security mission.[30] They are being expanded and given better equipment like very fast patrol boats. The Air Force and Navy are providing them more surveillance and patrol support, and some consideration is being given to giving the Boarder Guard surveillance helicopters, while the Navy is seeking suitable maritime patrol aircraft.

It is virtually impossible, however, for Saudi Arabia to fully secure its Gulf or Red Sea coasts against smuggling and infiltration by small craft. Traffic in the Gulf and Red Sea is simply too high, the coasts are too long, and sensors cannot track movements by dhows and small craft. The Saudi Navy, Border Guard, and National Guard are able to provide adequate security screening for key ports, desalination facilities, and petroleum export facilities with roughly two weeks of warning. Coverage is generally limited in peacetime.

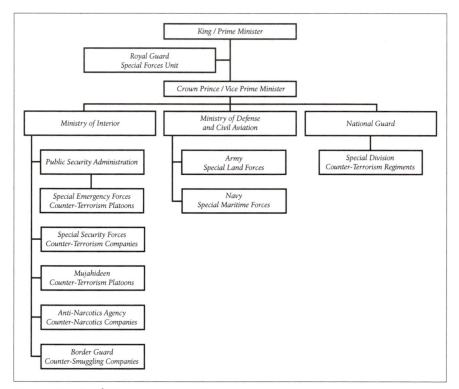

Figure 6.2: Saudi Counterterrorism Forces

Security and the Role of the Judicial System

Another aspect of the Saudi security apparatus, the Saudi civil and criminal legal system, has slowly been modernized, but it presents problems in terms of both efficient internal security operations and human rights. It is traditional and religious in character and is based on Shari'a as interpreted by Islamic practice under the Wahhabi order, which adheres to the Hanbali School of the Sunni branch of Islam.

The Shari'a courts exercise jurisdiction over common criminal cases and civil suits regarding marriage, divorce, child custody, and inheritance. These courts base judgments largely on the Qur'an and on the Sunna, another Islamic text. Cases involving relatively small penalties are tried in Shari'a summary courts; more serious crimes are adjudicated in Shari'a courts of common pleas. Appeals from Shari'a courts are made to the courts of appeal. The Saudi government permits Shiite Muslims to use their own legal tradition to adjudicate noncriminal cases within their community. Other civil proceedings, including those involving claims against the government and enforcement of foreign judgments, are held before specialized administrative tribunals, such as the Commission for the Settlement of Labor Disputes and the Board of Grievances.[31]

The Judicial System and Internal Security

The judicial system works differently when it deals with internal security issues. The Saudi government is still deeply concerned about the security of the military forces—although there have been no recent cases of active opposition within either the regular military forces or the paramilitary and security forces. The military justice system has jurisdiction over uniformed personnel and civil servants who are charged with violations of military regulations. The king, the crown prince, and the minister of defense and civil aviation review the decisions of courts-martial, and it is clear that serious cases get the direct attention of the senior leadership. Similarly, the Saudi government conducts closed trials for persons who may be political prisoners and in other cases has detained persons incommunicado for long periods while under investigation.

The U.S. State Department reports that there are several bodies that perform higher legal review functions:

The Supreme Judicial Council is not a court and may not reverse decisions made by a court of appeals. However, the council may review lower-court decisions and refer them back to the lower court for reconsideration. Only the Supreme Judicial Council may discipline or remove a judge. The king appoints the members of this council.

The Council of Senior Religious Scholars is an autonomous body of 20 senior religious jurists, including the minister of justice. It establishes the legal principles to guide lower-court judges in deciding cases.

Provincial governors have the authority to exercise leniency and reduce a judge's sentence.

The king reviews cases involving capital punishment. He has the authority to commute death sentences and grant pardons, except for capital crimes committed against individuals. In such cases, he may request the victim's next of kin to pardon the murderer—usually in return for compensation from the family or the king.

THE MUTAWWA'IN, OR RELIGIOUS POLICE

Saudi Arabia has a religious police called the Mutawwa'in, which is a force organized under the king in conjunction with the Islamic "clergy," or ulema. It is known in English as the Organization to Prevent Vice and Promote Virtue or Committees for Public Morality and is part of the government's Department of Virtue Propagation and Vice Prevention. It is primarily responsible for ensuring compliance with the precepts of Wahhabism, but it performs some security functions in dealing with religious extremists.[32] The Mutawaa'in enforce the public observances of religious practices, such as the closure of public establishments during prayer times. They have been known to exceed their authority with both Saudi and expatriates alike by undue harassment of both men and women in public places and trespassing into private homes.

The State Department reports that:

> The Mutawaa'in have the authority to detain persons for no more than 24 hours for violations of the strict standards of proper dress and behavior. However, they sometimes exceed this limit before delivering detainees to the police. Current procedures require a police officer to accompany the Mutawaa'in at the time of an arrest. The Mutawaa'in generally comply with this requirement. In the more conservative Riyadh district, however, there are continuing reports received of Mutawaa'in accosting, abusing, arresting, and detaining persons alleged to have violated dress and behavior standards. Mutawaa'in practices and incidents of abuse varied widely in different regions of the country, but were most numerous in the central Najd region. In certain areas, both the Mutawaa'in and religious vigilantes acting on their own harassed, assaulted, battered, arrested, and detained citizens and foreigners. The Government requires the Mutawaa'in to follow established procedures and to offer instruction in a polite manner; however, Mutawaa'in did not always comply with the requirements. The Government has not publicly criticized abuses by Mutawaa'in and religious vigilantes, but has sought to curtail these abuses.

It also reports that the Mutawaa'in enforce strict standards of social behavior, including the closing of commercial establishments during the five daily prayer observances, insisting on compliance with strict norms of public dress, and dispersing gatherings of women in public places. The Mutawaa'in frequently reproach Saudi and foreign women for failure to observe strict dress codes, and have arrested men and women found together who were not married or closely related. In November 1998, several Mutawaa'in attacked and killed an elderly Shiite prayer leader in Hofuf for calling the prayer according to the Shiite tradition. Mutawaa'in attempts to cover up the killing were unsuccessful. The State Department reports that the government reportedly investigated the incident but does not make public the results of any investigations involving Mutawaa'in personnel.

The level of Mutawwa'in activity has varied over time, and is difficult to predict. The government appointed a new and more compliant leader of the religious police after a series of raids on rich and influential Saudis in 1990, but their power grew strikingly after the Gulf War, as Saudi traditionalists reacted to the presence of U.S. and other Western forces, but seems to have peaked in the mid-1990s. The number of reports of harassment by the Mutawaa'in during the late 1990s remained relatively low in comparison with previous years, but the Mutawaa'in continues to intimidate, abuse, and detain citizens and foreigners of both sexes.

Some Saudi officials go so far as to describe the Mutawwa'in as a form of disguised unemployment for religious Saudis and state it is sharply overstaffed in some areas. One senior Saudi official went so far as to refer to the Mutawwa'in a "religious labor union more interested in their benefits than anything else." Other Saudis are more divided in their reaction. Some feel the Mutawwa'in perform a useful function in limiting the secularization of the Kingdom. Others see it as an outdated and overconservative annoyance.[33] Serious questions also remain about the degree to which the attitudes of organizations like the Mutawwa'in affected the safety of Saudi girls' schools and did or did not interfere in a school fire that killed 15 Saudi girls in March 2002.[34]

In late November 2002, Prince Nayef was sufficiently disturbed over continuing problems with the Mutawwa'in that he publicly took action to try to improve the conduct of the Department of Virtue Propagation and Vice Prevention. He called on the department to "hire well qualified people and not people of limited qualifications who act recklessly," to "gently deal with the people and avoid harshness, especially with young people." He announced a training institute was being set up and that the Mutawwa'in would operate with better training and discipline.[35]

In general, the Mutawwa'in seem to be more of a Saudi internal security problem than part of the solution. Saudis do not seem to be able to cite any examples of cases where the Mutawwa'in have played a role in limiting the activities of Islamic extremists and defending the core values of Islam against extremism or in defending religious values while aiding modernization and reform. To be blunt, they have been a "gentler and kinder" Taliban. They have carried out rote enforcement of Saudi religious practices while acting as a tacit endorsement of efforts to force compliance with Islam rather than persuade. As such, they often at least indirectly endorse Islamic extremism while lacking the intellectual depth, training, and experience to truly defend one of the world's great religions.

It should be noted, however, that there is another force called the Muja-hideen, whose operations are centered in Riyadh and that largely patrols it at night as a kind of religious vice squad. It has taken part in counterterrorism operations. This force is much more professional than the Mutawwa'in and is rarely seen or talked about. It is staffed by around 5,000 and is an independent service that reports administratively to Prince Nayef, the minister of interior, and operationally to the assistant minister for security affairs.

Chapter 7

Saudi Energy Security

E nergy security is only one of the security challenges Saudi Arabia faces, but it is certainly critical to both the Kingdom and the world as a whole. Saudi Arabia is the center of a region that now dominates the world's petroleum exports and whose importance will grow steadily over the coming decades. This inevitably makes Saudi Arabia a key potential target for anyone who wishes to use energy exports as a strategic weapon.

At the same time, Saudi Arabia's economic dependence on energy exports makes its energy facilities a potential target for direct attack, covert attack, and terrorism. Osama bin Laden has recognized this all too clearly. While al Qaeda has not previously attacked Saudi energy facilities directly, bin Laden announced that such attacks might be part of its future strategy in a tape issued in December 2004.[1]

THE ROLE OF THE GULF AND MIDDLE EAST IN GLOBAL ENERGY EXPORTS

Current estimates indicate that the Middle East and North Africa (MENA) have some 63 percent of all of the world's proven oil resources, and some 37 percent of its gas. In 2003 Saudi Arabia alone was estimated to have roughly 26 percent of the world's proven oil resources and 4 percent of its gas, Saudi Arabia also provided 12.55 percent of the entire world's oil production; the Gulf provided 28.72 percent, and the entire MENA region provide approximately 34 percent.[2] The Energy Information Agency (EIA) of the U.S. Department of Energy and the U.S. Geological Survey (USGS) estimate that Saudi Arabia now has the capacity to produce a maximum of 11.2 million barrels per day (bpd) of crude (with a sustained capacity of 10.6–10.8). The EIA estimates that these high oil reserves, and low incremental production costs, will ensure that Saudi Arabia and the Gulf region will dominate increases in oil production through at least 2015.[3]

The EIA estimates that Saudi Arabia alone will account for 4.2 million bpd of the total increase, Iraq for 1.6 million bpd, Kuwait for 1.3 million bpd, and the UAE for 1.2 million bpd by 2015 in its reference case projection. These four countries will account for 8.3 million bpd out of a worldwide total of 17.9 million bpd (46 percent). To put these figures in perspective, Russia will account for an increase of only 1.3 million bpd.[4]

The International Energy Agency (IEA) estimates that total conventional and nonconventional oil production will increase from 77 million bpd in 2002 to 121.3 million bpd in 2030. This is a total increase of 44.3 million bpd worldwide. The Middle East will account for 30.7 million bpd, or 69 percent of this total. The IEA also estimates that the rate of dependence on Middle East oil will increase steadily after 2010 as other fields are depleted in areas where new resources cannot be brought on line. It estimates that 29 million bpd, or 94 percent of the total 31 million bpd increase in OPEC production between 2010 and 2030, will come from Middle Eastern members of OPEC.[5]

In these estimates, and in virtually every other major forecast, Saudi Arabia is a key petroleum exporter and is central to a steadily more interdependent global economy. Saudi Arabia is also the only oil producer that has consistently sought to maintain surplus oil production capacity, with a nominal goal of 2 million bpd. This situation will not change in the foreseeable future.

There are, however, serious uncertainties in virtually every aspect of such estimates. For example, the claims MENA and Gulf countries make regarding their "proven reserves" have become highly political over the last few decades and may well be exaggerated. Nevertheless, the issue is not whether Saudi Arabia and the Gulf will play a critical role in world energy supplies; it is rather how much petroleum capacity they can develop and export. The Kingdom has roughly 80 oil and gas fields and more than 1,000 oil wells; however, more than 50 percent of the Kingdom's reserves are in only eight fields.[6]

Most estimates indicate that Saudi Arabia holds roughly one-quarter of the world's proven oil reserves, with a nominal figure of 261.90 billion barrels, according to the EIA, and may contain up to 1 trillion barrels of ultimately recoverable oil.[7]

Saudi sources have recently gone much higher. On December 27, 2004, Saudi Oil Minister Ali al-Naimi stated that the country's proven reserves can go up to 461 billion barrels in the next few years.[8] He reiterated this point on April 8, 2005. He was quoted as saying "There is a possibility that the Kingdom will increase its reserves by around 200 billion barrels, either through new finds or by increasing what it produces from existing fields. . . . These reserves enable the Kingdom to remain a major oil producer for between 70 and 100 years, even if it raises its production capacity to 15 million bpd, which may well happen during the next 15 years."[9] Increasing oil reserves by 200 billion barrels, however, continues to be an unverifiable possibility.

Changing Patterns in Import Dependence That Affect the Global Economy

This dependence will be easier to secure with a friendly and stable Iraq, but Saudi Arabia and the world have little choice. The EIA summarizes the trends in Gulf oil exports, as follows in its *International Energy Outlook for 2004*, and it should be noted that its estimates are based on favorable assumptions about increases in other fuels like gas, coal, nuclear and renewables, and favorable assumptions about increases in conversion efficiency, and other aspects of energy efficiency:[10]

> In 2001 industrialized countries imported 16.1 million barrels of oil per day from OPEC producers. . . . Of that total, 9.7 million barrels per day came from the Persian Gulf region. Oil movements to industrialized countries represented almost 65 percent of the total petroleum exported by OPEC member nations and almost 58 percent of all Persian Gulf exports.[11]

> By the end of the forecast period (2025), OPEC exports to industrialized countries are estimated to be about 11.5 million barrels per day higher than their 2001 level, and more than half the increase is expected to come from the Persian Gulf region.[12]

> Despite such a substantial increase, the share of total petroleum exports that goes to the industrialized nations in 2025 is projected to be almost 9 percent below their 2001 share, and the share of Persian Gulf exports going to the industrialized nations is projected to fall by about 13 percent. The significant shift expected in the balance of OPEC export shares between the industrialized and developing nations is a direct result of the economic growth anticipated for the developing nations of the world, especially those of Asia.

> OPEC petroleum exports to developing countries are expected to increase by more than 18.0 million barrels per day over the forecast period, with three-fourths of the increase going to the developing countries of Asia. China, alone, is likely to import about 6.6 million barrels per day from OPEC by 2025, virtually all of which is expected to come from Persian Gulf producers.

> North America's petroleum imports from the Persian Gulf are expected to double over the forecast period. At the same time, more than one-half of total North American imports in 2025 are expected to be from Atlantic Basin producers and refiners, with significant increases expected in crude oil imports anticipated from Latin American producers, including Venezuela, Brazil,

Colombia, and Mexico. West African producers, including Nigeria and Angola, are also expected to increase their export volumes to North America. Caribbean Basin refiners are expected to account for most of the increase in North American imports of refined products. With a moderate decline in North Sea production, Western Europe is expected to import increasing amounts from Persian Gulf producers and from OPEC member nations in both northern and western Africa. Substantial imports from the Caspian Basin are also expected.

Industrialized Asian nations are expected to increase their already-heavy dependence on Persian Gulf oil. The developing countries of the Pacific Rim are expected to almost double their total petroleum imports between 2001 and 2025.

While quantified estimates of export dependence are uncertain, its clear that it would take a massive breakthrough(s) in technology or discoveries of reserves outside the Middle East and North Africa to change these trends.

Dependence on MENA Export Security and High Rates of Energy Investment in the Region

Both the military security of the MENA region and its ability to achieve the necessary investment in new energy production are critical global strategic interests as well as vital strategic interests for Saudi Arabia and its neighbors. For example, some 40 percent of all world oil exports now pass through the Strait of Hormuz daily, and both EIA and IEA projections indicate this total will increase to around 60 percent by 2025–2030.[13]

The IEA projections, for example, indicate that Middle Eastern exports will total some 46 million bpd by 2030 and represent more than two-thirds of the world total. This means that the daily traffic in oil tankers will increase from 15 million bpd and 44 percent of global interregional trade in 2002 to 43 million bpd and 66 percent of global interregional trade in 2030. This means that the daily traffic in LNG carriers will increase from 28 BCM and 18 percent of global interregional trade in 2002 to 230 carriers and 34 percent of global interregional trade in 2030.[14] The IEA does, however, estimate that these increases would be some 11 percent lower if oil prices remained consistently high in constant dollars.

The International Energy Agency also estimates that imports will rise from 63 percent of total OECD demand for oil in 2002 to 85 percent in 2030. Some $3 trillion dollars must be invested in the oil sector from 2003 to 2030 to meet world demand for oil, and something approaching half of this total must be invested in the Middle East. Some $234 billion will be required for tankers and oil pipelines, and again, a substantial amount must go to the MENA area.[15]

The World Buys Oil in a Global Market, Not from Given Supplier Countries

Under most conditions, the normal day-to-day destination of MENA oil exports is strategically irrelevant. Oil is a global commodity, which is distributed to meet the needs of a global market based on the process of bids by importers acting in global competition. With the exception of differences in price because of crude type and transportation costs, all buyers compete equally for the global supply of available exports, and the direction and flow of exports changes according to marginal price relative to demand.

As a result, the percentage of oil that flows from the MENA region to the United States under normal market conditions has little strategic or economic importance. If a crisis occurs, or drastic changes take place in prices, every importing nation will have to pay the same globally determined price as any other nation, and the source(s) of U.S. imports will change accordingly. Moreover, the OECD nations are required to share all imports with other OECD countries in a crisis under the monitoring of the International Energy Agency.

The size of direct imports of petroleum is also only a partial measure of strategic dependence. The economy of every industrialized state is dependent on energy-intensive imports from Asia and other regions, and what comes around must literally go around. While the EIA and IEA do not make estimates of indirect imports of Middle Eastern oil in terms of the energy required to produce the finished goods, the United States, Europe, and Japan all import them from countries that are dependent on Middle Eastern exports.

To put this dependence in perspective, direct U.S. oil imports increased from an annual average of 7.9 million bpd in 1992 to 11.3 million bpd in 2002, and 2.6 MMBD worth of U.S. petroleum imports came directly from the Middle East in 2002.[16] If indirect U.S. imports, in the form of manufactured goods dependent on imports of Middle Eastern oil, were included, the resulting figure might well be 30 to 40 percent higher than the figure for direct imports.

SAUDI ARABIA'S IMPORTANCE TO ENERGY SECURITY

Regardless of all the uncertainties in global demand and of the uncertainties surrounding Saudi energy capacity, the Kingdom will continue to be central to any discussion of the energy market.

- **The largest oil reserves in the world:** Regardless of whether Saudi Arabia has 25 percent of the world's known reserves (260 billion barrels), Saudi Arabia will still dominate much of the world supply. Most oil-producing countries use the same methodology to calculate reserves. In broad terms, the uncertainties affecting Saudi resources affect all other major producers, particularly in the MENA region.

• **The largest oil producer in the world:** Saudi Arabia has produced 12.5 percent of world total production for the last decade and has been the only oil producer that has consistently sought to maintain surplus oil production. If it does encounter problems in maintaining and increasing capacity, virtually all exporters will encounter similar or greater problems.

• **An influential member of OPEC:** Saudi Arabia will continue to play a central role in the decisions of OPEC. Because of its immense reserves and influence over the other member states, especially the Gulf countries, the Kingdom has weight with the organization and the ability to change production hikes or cuts.

• **Largest spare capacity:** The Kingdom still seems to have approximately 1.5–2.0 million bpd of spare capacity. It claims to be "easily capable" of producing 15 million bpd in the next 15 years. Its ability to do so, as opposed to its willingness to do so, depends primarily on its ability to manage megaprojects and to attract and retain the skill sets needed, as well as its ability to procure the required steel, engineering services, drilling rigs, and so forth.

• **Central to Gulf security:** The Kingdom has the largest and most modern military and internal security apparatuses in the Gulf. Saudi Arabia continues to play an important role in the stability of the other Gulf Cooperation Council (GCC) states and in securing oil facilities from asymmetric attacks from extremists or conventional attacks from Iran.

Saudi holds one-quarter of the world's proven oil reserves, with 259.4 billion barrels (another 2.5 billion barrels are in the Saudi-Kuwait Neutral Zone) and may contain up to 1 trillion barrels of ultimately recoverable oil.[17]

The Kingdom has roughly 80 oil and gas fields and more than 1,000 oil wells. The Supreme Petroleum Council oversees the nationalized oil industry, the Saudi Arabian Oil Company (Saudi Aramco). Aramco claims that the average depletion rate for Saudi oil fields is 28 percent, with the giant Ghawar field having produced 48 percent of its proved reserves. Aramco also claims that, if anything, Saudi oil reserves are underestimated, not overestimated.[18]

But the EIA reports that outside analysts, notably Matthew Simmons of Houston-based Simmons and Company International, have disputed Aramco's optimistic assessments of Saudi oil reserves and future production, pointing to—among other things—more rapid depletion rates and a higher "water cut" than the Saudis claim. However, the EIA forecasts that Saudi oil production capacity could reach 18.2 million bbl/d by 2020 and 22.5 million bbl/d by 2025.[19]

Critical Saudi Energy Facilities

Saudi energy facilities have become far more costly and complex. The days of easy-to-produce fields are long over, and Saudi Aramco must now rely on the most sophisticated production techniques in the world and fund the most advanced network of production and recovery facilities.

Although Saudi Arabia has some 80 oil and gas fields,[20] more than half of its oil reserves are contained in eight fields, including the world's largest onshore and offshore fields, Ghawar and Safaniya, respectively. Ghawar is the world's largest oil field, with estimated remaining reserves of 70 billion barrels. Safaniya is the world's largest offshore oilfield, with estimated reserves of 35 billion barrels.

According to the EIA, Ghawar's main producing structures are, from north to south: Ain Dar, Shedgum, Uthmaniyah, Farzan, Ghawar, Al Udayliyah, Hawiyah, and Haradh. Ghawar alone accounts for about half of Saudi Arabia's total oil production capacity and could be a key target if any attack was made on Saudi fields. Safaniya, however, would be more attractive in terms of asymmetric attacks, because offshore fields are easier targets.

Saudi Arabia also produces a wide variety of crude oils, from heavy to super light. As is shown in Table 7.1, 65-70 percent of the country's aggregate oil production capacity is considered light gravity. The remainder is either medium or heavy, although the country is moving toward reducing the relative proportion of these two grades. Ghawar is the major producer of Arabian light crude. Arab Extra Light crude comes from Abqaiq, an enormous field, containing 17 billion barrels of proven reserves. Shaybah—with estimated reserves of 15 billion barrels—produces a mix of Arabian light and Arabian Extra Light.

Table 7.1: Saudi Maximum Production Capacity by Grade

Type of Crude	Million bpd
Arabian Super Light	0.250
Arabian Extra Light	1.400
Arabian Light	6.700
Arabian Medium	1.450
Arabian Heavy	1.200
Total	11.200

Source: Saudi National Security Assessment Project.

The current production capabilities of Saudi Arabia's oilfields are shown in Table 7.2. The EIA also reports that major efforts are under way to increase production capacity.

In March 2002, Aramco awarded major turnkey contracts to Italy's Snamprogetti ($630 million) and Technip-Coflexip ($360 million) aimed at increasing total Saudi oil production capacity by 800,000 bbl/d (500,000 bbl/d of Arabian light and 300,000 bbl/d of Arabian medium), by October 2004. The $1.2 billion project, known as the Qatif producing facilities development program (QPFDP), is located in the eastern part of the country near Dhahran, and will serve crude oil production from fields in the area. QPFDP involves construction of two gas-oil separation plants (GOSPs), as well as gas treatment and oil stabilization facilities. Qatif production is slated to replace production elsewhere in Saudi Arabia, not to boost overall capacity. In June 2004, Reuters reported that Saudi Arabia planned to bring on the first production from Qatif (and also from another field, Abu Safa), by July 2004. . . .

Another potential project, at the Khurais field, could increase Saudi production capacity by 800,000 bbl/d at a cost of $3 billion. This would involve installation of four GOSPs, with a capacity of 200,000 bbl/d each, at Khurais, which first came online in the 1960s but was mothballed by Aramco (along with several other fields—Abu Hadriya, Abu Jifan, Harmaliyah, and Khursaniyah) in the 1990s.

The $280 million Haradh-2 project aims to increase production capacity at the Haradh oil field to 900,000 bbl/d—triple current production—by 2006. This will involve adding a second, 300,000-bbl/d GOSP to Haradh (in addition to one 300,000-bbl/d GOSP inaugurated in January 2004), while shutting in some heavy oil production in the Ghawar area. Haradh also will produce significant volumes of non-associated natural gas, natural gas condensates (perhaps 170,000 bbl/d), and sulfur. . . .

Saudi Arabia's long-term goal is to develop its lighter crude reserves, including the Shaybah field located in the remote Empty Quarter area bordering the United Arab Emirates. Shaybah contains an estimated 15.7 billion barrels (or higher) of premium grade 41.6o API sweet (nearly sulfur-free) crude oil, with production potential believed to be 1 million bbl/d (output as of early April 2004 was around 560,000 bbl/d). Overall, the Shaybah project cost around $2.5 billion, with production starting in July 1998. According to Oil Minister Naimi (October 1999), the development of Shaybah showed that "the cost of adding . . . capacity—that is, all the infrastructure, producing and transportation facilities—necessary to produce one additional barrel of oil per day in Saudi Arabia is, at most, $5,000 compared to between $10,000 and $20,000 in most areas of the world. So both our current production costs, and the costs for developing more production capacity for the future, are probably the world's lowest." The Shaybah complex includes three gas/oil separation plants (GOSPs) and a 395-mile pipeline to connect the field to Abqaiq, Saudi Arabia's closest gathering center, for blending with Arab Light crude (Berri and Abqaiq streams). In addition to oil, Shaybah has a large natural gas "cap" (associated gas), with estimated reserves of 25 trillion cubic feet (Tcf). Gas production of 880 million cubic feet per day (Mmcf/d) is reinjected, along with natural gas liquids (NGLs). A possible gas recovery project could be implemented within 5 or 6 years, potentially for use in petrochemical production.[21]

Oil fields are large-area targets, with many redundant facilities. While fires can be set in many areas of a working field, including at oil wells, fires do not produce critical or lasting damage. Unless wells are attacked with explosives deep enough in the wellhead to result in permanent damage to the well, most facilities can be rapidly repaired.

There also, however, are larger items of equipment and central facilities that would do far more to interrupt production and many of which require months of manufacturing time to replace. Such facilities include central pumping facilities, gas-oil separators (GOSPs), and related power plants, water injection facilities, and desalination plants. Vulnerability also increases sharply if key targets in a field are attacked as a system, rather than as individual elements, and if expert assistance is available to saboteurs or attackers.

Table 7.2: Saudi Field Production

Facility	Million bpd
Abqaiq	0.450
Abu Safah	0.300
Safaniya	1.500
Shaybah	0.500
Ghawar	5.500
Qatif	0.500
Marjan	0.450
Berri	0.400
Zuluf	0.800
Khurais (mothballed)	0.150
Neutral Zone	0.350
Khursaniyah (mothballed)	0.100
Munifa	0.000
Hawtah	0.200
Total	11.200

Source: Saudi National Security Assessment Project.

THE SAUDI PIPELINE AND EXPORT SYSTEM

The Saudi pipeline and export system is both another key measure of capacity and a key potential vulnerability, although most pipeline facilities can be repaired relatively easily and quickly, with the exception of some pumping and control facilities. According to the EIA, the Saudi oil system is divided into a northern producing area and a southern producing area. Northern oil, except for crude from Safaniya and Zuluf, is stabilized at Ras al-Ju'aymah and Ras Tanura stabilizers to remove toxic hydrogen sulfide and then sent to refineries or the export terminals at Ras Tanura and Ras al-Ju'aymah.[22]

All the petroleum from the southern areas is pumped to Abqaiq for stabilization and from there to Ras Tanura and Ras al-Ju'aymah. The 5 million bpd East-West Crude Oil Pipeline (Petroline), operated by Saudi Aramco since 1984 (when it took over from Mobil), is used mainly to transport Arabian Light and Super Light to refineries in the Western Province and to Red Sea terminals for export to European markets.

The Saudi government expanded the Petroline in part to maintain Yanbu as a strategic option to Gulf port facilities in the event that exports were blocked at that end. Furthermore, it is clear that Petroline's capacity could be expanded significantly and that this would enhance the line's strategic value. Yanbu, however, remains a far less economic option for Saudi oil exports than Ras Tanura. Among other factors, shipments from Yanbu adds about five days roundtrip travel time for tankers through the Bab el Mandab strait to major customers in Asia compared to Ras Tanura (via the Strait of Hormuz).

According to Oil Minister Ali al-Naimi, the Petroline is only used at half capacity. Given this, as well as the desire to boost natural gas usage, Saudi Aramco has begun converting the line to natural gas pumping capability. The natural gas will supply Yanbu's petrochemical and power facilities.

The 290,000 bpd Abqaiq-Yanbu natural gas liquids pipeline runs parallel to the Petroline, which serves Yanbu's petrochemical plants. The Trans-Arabian Pipeline (Tapline) to Lebanon is mothballed, and the 1.65 million bpd, 48-inch Iraqi Pipeline across Saudi Arabia (IPSA), which runs parallel to the Petroline from pump station number three (there are 11 pumping stations along the Petroline, all using on-site gas turbine electric generators) to the port of Mu'ajjiz, just south of Yanbu, was closed indefinitely following the August 1990 Iraqi invasion of Kuwait. It was seized by the Saudi government in 2002, after Iraq failed to pay required upkeep fees for 12 years. Saudi Aramco has begun converting the ill-fated pipeline, which was built by the Iraqis during the Iran-Iraq War to bypass its damaged Gulf export facilities, but which operated for only six months, to natural gas pumping capability. The natural gas will supply Yanbu's petrochemical and power facilities.

Most of Saudi Arabia's crude oil is exported from the Gulf via the huge Abqaiq processing facility, which handles around two-thirds of the country's oil output. This makes it another key potential target, but there is no evidence of any bottleneck in increasing Saudi export capacity. Saudi Arabia also has several major oil terminals for loading its oil exports, which are listed in Table 7.3. Its primary oil-export terminals are located at Ras Tanura (5.5–6.0 million bpd capacity, the world's largest offshore oil loading facility) and Ras al-Ju'aymah (3.0–3.5 million bpd) on the Gulf, plus Yanbu (4.5–5.0 million bpd) on the Red Sea. Combined, these terminals can now handle from between 13 and 14 million bpd and demonstrate Saudi Arabia's ability to handle increased production capacity. Each of these terminals is, however, a major potential target for terrorist or asymmetric attacks.

Table 7.3:   Saudi Oil Terminals

Terminals	Descriptions
Ras Tanura	World's largest offshore oil loading facility, on the Gulf; 5.5–6 million bbl/d capacity
Yanbu	On the Red Sea, fed by Petroline; 4.5–5 million bbl/d capacity
Jubail, Ras al-Ju'aymah	On the Gulf northwest of Ras Tanura; 3–3.5 million bbl/d capacity
Jeddah	On the Red Sea south of Yanbu
Jizan	On the Red Sea, refined products
Ras al-Khafji	On the Gulf in the Saudi-Kuwaiti Neutral Zone, crude oil
Rabigh	On the Red Sea, north of Jeddah, crude oil and refined products
Zuluf	Offshore in the Gulf, linked to Zuluf oil field

Source: Saudi National Security Assessment Project.

Refineries and Product Facilities

Saudi's diversification and investment in "downstream" capacity get far less attention overseas than in Saudi Arabia. It is, however, both a measure of how serious Saudi Arabia is about maintaining and increasing capacity, creating new jobs, developing the Saudi economy, and creating the conditions for internal stability.

The Kingdom now has eight refineries, with a combined crude throughput capacity of roughly 1.75 million bpd, in addition to about 1.6 million bpd of overseas refining capacity. A 200,000 bpd fractionation component was completed at the Ras Tanura refinery in August 2003. There are plans to increase the Rabigh refinery's capacity to as much as 400,000 bpd and to upgrade its product slate from "low-value" heavy products to gasoline and kerosene. Another innovation will be the addition of an ethane cracker fed by natural gas from the Eastern Province through a converted oil line.

The Kingdom expects that domestic demand for refined products will reach 4 million bpd by 2010, a 10 percent per year increase.[23] Saudi Aramco has two joint ventures in the Kingdom's refineries: Sasref (320,000 bpd) refinery at Jubail, with Royal Dutch Shell, and Samref (400,000 bpd) in Yanbu, with Exxon Mobil Corp. The Kingdom plans to upgrade and expand its current plants, which could produce 2.1 million bpd with an estimated cost of $1.5–$2.0 billion. Aramco was also considering investing $4-$5 billion in revamping its Ras Tanura refinery and has signed a $6-$7 billion investment agreement with Japan's Sumitomo Chemical Co. to upgrade its refinery in Rabigh.[24]

Saudi Aramco has also said that it has been in talks with possible joint venture partners for an investment of $4–$5 billion to build a new refinery in Yanbu. The refinery will have a capacity of 400,000 bpd and would produce U.S. and European specification products. The Yanbu refinery is expected to run Arab Heavy Crude. It was reported that Hindustan Petroleum Corp Ltd. held "preliminary talks" with Aramco on building the refinery.[25] Other Indian companies have expressed interest in expanding the refinery, according to Aramco's vice president for refining, Khalid Al-Buainain. In 2004 the same plant was reported to be "under discussion" with Japanese companies to be developed as a refinery with a capacity of 800,000 bpd.[26]

It is clear from such plans that Saudi Arabia does count on a high level of sustained capacity. There is no direct correlation between downstream investment and total upstream capacity, but Saudi Aramco has a clear interest in investing in refining facilities both in and out of the Kingdom that are designed to process its heavy crude efficiently. Ethane-based petrochemical plants located in the Kingdom rank among the most profitable in the world.

Table 7.4:   Major Refineries

Refinery	Capacity Million bpd
Saudi Aramco-Rabigh	400,000
Ras Tanura	300,000
Yanbu	190,000
Riyadh	120,000
Jeddah	60,000
Saudi Aramco/Mobil-Yanbu	340,000
Petromin/Shell-al-Jubail	305,000
Arabian Oil Company-Ras al-Khafji	30,000

Source: Saudi National Security Assessment Project.

Natural Gas

While most outside studies focus on Saudi export capabilities, Saudi Arabia is becoming steadily more dependent on using its natural gas to free up oil for export and to provide the feedstock for petrochemical exports. This makes Saudi gas facilities another major potential energy target. The EIA describes current and planned scale of Saudi Gas facilities as follows:

> Using natural gas instead of oil domestically will help free up additional crude oil for export (OPEC quotas are on production, not exports). Overall, Saudi Arabia aims to triple natural gas output (to 15 Bcf/d) by 2009. To date, Saudi Arabia has not expressed great interest in exporting liquefied natural gas mainly due to doubts regarding economic viability and concerns that gas exports could compete with more lucrative oil exports. . . .

> Domestic demand is driving a \$4.5 billion expansion of the MGS, which was completed in 1984. The MGS feeds gas to the industrial cities of Yanbu on the Red Sea and Jubail, which combined account for 10% of the world's petrochemical production. Prior to the MGS, all of Saudi Arabia's natural gas output was flared. . . .

> Saudi Arabia's proven natural gas reserves are estimated at 224.7 trillion cubic feet (Tcf), ranking fourth in the world (after Russia, Iran, and Qatar), and up about 5 Tcf from 2002. Most (around 60%) of Saudi Arabia's currently proven natural gas reserves consist of associated gas, mainly from the onshore Ghawar field and the offshore Safaniya and Zuluf fields. The Ghawar oil field alone accounts for one-third of the country's proven natural gas reserves. . . .

> Only 15% of Saudi Arabia has been "adequately explored for gas," according to Aramco's vice president for new business development, Khalid al-Falih. Most new associated natural gas reserves discovered in the 1990s have been in fields that contain light crude oil, especially in the Najd region south of Riyadh. Most of Saudi Arabia's non-associated gas reserves (Mazalij, Al-Manjoura, Shaden, Niban, Tinat, Al-Waar, etc.) are located in the deep Khuff reservoir, which underlies the Ghawar oil field. Natural gas also is located in the countries extreme northwest, at Midyan, and in the Empty Quarter (Rub al Khali) in the country's southeastern desert. The Rub al Khali alone is believed to contain natural gas reserves as high as 300 Tcf.

> Another large natural gas field, called Dorra, is located offshore near the Khafji oil field in the Saudi-Kuwaiti Neutral Zone and may be developed by Japan's AOC. Dorra development is controversial, however, because part of it is also claimed by Iran (which calls the field Arash). The maritime border between Kuwait and Iran remain undemarcated, but Saudi Arabia reached an agreement with Kuwait in July 2000 to share Dorra equally. Currently, Iran is resisting any moves by Kuwait and Saudi Arabia to develop the field on their own. Iran and Kuwait have been discussing their offshore boundary since 2000. . . .

Gas development is slated to consume a large share of Aramco's budget (in late 1999, Aramco decided to invest $45 billion over 25 years on upstream gas development and processing facilities), and Aramco is aiming to add 3-5 Tcf of new non-associated natural gas reserves per year to meet rapid (5%–7% annual) gas demand growth. Non-associated gas development is desirable in particular because it guarantees a steady flow of gas regardless of oil output, which tends to fluctuate. Currently, non-associated gas accounts for 40% of Saudi Arabia's total gas reserves. . . .

Following cancellation of the SGI, Saudi Arabia repackaged the (gas) project as a series of smaller, more focused contracts, with better rates of return than previously offered. At the same time, the Saudis moved away from the integrated upstream/downstream gas, water, power, and petrochemical nature of the SGI, and instead specifically targeted upstream natural gas development in the area that had comprised Core Venture 3. Downstream and "midstream" elements of the SGI will now be handled separately, in large part by SABIC and Aramco. In July 2003, Saudi Arabia reached a tentative deal (officially signed on November 15) with Royal Dutch/Shell and Total on Blocks 5–9 and 82–85 in the Shaybah and Kidan areas of the "Empty Quarter" region. Besides the major European companies, Saudi Aramco—replacing ConocoPhillips—will have a 30% share in the $2 billion project. Shell will maintain a 40% share and Total the remaining 30%. The deal covers an area of 81,000 square miles.

In January 2004, Russia's Lukoil won a tender to explore for and produce non-associated natural gas in the Saudi Empty Quarter. Lukoil will operate in Block A, near Ghawar, as part of an 80/20 joint venture with Saudi Aramco. Also in January 2004, China's Sinopec won a tender for gas exploration and production in Block B, while an Eni-Repsol consortium was granted a license to operate in Block C. Under terms of the agreements, Aramco will take "sales quality gas" on a take-or-pay basis for $0.75 per million Btu, while condensates and natural gas liquids will be sold at international market rates (note: Saudi accession to the WTO will most likely require it to give up the dual pricing system for natural gas, and also to set up a comprehensive, transparent regulatory framework for the natural gas sector). In addition, the Saudi government will fund a pipeline connection from the country's Master Gas System (MGS) to contract delivery points.

Additional natural gas production is being encouraged as a feedstock for the country's growing petrochemical industry (at Yanbu and Jubail, for instance), as well as for electricity generation, desalination plants and other industrial establishments, and as a replacement for direct oil burning. In July 2003, Saudi Arabia invited more than 40 companies to bid on three onshore natural gas blocks in the South Ghawar area. As of December 2003, approximately 20–30 companies reportedly had expressed interest. . . .

In October 2002, construction was completed on a $4 billion, 1.4-billion-cubic-feet (Bcf)-per-day, non-associated gas processing plant at Hawiyah, located south of Dhahran and east of Riyadh near the giant Ghawar oil field. Hawiyah represents the largest Saudi natural gas project in more than 10 years, and the first to process only non-associated gas (from the deep Khuff and Jauf reservoirs). Hawiyah was officially inaugurated in October 2002, and reportedly is producing enough natural gas to free up around 260,000 bbl/d of Arabian Light crude oil for export.

Besides Hawiyah, Foster Wheeler has been managing a $2 billion project to build a new natural gas processing plant at Haradh, 120 miles southwest of Dhahran. The Haradh plant is similar in scope to one at Hawiyah. When completely online—reportedly all four trains were completed as of June 2003—total Saudi natural gas processing capability will increase by around 1.5 Bcf/day, to around 9.5 Bcf/day. Eventually, a $900–$1,100 million, 3,800-Mmcf/d "straddle plant"—a natural gas reprocessing plant located adjacent to a gas transmission line for the purpose of extracting light hydrocarbon liquids newly formed due to recurring compression and decompression of gas during transmission—may be built as well. If so, the straddle plant will likely service both Haradh and Hawiyah and increase Saudi NGL production. . . .

In other natural gas-related developments, a key pipeline project was completed in June 2000 to extend the MGS from the Eastern Province (which contains large potential gas and condensate reserves) to the capital, Riyadh, in the Central Province. This is part of a broader expansion of the existing gas transmission system in Saudi Arabia, reportedly to include the construction of around 1,200 miles of additional natural gas pipeline capacity (on top of 10,500 miles of oil, gas, condensate, products, and natural gas liquid pipelines currently in operation) by 2006.[27]

Petrochemicals

Petrochemicals are another source of vulnerability. SABIC, the largest nonoil industrial company in the Middle East, now accounts for about 10 percent of the world's petrochemical production.

Saudi Arabia also has wide-ranging plans for the expansion of its petrochemical production, using natural gas. In 2001 SABIC completed an ambitious expansion of the Yanbu petrochemical facility at a cost of $1 billion, making it the largest polyethylene plant in the world. In 2003 Saudi Aramco awarded a contract to Snamprogetti to construct new units at the facility. SABIC has also approved a loan for $1.15 billion to build a new petrochemical plant in the eastern industrial city of Jubail. The facility is slated to come on line in the second half of 2004 and is expected to produce 1 million tons of ethylene per year, in addition to olefins, polyethylene and glycol ethylene.

Strategic Reserves

Saudi Arabia has a strategic storage program. The Kingdom has increased its strategic storage capacity for oil products by several billion barrels. In August 2004, the Kingdom opened an underground storage facility in Jeddah, with a reported storage capacity of 945,000 barrels of crude oil and refined products. The purpose of the Saudi Strategic Storage Program is to ensure oil supplies during a crisis. So far, Saudi Arabia has invested more than $2.9 billion to build underground storage facilities in five sites: Riyadh, Jeddah, Abha, Medina, and Qasim. The facilities are connected via pipeline to the bulk plants and refineries.

Petroleum Infrastructure Security

While the previous analysis has focused on Saudi production capacity, this is scarcely the only issue affecting the Kingdom's level of exports. At least in the short run, terrorism may be much more of a threat to Saudi exports than any short-fall in production capacity. There have been many studies of energy security over the years, including studies by the CIA, EIA, and IRA. All have found that Saudi Arabia is a key petroleum exporter and central to a steadily more interdependent global economy. Saudi Arabia is also the only oil producer that has consistently sought to maintain surplus oil production capacity, with a nominal goal of 2 million bpd. This situation will not change in the foreseeable future.

While details of the Saudi security budget are classified, it is estimated to total more than $8 billion in 2004. Between 2002 and 2004, the Saudi government allocated approximately $1.2 billion to increase security at all of its energy facilities. At any one time, it is estimated that there are between 25,000 and 30,000 soldiers protecting the Kingdom's oil infrastructure. "For years, Saudi Arabia has recognized the importance of protecting its vital facilities, long before the recent terrorist actions. So we've always maintained a high level of security," says Abdullatif Othman, executive director of Saudi Aramco affairs.

As noted previously, unless wells are attacked with explosives deep enough in the wellhead to result in permanent damage to the well, most facilities can be rapidly repaired, although there are larger items of equipment and central facilities whose damage would do far more to interrupt production and many of which require months of manufacturing time to replace. Vulnerability also increases sharply if key targets in a field are attacked as a system, rather than as individual elements, and if expert assistance is available to saboteurs or attackers.

Recent Patterns of Vulnerability

Such concerns are not theoretical. On May 1, 2004, four attackers broke into the offices of ABB Lummus in Yanbu, a Saudi petrochemical compound, and killed six senior multinational workers and one Saudi. Al Qaeda claimed responsibility. The Yanbu attack was followed by a similar incident at the end of May at a residential complex in Al Khobar that killed 22 people, mainly foreigners. In the first few weeks of June 2004, several more foreign workers were killed, including one who was kidnapped and beheaded. Other terrorist plots have been foiled. In 2002 counterintelligence investigations uncovered a sabotage plot against the Ras Tanura terminal. Significantly, after interrogations of suspects, Saudi authorities determined that none of the company's employees were involved.

Al Qaeda sympathizers are not the only threat to the Saudi oil supply. There is also concern over the large Shiite Muslim population in the Eastern Province (Al Ahsa, where much of the petroleum infrastructure is located). In late 1979 and early 1980, riots among this group were alleged to have been inspired by taped messages of the late Ayatollah Khomeini. In 1996 Saudi Shiite terrorists, trained and financed by Iran's Revolutionary Guard, planted a truck bomb that killed 19 American Air Force personnel at the Khobar Towers near Dhahran, headquarters of Saudi Aramco. Shiites—which make up just under 50 percent of the labor force of Saudi Aramco and around 7.5 percent of Saudi Arabia's population—have suffered from economic, political, and religious discrimination. The Saudi government has recognized that this represents a potential security threat and has taken steps to address Shiite grievances.

The attacks in Yanbu and Al Khobar in the spring and summer of 2004 fanned fears about the vulnerability of Saudi Arabia's oil infrastructure, especially in the West, where the media was filled with almost daily reports about instability in the Kingdom and its repercussions on world energy markets. Following the attacks, a senior U.S. State Department official warned that Saudi economic facilities and infrastructure are likely targets of terrorists. And with oil prices at an all-time high, such fears gained new urgency in mid 2004. In fact, a "security premium" of at least several dollars was likely factored into the price of oil during that time.

It is important to note, however, that Saudi security agents were able to quickly cordon the industrial portions of the facility during the attack on Yanbu and force the terrorists away from the compounds and into the city proper, where they were quickly killed; the industrial complex was never in danger. Still, analysts point to several scenarios, which at the very least could destabilize Saudi oil production.

Improving Security Capabilities

Securing the Kingdom's energy infrastructure, which covers hundreds of square miles, is a complex and daunting task. The Kingdom's five enormous oil fields are connected by thousands of miles of pipeline. Ghawar, the world's largest field, is 150 miles long and 25 miles wide. The Kingdom has fortified its oil infrastructure security through the use of high tech surveillance systems and the creation of special security units, as well as deployment of members of various military and security forces.

Under the auspices of the Ministry of Interior, a special unit has been created to oversee security at the major oil facilities. This unit is made up of representatives from the Special Security Forces, Special Emergency Forces, the General Security Service (the domestic intelligence service), regular forces of the Public Security Administration (including police officers), the Petroleum Installation Security Force (PISF), specialized brigades of the National Guard, the Navy, and the Coast Guard.

In most cases, the Petroleum Installation Security Force (supplemented by specialized brigades of the National Guard) guards the wells and other important installations within a given facility. Members of the Special Emergency Forces and elements of the National Guard and regular police forces generally protect the perimeters of these installations. The Navy and Coast guard work to protect terminal docks and offshore fields, and the Air Force provides surveillance and protection from the air. Finally, threat assessment and intelligence gathering is conducted by the General Security Service and members of the Special Security Forces act as an elite antiterrorism squad.

An example of the intensive security at these facilities can be found at Abqaiq, the Kingdom's largest oil processing facility, and the largest crude stabilization plant in the world. Recently Abdallah Jumah, the CEO of Saudi Aramco, revealed that Abqaiq and other major installations are protected by approximately 5,000 security guards in the employ of Saudi Aramco. These guards work at key checkpoints and act as a police force within the compounds; the outer perimeter is defended by a specialized brigade of the National Guard and the Special Emergency Forces. At the heart of Abqaiq are 10 cylindrical towers within which hydro-desulphurization occurs (the process of making crude oil "sweeter"). Specialized units that work in cooperation with the perimeter forces cordon each tower.

Security is massive at Ghawar. The Petroleum Installation Security Force protects all major wells in the enormous complex. Outside each of the facilities stand National Guard personnel, as well as elements of the Special Emergency Forces. There is continuous air surveillance from helicopters and round the clock F15 patrols. On the perimeter, heavily equipped National Guard battalions stand guard.

Saudi Arabia's terminals are similarly well defended. On an average day, anywhere between 2.5 and 3 million barrels of oil flow through the Ras al-Ju'aymah terminal. From the main platform, the oil flows to five mooring buoys located offshore, each capable of transferring an estimated 1.5 to 2 million bpd to awaiting tankers. At Ras Tanura, the average capacity is 4.5 to 5 million bpd, with one platform alone handling 47 percent of the terminal's exports. Clearly, a successful attack on one of these terminals or on the off-loading platforms could be devastating. For this reason, security at these complexes is colossal and comprehensive. Each terminal and platform has its own specialized security units, composed of Saudi Aramco security forces and specialized units of the National Guard and the Ministry of Interior. The Coast Guard and components of the Navy protect the installations from the sea. The thousands of tankers entering and leaving these areas each year are escorted by naval ships and covered from the air. While security at the terminals and at sea may seem like a formidable task, six tankers per day are all that is required to export 9 million barrels. Pilots at the Dhahran Air Base (only 10 to 15 minutes flying time from Ras Tanura) are trained to defend against any hijacked aircraft.

Perhaps the weakest link in the system is the estimated 17,850 kilometers of pipeline in the Kingdom. While it is impossible to protect the entire length from sabotage, Saudi security forces have ensured that any damage can be quickly contained and repaired. The pipeline is monitored and controlled from a central command center at Saudi Aramco, so that any suspicious activity can be immediately investigated. In addition, the pipelines have always been fitted with emergency shutdown valves at approximately every kilometer. This greatly isolates the potential effect of any accidental or sabotage-induced leak. Specialized backup teams that can be quickly dispatched by helicopter to repair any damage are strategically located along the length of the line. Internal estimates reveal that in a worst-case scenario—where an entire section of pipeline is destroyed—repair teams could bring the pipeline back to normal operation within 36 hours (Saudi Arabia maintains the world's largest stockpile of repair pipeline, stored throughout the length of the pipeline).

OVERALL VULNERABILITY

It is impossible to completely eliminate the threat of terrorism against the Kingdom's energy infrastructure, and Saudi Arabia faces the threat of conventional military attack, asymmetric warfare, and proliferation as well. Given the recent security efforts by the Saudi government (much of which remains classified), the overlapping and redundant layers of defense around key installations, and the extensive disaster planning and drills that have taken place have significantly lessened the probability of any major attacks being carried out successfully.

Short of a spectacular strike on the scale of 9/11, or some form of systematic sabotage from inside Saudi Aramco or other key energy industries, most foreseeable assaults are likely to be quickly confined, and any resulting damage is likely to be repaired relatively quickly. Energy security will, however, be a continuing problem for Saudi Arabia and the world. Moreover, global energy use is expected to rise by more than 50 percent by 2025, and the security of Saudi energy exports will play a steadily more vital role in the world's economy.

Chapter 8

Military Reform

As has been touched upon earlier, Saudi Arabia's primary need for reform does not affect its security apparatus. It is rather the need for the kind of economic, social, and political reforms that will develop and diversify its economy and create jobs and economic opportunity for the country's rapidly growing population. Saudi Arabia's second priority is to create more effective internal security forces without creating a climate of repression and without creating new cells of terrorists or groups of extremists. The reform of the Saudi military is now a third priority, and the control of the cost of Saudi forces and especially Saudi arms imports has priority over reforms that enhance military effectiveness.

This does not mean, however, that Saudi military forces do not need continuing modernization and reform. Chapters 4 and 5 have already discussed many areas where change is needed or is already under way. Some are highly technical and specific, but there are broad themes as well.

SAUDI MILITARY DEVELOPMENT

The previous chapters have shown that Saudi Arabia is by far the strongest and most modern military power in the Gulf and the only force large enough to provide the support, training, C^{4}I/BM, and other specialized capabilities necessary to sustain modern land-air combat and provide the infrastructure for effective regional cooperation. Its military forces are now strong enough to deal with many low-intensity contingencies and limit the amount of U.S. reinforcements needed in low-intensity contingencies.

Yet, Saudi Arabia does remain vulnerable to threats from Iran. Iran may be moving toward moderation, but Saudi Arabia cannot ignore its conventional military capabilities or efforts to proliferate. Saudi Arabia is within five to seven minutes flying time from Iran, from the earliest point of detection by an AWACS to overflying key Saudi targets on the Gulf coast. Missile attacks would offer even less warning and present more problems for defense.

While Iran cannot bring the bulk of its land power to bear without major increases in amphibious lift, it can bring naval and air pressure to bear on tanker and air traffic through the Gulf and can threaten Saudi Arabia in other ways. "Wars of intimidation" will generally offer Iran more prospects of success than actual fighting, and Iran's ability to intimidate will increase as it develops its missile forces and its chemical, biological, radiological, and nuclear-warfare capabilities.

Cooperation with Other Southern Gulf States

The best way of dealing with these challenges is to go beyond simply reforming the Saudi armed forces, and to do so in the context of more effective efforts to develop collective security. The lack of effective military cooperation between the Kingdom, other moderate Gulf states, and its Arab neighbors outside the Gulf presents major problems for Saudi Arabia that are not easy to solve.

Saudi Arabia cannot turn to the rest of the Arab world for meaningful military support. The failure of the Damascus Declaration of 1992 to give Saudi Arabia any credible guarantee of Egyptian and Syrian reinforcements was the result of far more than Arab politics and Egyptian and Syrian demands for money. Neither Egypt nor Syria is organized to project effective combat forces. They lack most of the technological advantages of U.S. and Saudi forces, and they are not equipped and trained to provide the Saudi Air Force and Saudi Army with the mix of interoperable capabilities they need. Although they are Arab and Muslim, they also are states with separate interests, regional ambitions, and strategic objectives that often differ from those of Saudi Arabia.

This means Saudi Arabia badly needs to strengthen its cooperation with the countries of the Gulf Cooperation Council (GCC). As Chapter 3 has shown, however, there has been more progress in political and economic areas than in military areas. This is true even in the areas where the mission need for such progress is most obvious.

No one nation along the Southern Gulf coast can cover the entire air space in this region. Efforts to create a GCC-wide C^4I system for air defenses are making slow progress, but they are still in the early stages of development. The GCC has some progress in a few similar areas like military exercise training, air combat, and mine warfare, but this progress is equally slow and tentative in each case.

The GCC's longstanding failure to agree on effective plans for cooperation, interoperability, and integration has left the military role of the GCC a largely symbolic one. The GCC will only play a major role in regional security once it can develop integrated air defenses, integrated mine-warfare and maritime-surveillance capabilities, an ability to deal with Iranian surface and ASW forces, rapid reaction forces that can actually fight, and the ability to defend Kuwait and eastern Saudi Arabia against land attack.

Even if expanded military cooperation is not possible on a GCC-wide basis, Saudi Arabia must focus on finding ways to strengthen the defense of its northern border area and Kuwait. At a minimum, Saudi Arabia must work to:

- Create an effective planning system for collective defense and for the creation of interoperable forces with common C^4I/BM capabilities and interoperable infrastructure and sustainability.

- Provide the infrastructure, transportation, sustainability, training, and C^4I systems to rapidly deploy Saudi forces to support the joint land defense of the Kuwaiti/Northwestern Saudi borders and to reinforce other Gulf states, like Oman, in the event of any Iranian amphibious or airborne action.

- Create joint air defense and air attack capabilities with an emphasis on Saudi-Kuwaiti-Bahraini cooperation.

- Integrate the Saudi C^4I and sensor nets for air and naval combat, including BVR and night warfare, and link them to Kuwait, Bahrain, and the other Southern Gulf states.

- Create joint air and naval strike forces to deal with threats from Iran and Iraq.

- Develop a joint war fighting capability to provide minesweeping, naval-based air and antiship missile defenses to protect Gulf shipping, offshore facilities, ports, and coastal facilities.

- Establish effective cross-reinforcement and tactical mobility capabilities throughout the Kingdom, with special emphasis on the defense of Kuwait and the Saudi-Iraqi border. Emphasize forward defense and active maneuver warfare.

- Prepare for rapid over-the-horizon reinforcement by the United States and other Western powers. Work with the other Gulf states and the U.S. and other Western forces to find solutions to prepositioning on a GCC-wide basis and prepare Saudi bases for rapid over-the-horizon deployments and reinforcements in an emergency.

- Set up joint training, support, and infrastructure facilities with the other Southern Gulf states.

- Create common advanced training systems that develop a brigade and wing-level capability for combined arms and joint warfare, a capability that can support realistic field training exercises for Saudi and allied Southern Gulf forces of the kind practiced by U.S. and Israeli forces.

- Develop a common capability to provide urban and urban area security and to fight unconventional warfare and low-intensity combat.

- Begin development of a broadly based counterproliferation program.

Force Transformation and Mission-Oriented Procurement Priorities

The Kingdom must deal with broad internal challenges as well. The time is over when the Kingdom could spend its way out of its military development problems or could excuse the lack of overall balance and effectiveness in its forces on the grounds it was still in the early phases of force modernization and development.

Saudi Arabia needs to give its force-development efforts more focus in order to develop a comprehensive program of affordable force transformation that can better meet its future needs. In doing so, it must focus on procuring interoperable and/or standardized equipment to provide the capability to perform the following missions:

- Heavy armor, artillery, attack helicopters, and mobile air defense equipment for defense of the upper Gulf.

- Interoperable offensive air capability with standoff, all-weather precision weapons and antiarmor/antiship capability.

- Interoperable air defense equipment, including heavy surface-to-air missiles, BVR/AWX fighters, AEW and surveillance capability, ARM and ECM capability. (Growth to ATBM and cruise-missile defense capability.)

- Maritime surveillance systems and equipment for defense against maritime surveillance and unconventional warfare.

- Mine detection and clearing systems.

- Improved urban, area, and border security equipment for unconventional warfare and low-intensity conflict.

- Advanced training aids.

- Support and sustainment equipment.

Planning, Budgeting, and Procuring Balanced Forces

Money has long been a critical issue and will become steadily more important in the future. Saudi Arabia signed nearly $25 billion worth of new arms agreements between 1993 and 2000 and took delivery on $66 billion worth of military imports.[1] This is more than the Kingdom can afford, and Saudi Arabia needs to consolidate its modernization programs to reduce its number of different suppliers and major weapons types. It also needs to establish much more strict limits to its defense spending and make its spending more effective.

One key spending priority is the emphasis on mission capabilities just discussed; another is to give proper priority to readiness, training, and sustainability. This emphasis needs to be integrated into an effective Ministry of Defense and Aviation (MODA) planning, programming, and budgeting system that gives proper emphasis to funding jointness and balanced war fighting capability, rather than the procurement of new weapons. There needs to be a staff within each branch, service, and the MODA.

This means carefully monitoring current and planned rates of expenditure to ensure proper readiness and sustainability and making hard choices like going for PGMs and C⁴I/BM as substitutes for whole new platforms. It means stretching out procurements and not retaining obsolete weapons, and so forth. Hard choices are, after all, the essence of effective planning. A key beginning point is effective net assessment and creating a realistic set of goals and a planning, programming, and budgeting system to match.

Realistic Limits on Military Spending and Arms Purchases

Saudi Arabia is scarcely poor, but it needs to set firm and realistic limits on its military procurement spending. The goal for Saudi Arabian military procurement should not be simply to buy the best or most possible equipment, but rather to improve the overall holdings of combat forces in a balanced and evolutionary manner. It should be to reach the maximum possible interoperability with the power projection capabilities of U.S. land and air forces and to procure the training, munitions, and support facilities to deal with the threat from Iran.

RECASTING THE TERMS OF SAUDI ARMS BUYS. There is pressure on Saudi Arabia to make new major buys from many countries and manufacturers. Saudi Arabia has long been a lead customer, and virtually all countries have surplus manufacturing capacity, declining local markets, and a need for economies of scale. This has compounded the longstanding problems created by political pressure on the Kingdom to make arms purchases, efforts to sell developmental equipment before its regional performance is proven, efforts to sell without providing truly demanding demonstrations subject to adequate test and evaluation, and efforts to sell without demanding contract terms and penalties.

The reality is, however, that Saudi Arabia now has more limited requirements and operates in a buyers' market, where it has every incentive to be ruthless in putting pressure on selling countries and manufacturers to get the best possible terms. The trends in the conventional military threat discussed in Chapter 1 are easing the strain Saudi arms imports put on the Saudi national budget and the Saudi economy.

Waste versus Accountability. Outside critics have often exaggerated the level of waste and corruption in Saudi arms deals and military procurement. The Kingdom has generally bought the right arms and got a highly effective mix of weapons for its money. As will be discussed later, the terms of U.S. Foreign Military Sales (FMS) programs also places serious limits on the misuse of funds. In addition, European countries maintain audit programs that help to limit such problems.

The fact remains, however, that even relatively limited waste and corruption still involve major amounts of money—given the massive size of Saudi arms purchases. Furthermore, some very large Saudi arms deals like the Al Yamamah program, which started out as an integrated purchase of weapons, and services from Britain were structured in ways that involved complex follow-on deals and that led to charges about massive waste and corruption.

Such large-scale purchases have since been expanded to include buys from France and have layered new purchases on old in ways that have made accountability impossible. The original Al Yamamah program was signed in the mid-1980s and thereafter expanded to levels costing over $30–$35 billion, with off-budget outlays of roughly $3 billion a year. The program also had additional accountability problems caused by including the barter of oil for weapons and complex offset arrangements. Further spending has taken place since 2001 in ways that have led to new charges of waste and corruption.

Above all, the Kingdom needs to recognize that it can no longer afford military procurement efforts that emphasize political considerations and/or high-technology "glitter" over military effectiveness. Saudi Arabia needs long-term force plans and planning, programming, and budget systems that create stable and affordable force-development and defense-spending efforts. It needs to bring its manpower quality and sustainment capabilities into balance with its equipment. It needs to recognize that its effectiveness is heavily dependent on interoperability with U.S. and GCC forces.

There should never be another massive Saudi arms package deal with the United States or Europe of the kind that took place during the Gulf War or a purchase like Al Yamamah. Barring a future major war, purchases should be made and justified on a case-by-case basis, off budget and oil barter deals should be illegal, and all offset deals should be subject to annual public reporting with an independent accountant and auditor.

Saudi Arabia must also minimize the waste of funds on:

- Unique equipment types and one-of-a-kind modifications.
- "Glitter factor" weapons; "developmental" equipment and technology.
- Arms buys made from Europe for political purposes where there is no credible prospect that the seller country can project major land and air forces.
- Noninteroperable weapons and systems.
- Submarines and ASW systems.
- Major surface warfare ships.
- Major equipment for divided or "dual" forces.
- New types of equipment that increase the maintenance, sustainability, and training problem, or layer new types over old.
- New types of equipment that strain the financial and manpower resources of Saudi Arabia and overloaded military units that are already experiencing absorption and conversion problems in using the equipment they possess or have on order.

SHIFTING TO BETTER PROCUREMENT MANAGEMENT AND LONGER-TERM PLANNING. There seems to be a need for several reforms in Saudi arms purchases and offset programs. First, they are needed for maximum transparency and public exposure of the financial details of contracts and purchase arrangements to encourage public review and trust. Second, they are needed for annual public reporting on contract performance and the individual performance of offset programs. Third, they are needed for the creation of a major new independent audit function within the Ministry of Defense and Aviation, with investigative accounting responsibility, to review such programs. Fourth, such reforms are needed for the creation of a body similar to the U.S. General Accounting Office under the king to conduct such audits in the case of suspect or troubled programs. Finally, they are needed for the inclusion of detailed procurement data in the kind of public defense program and budget discussed earlier.

Through the late 1990s, major procurement planning tended to lurch from year to year and from major deal to major deal, rather than being part of a coherent future year plan and program budget. Force modernization also tended to focus on major weapons buys without coherent plans to provide suitable support, training, and sustainment. These problems were further compounded by layering service and support contracts over procurement contracts, exaggerating the cost-benefits of grossly overambitious offset contracts, and uncertain accounting for soft expenditures like transportation and overhead costs.

While Saudi Arabia has long had reasonably well-drafted five-year plans in its civil sector, the Saudi military and security structure seem to be behind the civil sector in practical planning, programming, and budgeting skills, and it's uncertain that they have established the proper lines of authority to implement coherent plans even if they are drafted.

Effective arms buys require hard choices and well-planned trade-offs, and Saudi Arabia is long past the point where it simply can throw money at the problem. It needs a stable long-term procurement plan that spends no more than 60–70 percent of what the Kingdom has averaged since the Gulf War, that limits total outstanding orders to $7–$8 billion, that focuses on its highest priorities for standardization and interoperability with the United States, and that ensures that Saudi Arabia does not buy a series of partly incompatible systems when it buys from other countries.

The solution would seem to be both a suitable procurement plan for MODA, integrated into its planning, programming, and budgeting (PPB) system, and a broader national procurement plan, where the combined procurement efforts of the regular forces, National Guard, and various security elements of the Ministry of Interior are integrated into a common plan. This, however, is far easier to call for than implement. The United States, for example, has never been able to create a stable or fully effective procurement plan for its Department of Defense, much less link it effectively to its PPB system, or to the overall mix of requirements for national security including homeland defense.

Saudi Arabia has the potential advantage that its forces and budgets are far smaller, but the complications in creating efficient government planning of any kind universally seem to be a function of the number of agencies involved, and not of scale of effort.

Possible Saudi Needs and Major Purchases by Service. There are many areas where Saudi Arabia will still need major future arms buys. Army procurement raises several issues. Many countries are attempting to sell Saudi Arabia advanced armor, including main battle tanks. For example, it has been reported that Saudi Arabia is negotiating with Pakistan to purchase hundreds of Al-Khalid battle tanks, MBT 2000s, and that they were getting ready to test it in the southern city of Sharurah.[2]

While the Kingdom continues to discuss buying such types of advanced modern tanks, there are also arguments against near-term purchases. The Saudi Army has problems in operating and sustaining its present mix of M-60s and M-1s, and some Saudi officers feel that making their existing mix of equipment as ready, sustainable, and effective as possible should have priority. One counterargument is that Saudi Arabia's French-made AMX-30s are obsolete, and many are in storage, but Saudi Army officers feel they are still suitable for the kind of lighter brigades Saudi Arabia needs in dealing with counterterrorism and border defense in an era where Saddam Hussein's Iraq no longer poses a threat, and Iran and Iraq have very slow rates of force modernization and do not pose a serious threat of invasion.

Saudi Arabia also eventually needs to rationalize its mix of other armored vehicles. However, there is no near-term threat that requires expensive purchases in these areas, and upgrading its M-113s is a possible alternative. The Army does not need more long-range, self-propelled artillery firepower, but it does need to support its existing systems with the kind of sensors, battle management, and fire-control systems that can best help Saudi ground forces defend their long borders with Yemen and Iraq, which are exceptionally difficult to secure against infiltration and smuggling. In the case of its antitank weapons, the Army will eventually need a new system to replace its LAWs and Dragons, but it can simply upgrade its TOW-1As to TOW-2s.

The Saudi Army does seem to need more attack and lift helicopters and has a comprehensive plan to modernize army aviation. Once again, however, it can afford a relatively slow and carefully phased modernization effort unless major changes take place in the threat.

As is the case with all of its services, however, the Saudi Army does need to fully fund training, readiness and sustainment procurement and give them priority over new weapons. Here, the Saudi Army and other land services may need to reexamine their level of reliance on the civil sector for transporters that can rapidly move armor and artillery long distances, and for support vehicles and services. This seems to be a cost-effective alternative to dependence on army combat and service support forces that are not needed in peacetime, but it does raise questions about the vulnerability of civilian systems and the ability to provide the support needed on a timely basis and with the experience and effectiveness required.

The past modernization of the Saudi Air Force and Air Defense Forces has sometimes been overambitious, as has the modernization of Saudi Arabia's land-based air defense forces. The end result, however, has been to create an advanced and modern air force by regional standards. Upgrading its existing aircraft, selective purchases, and an emphasis on new air munitions, avionics, and IT systems may well meet its future needs. For example, it has upgraded its five E-3A AWACS and taken delivery on a total of 12 AB-412TP search-and-rescue helicopters.

The Air Force has other priorities. Saudi Arabia underfunded the support of its F-15 force to the point in the late 1990s where pilots flew too few hours a month and did little demanding training. Restoring readiness is critical. This includes funding adequate maintenance and sustainability as well.

Saudi Arabia has had to largely convert its aging F-5s to the training mission and to ground some others—although it still gets good use from its RF-5s in missions like border surveillance. It is considering selling its F-5E-IIs and F-5Fs and buying either new aircraft like the Eurofighter, Rafale, or Joint Strike Fighter (JTF), or smaller numbers of new F-15s. The key question, however, is whether Saudi Arabia needs to make such purchases now or whether it can wait until the Eurofighter, Rafale, and JTF are fully proven configurations and their full purchase and life-cycle costs are known. Saudi Arabia no longer seems to be considering the F-16 as an alternative for acquisition, although it remains a highly capable aircraft relative to any current potential threat aircraft.

Buying maritime patrol aircraft may be the highest-priority need for new platforms in order to both free the E-3As for air combat missions and provide the Air Force and Navy with badly needed improvements in coastal surveillance and coverage of the Gulf and Red Sea. There are reports that Saudi Arabia and Pakistan are considering the joint purchase of 14 AEW&C planes based on Sweden's Saab 2000 and equipped with the Erieye radar and sensor suite by Ericsson Microwave Systems. Saudi Arabia may find this option more attractive than going to the United States for a new AWACS deal, and Pakistan needs AEW&C aircraft to counter the recent Indian purchase of Israeli planes, the Phalcon.[3]

Saudi Arabia's main requirement for its Air Defense Forces is the need to fund steady improvements in the netting of its air defense system and to upgrade its Patriots to the PAC-3 version to provide better cruise missile, theater ballistic missile, and UAV defense. The Kingdom has obtained shared early-warning systems with the United States, but U.S. Patriots are the only system with antimissile capabilities currently in Saudi Arabia's inventory.

The antiballistic missile systems Saudi Arabia may eventually need to purchase for wide-area defense against the most advanced Iranian missiles like the Shahab are not yet available from the United States, or from any other supplier. In spite of some claims about the performance of advanced variants of the Russia S-300 and S-400 systems, they present much the same limitations—if not more so—than the U.S. Patriot and enhanced Standard missiles.

Saudi Arabia plans only a limited naval modernization program once it takes delivery on the three French *Lafayette*-class frigates in 2001–2005 that it ordered during the 1990s. Some officers still want to buy submarines, although it is far from clear that the Navy can afford to buy and sustain them. Others would like to shift the Navy's modernization priorities to areas like mine warfare and to concentrate on filling in the gaps in U.S. Navy mission capabilities in the Gulf. This is an important change. Past Saudi naval imports often reflected more interest in prestige and in the "glitter factor" of having the best-armed large ships than in Saudi Arabia's mission priorities or real-world military effectiveness.

As has been noted earlier, the Saudi National Guard has modernized more slowly and has kept its arms imports in better balance with its readiness and ability to absorb them. At the same time, the challenges the Guard has faced have been far less serious than those facing the regular forces, and Saudi Arabia has not been able to bring its planning for the regular forces and guard together in a common programming, planning, and budgeting system or to rationalize their modernization and roles and missions in ways that both produce military synergy and ensure that the National Guard can meet Saudi Arabia's evolving internal security needs.

PURCHASE OF THE RAFALE? Following Crown Prince Abdullah's visit to Paris in April 2005, it was rumored that the Kingdom has been in discussion with France's Dassault Aviation for the purchase of 96 Rafale combat aircraft. According to press reports, the Kingdom and France have agreed "in principle" to finalize Saudi Arabia's purchase of 48 aircraft and an option to buy 48 more for €6.0 billion.[4]

Dassault played down the report and said that the aviation company has been in discussions with the Kingdom for years about the Rafale. It was reported that the Rafale A prototype was presented to Saudi Arabia in 1986.[5] The Kingdom unequivocally denied any discussions concerning the Rafale. The Saudi foreign minister, Prince Saud al-Faisal, was quoted as saying, "Prince Abdullah's visit was more significant than concluding commercial deals." When asked about any aircraft deal with France, Al-Faisal said, "No decisions have been taken on these issues and thus we were not able to sign deals during this visit."[6]

The Rafale is a twin-jet aircraft designed for short- and long-term missions. It is equipped for land and sea attacks, air defense, and air superiority. It can also be used for high accuracy strikes and nuclear strike deterrence. The Rafale has three models: the Rafale M is a single-seat aircraft and is made for the navy, the Rafale B is a two-seat plane and is made for the air force, and the Rafale C is a two-seat aircraft made for the air force.

The following descriptions of the Rafale aircraft were adapted from airforce-technology.com:[7]

- *Cockpit:* The cockpit has hands-on throttle and stick control (HOTAS). The cockpit is equipped with a head-up, wide-angle holographic display from Thales Avionique, which provides aircraft control data, mission data and firing cues. A collimated, multi-image head-level display presents tactical situation and sensor data, and two touch-screen lateral displays show the aircraft system parameters and mission data. The pilot also has a helmet-mounted sight and display. A Cursor Control Device (CCD) camera and on-board recorder record the image of the head-up display throughout the mission.

- *Weapons:* The Rafale can carry payloads of over nine tons on 14 hardpoints for the air force version, and 13 for the naval version. The range of weapons includes Mica, Magic, Sidewinder, ASRAAM and AMRAAM air-to-air missiles; Apache, AS30L, ALARM, HARM, Maverick and PGM100 air-to-ground missiles; and Exocet/AM39, Penguin 3 and Harpoon antiship missiles. For a strategic mission, the Rafale can deliver the MBDA (formerly Aerospatiale) ASMP stand-off nuclear missile. Main weapons are expected to be the MBDA (formerly Matra BAe Dynamics) MICA air-to-air missile, MBDA Storm Shadow/Scalp EG stand-off cruise missile and the MBDA (Aerospatiale) AS 30 laser-guided missile.

  From 2006, the Rafale will also be armed with the Sagem AASM precision-guided bomb, which has both GPS/inertial guidance and, optionally, imaging infrared terminal guidance.

  The Rafale has a twin-gun pod and a GIAT 30-mm DEFA 791B cannon, which can fire 2,500 rounds per minute.

  The Rafale is equipped with laser-designation pods for laser guidance of air-to-ground missiles.

- *Countermeasures:* The Rafale's electronic-warfare system is the Spectra from Thales. Spectra incorporate solid-state transmitter technology, radar warner, DAL laser warning receiver, missile warning, detection systems, and jammers.

- *Sensors:* The Rafale is equipped with an RBE2 radar, developed by Thales, which has look-down and shoot-down capability. The radar can track up to eight targets simultaneously and provides threat identification and prioritization. The optronic systems include the Thales/SAGEM OSF infrared search-and-track system, installed in the nose of the aircraft. The optronic suite carries out search, target identification, telemetry and automatic target discrimination and tracking.

- *Navigation and Communications:* The communications suite on the Rafale uses the Saturn onboard V/UHF radio, which is a second-generation, anti-jam tactical UHF radio for NATO. Saturn provides voice encryption in fast-frequency hopping mode. The aircraft is also equipped with fixed-frequency VHF/UHF radio for communications with civil air traffic control. A multifunction information distribution system (MIDS) terminal provides secure, high-data-rate tactical data exchange with NATO C2 stations, AWACS aircraft or naval ships.

  Rafale is equipped with a Thales TLS 2000 navigation receiver, which is used for the approach phase of flight. The TLS 2000 integrates the instrument landing system (ILS), microwave landing system (MLS) and VHF Omni-directional Radio-ranger (VOR) and marker functions.

  The radar altimeter is the AHV 17 altimeter from Thales, which is suitable for very low flight. The Rafale has a TACAN tactical air navigation receiver for en route navigation and as a landing aid.

  The Rafale has an SB25A combined interrogator-transponder developed by Thales. The SB25A is the first IFF using electronic scanning technology.

- *Engine:* The Rafale is powered by two M88-2 engines from SNECMA, each providing a thrust of 75kN. The aircraft is equipped for buddy-buddy refueling with a flight refueling hose reel and drogue pack. Messier-Dowty provides the "jumper" landing gear, designed to spring out when the aircraft is catapulted by the nose gear strut.

It is unclear if a deal was made on the Rafale or which model the Kingdom may purchase. Some experts have argued that this "agreement" with France is a reminder by the Saudis to the "British and U.S. governments that there are other options out there when it comes to buying combat aircraft. It reminds their allies how important they are. However, I don't believe there is the political will or funding to purchase new aircraft at this time."[8]

As is the case with any procurement or offset program, the Kingdom must focus how such a deal does or does not serve its overall strategic interests. It is far from clear that the Saudi Air Force needs any new aircraft at this time or what the threat is, given the disappearance of the Iraqi Air Force and the lack of modernization and growth in the Iranian and Yemeni Air Forces. If the deal is seen as important to the Kingdom's national defense, the contract must include proper training, munitions, and logistic support to ensure against waste and the "glitter factor." Saudi Arabia's prestige is enhanced not by adding another weapon system to its arsenal, but rather by developing the necessary jointness, interoperability, and sustainment in its armed forces.

UPGRADING THE RSAF's TORNADOS? In early 2005, the Royal Saudi Air Force (RSAF) had 85 Tornado IDSs (10 Tornado GR1 recce-attack equipped) and 22 Tornado ADVs. It was reported that in April 2005, three of the RSAF's Tornado IDS strike/attack aircraft were seen at a BAE Systems' facility in England. BAE said that the aircraft were in their Warton facility as part of the Al Yamamah support contract.[9]

Other experts, however, have argued that the Tornados' arrival in England is a prelude to an upgrade contract for the RSAF GR1 fleet. The three aircrafts, they said, were prototypes for the coming upgrade. The British Royal Air Forces adapted some modification to its fleet in 2003. The upgrades, while believed to be more extensive than what the RSAF may adapt, may give a good benchmark of any possible upgrade.[10]

The Tornado midlife upgrade, the GR4 configuration, which is an update from the GR1 model, based on lessons learned from the Tornado's performance in the Gulf War includes:[11]

- New avionics to improve navigation and flight performance, including more-advanced Global Positioning System equipment;
- FLR (forward-looking infrared), NVG (night-vision goggle capabilities), and laser-designation facilities to allow for precision bombing;
- A multifunctional pilot head-up display and head-down display of flight, navigation, attack, or other information such as thermal imaging projected on the pilot's forward field of view;
- Improved reconnaissance capabilities;
- Defensive aids subsystems to protect the aircraft from SAMs and radar-directed AA guns;
- Equipped with Sea Eagle antishipping missiles;
- A 1760 weapons bus controlling the release of new advanced missiles like Brimstone;
- Advanced short-range air-to-air missiles; and
- Storm Shadow stand-off cruise missiles.[12]

The GR4 was used by the British Air Force in Southern Watch as well as in the Iraq War. All indications are that the aircraft performed well. Its main role was ground medium- and low-level precision strikes. The upgraded Tornado aircraft are more stealthy planes. They have the capabilities to see in the dark, using their FLIR and NVG, fly in close formation, and at terrain-following height. These characteristics give the GR4 higher abilities of deep covert incursions.[13]

It is uncertain whether the Kingdom has agreed to upgrade its fleet, what types of updates it has agreed to, or the cost of the contract. If the rumors are true and the upgrades include most if not all the GR4 configurations, it might well be a cost-effective way of enhancing the RSAF stealth capabilities and giving the Kingdom an edge. However, as is the case with any weapon system, the Kingdom must improve its manpower training program, enhance its integrated C^4I and IS&R, and focus on building jointness and interoperability between the Saudi services, among its Gulf allies, and with power-projection partners such as the United States and the UK.

ENDING THE TURNKEY APPROACH: THE POSSIBLE ROLE OF TEST AND EVALUATION. One inter- esting concept raised by Saudi officers is to shift to far more reliance on Saudi test and evaluation. In the past, the Kingdom has tended to buy cutting-edge systems to try to offset the superior numbers of potential threats like Iran and Iraq. This has often forced it to buy systems before they are proven and tested, and often in configurations that do not fully meet Saudi needs.

Changes in the threat, the ability to modernize platforms rather than replace them, and the growing importance of information systems and smart munitions all combine to allow Saudi Arabia to wait until systems are proven and are deployed in the forces of seller countries and then demand samples for comparative test and evaluation. Such a shift from "turnkey buys" to "proof of performance" would require Saudi Arabia to create new staffs and facilities. As several senior Saudi officers point out, however, the cost would be far smaller than making even one significant error in a major procurement and would put far more pressure on seller countries and manufacturers to perform.

RESHAPING DEFENSE PLANNING, PROGRAMMING, BUDGETING, AND TRANSPARENCY

All of these points indicate that Saudi Arabia needs to make another reform in the way it shapes its defense plans, budgets, and purchases. Saudi Arabia is scarcely unique in keeping virtually all of the military, technical, and financial and management aspects of its arms deals secret. Virtually every country in the developing world does so, and the details of procurement and service contracts of many Western states are almost impossible for outsiders to obtain. The fact is, however, that virtually every war-fighting aspect of such contracts soon becomes public. There is no military or strategic reason for classifying the cost and structure of arms deals. In fact, there is even less reason to classify them than the total defense budget. The actual flow of arms and munitions is so public that attempts at secrecy are futile.

The past lack of transparency and accountability has been a serious problem in Saudi arms buys, as it has the tendency to create large contract programs that become open-ended purchasing programs. Secrecy does not aid effective planning or preserve the Kingdom's security. It instead encourages poor planning and budgeting, as well as corruption and cronyism. It encourages the failure to insist on plans that force the various military services to develop joint plans, demonstrate their effectiveness, and convince the Saudi people that they get the security their money should buy. It also makes it impossible to explain the need for the Kingdom's alliances, and the nature of the threats the Kingdom faces.

Open and transparent procurement budgeting is a solution to many of the resulting problems and puts pressure on both Saudi planners and seller countries and manufacturers. The creation of public defense plans, programs, and program budgets is one way to help reform the Kingdom's defense planning, programming, and budgeting system; to set a sustainable level of defense spending, and to build public confidence and trust. The Kingdom should also begin to issue white papers explaining major defense purchases, real-world progress in offset efforts, and other major security actions as another way to build that trust and reduce political pressure from outside countries over issues like major arms purchases.

Arms Sales and Security Assistance

Both the Saudi government and its foreign arms suppliers need to recognize that the majority of educated Saudis already ask serious questions about the value of Saudi Arabia's arms imports and the honesty of the procurement and delivery process. This questioning comes from senior Saudi officials and some junior members of the royal family as well as the public, and it is one of the few areas where Saudi Arabia's most progressive businessmen and technocrats and Islamic extremists agree in criticizing the Saudi government.

The time has passed when the Saudi government could deal with these problems with secrecy and silence. It needs to make its programs more public, bring them openly on budget, and demonstrate that it has accounting procedures that limit favoritism and commissions to levels that are broadly acceptable in Saudi society. One key way of doing this would be to make both the military budget and the procurement budget subject to the same review by the

Majlis as the rest of the Saudi budget and provide more details in the Saudi Arabia Monetary Agency budget data—some of the most sophisticated budget reporting in any Middle Eastern state. Such review could evolve with time and would take on added impact and legitimacy if part or all of the Majlis eventually became publicly elected.

Sellers have obligations as well. The West and other arms sellers have energy security needs and strategic interests far more important than arms sales. They must be careful in pressing for military sales in ways that do not meet vital Saudi security needs and that do not take Saudi Arabia's domestic economic problems and social needs into account. Saudi Arabia has long been the largest single customer for U.S. and European military exports. Saudi purchases have had the benefit of increasing interoperability and sustainability with British, French, and U.S. forces and of reducing the unit cost of equipment purchased by Western forces.

It is clear, however, that Saudi Arabia faces serious long-term constraints on what it can buy in the future, and that it will often have to make hard choices between the military desirability of standardization with Western power projection forces and the political need to buy arms from a range of friendly states.

Defense contractors will be defense contractors; they exist to sell regardless of need or merit. Governments, however, must act as governments and think first of their strategic interests. It is time that governments of Europe and the United States make it clear to the Saudi people that they emphasize Saudi security, military readiness, and effectiveness rather than exports and sales. They need to make it clear that that they are not pressuring Saudi Arabia to buy unnecessary arms, recognize Saudi Arabia's need to limit its purchases to the level Saudi Arabia can afford, and act to prevent corruption and ensure that arms buys are part of packages that include the proper support, training, munitions stocks, and sustainability.

Chapter 9

Internal Security Reform

S audi Arabia has taken a number of steps to improve its internal security and support the war on terrorism since September 11th. Saudi intelligence and the Saudi foreign ministry have conducted a detailed review of Saudi companies and charities operating in Pakistan and Central Asia. Saudi Arabia and the other Gulf Cooperation Council (GCC) countries also agreed to take new steps to control the flow of funds and money laundering at the GCC summit meeting on December 31, 2001.[1]

The Saudi government has arrested a number of individuals the United States suspects of supporting Osama bin Laden, as well as cracked down on its more extreme Islamists. While it has acted slowly because of the sensitivity Saudis show to any outside pressure and because of rising public anger over the Second Intifada, it issued orders blocking the assets of 66 persons, companies, groups, and charities on the U.S. watch list for entities linked to global terrorism in late October 2001.[2] Saudi Arabia agreed to sign the 1999 UN antiterrorism convention aimed at blocking the financial support of terrorists in early November 2001.[3] In December 2001, the foreign minister, Prince Saud al-Faisal, promised to punish Saudis criminally involved in al Qaeda terrorism.[4]

The government has acted to freeze bank accounts linked to suspected terrorists, and Saudi intelligence is now monitoring at least 150 accounts for terrorist activity. The Saudi Chamber of Commerce established a task force in January 2002 to develop a financial and administrative system for Saudi charities to ensure that their funds would not go to extremist causes, and the Saudi Arabian Monetary Agency (SAMA) is assisting Saudi banks to develop and computerize systems to track money laundering. The Saudi government is also drafting new laws to limit money-laundering activity.[5]

Another major institutional initiative is the creation of a specialized Financial Intelligence Unit (FIU) in the Ministry of Interior. This unit is specially tasked with handling money-laundering cases. A communication channel between the Ministry of Interior and SAMA on matters involving terrorist-financing activities has also been established.

SAUDI REFORMS TO THE INTERNAL SECURITY
APPARATUS BEFORE MAY 2003

Saudi Arabia issued a full list of the new actions it has taken to reshape these aspects of its security apparatus in early December 2002, and U.S. officials have confirmed the validity of this list. These measures can be summarized by category as follows:[6]

International Cooperation

- Supporting and implementing UN Security Council Resolution 1267 by freezing the funds and financial assets of the Taliban. Freezing the funds of the individuals listed in Security Council Resolution 1333. Signing the International Convention for Suppression and Financing of Terrorism based on Security Council Resolution 1373 and reporting on the implementation of the rules and procedures pertaining to this resolution; reporting to the Security Council on the implementation of Resolution 1390. Supporting and implementing Security Council Resolution 1368, of September 12, 2001, limiting the financing of terrorist activities.

- Maintaining a counterterrorism committee with the United States composed of intelligence and law enforcement personnel who meet regularly to share information and resources and to develop action plans to root out terrorist networks. Saudi Arabia has sought to strengthen cooperation between the Kingdom and the United States through reciprocal visits.

- Encouraging Saudi government departments and banks to participate in international seminars, conferences, and symposia on combating terrorist financing activities. Saudi Arabia has hosted such events and is a member of the GCC Financial Action Task Force (FATF).

- Completing and submitting the self-assessment questionnaire regarding the 40 recommendations of the FATF. Saudi Arabia has also submitted the self-assessment questionnaire regarding the eight Special Recommendations of the FATF.

- Having the Saudi Arabian Monetary Authority exchange information on money laundering-related activities with other banking supervisory authorities and with law enforcement agencies. SAMA has created a committee to carry out a self-assessment for compliance with the recommendations of the FATF, and these questionnaires have been submitted. Saudi Arabia has invited the FATF to conduct a mutual evaluation in April 2003.

- Signing a multilateral agreement under the auspices of the Arab League to fight terrorism.

- Submitting a report every 90 days on the initiatives and actions the Kingdom has taken to fight terrorism to the UN Security Council committees dealing with terrorism.
- Establishing formal communication points between the Ministry of Foreign Affairs and the permanent representative to the UN.

Arrests and Questioning of Suspects

- Saudi Arabia has questioned over 2,000 individuals for possible ties to al Qaeda. Many of these people fought in Afghanistan during the Soviet invasion as well as in Bosnia and Chechnya.
- Detaining up to 200 suspects out of this total for questioning and interrogation. Well over 100 were still held in detention in December 2002.
- Saudi intelligence and law enforcement agencies identified and arrested a cell composed of seven individuals linked to al Qaeda, the members of which were planning to carry out terrorist attacks against vital sites in the Kingdom. The cell leader was extradited from the Sudan. This cell was responsible for the attempt to shoot down American military planes at Prince Sultan Air Base, using a shoulder-launched surface-to-air missile.
- Saudi Arabia successfully negotiated with Iran for the extradition of 16 suspected al Qaeda members. These individuals are now in Saudi custody and are being questioned. The Iranian authorities handed over the al Qaeda fugitives, all Saudis, knowing that whatever intelligence was obtained from them during interrogation in Saudi Arabia would be passed on to the United States for use in the war against terrorism.
- Asking Interpol to arrest 750 people, many of whom are suspected of money-laundering, drug-trafficking, and terror-related activities. This figure includes 214 Saudis whose names appear in Interpol's database and expatriates who had fled Saudi Arabia.
- Helping to identify a network of more than 50 shell companies that Osama bin Laden used to move money around the world. The companies were located in the Middle East, Europe, Asia, and the Caribbean. A sophisticated financial network that weaved through more than 25 nations was uncovered and virtually shut down.

Legal and Regulatory Actions and Freezing Terrorist Assets and Combating Money Laundering

- Signing and joining the United Nations Convention against Illicit Trafficking of Narcotics and Psychotropic Substances in 1988.

- Freezing assets of Osama bin Laden in 1994.
- Establishing anti-money laundering units at the Ministry of Interior, SAMA, and Commercial Banks in 1995.
- Having SAMA issue "Guidelines for Prevention and Control of Money Laundering Activities" to Saudi Banks to implement "Know Your Customer Rules," maintain records of suspicious transactions, and report them to law enforcement officials in SAMA in 1995. ·
- Adopting 40 recommendations of the Financial Task force relating to banking control of money laundering that grew out of the G-7 meeting in 1988.
- Saudi banks to identify and freeze all assets relating to terrorist suspects and entities per the list issued by the United States government on September 23, 2001. Saudi banks have complied with the freeze requirements and have initiated investigation of transactions that suspects linked to al Qaeda may have undertaken in the past.
- Investigating bank accounts suspected to have been linked to terrorism. Saudi Arabia froze 33 accounts belonging to 3 individuals that total about $5,574,196.
- Establishing a special committee with personnel from the Ministry of Interior, Ministry of Foreign Affairs, the Intelligence Agency and SAMA to deal with requests from international bodies and countries with regards to combating terrorist financing.
- Reorienting the activities of the GCC Financial Action Task Force to deal with terrorism and creating a committee to carry out a self-assessment for compliance with the recommendations of the FATF.
- Joining finance ministers and central bank governors of the G-20 to develop an aggressive action plan directed at the routing out and freezing of terrorist assets worldwide.
- Having SAMA instruct Saudi banks to promptly establish a supervisory committee to closely monitor the threat posed by terrorism and to coordinate all efforts to freeze the assets of potential terrorists. The committee is composed of senior officers from banks responsible for risk control, audit, money-laundering units, legal affairs, and operations. The committee meets regularly in the presence of SAMA officials.
- Requiring Saudi banks to put in place mechanisms to respond to all relevant inquiries, both domestically and internationally, at the level of their chief executive officers, as well as at the level of the supervisory committee. To ensure proper coordination and effective response, all Saudi banks route their responses and relevant information via SAMA.

- Having the Ministry of Commerce issue Regulation #1312 aimed at preventing and combating money laundering in the nonfinancial sector. These regulations are aimed at manufacturing and trading sectors and also cover professional services such as accounting, legal, and consultancy services.

- Creating an institutional framework for combating money laundering, including the establishment of anti-money laundering units, with a trained and dedicated specialist staff. These units work with SAMA and law enforcement agencies. The government has also encouraged banks to bring money laundering-related experiences to the notice of various bank committees (chief operations officers, managing directors, fraud committees, and so forth) for exchange of information and joint actions.

- Creating a specialized Financial Intelligence Unit (FIU) in the Ministry of Interior. This unit is specially tasked with handling money-laundering cases. A new liaison group dealing with terrorist finances has been established between SAMA and the Ministry of Interior.

- Carrying out regular inspection of banks to ensure compliance with laws and regulations. Any violation or noncompliance is cause for serious actions and is referred to a bank's senior management and the board. Furthermore, the government has created a permanent committee of bank compliance officers to review regulations and guidelines and recommend improvements as well as to ensure all implementation issues are resolved.

- Freezing bank accounts suspected of links to terrorists.

- Using the interbanking system in Saudi Arabia to identify possible sources of funding of terrorism.

- Supporting UN resolutions, such as UN Security Council Resolution 1368 to limit the financing of terrorist activities.

- Working with the United States and other countries to block more than $70 million in possible terrorist assets in Saudi Arabia and other countries.

- Quietly providing data on suspect private Saudi accounts in Switzerland, Liechtenstein, Luxembourg, Denmark, and Sweden.

- Directing SAMA to issue rules "Governing the Opening of Bank Accounts" and "General Operational Guidelines" in May 2002 to protect banks against money-laundering activities. For instance, Saudi banks are not permitted to open bank accounts for nonresident individuals without specific approval from SAMA. Banks are required to apply strict rules, and any noncustomer business has to be fully documented.

- Making significant new efforts to train staff in financial institutions and the security and investigations departments in the Ministry of Interior as well as others involved in compliance and law. Special training programs have been developed for bankers, prosecutors, judges, customs officers, and other officials from government departments and agencies. Furthermore, the Prince Nayef Security Academy, King Fahd Security Faculty, and Public Security Training City offer training programs.

- Establishing a permanent committee of representatives of seven ministries and government agencies to manage all legal and other issues related to money laundering activities.

- Directing SAMA to organize a conference with the Riyadh Interpol for the First Asian Regional meeting in cooperation with law enforcement agencies and financial institutions during January 28–30, 2002.

- Having the Council of Saudi Chambers of Commerce and Industry, in cooperation with SAMA, conduct an International Conference on Prevention and Detection of Fraud, Economic Crimes, and Money Laundering during May 13–14, 2002.

- Directing Saudi banks and SAMA to computerize reported cases to identify trends in money-laundering activities to assist in policymaking and other initiatives.

Actions Taken in Regard to Charitable Organizations

- Creating a High Commission for the Oversight of Charities to look at ways to regulate charities, help them put financial control mechanisms and procedures in place, require that charities conduct audits, and review them. A department will be set up that will grow out of the high commission to maintain suitable review and controls. This will compensate for the fact that Saudi Arabia does not have an income tax and does not have the same tax-related review of expenditures common in the West.

- Requiring that charitable activities that extend outside Saudi Arabia be reported to the Saudi government and are routinely monitored and that charitable activities outside Saudi Arabia be reported to the Foreign Ministry.

- Taking joint action with the United States to freeze the assets of, Wa'el Hamza Julaidan, a Saudi fugitive and a close aide of bin Laden, who is believed to have funneled money to al Qaeda. Julaidan served as the director of the Rabita Trust and other organizations.

- Entering the final process of setting up operational procedures under the High Commission for the Oversight of Charities to manage contributions and donations to and from the charities.

- Auditing all charitable groups to ensure there are no links to suspected organizations since September 11, 2001.

- Issuing new guidelines and regulations, including financial control mechanisms to make sure terrorist and extremist organizations cannot take advantage of legitimate charities.

- Setting up the Higher Saudi Association for Relief and Charity to oversee the distribution of donations and guarantee they are channeled to the needy.

- Strengthening the role of the Saudi and U.S. counterterrorism committee composed of intelligence and law enforcement personnel who meet regularly to share information and resources on the misuse of charities and charitable funds and to develop plans of action to root out terrorist networks.

- Freezing bank accounts involving the flow of charitable funds that are suspected of being linked to terrorism.

- Working with the U.S. Treasury Department to block the accounts of the Somalia and Bosnia branches of the Saudi Arabia-based Al-Haramain Islamic Foundation in March 2002. While the Saudi headquarters for this private charitable entity is dedicated to helping those in need, the United States and Saudi Arabia determined that the Somalia and Bosnia branches of the organization engaged in supporting terrorist activities and terrorist organizations such as al Qaeda, AIAI (al-Itihaad al-Islamiya), and others.

SAUDI INTERNAL SECURITY REFORMS SINCE MAY 2003

The Saudi security dynamic changed again as a result of the events of 2003. This increase in Saudi activity is shown in the following chronology of events that took place during 2003:

- In February 2003, the Saudi Arabian Monetary Agency (SAMA) began to implement a major technical program to train judges and investigators on legal matters, including terror financing and money-laundering methods, international requirements for financial secrecy, and the methods followed by criminals to exchange information.

- On May 12, 2003, a series of tragic bombings took place in Riyadh. Saudi Arabia reacted with a series of new efforts to combat terrorism, and more than 200 suspects were arrested in connection with the Riyadh bombings between May and September 2003. Since September 11, Saudi Arabia has questioned thousands of suspects and arrested more than 600 individuals with suspected ties to terrorism:

— In May 2003, three clerics, Ali Fahd al-Khudair, Ahmed Hamoud Mufreh al-Khaledi, and Nasir Ahmed al-Fuhaid, were arrested after calling for support of the terrorists who carried out the Riyadh attacks. In November 2003, Ali Fahd al-Khudair recanted his religions opinions on Saudi TV. Shortly after, a second cleric, Nasir Ahmed al-Fuhaid, recanted and withdrew his religious opinions describing them as a "grave mistake." On December 16, 2003, Ahmed Hamoud Mufreh al-Khaledi became the third cleric to recant on national television.

— Eleven suspects were taken into custody on May 27 and May 28 in the city of Medina. Weapons, false identity cards and bomb-making materials were confiscated. In addition, Saudi national Abdulmonim Ali Mahfouz al-Ghamdi was arrested following a car chase. Three non-Saudi women without identity cards, who were in the car he was driving, were detained.

— Yusef Salih Fahad al-Ayeri, aka Swift Sword, a major al Qaeda operational planner and fundraiser, was killed on May 31 while fleeing from a security patrol.

— Ali Abd-al Rahman al-Fagasi al-Ghamdi, aka Abu Bakr al-Azdi, surrendered to Saudi authorities. al-Ghamdi, considered one of the top al Qaeda operatives in Saudi Arabia, is suspected of being one of the masterminds of 12 May bombings in Riyadh.

— Turki Nasser Mishaal Aldandany, another top al Qaeda operative and one of the masterminds of the 12 May bombings, was killed on 3 July along with three other suspects in a gun battle with security forces that had them surrounded.

— Saudi security forces raided a terrorist cell on June 14, in the Alattas building in the Khalidiya neighborhood of Mecca. Two Saudi police officers and five suspects were killed in a shootout. Twelve suspects were arrested, and a number of booby-trapped Qur'ans and 72 home-made bombs, in addition to weapons, ammunition, and masks were confiscated.

— In July 21, the Ministry of Interior announced that Saudi authorities had defused terrorist operations that were about to be carried out against vital installations and had arrested 16 members of a number of terrorist cells after searching their hideouts in farms and houses in

Riyadh Province, Qasim Province, 220 miles north of Riyadh, and the Eastern Province. In addition, underground storage facilities were found at these farms and homes containing bags, weighing over 20 tons, filled with chemicals used in the making of explosives.

— Three men were arrested on July 25 at a checkpoint in Mecca for possessing printed material that included a "religious edict" in support of terrorist acts against Western targets.

— On July 28, Saudi security forces killed six terrorist suspects and injured one in a gunfight at a farm in Qasim Province, 220 miles north of Riyadh. Two Saudi security officers were killed and eight suffered minor injuries. Four people who harbored the suspects were arrested. Nine security officers have been killed and 19 injured in counterterrorism activities since May 12.

• In May 2003, SAMA issued instructions to all Saudi financial institutions to strictly implement 40 recommendations of the FATF regarding money laundering and the numerous recommendations regarding terror financing. Furthermore, SAMA issued instructions to all Saudi financial institutions prohibiting the transfer of any funds by charitable organizations outside the Kingdom. SAMA has also created a committee to carry out self-assessment for compliance with the FATF recommendations and these self-assessment questionnaires have been submitted. The FATF conducted a mutual evaluation on September 21–25, 2003.

• In May 2003, a Saudi-U.S. task force was organized from across law enforcement and intelligence agencies to work side by side to share "real-time" intelligence and conduct joint operations in the fights against terrorism. Saudi authorities worked closely with U.S. and British law enforcement agents who came to the Kingdom to assist in the investigation. The U.S. ambassador to Saudi Arabia, Robert Jordan, described the cooperation of Saudi investigators with the U.S. law enforcement representatives as "superb."

Saudi Arabia redeployed Special Forces to enhance security and counterterrorism efforts.

• In May 2003, SAMA distributed entitled "Rules Governing Anti-Monetary Laundering and Combating Terrorist Financing" to all banks and financial institutions in Saudi Arabia, requiring the full and immediate implementation of nine new polices and procedures. The new regulations include the following:

— All bank accounts of charitable or welfare societies must be consolidated into a single account for each such society. SAMA may give permission for a subsidiary account if necessary, but such an account can only be used to receive, not to withdraw or transfer, funds.

— Deposits in these accounts will be acceptable only after the depositor provides the bank with identification and all other required information for verification.

— No ATM or credit cards can be issued for these accounts. No checks and drafts are permitted from the charitable institution's account, and all checks and drafts are to be in favor of legitimate beneficiaries and for deposits in a bank account only.

— No charitable or welfare society can open or operate these bank accounts without first presenting a valid copy of the required license.

— No overseas fund transfers allowed from these bank accounts.

— SAMA's approval is required to open a bank account.

— Only two individuals who are authorized by the board of a charitable institution shall be allowed to operate the main account.

— Another major institutional initiative is the creation of a specialized Financial Intelligence Unit in the Security and Drug Control Department of the Ministry of Interior. This unit is specially tasked with handling money-laundering cases. A communication channel between the Ministry of Interior and SAMA on matters involving terrorist-financing activities had also been established.

• In August 2003, the Council of Ministers approved new legislation that puts in place harsh penalties for the crime of money laundering and terror financing. This legislation requires jail sentences of up to 15 years and fines up to $1.8 million for offenders. The new law:

— Bans financial transaction with unidentified parties,

— Requires banks to maintain records of transactions for up to 10 years,

— Establishes intelligence units to investigate suspicious transactions,

— Sets up international cooperation on money-laundering issues with countries with formal agreements have been signed.

• In August 2003, Saudi Arabia and the United States established another joint task force aimed at combating the financing of terrorism. The task force, which was initiated by Crown Prince Abdullah, is further indication of the Kingdom's commitment to the war on terrorism and its close cooperation with the United States in eradicating terrorists and their supporters.

— On September 23, 2003, security forces surrounded a group of suspected terrorists in an apartment in the city of Jizan. During a gun battle, one security officer was killed and four officers injured. Two suspects were arrested and one killed. The suspects were armed with machine guns and pistols and a large quantity of ammunition.

— On October 5, 2003, security forces arrested three suspects during a raid in the desert to the east of Riyadh.

— On October 8, 2003, security forces raided a farm in the northern Muleda area of Qasim Province and were able to arrest a suspect. Three other suspects fled the scene. Two security officers suffered injuries.

— On October 20, 2003, security forces raided several terrorist cells in various parts of the country, including the city of Riyadh, the Al Majma'a District in Riyadh Province, Mecca Province, the Jeddah District of Mecca Province, and Qasim Province. Security forces confiscated items, including C4 plastic explosives, homemade bombs, gas masks, and large quantities of assault rifles and ammunition.

— On November 3, 2003, Saudi police arrested six suspected al Qaeda militants after a shootout in the holy city of Mecca. The raid on an apartment triggered a shootout that left two suspected terrorists dead, and one security officer wounded.

— On November 6, 2003, security forces investigating a suspected terrorist cell in the Al Swaidi district of Riyadh came under fire from the suspects, who attempted to flee while attacking security forces with machine guns and bombs. In the exchange of fire, one terrorist was killed and eight of the security officers suffered minor injuries. On the same day, in the Al Shara'ei district of Mecca, two terrorist suspects, who were surrounded by security forces, used homemade bombs to blow themselves up. Their suicide followed a firefight during which they refused to surrender when requested by the security officers.

— On November 20, 2003, Abdullah bin Atiyyah bin Hudeid al-Salami surrendered himself to security authorities. He was wanted for suspected terrorist activities.

— On November 25, 2003, a car bomb plot was foiled in Riyadh. The encounter with security forces led to the deaths of two wanted terrorist suspects: Abdulmohsin Abdulaziz al-Shabanat, who was killed in the exchange of fire, and Mosaed Mohammad Dheedan Alsobaiee, who committed suicide by detonating the hand grenade he was carrying.

The vehicle that was seized was loaded with explosives and camouflaged as a military vehicle.

— On November 26, 2003, a suspected terrorist was arrested. The suspect's hiding place was linked to the terrorist cell involved in the November 9 car bombing at the Al Muhayya residential complex in Riyadh. Search of the hiding place revealed large quantities of arms and documents. Items discovered by security forces included one SAM-7 surface-to-air missile, five rocket-propelled grenade launchers, 384 kilograms of the powerful explosive RDX, 89 detonators, 20 hand grenades, 8 AK-47 assault rifles, 41 AK-47 magazines, and 16,800 rounds of ammunition. Also recovered were four wireless communication devices, three computers, computer disks and CDs, and SR 94,395 in cash, as well as numerous identity cards and leaflets calling for the perpetration of acts of terror.

— On December 6, 2003, the Ministry of Interior published the names and photos of 26 suspects wanted by security forces in connection with the terrorist incidents that had taken place in the Kingdom in the previous few months, urging them to surrender to the authorities. The ministry called on all citizens and residents to report information they may have about any of the wanted suspects. Immediate financial rewards of up to $1.9 million were offered for information leading to the arrest of any wanted suspect, or any other terrorist elements and cells.

— On December 8, 2003, the Ministry of Interior announced that Ibrahim Mohammad Abdullah al-Rayyes, whose name was on the December 6 list, had been killed by security forces. The ministry statement praised citizens' cooperation with the security forces, who are pursuing those wanted and those who are trying to undermine the country's security and safety.

— On December 30, 2003, Mansour ibn Muhammad Faqeeh, whose name had been published in a December 6 list of 26 wanted terrorist suspects, surrendered to security authorities.

— By December 2003, Saudi security forces had conducted over 158 raids on various terrorist elements and groups.

— In December 2003, Saudi Arabia and the United States took steps to designate two organizations as financiers of terrorism under United Nations Security Council Resolution 1267 (1999). These organizations are the Bosnia-based Vazir and the Liechtenstein-based Hochburg AG.

— On January 22, 2004, in a joint press conference, U.S. Treasury Secretary John W. Snow and Adel al-Jubeir, foreign affairs adviser to Crown Prince Abdullah, called upon the United Nations Sanctions Committee to designate four branch offices of the Al-Haramain Islamic Foundation as financial supporters of terrorism. This was the fourth joint action taken against terrorist financing by the U.S. Treasury Department and the Kingdom of Saudi Arabia.

PROSPECTS FOR FURTHER INTERNAL SECURITY REFORMS

It will take at least several years for Saudi Arabia to come fully to grips with current terrorist threats. Its short-term successes have not removed cadres that are well equipped with arms and explosives, and past experience indicates that extremists and terrorists will soon change tactics, acquire better intelligence, and become far more sophisticated in concealing their existence and affiliations.

New terrorists and extremists will infiltrate from the outside, and conflicts like the insurgency in Iraq will inevitably attract, indoctrinate, and train new generations of Saudi activists and extremists. Like the broader war on terrorism, Saudi Arabia faces at least a low-level threat that will be generational in character and which will probably exist in some form for the next decade.

Saudi Arabia can only move so quickly. It must maintain popular support, and many of the necessary social and educational reforms to address the problems that created these threats will take a half a decade to address. In the interim, there are bound to be more successful terrorist attacks. Almost inevitably, the Kingdom's pace of change—an emphasis on co-option versus direct action—will also prolong tensions with the United States.

As yet, there seems to be little broad social support for violent extremism anywhere in the Kingdom. To the extent there are relevant public opinion surveys, they show that young Saudis are far more interested in education, jobs and a career than any form of radicalism, and that the most polarizing political issue is the Arab-Israeli conflict and not religion. The situation seems far closer to the early phases of the low-level "Armed Islamic Group" (AIG) threat to Egypt than to the kind of threat that could overthrow the monarchy. It is a major warning that both better security methods and reforms are needed, not that the government is at risk or that investments in Saudi Arabia should be assigned a much higher level of risk.

It is clear, however, that the Saudi government must continue to steadily do more to come to grips with security problems like Islamic extremism while it simultaneously continues to liberalize its overall internal security arrangements. It must also create and enforce a more modern version of the rule of law.

No one can argue with Saudi advocacy of Islam and the conservative practices of the Wahhabi sect when these are so clearly the choice of the Saudi people. Everyone can argue with the thesis that extremists can use God to advocate violence, terrorism, and actions that kill innocent civilians. The same is true of halting religious practices that teach intolerance and hatred, regardless of whether such practices are defended in the name of Islam, Judaism, Christianity, or any other faith. The Saudi government needs to aggressively and consistently enforce its own policies in those areas.

There is no inherent dilemma between improving intelligence and the security services and liberalization. More modern security and legal procedures can improve the quality of investigations, intelligence gathering, and warning without preventing reductions in censorship and government controls, more tolerance of the Saudi Shiite and practices of foreigner on Saudi soil, and methods of arrest and trial that guarantee more rights. Past progress in these areas has also shown that the necessary rate of progress can be made on Saudi terms and in ways that preserve Saudi custom.

There are also five key problems that Saudi Arabia must face in terms of cooperation with the United States and other key actors in the broader war on terrorism:

- *Counterterrorism cooperation must steadily improve at every level.* Although counterterrorism has improved drastically, the Kingdom must continue its internal or external progress on promised reforms, fully implement the measures under way, and pay more attention to the need to reshape its approach to Islamic causes outside Saudi Arabia in ways that support reform, moderation, and tolerance.

- The level of popular tension between the United States and Saudi Arabia has reached the point where it actively encourages Saudi hostility to the United States in ways that aid extremists and terrorists. This has been compounded by a failure to create immigration and visa procedures that combine protection against terrorists with rapid and effective procedures for encouraging legitimate cultural, business, medical and student entrants to the United States. The United States badly needs to reshape its focus on counterterrorism to strengthen the ties between the United States and Saudi and Arab moderates throughout the world, to ensure that students continue to be educated in the United States, and to ensure that legitimate medical cases are screened and expedited on a humanitarian basis.

- The Arab-Israeli conflict—and Israeli-Palestinian War in particular—has created serious tensions between the United States and Saudi Arabia, and the Arab world and the West. Both Saudi Arabia and the United States are going to have to live with this fact, and inevitably, most Saudis will see movements like Hamas and the Hezbollah more as "liberators" or "freedom fighters" than as terrorists. Whatever the U.S. and Saudi governments say in public about this aspect of the war on terrorism, there will be inevitable limits to their cooperation. This will, inevitably, lead to Israeli and pro-Israel demands for Saudi action in dealing with such groups that Saudi Arabia will not comply with, triggering more political and media attacks against Saudi Arabia. Equal hostility will exist in Saudi Arabia over U.S. unconditional support to Israel. No amount of pressure can resolve this situation. Strong parallel efforts to revitalize the Arab-Israeli peace process can, to some extent, ameliorate it.

- The fall of Saddam Hussein's regime and the rise of active terrorism within Saudi Arabia are key factors that illustrate the need to recast Saudi security in the broadest sense. Saudi security efforts now cost so much that they are a serious threat to Saudi security. They also indicate that the United States needs to actively help Saudi Arabia to refocus its security efforts on internal security—with is generally an order of magnitude cheaper than a conventional military build-up—and shift resources to economic growth and social programs.

- Saudi Arabia needs to coordinate a policy to make sure Iran does not get nuclear weapons, and if it does, to create deterrence either through an anti-missile defense or any other means necessary. The Kingdom is worried about Iran controlling the Shiite majority of Iraq, and if it goes nuclear, two hostile countries will surround the Kingdom. This alliance will not only impose an external threat on Saudi Arabia, but also potentially will bring about an increase in the incitements of the Shiite minority in the Eastern Province. The Saudis will have to find a deterrent system if they feel that they cannot rely on U.S. protection anymore.

Finally, the longer term key to U.S. and Western efforts to help Saudi Arabia fight terrorism is not government-to-government cooperation in counterterrorism, but rather cooperation between the Saudi and U.S. private sectors. It is investment and trade that create jobs in Saudi Arabia and reduces the social and economic pressures that help encourage extremism and terrorism. Saudi Arabia needs to be more realistic about the return on investment, risk premiums, contract structures, and security necessary to create suitable incentive for

U.S. and foreign investment at the level and speed required. The United States, however, must do more to assist U.S. industry and may have to provide some form of guarantees. A "business as usual" approach will not do.

Chapter 10

The Broader Priorities for Security Reform

The analysis in this book has focused on military and internal security developments in the Kingdom. These are the conventional areas dealt with in national security analysis, and the Kingdom faces serious challenges in both areas. The fall of Saddam Hussein's regime has left many security challenges, and the rise of Islamist extremism and violence poses a whole new series of internal security challenges. The preceding chapters have described both considerable ongoing progress in meeting these challenges and many areas where further reforms and changes are needed.

As has been discussed in virtually every chapter, however, Saudi security also requires a broad process of continuing evolutionary reform of the Kingdom's political, economic, and social systems, not just reform of the Saudi military, internal security, and intelligence services.

The health of the Saudi economy, and coming to grips with the Kingdom's problems with education, Saudization, youth employment, and demographics are the true keys to security. So is a level of political progress that expands the role ordinary Saudis can play in government and in making further reductions in sources of social unrest like corruption. Even the best counterterrorist operations can only deal with the small fraction of the Saudi population that represents violent extremists. True internal security is based on popular support.

The West has been quick to recognize the problems in Saudi Arabia and slow to recognize that progress both is under way and has had the support of the Saudi leadership in many areas. For example, King Fahd has made reforms a clear national priority. In his speech at the annual meeting of the Shura Council in Riyadh in 2003, he underscored the Saudi government's commitment to reform. The king reaffirmed the government's commitment in fighting terrorism, poverty, and unemployment. He also gave his approval for the establishment of a nongovernmental body that would focus on human rights, saying, "this development will make the efforts of the state and citizens come together to protect man's dignity." Furthermore, he pledged to eliminate administrative corruption.

There is little evidence of any serious split between members of the royal family and Saudi ministers over the broad need to move forward. There have been many debates and disagreements over how fast to move and in what areas. There is a clear need to find a better balance between moving too slowly, the risk of revolutionary or destabilizing change, and the clear need to evolve.

The momentum and consistency behind reform efforts is, however, a problem. Crown Prince Abdullah, many other senior princes, and many Saudi ministers and technocrats have consistently supported the need for reform. At the same time, there have been many debates over how quickly the Kingdom should move and in what areas. The struggle against terrorism has led Saudi Arabia to overreact in enforcing internal security measures, and Saudi leaders are not willing to confront Saudi Arabia's conservative majority and clergy where this seems likely to cause internal unrest or increase support for Islamic extremists. Legitimate Saudi reformers have been arrested, and others are cautious in speaking out.

The right kind of Western pressure—pressure that quietly and steadily supports Saudi reformers—can help. The wrong kind of pressure is counterproductive. Far too few outside Saudi Arabia understand that it must move at the pace a conservative clergy and people allow, and that the government must make constant trade-offs and choices to find the path of reform that has the broadest popular support. Calls for reform in Western terms at a Western pace are also highly counterproductive. They are used by conservatives to make the Saudi reformers who actually live in the Kingdom and try to accomplish something seem tools of the West. This is why the government of Saudi Arabia has consistently emphasized that its efforts toward reform have been driven by domestic need and not by foreign pressure.

Political Reform

Saudis would be among the first to state that the Kingdom has as many faults as any other nation and that far more political, economic, and social reform is needed than has taken place to date. Nevertheless, Saudi Arabia has made progress in several areas of reform since the late 1990s. It has focused on four areas of internal reforms: political, economic, administrative, and social.

While there have been some significant problems and setbacks, the process of reform has increased in intensity and speed in recent years. Furthermore, the most senior members of the royal family have consistently restated their commitment to reform since the outbreak of major terrorist attacks in 2003.

King Fahd summarized many of the reforms that are needed in a speech on May 17, 2003, in which he emphasized the need for administrative reform and the introduction of an electoral system to increase citizens' participation in the political system. He also reiterated the Kingdom's determination to fight terrorism and the need for further international cooperation. Crown Prince Abdullah has repeatedly called for reform, and Prince Saud al-Faisal, the Saudi foreign minister, has described the reform process as follows:

> Saudi Arabia is undergoing a process of reform that started some time ago. It is doing it to please the people of the country, to respond of the needs of the country. It is not doing it to get a report of good behavior.... Our country needs reforms and they are needed for serving the people of this country. And so the reforms are indigenous... the timing of their implementation depends on what is possible and what is achievable according to the ability and the consensus that we can achieve for this reform.... We want to maintain the unity and the cohesion of our society.

Shura Council

Progress has been slow on political reform, but Saudi Arabia is moving forward. In September 1992, King Fahd introduced the Basic Law, the Consultative Council, the Majlis Al-Shura, and the regional assemblies. The idea behind all the reform is to gradually increase citizen participation in the political system. The Basic Law is designed to function as a constitution and to ensure the rights of citizens.

The Majlis Al-Shura was established on December 29, 1993, as a 60-member appointed council. The number of members has increased three times. First, in 1997 the Majlis Al-Shura membership became 90; second, in 2001 the number increased to 120; and in 2005, the Shura membership was increased to 150. The council was to provide an institutional framework for more citizen inclusion and to introduce more transparency in the political decision making.

The Shura Council has grown in statue and respect since its inception in the early 1990s. It is seen as a first step in this decade-long political reform and as being in agreement with the Islamic and Arab traditions of the Kingdom.

Crown Prince Abdullah was asked about the possibility of electing some of the Shura Council, and did not reject the idea. He stated that, "if [the election time] comes and the Saudi people deem they are warranted, we will not fail." However, he cautioned against moving too fast, which might have a negative impact on the social cohesion of the state.

Defense Minister Prince Sultan has discussed elections, but he has also argued that early elections could bring unfit individuals into government, such as the illiterate. (The Shura Council is currently a highly educated group, with a majority of its members holding doctoral degrees.)

These statements illustrate the widely contrasting views held by some government officials over how to move forward. Saudi Arabia needs to find a way to reconcile these opposing visions to ensure that all of its citizens have the opportunity to participate in the government institutions that represent them. Nevertheless, the senior leadership does seem content with the notion that Shura Council elections will eventually come to pass. As Foreign Minister Prince Saud al-Faisal has said, "[In Saudi Arabia], real reform is being done with the intention of keeping social cohesion and unity of the country together. We are not playing experiments in labs. We believe we are going at it with the ear of our leaders to the heartbeat of the people, what they expect, what they need and how far they want to go."

Regional Assemblies

The institutionalization of decision making has been extended to the regional level by the introduction of the regional assemblies in all of the 13 regions shown in Figure 10.1. The governor of the province chairs the assemblies, with the vice governor acting as the vice chairman. The remaining members are appointed from notable people who live in the province and who are at least 30 years old. The Basic Law gives the regional assemblies the duties of studying the implementation of the development plan, setting priorities in terms of the needs of their region, and studying the rural and urban organizational layouts.

Since their inception in 1993, the regional assemblies have not only increased the participation of citizens, but they also have had a tangible influence on the development of their provinces.

Municipal Elections

On October 29, 2003, the Kingdom approved a plan to introduce local municipal elections. The plan called for elections of half of the members of the 178 municipal councils around the Kingdom, and by July 10, 2004, the Kingdom announced the basic regulations of the elections.

The Kingdom has started an awareness campaign to educate the public about the process, however, and announced the requirements to become a candidate, as follows:[1]

- That he is a Saudi by blood or birth, or has held Saudi citizenship for not less than 10 years,
- That he is over the age of 25 years,
- That he is a permanent resident within the boundaries of the municipality,

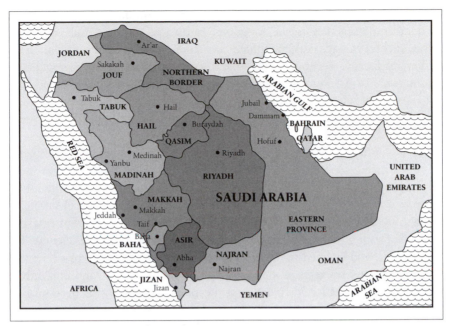

Figure 10.1: Map of the 13 Provinces with Their Capitals

Source: The Saudi embassy in Washington, D.C.

- That he has not been convicted of any illegal act or felony and that if he has been in jail, it must have been more than 5 years ago,
- That he has not been fired from public service for improper behavior unless it was at least five years ago,
- That he is familiar with the province and its people and is literate,
- That he has never filed for bankruptcy.

Prince Mitiab bin Abdullah, the minister of municipal and rural affairs announced the creation of a committee to supervise the election process. These phases of the elections are shown below in Table 10.1.

Table 10.1: Municipal Elections Phases

Phase	Provinces	Voter Registration	Election Day
One	Riyadh	11/23/2004-11/22/2004	02/10/2005
Two	Eastern, Asir, Baha, Jizan, and Najran	12/14/2004-01/12/2005	03/03/2005
Three	Mecca, Medina, Qasim, Al Jouf, the Northern Border Region, Tabuk and Hail	02/15/2005-03/16/2005	04/21/2005

Source: Saudi Arabian Ministry of Municipalities.

The results of the municipal elections were a testing ground for the institution of democratic practices in the Kingdom. Municipal councils deal with local issues such as garbage collection, road construction, and other local matters. If successful locally, elections could follow for assemblies at the regional and national levels. As Shura Council member Abdulmuhsin al-Akkas said, the goal is to teach Saudis how to "disagree by peaceful means." By the end of 2004, government banners lined the roads of major cities, informing residents where to register to vote.

Women were not permitted to vote in the first round of elections. Lobbying by senior members in the religious establishment appears to have had an effect on the municipal elections. Prince Nayef announced that women would not be permitted to vote or run for office in Saudi Arabia's first nationwide elections. "I don't think that women's participation is possible," he told a Kuwaiti newspaper. The Saudi government cited logistical and administrative restrictions for the decision and claimed that there was an insufficient number of women to run the women-only registration centers and polling stations, and that only a fraction of the Kingdom's women had the photo identity cards necessary to vote.

Many women, however, have resisted applying for the I.D. cards, which were first introduced in 2001, insisting the photographs would display their unveiled faces. Issuing voter cards with or without photos is one obvious solution. In any case, many Saudis feel it would be in the Kingdom's interest to allow women to participate in the next round of elections, which will occur in 2009.

Voter registration went smoothly, but not without obstacles. The process gained some rare public support from high-ranking royal family members. To raise awareness and encourage Saudi citizens to participate in the municipal elections, princes have appeared in person to register themselves. Prince Khalid al-Faisal, the governor of Asir, after his appearance at a registration station, said "I believe that future [public] participation in the country will depend on the success of this experience."[2]

However, the turnout for registration, despite the public support from the royal family, has been less than expected. In Riyadh Province, out of the 400,000–700,000 eligible voters, only 149,000 men registered. The turnout was larger, though, in the Eastern Prince, which has large numbers of Saudi Shiites. Skepticism about the elections runs high among people who don't think that this concession by the royal family was sincere and those who believe that the elections did not conform with their traditions.[3]

Mohsen al-Awaji, a former member of the opposition, who continues to be a vocal critic of the Saudi leadership, was quoted as saying, "We should be choosing our leaders from top to bottom, not voting for a council that has no powers and whose main job in most people's minds is collecting garbage." He argued that some Saudis did not register to vote because they were rejecting the idea of the election.[4]

Prince Mansour bin Mitab said,[5] "Turnout is the aspect we are least concerned about. The most important thing is integrity, international standards and that we institutionalize elections as a process." Furthermore, reformers in the Kingdom are looking ahead to what comes after the elections. A Saudi lawyer was quoted as saying that "Any election changes the social awareness of the people participating in it. But it is important to realize that we still don't know what the future of reform is. Beyond these elections, no one has spelled out the agenda."[6]

Regional Reform

Saudi Arabia has encouraged reform across the Arab world by introducing a "Charter to Reform the Arab Position" in January 2003, which encourages internal reforms and emphasizes the importance of reform to the future of the Arab world. The charter calls for the creation of a Greater Arab Free Trade Zone by the end of 2005. In addition, at the end of the Arab League Summit in Tunis in May 2004, 21 members signed the "Tunis Declaration," which pledges to carry out social reforms, promote democracy, expand popular participation in politics and public affairs, and reinforce women's rights.[7]

ECONOMIC REFORM

Economic reform is vital, whether or not Saudi Arabia has continued years of high oil revenues. Once again, senior Saudi leaders recognize this need. In his May 2003 speech at the Shura Council, King Fahd made clear that the Saudi reform program was based on domestic initiatives, not foreign influence, and, in the economic sphere, were targeted at enhancing and diversifying economic activity inside the Kingdom. He noted that easing and streamlining foreign investment opportunity, privatizing the economy, boosting tourism, revising the tax code, and reforming the capital markets would be instrumental in achieving this goal. He also stated that addressing the issues of poverty and unemployment through Saudization of jobs was of particular concern.

Progress remains slow in many areas, but the Kingdom has continued its reform efforts in spite of high oil revenues over the last few years as well as its high growth rates as a result of the rise in oil prices. It has embarked on strengthening economic ties with the European Union (EU) and the United States and continued its ambition to join the World Trade Organization (WTO).

The Saudi economy has been growing rapidly in the early 2000s, and reached rates as high as 6.4 percent in 2003. The minister of finance, Ibrahim al-Assaf, has projected equally high rates for 2004. Asked if terror attacks had resulted in an outflow of capital from the country, he replied,[8] "Absolutely not. It has been the other way around; we have an increase in liquidity." Dr. Al-Assaf cited the vigorous performance of the stock market and stated that Saudi Arabia's financial sector, including the insurance industry, had become a "driving force" in the economy.

Saudi Arabia has made efforts to deal with its rising unemployment rate and the rapid increases in its population—two areas with serious national security implications. It has sought to diversify its economy away from the petroleum sector, to encourage foreign investment, to strength Saudization, and to revise the tax code. There already has been considerable diversification in the Saudi economy. The oil sector provided 35 percent of GDP in 2004, compared to 65 percent of GDP in 1974, although these figures are misleading, because petrochemicals and other petroleum-related products are not included in the petroleum sector statistics, and the growth of the service and manufacturing sectors is heavily linked to petroleum products and revenues.

Investment Environment and Capital Markets

The Kingdom has sought to make its investment environment more hospitable for foreigners and citizens alike. Once again, the Saudi officials involved recognize that the pace has sometimes been slow and much more needs to be done. Laws and regulations have been passed, however, to protect investors and to make the process more transparent. In April 2000, the Kingdom announced its new Foreign Investment Law, which created the Saudi Arabia General Investment Authority (SAGIA) to encourage, streamline, and monitor investment activities.

The General Investment Authority was created to streamline the foreign investment applications process. The authority was charged with responding to an application within 30 days, and, if it failed to do so, the license would automatically be issued. In addition, if a license was denied, the foreign investor had the right to appeal that decision.

The Foreign Investment Law has fostered a great deal of economic activity. In June 2001, the Saudi Arabian General Investment Authority released one-year statistics on the effect of this initiative that showed considerable results: a total of $7.6 billion worth of foreign investment permits had been issued, and SAGIA had issued permits for 91 projects, with a total value of $8.1 billion. Foreign investors had accounted for 93.6 percent of this value. As evidence that the trend was being sustained, the assessment noted that $366 million worth of projects were approved in the month of May 2001 alone.

In June 2002, the SAGIA approved several changes in the Foreign Investment Law of 2000 that were primarily aimed at making the rules more business friendly. The changes gave foreign investors increased flexibility and strengthened the legal backing of their rights in the Kingdom, especially in the areas of property ownership, parity with national companies, and avoiding double taxation.

Furthermore, the Kingdom has opened many sectors to foreign investors. For example, in December 2001, the Saudi Communications Commission (SCC) was created as a body to open up the telecommunications sector to foreign investors. In February 2003, the Supreme Economic Council (SEC) opened up the following sectors for foreign investment: electricity, insurance, television and radio studios, advertising and public relations, and press services and foreign media offices.

The upgrading of the capital market system is vital to the continuing economic reform program. In May 2002, in a key address to the Eighth Conference for Investment and Arab Capital Markets in Beirut, Saudi oil minister Ali al-Naimi told the conferees "that the structural changes towards privatization and financial and economic reforms and adaptation to the requirements of globalization in both their commercial and financial dimensions currently being witnessed by our economies make the role of Arab capital markets pivotal in facilitating structural reform operations."

On June 16, 2003, the Council of Ministers passed the Saudi Arabian Capital Market Law to strengthen the economy and increase citizen participation in the capital market. It established the Saudi Arabian Capital Markets Authority to protect, ensure fair business, promote and develop the capital market, license brokers, and offer securities to the public. The law also created the Saudi Arabian Stock Exchange (SASE) to act as a depository center to the Kingdom.

The Saudi stock market has experienced high growth over the past decade. Its trading volume has grown by 300.7 percent in one year. The value of shares traded was $35.73 billion in November 2002, and in November 2003 it was $143.2 billion. The development of the Saudi Stock market can be seen in more detail in Figure 10.2.

The reforms in the investment and capital market laws should also help the Saudi position toward achieving its goal of joining the WTO. Furthermore, the Kingdom has reformed other areas of its economy. Those reforms include:

- The approval of a 65-Article Patent Law by the Council of Ministers on July 17, 2004. The new law satisfies the TRIPS, Trade-Related Aspects of Intellectual Property Rights, and the Paris Agreement for Industrial Prop-

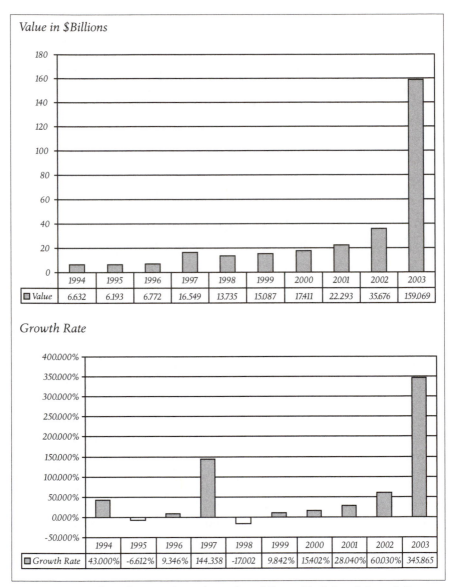

Value in $Billions

	1994	1995	1996	1997	1998	1999	2000	2001	2002	2003
☐ Value	6.632	6.193	6.772	16.549	13.735	15.087	17.411	22.293	35.676	159.069

Growth Rate

	1994	1995	1996	1997	1998	1999	2000	2001	2002	2003
☐ Growth Rate	43.000%	-6.612%	9.346%	144.358	-17.002	9.842%	15.402%	28.040%	60.030%	345.865

Figure 10.2: Saudi Arabian Stock Market Value of Shares Traded and Growth Rates: 1994–2004

Source: Tadawul Annual Report 2004.

erty. This law covers four categories of intellectual properties: patents, lay-out designing of integrated circuits, variety of plants in the field of agriculture, and industrial designing.[9]

- On June 9, 2003, the Council of Ministers endorsed a 28-Article Copyright Law, which meets TRIPS. The Kingdom has also joined the Universal Copyright Convention and the Berne Convention for the Protection of Literary and Artistic Works.

- On July 5, 2004, the Council of Saudi Chambers of Commerce and Industry (CSCCI) announced plans to set up a center to prepare Saudi business once the Kingdom joins the WTO.

Transparency

The Saudi government and bureaucracy have been slow to act in some areas, but Saudi reformers do see transparency and openness of operations as key elements in the successful liberalization of the Kingdom's economy. The government also recognizes the role transparency can play in attracting domestic and foreign investors. Basic access to the open exchange of information remains of prime importance—the Internet is now available without interference to 80 percent of Saudi Arabia's population—and a linchpin of the Kingdom's economic and political reform programs. Steps toward transparency include:

- The Ministry of Labor has approved the establishment of "work committees" in each business or office where the number of Saudi workers exceeds 100. This has given the green light to setting up the first elements of "trade unions" for some 3 million Saudi workers, which will enhance the communications with and information available to the workforce.

- In October 2001, long before more institutionalized initiatives were taken in investment and trade, the Saudi Arabian Monetary Agency introduced a new, electronic-based trading platform, known as *Tadawul,* to provide up-to-the-minute price, volume, and company information for a continuous, order-driven stock market. The goal was to break out of the paper transaction world and attract new investors with a far more transparent and efficient stock trading system.

- In September 2003, the Council of Ministers amended a royal decree on the maximum duration of a government representative's membership on the board of directors of public corporations, which, over time, should effectively reduce the undue individual influence these officials can establish and maintain on these boards. Such representatives, with the exception of high-level executives of the corporations, were now limited to a three-year term, with a single extension possible.

Privatization

Privatization is not a substitute for a strong, self-initiating private sector. Selling off state assets can actually drain capital into areas where it is not possible to sell services at competitive market prices, overemployment is seen as a political necessity, and inheriting a large, inefficient state structure is as much a curse as a blessing. The right kind of privatization can, however, help free the state of the burden of the economy and the economy of the burden of the state.

Crown Prince Abdullah set the right priorities on May 13, 2002, when he said,[10] "I wish to make clear that the government of Saudi Arabia has since the very beginning been extremely supportive of the private economic sector." As part of strengthening the private sector, encouraging employment, and boosting economic development, the Kingdom has been privatizing many of the public sectors through a phased program. The government privatizes parts of the sector, and then the public ownership is decreased over time. For example, when the Saudi Telecom Company was privatized in December 2002, 30 percent of its outstanding shares were sold to private investors, which raised more than $4 billion, but the rest remains owned by the government and will be eventually privatized.[11]

In November 2002, the Supreme Economic Council announced the plan to privatize as many as 20 sectors, including telecommunications; civil aviation; desalination; highway management; railways; sports clubs; health services; government hotels; municipal services; education services; operation and management of social service centers; Saudi employment services; agricultural services; construction and management of public abattoirs, public parks and recreation centers; and cleaning and waste collection.[12]

More privatization projects have been announced; a chronology of such privatization efforts since mid 2002 is as follows:

- *June 2002:* a health bill that includes privatization of some government run hospitals was approved by the Council of Ministers.
- *January 2003:* Dr. Khaled al-Otaibi, director general of posts at the Ministry of Posts, Telegraphs, and Telephones, announced that the privatization of the postal services has been going according to plan, which includes 100 private agencies.
- *January 2003:* the Cabinet passed a tax cut on foreign firms from 45 percent to 20 percent and a fixed tax rate of 30 percent on natural gas.
- *June 2003:* the SEC approved the "eventual" privatization of the aviation sector.
- *August 2003:* urban transportation privatization was announced.

- *September 2003:* foreign and domestic companies were invited to bid for an $8 billion project in the water desalination and electricity sectors.

- *October 2003:* the Joint Stock Company for Medical Care was established to manage and own health facilities.

- *October 2003:* the privatization of domestic and international airport operation—except for security and auditing functions—was announced by the Saudi Civil Aviation Commission.

- *March 2004:* the Communications and Information Technology Commission (CITC) announced that it has approved the purchase of up to 49 percent of a new GSM mobile company.

- *April 2004:* The general president of the Saudi Railways Organization (SRO), Khaled al-Yahya, confirmed that three major rail projects have been approved by the SEC. The projects include the extension of the Damman-Riyadh line, a line connecting Mecca, Medina, and Jeddah, and a line linking Riyadh, Qasim, and the Northern Border Province.

- *May 2004:* the SEC started privatizing Ma'aden, a Saudi mining company.

- *May 2004:* the SEC opened up the sales for shares of the National Company for Cooperative Insurance (NCCI), which has $66.7 million capital.

- *June 2004:* the mayor of Jeddah announced the opening up of projects in the development of satellite towns around Jeddah to private companies.

The Government Budget and Public Debt

Since 1982, the Kingdom has been running high budget deficits due to low oil prices, mismanagement, and high defense spending. Figure 10.3 shows that the year 2000 was the first year Saudi Arabia enjoyed a surplus, and since that year, with the exception of 2001, the Saudi budget has been either in balance or in surplus.

In 2004 government revenues totaled $104.8 billion, while government spending was $78.7 billion. The government announced that the $26.1 billion surplus would be spent on two broad areas. First, $15.2 billion would be used to pay down the Kingdom's public debt. This payment would decrease the government's domestic liability from $178.6 billion to $163.7 billion, 66 percent of GDP down from 119 percent of GDP in 1999. Saudi economists think that paying down the Kingdom's debt would increase outside investors' confidence in the soundness of the economic structure of the economy.[13]

In addition to paying down the debt, $10.9 billion will be spent on new development projects. Some of the surplus will go to the Saudi Real Estate Fund and the Saudi Credit Bank, aimed at financing new business ventures.

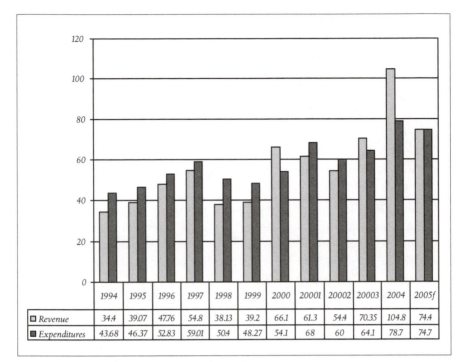

	1994	1995	1996	1997	1998	1999	2000	20001	20002	20003	2004	2005f
☐ Revenue	34.4	39.07	47.76	54.8	38.13	39.2	66.1	61.3	54.4	70.35	104.8	74.4
■ Expenditures	43.68	46.37	52.83	59.01	50.4	48.27	54.1	68	60	64.1	78.7	74.7

Figure 10.3: Saudi Arabian Budget Balance: 1994–2005

Source: Brad Bourland, *Saudi Arabia's Budget Performance,* various editions. The numbers for 2005 are forecasted by the SMBA.

The Kingdom hopes to rebuild its infrastructure, which has not been renewed since the 1980s. This new spending, if managed well, will boost the construction sector and reenergize the real estate market.[14]

The combination of paying down the public debt and building up the Kingdom's foreign assets represent the best fiscal and debt portfolio since the early 1980s. This growth resulted from or coincided with three major shifts. First, Saudi Arabia enjoyed low interest rates, which increased lending by 26 percent—increasing liquidity and investment in the Kingdom. Second, major ventures were started in the water, gas, power, and petrochemical sectors. Third, Saudi Arabia witnessed three major IPOs: Saudi Telecoms (STC), Sahara Petrochemicals, and Ettisalat. These IPOs increased the investment inflow to the Saudi capital markets and spurred real economic growth.

While the fiscal year of 2004 was a year of budget surplus and a 19 percent nominal GDP growth, the real GDP growth was only 4.7 percent. In addition, the fiscal health of the Kingdom will face many fiscal challenges in the future. Large entitlement programs, subsidies and debt to domestic farmers, and large spending on domestic security still put a lot of strain on the government budget.

As Figure 10.4 shows, the Kingdom still suffers from a $163.7 domestic debt. While, the economic growth in 2004 resulted from many factors other than the hike in oil prices, the Kingdom's economy is still highly dependent on oil. Saudi Arabia has to diversify its economy away from oil and the uncertainty of the volatile energy global market. It is still unclear how future surpluses will be used or how these budgetary reforms will translate into real long-term commitment to financial transparency and reforming the relevant governmental agencies.

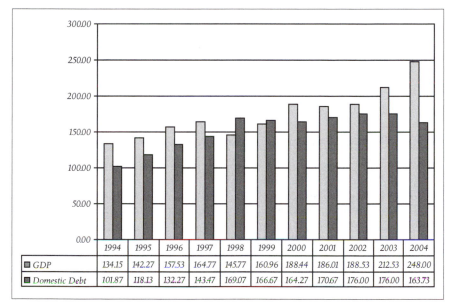

	1994	1995	1996	1997	1998	1999	2000	2001	2002	2003	2004
■ GDP	134.15	142.27	157.53	164.77	145.77	160.96	188.44	186.01	188.53	212.53	248.00
■ Domestic Debt	101.87	118.13	132.27	143.47	169.07	166.67	164.27	170.67	176.00	176.00	163.73

Figure 10.4: Saudi Arabia's Domestic Debt: 1994–2004

Source: Brad Bourland, Saudi Arabia's Budget Performance and Economy Watch, various editions.

Addressing the Unemployment Problem

Demographics have already made employment a critical issue, and the problem will grow steadily for at least the next quarter century because of existing population momentum. During the 1980–2000 period, the Saudi population increased from 12 million to 20 million. In 2002 the Saudi labor force was 3.15 million people, and the official unemployment figure is 9.6 percent.

The latest census of 2004 found that the population is 22,673,538 people. Of those, 16,529,302 are Saudis and 6,144,236 are expatriates. The number of foreign laborers is approximately 2 million less than earlier expected. Furthermore, only 15 percent of the foreign workers fall in the category of skilled workers. Most of them work in agriculture, cleaning, and domestic service.[15]

The official unemployment estimate severely undercounts the number of Saudis who need jobs and does not attempt to estimate nonproductive jobs or disguised unemployment. The real unemployment figure is probably as high as 25 percent and probably is distinctly higher among Saudi young men. The figure also makes no serious allowance for the number of women who would seek work if the opportunity was provided, and whose productivity is needed at a time when more women graduate from secondary school and universities than men do and do so in more practical subjects. The truth is that the Kingdom has a major unemployment problem even in a time of booming oil revenues, and it is growing more rapidly, with as many as 350,000 workers entering the workforce every year.[16]

In January 2005, following an employment campaign in the Kingdom, the Ministry of Labor announced that the number of Saudi males who did not have a job and were seeking one totaled 180,500. While the Minister of Labor argued that this number should be adapted as the official unemployment number, it's not very reliable. It is unclear what methodology the employment campaign used. Further, such campaigns tend to have a self-selection bias, which makes any deductive conclusion about the actual number of unemployed invalid.[17]

Saudi Arabia has enacted some reforms in its approach to this problem that include job training, Saudization, job creation, employment of women, and the creation of a fund to help Saudi citizens achieve economic independence. The Kingdom's efforts in economic liberalization, diversification, and privatization are also seen as key steps in creating more private sector jobs for young Saudis.

The Kingdom has augmented these reforms with the creation of the National Program for Training and Employment to prepare Saudis entering the job market to be more competitive, especially against a cheap foreign labor force. In addition, on July 8, 2004, Saudi Arabia announced the creation of a "Centennial Fund" to help Saudi workers—men and women—set up small- and medium-size business enterprises. The fund was also paired with Saudi General Investment Authority to assist entrepreneurs to translate their ideas into viable businesses.

Saudi Arabia has also invested in increasing women's participation in the workforce. An estimate by the Work Bank put the increase in women's participation in the workforce at 640 percent since the 1960s.[18] In 2002, 15 percent of the Saudi labor force, 465,000, were Saudi women, who were part owners in 22,000 businesses, including the accounting, banking, computer training, automotive, and many high tech sectors.

The fact remains, however, that a majority of private-sector jobs in the Kingdom are filled by a cheap foreign labor force. Saudi nationals compose 65 percent of the 7 million-strong labor force—but only 5 percent of the private-sector jobs.

The Kingdom has set a goal to increase the share of Saudi nationals in the workforce to 70 percent by 2010. To increase the share of nationals in the labor force, the Ministry of Labor chairs the board of the General Organization for Technical Education and Vocational Training and Manpower Development Fund. The fund aims at preparing Saudi youths to compete against cheap foreign labor through covering the expenses of job training.

Saudi Arabia is providing the incentives and the job training to Saudi citizens to become more competitive in the job market, and part of this is the Saudization program, but progress does not match need. Table 10.2 gives the results of a survey of businesses conducted by the Ministry of Planning. It gives the top reasons for not hiring Saudis, and as we can see the top two reasons given are that Saudis are not interested in these jobs and that it's cheaper to hire non-Saudis.

Table 10.2: Reasons for Hiring Non-Saudis

Reason	% of Firms
Saudis are not interested in these jobs	48.3
Non-Saudis require lower wages	47.4
Non-Saudis are more experienced/skilled	34.5
Available Saudis are not qualified	25.4
Saudis are not available	14.2
Other	3.9
Lack of employment agencies	3.4
Saudis are not committed to work	1.3
Saudis insist on management positions	0.4

Source: Ministry of Planning, *Private Establishment Survey*, table 3.16, 1999. Adapted from Girgis (2002).

The non-Saudi labor force was 3.09 million in 2002. In 2001 the Ministry of Labor and Social Affairs called for a reduction in the foreign workforce by 150,000 a year to achieve a goal of fewer than one million foreign workers by the year 2030. The Saudi government also started to crack down on illegal workers. It has deported many, fined their sponsors, and has also made it harder to import foreign labor.

The Minister of Labor argued that the average salary of an expatriate is SR 1,133 compared to SR 3,495 earned by a Saudi national on average. To further reduce the demand for and the supply of foreign labor, the Ministry of Labor is proposing levying income tax on expatriates and increasing the fees on visa applications.[19]

Furthermore, Saudi Arabia has set specific goals for Saudizing many of its sectors, including the retail sector, taxi drivers, jewelry shops, and so forth, in addition to opening new sectors such as tourism. By 2006, the Kingdom hopes to restrict commercial activities in up to 25 sectors, and study is under way to add at least 10 more categories, Ghazi al-Gosaibi, the minister of labor, said. According to the Kingdom's official statistics, 80 percent of accounting and translating jobs have been Saudized, as of early 2005. While once a sector is Saudized, new foreign labor is prohibited from entering the Kingdom, but those who are on job are staying until their visa expires and they train those who are taking their spot.[20]

As a result, Saudization programs have had some positive effects by increasing the share of Saudis in the workforce—and this can be seen in Figure 10.5.

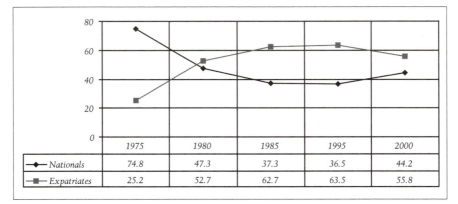

	1975	1980	1985	1995	2000
◆ Nationals	74.8	47.3	37.3	36.5	44.2
■ Expatriates	25.2	52.7	62.7	63.5	55.8

Figure 10.5: Share of Saudi Nationals in Workforce: 1975–2000

Source: Maurice Girgis, "Would National and Asians Replace Arab Workers in the GCC?," p.12.

The government recognizes that problems exist with the Saudization policy. Specifically, this has been an obstacle in the Kingdom's accession to the WTO, which, along with the International Labor Organization (ILO), has called on Saudi Arabia to allow workers to organize, to institute greater female employment, to end job discrimination, and to promote free movement of labor. But the government continues to work toward overcoming these challenges.

The government has set up the Human Resources Development Fund (HRDF) to encourage companies to train and employ Saudi youths through a cost-sharing system as well as the General Organization for Technical Education and Vocational Training (GOTEVOT), a government-funded national training program that has established training standards to improve the employability of young Saudis. Notwithstanding these advancements, there will still be 10 million foreign workers out of a projected 39 million workers in the Kingdom in 2030.

Corruption is hindering and in some cases threatening the reform program. Many officials benefit from the existing order and in some cases actively hinder reform. Corruption in military procurement and construction is rampant. Efforts to "Saudize" the workforce have run into problems, because many business people profit from cheap foreign labor.

This helps explain why the crown prince has made uprooting corruption a primary goal. One way this message has been sent is through rewarding those who report abuses. For instance, Abdul Aziz Nirza, the senior official responsible for licensing medication, was recently granted the highest honor in the Kingdom when he turned down a 10 million riyal bribe from a pharmaceutical firm attempting to bypass the standard route for licensing medication.

In another incident, the Saudi telecommunications minister, Dr. Ali al-Johani, was removed from his post by the crown prince for allegedly accepting between $15 and $21 million, as well as other favors, from an arrangement involving a partner of Lucent Technologies and its affiliates. Lucent also arranged for donations to be paid to a prominent cancer center on the minister's behalf. Al-Johani, who was responsible for awarding billions in government contacts, had purportedly been courted by the U.S. telecom giant that had incidentally won more than $5 billion in Saudi contracts. Although the government takes such episodes seriously, corruption is endemic in Saudi society and is unlikely to be eliminated any time soon.

Accession to the WTO and Free Trade

Saudi Arabia has long aimed for stronger economic ties within the Gulf region. At the same time, the country continues to look beyond the region to membership in the World Trade Organization and seeks new opportunities to widen its participation in regional trade arrangements. For instance, in March 1999, the Minister of Industry and Electricity called for an Arab economic and industrial bloc in the form of an Arab free trade zone that would strengthen the position of the Arab states in the global marketplace—a proposal that was moved forward at the Arab Summit meeting of March 2002.

In January 2001, the Saudi Cabinet notified the Gulf Cooperation Council that it was prepared to start implementing the GCC decision to establish a member-state customs federation as early as 2005. Further, at its July 3, 2002, weekly meeting, the Saudi Cabinet announced that it had agreed to the moving up of the beginning of the GCC Customs Union to January 2003, including the issuing of a united GCC currency starting in 2010.

The Kingdom has signed 35 bilateral trade agreements with WTO members and has been trying to become a WTO member since the organization's creation in 1996. Many of the economic and commercial law reforms are part of the requirements of the WTO. For example, the Foreign Investment Law gives foreigners the ability to have 100 percent ownership in the Kingdom, and Saudi Arabia has reduced in custom tariffs on foreign investment.

On July 5, 2004, the Saudi Council for Chambers of Commerce announced that they will provide technical training and support to Saudi companies to prepare them for the Kingdom's accession into the WTO, which Saudi Arabia hopes to achieve with the help of the United States.

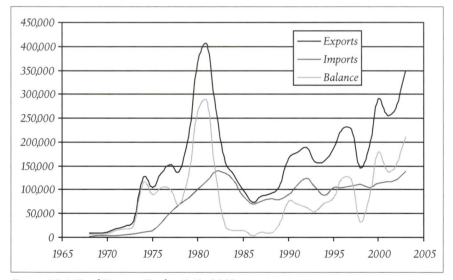

Figure 10.6: Total Foreign Trade: 1969–2003

Source: Saudi Arabian Monetary Authority.

Saudi Arabia and the European Union signed a bilateral trade agreement August 31, 2003. This added the EU to a growing list of countries and communities with whom Saudi Arabia has signed trade agreements, including Argentina, Australia, Brazil, Canada, China, Cuba, the Czech Republic, Ecuador, the European Union, Hungary, India, Japan, Kyrgyzstan, Latvia, Malaysia, Mexico, New Zealand, Norway, Pakistan, Paraguay, Poland, Slovakia, South Africa, South Korea, Sri Lanka, Switzerland, Taiwan, Turkey, Uruguay, and Venezuela.

Saudi Arabia has long expressed its interest in initiating the economic changes necessary for the Kingdom to join the WTO. Determined to meet WTO-membership obligations, the Kingdom has, since formulation of the 2000–2005 Saudi Development Plan, accelerated the pace of the Saudi economy toward participation in the global economy and privatization, enhanced technological developments in the Kingdom, and expanded its production base.

Since 2003 Saudi leaders have actively linked WTO membership to the country's liberalization and economic reform activities. Thus, the Saudi commerce minister, Dr. Hashim bin Abdullah Yamani, told[21] the fifth WTO ministerial conference in September 2003, "Saudi Arabia is ready to compete in a globalized economy. To prepare itself, the Kingdom has substantially completed a major restructuring strategy and an economic reform program, the center piece of which is the key role of the private sector in economic activity." In February 2004, Dr. Yamani reported[22] to the WTO that the Kingdom had "accomplished a great deal on the path of economic reform," including "the restructuring of governmental establishments, and the issuance of regulations relating to WTO agreements, including protection of intellectual property rights, import licenses, health measures, customs evaluation and technical barriers to trade."

However, recent negotiations on the issue of market access for U.S. insurance companies have impeded the WTO accession process. At a September 13, 2004, meeting in Geneva, Saudi negotiators seemed unwilling to bring about any changes in the Kingdom's insurance regulations. Saudi Arabia also dismissed the possibility of allowing American insurance companies to open branches in the country. A review is under way by a Saudi committee to consider the demands and objections raised by the United States.[23]

Economic Diversification

Saudi Arabia regards diversification, in close conjunction with privatization, as a key element of its economic reform program, with emphasis given to the fields of tourism, agriculture, transportation, telecommunications, and electricity production. The commerce minister noted this policy in a September 2002 speech at the Johannesburg World Summit on sustainable development when he noted that "the Kingdom of Saudi Arabia must implement the economic reform plan, expand the economic base program, and diversify gross domestic product resources in order to face the challenges of development and compete with the tremendous technical capabilities and know-how of giant multinational companies and other countries."

The Saudi economy has diversified significantly over the past three decades. This shift away from dependence on the petroleum sector has been led by the production of natural gas, banking, construction materials, mining, and pharmaceuticals.

Saudi Arabia has the fourth largest natural gas reserves in the world; it aims to expand its capacity from 3 billion to 7 billion cubic feet. In addition, Saudi Arabia is the largest producer of construction materials, which is its largest nonoil sector industry. The National Commercial Bank reported that the construction materials sector contributes $12 billion to the Kingdom's economy.

Another growing sector is the Pharmaceuticals market, which is worth $1.17 billion. It is estimated to have a growth rate of 15 percent per year. In addition, there was a 47 percent increase in U.S. pharmaceutical exports to the Kingdom, to the tune of $82 million worth of exports.

The 1999–2000 *Year of Organization Building* in the Kingdom was capped off by the establishment of a holding company, the International Investment Company, to promote joint investment in a whole range of trade and commerce both inside and outside the country and by the creation of the Supreme Commission for Tourism (SCT), with the goal both of diversifying its income base and increasing job opportunities for Saudi citizens.

Because Saudi Arabia bases its diversification strategy on mobilizing private domestic and foreign investment, the Kingdom believes that specific diversification initiatives cannot be separated from the reform plan's privatization initiatives. Since 2002, initiatives to broaden the base of and private involvement in the economy and to expand the non-oil-related sectors of the economy have included: The opening of sectors of postal services, desalination, and railways to domestic and foreign investments by the SEC and a call for the selling of government stock holdings in Saudi companies. Under this initiative, the state-run postal services were transferred to a joint public-private organization, the Saudi Post Authority (SAPA); the private sector was invited to invest in the Kingdom's water desalination plants; and a $12 billion railway project linking the east and west coasts of the country as well as construction of a 1,300-kilometer railway for the transport of phosphates and other minerals from the northwest to processing plants in the east were opened to private investment.

In December 2002 the Saudi Cabinet approved 20 key and diversified public enterprises and sectors, including all or aspects of water and sewage, desalination, communications; air transportation, railways, roads, airport services, mail services, grain silos and flour mills, port services, services of the industrial cities, government-owned hotels, sports clubs, municipality services, cleaning and waste removal, education services, social services, agricultural services, and health services.

In terms of diversification, Saudi Arabia has given extra emphasis to the agricultural sector. Investment opportunities have been specifically prepared in the agricultural field with the help of specialized experts from the International Fund for Agricultural development, the World Bank, and the Islamic Bank for development. These efforts have included inclusion of Saudi Arabia in such regional initiatives as foundation of a GCC Customs Federation and the easing of the flow of imported agricultural and livestock commodities among GCC member states.

Social Reform

As is the case with economic and political reforms, social reforms in Saudi Arabia have been slow and have been tailored to the pace dictated by the Kingdom's tradition and culture. Nevertheless, social reforms touch many aspects of Saudi civil society, including human rights, women's rights, religious tolerance, and education. There has been enough progress to at least begin to ease the social tensions that act as a potential source of internal instability and extremism.

Human Rights

Saudi Arabia now faces the problem of advancing human rights and the rule of law while it is under attack by terrorists. There also is considerable popular resistance to some forms of reform, and the Kingdom's leadership must move at the pace that Saudi society and religious beliefs allow. This has not, however, prevented Saudi Arabia from moving forward.

Reforms in the areas of human rights have involved changing or amending current laws and allowing greater freedom of expression. There will be more on the judicial reform in the Administrative Reform section, but the following are a few of them:

- The Law of Procedure before Shari Courts was passed in September 2001 to ensure the rights of defendants for legal representation. It outlines the rules for police, evidence, and expert procedures.

- The Code of Law Practice was passed in January 2002. It outlines the requirements to become an attorney and the protection under the law for an attorney.

- The Criminal Procedure Law is a 225-article bill, approved in May 2002, that protects defendants and suspects before the courts and the government. It also outlines the rights of defendants with regard to interrogation, investigation, and incarceration.

King Fahd approved the first human rights organization, the National Human Rights Association (NHRA), in March 2004. NHRA adopted the "Riyadh Declaration," which was the result of a national conference on human rights held in Iraq in October 2003 and which affirmed that the foundation of human rights is the respect for human life and dignity; that a human being deserves respect regardless of race, color, or sex; that holding a person in custody without legal basis is forbidden in Islam; and that Islam requires tolerance of other faiths. It also called for a healthy balance between technological advances and social and traditional values.

Saudi Arabia still enforces a heavy degree of de facto censorship on its media. Nevertheless, several developments have encouraged freedom of expression, and a free press, since 2001:

- *July 17, 2001:* the Kingdom passed a 30-article law that argued for restructuring the press industry and granted journalists the ability to unionize.
- *February 24, 2004:* The Saudi Journalist Association (SJA) was established, which aimed to protect journalists' rights in the Kingdom.
- *March 2004:* The Shura Council passed a resolution urging the Ministry of Communication to grant journalists greater freedoms and to open up the press industry to private investment.
- *June 7, 2004:* The SJA elected a nine-member board, including two women.

On March 29, 2004, the Shura Council passed several resolutions concerning the Ministry of Culture and Information, urging the ministry to encourage greater freedom of the press in Saudi media and to open up opportunities for investment in the media to the Saudi private sector. In June 2004, hundreds of journalists participated in elections for the Saudi Journalists Association, the first of its kind held in Riyadh. The minister of culture and information, Dr. Fouad al-Farsy, said that, "the Ministry is ready to cooperate with the association to realize the hopes and aspirations of all journalists."

The reality, however, has been quite different. Despite his statements, Dr. al-Farsy has done very little to actually protect the independence of journalists within the Kingdom. Many complain that his promises have been unfulfilled. In addition, the ministry is thought to have interfered with the election of the chairman of the board of the Journalists Association, undermining the organization's credibility to the point where many prominent reform-minded journalists refuse to take part. Until these issues are addressed, the organization will not fulfill its mission.

In addition, press freedom remains shaky. According to the Committee to Protect Journalists, in April 2004, a contributor for the *Al-Sharq Al-Awsat* newspaper was arrested for criticizing the arrest of a group of reformers. Several others have been detained on similar grounds. In another instance, the government arrested a Saudi poet who wrote a poem describing certain members of Saudi judiciary as "the corruption makers on earth." The editor of the *Al-Madina* newspaper, which published the poem, was dismissed from his post.[24]

Other efforts at reform are under way. In June 2003, the King Abdul Aziz Library convened the first national dialogue meeting, the National Forum for Intellectual Dialogue, which lasted for four days and drew religious scholars and intellectuals from every portion of society. The group later met with Crown Prince Abdullah and presented him with a summary of their discussion, which emphasized rational debate, frankness, and objectivity, while highlighting the importance of moderate language when discussing Islamic issues.

National Dialogue

The Saudi leadership has realized that Saudi society as a whole must be convinced of the need for any given aspect of the Saudi reform agenda, especially the social aspects. On August 23, 2003, Crown Prince Abdullah announced the establishment of the King Abdul Aziz Center for National Dialogues. Its goals were the advancement of an open and free exchange of ideas about a variety of subjects, as Prince Saud al-Faisal said on February 19, 2004, "including, but not limited to, reassessment of the standards of education; dealing with the emergence of extremism; the essential role women should play in society; and institutional development. Diversity and tolerance are the guiding principles."[25]

Three conferences or rounds of talks have taken place, where over 60 Saudi intellectuals, including women, participated in a discussion on many subjects, including "the Relationship between Ruler and Ruled, Rights and Duties of Citizens and Their Relationship with Extremism." Crown Prince Abdullah said of the conference,[26] "I have no doubt that the establishment of the Center and the continuation of dialogue within its boundaries will become a historic achievement that contributes to the creation of a channel for objective expression that would have an effective impact in combating extremism and fostering a pure atmosphere that could give birth to wise position and illuminating ideas that reject terrorism and terrorist thought."

These dialogues are still in their early stages and often have problems or do not lead to actions that follow up on words. Nevertheless, they play an important role in bringing together members of Saudi society who would not otherwise interact. At a recent meeting, a hard-core Salafi cleric sat between the head of the Sufi movement in Riyadh and a prominent Shiite cleric. However, the road to mutual respect and understanding will not be smooth. In a telling gesture, the Salafi cleric hid his face when cameras tried to capture this historic meeting.

Women's Rights and Values

Saudi Arabia can only reform its economy and make full use of the talents of all of its people, if it expands women's participation in the workforce and ensures their equal treatment under the law. Progress remains slow, but the Kingdom signed the Convention on the Elimination of All Forms of Discrimination against Women (CEDAW) on September 7, 2004. Other reforms include:

- *January 2001:* Thoraya Obaid was appointed as the first Saudi woman executive director of the UN Population Fund and the undersecretary general for population affairs at the UN.

- *March 2003:* The government announced a plan to increase the participation of women in the technological, automotive, and industrial manufacturing sectors.

- *October 2003:* An advisory working group was commissioned to study women's voting rights issue.

- *December 2003:* Crown Prince Abdullah received a petition from 300 Saudi women calling for the creation of a higher council for women dealing with special rules concerning the family and divorce, the elimination of the requirement that women must have a supervisor, and the ability for women to transfer property after the death of the inheritor.

- *March 2004:* A law was enacted by the Shura Council to ensure the right of *everyone* 21 or older to vote and to open up many of the public sector jobs for women.

- *June 1, 2004:* The Council of Ministers introduced a nine-point plan that urged the creation of more job opportunities for women and to review and develop current labor and maternity laws in many of the ministries.

- *June 2004:* A deal between a Saudi company and two Chinese and Malaysian firms was signed to build Saudi Arabia's first industrial city for women in Jeddah. In two years, the city will train 20,000 women in many industrial jobs.

- *November 29, 2004:* Saudi businesswomen voted directly in the elections for the Riyadh Chamber of Commerce and Industry (RCCI) board for the first time. Princess Haila al-Farhan, the director of the women's section of the RCCI, said that 2,750 women registered with RCCI.

In December 2001, the Saudi Interior Ministry, rejecting the insistence of conservative clerics that the practice violated Saudi custom, began issuing identity cards to women. To qualify for an identity card, a woman must be 22 years old, she should have the written consent of her guardian as well as a letter from her employer (if she is employed), and she must provide a picture of herself with her hair covered and her face clear of makeup.

On October 2003, an advisory working group established by Crown Prince Abdullah to study challenges to the Kingdom proposed the implementation of municipal elections with full voting rights for women. In a poll of 15,000 Saudis, municipal elections were endorsed in all regions (78.5 percent was the lowest figure in favor). On the more sensitive issue of women's right to vote, only 3 out of 13 regions were opposed.

Although the emerging debate on women's rights is encouraging, severe forms of discrimination and restrictions on personal freedoms still persist— affecting women from all walks of life and in virtually every aspect of their daily lives. Women are still denied fundamental liberties such as voting rights (despite the enactment of a law stating that anyone over 21 should be permitted to vote), driving privileges and the opportunity for travel and study abroad unless accompanied by a male chaperon. Although there are plans to open the major industries to women, including law, diplomacy and the public sector, women are making little headway in finding employment in private enterprise. Working women in the Kingdom, many of whom are expatriates, compose only about 14 percent of the workforce and are paid less than foreign male workers.[27]

Educational Reform

Saudi education reform is vital to both fighting the kind of hatred and violence preached by Islamic extremist "deviants" and creating effective employment and economic reform. The Kingdom has 8 public universities, more than 100 colleges and more than 26,000 schools. In 1970 there were 2,500 college graduates a year, but now there are 200,000. Saudi Arabia has one of the lowest students-to-teacher ratios of 12.5 to 1. The Kingdom's literacy rate has gone from 25 percent to 90 percent in two generations.

Educational reform has become an area of steadily growing importance in the post-9/11, post-May 2003 era and involves a variety of policies designed to rid the Kingdom's schools of extremist teachings and to improve the national curriculum to better prepare students for the job market of the 21st century. Textbooks and curricula are being updated, and two pilot programs to experiment with new teaching methods and teacher training manuals have been established in Riyadh and Jeddah.

There is an effort within the government to assure that the Islam being taught and practiced is one that espouses the core principles of the religion—peace, tolerance, moderation, and wisdom. The Ministry of Islamic Affairs has initiated a comprehensive three-year program aimed at educating imams and monitoring religious education to safeguard against extremism and intolerance.

In September 2004, Education Minister Mohammad al-Rasheed announced that extremists would no longer be eligible to teach in Saudi schools in the future. Addressing critics' fears that extremists indoctrinate the Kingdom's youths with extremist ideas and intolerance he said, "We will not allow any extremist or fanatic to work in the field of education as not to spoil the minds of our sons and daughters or sway them toward un-Islamic actions."[28] The Kingdom started dismissing teachers with extremist ideologies. For example, the Ministry of Education has reportedly banned a teacher in Taif for spending "the last 15 minutes of his teaching session to read and explain the holy Qur'an in a wrong way instead of teaching English," Al-Watan quoted the principal of the school as saying.[29]

In an effort to distance the country's educational curriculum from the influence of extremist religious authorities, Saudi Arabia has initiated a variety of other reforms. The current pro-reform environment began in 2000 when a 30-member committee of education experts reviewed the country's curricula and made recommendations for educational development. In February 2003, officials began editing controversial chapters in the country's textbooks. Dr. Khaled al-Awwad, deputy minister of education, will be overseeing the printing of a series of revised textbooks in a wide array of subjects, including social science, mathematics, and science. Various committees have been assigned to write different books, with at least one special committee working on each subject.

In a December 2003 summit of the Gulf Cooperation Council, the Saudi government pledged to reform religious education across the region. The Shura Council also passed an education bill that explicitly calls for a new emphasis on moderation in classes on religion. The Shura Council bill stresses that moderation is a principle of Islam, which supports "training students to engage in dialogue." Secretary general of the Shura Council, Hamud al-Badr, also said that the goal of the bill is to teach moderation in Islam.

Finally, the Ministry of Islamic Affairs has initiated a three-year program to educate imams and monitor religious education to ensure moderation. Two thousand imams who have violated prohibitions against the preaching of intolerance have been suspended from their positions, and 1,500 have been referred to these educational programs.

Saudi Arabia realizes the need to reform its educational system to cope with the exploding demographics and a globally competitive job market. The Kingdom has taken several initiatives geared toward improving the curriculum and textbooks to prepare students for the practical and high-paying job, as well as to avoid inflammatory teachings.

- In February 2002, Saudi Arabia initiated a process of evaluating and assessing its school curriculum. This audit determined that about 5 percent of textbooks contained possibly offensive language. A program was put into place to eliminate such material, and textbooks and curricula have been updated and modernized. Two pilot programs, one in Riyadh and one in Jeddah, have been established to experiment with new teaching methods.

- Student councils are being set up in public schools to begin educating young Saudis about civic responsibilities and participatory governance.

- In August 2002, the Department of Statistics reported that 93.2 percent of Saudi women and 89.2 percent of Saudi men are literate.

- Saudi Arabia is open to foreign investment for private higher education.

- In October 2003, Dr. Maha Abdullah Orkubi was appointed dean of the Jeddah branch of the Arab Open University (AOU), the first time for a Saudi woman to be appointed to such a senior academic position.

- In December 2003, Crown Prince Abdullah ordered a review of the country's education system. His motivation in pursuing reforms of the system was to put greater emphasis on the need to give scientific training to Saudi students and to expand opportunities for employment. Prince Sultan was named chair of the ministerial supervisory committee tasked with overseeing the process of educational reform. The committee, which worked with a number of subcommittees made up of education experts, has completed a study of the country's education system and forwarded its recommendations for reform to a decision-making group that includes Prince Sultan. Involved in the study were members of the Shura Council, several ministers and the president of the General Presidency for Two Holy Mosques Affairs.

- Saudi Arabia has introduced English-language classes to the sixth grade for the 2004–2005 academic year to improve English-language teaching at intermediate and secondary schools.

- The Saudi government realizes that those on the frontlines of education—the ministers, administrators, professors, and teachers—are the best source for recommendations on how to improve the Saudi school system. Therefore, the government has opened its doors to internal criticism and recommendations from education officials and employees. Many of these critics' comments are aimed directly at limiting the influence of extremist clerics in the educational system.

Religious Reform and Tolerance

It has already been suggested that Saudi Arabia must meet the ideological and religious challenge posed by Islamist extremists, or what the Kingdom calls "deviants," head on. The rise of neo-Salafi radicals risks twisting one of the world's great religions into a source of violence that can destabilize Islamic nations, create major tensions with all non-Islamic states and cultures, and block all progress and reform at a time when demographic and social pressure make this vital in virtually every Arab and Islamic state—and certainly in Saudi Arabia.

Saudi Arabia has a unique religious status that inevitably shapes both its current social and cultural attitudes and the nature of political and social reform. It is the birthplace of Islam and the host nation to the annual Hajj. As the site of the two holy mosques, and Islam's most sacred shrine, the Ka'aba, the Kingdom holds enormous significance for Muslims worldwide.

Islam not only guides the lives of the people of Saudi Arabia, but Islamic tradition pervades the policies and functions of government as well. The Qur'an is the constitution of the Kingdom, and the Shari'a is the basis of the Saudi legal system. Given its special significance, Saudi Arabia takes seriously its role as a leader in the pursuit of worldwide Islamic solidarity. It is host to the Muslim World League and the Organization of the Islamic Conference, institutions committed to the preservation of Islamic interests.

Change in Saudi religious practices will come slowly and have to be based on popular consensus; not pressures from outside the Islamic world. Nevertheless, the government is pursuing religious developments that include increasing religious tolerance, removing extremist elements, and reviewing global Islamic policies to ensure they are in line with the tolerant Islam practiced by the vast majority of the Saudi people. And while the Saudi government has made progress on these fronts, there are several areas where reform lags behind what is necessary.

There is no reason that Saudi Arabia should always copy Western approaches to internal security and law enforcement as it makes the necessary changes. The Kingdom can preserve its Islamic character and still take the necessary steps to end support for violent Islamic extremism both within and outside Saudi Arabia. Similarly, Saudi Arabia can also do much to liberalize and improve human rights without giving up its own national cultural traditions and still act to suppress terrorist and extremist activity.

The Saudi government needs to be more proactive in encouraging Saudi clerics and scholars to challenge extremist voices directly, loudly, and at every level. Saudi clerics and scholars should act on their own. They cannot stand by and ignore the reality of the risks involved, or the level and kind of violence that is taking place. They may have reasons to be angry at the United States and the West, or to disagree with the government, but these are not reasons to tolerate a threat to Islam and all its fundamental values.

Nevertheless, Saudi economic and political reform cannot take place without sufficient religious and social reform, and without sufficient tolerance of modern media and communications, to allow Saudi Arabia to compete in global economic terms. Saudi Arabia must become a more open society and one where its young men and women are fully prepared to compete in the market place with global efficiency. This is not a need based on the moral and ethical need to improve human rights—valid as such issues are—it is a pragmatic need that is vital to Saudi Arabia's future development and growth.

Religious Tolerance and Diversity

Saudi Arabia is actually a mosaic of religious beliefs, despite the identification of the nation with the Sunni form of Islam. Within the Sunni majority (90 percent of the population), the predominant strand is Salafi. However, Hanafi and Shafei Sunnis have sizable followings in the Western provinces of the Kingdom. In addition, there are two main groups of Shiites: the "duodecimains" (twelvers), who reside primarily in the Eastern Province; and the Ismailis ("seveners"), who live mainly in the Southern Province of Najran.

The word Salafi comes from the Arabic *Salaf*, a term for the companions of Prophet Mohammad. Modern usage is derived from the phrase *minhaj al-Salaf*, or "method of the early Muslims." The modern Salafi regard the first three generations of Muslims, *al Salaf al Salih* ("pious predecessors"), including the Prophet Mohammad and the "Companions," as perfect examples of prime authority. So-called Wahhabism is a traditionalist movement of Sunni Islam founded by Sheikh Muhammad ibn Abd al-Wahhab (1703–1792) and is derived from the Hanbali school of Islam, which is the official practice in the Kingdom. Wahhabism is regarded, especially in the West, as an intolerant version of Islam and is considered to be at the heart of the radical Islamist ideology that encourages terror.

Shiites believe that Ali—the son-in-law of the Prophet Mohammad—and his descendents are the true imams. Shiites account for 10 percent of the population, with most of them concentrated in the oil-rich Eastern Province. They are prevalent in the middle class in liberal professions as well as the private business sector. However, of the top 400 government positions, only one—undersecretary of state—is held by a Shiite. And of the 120 members of the Shura Council, only two are Shiites.

Saudi Shiites have been making demands for greater tolerance in Saudi Arabia over the last few years. In April 2003, a delegation traveled to Riyadh to present the Crown Prince Abdullah with a petition, signed by 450 Shiites, that made a number of requests. These requests included the recognition of Shiism as a legitimate form of Islam, the removal of anti-Shiite rhetoric from educational textbooks, the right to own and manage their own mosques, and the opening of more public and private employment opportunities to Shiites. The government has granted some of these requests and is in the process of reviewing others.

While the Saudi government has taken some steps to increase religious tolerance in the Kingdom, much more needs to be done. Various meetings have taken place between religious leaders of different denominations at the King Abdul Aziz Center for National Dialogue.

Extremist clerics preaching hate against the Shiites and other religions have been removed from their positions and ordered to undergo retraining. In response to the complaint that it is difficult for Shiites to obtain permits to build new mosques, the granting of new mosque permits has increased recently. The official statement from the conference on "Human Rights in Peace and War" declared, among other things, that tolerance of faith is required by Islam, which also prohibits coercing people to follow a certain religion.

Nevertheless, intolerance is still a "particular concern" in a country that bans the public practice of all other religions except Islam. More than half a million Christians, Buddhists, and others working in the Kingdom have often been forced to secretly move from house to house in order to worship.[30] In one instance, 14 foreign nationals were arrested in the city of Jeddah over a seven-week period from July to September 2001. The arrests followed a raid at the home of an Indian national whose personal computer, containing the names of other Christians in the city, was seized. It is alleged that the raid led to further arrests.

Non-Muslims are not the only victims of intolerance. A report issued by the United States Commission on International Religious Freedom (USCIRF) gave singular consideration to the activities of the Saudi religious police, the Mutawwa'in, "whose powers are vaguely defined and exercised in ways that violate the religious freedom of others." The government "vigorously enforces its prohibition" against anyone who does not adhere to the official interpretation of Islam. The Mutawwa'in's control extends to the appointment of clergy, and the regulation of sermons and religious educational content.[31]

The Role of the Ulema

The ulema is the community of religious leaders trained in Islam and in the interpretation and application of Shari'a (Islamic law), *Fiqh* (Islamic jurisprudence), and Islamic sciences and doctrines. They are responsible for guiding the spiritual and intellectual life of the *umma* (Muslim community). The ulema and the government work closely to assure the religious health of the nation.

This political-religious alliance serves to underline the concept that the state and religion are inseparable in an Islamic country. The Kingdom is an Islamic state governed by the Qur'an, and as such the ulema play a prominent role in its government and administration. They are most influential in the following areas:

- The judicial system of Saudi Arabia.
- The implementation of the rules of the Shari'a Religious Guidance Group.
- Religious education.
- Religious jurisprudence.
- Preaching and spiritual guidance.
- Religious supervision of all mosques in the Kingdom.
- Propagation of Islam abroad.
- Scientific and Islamic research.
- Notaries public.

While the ulema have no formal prescribed powers in the Kingdom, many leading members occupy prominent places in a variety of organizations and are chosen by the senior leadership. These include:

- Council of the Assembly of Senior Ulema (Majlis Hay'at Kibar al-Ulema)
- The Higher Council for Justice (Al-Majlis al-Aali li'l-Qada)
- The Ministry of Islamic Affairs and Endowments
- Committee for the Prevention of Vice and Propagation of Virtue

Most religious leaders in the Kingdom reject violence and extremism and are mainly concerned with the implementation of policies in accordance with Islamic law. In August 2004, The Council of Senior Clerics said in a statement that taking part in terrorist acts is "a dangerous criminal act . . . punishable by Islamic law." The statement continued, "[Terrorism] is an act of sabotage, and an absolute aberration [Those behind recent attacks and plots] shouldn't have been moved by corrupt statements and slogans that cause division and corrupt the nation. [Violent acts have] no religious grounds."

The religious leadership of the Kingdom is conservative, not radical. Most of the senior leaders in the religious establishment work with the government to ensure that Islamic values are reflected in the regulations and procedures of the Kingdom and are consulted on every major issue. These clerics devote their lives to the application of the Qur'an and Sunna and are specialists in the religious sciences. They act as the educators and the religious and moral guides of the Muslim community, and while they may sometimes oppose reform or seek to delay it, they also act as a powerful stabilizing force in dealing with extremism and terrorism.

There is, however, a fringe element within the religious establishment that espouses extremist views. For example, as American troops were preparing to launch a major assault on the insurgents in Fallujah on November 2004, 26 prominent Saudi religious scholars, in an open letter to the people of Iraq, urged the Iraqis to support a "jihad' against U.S.-led forces. Prince Turki al-Faisal denounced the scholars, saying, "They are a tiny extremist minority who have put this letter out in deliberate defiance of much more authoritative edicts calling for peace and stability in the region and urging the Iraqi people to unite behind their government." He went on to emphasize, "they did not represent the views of the overwhelming majority of Saudis or senior religious scholars in the Kingdom."[32] Crown Prince Abdullah declared that terrorists and their sympathizers were responsible for sullying the image of Islam and Muslims worldwide, saying, "Now everybody looks at Muslims, Arabs, Saudis and others as criminals. In fact, we have nothing to do with the crimes." He added that al Qaeda and its surrogates would be "defeated no matter how long it takes."[33]

Similarly, Sheikh Saleh al-Luhaidan, head of the Higher Judicial Council, called for the prosecution of teachers and clerics who encourage Saudi youths to fight against the U.S.-led coalition in Iraq, saying, "The authorities should question and hold accountable the authors of the statements and edicts which make the people feel that fighting in Iraq is a heroic and religiously legitimate act." He went on to say that, donating money to the cause "is only bound to aggravate the situation," and that the Kingdom did not want to "repeat in Iraq the same mistakes committed in Afghanistan."[34]

Efforts are in progress to moderate these voices. For instance, the government has taken numerous steps toward curbing the influence of extremist religious leaders in the Kingdom. Through Sheikh Saleh al-Asheikh, minister of Islamic affairs, restrictions have been placed on unauthorized persons from making speeches at mosques. This order is part of a new program for the maintenance of mosques and their employees. In it, speakers are warned against making provocative speeches and inciting violence or hatred. Further, the order declares that mosques are meant for prayer, guidance and other devotional activities and should not be used as "political platforms." Clerics are also cautioned against reciting poems praising those who advocate violence or intolerance. Violators are subject to severe punishment, including removal from office.

In 2003 an estimated two thousand imams who had violated prohibitions against preaching intolerance were enrolled in orientation courses to increase their awareness of Prophet Mohammad's definition of Muslims ("We are a people of the middle"). The Ministry of Islamic Affairs has begun a three-year program to educate religious leaders and monitor activities in mosques and religious schools with a view toward eradicating extremism and intolerance.

In a speech to a body of high-ranking religious scholars, King Fahd said, "Scholars must highlight the dangers which extremism poses to the Muslim faith and conduct." He called on religious leaders to unite and "correct the flaws in the thinking of some Muslims through dialogue in seminars, conferences and the media." The king also urged them to condemn "aberrant fatwas" that legitimized militancy and suicide attacks.

In May 2003, three clerics were arrested for violating recent proclamations against incendiary speeches and activities. Ali Fahd al-Khudair, Nasir Ahmed al-Fuhaid and Ahmed Hamoud Mufreh al-Khaledi were taken into custody in Medina. Among other charges, the three were accused of using the Internet to incite extremist thought and encouraging violence. The government has vowed to crack down on anyone spreading incendiary ideas. Commenting on the arrest, Interior Minister Prince Nayef said, "Those who claim to be clerics and issue religious edicts are far from that. In reality, they are worthless."

There is a good indication that the government crackdown is having an effect in that some clergy are reassessing their former positions. Al-Khudair, al-Al-Fuhaid, and Al-Khaledi have all retracted their previous fatwas calling for armed resistance against the government. Al-Khaledi was quoted as telling his followers, "Put down your weapons and forsake your extreme ideas."

On April 28, 2004, speaking at the Council on Foreign Relations, Foreign Minister Prince Saud al-Faisal warned against attacking the Kingdom's religious establishment and blamed them for a rise in religious extremism. Emphasizing the critical role of the ulema in combating terrorism, Prince Saud said, "It is the religious establishment in Saudi Arabia that, in fact, is proving to be the body most qualified to delegitimize al Qaeda's claims, the very religious community that is being attacked and discredited."

Islamic Policies

The problems of Saudi private and charitable contributions to extremist and terrorist groups also need to be put in broader perspective. Saudi Arabia's commitment to the Muslim community has taken many forms, and much of it has acted to help encourage stability inside Saudi Arabia and elsewhere in the Islamic world. The Kingdom has provided tens of billions of dollars in aid to Muslims over many years. To accommodate the Hajj pilgrims, a vast network of airports, seaports, roads, and facilities have been built. The government has invested large sums of money in the expansion of two holy mosques in Mecca and Medina and is active in its endeavors to promote the interests of Muslims in all nations.

The Kingdom is a founding member of the Organization of the Islamic Conference (OIC), which is based in Jeddah and was formed in 1969. The OIC is an international organ, with a permanent delegation to the United Nations. Consisting of 57 members, the OIC is dedicated to serving the interests and security of the world's 1.3 billion Muslims. Saudi Arabia is also a member of the Islamic Organization for Science, Technology, and Development.

Saudi Arabia has played an important role in supporting economic and social development plans in developing countries in general and in Islamic countries in particular. The Kingdom allocates a substantial portion of its GNP to assisting countries in their development programs. Development assistance and loans provided by the Kingdom to developing countries that are members of the OIC have amounted to approximately $77 billion over the past 15 years. In some years, assistance has amounted to 6 percent of the GNP, surpassing in relative terms the contributions of industrial countries as a whole.

Saudi Arabia is the largest contributor to the Islamic Development Bank, which is headquartered in Jeddah. The purpose of the bank is to promote economic development and social progress of member countries and Muslim communities. The bank has also established special funds and trust funds for Muslim communities in nonmember countries. Saudi Arabia is also a generous contributor to the Islamic Development Fund that provides economic assistance for community infrastructure projects.

Saudi charity has also had positive, as well as negative effect. Saudi Arabia has undertaken a wide range of programs to aid Muslims in non-Muslim countries. The Kingdom has established Islamic centers and mosques in areas with large Muslim populations. Special organizations serving Muslims inside and outside the Islamic world include the Muslim World League, the World Assembly of Muslim Youth, and the King Faisal Foundation. The Kingdom has also established special organizations such as the International Islamic Relief Organization and the Higher Committee for the Collection of Donations for Muslims in the Balkans, as well as a variety of social and cultural organizations. These bodies are active throughout the world supporting religious, political, and social causes and are dedicated to serving the disadvantaged regardless of religion.

The Kingdom is active in establishing Muslim educational centers throughout the Islamic world. Saudi Arabia has provided scholarships for outstanding students from Muslim minority communities to study at Saudi universities. Currently, there are thousands of such students studying at universities in Mecca and Medina.

To promote a better understanding of Islam among non-Muslims, the Saudi government has provided funding for the creation of Islamic studies departments at major universities in the United States and Europe. The best known of these departments are at Harvard University Law School, the University of California at Berkeley, and the Universities of London and Moscow. The Kingdom also operates Islamic academies in North America and Europe that offer a comprehensive curriculum in both Arabic and the local languages. Currently, there are institutions located in Washington, D.C.; London; Bonn; and Moscow. Plans are already under way to establish others in southern California.

Crown Prince Abdullah recently issued a statement at a gathering of young people from around the world urging them to reject extremism, saying,[35] "It is your responsibility, when you return to your nations, to counsel people to employ wisdom, patience and reason in dealing with issues."

In October 2002, Saudi Arabia, along with other GCC states, issued a joint declaration pledging "unequivocal support" for all initiatives to combat terrorism. The ministers expressed their confidence in the constructive role the Kingdom was playing in working for peace and security in the world.

In February 2003, Saudi Arabia's Council of Senior Ulema issued an edict condemning attacks on non-Muslims in the Kingdom and elsewhere. The edict also denounced those who judged people as "infidels" and targeted them for violence. The religious leaders warned against following those who harbor deviant beliefs and misguided ideologies and stressed that it was the obligation of Muslims worldwide to join the fight against such extremist tendencies.

On April 20, 2004, the Kingdom organized an international conference in Riyadh with the theme "Islam's Position on Terrorism." Nearly 120 researchers and scholars from around the world took part in the program. The attendees sought to examine the Islamic position on violence and extremism and to formulate scientific, psychological, and social recommendations to combat the development of terrorism and extremism.

Administrative and Governance Reform

Saudi Arabia has stated that it is pursuing administrative reforms of government agencies to "improve [the] system of the government," to achieve the goals of expanding electoral institutions and procedures, and to enhance human rights, women's rights, and religious tolerance. The proposed reforms include changes in the structure, responsibilities and monitoring of the various ministries, improvements or initiations in the various councils, authorities, commissions, companies, and departments that oversee and/or conduct official activities in the Kingdom and legal innovations that assure the smooth, progressive, and fair operations of the copyright, trademark, customs, economic, judicial, insurance, criminal procedure, census, statistical, and taxation system and processes.

However, administrative reform needs to be hastened. Coordination between the various reforms and government bodies working on them is not as vigorous as it should be. In some cases, it is nonexistent. For example, the Ministry of Islamic Affairs and the Ministry of Foreign Affairs have a history of issuing contradictory statements on progress toward monitoring charities.

Ministerial Reforms

In October 2003, King Fahd ordered the reform of almost each of the Kingdom's ministries. This included merging and restructuring ministries to limit waste and to streamline their work to make them more efficient in meeting the challenges outlined earlier. The results of the ministerial reforms are as follows:

- *Ministry of Commerce and Industry:* This ministry is the result of a merger of the Ministry of Commerce and the Ministry of Industry and Electricity. It oversees food qualities, consumer protection, commercial registration, labeling regulation, hotel oversight, bilateral trade agreements, and WTO accession. In addition, it is spearheading the Kingdom's e-governance and e-commerce efforts, regulates the current industrial cities in Jubail and Yanbu, and plans to build new ones in Asir, Medina, Jouf, Tabuk, Hail, and Najran.

- *Ministry of Water and Electricity (MoWE):* This ministry is the result of a merger of the Ministry of Industry and Electricity and the Ministry of Water and Agriculture. A new Ministry of Agriculture was also created at this time. MoWE's responsibilities include generating, transmitting, and regulating electricity; creating a network to deliver water to all parts of the country, and regulating water-digging licenses, private investment, and water tariffs.

MoWE provided SR285 million to study ground water reserves in the Kingdom. The Kingdom is the world's largest producer of desalinated water, with 27 plants that provide drinkable water to many urban and industrial areas and which meets 70 percent of Saudi Arabia's water demand.

The Kingdom has instituted such water conservation programs as educating the public to reduce water waste. Farming constitutes 90 percent of water consumption, taking some to 20 billion cubic meters of water. A national water plan is being studied by Saudi Arabia and the World Bank. The results of this will be published in 2005–2006.

- *Ministry of Planning and National Economy:* This ministry is the result of a merger of the Ministry of Planning and the Ministry of National Economy and Finance, during which a new Ministry of Finance was created. The Ministry of Planning and National Economy is responsible for managing and planning the five-year development plans, publishing reports on the Saudi economy, collecting demographic data, maintaining the national economy, and estimating the national state budget.

- *Ministry of Culture and Information:* the Ministry of Information was expanded to oversee cultural organizations that were under the control of the General Presidency of Youth and Welfare such as cultural centers, literary and artistic clubs, and public libraries. In addition, it is still responsible for media broadcasting, domestic and foreign press—including the Saudi Press Agency, and the publication of print materials.

- *Ministry of Communications and Information Technology:* This ministry was created by restructuring the Ministry of Posts, Telegraphs, and Telephones. The new ministry's responsibilities include the monitoring and managing of all forms of modern communications. In addition, it has seen some reforms, such as: In January 1996 it oversaw the launch of GSM in 45 cities, and currently there are 5.5 million subscribers; in May 1998, Saudi Telecom was privatized; in 1999 Internet service was introduced to the Kingdom, and by 2003 there were 21 ISP's; in 2003 the Saudi postal service was privatized; in December 2002, the Kingdom launched its third satellite, which was designed and built by Saudi scientists at the Institute of Space Research.

- *Ministry of National Education:* This ministry previously was named the Ministry of Knowledge; it oversees public education at all levels K-12, educational services in the Saudi Arabia National Guard (SANG) and Ministry of Defense and Aviation (MODA), and educational services for the handicapped and the disabled.

- *Ministry of Civil Service:* This ministry was established in 1999 to oversee civil servants' recruitment, employment, and training.

- *Ministry of Labor:* This ministry was part of the Ministry of Labor and Social Affairs until March 22, 2004. Furthermore, the Manpower Council was moved under the Ministry of Labor, and its responsibilities include solving the unemployment problem, settling labor disputes, regulating labor visas, and implementing the Saudization of the labor force, which is delved into further under the Economic Reform section.

- *Ministry of Social Affairs:* This ministry was part of the Ministry of Labor and Social Affairs until March 22, 2004. Its responsibilities include social insurance, charities, and social research.

- *Ministry of Transport:* This ministry used to be named the Ministry of Communications; it is responsible for all transportation in the Kingdom (except aviation) and the road infrastructure. It also chairs the Saudi Arabian Railways Organization.

- *Ministry of Municipalities:* This ministry took over the responsibilities of the Ministry of Housing and Public Utilities. Its responsibilities include overseeing the development and planning of villages, regulating the standards of the housing, providing public utilities at the municipalities, and controlling public land.

Other Governmental Reforms

In addition to ministerial reforms, the Kingdom has created new councils and dissolved some to eliminate bureaucracy. The following is a list of organizational reforms in some of the prominent councils and their responsibilities:

- *Supreme Economic Council (SEC):* Created in August 1999, it is chaired by Crown Prince Abdullah and many prominent Saudis from the private sector and former officials set on it. Some of its several responsibilities include developing economic policy and promoting coordination among various government entities.

- *Supreme Council for Petroleum and Minerals (SCPM):* Established in January 2000. This 11-member council was given the responsibility of all issues concerning the energy sector, including Saudi Aramco oil policy, five-year oil plans, oil exploration, and oil investment.

- *Saudi Arabian General Investment Authority (SAGIA):* Created in April 2000 to promote and oversee domestic and foreign investment in the Kingdom. It has monitored, promoted, and conducted studies about the investment climate in the Kingdom. SAGIA has issued investment licenses worth more than $13.71 billion.

- *Saudi Arabian Capital Markets Authority (SACMA):* Established in June 2003 following the passage of the Capital Market Law by the Council of Ministers. It is set up to regulate, register, and monitor all issues dealing with capital markets such as buying and selling securities and mergers and acquisitions.

- *Saudi Arabian Stock Exchange (SASE):* This is the Kingdom's stock market, which it has been developing since 1984. In October 2001, an electronic-based trading, clearing, and settlement structure was created, *Tadawul.*

- *Food and Drugs Authority (FDA):* Created in March 2003 to monitor, regulate, and establish standards for food and drug safety to protect consumers.

- *Supreme Council for Tourism (SCT):* Established in April 2000 to develop the tourism industry in the Kingdom. The government raises about $2 billion per annum from tourism. SCT aims to transform the Kingdom into an attractive tourist destination, especially for Saudis to travel within their country. Saudi nationals spend an estimated $15 billion a year on tourism outside the Kingdom.

- *National Commission for Relief and Charitable Works Abroad:* Created in February 2004 to monitor all charitable works and avoid the chance of funds being diverted into terrorism. It is being chaired by the minister of foreign affairs, Prince Saud al-Faisal. It has started enforcing the regulation that charities have to be audited. A financial intelligence unit was created to coordinate all aspects of money tracking.

- *Department of Public Statistics:* Created in July 2002 to provide better information for domestic agencies, the Saudi public, and the international community, including the census system.

- *Electricity Regulatory Authority:* Created in November 2001 to act as an independent regulatory body on all issues dealing with electricity.

Judicial and Legal Reform

Much still needs to be done in reforming the Saudi legal system, but the Kingdom has passed and implemented legal and judicial reforms aimed at improving three major areas:

- *Intellectual Property Rights:* These reforms were signed to encourage innovation, attract new investments from abroad, and prepare the Kingdom to its accession to the WTO by meeting such standards as TRIPS. Laws have been passed to protect intellectual property rights such as:

  — On June 9, 2003, a 28-article *Copyright Law* was passed by the council of Ministers. It protects print publications, software, DVDs, lectures, recording, and art work.

  — On August 5, 2002, a *Trademark Law* was approved by the Council of Ministers to cover any distinguishable and visible signs. Complaints can be heard by the Board of Grievances.

  — On May 10, 2004, a 65-article *Protection Bill* was approved by the Shura Council to regulate patents on new inventions.

- *Judicial Regulations:* These regulations were reformed to ensure a fair justice system that protects human rights and defendant's rights under the law. The following regulations were passed recently by the Kingdom:

  — In September 2001, the Kingdom passed the *Law of Procedure Before Shari'a Courts,* which grants defendants the right to legal representation and outlines the rules of pleas, evidence, and experts' opinions.

  — In January 2002, the Kingdom implemented the *Code of Law Practice,* which outlines the requirements to become an attorney in the Kingdom.

  — In May 2002, the *Criminal Procedure Law,* a 225-article bill, was approved. It protects defendants and suspects before the courts and the government. It also outlines the rights of defendants with regard to interrogation, investigation, and incarceration.

- *Commercial Legislation:* We have touched on commercial law reforms in the Economic Reform section, but the following is a summary of the reform in commercial laws that have taken place recently:

  — On June 6, 2003, the *Capital Markets Law* was approved by the Council of Ministers. This law defines and regulates the capital markets in the Kingdom. It also created the Saudi Arabian Stock Market Exchange.

  — On April 10, 2002, a new Foreign Investment Law was approved by the Council of Ministers. The new law included reforming laws dealing with foreign investment, cut capital gain taxes paid by foreign firms, and established the General Investment Authority (GIA) to regulate and evaluate licenses to foreign investment.

— On July 14, 2003, a new *Insurance Law* was passed in the Kingdom
   that gave the Saudi Arabian Monetary Agency (SAMA) the power to
   regulate the insurance industry, which is composed of 190 firms.

OVERALL PROGRESS IN REFORM

This discussion of Saudi reform efforts needs to be viewed in several different
ways. The first way is that Saudi Arabia is not a static nation that is ignoring
the need for reform or fails to move forward.

The second way is that the pace of reform to date has not kept up with the
demographic and economic pressures on the Kingdom—both of which would
grow much worse if any major drop took place in the exceptionally high oil
prices in recent years and Saudi Arabia's oil export income. Vital as some
aspects of military and security reform are, they cannot compensate for the failure to increase the current pace of the Kingdom's reform efforts.

The third way of looking at reform is one touched upon earlier. Saudi Arabia must take the attitude of its people and key elites into account, even when
they are conservative and are opposed to some forms of reform. One of the iro-
nies of outside calls for reform, and even some calls by Saudi reformers, is that
many simultaneously call for instant democracy and then for reforms in many
other areas that the Saudi people, as yet, do not support or have no broad consensus in favor of action. Reform must evolve, not be suddenly imposed.

In an October 7, 2004, interview, U.S. senator Joseph Biden strongly criticized the educational system in the Kingdom and in the Saudi-sponsored
schools abroad and commented on what he called a general lack of "concrete
steps" toward reform.[36] He did, however, concede that the process of modernization and democratic reforms was difficult and needed to be implemented
internally rather than imposed from the outside, a sentiment that is shared by
many within the Saudi government. Washington has also strongly denounced
the imprisonment of Saudi reform advocates who were arrested for openly criticizing the Kingdom's rigorous religious atmosphere and slow pace of reform.
The U.S. State Department condemned the arrests as "inconsistent with the
kind of forward progress that reform-minded people are looking for."[37]

Recently, 15–21 Saudis, including a woman, protested against the government in Riyadh and Jeddah. It is reported that the protests were called for by
the Saudi opposition in London. Saudi forces arrested 15 and sentenced some
to up to 6 months in prison and up to 225 lashes.[38] While the opposition
claimed that thousands of people were protesting, it was in fact not more than
several people in both cities and had very little impact.

A Saudi academic, Dr. Khalid al-Dakhil, argued that while the focus of the Kingdom in 2003 was reform, Saudi "officials stopped talking about reform the way they used to." He pointed out arrests of reformists, and the new law, issued recently, that criminalized the signing of petitions by government employees or criticizing the government in the press. Infractions are punishable by dismissal or prison. Professor al-Dakhil wrote, "A split over the proposed reforms had been developing within the government for quite some time. A final agreement between the two parties, it would seem, could not have been reached before the government dealt with the terrorist bombings. But as soon as it started to get the upper hand on this war, the government felt justified to silence any call for reform. Does this mean that reform represents for the authorities as much of a threat as terrorism does? It should not."[39]

However, Shura Council member, Dr. Ihsan Buhaleega insists that, the government's commitment to reform is "evident" in the fact that some Saudi citizens will be voting in the coming election, and efforts are being directed at "improving people's lives" by expanding social services and fighting unemployment.[40]

The problem for both Saudi Arabia and its friends is to find the right balance and the right pace. As is the case with every country in the world, this means finding solutions tailored to a given nation, and that encourages practical reform from within. The West, in particular, must be sensitive to the fact that noisy calls for instant reform from the outside, rather than quiet support for Saudi reformers, can do more to alienate Saudis than encourage them. This is particularly true if outside calls for reform ignore the religious character of Saudi Arabia and the all too present threat of Islamic extremism and terrorism.

It ultimately will be as difficult for Saudis as for foreigners to find the narrow line between stepping up the pace of reform and trying to force the pace beyond its practical limits. In both cases, a quiet consistency is likely to be far more productive than episodic and politically impractical calls for instant progress. Prince Mansour bin Mitab, the head of the election committee, said, "When we talk about reform, it requires not just government will. There is a spectrum where on the far right people want minor slow, incremental changes and on the far left they want a big jump. The challenge is how to deal with these differences."[41]

Notes

Chapter 1

1. Joel Brinkley, "Saudis Blame U.S. and Its Role in Iraq for Rise of Terror," *New York Times,* October 14, 2004.

2. Barry Schweid, "Saudi Plan for Muslim Forces Rejected," *Associated Press,* October 19, 2004.

3. Unless otherwise stated, the numbers for military manpower and equipment used in this report are adapted by the authors from the 2003–2004 and 2004–2005 editions of the International Institute for Strategic Studies (IISS), *Military Balance* (London: IISS).

4. Department of Defense, *Iraq Weekly Status Report,* November 3, 2004, and information provided from MNSTC-I.

5. U.S. State Department, *World Military Expenditures and Arms Transfers, 1999–2000* (Washington, DC, 2000), p. 77.

6. The counts of Iran's military manpower, weapons numbers and types, force strength, and defense expenditures in this report rely heavily on various editions of the IISS, *Military Balance.* These figures are taken from *Military Balance, 2004–2005,* pp. 354–55.

7. U.S. State Department, *World Military Expenditures and Arms Transfers, 1999–2000,* p. 77.

8. Richard F. Grimmett, *Conventional Arms Transfer to Developing Nations* (Washington, DC: Congressional Research Service, CRS RL32547, August 26, 2004), pp. 50 and 61.

9. Ibid.

10. Adapted from EIA, "World Oil Transit Chokepoints," June 2004, *http://www.eia.doe.gov/emeu/cabs/choke.html.*

11. The Suez Canal is not seen as a threat to Saudi Arabia in this analysis. It is, however, a major choke point. The EIA notes that:

    ...some 3.8 million MMBD flowed through the Canal and Sumed Pipeline complex in 2003. "Of this total, the Sumed Pipeline transported 2.5 million bbl/d of oil northbound (nearly all from Saudi Arabia) and the Suez Canal about 1.3 MMBD.

In 2003, about 2,800 oil tankers passed through the Suez Canal carrying 1.3 million bbl/d of oil. This represented a 26% increase in oil shipments from 2002 levels, when 2,500 ships transported about 1.0 million bbl/d of oil through the canal. Oil historically has represented about 25 percent of Suez Canal revenues. Currently, the Suez Canal can accommodate Suezmax class tankers with drafts of up to 62 feet and 200,000-dead-weight-ton maximum cargos. In 2001, the Suez Canal Authority (SCA) launched a 5-year program to reduce tanker transit times (from 14 hours to 11 hours) through the Canal. The SCA also is moving ahead with a 10-year project to widen and deepen the Canal, so that by 2010 it can accommodate Very-Large-Crude-Carrier (VLCC) and Ultra-Large-Crude-Carrier (ULCC) class tankers with oil cargos of up to 350,000 dead-weight-tons.

The Sumed pipeline, with a capacity of about 2.5 million bbl/d, links the Ain Sukhna terminal on the Gulf of Suez with Sidi Kerir on the Mediterranean. Sumed consists of two parallel 42-inch lines, and is owned by Arab Petroleum Pipeline Co., a joint venture of EGPC (50%), Saudi Aramco (15%), Abu Dhabi's ADNOC (15%), three Kuwaiti companies (15% total), and Qatar's QGPC (5%). The pipeline has been in operation since January 1977, and has served as an alternative to the Suez Canal to transport loads from tankers that are too large to pass fully laden through the canal.

12. EIA, "World Oil Transit Chokepoints," June 2004, *http://www.eia.doe.gov/emeu/cabs/choke.html*.

13. Robin Wright and Peter Baker, "Iraq, Jordan See Threat to Election from Iran," *Washington Post,* December 1, 2004, p 1.

14. Ibid.

15. "Iran Announces Largest War Games Exercise 'Ever' Near Iraq Borders," *Associated Press,* December 3, 2004.

16. U.S. State Department, *World Military Expenditures and Arms Transfers, 1999–2000,* p. 77.

17. The counts of Iran's military manpower, weapons numbers and types, force strength, and defense expenditures in this report rely heavily on various editions of the IISS, *Military Balance*. These figures are taken from *The Military Balance, 2004–2005,* pp. 354–55.

18. Grimmett, pp. 50 and 61.

19. U.S. State Department, *World Military Expenditures and Arms Transfers, 1999–2000,* p. 77.

20. IISS, *The Military Balance,* 1997–98 and 2004–2005 editions; *Jane's Sentinel: The Gulf States,* "Iran," various editions.

21. There are reports that the lighter and smaller formations in the Regular Army include an airmobile forces group created since the Iran-Iraq War, which includes the 29th Special Forces Division, formed in 1993–94, and the 55th paratroop division. There are also reports that the Regular Army and IRGC commando forces are loosely integrated into a corps of up to 30,000 men with integrated helicopter lift

and air assault capabilities. The airborne and special forces are trained at a facility in Shiraz. These reports are not correct. Note that detailed unit identifications for Iranian forces differ sharply from source to source. It is unclear that such identifications are accurate, and now dated wartime titles and numbers are often published, sometimes confusing brigade numbers with division numbers.

22. No reliable data exist on the size and number of Iran's smaller independent formations.

23. See *Jane's Armor and Artillery, 2002–2003* (London, Jane's Information Group), pp. 47–54.

24. The estimates of Iran's AFV and APC strength are based on interviews with Israeli, British, and U.S. civilian experts and the IISS, *Military Balance*, "Iran," various editions; *Jane's Sentinel: The Gulf States*, "Iran," various editions.

25. See *Jane's Armor and Artillery, 2002–2003*, p. 173.

26. Christopher Foss, "Iran Reveals Up-Armoured Boraq Carrier," *Jane's Defence Weekly*, April 9, 2003, http://jdw.janes.com, accessed January 8, 2004. See *Jane's Armor and Artillery, 2001–2003*, pp. 309–31.

27. Lyubov Pronima, "U.S. Sanctions Russian Firm for Alleged Iran Sales," *Defense News*, September 22, 2003, p. 12.

28. Riad Kahwah and Barabara Opall-Rome, "Hizbollah: Iran's Battle Lab," *Defense News*, December 13, 2004, pp. 1 and 6.

29. Dough Richardson, "Iran's Raad Cruise Missile Enters Production," *Jane's Missiles and Rockets*.

30. *Jane's Defence Weekly*, January 15, 2003, http://jdw.janes.com, accessed January 8, 2004.

31. *International Defense Review*, July 1996, pp. 22–26; Anthony H. Cordesman, "Iran's Weapons of Mass Destruction," CSIS, April 1997.

32. Amir Taheir, "The Mullah's Playground," *Wall Street Journal*, December 7, 2004, p. A10.

33. Reuters, "Iran Denies Missile Cooperation with North Korea, " February 1995.

34. This assessment draws upon a number of sources. Key sources include Global Security, "Shahab 3. Zelzal 3," *http://www.globalsecurity.org/wmd/world/iran/shahab-3.htm*, last modified November 23, 2004—10:57; Global Security, Shahab-4, *http://www.globalsecurity.org/wmd/world/iran/shahab-4.htm*, last modified November 23, 2004—10:57; Missilethreat.com, a project of the Claremont Institute, *http://www.missilethreat.com/missiles/shabab-3_iran.html*, accessed November 25, 2004; Missilethreat.com, "Shahab 4," Project of the Claremont Institute, *http://www.missilethreat.com/missiles/shabab-4_iran.html*, accessed November 25, 2004; and Federation of American Scientists, "Shahab-3/Zezal-3," *http://www.fas.org/nuke/guide/iran/missile/shahab-3.htm*, last updated May 13, 2003, 03:38:11 AM.

35. globalsecurity.org

36. "Unclassified Report to Congress on Acquisition of Technology Relating to Weapons of Mass Destruction and Advanced Converted Munitions," January 1–June 30, 2003. Presented to Congress November 10, 2003.

37. "News," Spacewar.com, September 20, 2004; *Haaretz,* September 20, 2004.

38. "Iran Boasts Shahab-3 Is in Mass Production," *Jane's Missiles and Rockets,* November 19, 2004.

39. Jane's Islamic Affairs Analyst, "Iran threatens to Abandon the NPT," September 29, 2004.

40. Douglas Jehl, "Iran Reportedly Hides Work on a Long-Range Missile," *New York Times,* December 2, 2004.

41. Douglas Jehl, "Iran Is Said to Work on New Missile," *International Herald Tribune,* December 2, 2004, p. 7; Jehl, "Iran Reportedly Hides Work."

42. "Iran Enhances Existing Weaponry by Optimizing Shahab-3 Ballistic Missile," *Jane's Missiles and Rockets,* January 20, 2004.

43. Bill Gertz, "US Told of Iranian Effort to Create Nuclear Warhead," *Washington Times,* December 2, 2004, p. 3.

44. Kahwah and Opall-Rome, "Hizbollah: Iran's Battle Lab," pp. 1 and 6.

45. Amir Taheir, "The Mullah's Playground," *Wall Street Journal,* December 7, 2004, p. A10.

46. The estimates of such holdings of rockets are now in the thousands, but the numbers are very uncertain. Dollar estimates of what are significant arms shipments are little more than analytic rubbish, based on cost methods that border on the absurd, but significant shipments are known to have taken place.

47. "Iran Enhances Existing Weaponry by Optimizing Shahab-3 Ballistic Missile," *Jane's Missiles and Rockets,* January 20, 2004.

48. See *Time,* March 21, 1994, pp. 50–54; November 11, 1996, pp. 78–82. Also see *Washington Post,* November 21, 1993, p. A-1; August 22, 1994, p. A-17; October 28, 1994, p. A-17; November 27, 1994, p. A-30; April 11, 1997, p. A-1; April 14, 1997, p. A-1. *Los Angeles Times,* November 3, 1994, pp. A-1, A-12. *Deutsche Presse Agentur,* April 17, 1997, 11:02. *Reuters,* April 16, 1997. *BC Cycle,* April 17, 1997. *The European,* April 17, 1997, p. 13. *The Guardian,* October 30, 1993, p. 13; August 24, 1996, p. 16; April 16, 1997, p. 10. *New York Times,* April 11, 1997, p. A1. *Associated Press,* April 14, 1997, 18:37. *Jane's Defence Weekly,* June 5, 1996, p. 15. *Agence France Press,* April 15, 1997, 15:13. BBC, April 14, 1997, ME/D2892/MED. *Deutscher Depeschen* via ADN, April 12, 1997, 0743. *Washington Times,* April 11, 1997, p. A22.

49. For typical reporting by officers of the IRGC on this issue, see the comments of its acting commander in chief, Brig. Gen. Seyyed Rahim Safavi, speaking to reporters during IRGC week (December 20–26, 1995). FBIS-NES-95-250, December 25, 1995, IRNA 1406 GMT.

50. Interviews and *Washington Times,* May 12, 1997, p. A-13; October 11, 1997, p. A-6. *Jane's Defence Weekly,* June 25, 1997, p. 14; October 1, 1997, p. 19. *Reuters,* July 3, 1997, 0452; July 9, 1997, 1655; September 28, 1997, 0417; October 6, 1997, 1600.

51. The reader should be aware that much of the information relating to the Quds is highly uncertain and is drawn from Israeli sources. Also, however, see the article from the Jordanian publication *Al-Hadath* in FBIS-NES-96-108, May 27, 1996, p. 9; and in *Al-Sharq Al-Awsat,* FBIS-NES-96-110, June 5, 1996, pp. 1,4; A. J. Venter, "Iran Still Exporting Terrorism," *Jane's Intelligence Review,* November, 1997, pp. 511–16.

52. *New York Times,* May 17, 1998, p. A-15; *Washington Times,* May 17, 1998, p. A-13; *Washington Post,* May 21, 1998, p. A-29.

53. Venter, "Iran Still Exporting Terrorism," pp. 511–16.

54. "Iran," *Jane's Sentinel Security Assessment,* 29 October 2001.

55. *World Missiles Briefing,* Teal Group Corporation.

56. *Jane's Defence Weekly,* June 25, 1997, p. 3; *Associated Press,* June 17, 1997, 1751; *United Press,* June 17, 1997, 0428; *International Defense Review,* June 1996, p. 17.

57. *Jane's Fighting Ships, 2002–2003* (London: Jane's Information Group), pp. 336–43.

58. Ibid.

59. *Washington Times,* March 27, 1996, p. A-1.

60. *Defense News,* January 17, 1994, pp. 1, 29.

61. *Jane's Fighting Ships, 2002–2003,* pp. 336–43.

62. Only two torpedo tubes can fire wire-guided torpedoes. *Defense News,* January 17, 1994, pp. 1, 29.

63. *Jane's Fighting Ships, 2002–2003,* pp. 336–43.

64. See David Miller, "Submarines in the Gulf," *Military Technology* (June 1993), pp. 42–45, and David Markov, "More Details Surface of Rubin's 'Kilo' Plans," *Jane's Intelligence Review* (May 1997), pp. 209–15.

65. In addition to the sources listed at the start of this section, these assessments are based on various interviews; various editions of the IISS *Military Balance;* the *Jaffee Center Middle East Balance;* "Iran," *Jane's Sentinel: The Gulf States;* and *Jane's Defence Weekly,* July 11, 1987, p. 15.

66. A. Kozhikov and D. Kaliyeva, "The Military Political Situation in the Caspian Region," *Central Asia's Affairs* 3 No 3, December 2003.

67. Ibid.

68. "Iran," *Jane's Sentinel Security Assessment—The Gulf States, Armed Forces,* October 7, 2004.

69. The range of aircraft numbers shown reflects the broad uncertainties affecting the number of Iran's aircraft that are operational in any realistic sense. Many aircraft counted, however, cannot engage in sustained combat sorties in an extended air campaign. The numbers are drawn largely from interviews; *Jane's Intelligence*

Review, Special Report No. 6, May 1995; "Iran," *Jane's Sentinel—The Gulf Staffs,* various editions; the IISS, "Iran," *Military Balance,* various editions; Andrew Rathmell, *The Changing Balance in the Gulf* (London: Royal United Services Institute, Whitehall Papers 38, 1996); Dr. Andrew Rathmell, "Iran's Rearmament: How Great a Threat?," *Jane's Intelligence Review* (July 1994), pp. 317–22; *Jane's World Air Forces* (CD-ROM).

70. *Wall Street Journal,* February 10, 1995, p. 19; *Washington Times,* February 10, 1995, p. A-19.

71. *Jane's All the World's Aircraft, 2002–2003* (London: Jane's Information Group), pp. 259–63.

72. Robert Hewson, "Iran's New Combat Aircraft Waits in the Wings," *Jane's Defence Weekly,* November 20, 2002, p. 15. *Jane's All the World's Aircraft, 2002–2003,* pp. 259–63.

73. *Jane's All the World's Aircraft, 2002–2003,* pp. 259–63.

74. Periscope, Nations/Alliances/Geographic Regions/Middle East/North Africa, Plans and Programs.

75. Reports that the IRGC is operating F-7 fighters do not seem to be correct.

76. *Reuters,* June 12, 1996, 17:33.

77. "Iran Reveals Shahab Thaqeb SAM Details," *Jane's Defence Weekly,* September 4, 2002, http://jdw.janes.com, accessed January 9, 2004.

78. Based on interviews with British, Israeli, and U.S. experts, and Anthony H. Cordesman, *Iran and Iraq: The Threat from the Northern Gulf* (Boulder, CO: Westview, 1994); Anthony H. Cordesman and Ahmed S. Hashim, *Iran: The Dilemmas of Dual Containment* (Boulder, CO: Westview, 1997); IISS, "Iran," *Military Balance,* various editions; "Iran," *Jane's Sentinel: The Gulf States,* various editions; USNI Data Base; Anoushiravan Ehteshami, "Iran's National Strategy," *International Defense Review* (April 1994), pp. 29–37; "Military Technology," *World Defense Almanac: The Balance of Military Power* 17, no. 1 (1993), ISSN 0722-3226, pp. 139–42; working data from the Jaffee Center for Strategic Studies; Rathmell, "Iran's Rearmament," pp. 317–22; Ahmed Hashim, "The Crisis of the Iranian State," Adelphi Paper 296, London, IISS, Oxford, July 1995, pp. 7–30 and 50–70; Rathmell, *Changing Military Balance,* pp. 9–23; Michael Eisenstadt, *Iranian Military Power, Capabilities and Intentions* (Washington, DC: Washington Institute, 1996), pp. 9–65; and Anoushiravan Enreshami, "Iran Strives to Regain Military Might," *International Defense Review* (July 1996), pp. 22–26.

79. *Jane's Defence Weekly,* September 4, 1996, p. 4.

80. EIA, "Persian Gulf Fact Sheet," September 2004, *http://www.eia.doe.gov/emeu/cabs/pgulf.html.*

81. See *http://www.eia.doe.gov/emeu/security/choke.html#HORMUZ.* The EIA estimates that some 13 MMBD flowed through the Strait in 2002. The IEA puts the figure at 15 MMBD in 2003. Both agencies indicate that the amount of oil moving by tanker

will increase steadily as Asian demand consumes a larger and larger share of total exports.

Closure of the Strait of Hormuz would require use of longer alternate routes (if available) at increased transportation costs. Such routes include the 5 million-bbl/d capacity Petroline (East-West Pipeline) and the 290,000-bbl/d Abqaiq-Yanbu natural gas liquids line across Saudi Arabia to the Red Sea. Theoretically, the 1.65-MMBD Iraqi Pipeline across Saudi Arabia (IPSA) also could be used, more oil could be pumped north to Ceyhan (in Turkey), and the 0.5 million-bbl/d Tapline to Lebanon could be reactivated.

82. EIA, "UAE Country Brief," February 2004, *http://www.eia.doe.gov/emeu/cabs/uae.html.*

83. *Arab News,* December 6, 2004, p. 1; *Middle East Economic Digest,* 12–18 November, 2004, p. 44.

84. *Middle East Economic Digest,* 12–18 November, 2004, p. 44.

85. EIA, "Saudi Country Brief," June 2004, *http://www.eia.doe.gov/emeu/cabs/saudi.html,* accessed November 11, 2004.

86. Ibid.

87. International Energy Agency, "Oil Market Outlook," *World Energy Outlook, 2004,* OECD/IEA, Paris, October 2004, table 3.7 and 3.8.

88. International Energy Agency, "Oil Market Outlook," *World Energy Outlook, 2004* (Paris: OECD/IEA, October 2004), chapter 3.

89. *Washington Post,* November 18, 2004, p. A-1.

90. Shirley Kan, "China's Proliferation of Weapons of Mass Destruction," Congressional Research Service, March 1, 2002, CRS IB 9256.

91. Merav Zafary, "Iranian Biological and Chemical Weapons Profile Study," Center for Nonproliferation Studies, Monterey Institute of International Studies, February 2001.

92. "Iran," *Jane's Sentinel Security Assessment-The Gulf States, Armed Forces,* October 7, 2004.

93. The following list summarizes the far more comprehensive descriptions of Iranian nuclear facilities developed by Global Security, headed by John Pike. The full analysis for Iranian facilities can be found at the Global Security Web site, Iran Nuclear Facilities, *http//www.globalsecurity.org/wmd/world/iran/nuke-fac.htm.*

94. All IAEA quotes are taken from the report by the director general to the board of governors, "Implementation of the NPT Safeguards Agreement in the Islamic Republic of Iran," IAEA, GOV 2004/83, November 15, 2004.

95. IAE A Report by director General, "Implementation of NPT Safeguards Agreement in the Islamic Republic of Iran." November 15, 2004

96. All IAEA quotes are taken from the report by the director general to the board of governors, "Implementation of the NPT Safeguards Agreement in the Islamic Republic of Iran," IAEA, GOV 2004/83, November 15, 2004.

97. Global Security notes that "According to Paul Leventhal of the Nuclear Control Institute, if Iran were to withdraw from the Nonproliferation Treaty and renounce the agreement with Russia, the Bushehr reactor could produce a quarter ton of plutonium per year, which Leventhal says is enough for at least 30 atomic bombs. Normally for electrical power production the uranium fuel remains in the reactor for three to four years, which produces a plutonium of 60 percent or less Pu-239, 25 percent or more Pu-240, 10 percent or more Pu-241, and a few percent Pu-242. The Pu-240 has a high spontaneous rate of fission, and the amount of Pu-240 in weapons-grade plutonium generally does not exceed 6 percent, with the remaining 93 percent Pu-239. Higher concentrations of Pu-240 can result in pre-detonation of the weapon, significantly reducing yield and reliability. For the production of weapons-grade plutonium with lower Pu-240 concentrations, the fuel rods in a reactor have to be changed frequently, about every four months or less."

98. IAEA Report by Director General, "Implementation of NPT Safeguards Agreement in the Islamic Republic of Iran." November 15, 2004.

99. IAEA, "Implementation of the NPT Safeguards Agreement in the Islamic Republic of Iran."

100. Ibid.

101. *Saudi Gazette,* December 6, 2004, p. 8; *Arab News,* December 6, 2004, p. 5; *International Herald Tribune,* December 3, 2004, p. 4; *Daily Star,* December 3, 2004, p. 7.

102. IAEA, "Implementation of the NPT Safeguards Agreement in the Islamic Republic of Iran."

103. *Saudi Gazette,* December 6, 2004, p. 8; *Arab News,* December 6, 2004, p. 5; *International Herald Tribune,* December 3, 2004, p. 4; *Daily Star,* December 3, 2004, p. 7.

104. IAEA, "Implementation of the NPT Safeguards Agreement in the Islamic Republic of Iran."

105. Ibid.

106. David Sanger, "Pakistan Found to Aid Iran Nuclear Efforts," *New York Times,* September 2, 2004.

107. "Text of EU-Iran nuclear agreement," *Albawaba,* November 15, 2004. Available at http://www.albawaba.com/news/index.php3?sid=288927&lang=e&dir=news.

108. George Jahn, "Iran Satisfies IAEA Regarding Enrichment," *Associated Press,* November 15, 2004.

109. Ali Akbar Dareini, "Iran Suspends Uranium Enrichment," *Associated Press,* November 22, 2004.

110. IAEA, "Implementation of the NPT Safeguards Agreement in the Islamic Republic of Iran."

111. "Iran Declaration," http://news.bbc.co.uk/1/hiworld/middle_east/3211036; International Crisis Group, "Iran: Where Next on the Nuclear Standoff," *Middle East Briefing,* Amman/Brussels, November 24, 2004, pp. 2–3.

112. *Guardian,* June 28, 2004.

113. International Crisis Group, "Iran: Where Next on the Nuclear Standoff," *Middle East Briefing,* Amman/Brussels, November 24, 2004, p. 15; *Jane's Intelligence Review,* August 19, 2004; *UPI,* August 9, 2004.

114. Robin Wright and Keith Richburg, "Powell Says Iran Is Pursuing Bomb." *Washington Post,* November 18, 2004. p. A01.

115. Gertz, "US Told of Iranian Effort to Create Nuclear Warhead," p. 3.

116. Alrashid, Abdulrahman, "Yes We Are Afraid of the Iranian Uranium." *Al-Sharq Al-Awsat,* October 8, 2003.

117. Speech at the annual USCENTCOM conference, June 26, 1997.

118. *Los Angeles Times,* March 17, 1992, p. 1.

119. *New York Times,* November 30, 1992, pp. A-1 and A-6, January 5, 1995, p. A-10; *Washington Times,* January 6, 1995, p. A-15.

120. *New York Times,* January 10, 1995, p. A-3; *Jane's Intelligence Review,* "Iran's Weapons of Mass Destruction," Special Report Number 6, May 1995, pp. 4–14; Gerald White, *The Risk Report* 1, no. 7 (September 1995); *Jane's Intelligence Review,* October, 1995, p. 452.

121. *Associated Press,* May 5, 1997, 01:26.

122. *Chalk Times,* January 10, 1995, p. 31; *Washington Times,* January 19, 1995, p. A-18.

123. Rodney W. Jones and Mark G. McDonough with Toby Dalton and Gregory Koblentz, *Tracking Nuclear Proliferation: A Guide in Maps and Charts, 1998.* Carnegie Endowment for International Peace (CEIP), 1999.

124. http://www.defenselink.mil/pubs/prolif97/graphics.html.

125. *Washington Times,* July 29, 1998, p. A-12.

126. Nonproliferation Center, Director of Central Intelligence, Unclassified Report to Congress on the Acquisition of Technology Relating to Weapons of Mass Destruction and Advanced Conventional Munitions 1 January through 30 June 1999. This report is issued in response to a Congressionally directed action in Section 721 of the FY 97 Intelligence Authorization Act, which requires: "(a) Not later than 6 months after the date of the enactment of this Act, and every 6 months thereafter, the Director of Central Intelligence shall submit to Congress a report on (1) the acquisition by foreign countries during the preceding 6 months of dual-use and other technology useful for the development or production of weapons of mass destruction (including nuclear weapons, chemical weapons, and biological weapons) and advanced conventional munitions; and (2) trends in the acquisition of such technology by such countries." At the DCI's request, the DCI Nonproliferation Center (NPC) drafts this report and coordinates it throughout the Intelligence

Community. As directed by Section 721, subsection (b) of the Act, it is unclassified. As such, the report does not present the details of the Intelligence Community's assessments of weapons of mass destruction and advanced conventional munitions programs that are available in other classified reports and briefings for the Congress.

127. *New York Times,* January 17, 2000, p. A-1 and A-8; *Bloomberg News,* January 17, 2000, 08:28; *Reuters,* January 17, 2000, 13:53; *Associated Press,* January 18, 2000, 0211.

128. *Reuters,* January 24, 2000, 18:55; January 26, 2000, 11:21.

129. *Reuters,* January 24, 2000, 18:32.

130. Director of Central Intelligence, "Unclassified Report to Congress on the Acquisition of Technology Relating to Weapons of Mass Destruction and Advanced Conventional Munitions, 1 July through 31 December 2003," CIA, 2004, *http://www.cia.gov/cia/reports/721_reports/july_dec2003.htm.*

131. *Jane's Intelligence Review,* August 19, 2004; International Crisis Group, "Iran: Where Next on the Nuclear Standoff," *Middle East Briefing,* November 24, 2004, p. 15.

132. *Washington Times,* May 17, 1995, p. A-15; Office of the Secretary of Defense, *Proliferation: Threat and Response* (Washington, DC: Department of Defense, April, 1996), pp. 12–16.

133. Gertz, "US Told of Iranian Effort to Create Nuclear Warhead," p. 3; Jehl, "Iran is Said to Work on New Missile," p. 7; Jehl, "Iran Reportedly Hides Work on a Long-Range Missile."

134. Most experts feel Iran has not made significant progress in any covert reactor program large enough to produce weapons materials, or in laser isotope separation.

135. *New York Times,* May 14, 1995; *Washington Post,* November 5, 1997, p. A-1.

136. For interesting insights into possible scenarios and their implications, see Anthony H. Cordesman, "Terrorism and the Threat from Weapons of Mass Destruction in the Middle East: The Problem of Paradigm Shift" (Washington, DC: CSIS, October 17, 1996); Brad Roberts, *Terrorism with Chemical and Biological Weapons, Calibrating Risks and Responses* (Alexandria, VA: Chemical and Biological Weapons Control Institute, 1997); Shai Feldman, *Nuclear Weapons and Arms Control in the Middle East* (Cambridge, MA: MIT Press, 1997).

CHAPTER 2

1. "Saudi Arabia, A Chronology of the Country's History and Key Events in US-Saudi Relationship," *http://www.pbs.org.*

2. "In al-Qaeda's Sights," *Council on Foreign Relations,* November 11, 2003, *www.cfr.org/background/saudi_terror.php;* "Al-Qaeda," Wikpedia, *www.en.wikipedia.org.*

3. "Al-Qaeda," *www.globalsecurity.org.*

4. Adapted from work by Douglas Baldwin.

5. AFP, "Saudi Vows No Rest Until Killers Are Caught," November 10, 2003.

6. "Saudi Arabia Seeks to Portray Captured al-Qaeda Militants in Humiliating Light," *Associated Press,* September 10, 2004.

7. Mahmoud Ahmad, "Al-Qaeda Operatives Are an Ignorant Lot, Say Former Members," *Arab News,* October 3, 2004.

8. *Arab News,* January 1, 2005.

9. Abdullah al-Shihri, "Saudi Police Hunt Suspects in Attack," *Associated Press,* December 30, 2004.

10. "Al-Qaeda: Riyadh Attack Targeted Interior Minister," *Daily Star,* January 5, 2005. Available at: *http://www.dailystar.com.lb/article.asp?edition_id=10&categ_id=2 &article_id=11522*

11. Ibid.

12. Faiza Saleh Ambah, "Victims Provide Details on Saudi Attack," *Associated Press,* December 7, 2004.

13. The following analysis of the bin Laden tape draws on the work of Shaun Waterman, *UPI* Homeland and National Security Editor.

14. Middle East Media Research Institute (MEMRI), December 30, 2004.

15. Craig Whitlock, "Al-Qaeda Shifts Its Strategy in Saudi Arabia," *Washington Post,* December 19, 2004.

16. "US Consulate Attackers Are Vilified," www.news.scotsman.com

17. Nawaf Obaid, "Independent Saudi Poll Reveals Major Changes in the Kingdom." June–December 2003.

18. AP, May 8, 2004, "Saudi Prinice Urges Shunning of Terrorists."

19. Abdul Wahab Bashir, "Kingdom Has No Plans to Close Down Charities," *Arab News,* January 1, 2005, p. 2.

20. Abdul Wahab Bashir, "Amnesty Is a Sign of Strength, Says Nayef," *Arab News,* June 28, 2004.

21. "Saudi Frees Suspects Who Surrendered Under Amnesty," *Reuters,* November 11, 2004.

22. Abdul Wahab Bashir, "2-Month Amnesty for Weapons Handover," *Arab News,* June 30, 2004.

23. Bouchaib Silm, "Countering Terror with an Amnesty: Why It Makes Sense," *The Straits Times,* September 15, 2004.

24. "Saudi Paper Published 'Confession' by Unidentified Militant," BBC Monitoring, Middle East, October 24, 2004.

25. Rawya Regeh, "Fathers of Saudi Militants Appear on Television to Condemn Terror," *Associated Press,* December 5, 2004.

26. Dominic Evans, "Saudi Militants Say Jailers 'Like Family,'" *Reuters*, December 15, 2004.

27. "Bi-partisan Panel Commends U.S. and Saudi Efforts to Disrupt Terrorist Financing, But Says More Progress Is Needed," Council on Foreign Relations, www.cfr.org.

28. "Saudi Charity Remains Open Despite Govt Orders to Close It," *Associated Press*, October 14, 2004; "Senate Banking Hearing Challenges Saudi Cooperation on Terror Financing," C&O Special Report, October 4, 2004.

29. Diala Saadeh, "Saudi Steps Up Charity Monitoring During Ramadan," *Reuters*, October 26, 2004.

30. "Saudi Arabia Cited for Helpful Role in Combating Terrorist Financing," C&O Special Report, October 4, 2004.

31. Scott Macleod, Interview with *Time* magazine, "The Saudis Respond," September 10, 2003.

32. Essam Al-Ghalib, "Kingdom, Iraq Set to Restore Diplomatic Relations," Arab News, July 29, 2004.

33. "Saudi Prince Gets Libel Damages," BBC News, December 6, 2004.

34. "Saudi Says Stops Nearly One Milo at Borders," *Reuters*, September 21, 2004.

35. Ali Akbar Dareini, "Ways to Stop Iraq Infiltrators Sought," *Associated Press*, December 1, 2004.

36. "Kroll Sees Terror, Political Risk in Saudi Rising," *Reuters*, September 22, 2004.

37. "Saudi Arabia: Who Are the Islamists?," International Crisis Group-ICG Report, September 21, 2004; George Friedman, "Saudi Arabia: A Balancing Act," January 30, 2004, www.Stratfor.com.

Chapter 3

1. *Jane's Sentinel Security Assessment,* August 27, 2004.

2. Richard F. Grimmett, *Conventional Arms Transfer to Developing Nations, 1996–2003* (Washington, DC: Congressional Research Service, CRS RL32547, August 26, 2004), pp. 52 and 65.

3. The Estimate, a bi-weekly newsletter, "Political 8 Security Intelligence Analysis of the Islamic World and its Neighbors." January 25, 2002, p. 4. www.theestimate.com.

4. Grimmett, pp. 52 and 65.

Chapter 4

1. David E. Long, *The Kingdom of Saudi Arabia* (University Press of Florida, 1997), pp. 35–38.

2. Royal Embassy of Saudi Arabia, "Government Official's Biographies: His Royal Highness Prince Sultan bin Abdul Aziz Al Saud," available from *http://www.saudi-embassy.net/gov_profile/bio_sultan.html*, accessed on May 30, 2002.

3. Joseph A. Kechichian, *Succession in Saudi Arabia* (New York: Palgrave, 2001), p. 79.

4. Based on the work of Richard F. Grimmett in various editions of *Conventional Arms Transfer to Developing Nations* (Washington, DC: Congressional Research Service).

5. *Reuters,* May 14, 1996; *Jane's Defence Weekly,* May 22, 1996, p. 4.

6. *Defense News,* "U.S. Lifts Ban on Military Equipment to Yemen: U.S. Official," *http://www.defensenews.com/story.php?F=3150933&C=mideast*, accessed on September 2, 2004.

7. Exchange rate of 3.75 Saudi Riyal to $US1.

8. Department of State, *Annual Report on Military Expenditures, 1999,* submitted to the Committee on Appropriations of the U.S. Senate and the Committee on Appropriations of the U.S. House of Representatives, July 27, 2000, in accordance with section 511(b) of the Foreign Operations, Export Financing, and Related Programs Appropriations Act, 1993.

9. IISS, *Military Balance* for 2003–2004 and 2004–2005 (London: IISS).

10. IISS, *Military Balance,* various editions. This number includes the National Guard.

11. The FY1988 budget was planned to have a $10 billion deficit, with $8 billion in foreign borrowing. It involved the first foreign borrowing in 25 years and the first increase in taxes in eight years—all on foreign businesses. The actual budget reached a $15–17 billion deficit by the year's end, with some $10 billion in financing. *Economist,* January 16, 1988, p. 59; *Defense News,* January 18, 1988, p. 4.

12. Based on various editions of the CIA *World Factbook.* Some of the differences between these estimates may, however, reflect differences in the CIA definition of GDP and military expenditures.

13. *Report on Allied Contributions to the Common Defense, March 2001, June 2002, July 2003,* Report to the U.S. Congress by the Secretary of Defense. Available at *http://www.defenselink.mil/pubs/allied.html*.

14. Interview with official of the Office of the Secretary of Defense, February 2001.

15. *Defense News,* November 20–26, 1995, p. 27.

16. Grimmett, *Conventional Arms Transfers to the Third World,* 1985–92 edition, pp. 59 and 69; 1989–96 edition, pp. 53 and 65; and 1992–96 edition, pp. 47–49 and 58–60.

17. Grimmett, *Conventional Arms Transfers,* 1996–2003 edition, pp. 50 and 61

18. Grimmett, *Conventional Arms Transfers,* 1989–96 edition, pp. 53 and 65–66.

19. Grimmett, *Conventional Arms Transfers,* 1996–2003 edition, pp. 53 and 51–61.

20. Grimmett, *Conventional Arms Transfers,* 1996–2000 edition, pp. 50 and 61.

21. Arms Control and Disarmament Agency (ACDA), *World Military Expenditures and Arms Transfers, 1989* (Washington, DC: GPO, 1990), table II; ACDA printout dated May 14, 1996; Arms Control and Disarmament Agency (ACDA), *World Military Expenditures and Arms Transfers, 1996* (Washington, DC: GPO, 1997), table II; and U.S. State Department, *World Military Expenditures and Arms Transfers, 1998* (Washington, DC: Bureau of Arms Control, 1999).

22. See ACDA, "High Costs of the Persian Gulf War," *World Military Expenditures and Arms Transfers, 1987* (Washington, DC: GPO, 1988), pp. 21–23; ACDA printout dated May 14, 1996; and Grimmett, *Trends in Conventional Arms Transfers, 1982–89* edition.

23. Estimates based on data provided by Richard F. Grimmett of the Congressional Research Service.

24. ACDA, *World Military Expenditures and Arms Transfers, 1989*; ACDA, *World Military Expenditures and Arms Transfers, 1996*; U.S. State Department, *World Military Expenditures and Arms Transfers, 1998*.

25. These data are all taken from the 1988-96 editions of Grimmett, *Conventional Arms Transfers to Developing Nations*.

26. Grimmett, *Conventional Arms Transfer, 1996–2000*, pp. 50 and 61.

27. Ibid.

Chapter 5

1. This refers to Iraq's forces as of March 2003, before the war started.

2. IISS, *Military Balance,* various editions.

3. *Jane's Sentinel Security Assessment—The Gulf States,* November 14, 2003.

4. The IISS reports 90 GCT-1s, but Giat only reports the sale of 51.

5. David Long, *The Kingdom of Saudi Arabia* (Gainesville: University Press of Florida, 1997).

6. Larry R. Allen and Fred W. Bucher, "Modernizing the Saudi Guard," http://www.army.mil/soldiers/march95/p28.html, accessed on September 3, 2004.

7. Robin Hughes, *Jane's Defence Weekly,* December 3, 2003.

8. *Jane's Defense Weekly,* August 7, 2002, p. 16.

9. Richard Scott, "Sawari II Frigates Set Sail," *Jane's Navy International,* January 1, 2005.

10. Naval-Technonogy.Com, available at *http://www.naval-technology.com/projects/al_riyadh*, accessed January 21, 2005.

11. Scott, "Sawari II Frigates Set Sail"; Naval-Technology.com, accessed January 21, 2005.

12. Scott, "Sawari II Frigates Set Sail."

13. Richard Scott, "New Saudi Frigates to Receive Oto Melara Guns," *Jane's Defence Weekly,* November 27, 2002, *http://jdw.janes.com*, accessed January 9, 2004.

14. Ibid.

15. "Nations/Alliances/Geographic Regions Middle/East/North Africa—Saudi Arabia," *Periscope.*

16. J. A. C. Lewis, "Saudis Move Closer to NH 90 Purchase for Navy," *Jane's Defence Weekly,* December 24, 2003, *http://jdw.janes.com*, accessed January 8, 2004.

17. Ibid.

18. Based on *Jane's Fighting Ships,* 1996–97, 1999–2000, and 2000–2001; IISS, *Military Balance,* 1996–97 and 1999–2000 and 2001–2002.

19. USCENTCOM, *Atlas,* 1996, MacDill Air Force Base, USCENTCOM, 1997; and the IISS, *Military Balance,* various editions.

20. Ibid.

21. *Defense News,* September 9, 1996, p. 26.

22. *Defense News,* March 17, 1997, p. 3; *Associated Press,* May 12, 1997, 0251; *Jane's Defence Weekly,* July 30, 1997, p. 17.

23. Patrick Clawson, "Nuclear Proliferation in the Middle East: Who Is Next after Iran?" The Washington Institute for Near East Policy, April 2003.

24. Ed Blanche, "Gulf-Saudi Arabia's Nuclear Footprint," *Jane's Islamic Affair Analyst,* September 1, 2003.

25. *http://www.globalsecurity.org/wmd/world/saudi*, accessed on September 15, 2004.

26. *Associated Press,* May 12, 1997, 0251.

27. Ibid.

28. U.S. experts have never monitored a test of the conventional version of the missile. CEP stands for circular error probable and is an indication of a missile's accuracy. The figure represents the radius of a circle in which half the warheads are expected to fall. It should be noted, however, that the theoretical figures apply only to missiles that operate perfectly up to the point the missile has left the launcher and at least its first booster and guidance system are operating perfectly. Operational CEPs can only be "guesstimated," but they will be much lower. Missiles generally do not have fail-safe warheads. A substantial number will have partial failures and deliver their warhead far from their intended targets. *Jane's Defence Weekly,* October 1, 1990, pp. 744-46; Fred Donovan, "Mideast Missile Flexing," *Arms Control Today* (May 1990), p. 31; Shuey, Lenhart, Snyder, Donnelley, Mielke, and Moteff, *Missile Proliferation: Survey of Emerging Missile Forces* (Washington, DC: Congressional Research Service, Report 88-642F, February 9, 1989).

29. *Jane's Defence Weekly,* October 1, 1990, pp. 744–46, July 30, 1997, p. 17; Donovan, "Mideast Missile Flexing," p. 31; Shuey et al., *Missile Proliferation.*

30. *Associated Press,* May 12, 1997, 0251; *Jane's Defence Weekly,* July 30, 1997, p. 17.

31. *Jane's Defence Weekly,* October 1, 1988, pp. 744-55, July 30, 1997, p. 17; *Associated Press,* May 12, 1997, 0251.

32. *Jane's Defence Weekly,* October 1, 1990, pp. 744–46.

33. *Washington Times,* October 4, 1988, p. A-2; *Christian Science Monitor,* October 8, 1988, p. 2.

34. Shuey et al., *Missile Proliferation.,* pp. 64–65.

35. The warhead could also be enhanced with submunitions, a proximity fuse to detonate before impact to give an optimum burst pattern and widen the area covered by shrapnel, and a time-delay fuse to allow the warhead to fully penetrate a building before exploding. Shuey et al., *Missile Proliferation,* pp. 23–24.

36. *Jane's Defence Weekly,* July 30, 1997, p.17.

37. *Jane's Defence Weekly,* June 16, 1999, p.14.

38. Ibid.

Chapter 6

1. *Ain AlYaqeen,* November 29, 2002. http://www.ain-al-yaqeen.com/issues/20021129/feat6en.htm, accessed on September 8, 2004.

2. Author interviews in Saudi Arabia in 2000.

3. *Associated Press,* December 30, 2001, 1928; *Reuters,* December 29, 2001, 1802; *Saudi Arabia* 18, no. 10 (October 2001), pp. 1–4.

4. This chronology is taken from work by the National Council on U.S.-Arab Relations. A far more detailed version, with detailed references to the events in appendix 1, can be found at *http://www.saudi-us-relations.org/Fact_Sheets/TimelineTerrorism. html.*

5. *Gulf News,* February 19, 2004, *http://www.gulf-news.com/Articles/news.asp?Article ID=111432*

6. Various sources were used for this chronology. Including many wire stories, some of the documents provided by the Saudi embassy, and (1) *http://timelines.ws/countries/ SAUDIARABIA.HTML,* accessed September 29, 2004; (2) *http://www.saudi-us-relations.org/Fact_Sheets/TimelineTerrorism.html,* accessed January 26, 2005; and (3) *http://www.arabnews.com/?page=1&section=0&article=43846&d=26&m=4&y= 2004,* accessed September 28, 2004.

7. Claude Salhani, "Game Over for Saudi Terrorists," *UPI,* August 31, 2004.

8. Scott Wilson, "Saudis Fight Militancy with Jobs," *Washington Post,* August 31, 2004.

9. Ibid.

10. Claude Salhani, "Analysis: Saudi's New Weapon—Reform," *UPI,* September 7, 2004.

11. Prince Nayef is 68 years old. Like Fahd, Abdullah, and Nawaf, he is a son of King Abdul Aziz.

12. These comments are based on an English transcript and summary provided in e-mail form by the Saudi embassy in Washington, D.C., on December 5, 2002.

13. Ibid.

14. *Gulf Daily News, http://www.gulf-daily-news.com/arc_Articles.asp?Article=90497& Sn=WORL&IssueID=27163*, accessed September 16, 2004.

15. Ed Blanche, "Saudi Extremists Target Intelligence Chiefs," *Jane's Intelligence Review,* February 1, 2004.

16. Prince Nawaf is a son of King Abd al-Aziz, and the uncle of Prince Turki. Prince Turki is brother of Prince Saud al-Faisal, the foreign minister, and son of the late King Faisal.

17. See Simon Henderson, "The Saudis: Friend or Foe?," *Wall Street Journal,* October 22, 2001, as provided by e-mail in *publications@washingtoninstitute.org*. Also see *The Estimate* 8, no. 16 (September 7, 2001), p. 1.

18. *Arab News.* July 8, 2001, available at *http://www.arabnews.com/article.asp?ID=3823*.

19. "The Kingdom of Saudi Arabia's Experience in Fighting Drug and Arms Smuggling and the Relationship between Terrorism and Arms Table 5 and 6," a working paper submitted at the Counterterrorism International Conference, Riyadh, 5–8 February, 2005.

20. Ibid.

21. *Defense News,* November 11, 1991, p. 36; *Washington Technology,* September 24, 1992, p. 1.

22. "Security and Foreign Forces, Saudi Arabia," *Jane's Sentinel Security Assessment— The Gulf States,* December 23, 2004.

23. Jonathan Fenby, "Chirac takes Charge to Clinch E7BN Franco-Saudi Arms Deal," *Sunday Business Group,* May 2, 2004, p. 7.

24. Herve Gattegno, "The Saudi Contract that Pits Mr. Chirac against Mr. Sarkozy," *Le Monde,* April 15, 2005.

25. Fenby, "Chirac Takes Charge," p. 7.

26. Ibid.

27. Douglas Barrie, Michael A. Taverna, and Robert Wall, "Singapore Sling: Eurofighter Typhoon Drops from Singaporean Short List, Faces Potential Competition in Saudi Arabia," *Aviation Week & Space Technology,* April 25, 2005.

28. "Dassault Steps Up Negotiating Sale of Rafale Airplanes to Riyadh," *Le Monde,* April 16, 2005.

29. Barrie, Taverna, and Wall, "Singapore Sling."

30. This analysis draws heavily on interviews, various annual editions of the IISS, *Military Balance*; and *Jane's Sentinel—The Gulf States, 1997.*

31. This text is modified from text provided in the U.S. State Department, *Country Report on Human Rights Practices, http://www.state.gov/www/global/human_rights/ 1999_ hrp_report/saudiara.html*, and U.S. State Department, "Saudi Arabia," *1999 Country Reports on Human Rights Practices*, released by the Bureau of Democracy, Human Rights, and Labor, U.S. Department of State, February 25, 2000.

32. Ibid., and other editions of this report series.

33. The Ministry of Islamic Affairs funds the Mutawaa'in, and the general president of the Mutawaa'in holds the rank of cabinet minister. The ministry also pays the salaries of imams (prayer leaders) and others who work in the mosques. During 1999 foreign imams were barred from leading worship during the most heavily attended prayer times and prohibited from delivering sermons during Friday congregational prayers. The government claims that its actions were part of its Saudization plan to replace foreign workers with citizens.

34. *Associated Press,* March 18, 2002, 0650, March 25, 2002, 1225; *Reuters,* March 12, 2002, 0430.

35. These comments are based on an English transcript and summary provided in e-mail form by the Saudi embassy in Washington, D.C., on December 5, 2002.

CHAPTER 7

1. See the detailed discussion in chapter 2.

2. Estimates differ according to source, the last comprehensive U.S. Geological Survey analysis was performed in 2000 and was seriously limited by the fact that many countries were affected by war or internal turmoil and declared reserves without explaining them or provided data by field. Standard estimates of reserves by non-U.S. government sources like those in the *Oil and Gas Journal* and *World Oil* do not adjust reported data according to a standardized methodology or adjust for the large number of countries that never alter their estimates of reserves for actual production. For example, 6 of the 10 nations with the largest proven reserves are in the MENA region. An International Energy Agency analysis shows a range of 259–263 billion barrels for Saudi Arabia, 105–133 billion barrels for Iran, 66–98 billion for the UAE, and 31–29 billion for Libya. The figure of 115 billion for Iraq is consistent only because it is a figure announced in the past by the Iraqi government and there are no accurate, verified estimates. To put these figures in perspective, the range for Russia is 60–69 billion, 25–35 billion for Nigeria, 23–21 billion for the United States, and 52–78 billion for Venezuela. International Energy Agency, "Oil Market Outlook," *World Energy Outlook* (Paris: OECD/IEA, October 2004), table 3.2.

   Estimates alter radically if an unconventional oil reserve like Canadian tar sands are included. The Middle East has only about 1 percent of the world's known reserves of oil shales, extra heavy oil, tar sands, and bitumen. Canada has 36 percent, the United States has 32 percent, and Venezuela has 19 percent. The rest of the world has only 12 percent. The cost effectiveness of producing most of these reserves and the environmental impact of doing so are highly uncertain, however, even at high oil prices. Ibid., figure 3.13.

Reserve estimates also change radically if ultimately recoverable reserves are included, and not simply proven reserves. Some estimates put the total for such reserves at around 2.5 times the figure for proven reserves. For example, the IEA estimate for the Middle East drops from around 60 percent to 23 percent. Such estimates are speculative however, in terms of both their existence and recovery price and do not have significant impact on estimates of production capacity through the 2025–2030 period. They also ignore gas and gas liquids. The Middle Eastern share of undiscovered oil and gas resources rises to 27 percent based on existing data.

Such estimates are also heavily biased by the fact that so little experimental drilling searching for new fields occurred in the Middle East between 1992 and 2002. The IEA estimates than only 3 percent of some 28,000 wildcat explorations for new fields worldwide took place in the Middle East during that period. Some 50 Saudi fields, with 70 percent of the reserves that are proven, still await development. Ibid., figure 3.15.

3. Guy Caruso, "US Oil Markets and the Middle East, DOE/EIA," October 20, 2004.

4. Ibid.

5. IEA estimate in the *World Energy Outlook for 2005,* table 3.5, and analyzed in chapter 3.

6. EIA/DOE, *Saudi Arabia, Country Study, January 2005, http://www.eia.doe.gov/emeu/cabs/saudi.html.*

7. Ibid.

8. Ibid.

9. Nasser Al-Salti, "Kingdom Oil Reserves May Go Up by 200 Billion Barrels, Naimi Says," *Arab News,* April 7, 2005.

10. The DOE/EIA, *International Energy Outlook for 2004* can be found at *http://www.eia.doe.gov/oiaf/ieo/download.html.*

11. See *http://www.eia.doe.gov/emeu/cabs/pgulf.html.* In 2003 Persian Gulf countries had estimated net oil exports of 17.2 million barrels a day (MMBD) of oil (see pie chart). Saudi Arabia exported the most oil of any Persian Gulf country in 2003, with an estimated 8.40 MMBD (49 percent of the total). Also, Iran had estimated net exports of about 2.6 MMBD (15 percent), followed by the United Arab Emirates (2.4 MMBD—14 percent), Kuwait (2 MMBD—12 percent), Iraq (0.9 MMBD—9 percent), Qatar (0.9 MMBD—5 percent), and Bahrain (0.01 MMBD—0.1 percent).

U.S. gross oil imports from the Persian Gulf rose during 2003 to 2.5 MMBD (almost all of which was crude), from 2.3 MMBD in 2002. The vast majority of Persian Gulf oil imported by the United States came from Saudi Arabia (71 percent), with significant amounts also coming from Iraq (19 percent), Kuwait (9 percent), and small amounts (less than 1 percent of the total) from Qatar and the United Arab Emirates. Iraqi oil exports to the United States rose slightly in 2003, to

481,000 bbl/d, compared to 442,000 bbl/d in 2002. Saudi exports rose from 1.55 MMBD in 2002 to 1.77 MMBD in 2003. Overall, the Persian Gulf accounted for about 22 percent of U.S. net oil imports and 12 percent of U.S. oil consumption, in 2003.

Western Europe (defined as European countries belonging to the Organization for Economic Cooperation and Development—OECD) averaged 2.6 MMBD of oil imports from the Persian Gulf during 2003, an increase of about 0.2 MMBD from the same period in 2002. The largest share of Persian Gulf oil exports to Western Europe came from Saudi Arabia (52 percent), with significant amounts also coming from Iran (33 percent), Iraq (7 percent), and Kuwait (6 percent).

Japan averaged 4.2 MMBD of net oil imports from the Persian Gulf during 2003. Japan's dependence on the Persian Gulf for its oil supplies increased sharply since the low point of 57 percent in 1988 to a high of 78 percent in 2003. About 30 percent of Japan's Persian Gulf imports in 2003 came from Saudi Arabia, 29 percent from the United Arab Emirates, 17 percent from Iran, 12 percent from Kuwait, 11 percent from Qatar, and around 1 percent from Bahrain and Iraq combined. Japan's oil imports from the Persian Gulf as a percentage of demand continued to rise to new highs, reaching 78 percent in 2003.

12. Estimates by country are necessarily uncertain. The *International Energy Outlook for 2004* estimate of production capacity in MMBD for MENA countries is as follows:

Country	2001	2010 Reference	2010 High Price	2020 Reference	2020 High Price	2025 Reference	2025 High Price
Iran	3.7	4.0	3.5	4.7	3.8	4.9	4.3
Iraq	2.8	3.7	2.9	5.3	3.7	6.6	4.6
Kuwait	2.3	3.7	2.3	4.4	2.9	5.0	3.4
Qatar	0.6	0.6	0.6	0.8	0.7	0.8	0.7
Saudi Arabia	10.2	13.2	9.4	18.2	12.9	22.5	16.0
UAE	2.7	3.3	2.7	4.6	3.3	5.2	3.9
Total Gulf	22.4	27.9	21.4	38.0	27.3	45.0	32.9
Algeria	1.6	2.0	1.6	2.4	2.0	2.7	2.2
Libya	1.7	2.0	1.7	2.6	2.1	2.9	2.4
Other Middle East	2.0	2.2	2.4	2.6	2.9	2.8	3.1
Total Other	4.3	6.2	5.7	7.6	7.0	8.4	7.7
Total MENA	26.7	34.1	26.1	45.6	34.3	53.4	40.6
Total World	79.3	95.1	90.0	114.9	107.2	126.1	117.3
(United States)	9.0	9.5	9.9	8.9	9.6	8.6	9.0

OPEC data are labeled confidential but are very similar. The IEA does not provide country-by-country estimates, but uses very similar models with similar results. It estimates total world production was 77 MMBD in 2002, and will increase to 121 MMBD in 2030. If one looks at the data for the Middle East, the latest IEA estimates are as follows:

The IEA estimate in the *World Energy Outlook for 2004,* table 3.5, is:

	2002	2010	2020	2030	Avg. Annual Growth
OPEC Middle East	19.0	22.5	37.4	51.8	3.6%
Other Middle East	2.1	1.8	1.4	1.0	-2.7%
Total	21.1	24.3	38.8	52.8	
Nonconventional Oil (Worldwide)	1.6	3.8	6.1	10.1	6.7%
World	77.0	90.4	106.7	121.3	1.6%

13. See *http://www.eia.doe.gov/emeu/security/choke.html#HORMUZ.* The strait is the narrow passage between Iran and Oman that connects the Persian Gulf with the Gulf of Oman and the Arabian Sea. It consists of two-mile-wide channels for inbound and outbound tanker traffic, as well as a two-mile-wide buffer zone. The EIA estimates that some 13 MMBD flowed through the Strait in 2002. The IEA puts the figure at 15 MMBD in 2003. Both agencies indicate that the amount of oil moving by tanker will increase steadily as Asian demand consumes a larger and larger share of total exports.

Closure of the Strait of Hormuz would require use of longer alternate routes (if available) at increased transportation costs. Such routes include the 5 million-bbl/d capacity Petroline (East-West Pipeline) and the 290,000-bbl/d Abqaiq-Yanbu natural gas liquids line across Saudi Arabia to the Red Sea. Theoretically, the 1.65-MMBD Iraqi Pipeline across Saudi Arabia (IPSA) also could be used, more oil could be pumped north to Ceyhan (Turkey), and the 0.5 million-bbl/d Tapline to Lebanon could be reactivated.

14. IEA, "Oil Market Outlook," *World Energy Outlook, 2004,* tables 3.7 and 3.8.

15. Ibid., chapter 3.

16. BP/Amoco, *BP Statistical Review of World Energy* (London: BP, 2003), p. 17.

17. See EIA/DOE, *Saudi Arabia, Country Study, June 2004.*

18. Ibid.

19. Ibid.

20. EIA/DOE, *Saudi Arabia, Country Study, January 2005.*

21. EIA/DOE, *Saudi Arabia, Country Study, June 2004.*

22. EIA/DOE, *Saudi Arabia, Country Study, January 2005.*

23. "Saudi Aramco Plans New Yanbu' Refinery, Integrated Ras Tanura Ptechems Plant," *Middle East Economic Survey,* April 10, 2005.

24. "Saudis to Build New Export Refinery," *Reuters,* April 5, 2005.

25. Ibid.

26. "Saudi Aramco Plans New Yanbu' Refinery."

27. EIA/DOE, *Saudi Arabia, Country Study, June 2004.*

Chapter 8

1. Grimmett, *Conventional Arms Transfers, 1993–2000,* pp. CRS-47, 48, 58, 59.

2. *Jane's Defence Weekly,* September 22, 2004.

3. "Saudi Arabia, Pakistan Eye Joint AEW Buy," *Defense News,* November 1, 2004.

4. Jean-Pierre Neu, "Saudis Pledge to Buy French Jets in Ä6.0 Deal," *The Financial Times,* April 15, 2005.

5. Ibid.

6. P. K. Abdul Ghafour, "No Arms Deals during French Visit, Says Saud," *Arab News,* April 18, 2005.

7. Airforce-Technology.com, available at *http://www.airforce-technology.com/projects/ rafale/,* accessed on May 5, 2005.

8. Andrew Chuter and Pierre Tran, "Saudi Aircraft Moves Prompt Speculation about Ties with UK," *Defense News,* April 25, 2005. p. 4.

9. Ibid.

10. Ibid.

11. Ibid.

12. Ibid. Also, *http://www.answers.com/main/ntquery?method=4&dsid=2222&dekey= RAF+Tornado+GR4&gwp=8&curtab=2222_1;* and *http://www.globalsecurity.org/ military/world/europe/tornado.htm,* accessed on May 6, 2005.

13. Ibid.

Chapter 9

1. *Wall Street Journal,* February 5, 2002.

2. *Reuters,* October 31, 2001, 1255.

3. *Associated Press,* November 6, 2001, 0617.

4. *Washington Post,* December 8, 2001, p. A-3.

5. *Washington Times,* February 8, 2002, p. 18; *Wall Street Journal,* February 5, 2002.

6. Embassy of Saudi Arabia, "Initiatives and Actions Taken by the Kingdom of Saudi Arabia in the Financial Area to Combat Terrorism," December 3, 2002.

CHAPTER 10

1. Riyad Qusti, "No Foreign Observers for Elections: Riyadh Mayor," *Arab News*, November 22, 2004.

2. William Wallis, "Royal Seal of Approval for Polls Fails to Stir Public," *Financial Times*, January 21, 2005.

3. Ibid.

4. Faiza Saleh Ambah, "Saudi Candidates Learn Politics," *Christian Science Monitor*, January 12, 2005.

5. Wallis, "Royal Seal of Approval."

6. Ibid.

7. The Royal Embassy of Saudi Arabia, "Political and Economic Reform in the Kingdom of Saudi Arabia," Washington, D.C., September 2004.

8. Barry Moody and Dominic Evans Reuters; May 13, 2004.

9. "Patent law effective as of September 15, 2004. Available at: *http://www.sagia.gov.sa/innerpage.asp?ContentID=7&Lang=en&NewsID=350*, accessed November 23, 2004.

10. Report by Saudi Embassy Washington; "Political and Economic Reform in the Kingdom of Saudi Arabia," December, 2003.

11. Saudi embassy, "Political and Economic Reform."

12. Ibid.

13. "Saudi Arabia Pays Down Debt, Sees Sustained Financial Strength in 2005," *Middle East Economic Survey*, January 17, 2005.

14. Brad Bourland, "Saudi Arabia's 2005 Budget, 2004 Performance, " Saudi American Bank, December 11, 2004, and "Saudi Arabia Pays Down Debt."

15. P. K. Abdul Ghafour, "Census Finds Expat Numbers Below Estimate," *Arab News*, November 26, 2004.

16. The General Statistics Department announced new population statistics on November 26, 2004, stating that preliminary results of this year's general census estimates the total number of expatriates in the Kingdom as 6.14 million. This figure is much lower than the 8.8 million official figure given earlier by the labor minister. According to the census, which started 15 September, the Kingdom's total population is more than 22 million. The department added that there are 8,285,662 male Saudis, who represent 50.1 percent of the total Saudi population, while the number of Saudi females is 8,243,640. According to the last census taken in 1992, the population of Saudi Arabia amounted to 12,304,000 Saudis and 4,625,000 foreigners. Riyadh and Jeddah had populations of more than two million each.

17. Abdul Wahab Bashir, "Jobless Figure Put at 180,433," *Arab News*, January 13, 2005.

18. "Saudi Business Women to Participate in Dubai Conference." *Arab News*, November 24, 2004.

19. Javid Hassan, "Move to Saudize Ten More Job Catgories," *Arab News,* January 6, 2005.

20. Ibid.

21. WTO, Ministerial Conference, fifth session; September 10–14, 2003, "Statement by HE Dr. Hashim Yamani."

22. Ibid.

23. "Insurance Hurdle in Saudi-US WTO Talks," *Saudi Gazette.*

24. "Saudi Arabia Arrests Poet for Criticizing Corruption," *Arab News,* March 21, 2004.

25. Saudi embassy, "Political and Economic Reform," p. 4.

26. Saudi Embassy, Washington, DC, August 3, 2003.

27. "Urbanization and Development," *http://www.countrystudies.us/saudi-arabia*

28. Abdullah al-Shihri, "Saudis: Fanatics May Not be Teachers," *Associated Press,* September 7, 2004.

29. "Saudi Teacher Banned over Extremist Idea," *UPI,* November 29, 2004.

30. Howard Schneider, "When Islam Meets the Modern Economy," *http://www.washingtonpost.com.*

31. Editorial, *Manila Times, http://www.manilatimes.*

32. Brian Whitaker, "Militants Call for Muslim Uprising," *Guardian,* November 11, 2004.

33. P. K. Abdul Ghafour, "Terrorists Tarnish Image of Islam, says, Abdullah," *Arab News,* November 21, 2004.

34. "Saudi Edicts Urging Iraq Fight Criticized, " *Associated Press,* November 20, 2004.

35. Saudi Embassy, Washington, DC, Press Release, February 4, 2003.

36. "Interview with Senator Joseph Biden," *Wide Angle PBS,* October 7, 2004.

37. Donna Abu-Nasr, "Saudi Reformist Demanding Openness Refuse to Proceed with Court Hearing," *Associated Press,* October, 4, 2004.

38. Abdullah Al-Shihri, "15 Saudi Protesters Get Prison Sentence, Lashing," *Associated Press,* January 14, 2005.

39. Khalid al-Dakhil, "Quiet Time," *New York Times,* November 27, 2004.

40. Faiza Saleh Ambah, "Moves toward Reform Wane in Saudi Arabia, " *Christian Science Monitor,* October 4, 2004.

41. Faiza Saleh Ambah, "Saudi Candidates Learn Politics," *Christian Science Monitor,* January 12, 2005.

About the Authors

Anthony H. Cordesman holds the Arleigh A. Burke Chair in Strategy at CSIS. He is also a national security analyst for ABC News and a frequent commentator on National Public Radio and the BBC. The author of more than 30 books on U.S. security policy, energy policy, and the Middle East, his most recent publications include *The War after the War: Strategic Lessons of Iraq and Afghanistan* (CSIS, 2004); *The Military Balance in the Middle East* (Praeger, 2004); *Energy Developments in the Middle East* (Praeger, 2004); and *The Iraq War: Strategy, Tactics, and Military Lessons* (CSIS, 2003).

Nawaf Obaid is a Saudi national security and intelligence consultant based in Riyadh, Saudi Arabia. He is currently the managing director of the Saudi National Security Assessment Project. He was a former senior research fellow at The Washington Institute for Near East Policy (WINEP). He also was the project director for the study, "Sino-Saudi Energy Rapprochement and the Implications for US National Security," conducted for the adviser and director for net assessments to the U.S. Secretary of Defense. His studies, reports, and opinion pieces in newspapers such as the *Washington Post*, the *New York Times,* and the *International Herald Tribune* can be downloaded from the Internet by doing a name search.

He is the author of a book on Saudi oil policy, *The Oil Kingdom at 100: Petroleum Policymaking in Saudi Arabia* (WINEP Editions), and is currently writing a new one, *The Struggle for the Saudi Soul: Royalty, Islamic Militancy and Reform in the Kingdom,* to be published in 2005. He has a BS from Georgetown University's School of Foreign Service, an MA from Harvard University's Kennedy School of Government, and has completed doctoral courses at MIT's security studies program.